New Perspectives on

XML

2nd Edition

Comprehensive

Patrick Carey

Carey Associates, Inc.

COURSE TECHNOLOGY
CENGAGE Learning™

Australia • Brazil • Japan • Korea • Mexico • Singapore • Spain • United Kingdom • United States

COURSE TECHNOLOGY
CENGAGE Learning™

New Perspectives on XML, 2nd Edition—Comprehensive
Course Technology, Cengage Learning

Executive Editor: Rachel Goldberg

Product Manager: Donna Gridley

Associate Product Manager: Janine Tangney

Editorial Assistant: Rebecca Padrick

Marketing Manager: Joy Stark

Developmental Editor: Sasha Vodnik

QA Manuscript Reviewers: Burt LaFountain, Christian Kunciw, Danielle Shaw, Susan Whalen

Senior Production Editor: Catherine G. DiMassa

Composition: GEX Publishing Services

Text Designer: Steve Deschene

Cover Designer: Nancy Goulet

Cover Artist: Helmick & Schechter Sculpture www.handsart.net

For product information and technology assistance, contact us at
Cengage Learning Customer & Sales Support, 1-800-354-9706
For permission to use material from this text or product, submit all requests online at **www.cengage.com/permissions**
Further permissions questions can be emailed to
permissionrequest@cengage.com

ISBN-13: 978-1-4188-6064-6

ISBN-10: 1-4188-6064-6

Course Technology
25 Thomson Place
Boston, Massachusetts 02210
USA

Cengage Learning is a leading provider of customized learning solutions with office locations around the globe, including Singapore, the United Kingdom, Australia, Mexico, Brazil, and Japan. Locate your local office at:
international.cengage.com/region

Cengage Learning products are represented in Canada by Nelson Education, Ltd.

To learn more about Course Technology, visit **www.cengage.com/coursetechnology**.

To learn more about Cengage Learning, visit **www.cengage.com**.

Purchase any of our products at your local bookstore or at our preferred online store **www.ichapters.com**.

Disclaimer
Any fictional URLs used throughout this book are intended for instructional purposes only. At the time this book was printed, any such URLs were fictional and not belonging to any real persons or companies.

Some of the product names and company names used in this book have been used for identification purposes only and may be trademarks or registered trademarks of their respective manufacturers and sellers.

Printed in the United States of America
6 7 8 9 10

Preface

Real, Thought-Provoking, Engaging, Dynamic, Interactive—these are just a few of the words that are used to describe the New Perspectives Series' approach to learning and building computer skills.

Without our critical-thinking and problem-solving methodology, computer skills could be learned but not retained. By teaching with a case-based approach, the New Perspectives Series challenges students to apply what they've learned to real-life situations.

Our ever-growing community of users understands why they're learning what they're learning. Now you can too!

See what instructors and students are saying about the best-selling New Perspectives Series:

"First of all, I just have to say that I wish that all of my textbooks were written in the style of the New Perspectives Series. I am using these titles for all of the courses that I teach that have a book available."
— Diana Kokoska, University of Maine at Augusta

"The New Perspectives format is a pleasure to use. The Quick Checks and the tutorial Review Assignments help students view topics from a real-world perspective."
— Craig Shaw, Central Community College—Hastings

"We have been using the New Perspectives Series for several years and are pleased with it. Step-by-step instructions, end-of-chapter projects, and color screenshots are positives."
— Michael J. Losacco, College of DuPage

...and about New Perspectives on XML:

"This is, by far, the best treatment of namespaces I've ever seen in any text."
—Lisa Macon, Valencia Community College

www.course.com/NewPerspectives

Why *New Perspectives* will work for you

Context
Each tutorial begins with a problem presented in a "real-world" case that is meaningful to students. The case sets the scene to help students understand what they will do in the tutorial.

Hands-on Approach
Each tutorial is divided into manageable sessions that combine reading and hands-on, step-by-step work. Screenshots—now 20% larger for enhanced readability—help guide students through the steps. **Trouble?** tips anticipate common mistakes or problems to help students stay on track and continue with the tutorial.

Review

Review
In New Perspectives, retention is a key component to learning. At the end of each session, a series of Quick Check questions helps students test their understanding of the concepts before moving on. And now each tutorial contains an end-of-tutorial summary and a list of key terms for further reinforcement.

Apply

Assessment
Engaging and challenging Review Assignments and Case Problems have always been a hallmark feature of the New Perspectives Series. Now we've added new features to make them more accessible! Colorful icons and brief descriptions accompany the exercises, making it easy to understand, at a glance, both the goal and level of challenge a particular assignment holds.

Reference Window

Task Reference

Reference
While contextual learning is excellent for retention, there are times when students will want a high-level understanding of how to accomplish a task. Within each tutorial, Reference Windows appear before a set of steps to provide a succinct summary and preview of how to perform a task. In addition, a Task Reference at the back of the book provides quick access to information on how to carry out common tasks. Finally, each book includes a combination Glossary/Index to promote easy reference of material.

Student Online Companion
This book has an accompanying online companion Web site designed to enhance learning. Go to www.course.com/carey to find:
- Additional content for further exploration
- List of URLs from the book
- Student Data Files
- Links to software
- Student Edition Labs—These online interactive labs offer students hands-on practice and reinforcement of skills and concepts relating Web and Internet topics.
- Information about other Patrick Carey products

www.course.com/NewPerspectives

New Perspectives offers an entire system of instruction

The New Perspectives Series is more than just a handful of books. It's a complete system of offerings:

New Perspectives catalog
Our online catalog is never out of date! Go to the catalog link on our Web site to check out our available titles, request a desk copy, download a book preview, or locate online files.

Coverage to meet your needs!
Whether you're looking for just a small amount of coverage or enough to fill a semester-long class, we can provide you with a textbook that meets your needs.

- Brief books typically cover the essential skills in just 2 to 4 tutorials.
- Introductory books build and expand on those skills and contain an average of 5 to 8 tutorials.
- Comprehensive books are great for a full-semester class, and contain 9 to 12+ tutorials.
- Power Users or Advanced books are perfect for a highly accelerated introductory class or a second course in a given topic.

So if the book you're holding does not provide the right amount of coverage for you, there's probably another offering available. Go to our Web site or contact your Course Technology sales representative to find out what else we offer.

Instructor Resources
We offer more than just a book. We have all the tools you need to enhance your lectures, check students' work, and generate exams in a new, easier-to-use and completely revised package. This book's Instructor's Manual, ExamView testbank, PowerPoint presentations, data files, solution files, figure files, and a sample syllabus are all available on a single CD-ROM or for downloading at www.course.com.

How will your students master Computer Concepts and Microsoft Office?
Add more muscle and flexibility to your course with SAM (Skills Assessment Manager)! SAM adds the power of skill-based assessment and the award-winning SAM classroom administration system to your course, putting you in control of how you deliver exams and training.

By adding SAM to your curriculum, you can:

- Reinforce your students' knowledge of key computer concepts and application skills with hands-on exercises.
- Allow your students to "learn by listening," with access to rich audio in their training
- Build hands-on computer concepts exams from a test bank of more than 200 skill-based concepts, windows, and applications tasks.
- Schedule your students' training and testing exercises with powerful administrative tools.
- Track student exam grades and training progress using more than one dozen student and classroom reports.

Teach your introductory course with the simplicity of a single system! You can now administer your entire Computer Concepts and Microsoft Office course through the SAM platform. For more information on the SAM administration system, SAM Computer Concepts, and other SAM products, please visit http://www.course.com/sam.

Distance Learning
Enhance your course with any of our online learning platforms. Go to www.course.com or speak with your Course Technology sales representative to find the platform or the content that's right for you.

www.course.com/NewPerspectives

About This Book

This book provides comprehensive instruction in basic to advanced concepts of XML, using a practical, step-by-step approach.

- Teaches students XML using a simple text editor and Web browsers to view the completed document
- Allows students to work with different XML vocabularies including XHTML, MathML, and RSS
- Shows students how to validate XML documents using DTDs and schemas
- Presents how to use CSS, XSLT, and XPath to transform XML documents into a variety of output formats
- Covers data binding and the Document Object Model under both the W3C and Internet Explorer DOMs
- Includes an enhanced Online Companion with additional material
- Visit www.course.com/carey to find the latest information on best-selling products by Patrick Carey

Acknowledgments

I would like to thank the people who worked so hard to make this book possible. Special thanks to Sasha Vodnik for his excellent suggestions and ideas in developing this material and to Donna Gridley, the Product Manager who worked so hard in overseeing this project, keeping it on task and on target. Other people at Course Technology who deserve credit are Rachel Goldberg, Executive Editor; Janine Tangney, Associate Product Manager; Cathie DiMassa, Senior Production Editor; and Quality Assurance Testers Burt LaFountain, Christian Kunciw, Susan Whalen, and Danielle Shaw.

Feedback is an important part of writing any book, and thanks go to the following reviewers for their ideas and comments: Lisa Macon, Valencia Community College; George Jackson, Collin County Community College; Allen Schmidt, Madison Area Technical College; Dorothy Harman, Tarrant County College; Cheryl Jordan, San Juan College; and Mary Lee Herrmann, Hagerstown Community College.

Special thanks also go to the members of our New Perspectives HTML Advisory Committee: Dr. Nazih Abdallah, University of Central Florida; Liz Drake, Santa Fe Community College; Ric Heishman, Northern Virginia Community College, Manassas Campus; George Jackson, Collin County Community College District; David Jampole, Bossier Parrish Community College; Eric Kisling, Indiana University; Diana Kokoska, University of Maine Augusta; William Lomerson, Northwestern State University–Natchitoches; Lisa Macon, Valencia Community College; David Ray, Jones County Junior College; Lo-An Tabar-Gaul, Mesa Community College; Sandi Watkins, Foothill College; and Zachary Wong, Sonoma State University.

I want to thank my wife Joan for her love and encouragement, and my six children: John Paul, Thomas, Peter, Michael, Stephen, and Catherine, to whom this book is dedicated.

—Patrick Carey

Brief Contents

Table of Contents

New Perspectives on
XML

Read This Before You Begin: Tutorials 1–4

To the Student

Data Files

To complete the Level I XML Tutorials (Tutorials 1–4), you need the starting student Data Files. Your instructor will either provide you with these Data Files or ask you to obtain them yourself.

The Level I XML Tutorials require the folders shown to complete the Tutorials, Review Assignments, and Case Problems. You will need to copy these folders from a file server, a standalone computer, or the Web to the drive and folder where you will be storing your Data Files.

Your instructor will tell you which computer, drive letter, and folder(s) contain the files you need. You can also download the files by going to www.course.com; see the inside back or front cover for more information on downloading the files, or ask your instructor or technical support person for assistance.

▼ **XML**
Tutorial.01x
Tutorial.02x
Tutorial.03x
Tutorial.04x

▼ **Student Online Companion**
The Student Online Companion can be found at www.course.com/carey. It contains additional information to supplement what you are learning in the text, as well as links to downloads and other tools.

To the Instructor

The Data Files are available on the Instructor Resources CD for this title. Follow the instructions in the Help file on the CD to install the programs to your network or standalone computer. See the "To the Student" section above for information on how to set up the Data Files that accompany this text.

You are granted a license to copy the Data Files to any computer or computer network used by students who have purchased this book.

System Requirements

If you are going to work through this book using your own computer, you need:

- **System Requirements** You will need a basic text editor, the current version of the Internet Explorer, Netscape, Firefox, or Safari Web browsers, and an XML validator. This book assumes that you will be using the free non-commercial version of Exchanger

XML to validate your XML documents, but you may use another application if that application is not available. Exchanger XML Lite can be run on most operating systems.

- **Data Files** You will not be able to complete the tutorials or exercises in this book using your own computer until you have the necessary starting Data Files.

Objectives

Session 1.1
- Describe the history and theory of SGML, HTML, and XML
- Define the limits of HTML as an information source
- Understand XML vocabularies
- Define well-formed and valid XML documents

Session 1.2
- Describe the basic structure of an XML document
- Create an XML declaration
- Work with XML comments
- Create XML elements and attributes
- Work with character and entity references
- Describe how XML handles character data, parsed character data, and white space

Session 1.3
- Work with XML parsers
- Understand how Web browsers work with XML documents
- Apply a style sheet to an XML document
- Create an XML processing instruction

Creating an XML Document

Developing an XML Document for the Jazz Warehouse

Case

The Jazz Warehouse

The Jazz Warehouse in Kansas City specializes in jazz recordings and collectibles. The store is famous for locating hard-to-find records, but also carries current releases.

The Jazz Warehouse has had recent success in offering items on the World Wide Web. Richard Brooks manages the Jazz Warehouse's Web site. Recently he has investigated XML as a potential means of organizing information about the store's collection and special offerings. He's learned that XML has some advantages in presenting structured content like the descriptions of some of the store's collectibles. Data stored in an XML document can be integrated with the store's Web site, and through the use of style sheets, he can present XML data in a way that would be attractive to potential customers.

Richard believes that the company will eventually move from a Web site that relies solely on HTML to a combination of HTML, XML, and style sheets. To move in that direction, he would like to start investigating how to display the company's recording inventory using XML. He has asked for your help in creating a small demonstration document for this purpose.

Student Data Files

▼tutorial.01x

▽ tutorial folder	▽ review folder	▽ case1 folder
jw.css	rare.txt	faq.txt
	jw2.css	faq.css

▽ case2 folder	▽ case3 folder	▽ case4 folder
hamlet.txt	stafftxt.xml	accounts.txt
plays.css	staff.css	delton.css

Session 1.1

Introducing XML

You and Richard meet to discuss how he can use XML to organize the content of the Jazz Warehouse Web site. First, Richard wants to know what XML is and how it can help his business.

XML stands for **Extensible Markup Language**. A **markup language** describes the structure and content of data. The term **extensible** means capable of being extended and modified. Thus XML is a markup language that can be extended and modified to match the needs of the author and the data content. The following short history lesson may help you better understand how XML fits in with the technologies of today.

A Short History of XML

XML has its roots in the **Standard Generalized Markup Language** (**SGML**), a language introduced in 1980 that describes the structure and content of any machine-readable information. SGML is **device-independent** and **system-independent**, meaning that documents written in SGML can be used, in theory, on almost any type of device under almost any type of operating system. SGML has been the chosen vehicle for creating structured documents in businesses and government organizations of all sizes. For example, think of the daunting task of documenting all of the parts used in a jet airplane, while at the same time creating a structure that engineers, mechanics, and developers can use to quickly retrieve and edit that information. SGML provides tools to manage documentation projects of this magnitude.

However, because of its power, scope, and flexibility, SGML is a difficult language to learn and apply. The official specification for SGML is over 150 pages long and covers some scenarios and cases that are rarely encountered by even the most experienced programmer. Thus the use of SGML is often limited to those organizations that can afford the cost and overhead of maintaining complex SGML environments. For example, SGML would not be suited for the World Wide Web, where Web page authors need a language that is easy to use.

SGML is more often used in creating **SGML applications**, which are markup languages based on the SGML architecture that can be applied to specific, not general, types of information. One such SGML application is **Hypertext Markup Language (HTML)**, which is used to create Web pages. Since HTML is an SGML application, it shares several of the properties of SGML, such as device-independence, but without the expensive overhead.

The success of the World Wide Web is due in no small part to HTML. HTML allows Web authors to easily design documents that can be displayed on different Web browsers running on a wide variety of operating systems. Creating Web sites with HTML is a straightforward process that does not require extensive programming experience. Since HTML files are simple text files, a Web page can be created and modified using no more than a basic text editor. This ease of use has made HTML popular with many different types of users. Millions of Web sites, including the Jazz Warehouse's Web site, were created with HTML, and it seems likely that HTML will continue to be an important language of the Web for a long time to come.

The Limits of HTML

Despite its popularity, HTML is not without limitations and flaws that frustrate Web developers. One of the major problems occurred when the Web became a primary source for information storage and retrieval, a task for which HTML was not designed. For example, if Richard wants to display information on a music title sold by the Jazz Warehouse, he might create a Web page containing the following HTML code:

```
<h2>Kind of Blue</h2>
<h3>Miles Davis</h3>
<ol>
    <li>So What (9:22)</li>
    <li>Freddie Freeloader (9:46)</li>
    <li>Blue in Green (5:37)</li>
    <li>All Blues (11:33)</li>
    <li>Flamenco Sketches (9:26)</li>
</ol>
```

This document has two headings: an h2 heading for the music title "Kind of Blue", and an h3 heading for the artist "Miles Davis". In addition, the document contains an ordered list describing each music track in the title, with the length of each track indicated in parenthesis. While the h2, h3, and other elements in this document provide information to the browser about how the page is structured, they don't tell us anything about the information the page contains. After all, this same document structure could be used in the following grocery page:

```
<h2>HiValue Foods</h2>
<h3>Fresh Produce</h3>
<ol>
    <li>Apples ($1.99/bag)</li>
    <li>Grapes ($1.49/bag)</li>
    <li>Onions ($1.99/bag)</li>
    <li>Red Leaf Lettuce ($0.50/bunch)</li>
    <li>Mushrooms ($0.79/carton)</li>
</ol>
```

As long as your only concern is placing text on a Web page, it makes no difference whether your page is about music or mushrooms. However, if Richard wants to implement a search engine that can quickly scan this document and extract information about the artist or music tracks, it would help if the document structure told the search engine something about the document content. Without being able to determine whether a particular tag refers to the title, music track, price, or artist, it's difficult to locate the precise piece of information that Richard might want.

A second limitation of HTML for data storage is that it is not extensible, and therefore can't be expanded to accommodate different types of information. In some cases, browser manufacturers have expanded the versions of HTML they support to offer new features, as Netscape did by introducing frames and as Internet Explorer did by offering inline frames. However, nothing in the language enables an individual Web author to expand the scope of HTML to meet the needs of a particular Web site.

One result of these browser modifications to HTML was a confusing mix of competing HTML standards—often one for each browser and, indeed, each browser version. While the innovations offered by Netscape, Internet Explorer, and others did much to increase the scope, power, and popularity of HTML, they did so at the expense of clarity. Web authors could not easily create Web sites without taking into account all of the browser differences.

A final limitation of HTML is that it can be inconsistently applied. For example, some browsers require all attribute values to be enclosed within quotes, while other browsers will accept attribute values with or without the enclosing quotation marks. Some browsers require all paragraphs to include an ending </p> tag, but others do not. While this lack of enforced standards can make it easier to write HTML code, it also means that code read by one browser may be rejected by another. Moreover, some browser code has become bloated as it has evolved to accommodate all of the various lapses in HTML syntax perpetrated by some Web authors and editing programs.

Thus, there were several reasons to look for a new language standard that would more easily extend to new information types, be customizable, and also require stricter adherence to the syntax of the language. This language was to be XML.

Exploring the Concepts behind XML

XML can be thought of as "SGML light." Like SGML, it is a language used to create other markup languages, but it does not have SGML's complexity and expansiveness. The standards for XML are developed and maintained by the **World Wide Web Consortium**, or **W3C**, an organization created in 1994 to develop common protocols and standards for sharing information on the World Wide Web. You can learn more about the W3C and view specifications for XML, HTML, and other languages at *http://www.w3.org*.

XML Design Goals

When it started planning the language, the W3C established ten primary design goals for XML:

1. XML must be easily usable over the Internet.
   Since the Web is one of the major sources of information sharing, XML had to be compatible with the major Web protocols such as HTTP and MIME.
2. XML must support a wide variety of applications.
   XML should not be limited to the Web: it must also be effective for other applications, such as databases, word processing, spreadsheets, financial transactions, and voice mail.
3. XML must be compatible with SGML.
   Because XML is a subset of SGML, many of the software tools developed for SGML should be adaptable for XML.
4. It must be easy to write programs that process XML documents.
   One of HTML's greatest strengths is its simplicity. XML should emulate this characteristic by making it easy for even nonprogrammers to write XML code.
5. The number of optional features in XML must be kept to the absolute minimum, ideally zero.
   SGML supports a wide range of optional features, which means that SGML software can be large and cumbersome. XML should remove this aspect of SGML, which would make it a more suitable development tool for Web sites, especially for those of small organizations like the Jazz Warehouse.
6. XML documents should be clear and easily understandable by nonprogrammers.
   Like HTML documents, XML documents should be text files. The contents of an XML document should follow a logical, tree-like structure. As you'll see later, XML authors can specify element names whose meanings are intuitively clear to anyone reading the XML code.
7. The XML design should be prepared quickly.

XML was only going to be a viable alternative to HTML if the Web community adopted it as a standard. For that to happen, W3C had to quickly settle on a design for XML before other competing standards emerged.

8. The design of XML must be exact and concise.

 The specifications for XML should not be as all encompassing and sprawling as SGML.

9. XML documents must be easy to create.

 For XML to be practical, XML documents needed to be as easy to create as HTML documents.

10. Terseness in XML markup is of minimal importance.

 As improvements in bandwidth have speeded up data exchange over the Internet, terseness (keeping document size small) was not as important as making document code understandable and easy to use.

Creating an XML Vocabulary

Like SGML, XML can be used to create **XML applications** or **vocabularies**, which are markup languages tailored to contain specific pieces of information. If Richard wanted to create a vocabulary for the works in the Jazz Warehouse music catalog, he might use XML to store the album information shown above in the following format:

```
<title>Kind of Blue</title>
<artist>Miles Davis</artist>
<tracks>
   <track length="9:22">So What</track>
   <track length="9:46">Freddie Freeloader</track>
   <track length="5:37">Blue in Green</track>
   <track length="11:33">All Blues</track>
   <track length="9:26">Flamenco Sketches</track>
</tracks>
```

We'll explore the structure and syntax of this document further in the next session, but even without knowing much about XML yet you can already infer a lot about the type of information this document contains. You can quickly see that this file contains data on a title named *Kind of Blue* by the artist Miles Davis and that the title has five tracks, starting with "So What" and concluding with "Flamenco Sketches." The track element also contains a length attribute that specifies the length of the track in minutes and seconds.

 The title, artist, tracks, and track elements in this example do not come from any particular XML specification; rather, they are custom elements that Richard might create specifically for one of the Jazz Warehouse documents.

 Richard could create additional elements describing things such as the selling price of the work, the publishing label, and the date the title was recorded. In this way, Richard can create his own XML vocabulary that deals specifically with music, track, and artist data.

Standard XML Vocabularies

If Richard wanted to share the vocabulary that he uses for the Jazz Warehouse with other music sellers, he might use a standard vocabulary that is accepted throughout the industry. As XML has grown in popularity, standard vocabularies have been developed across a wide range of disciplines.

For example, chemists need to describe chemical structures containing hundreds of atoms bonded to other atoms and molecules. To meet this need, an XML vocabulary called the **Chemical Markup Language** (**CML**) was developed, which codes molecular information. Figure 1-1 shows an example of a CML document used to store information on the ammonia molecule.

Figure 1-1 **Ammonia molecule described using CML**

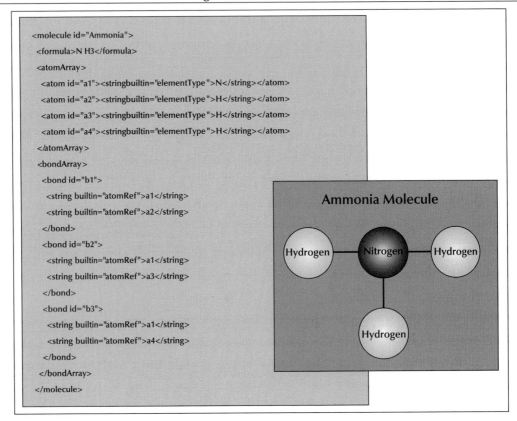

```
<molecule id="Ammonia">
 <formula>N H3</formula>
 <atomArray>
  <atom id="a1"><stringbuiltin="elementType">N</string></atom>
  <atom id="a2"><stringbuiltin="elementType">H</string></atom>
  <atom id="a3"><stringbuiltin="elementType">H</string></atom>
  <atom id="a4"><stringbuiltin="elementType">H</string></atom>
 </atomArray>
 <bondArray>
  <bond id="b1">
   <string builtin="atomRef">a1</string>
   <string builtin="atomRef">a2</string>
  </bond>
  <bond id="b2">
   <string builtin="atomRef">a1</string>
   <string builtin="atomRef">a3</string>
  </bond>
  <bond id="b3">
   <string builtin="atomRef">a1</string>
   <string builtin="atomRef">a4</string>
  </bond>
 </bondArray>
</molecule>
```

Another XML application, **MathML**, is used to store and evaluate mathematical operations, constants, and equations. XML vocabularies have even been developed that describe music notation and lyrics. Figure 1-2 lists a few of the many vocabularies that have been developed using XML.

XML vocabularies ◄ **Figure 1-2**

XML Vocabulary	Description
Channel Definition Format (CDF)	Automatic delivery of information from Web publishers to PCs, PDAs, cell phones, and other information devices
Chemical Markup Language (CML)	Coding of molecular and chemical information
Extensible Hypertext Markup Language (XHTML)	HTML written as an XML application
Mathematical Markup Language (MathML)	Presentation and evaluation of mathematical equations and operations
Musical Markup Language (MML)	Display and organization of music notation and lyrics
Open Financial Exchange (OFX)	Exchange of financial data between financial institutions, businesses, and consumers via the Internet
Real Simple Syndication (RSS)	Distribution of news headlines and syndicated columns
Synchronized Multimedia Integration Language (SMIL)	Editing of interactive audiovisual presentations involving streaming audio, video, text, and any other media type
Voice Markup Language (VoiceXML)	Creation of audio dialogues that feature synthesized speech, digitized audio, and speech recognition

One of the more important XML vocabularies is **XHTML** or the **Extensible Hypertext Markup Language**, which is a reformulation of HTML as an XML application. You'll examine some of the properties of XHTML as you learn more about XML in the upcoming tutorials.

You might find all of these acronyms and languages a bit overwhelming. Figure 1-3 shows the relationship between SGML, HTML, and XML, along with some of the various applications associated with SGML and XML.

Markup languages and vocabularies ◄ **Figure 1-3**

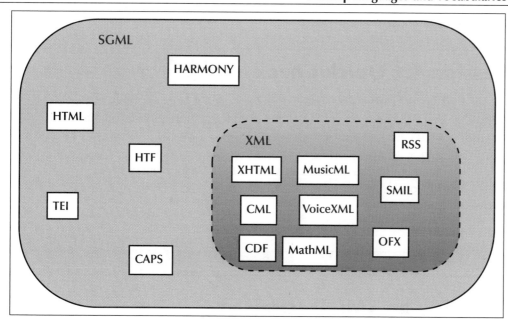

DTDs and Schemas

In order for different users to effectively share a vocabulary, rules have to be developed that specifically control what code and content a document from that vocabulary may have. This is done by attaching either a **document type definition** (**DTD**) or a **schema** to the XML document containing the data. Both DTDs and schemas contain rules for how data in a document vocabulary should be structured. For example, Richard can create a DTD or schema to require his documents to list the title, the artist, a list of tracks, and the price of each piece of music in the Jazz Warehouse inventory. DTDs and schemas are not required, but they can be helpful to ensure that your XML documents follow a specific vocabulary. The standard vocabularies listed in Figure 1-2 all have DTDs to ensure that people in a given industry or area all work from the same guidelines.

To create a DTD or a schema, you only need access to a text editor. Both DTDs and schemas can be accessed as external text files. DTDs can also be included within XML documents. You'll explore how to create DTDs and schemas in Tutorials 3 and 4.

Well-Formed and Valid XML Documents

To measure a document's compliance with XML rules, it can be tested against two standards: whether it is well-formed, and whether it is valid. A **well-formed document** contains no syntax errors and satisfies the general specifications for XML code as laid out by the W3C. At a minimum, an XML document must be well-formed or it will not be readable by programs that process XML code.

If an XML document is part of a vocabulary with a defined DTD or schema, it also needs to be tested to ensure that it satisfies the rules of that vocabulary. An XML document that satisfies the rules of a DTD or schema (in addition to being well-formed) is said to be a **valid document**. In this tutorial you'll look only at the basic syntax rules of XML in order to create well-formed documents. You'll learn how to create valid documents in the tutorials covering DTDs and schemas.

You're finished with your overview of XML's history and its relationship to other markup languages. In the next session, you'll start working on your first XML document for the Jazz Warehouse.

Review

Session 1.1 Quick Check

1. Define the term 'extensible.' How does the concept of extensibility relate to XML?
2. What is SGML and why was SGML not used for authoring pages on the World Wide Web?
3. What is an SGML application? Give one example.
4. Name three limitations of HTML that led to the development of XML.
5. What is a vocabulary?
6. What is MathML?

Session 1.2

Creating an XML Document

Now that you are familiar with the history and theory of XML, you are ready to create your first XML document. Like HTML documents, XML documents can be created with a basic text editor such as Notepad or TextEdit. More sophisticated XML editors are available that can make it easier to design documents, but they are not required for the Jazz Warehouse project.

The Structure of an XML Document

An XML document consists of three parts: the prolog, the document body, and the epilog. The **prolog** includes the following parts:

• An XML declaration indicating that the document is written in the language of XML
• Comment lines used to provide additional information about the document contents (optional)
• Processing instructions to be run by the program reading the XML document (optional)
• A document type declaration to provide information about the rules used in the document's vocabulary (optional).

After the prolog is the **document body**, which contains the document's content in a hierarchical tree structure. An optional **epilog** occurs after the document body and contains any final comments or processing instructions.

The XML Declaration

The first part of the prolog (and thus the first line in any XML document) is the **XML declaration** signaling to the program reading the file that the document is written in XML, and providing information about how that code is to be interpreted by the program. The syntax of the XML declaration is

```
<?xml version="version number" encoding="encoding type"
standalone="yes|no" ?>
```

where *version number* is the version of the XML specification being used in the document and *encoding type* identifies the character set used in the document.

The default version value is "1.0". You can also specify a version value of "1.1"; however, there is not a lot of difference between 1.0 and 1.1 specifications, and at the time of this writing, only a few programs completely support XML 1.1.

Because different languages use different character sets, the *encoding type* declaration allows XML to be used across a range of written languages. The default encoding scheme is "UTF-8", which matches most English language characters; however, if your XML document contains special characters such as ö or α, you may need to use an extended character set. For example, setting the encoding value to "ISO-8859-1" tells a program reading the document that characters from the ISO-8859-1 (Latin-1) character set are being used in the document; this character set includes many characters from non-English Western European languages.

Finally, the standalone attribute indicates whether the document contains any references to external files. If so, such references usually point to DTDs contained in external files. A standalone value of "yes" indicates that the document is self-contained, and a value of "no" indicates that the document requires additional information from external documents. The default value is "no".

A sample XML declaration therefore might appear as follows:

```
<?xml version="1.0" encoding="UTF-8" standalone="yes" ?>
```

This declaration indicates that the XML version is 1.0, the UTF-8 (English language) encoding scheme is being used, and the document is self-contained. If you instead entered the XML declaration

```
<?xml version="1.0" ?>
```

a processor would apply the UTF-8 encoding scheme and assume that the document has a standalone value of "no" by default.

It is important to remember that XML is case sensitive. You cannot change the code to uppercase letters. The code

```
<?XML VERSION="1.0" ENCODING="UTF-8" STANDALONE="YES" ?>
```

would result in an error because the code is entered in uppercase. In addition, you cannot drop the quotation marks around the values in a declaration. An XML declaration of

```
<?xml version=1.0 encoding=UTF-8 standalone=no ?>
```

would also result in an error because it is missing the quotation marks around the attribute values.

Reference Window **Creating an XML Declaration**

- To create an XML declaration, enter the following code in the first line of an XML document:
  ```
  <?xml version="version number" encoding="encoding type"
  standalone="yes|no" ?>
  ```
- where *version number* is the version of the XML specification being used in the document, *encoding type* identifies the character codes used in the document, and the standalone attribute indicates whether the XML parser needs to access external files when parsing the document.

Now that you've seen how to structure an XML declaration, you can start creating your first XML document by writing the prolog for an XML document to be used by the Jazz Warehouse.

To create the prolog:

1. Use your text editor to open a blank document.

   Trouble? Your instructor may direct you to use an XML editor. If you don't know how to use your text or XML editor, talk to your instructor or technical resource person.

2. Type the following line of code into your document:

   ```
   <?xml version="1.0" encoding="UTF-8" standalone="yes" ?>
   ```

3. Save your document as **jazz.xml** in the tutorial.01x/tutorial folder.

   Trouble? Windows Notepad automatically assigns the ".txt" extension to text files. To specify the ".xml" extension, type "jazz.xml" in the File name box, click "All Files" from the Save as Type drop-down list box, and then click the Save button.

   Trouble? If you use a word processor like Microsoft Word, you must save the document as a text file (with the ".xml" extension) and not in the word processor's native format.

Inserting Comments

Richard wants you to include information in the document about its purpose and contents. One way of doing this is with comments. Comments may appear anywhere in an XML document, although it's a good idea to insert a comment somewhere in the pro- log (after the XML declaration) to provide additional information about what the docu- ment will be used for and how it was created. Comments are ignored by programs reading the document and do not affect the document's content or structure.

XML comments follow the same syntax as HTML comments:

```
<!-- comment text -->
```

where `comment text` is the text of the comment. Add a comment to the jazz.xml file.

To add a comment to an XML document:

1. In your text editor, insert the following line below the XML declaration you just entered:

   ```
   <!-- This document contains data on Jazz Warehouse special
   offers -->
   ```

2. Save your changes to the jazz.xml document.

This completes your initial work on the prolog. Now you can focus your attention on the contents of the document body.

Working with Elements

The document body consists of the elements to be stored in the document. **Elements** are the basic building blocks of XML files, containing data to be stored in the document. The content is stored between an **opening tag** and a **closing tag**. The syntax of an XML ele- ment is

```
<element>content</element>
```

where `element` is the name given to the element, `content` represents the content of the element, `<element>` is the opening tag, and `</element>` is the closing tag. Element names are usually selected by XML authors to be descriptive of element contents. As you saw in the last session, Richard can store the name of an artist using the following line
of code:

```
<artist>Miles Davis</artist>
```

There are a few important points to remember about XML elements:

- Element names are case sensitive.
- Element names must begin with a letter or the underscore character (_) and may not contain blank spaces (e.g., you cannot name an element "First Name," but you can name it "First_Name").
- Element names cannot begin with the letters "xml" because those characters are reserved for special XML commands.
- The name in an element's closing tag must match the name in the opening tag.

For example, the following element text would result in an error because the opening tag is capitalized and the closing tag is not, meaning that they are not recognized as the opening and closing tags for the same element:

```
<ARTIST>Miles Davis</artist>
```

Empty Elements

Not all elements contain content. An **open element** or **empty element** is an element that contains no content. Empty element tags are entered using a **one-sided tag** obeying the syntax

```
<element />
```

where *element* is the name of the empty element. Note that an empty element consists of a single tag—there are no opening and closing tags.

If you are familiar with HTML, you already recognize empty elements as similar to HTML's collection of empty elements, such as the <hr /> tag for horizontal lines or the <img /> tag for inline graphics.

If empty elements contain no content, why use them in an XML document? One reason is to mark certain sections of the document for programs reading it. For example, Richard might want to use an empty element to distinguish one group of music titles from another. As you'll see later, empty elements can also contain attributes that can be used to store information.

Reference Window	**Creating XML Elements**

- To create an XML element, use the syntax
    ```
    <element>content</element>
    ```
  where *element* is the name given to the element, *content* represents the content of the element, *<element>* is the element's opening tag, and *</element>* is the closing tag.
- To create an empty or open element, use the syntax
    ```
    ```

Nesting Elements

In addition to content, elements can also contain other elements. An element contained within another element is said to be **nested**. In the following example, multiple track elements are nested within the tracks element:

```
<tracks>
     <track>So What (9:22)</track>
     <track>Freddie Freeloader (9:46)</track>
     <track>Blue in Green (5:37)</track>
     <track>All Blues (11:33)</track>
     <track>Flamenco Sketches (9:26)</track>
</tracks>
```

XML uses familial names to refer to the hierarchical relationships between elements. Thus, a nested element is a **child element** of its **parent element**. Elements that are side-by-side in a document's hierarchy are **sibling elements**. In the above code, each track element is a sibling of the other track elements, and each is a child of the tracks element.

One common syntactical error in creating an XML document is to improperly nest one element within another. XML does not allow the opening and closing tags of parent and child elements to overlap. Thus, the XML code

```
<title>Kind of Blue <artist>Miles Davis</title></artist>
```

would result in an error because the title element—the parent—is closed before the artist element, which is the child. You can think of a parent element as a container that must completely contain all of its child elements.

The Element Hierarchy

The familial relationship of parent, child, and sibling extends throughout the entire document body. All of the elements in the body are children of a single element called the **root element** or **document element.** Figure 1-4 shows a sample XML document with its hierarchy represented in a tree diagram. The root element in this document is the items element. Note that the XML declaration and comments are *not* included in the tree structure of the document body.

| Code for an XML document along with its corresponding tree diagram | Figure 1-4 |

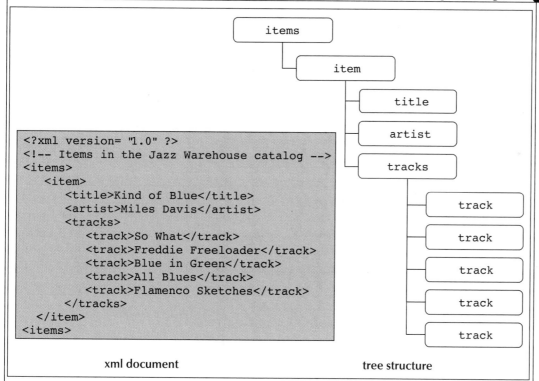

```
<?xml version= "1.0" ?>
<!-- Items in the Jazz Warehouse catalog -->
<items>
   <item>
      <title>Kind of Blue</title>
      <artist>Miles Davis</artist>
      <tracks>
         <track>So What</track>
         <track>Freddie Freeloader</track>
         <track>Blue in Green</track>
         <track>All Blues</track>
         <track>Flamenco Sketches</track>
      </tracks>
   </item>
<items>
```

xml document   tree structure

If an XML document does not include a root element, it is not considered well-formed and is rejected. The following document code is *not* well-formed because it lacks a root element containing all other elements in the document body:

```
<?xml version="1.0" ?>
<!-- Items in the Jazz Warehouse catalog -->
<title>Kind of Blue</title>
<artist>Miles Davis</artist>
<tracks>
   <track>So What</track>
   <track>Freddie Freeloader</track>
   <track>Blue in Green</track>
```

```
        <track>All Blues</track>
        <track>Flamenco Sketches</track>
</tracks>
```

Charting the Element Hierarchy

A quick way to view the overall structure of a document body is to chart the elements in a tree structure like the one shown in Figure 1-4. This can become confusing, however, when a single element has several children of the same type. For example, the tracks element in Figure 1-4 has five track elements within it. Other music titles may have a different number of track elements using this layout. It would be useful to have a general tree diagram that indicates whether a particular child element can occur zero, once, or several times within a parent. Figure 1-5 displays the shorthand code you'll see in the tree diagrams in this book to indicate the general structure of the document body.

| Figure 1-5 | Charting the number of child elements |

Symbol	Description	Chart	Interpretation
[none]	The parent contains a single occurrence of the child element.	item → title	An item can only have one title
?	The child element occurs once or not at all.	title → ? tracks	A title may or may not have a collection of tracks
*	The child element occurs any number of times.	items → * item	The items element can contain zero or more item elements
+	The child element occurs at least once.	tracks → + track	The tracks collection must contain at least one music track

Figure 1-6 shows how to apply these symbols to the XML document that you'll create for the Jazz Warehouse. According to this chart, the jazz document can contain any number of items, but each item needs to have one title, at least one artist, and may or may not list the music tracks. If there is a tracks collection it must contain at least one track.

Charting the jazz.xml document Figure 1-6

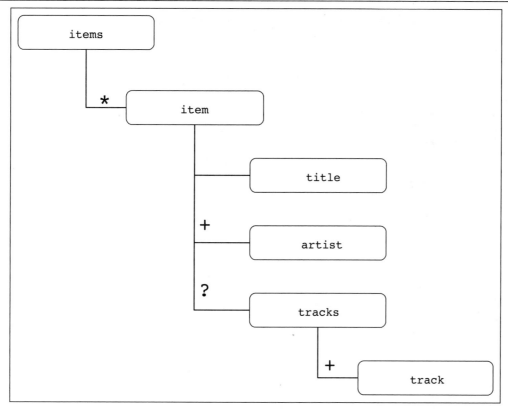

The symbols ?, *, and +, were not chosen at random. They are part of the code used in creating DTDs to validate XML documents. Using these symbols in a tree diagram will prepare you to learn more about DTDs in Tutorial 3.

Writing the Document Body

Now that you've reviewed some of the features of XML elements, you're ready to use them in an XML document. You have already begun creating the jazz.xml file, which describes the company's monthly specials. Richard would like you to add information on the music titles shown in Figure 1-7 to this file. XML allows authors to choose their own element names, so Richard has chosen appropriate names for the elements in his document.

Figure 1-7	Music titles for the Jazz Warehouse monthly specials

Title	Artist	Tracks
Kind of Blue	Miles Davis	So What
		Freddie Freeloader
		Blue in Green
		All Blues
		Flamenco Sketches
Cookin'	Miles Davis	My Funny Valentine
		Blues by Five
		Airegin
		Tune-Up
Blue Train	John Coltrane	Blue Train
		Moment's Notice
		Locomotion
		I'm Old Fashioned
		Lazy Bird

Add this information to the jazz.xml document using items as the root element of the document and placing each music title in a separate item element. You'll indent each child element a few spaces from its parent. This is a common practice to make XML code more readable and has no impact on how the code is interpreted.

To add these elements to the XML document:

1. Return to the **jazz.xml** document in your text editor.

2. Below the comment line, insert the following code for the document body:

```
<items>
   <item>
      <title>Kind of Blue</title>
      <artist>Miles Davis</artist>
      <tracks>
         <track>So What</track>
         <track>Freddie Freeloader</track>
         <track>Blue in Green</track>
         <track>All Blues</track>
         <track>Flamenco Sketches</track>
      </tracks>
   </item>
   <item>
      <title>Cookin'</title>
      <artist>Miles Davis</artist>
      <tracks>
         <track>My Funny Valentine</track>
         <track>Blues by Five</track>
         <track>Airegin</track>
         <track>Tune-Up</track>
      </tracks>
   </item>
   <item>
      <title>Blue Train</title>
      <artist>John Coltrane</artist>
      <tracks>
         <track>Blue Train</track>
         <track>Moment's Notice</track>
         <track>Locomotion</track>
```

```
            <track>I'm Old Fashioned</track>
            <track>Lazy Bird</track>
         </tracks>
      </item>
</items>
```

Figure 1-8 shows the complete contents of the jazz.xml file.

Document body for jazz.xml ◄ **Figure 1-8**

```
<?xml version="1.0" encoding="UTF-8" standalone="yes" ?>
<!-- This document contains data on Jazz Warehouse special offers -->

<items>
   <item>
      <title>Kind of Blue</title>
      <artist>Miles Davis</artist>
      <tracks>
         <track>So What</track>
         <track>Freddie Freeloader</track>
         <track>Blue in Green</track>
         <track>All Blues</track>
         <track>Flamenco Sketches</track>
      </tracks>
   </item>
   <item>
      <title>Cookin'</title>
      <artist>Miles Davis</artist>
      <tracks>
         <track>My Funny Valentine</track>
         <track>Blues by Five</track>
         <track>Airegin</track>
         <track>Tune-Up</track>
      </tracks>
   </item>
   <item>
      <title>Blue Train</title>
      <artist>John Coltrane</artist>
      <tracks>
         <track>Blue Train</track>
         <track>Moment's Notice</track>
         <track>Locomotion</track>
         <track>I'm Old Fashioned</track>
         <track>Lazy Bird</track>
      </tracks>
   </item>
</items>
```

► **3.** Save your changes to the file.

Working with Attributes

Every element in an XML document can contain one or more attributes. An **attribute** describes a feature or characteristic of an element. The syntax for adding an attribute to an element is

```
<element attribute="value"> ... </element>
```

or in the case of an empty element

```
<element attribute="value" />
```

Here, attribute is the attribute's name and *value* is the attribute's value. Attribute values are text strings, and thus must always be enclosed within either single or double quotes. For example, if Richard wants to include the length of each music track as an attribute of the track element, he could enter the following code:

```
<track length="9:22">So What</track>
```

Because they're considered text strings, attribute values may contain spaces and almost any character other than angle brackets (< and >). You can choose any name for an attribute, subject to the following constraints:

- The attribute name must begin with a letter or underscore (_).
- Spaces are not allowed in attribute names.
- Attribute names should not begin with the text string "xml".
- An attribute name can appear only once within an element.

Finally, like all of XML, attribute names are case sensitive. Thus, an attribute named "Length" is considered distinct from an attribute named "length".

| Reference Window | **Adding an Attribute to an Element** |

- To add an attribute to an element, use the syntax
  ```
  <element attribute="value"> ... </element>
  ```
  or
  ```
  <element attribute="value" />
  ```
  where *attribute* is the attribute's name and *value* is the attribute's value.

Richard has decided that he would like to include the length of each music track as an attribute of the track. Figure 1-9 shows the track lengths for the items in the jazz.xml file.

| Figure 1-9 | **Track lengths** |

Track	Length
So What	9:22
Freddie Freeloader	9:46
Blue in Green	5:37
All Blues	11:33
Flamenco Sketches	9:26
My Funny Valentine	5:57
Blues by Five	9:53
Airegin	4:22
Tune-Up	13:03
Blue Train	10:39
Moment's Notice	9:06
Locomotion	7:11
I'm Old Fashioned	7:55
Lazy Bird	7:03

Add each track length to the jazz.xml file as a length attribute of the corresponding track element.

To add the length attribute to each track element:

▶ 1. Locate the track element for the *So What* track, and within the opening tag insert the attribute **length = "9:22"**.

2. Insert the attribute **length = "9:46"** within the opening tag for the *Freddie Freeloader* track.

3. Add the length values to the remaining track elements in the document using Figure 1-9 as your guide. Figure 1-10 shows the revised contents of the jazz.xml file.

Length attributes added to document body **Figure 1-10**

```
<item>
    <title>Kind of Blue</title>
    <artist>Miles Davis</artist>
    <tracks>
        <track length="9:22">So What</track>
        <track length="9:46">Freddie Freeloader</track>
        <track length="5:37">Blue in Green</track>
        <track length="11:33">All Blues</track>
        <track length="9:26">Flamenco Sketches</track>
    </tracks>
</item>
<item>
    <title>Cookin'</title>
    <artist>Miles Davis</artist>
    <tracks>
        <track length="5:57">My Funny Valentine</track>
        <track length="9:53">Blues by Five</track>
        <track length="4:22">Airegin</track>
        <track length="13:03">Tune-Up</track>
    </tracks>
</item>
<item>
    <title>Blue Train</title>
    <artist>John Coltrane</artist>
    <tracks>
        <track length="10:39">Blue Train</track>
        <track length="9:06">Moment's Notice</track>
        <track length="7:11">Locomotion</track>
        <track length="7:55">I'm Old Fashioned</track>
        <track length="7:03">Lazy Bird</track>
    </tracks>
</item>
```

It's not always clear when to use attribute values rather than inserting a new element. For example, you could have placed the length information above as a child element of the track element using the following form:

```
<track>
    <track_title>So What</track_title>
    <length>9:22</length>
</track>
```

Some argue that attributes should never be used because they add to the document's complexity, and information would be more easily accessible by programs reading a document if it were placed within an element rather than an attribute.

A rule of thumb is that if all of the XML tags (and their attributes) were removed from a document, the remaining text would comprise the document's content or information. If, under this scenario, an attribute value is something you would want displayed, it should really be placed in an element. However, if the attribute is not necessary to understanding the document content, you can safely keep it as an attribute.

Another rule of thumb is that attributes should be used to describe data but not as data themselves. However, this can be a difficult distinction to make in most cases.

Using Character and Entity References

Now Richard would like you to include the selling price of each music title. Because the Jazz Warehouse has a sizable customer base in Great Britain, the XML document needs to include the selling price in both U.S. dollars ($) and British pounds (£). Figure 1-11 displays the cost of the CDs in each currency.

Figure 1-11	Music title prices

Title	US Price	UK Price
Kind of Blue	$11.99	£8.39
Cookin'	$7.99	£5.59
Blue Train	$8.99	£6.29

To add this information, you have to include the £ symbol in the XML document to represent British pounds. To insert characters like the £ symbol, which is not available on a standard U.S. keyboard, you use a **character reference**. The syntax for a character reference is

&#nnn;

where nnn is a character number from the ISO/IEC character set. The **ISO/IEC character set** is an international numbering system for referencing characters from virtually any language. Since it can be difficult to remember the character numbers for different symbols, some symbols can also be identified using an **entity reference** using the syntax:

&#entity;

where entity is the name assigned to the symbol.

Character references in XML work the same as character references in HTML. Figure 1-12 lists a few of the commonly used character and entity references.

Figure 1-12	Character and entity references

Symbol	Character Reference	Entity Reference	Description
©	&#169;		Copyright symbol
®	&#174;		Registered trademark symbol
™	&#153;		Trademark symbol
<	&#60;	&lt;	Less than symbol
>	&#62;	&gt;	Greater than symbol
&	&#38;	&amp;	Ampersand
"	&#22;	&quot;	Double quote
'	&#27;	&apos;	Apostrophe (single quote)
£	&#163;		Pound sign
€	&#128;		Euro sign
¥	&#165;		Yen sign

The appendix contains character and entity references for the first 256 characters in the ISO/IEC character set. Note that not all characters have both reference numbers and names.

Inserting Character and Entity References

- To insert a character reference into an XML document, use
  `&#nnn;`
  where *nnn* is a character reference number from the ISO/IEC character set.
- To insert an entity reference, use
  `&#entity;`
  where *entity* is a recognized entity name.

A common mistake in XML documents is to forget that the ampersand symbol (&) is interpreted by the XML processor as a character reference and not as a character. For example, the code

```
<artist>Miles Davis & John Coltrane</artist>
```

results in an error message because the & symbol is not followed by a recognized character reference number or entity name. To avoid this problem, you need to use the & or & character reference in place of the ampersand symbol:

```
<artist>Miles Davis &amp; John Coltrane</artist>
```

Character references are sometimes used to store the text of HTML code within an XML element. For example, to store the HTML tag <img src="logo.gif" /> in an element named htmlcode, you need to use character references to reference the < and > symbols contained in the HTML tag. The following code accomplishes this:

```
<htmlcode>&#60;img src="logo.gif" /&#62;</htmlcode>
```

The code

```
<htmlcode><img src="logo.gif" /></htmlcode>
```

would not give the same result because an XML processor would attempt to interpret <img src="logo.gif" /> as an empty element within the document and *not* as part of the document's content.

The character reference for the £ symbol is £. Use this character reference now to add British currency information to the jazz.xml document.

To insert price information into the document:

1. Within the jazz.xml file, insert the following elements directly after the title element for *Kind of Blue*:

   ```
   <priceus>US: $11.99</priceus>
   <priceuk>UK: &#163;8.39</priceuk>
   ```

2. After the title element for *Cookin'* add the following priceus and priceuk elements:

   ```
   <priceus>US: $7.99</priceus>
   <priceuk>UK: &#163;5.59</priceuk>
   ```

3. After the title element for *Blue Train* insert the following elements:

   ```
   <priceus>US: $8.99</priceus>
   <priceuk>UK: &#163;6.29</priceuk>
   ```

   Figure 1-13 shows the revised jazz.xml file.

Figure 1-13

Price information inserted using character references

```
<item>
    <title>Kind of Blue</title>
    <priceus>US: $11.99</priceus>
    <priceuk>UK: &#163;8.39</priceuk>
    <artist>Miles Davis</artist>
    <tracks>
        <track length="9:22">So What</track>
        <track length="9:46">Freddie Freeloader</track>
        <track length="5:37">Blue in Green</track>
        <track length="11:33">All Blues</track>
        <track length="9:26">Flamenco Sketches</track>
    </tracks>
</item>
<item>
    <title>Cookin'</title>
    <priceus>US: $7.99</priceus>
    <priceuk>UK: &#163;5.59</priceuk>
    <artist>Miles Davis</artist>
    <tracks>
        <track length="5:57">My Funny Valentine</track>
        <track length="9:53">Blues by Five</track>
        <track length="4:22">Airegin</track>
        <track length="13:03">Tune-Up</track>
    </tracks>
</item>
<item>
    <title>Blue Train</title>
    <priceus>US: $8.99</priceus>
    <priceuk>UK: &#163;6.29</priceuk>
    <artist>John Coltrane</artist>
    <tracks>
        <track length="10:39">Blue Train</track>
        <track length="9:06">Moment's Notice</track>
        <track length="7:11">Locomotion</track>
        <track length="7:55">I'm Old Fashioned</track>
        <track length="7:03">Lazy Bird</track>
    </tracks>
</item>
```

4. Save your changes to the file.

Understanding Text Characters and White Space

As you've seen from working on the jazz.xml file, XML documents consist only of text characters. However, text characters fall into three categories: parsed character data, character data, and white space. In order to appreciate how programs like browsers interpret XML documents, it's important to understand the distinctions between these categories.

Parsed Character Data

Parsed character data, or **pcdata**, consists of all those characters that XML treats as parts of the code of XML document. This includes characters found in

- the XML declaration
- the opening and closing tags of an element
- empty element tags
- character or entity references
- comments

Parsed character data is also found in other XML features that you'll learn about in later tutorials, such as processing instructions and document type declarations.

The presence of pcdata can cause unexpected errors to occur within a document. Since elements may contain other elements, XML treats any element content as potential pcdata. This means that symbols like &, <, or >—which are all used in creating markup tags or entity references—are parsed by programs reading the document. Thus, the line

```
<temperature> >100 degrees </temperature>
```

would result in an error: the ">" symbol in the temperature value is viewed as the end of a markup tag, and without any accompanying markup tag characters, the document is rejected as not well-formed. To avoid to this problem, you would have to replace the ">" symbol with either the character reference > or the entity reference >. The correct temperature value would then be entered as

```
<temperature> &gt;100 degrees </temperature>
```

Character Data

Once you remove parsed character data, the symbols remaining constitute a document's actual content, known as **character data**. Character data is not processed, but is treated as pure data content. One of the purposes of character and entity references is to convert pcdata into character data. Thus, when the program reading an XML document encounters an entity reference like > it converts it to the corresponding character data symbol—in this case, ">".

White Space

The third type of character that an XML document can contain is white space. **White space** refers to any space (from pressing the spacebar), new line character (from pressing the Enter key), or tab character (from pressing the Tab key) in a document. One of the questions in dealing with the text of an XML document is determining whether white space represents actual content or is used to make the code more readable. For example, the code in Figure 1-8 is indented to make it more readable, but this should not have any impact on the document content or structure.

If you're familiar with HTML, you may know that HTML applies **white space stripping**, in which consecutive occurrences of white space are treated as a single space. Thus, the HTML code

```
<p>This is     a
          paragraph</p>
```

is treated the same as

```
<p>This is a paragraph</p>
```

HTML uses white space stripping to allow HTML authors to format documents to be readable without affecting the appearance of documents in users' browsers. White space is treated slightly differently in XML, however. There is no white space stripping for element content, which means that the content of the XML element

```
<paragraph>This is     a
          paragraph</paragraph>
```

is treated as

```
This is     a
          paragraph
```

preserving both the new line character and all of the blank spaces. Be aware however, that is not the case when a document is read through the Internet Explorer browser. Internet Explorer transforms XML code into HTML, and in the process applies white space stripping to any element content.

When white space appears in places other than element content, XML treats it in the following manner:

- White space is ignored when it is the only character data between element tags (this allows XML authors to format their documents to be readable without affecting the content or structure).
- White space is ignored within a document's prolog and epilog and within any element tags.
- White space within an attribute value is not ignored and is treated as part of the attribute value.

In summary, these rules mean that white space is ignored unless it is part of the document's data.

Creating a CDATA Section

Sometimes an XML document needs to store large blocks of text containing the < and > symbols—for example, think of placing a tutorial about HTML in an XML document! In this case, it would be cumbersome to replace all of the < and > symbols with the < and > character references, and the code itself would be difficult to read.

As an alternative to using character references, you can place large blocks of text in a CDATA section. A **CDATA section** is a large of block text that XML treats as character data only. The syntax for creating a CDATA section is

```
<![CDATA[
      character data
]]>
```

A CDATA section may contain most markup characters, such as <, >, and &, and these characters are interpreted by XML parsers as text rather than markup commands. A CDATA section

- may be placed anywhere within in a document
- cannot be nested within other CDATA sections
- cannot be empty

The only sequence of symbols that may not occur within a CDATA section is "]]>" because this is the marker ending the CDATA section.

The following example shows an element named htmlcode containing a CDATA section used to store several HTML tags:

```
<htmlcode>
   <![CDATA[
      <h1>The Jazz Warehouse</h1>
      <h2>Your Online Store for Jazz Music</h2>
   ]]>
</htmlcode>
```

The text in this example is treated by XML as character data, not pcdata; thus, a processor would not read the <h1> and <h2> characters as element tags. You might find it useful to place any large block of text within a CDATA section to protect yourself from inadvertently inserting a character that would be misinterpreted by an XML processor (such as the ampersand symbol).

Richard would like you to insert a message element into the jazz.xml file that describes the purpose and content of the document. You decide to use a CDATA section for this task.

To create a CDATA section:

▶ **1.** After the <items> tag near the top of the jazz.xml file, insert the following lines of code:

```
<message>
<![CDATA[
    Here are some of the latest specials from the Jazz Warehouse.
    Please note that all Miles Davis & John Coltrane CDs will be
    on sale for the month of March.
]]>
</message>
```

Figure 1-14 shows the updated code for the jazz.xml file.

Code for the CDATA section ◀ **Figure 1-14**

```
<items>
    <message>
    <![CDATA[
        Here are some of the latest specials from the Jazz Warehouse.
        Please note that all Miles Davis & John Coltrane CDs will be
        on sale for the month of March.
    ]]>
    </message>
    <item>
        <title>Kind of Blue</title>
        <priceus>US: $11.99</price>
        <priceuk>UK: &#163;8.39</priceuk>
        <artist>Miles Davis</artist>
        <tracks>
            <track length="9:22">So What</track>
            <track length="9:46">Freddie Freeloader</track>
            <track length="5:37">Blue in Green</track>
            <track length="11:33">All Blues</track>
            <track length="9:26">Flamenco Sketches</track>
        </tracks>
    </item>
```

▶ **2.** Save your changes to the file.

▶ **3.** If you're going to take a break before working on the next session, you may close your text editor.

You've completed your work on Richard's XML document. In the next session, you'll learn how to display the document in a Web browser and how to format the output.

Session 1.2 Quick Check

Review

1. What are the three parts of an XML document?
2. What XML declaration would you enter to specify that your XML document supports version 1.0, uses the ISO-8859-1 encoding scheme, and does not require information from other documents?
3. What XML code would you enter to insert the comment "Values extracted from the JW database" into your XML document?
4. Why is the following code in error?

   ```
   <Title>Kind of Blue</title>
   ```
5. What is the root element?
6. What is an empty element?
7. Name three ways to insert the ampersand (&) symbol into the content of your XML document.
8. What is the difference between character data and parsed character data?

Session 1.3

Processing an XML Document

In the last session, you created your first XML document. In this session, you'll learn how to display the contents of that document.

XML Parsers

When an XML document is created, it needs to be evaluated by a program known as an **XML processor** or **XML parser**. Part of the function of a parser is to interpret a document's code and verify that it satisfies all of the XML specifications for document structure and syntax. XML parsers are strict. If one tag is omitted or a character is lowercase when it should be uppercase, a parser reports an error and rejects the document. This may seem excessive, but that rigidity was built into XML to eliminate the aspect of HTML that gave Web browsers wide discretion in interpreting HTML code. The end result is that XML code accepted by one parser should be accepted by other parsers. The other role of an XML parser is to interpret pcdata in a document and resolve any character or entity references.

Once an XML document is parsed, the XML parser may also be able to display the document's contents to the user. Figure 1-15 outlines the complete process from document creation to final presentation.

| Figure 1-15 | Parsing an XML document |

The author writes an XML document in an XML editor.

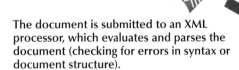
The document is submitted to an XML processor, which evaluates and parses the document (checking for errors in syntax or document structure).

The processed document is then displayed to the user in whatever format is used by the XML processor.

Web Browsers

Most current browsers include an XML parser of some type. Microsoft developed an XML parser called **MSXML** for its Internet Explorer browser. MSXML was introduced as an add-on for Internet Explorer version 4.0, and then was built directly into the Web browser for Internet Explorer versions 5.0 and above. The current release of MSXML is MSXML 4.0. Starting with version 6.0, Netscape also includes a built-in XML parser, as do Firefox and version 8.0 of Opera.

When an XML document is submitted to a browser, the browser first checks for syntax errors. If it finds none, the browser displays the contents of the document. Older browsers might display only the data content, while more current browsers display both the data and the document structure. Current browsers usually display XML documents in an expandable/collapsible outline format that allows users to hide nested elements. The various parts of the document may be color coded, making it easier to read and interpret.

To see how Richard's document is displayed, open it in your Web browser.

To display the jazz.xml file in a Web browser:

1. Start your Web browser and open the **jazz.xml** file from the tutorial.01x/tutorial folder.

   Figure 1-16 shows the contents of the file as it appears within Internet Explorer 6.0. Note that the character reference you used for the British pound (£) shows up as £ when the page is parsed by the browser.

   Trouble? If Internet Explorer displays a yellow information bar, click Allow Blocked Content, then click Yes in the Security Warning dialog box to fully display the file.

Figure 1-16 **Viewing an XML document in a browser**

```
<?xml version="1.0" encoding="UTF-8" standalone="yes" ?>
<!-- This document contains data on Jazz Warehouse special offers  -->
- <items>
  - <message>
    - <![CDATA[
            Here are some of the latest specials from the Jazz Warehouse.
            Please note that all Miles Davis & John Coltrane CDs will be
            on sale for the month of March.

      ]]>
    </message>
  - <item>
      <title>Kind of Blue</title>
      <priceus>US: $11.99</priceus>
      <priceuk>UK: £8.39</priceuk>
      <artist>Miles Davis</artist>
    - <tracks>
        <track length="9:22">So What</track>
        <track length="9:46">Freddie Freeloader</track>
        <track length="5:37">Blue in Green</track>
        <track length="11:33">All Blues</track>
        <track length="9:26">Flamenco Sketches</track>
      </tracks>
    </item>
  - <item>
      <title>Cookin'</title>
      <priceus>US: $7.99</priceus>
      <priceuk>UK: £5.59</priceuk>
      <artist>Miles Davis</artist>
    - <tracks>
        <track length="5:57">My Funny Valentine</track>
        <track length="9:53">Blues by Five</track>
        <track length="4:22">Airegin</track>
        <track length="13:03">Tune-Up</track>
      </tracks>
    </item>
  - <item>
      <title>Blue Train</title>
      <priceus>US: $8.99</priceus>
      <priceuk>UK: £6.29</priceuk>
      <artist>John Coltrane</artist>
    - <tracks>
        <track length="10:39">Blue Train</track>
        <track length="9:06">Moment's Notice</track>
        <track length="7:11">Locomotion</track>
        <track length="7:55">I'm Old Fashioned</track>
        <track length="7:03">Lazy Bird</track>
      </tracks>
    </item>
  </items>
```

Trouble? Depending on your browser and browser version, the jazz.xml file may look different from that shown in Figure 1-16.

Trouble? If you are running Internet Explorer for Windows, XML documents may be associated with Notepad or another application other than the Internet Explorer browser. To open an XML document in IE: 1) Go to Windows Explorer and locate the file; 2) Right-click the file icon and click Open With from the shortcut menu; 3) Click Internet Explorer from the list of available programs.

2. If you are running a browser that displays the contents of the document in outline form, click the **minus (–)** symbols in front of the <item> tags.

The browser collapses the elements nested within the <item> tags (see Figure 1-17).

Document hierarchy with item contents collapsed ◀ **Figure 1-17**

```
<?xml version="1.0" encoding="UTF-8" standalone="yes" ?>
<!-- This document contains data on Jazz Warehouse special offers  -->
- <items>
  - <message>
    - <![CDATA[
            Here are some of the latest specials from the Jazz Warehouse.
            Please note that all Miles Davis & John Coltrane CDs will be
            on sale for the month of March.

      ]]>
    </message>
  + <item>
  + <item>
  + <item>
  </items>
```

Click the plus symbols to redisplay contents of item elements

3. Click the **plus (+)** symbols to expand the content and display the contents of the <item> elements.

Having viewed the XML files with a Web browser, Richard would like to see how browsers check for errors. He asks that you intentionally introduce an error into the jazz. xml file to verify that the error is flagged by his browser.

To test for errors in the XML document:

1. If necessary, reopen the **jazz.xml** file in your text editor.

2. Change the last line of the file from </items> to **</ITEMS>**.

   This change violates the rule that all elements must have a starting and ending tag. The <items> tag at the top of the file has no corresponding ending </items> tag because XML is case sensitive.

3. Save your changes to the file and refresh or reload **jazz.xml** in your Web browser.

   If you browser contains a validating parser, it displays an error message similar to the one shown in Figure 1-18.

Error message produced by a document that is not well-formed ◀ **Figure 1-18**

The XML page cannot be displayed

Cannot view XML input using XSL style sheet. Please correct the error and then click the Refresh button, or try again later.

End tag 'ITEMS' does not match the start tag 'items'. Error processing resource 'file:///C:/Documents and Settings/...

```
</ITEMS>
--^
```

4. Return to the jazz.xml file in your text editor and change </ITEMS> back to **</items>**.

5. Save your changes to the file and then reload or refresh **jazz.xml** in your Web browser. Verify that the browser once again displays the document contents without errors.

Formatting XML Data

Richard appreciates your work on the XML document. He would like to share this type of information with other users and place it on the World Wide Web, but first he needs to have the data formatted in a visually attractive way. He does not want to display the contents in the default hierarchical format shown in Figure 1-16.

Unlike HTML documents, XML documents do not include any information about how they should be rendered. Rendering is determined solely by the parser processing the document. Because an XML document doesn't indicate how its data is to be formatted or displayed, you have to link the document to a style sheet if you want to have control over the document's appearance. The XML document and the style sheet are then combined by an XML parser to render a single formatted document (see Figure 1-19).

Figure 1-19 ▶ **Combining an XML document and a style sheet**

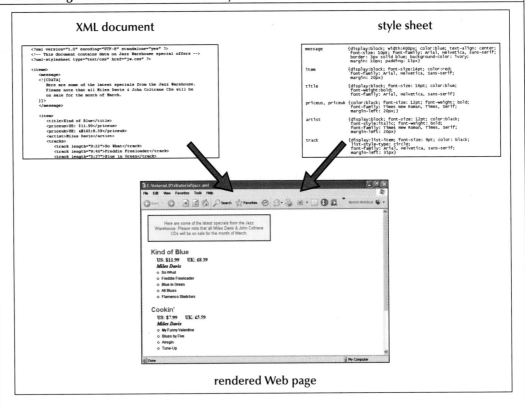

rendered Web page

Style Sheet Languages

Two main style sheet languages are used with XML documents. **Cascading Style Sheets** (**CSS**) is the standard developed for use with HTML on the World Wide Web. CSS is supported by most browsers and is relatively easy to learn and use. If you've used CSS with Web sites, you will find that you can easily apply your knowledge to XML documents.

Extensible Stylesheet Language (**XSL**) is a style sheet language developed for XML. XSL is actually an XML vocabulary that can be used to transform XML content into other document formats, such as HTML or formats used by word processors. While these features make XSL more powerful than CSS, it is not as easy to use as CSS, and does not have the same degree of browser support as CSS at this time. The outline form of Richard's document in Figure 1-16 is actually the XML document as transformed by an XSL style sheet. To override the default styles, you have to specify a different style sheet.

Applying a Style to an Element

Since Richard is interested in formatting the jazz.xml document for use only on the Web, you decide to apply a cascading style sheet to the document. CSS creates styles using the following syntax:

```
selector {attribute1:value1; attribute2:value2; ...}
```

where `selector` identifies an element (or a set of elements with each element separated by commas) from the XML document, and `attribute` and `value1`, `value2`, etc. are the style attributes and attribute values to be applied to the element. For example, to display the text of the artist element in a red boldface type, you would enter the following style declaration in a cascading style sheet:

```
artist {color:red; font-weight: bold}
```

Richard has already generated a style sheet for the elements of the jazz.xml file and stored the styles in an external style sheet named jw.css. The contents of the jw.css file are shown in Figure 1-20.

The jw.css style sheet ◄ Figure 1-20

```
message            {display:block; width:400px; color:blue; text-align: center;
                    font-size: 10pt; font-family: Arial, Helvetica, sans-serif;
                    border: 3px solid blue; background-color: ivory;
                    margin: 10px; padding: 15px}

item               {display:block; font-size:14pt; color:red;
                    font-family: Arial, Helvetica, Sans-serif;
                    margin: 20px}

title              {display:block; font-size: 16pt; color:blue;
                    font-weight:bold;
                    font-family: Arial, Helvetica, sans-serif}

priceus, priceuk   {color:black; font-size: 12pt; font-weight: bold;
                    font-family: Times New Roman, Times, serif;
                    margin-left: 20px; }

artist             {display:block; font-size: 12pt; color:black;
                    font-style:italic; font-weight: bold;
                    font-family: Times New Roman, Times, serif;
                    margin-left: 20px}

track              {display:list-item; font-size: 9pt; color: black;
                    list-style-type: circle;
                    font-family: Arial, Helvetica, sans-serif;
                    margin-left: 35px}
```

Inserting a Processing Instruction

Once you have created a style sheet, you create a link from the XML document to the style sheet through the use of a processing instruction. A **processing instruction** is a command that provides an instruction to XML parsers. Processing instructions have the general form

```
<?target instruction ?>
```

where `target` identifies the program (or object) to which the processing instruction is directed, and `instruction` is information that the document passes on to the parser for processing. Usually the instruction takes the form of attributes and attribute values. For example, the processing instruction to access and link the contents of an XML document to a style sheet is

```
<?xml-stylesheet type="style" href="url" ?>
```

where `style` is the type of style sheet the XML processor will be accessing and `url` is the name and location of the style sheet. Here, "xml-stylesheet" is the processing instruction's target and the other items within the tag are processing instructions that identify the type and location of the style sheet. For a cascading style sheet, `style` should be "text/css".

Reference Window

Attaching a Style Sheet to an XML Document

- To attach a cascading style sheet to an XML document, insert the following command within the XML document's prolog:

    ```
    <?xml-stylesheet type="text/css" href="url" ?>
    ```
    where `url` is the name and location of the CSS file.

Add a processing instruction to the jazz.xml file to access the styles in the jw.css Cascading Style Sheet.

To link the jw.css style sheet to the jazz.xml file:

1. Return to the **jazz.xml** file in your text editor.

2. Below the comment in the prolog, insert the following processing instruction (see Figure 1-21):

    ```
    <?xml-stylesheet type="text/css" href="jw.css" ?>
    ```

Figure 1-21 ▶ Adding a processing instruction

```
<?xml version="1.0" encoding="UTF-8" standalone="yes" ?>
<!-- This document contains data on Jazz Warehouse special offers -->
<?xml-stylesheet type="text/css" href="jw.css" ?>

<items>
   <message>
   <![CDATA[
       Here are some of the latest specials from the Jazz Warehouse.
       Please note that all Miles Davis & John Coltrane CDs will be
       on sale for the month of March.
   ]]>
   </message>
```

3. Close the file, saving your changes.

4. Reopen or refresh the **jazz.xml** file in your Web browser.

Figure 1-22 shows the contents of jazz.xml with the jw.css style sheet applied to the file's contents. Note that the browser uses the specified style sheet in place of its default styles.

The jazz.xml document formatted with the jw.css style sheet   **Figure 1-22**

Here are some of the latest specials from the Jazz Warehouse. Please note that all Miles Davis & John Coltrane CDs will be on sale for the month of March.

Kind of Blue
US: $11.99   UK: £8.39
Miles Davis
- So What
- Freddie Freeloader
- Blue in Green
- All Blues
- Flamenco Sketches

Cookin'
US: $7.99   UK: £5.59
Miles Davis
- My Funny Valentine
- Blues by Five
- Airegin
- Tune-Up

Blue Train
US: $8.99   UK: £6.29
John Coltrane
- Blue Train
- Moment's Notice
- Locomotion
- I'm Old Fashioned
- Lazy Bird

Trouble? If you are viewing this file using Internet Explorer 5.5 or earlier, the music tracks might not be displayed in a bulleted list.

You show Richard the formatted document and he tells you that it's just what he is looking for. Richard will show your work to the other members of his Web team, and they'll get back to you if they need more XML documents created in the future.

Session 1.3 Quick Check

Review

1. What is an XML parser?
2. What happens if you attempt to open an XML document that contains syntax errors in an XML parser?
3. What do you need in order to format the contents of an XML document?
4. What CSS style declaration would you enter to display the TITLE element in a bold font?
5. What is a processing instruction?
6. What XML code would you enter to display an XML document using the standard.css cascading style sheet?

Review

Tutorial Summary

In this tutorial you were introduced to the XML markup language. In the first session, you studied the background and theory behind XML. You learned how XML relates to SGML and HTML. You also saw how XML can be used to create vocabularies for specialized pieces of information. In the second session, you created your first XML document and learned how to work with elements and attributes. The second session also discussed how to work with character data, parsed character data, and white space in your XML documents. You also saw how to use entities to insert characters not found on your keyboard. The third session introduced the use of XML parsers and Web browsers to display the contents of an XML document. The tutorial concluded with a look at the use of external style sheets with XML.

Key Terms

attribute	Extensible Hypertext	schema
Cascading Style Sheets	Markup Language	SGML
CDATA section	Extensible Markup	SGML application
character data	Language	sibling element
character reference	Extensible Stylesheet	Standard Generalized
Chemical Markup	Language	Markup Language
Language	HTML	system-independent
child element	Hypertext Markup	valid document
closing tag	Language	W3C
CML	ISO/IEC character set	well-formed document
CSS	markup language	white space
device-independent	MathML	white space stripping
document body	MSXML	World Wide Web
document element	nested	Consortium
document type	one-sided tag	XHTML
definition	open element	XML
DTD	opening tag	XML application
element	parent element	XML declaration
empty element	parsed character data	XML parser
entity reference	pcdata	XML processor
epilog	processing instruction	XML vocabulary
extensible	prolog	XSL
	root element	

Practice

Practice the skills you learned in the tutorial using the same case scenario.

Review Assignments

Data files needed for this Review Assignment: jw2.css, rare.txt

Richard has returned with another document that he wants you to create for the Jazz Warehouse. This document contains a list of hard-to-find recordings that the Jazz Warehouse has recently acquired. Richard has saved the information in a text file and needs you to convert the document to XML. Figure 1-23 shows the structure of the document that he wants you to create.

Figure 1-23

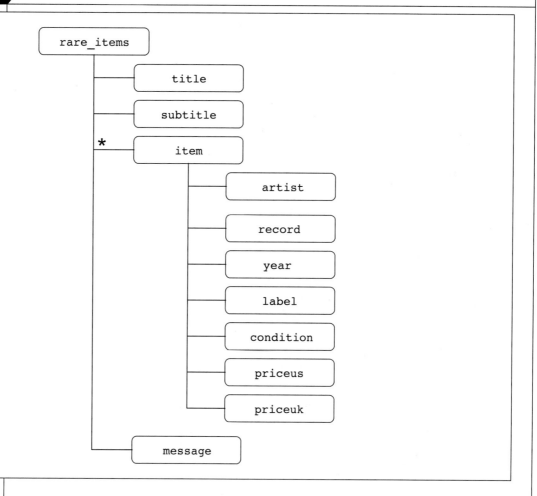

He also would like you to display the document using the jw2.css style sheet, which he is also providing. Figure 1-24 shows a preview of the rendered XML document.

Figure 1-24

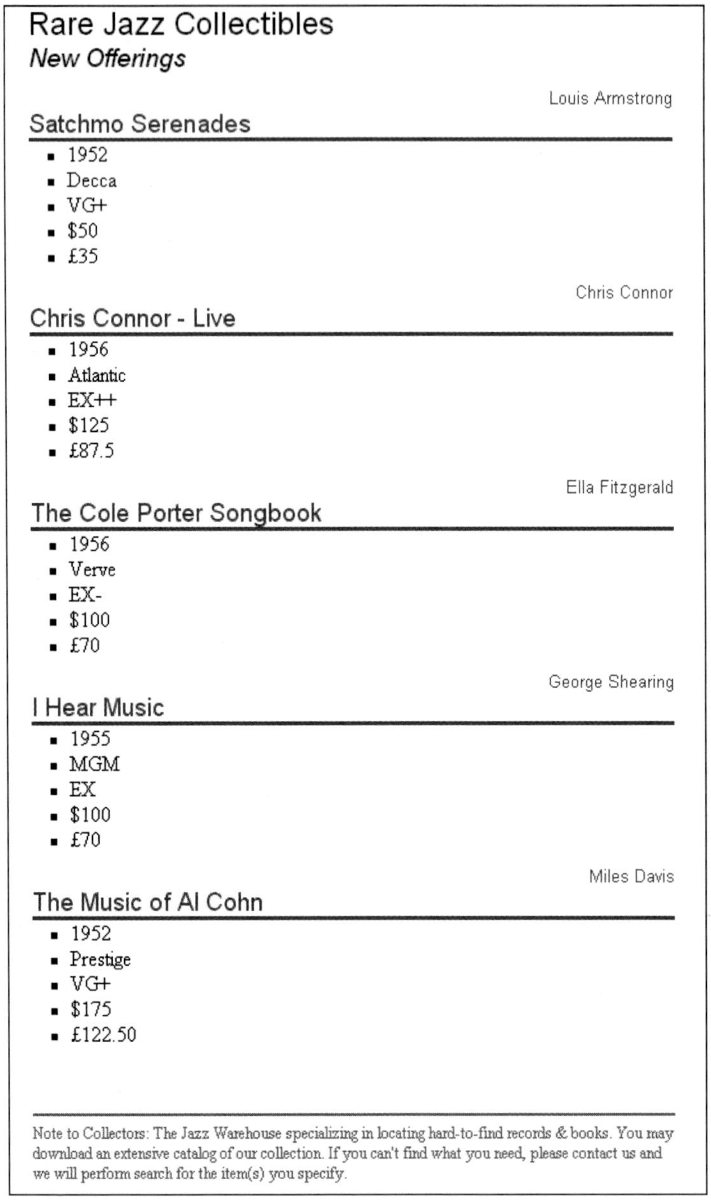

Rare Jazz Collectibles
New Offerings

Louis Armstrong

Satchmo Serenades
- 1952
- Decca
- VG+
- $50
- £35

Chris Connor

Chris Connor - Live
- 1956
- Atlantic
- EX++
- $125
- £87.5

Ella Fitzgerald

The Cole Porter Songbook
- 1956
- Verve
- EX-
- $100
- £70

George Shearing

I Hear Music
- 1955
- MGM
- EX
- $100
- £70

Miles Davis

The Music of Al Cohn
- 1952
- Prestige
- VG+
- $175
- £122.50

Note to Collectors: The Jazz Warehouse specializing in locating hard-to-find records & books. You may download an extensive catalog of our collection. If you can't find what you need, please contact us and we will perform search for the item(s) you specify.

To complete this task:

1. Using your text editor, open **rare.txt**, located in the tutorial.01x/review folder. Save the document as **rare.xml**.
2. Create a prolog at the top of the document, indicating that this is an XML document using the UTF-8 encoding scheme and that it is a standalone document.
3. Below the XML declaration, insert the following comment: "Jazz collectibles, recently acquired." Add additional comment lines containing your name as the page's author and the current date.
4. Enclose the document content in a root element named rare_items.
5. Create an element named title enclosing the title of the document, "Rare Jazz Collectibles".
6. Create an element named subtitle enclosing the subtitle "New Offerings."

7. There are five new recordings that the Jazz Warehouse needs to include in this document. Place each recording within an element named item and then include the following child elements:
    - name of the artist
    - name of the album
    - year the album was released
    - album label
    - condition of the album
    - selling price of the album in dollars
    - selling price of the album in pounds

   Enter element tags for each of these items using the following element names: artist, record, year, label, condition, priceus, and priceuk.

8. Richard was not able to type the symbols for British pounds in his original text document. Instead he used a capital "L". Replace each occurrence with a character reference to the British pound, £.

9. At the bottom of the file is a message to record collectors. Enclose this message in a CDATA section and place it within an element named message.

10. Add a processing instruction to the document's prolog to attach the document to the jw2.css style sheet.

11. Open **rare.xml** in your Web browser.

12. Submit your completed assignment to your instructor.

Case Problem 1

Apply

Use the skills you earned in this tutorial o create a FAQ docu- ment for a computer manufacturer

Data files needed for this Case Problem: faq.css, faq.txt

Jackson Electronics   Located in Santa Fe, NM, Jackson Electronics is a privately held manufacturer of consumer digital products such as scanners, printers, and digital cameras. Originally founded by Pete Jackson in 1948 as an office supply store, Jackson Electronics has thrived over the years with innovative thinking and effective use of cutting-edge technology. Alison Greely is one of the Webmasters for the Jackson Electronics Web site. Her primary responsibility is to maintain information on the frequently asked questions (FAQs) section of the site. Alison would like to convert her documents into XML format and has asked for your help. She has given you a text file containing FAQs for two of Jackson Electronics' products: the ScanMaster scanner and the DigiCam digital camera. Figure 1-25 shows the structure she would like to apply to the text in her file.

Figure 1-25

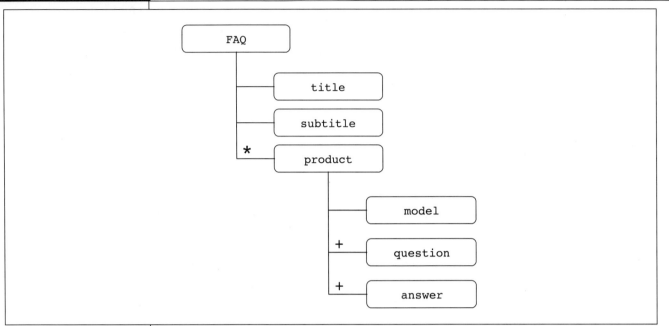

She would like this text file converted to an XML document and then linked to a cascading style sheet. Figure 1-26 shows a preview of the document rendered in a Web browser.

Figure 1-26

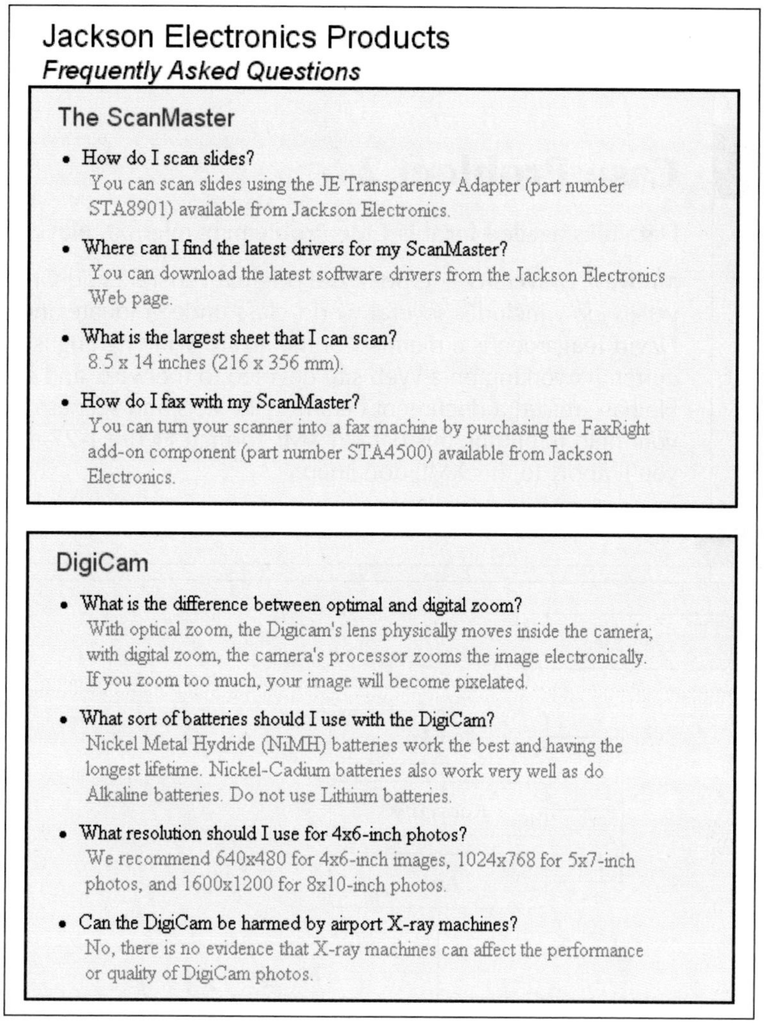

Jackson Electronics Products
Frequently Asked Questions

The ScanMaster

- How do I scan slides?
  You can scan slides using the JE Transparency Adapter (part number STA8901) available from Jackson Electronics.

- Where can I find the latest drivers for my ScanMaster?
  You can download the latest software drivers from the Jackson Electronics Web page.

- What is the largest sheet that I can scan?
  8.5 x 14 inches (216 x 356 mm).

- How do I fax with my ScanMaster?
  You can turn your scanner into a fax machine by purchasing the FaxRight add-on component (part number STA4500) available from Jackson Electronics.

DigiCam

- What is the difference between optimal and digital zoom?
  With optical zoom, the Digicam's lens physically moves inside the camera; with digital zoom, the camera's processor zooms the image electronically. If you zoom too much, your image will become pixelated.

- What sort of batteries should I use with the DigiCam?
  Nickel Metal Hydride (NiMH) batteries work the best and having the longest lifetime. Nickel-Cadium batteries also work very well as do Alkaline batteries. Do not use Lithium batteries.

- What resolution should I use for 4x6-inch photos?
  We recommend 640x480 for 4x6-inch images, 1024x768 for 5x7-inch photos, and 1600x1200 for 8x10-inch photos.

- Can the DigiCam be harmed by airport X-ray machines?
  No, there is no evidence that X-ray machines can affect the performance or quality of DigiCam photos.

To complete this task:

1. Using your text editor, open **faq.txt** from the tutorial.01x/case1 folder. Save the document as **faq.xml**.

2. Create a prolog at the top of the document, indicating that this is an XML document using version 1.0 of XML. You do not need to include any other information in the XML declaration.

3. After the XML declaration, insert the following comment: "ScanMaster and DigiCam FAQ." Add two more comments containing your name and the date.

4. Create a root element named FAQ.

5. Enclose the text "Jackson Electronics Products" in a title element, and set the text "Frequently Asked Questions" in an element named subtitle.

6. Create two product elements. Within each product element, insert a model element containing the name of the product.

7. Within the product elements, enclose each question in the text file within a question element.

8. Also within the product elements, enclose each answer in the document within an answer element, and place the text of those answers within a CDATA section.

9. Add a processing instruction to the prolog to apply the faq.css style sheet to this document.
10. Save your changes and open the **faq.xml** document in your Web browser.
11. Submit your completed project to your instructor.

Apply

Use the skills you learned in this tutorial to store data about Shakespeare in an XML document

Case Problem 2

Data files needed for this Case Problem: hamlet.txt, plays.css

Midwest University   One of the original Federal Land Grant Universities, Midwest University now includes several world-class undergraduate and graduate programs. Professor David Teagarden is a member of the award-winning English department at MU. He is currently working on a Web site devoted to the work and life of William Shakespeare. He has created a document detailing the acts and scenes of *Hamlet* and has asked for your help in putting this data in XML format. Figure 1-27 shows the tree structure that you'll apply to this XML document.

Figure 1-27

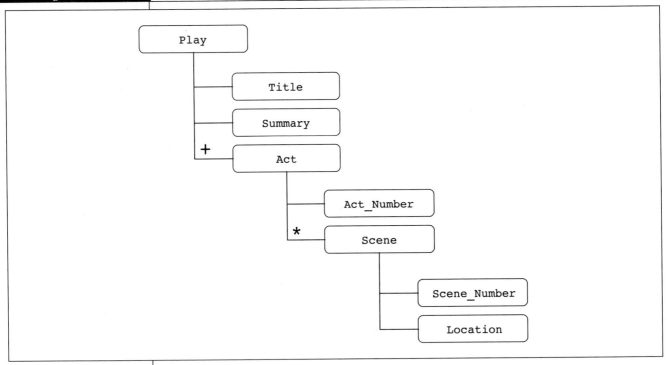

A style sheet has also been provided for you to display the *Hamlet* summary on the Web. Figure 1-28 shows a preview of the rendered Web page.

Figure 1-28

Hamlet

One of the greatest plays ever written in the English language, Hamlet is the story of the young Danish prince, Hamlet, who learns that his father was killed by his uncle and that the throne of Denmark is now held by this usurper and a murderer. Though filled with grief and the desire for revenge, Hamlet delays action until he is certain of his uncle's guilt. Hamlet hires a theater troupe to stage a play that re-enacts the events of his father's murder, hoping to determine the truth by watching the reaction of his uncle to the play. Hamlet's suspicions are confirmed when the king flees from the performance. As he moves to take revenge upon his uncle, Hamlet errs by killing the king's advisor, Polonius, and is banished from Denmark. Hamlet returns and kills the king, but he and his mother die by poison in the act. The play ends in tragedy but with the promise of immortality for Hamlet through his soldier's funeral and the recording of his story by his friend Horatio.

Act 1
- **Scene i:** Elsinore. A platform before the castle.
- **Scene ii:** A room of state in the castle.
- **Scene iii:** A room in Polonius' house.
- **Scene iv:** The platform.
- **Scene v:** Another part of the platform.

Act 2
- **Scene i:** A room in POLONIUS' house.
- **Scene ii:** A room in the castle.

Act 3
- **Scene i:** A room in the castle.
- **Scene ii:** A hall in the castle.
- **Scene iii:** A room in the castle.
- **Scene iv:** The Queen's closet.

Act 4
- **Scene i:** A room in the castle.
- **Scene ii:** Another room in the castle.
- **Scene iii:** Another room in the castle.
- **Scene iv:** A plain in Denmark.
- **Scene v:** Elsinore. A room in the castle.
- **Scene vi:** Another room in the castle.
- **Scene vii:** Another room in the castle.

Act 5
- **Scene i:** A churchyard.
- **Scene ii:** A hall in the castle.

To complete this task:

1. Start your text editor and open the **hamlet.txt** file from the tutorial.01x/case2 folder. Save the document as **hamlet.xml**.

2. Create a prolog at the top of the document, indicating that this is an XML document using version 1.0 of XML. You do not need to include any other information in the XML declaration.

3. Add comments that include your name and the current date.

4. Enclose the entire document content in a root element named Play.

5. Place the title of the play in an element named Title. The Title element should be the first child of the Play element.

6. Add an attribute to the Title element named "type". Set the value of the type attribute to "Tragedy".

7. Place the summary of the play in a CDATA section within a Summary element.

8. Place all of the information about each act of the play within an Act element. Place the name of each act (Act 1, Act 2, and so forth) within an Act_Number element.

9. Place all of the information about each scene of the play within a Scene element nested within each Act element. Place the name of each scene (Scene i, Scene ii, and so forth) within a Scene_Number element. Place the location of each scene within a Location element.

10. Create a processing instruction to attach the plays.css style sheet to this document.

11. Save your changes to the file and open it in your Web browser. Verify that the rendered page resembles that shown in Figure 1-28.

12. Submit your completed assignment to your instructor.

Case Problem 3

Challenge

Explore how to create a well-formed XML document

Data files needed for this Case Problem: staff.css, stafftxt.xml

Biotech, Inc. Located in Dallas, TX, Biotech, Inc. (BI) was created in April 2002 as a result of the merger of four smaller biotechnology research concerns. Linda Abrahams is a human resource representative for BI. Most recently, she has been entering employee data into an XML document and is running into a few problems. When she opened the document in her Web browser, the browser reported several syntax errors. Linda doesn't know how to solve the problem and has sought your help in cleaning up her code.

To complete this task:

1. Start your text editor and open the **stafftxt.xml** file from the tutorial.01x/case3 folder. Enter ***your name*** and ***the date*** in the comment section of the document. Save the file as **staff.xml**.

2. Open the **staff.xml** file in your Web browser.

Explore

3. Your Web browser reports syntax errors with the document. Using the information from the browser, locate and fix the errors. (*Note:* Your browser will report only one error at a time. After you fix one error and reload the file, the browser then displays the next error in the file, if one exists.)

4. Once you've fixed all of the syntactical errors, link the staff.xml document to the staff.css cascading style sheet.

5. Add a gender attribute to each Employee element in the document. Set the value of the gender attribute to "male" for male employees and "female" for female employees.

6. Reopen the staff.xml file in your Web browser.

Explore

7. Draw the tree structure for the contents of the staff.xml file.

8. Submit your completed assignment to your instructor.

Case Problem 4

Create

Test your knowledge of XML by creating an XML document for a life insurance company

Data files needed for this Case Problem: accounts.txt, delton.css

Delton Mutual Life Brian Carlson is an accounts manager for Delton Mutual Life and has created a text document containing personnel information for all the accounts in his portfolio. He would like your help in converting his text file to an XML document and then displaying that information in a Web page.

To complete this task:

1. Using the contents of the **accounts.txt** file, create an XML document named **accounts.xml** saved to the tutorial.01x/case4 folder.

2. The accounts.xml file should contain the following items:
   - The root element of the document should be named Accounts. The Accounts element should contain multiple occurrences of a child element named Client.
   - The Client element should have five child elements: Name, Address, Phone, E-mail, and Account_Total.
   - The Client element should have a single attribute named ID containing the customer ID number of each person (customer ID numbers begin with the letters "CS" followed by four digits).
   - The Name element should contain two child elements named First and Last, storing the first and last names of each person in Brian's accounts list.
   - The Address element should contain the following child elements: Street, City, State, and Zip, which contain the individual parts of the client's address.
   - The Phone element should contain the client's phone number.
   - The E-mail element should contain the client's e-mail address.
   - The Account_Total element should contain the current amount of money each client has invested with Delton Mutual Life.

3. Within the document's prolog, insert a comment describing the purpose of the document. Include your name and the date in the comment text.

4. Attach the accounts.xml file to a cascading style sheet named delton.css.

5. Open **accounts.xml** in your Web browser.

6. Submit your completed assignment to your instructor.

Review

Quick Check Answers

Session 1.1

1. Extensible means capable of being extended and modified. XML can be expanded by creating new elements and attributes for different pieces of information, and by allowing authors to create vocabularies tailored to specific information sources.

2. SGML stands for Standard Generalized Markup Language, which describes the structure and content of any machine-readable information and is device-independent and system-independent. While SGML was used to develop HTML, SGML is complicated and requires a complex environment, while Web page authors need a language that is easy to learn, manage, and implement.

3. An SGML application is a markup language created using SGML. HTML is one example of an SGML application.

4. HTML is not designed to describe information, HTML is not easily extended to different types of information, and HTML does not impose rigid standards for syntax and can therefore be inconsistently applied.

5. A vocabulary is a markup language tailored to contain a specific type of information.

6. An XML vocabulary used for presentation and evaluation of mathematical equations and operations

Session 1.2

1. the prolog, document body, and epilog
2. `<?xml version="1.0" encoding="ISO-8859-1" standalone="yes" ?>`
3. `<!-- Values extracted from the JW database -->`
4. The case of the opening and closing tags does not match.
5. The element at the top of the document hierarchy; all other elements in the document are children of the root element
6. An empty element contains no content, though it might contain one or more attributes whose values might be used by XML parsers.
7. Using a CDATA section, or using the `&#38;` or `&amp;` character references
8. Parsed character data, or pcdata, consists of all those characters that XML treats as parts of markup tags. Once you remove parsed character data, the symbols remaining constitute a document's actual content, known as character data.

Session 1.3

1. A program that reads an XML document and is able to test whether it is well-formed, and in some cases valid.
2. The parser reports an error and rejects the document.
3. A style sheet (usually a CSS or XSL style sheet)
4. `TITLE {font-weight: bold}`
5. A processing instruction is a command that provides instructions to be run by XML parsers.
6. `<?xml-stylesheet type="text/css" href="standard.css" ?>`

Objectives

Session 2.1
- Understand compound documents and the problem of name collision
- Declare a namespace for an XML vocabulary
- Apply a namespace to an element
- Create a default namespace
- Apply a namespace to an attribute

Session 2.2
- Declare a namespace within a CSS style sheet
- Apply a namespace to a style selector
- Use the escape character to apply a namespace to a selector
- Create a compound document containing XML and XHTML elements and attributes

Working with Namespaces

Combining XML Vocabularies in a Compound Document

Case

Jackson Electronics

Gail Oglund is an information technician at one of the assembly plants for Jackson Electronics, a manufacturer of computers and peripherals. Part of Gail's job is to design and create reports for manufacturing orders. Gail needs to compare the orders for printers, computers, and other products against the parts on hand needed to assemble them.

Recently the company has been looking at storing manufacturing information in XML documents. Several XML vocabularies have been developed for this task. One vocabulary is used to track the quantity of each part currently available at the assembly plant. Another vocabulary is used to record the assembled models that the plant must produce during the current week.

Gail would like to be able to produce a single document that combines information from both vocabularies. She also wants to display the document as a Web page on the plant's intranet, so the finished document needs to include elements from the XHTML vocabulary as well. Gail has come to you for help in producing a sample document that she can use as a model for future projects.

Student Data Files

▼tutorial.02x

▽ **tutorial folder**
- modtxt.css
- ordtxt.xml
- partstxt.css
- reptxt.htm
- + 2 XML documents
- + 1 CSS style sheet
- + 1 graphic file

▽ **review folder**
- filestxt.css
- pr205txt.htm
- printtxt.css
- + 2 XML documents
- + 1 CSS style sheet
- + 1 HTML file
- + 2 graphic files

▽ **case1 folder**
- agtxt.css
- conttxt.css
- reptxt.htm
- + 2 XML documents
- + 1 CSS style sheet
- + 1 graphic file

Session 2.1

Combining XML Vocabularies

At the Jackson Electronics assembly plant where Gail works, XML vocabularies have been developed for several tasks. One vocabulary was created to track the numbers of parts currently available at the plant, and another was created to store the orders that have to be assembled.

The tree structure of the vocabulary for tracking available parts is shown in Figure 2-1. The elements in this vocabulary include the title of each part, the part description, and the number of each part currently in stock. Gail has stored data on the parts required to assemble Jackson Electronics' Laser4C color printer in the parts.xml file.

| Figure 2-1 | Tree structure of the parts vocabulary |

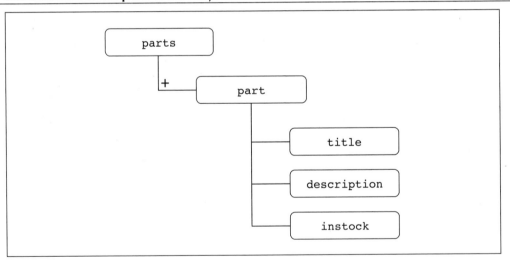

Gail has created an accompanying external CSS style sheet for this document in the parts.css file. Figure 2-2 shows the Web page that is generated when the style sheet is applied to the parts.xml file.

The style sheet and contents of parts.xml ◄ Figure 2-2

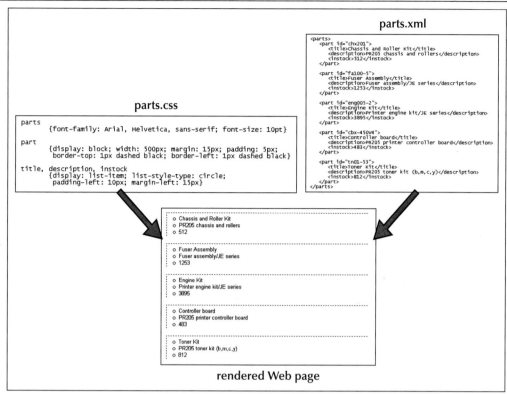

The tree structure for the vocabulary containing information on Jackson Electronics' models is shown in Figure 2-3. The vocabulary contains elements for a model's title, description, type, the number of models that need to be assembled, and the parts required for the assembly. Gail has used this vocabulary to create a document showing the order information for the Laser4C printer. She has stored this information in the model.xml file.

Tree structure of the model vocabulary ◄ Figure 2-3

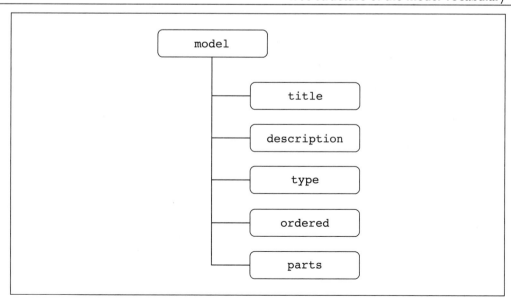

Gail has created a CSS style sheet for this document as well. Figure 2-4 shows the Web page that is generated when the style sheet is applied to the model.xml document.

Figure 2-4

The style sheet and content of the model.xml document

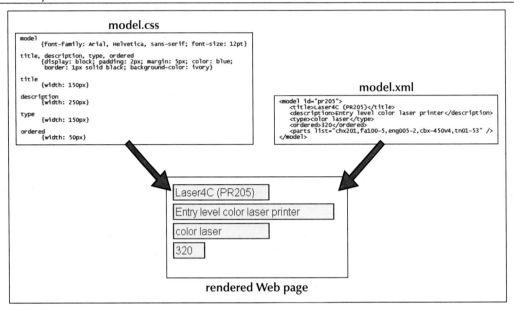

rendered Web page

Gail wants to combine her two XML documents in a single report so she can see at a glance how many models of the Laser4C printer are on order and how many of the necessary parts are available to meet those orders. She also wants her report to include the usual features found in Web pages, such as headings, tables, inline images, and descriptive text. Figure 2-5 shows a preview of how she wants the page to appear.

Proposed report page combining multiple vocabularies ◀ Figure 2-5

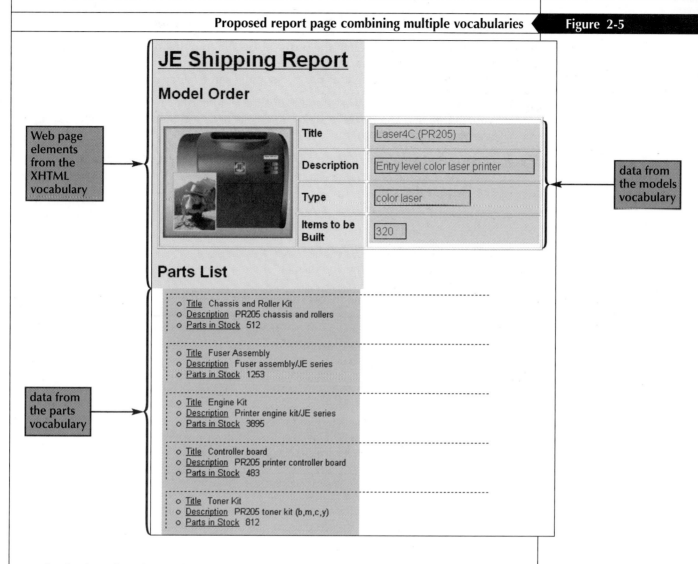

The final product that Gail wants to produce needs to include elements from three XML vocabularies: the parts vocabulary, the models vocabulary, and the XHTML vocabulary. All of these vocabularies need to coexist peacefully in the same document, and the various style sheets applied to the elements also need to work together. A document that combines several vocabularies is known as a **compound document**. Eventually, the compound document that Gail is preparing will be automatically generated by a script running off a server, but for now Gail wants you to create the prototype manually as a model for the programmers.

Creating a Compound Document

You'll start by combining the elements from just the parts and model vocabularies. The document combining these two vocabularies will be stored in a new file named order. xml. Since you'll also be working with the parts.css and model.css style sheets to complete Gail's project, you'll have to open those documents as well and link them to order. xml. Create all three files now.

To create the parts.css, model.css, and order.xml files:

► 1. Use your text editor to open the **partstxt.css** file from the tutorial.02x/tutorial folder. Enter *your name* and *the date* in the comment section at the top of the file. Close the file, saving it as **parts.css** in the same folder.

► 2. Open **modtxt.css** from the tutorial.02x/tutorial folder in your text editor. Enter *your name* and *the date* in the comment section, and then close the file, saving it as **model.css**.

► 3. Open **ordtxt.xml** from the tutorial.02x/tutorial folder in your text editor. Again enter *your name* and *the date* in the comment section at the top of the file. Save the file as **order.xml**.

► 4. At the bottom of the order.xml file, insert the following two processing instructions to link order.xml to the parts.css and model.css style sheets (see Figure 2-6):

```
<?xml-stylesheet type="text/css" href="parts.css" ?>
<?xml-stylesheet type="text/css" href="model.css" ?>
```

| Figure 2-6 | Linking to the parts.css and model.css style sheets |

```
<?xml version="1.0" encoding="UTF-8" standalone="yes" ?>
<!--
    New Perspectives on XML
    Tutorial 2
    Tutorial Case

    Jackson Electronics Order Report
    Author: Gail Oglund
    Date:   3/1/2008

    Filename:        order.xml
    Supporting Files: model.css, parts.css
-->

<?xml-stylesheet type="text/css" href="parts.css" ?>
<?xml-stylesheet type="text/css" href="model.css" ?>
```

Next you'll copy and paste the elements from the model.xml and parts.xml documents into the order.xml document. The structure of the order.xml document that you'll create is shown in Figure 2-7.

Structure of the order.xml document ◀ **Figure** 2-7

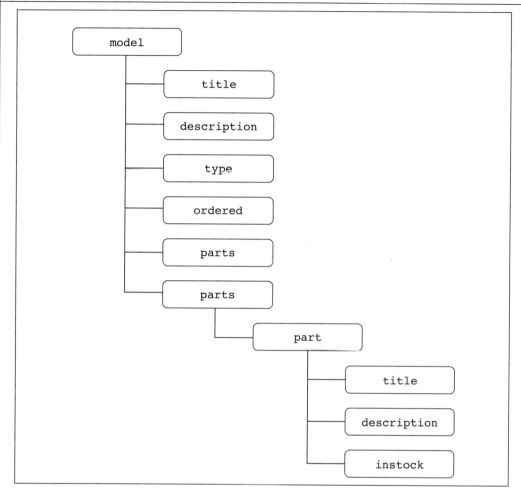

To copy and paste from the model.xml and order.xml files:

▶ **1.** In your text editor, open the **model.xml** file from the tutorial.02x/tutorial folder.

▶ **2.** Copy the contents of the document from the opening <model> tag to the closing </model> tag. Close the model.xml file.

▶ **3.** Return to the **order.xml** file in your text editor and paste the model.xml elements at the bottom of the file.

▶ **4.** In your text editor, open the **parts.xml** file from the tutorial.02x/tutorial folder.

▶ **5.** Copy the contents of the document from the opening <parts> tag to the closing </parts> tag. Close the parts.xml file.

▶ **6.** Return to the **order.xml** file and paste the parts elements into the document directly before the closing </model> tag. Figure 2-8 shows the revised contents of the order.xml file.

Figure 2-8 ▸ **The compound order.xml document**

```
<model id="pr205">
    <title>Laser4C (PR205)</title>
    <description>Entry level color laser printer</description>
    <type>color laser</type>
    <ordered>320</ordered>
    <parts list="chx201,fa100-5,eng005-2,cbx-450V4,tn01-53" />

    <parts>
        <part id="chx201">
            <title>Chassis and Roller Kit</title>
            <description>PR205 chassis and rollers</description>
            <instock>512</instock>
        </part>

        <part id="fa100-5">
            <title>Fuser Assembly</title>
            <description>Fuser assembly/JE series</description>
            <instock>1253</instock>
        </part>

        <part id="eng005-2">
            <title>Engine Kit</title>
            <description>Printer engine kit/JE series</description>
            <instock>3895</instock>
        </part>

        <part id="cbx-450V4">
            <title>Controller board</title>
            <description>PR205 printer controller board</description>
            <instock>483</instock>
        </part>

        <part id="tn01-53">
            <title>Toner Kit</title>
            <description>PR205 toner kit (b,m,c,y)</description>
            <instock>812</instock>
        </part>
    </parts>

</model>
```

Now check the appearance of this compound document in your Web browser.

To view the compound document:

▸ **1.** Save your changes to the **order.xml** file.

▸ **2.** Open **order.xml** in your Web browser. Figure 2-9 shows the rendered Web page.

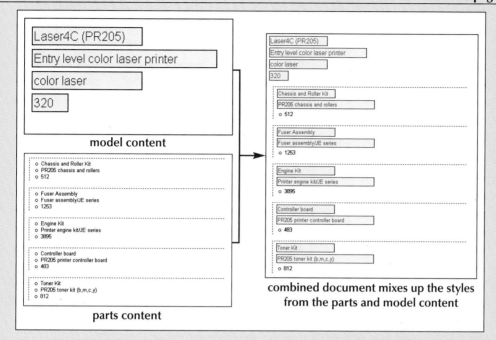

model content

parts content

combined document mixes up the styles
from the parts and model content

Trouble? If your browser does not display the rendered Web page, but instead displays the contents of the XML document in outline format, you may have made a mistake in entering the <?xml-stylesheet ...> processing instructions. Check your code against that shown in Figure 2-6.

Clearly, the styles applied to the compound document are quite different from the styles applied to the two individual documents shown earlier in Figures 2-2 and 2-4. Specifically, the styles used for each part's title and description have changed. What went wrong? The problem that Gail has run into by combining documents from two different XML vocabularies is called name collision.

Understanding Name Collision

You may have noticed in the structures of the parts and models vocabularies that several names are repeated. For instance, both vocabularies use the title and description names. In the parts vocabulary, these elements describe a particular part, while in the models vocabulary they are used to describe a fully assembled model. The parts element is also used in both vocabularies in different ways. In the parts vocabulary, the parts element contains a collection of part elements. In the models vocabulary, the parts element is an empty element containing an attribute listing the part element ids. The duplication of these element names is an example of **name collision**, which occurs when the same element name is used from different XML vocabularies within the same compound document (see Figure 2-10). When you combined the contents of the model.xml and parts.xml documents, the styles associated with the element names from the different vocabularies got mixed up, and the combined Web page looked nothing like the individual Web pages.

Figure 2-10 ▶ **Name collision in the order.xml document**

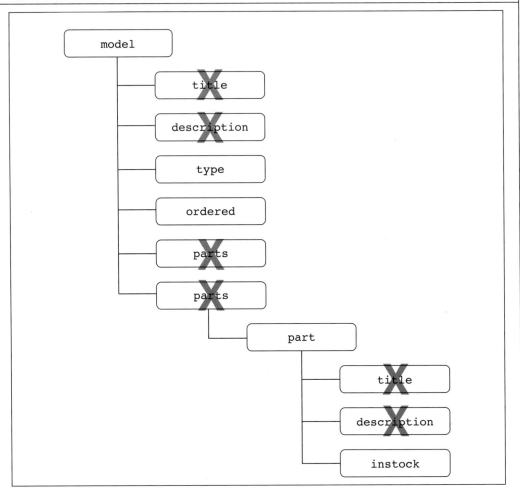

It is true that the plant could've been more careful in choosing the element names so as to prevent name collisions between different vocabularies. However, name collisions are often unavoidable. After all, one of the benefits of XML vocabularies is the ability to use simple element names to describe data. Creating complex element names to avoid name collision would eliminate one of the benefits of XML.

Moreover, there are other XML vocabularies such as XHTML over which Gail has no control. XHTML element names like title, name, first, last, or address are certain to be found in the thousands of XML vocabularies currently available.

Gail could avoid combining elements from different vocabularies in the same document in order to avoid name collisions; however, this would make XML a poor information tool.

Instead, Gail needs a mechanism that distinguishes elements from one vocabulary from elements in another vocabulary. XML provides such a mechanism with namespaces.

Working with Namespaces

A **namespace** is a defined collection of element and attribute names. For example, the collection of element and attribute names from Gail's models vocabulary could define a single namespace. Likewise, the element and attribute names from the parts vocabulary could constitute a different namespace. Applying a namespace to an XML document involves two steps:

1. Declaring the namespace
2. Identifying the elements and attributes within the document that belong to that namespace

You'll start by looking at how to declare a namespace.

Declaring a Namespace

To declare a namespace you add the following attribute to an element within an XML document:

```
xmlns:prefix="uri"
```

where *prefix* is a string of characters that you'll add to element and attribute names to associate them with the declared namespace, and *uri* is a **Uniform Resource Identifier (URI)**—a string of characters that uniquely identifies a resource, which in this case is the declared namespace. For example, the following code declares a namespace within the model element. The prefix of this namespace is "mod" and the namespace's URI is *http://jacksonelect.com/models*:

```
<model xmlns:mod="http://jacksonelect.com/models">
```

There is no limit to the number of namespace attributes that can be declared within an element. Once a namespace has been declared, it can be applied to any descendant of the element. Since you often want to make a namespace available to all elements within a document, some XML authors add all namespace declarations to the document's root element.

Declaring a Namespace	Reference Window

- To declare a namespace, add the following attribute to an element in the document:
  ```
  xmlns:prefix="uri"
  ```
  where `prefix` is the namespace prefix and `uri` is the URI of the namespace. The namespace is applied to the element containing the xmlns attribute, as well as to its descendant elements.
- To declare a default namespace, add the xmlns attribute without a prefix as follows:
  ```
  xmlns="uri"
  ```

Understanding URIs

Before exploring how to apply a declared namespace to a document, start by taking a closer look at the namespace's URI. The URI in the above code looks like a Web address you might use in creating a link to a Web site; however, that's not its purpose. The purpose of a URI is to provide a unique string of characters identifying a resource.

One version of a URI is a **Uniform Resource Locator** or **URL**, which is used to identify the location of a resource (such as a Web page) on the Web. There is a good reason to use URLs as a basis for identifying namespaces. If an XML vocabulary is made widely available, the namespace associated with that vocabulary needs to be unique. URLs serve as a built-in mechanism on the Web for generating unique addresses. For example, the home page of Gail's company, Jackson Electronics, has a Web address of

```
http://www.jacksonelect.com
```

providing customers a unique location to access all of Jackson Electronics' online services and products. Thus, if you want to ensure the uniqueness of any namespaces associated with the vocabularies developed for Jackson Electronics documents, it makes sense to use the Jackson Electronics Web address as a foundation. In the case of the models namespace, you could use the URL "http://jacksonelect.com/models". Note that the URL doesn't actually have to point to a real site on the Web; however, it's often helpful to place documentation at the Web page used in the URL.

Another type of URI is a **Uniform Resource Name** or **URN**. A URN provides a persistent name for a resource, independent of that resource's location. URNs take the form

```
urn:NID:NSS
```

where *NID* is the namespace identifier and *NSS* is a text string specific to that namespace. The *NID* indicates how to interpret the text string in the *NSS*. For example, the following URN uniquely identifies a book by its ISBN number:

```
urn:isbn:0-619-01969-7
```

If a URL can be thought of as a unique address of a specific location, a URN can be thought of as a unique name that is associated with a specific item. Currently URNs are rarely used in place of URLs, but this may change in the future.

Using URLs or URNs is widely accepted in declaring namespaces, but nothing prevents you from using almost any unique string identifier, such as "JacksonElectronics-ModelNS" or "PR205X299x". The main requirement is that a URI be unique so as not to be confused with the URIs of other namespaces.

After reviewing the material on namespaces, you and Gail agree to create namespaces for the parts and models vocabularies. You decide to declare both namespaces in the root element of the order.xml document, assigning "mod" as the prefix for the models namespace and "pa" as the prefix for elements in the parts namespace. The URIs for the two namespaces will be "http://jacksonelect.com/models" and "http://jacksonelect.com/parts" respectively. These URLs do not point to actual sites on the Web, but they will fulfill Gail's desire to have unique URIs for the namespaces.

To declare the models and parts namespaces:

1. Return to **order.xml** file in your text editor.

2. Within the opening <model> tag, insert the following namespace declarations (see Figure 2-11):

```
xmlns:mod="http://jacksonelect.com/models"
xmlns:pa="http://jacksonelect.com/parts"
```

Figure 2-11 | **Declaring the models and parts namespaces**

```
<model id="pr205" xmlns:mod="http://jacksonelect.com/models"
                   xmlns:pa="http://jacksonelect.com/parts">
   <title>Laser4C (PR205)</title>
   <description>Entry level color laser printer</description>
   <type>color laser</type>
   <ordered>320</ordered>
   <parts list="chx201,fa100-5,eng005-2,cbx-450v4,tn01-53" />
```

Now that you've declared the two namespaces, you have to indicate which elements in the document belong to those namespaces.

Applying a Namespace to Elements

To apply an XML namespace, you give elements and attributes qualified names. A **qualified name** or **qname** is an element name consisting of two parts: the **namespace prefix** that identifies the namespace, and the **local part** or **local name** that identifies the element or attribute within that namespace. An **unqualified name** is a name without a namespace reference. The general form for applying a qualified name to a two-sided tag is

```
<prefix:element> ... </prefix:element>
```

where *prefix* is the namespace prefix and *element* is the local part. Up to now, you've worked only with unqualified names. To change the element names in the model.xml document into qualified names, you could declare and apply the following namespace prefixes:

```
<mod:model xmlns:mod="http://jacksonelect.com/models">
    <mod:title>Laser4C (PR205)</mod:title>
    <mod:description>Entry level color laser printer</mod:description>
    <mod:type>color laser</mod:type>
    <mod:ordered>320</mod:ordered>
    <mod:parts list="chx201,fa100-5,eng005-2,cbx-450V4,tn01-53" />
</mod:model>
```

Note that the opening <model> tag includes both the namespace prefix and the xmlns attribute to declare the namespace. This indicates that the model element is also part of the namespace that it declares.

In Gail's order.xml document, the mod prefix is used for elements from the models namespace and the pa prefix is used for elements from the parts namespace. Apply these namespaces to the document.

To apply the models and parts namespaces:

▶ 1. Add the **mod:** prefix to the opening and closing tags of each element in the models namespace (see Figure 2-12).

Applying the models namespace prefix   Figure 2-12

```
<mod:model id="pr205" xmlns:mod="http://jacksonelect.com/models"
               xmlns:pa="http://jacksonelect.com/parts">
    <mod:title>Laser4C (PR205)</mod:title>
    <mod:description>Entry level color laser printer</mod:description>
    <mod:type>color laser</mod:type>
    <mod:ordered>320</mod:ordered>
    <mod:parts list="chx201,fa100-5,eng005-2,cbx-450V4,tn01-53" />

    <parts>
        <part id="chx201">
            <title>Chassis and Roller Kit</title>
            <description>PR205 chassis and rollers</description>
            <instock>512</instock>
        </part>

        <part id="fa100-5">
            <title>Fuser Assembly</title>
            <description>Fuser assembly/JE series</description>
            <instock>1253</instock>
        </part>

        <part id="eng005-2">
            <title>Engine Kit</title>
            <description>Printer engine kit/JE series</description>
            <instock>3895</instock>
        </part>

        <part id="cbx-450V4">
            <title>Controller board</title>
            <description>PR205 printer controller board</description>
            <instock>483</instock>
        </part>

        <part id="tn01-53">
            <title>Toner Kit</title>
            <description>PR205 toner kit (b,m,c,y)</description>
            <instock>812</instock>
        </part>
    </parts>

</mod:model>
```

> **2.** Add the **pa:** prefix to the opening and closing tags of each element in the parts namespace (see Figure 2-13).

Figure 2-13 | **Applying the parts namespace prefix**

```
<mod:model id="pr205" xmlns:mod="http://jacksonelect.com/models"
             xmlns:pa="http://jacksonelect.com/parts">
 <mod:title>Laser4C (PR205)</mod:title>
 <mod:description>Entry level color laser printer</mod:description>
 <mod:type>color laser</mod:type>
 <mod:ordered>320</mod:ordered>
 <mod:parts list="chx201,fa100-5,eng005-2,cbx-450v4,tn01-53" />

 <pa:parts>
   <pa:part id="chx201">
       <pa:title>Chassis and Roller Kit</pa:title>
       <pa:description>PR205 chassis and rollers</pa:description>
       <pa:instock>512</pa:instock>
   </pa:part>

   <pa:part id="fa100-5">
       <pa:title>Fuser Assembly</pa:title>
       <pa:description>Fuser assembly/JE series</pa:description>
       <pa:instock>1253</pa:instock>
   </pa:part>

   <pa:part id="eng005-2">
       <pa:title>Engine Kit</pa:title>
       <pa:description>Printer engine kit/JE series</pa:description>
       <pa:instock>3895</pa:instock>
   </pa:part>

   <pa:part id="cbx-450v4">
       <pa:title>Controller board</pa:title>
       <pa:description>PR205 printer controller board</pa:description>
       <pa:instock>483</pa:instock>
   </pa:part>

   <pa:part id="tn01-53">
       <pa:title>Toner Kit</pa:title>
       <pa:description>PR205 toner kit (b,m,c,y)</pa:description>
       <pa:instock>812</pa:instock>
   </pa:part>
 </pa:parts>

</mod:model>
```

> **3.** Save your changes to the order.xml file. If you intend to take a break before starting the next session, you may close the file now.

Since you've added several namespace prefixes to the various elements in the order. xml document, it's a good idea to verify that you have not added any syntax errors to the file. You can do this by reloading the file in your Web browser.

To check for syntax errors in the order.xml file:

> **1.** Reload or refresh **order.xml** in your Web browser.
>
> If you are using Netscape, Opera, or Firefox, the Web page should look unchanged from that shown earlier in Figure 2-9. If you are running Internet Explorer, you should see the data content of the order.xml file without any formatting at all (see Figure 2-14).

Figure 2-14 | **The order.xml file as it appears in Internet Explorer Version 6.0**

Laser4C (PR205) Entry level color laser printer color laser 320 Chassis and Roller Kit PR205 chassis and rollers 512 Fuser Assembly Fuser assembly/JE series 1253 Engine Kit Printer engine kit/JE series 3895 Controller board PR205 printer controller board 483 Toner Kit PR205 toner kit (b,m,c,y) 812

> **Trouble?** If your browser reports a syntax error, you may have neglected to include all of the namespace prefixes shown in Figures 2-12 and 2-13. Return to the order.xml file in your text editor and verify that you have included all of the prefixes, including the prefixes in the closing tags.

▶ **2.** If you plan on taking a break before the next session, you may close your Web browser.

Applying a Default Namespace

While you used namespace prefixes for all of the elements in the order.xml document, this is not always required. You can declare a **default namespace** by omitting the prefix in the namespace declaration. Any descendant element or attribute is then considered part of this namespace unless a different namespace is declared within one of the child elements. Thus, the syntax to create a default namespace is

```
<element xmlns="uri"> ... </element>
```

To define the model namespace as the default namespace for model elements, for example, you could enter the following code:

```
<model xmlns="http://jacksonelect.com/models">
    <title>Laser4C (PR205)</title>
    <description>Entry level color laser printer</description>
    <type>color laser</type>
    <ordered>320</ordered>
    <parts list="chx201,fa100-5,eng005-2,cbx-450V4,tn01-53" />
</model>
```

In this case, all of the elements, including the model element, are considered to be part of the models namespace. The advantage of default namespaces is that they make the code easier to read because you do not have to add the namespace prefix to each element. The disadvantage, however, is that an element's namespace is not readily apparent from the code. Still, many compound documents use a default namespace that covers most of the elements in the document, with elements from other XML vocabularies assigned namespace prefixes.

Working with Attributes

Like an element name, an attribute can be qualified by adding a namespace prefix. The syntax to qualify an attribute is

```
<element prefix:attribute="value"> ... </element>
```

where *prefix* is the namespace prefix and *attribute* is the attribute name. For example, the following code assigns both the model element and id attribute to the same namespace:

```
<mod:model xmlns:mod="http://jacksonelect.com/models"
          mod:id="pr205">
...
</mod:model>
```

Unlike element names, there is no default namespace for attribute names. Default namespaces apply to elements, but not to attributes. An attribute name without a prefix is assumed to belong to the same namespace as the element that contains it. Thus, the id attribute in the following code is automatically assumed to belong to the models namespace, even though it lacks the mod prefix:

```
<mod:model xmlns:mod="http://jacksonelect.com/models"
          id="pr205">
...
</mod:model>
```

Since an attribute is automatically associated with the namespace of its element, why would you ever need to qualify an attribute name? In most cases you don't. The only exception occurs when an attribute from one namespace needs to be used in an element from another namespace. For example, XHTML uses the class attribute to associate elements belonging to a common group or class. You could attach the class attribute from the XHTML namespace to elements from other namespaces. Since the class attribute is often used in Cascading Style Sheets to apply common formats to groups of elements, using the class attribute in other XML elements would allow this feature of CSS to be applied to those elements as well.

For Gail's document, there is no need to assign attributes to namespaces, so you will not add this feature to the order.xml file.

Reference Window	**Applying a Namespace**

- To apply a namespace to an element, add the namespace prefix to the element's opening and closing tags:
  ```
  <prefix:element> ... </prefix:element>
  ```
  where *prefix* is the namespace prefix and *element* is the local part of the qualified element name. If no *prefix* is specified, the element is assumed to be part of the default namespace.
- To apply a namespace to an attribute, add the namespace prefix to the attribute name:
  ```
  <element prefix:attribute="value"> ... </element>
  ```
  where *attribute* is the attribute name. An attribute is by default part of the namespace of its associated element.

Gail is pleased with the work that you've done applying namespaces to her document, but she wonders why it has not had an effect on the appearance of the Web page in some of her browsers, and has entirely removed the formatting in Internet Explorer. In the next session, you'll address this problem by applying namespaces to the styles in CSS style sheets.

Review	# Session 2.1 Quick Check

1. What is a name collision?
2. What is a namespace? How do namespaces prevent the problem of name collisions?
3. What attribute would you add to a document's root element to declare a namespace with the URI "http://ns.doc.book" and the prefix "book"?
4. How would you modify the code "<author>David Stevens</author>" to indicate that the element belongs to the book namespace declared in the previous question?
5. What attribute would you add to the root element in Question 3 to make the book namespace the default namespace for the document?
6. How would you change the code "<book isbn="0-1969-7">Blue Moon</book>" to explicitly indicate that the isbn attribute belongs to the book namespace?

Session 2.2

Adding a Namespace to a Style Sheet

Having added namespaces to Gail's document, your next task is to add namespace support to the style sheets she designed. Recall from Tutorial 1 that to apply a CSS style to an XML element you use the following style declaration:

```
selector {attribute1:value1; attribute2:value2; ...}
```

where *selector* represents the name or names of elements in the XML document. Thus, to set the width of the title element, you could enter the following style declaration:

```
title {width: 150px}
```

If an element has a qualified name such as mod:title, you might be tempted to include the prefix in the selector name as follows:

```
mod:title {width: 150px}
```

However, this doesn't work for Cascading Style Sheets because CSS reserves the colon character for pseudo-elements and pseudo-classes. Instead, you have to declare a namespace in the style sheet and then reference that namespace in the selector.

Declaring a Namespace

To declare a namespace in a style sheet, you add the following rule to the style sheet file:

```
@namespace prefix url(uri);
```

where *prefix* is the namespace prefix and *uri* is the URI of the namespace. Both the prefix and URI must match the prefix and URI used in the XML document. Thus, to declare the models namespace in Gail's style sheet, you would add the following rule:

```
@namespace mod url(http://jacksonelect.com/models);
```

Note that the prefix (mod) and the URI (http://jacksonelect.com/models) match the prefix and URI you entered in the last session.

As with XML documents, the namespace prefix is optional. If the namespace prefix is omitted, then the URI in the @namespace rule is considered to be the default namespace for the selectors in the style sheet. Any @namespace rules in the style sheet must come after all @import and @charset rules and before any style declarations. If a namespace prefix is declared more than once, only the last instance is used in the style sheet.

Applying a Namespace to a Selector

Once you've declared a namespace in a style sheet, you can associate selectors with that namespace by adding the namespace prefix to each selector name using the syntax

```
prefix|selector {attribute1:value1; attribute2:value2; ...}
```

For example, the style declaration

```
mod|title {width: 150px}
```

applies the width style to all title elements that belong to the models namespace. You can also use the wildcard symbol (*) to apply a style to any element within a namespace or to elements across different namespaces. For example, the style declaration

```
mod|* {font-size: 12pt}
```

applies the font-size style to any element within the models namespace. Similarly, the declaration

```
*|title {width: 150px}
```

sets a width of 150 pixels to any element named title from any namespace. If you omit the namespace prefix from a selector, its style is also applied to all namespaces. Thus, the declaration

```
title {width: 150px}
```

would apply to all elements named title in any namespace. This is the reason that the styles from the style sheets got mixed up in Gail's Web page. Because of the name collisions, the browser applies the style from one namespace to elements in another namespace. Now that you know how to distinguish namespaces, however, this will not be a problem.

Now that you've seen how to define a namespace for style sheets, you decide to add @namespace rules to the style sheets in the model.css and parts.css files.

To add namespaces to the model.css and parts.css style sheets:

1. Reopen the **model.css** style sheet in your text editor.

2. Directly after the opening comment tags, insert the following namespace declaration:

   `@namespace mod url(http://jacksonelect.com/models);`

3. Add the namespace prefix **modl** to each selector in the style sheet as shown in Figure 2-15.

Figure 2-15	Applying the models namespace to the style sheet

```
@namespace mod url(http://jacksonelect.com/models);

mod|model
       {font-family: Arial, Helvetica, sans-serif; font-size: 12pt}

mod|title, mod|description, mod|type, mod|ordered
       {display: block; padding: 2px; margin: 5px; color: blue;
        border: 1px solid black; background-color: ivory}

mod|title
       {width: 150px}

mod|description
       {width: 250px}

mod|type
       {width: 150px}

mod|ordered
       {width: 50px}
```

4. Save your changes to the file.

5. Open the **parts.css** style sheet in your text editor and, directly above the first style declaration, insert the following namespace declaration:

   `@namespace pa url(http://jacksonelect.com/parts);`

6. Add the namespace prefix **pal** to each selector in the style sheet (see Figure 2-16):

Applying the parts namespace to the style sheet ◀ Figure 2-16

```
@namespace pa url(http://jacksonelect.com/parts);

pa|parts
        {font-family: Arial, Helvetica, sans-serif; font-size: 10pt}

pa|part
        {display: block; width: 500px; margin: 15px; padding: 5px;
         border-top: 1px dashed black; border-left: 1px dashed black}

pa|title, pa|description, pa|instock
        {display: list-item; list-style-type: circle;
         padding-left: 10px; margin-left: 15px}
```

7. Save your changes to the style sheet.

Defining Namespaces with the Escape Character

Not all browsers support the use of the @namespace rule. When the specifications for XML 1.0 were first posted, there was no support for namespaces; thus, there were several competing proposals for adding namespace support to XML and CSS. A proposal which was not adopted but which was implemented in the Internet Explorer browser was to insert the backslash escape character (\) before the namespace prefix in CSS style sheets. Thus, for Internet Explorer to apply a style to an element from a particular namespace, you use the declaration

```
prefix\:selector {attribute1:value1; attribute2:value2; ...}
```

where *prefix* is the namespace prefix used in the XML document. For example, the declaration for the title element in the models namespace would appear as

```
mod\:title {width: 150px}
```

You can apply the same style to several elements in the namespace by using the * symbol. Thus, the declaration

```
mod\:* {width: 150px}
```

sets the width of all elements in the models namespace to 150 pixels.

Browsers like Firefox, Opera, and Netscape do not support this method with XML documents; thus, if you want to support the widest range of browsers, you have to duplicate the styles in the style sheet using both methods. Gail wants the style sheets to work across a wide range of browsers, so you agree to add style declarations using the escape character format.

To apply the escape character format to the style sheets:

1. Return to the **model.css** style sheet in your text editor.

2. Copy the six style declarations in the document.

3. Paste the copied declarations below the comment "Insert CSS namespace escape styles here."

4. Change the format of the namespace prefixes from | to **\:** in each of the pasted style declarations, as shown in Figure 2-17.

Figure 2-17 ▸ **Using the escape character in the model.css style sheet**

```
/* Insert CSS namespace escape styles here */

mod\:model
        {font-family: Arial, Helvetica, sans-serif; font-size: 12pt}
mod\:title, mod\:description, mod\:type, mod\:ordered
        {display: block; padding: 2px; margin: 5px; color: blue;
         border: 1px solid black; background-color: ivory}

mod\:title
        {width: 150px}

mod\:description
        {width: 250px}

mod\:type
        {width: 150px}

mod\:ordered
        {width: 50px}
```

▸ **5.** Close the model.css file, saving your changes.

▸ **6.** Return to the **parts.css** style sheet in your text editor and copy the three style declarations. Paste the copied text at the bottom of the file.

▸ **7.** Change the format of the pasted declarations from | to **\:** as shown in Figure 2-18.

Figure 2-18 ▸ **Using the escape character in the parts.css style sheet**

```
/* Insert CSS namespace escape styles here */

pa\:parts
        {font-family: Arial, Helvetica, sans-serif; font-size: 10pt}

pa\:part
        {display: block; width: 500px; margin: 15px; padding: 5px;
         border-top: 1px dashed black; border-left: 1px dashed black}

pa\:title, pa\:description, pa\:instock
        {display: list-item; list-style-type: circle;
         padding-left: 10px; margin-left: 15px}
```

▸ **8.** Close parts.css, saving your changes.

Now that you've added namespace support (using both methods) to the model.css and parts.css style sheets, test that your Web browser displays the appropriate styles for combined elements in the order.xml document.

▸ **9.** Use your Web browser to open the **order.xml** file.

As shown in Figure 2-19, styles for the elements in the models and parts namespaces are correctly applied. Compare this page with the one shown earlier in Figure 2-9, in which the styles were mixed up between the two namespaces.

Web page combining styles from both namespaces ◄ Figure 2-19

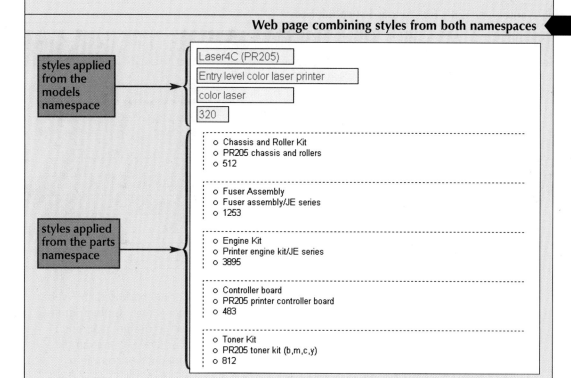

You show the Web page to Gail. She's pleased that you were able to work out the problems with the style sheets and the namespaces. The Web page as it currently stands contains all of the data that Gail wants; however, it does not contain any descriptive text. Gail wants you to add a third XML vocabulary to the document—one that includes page elements that describe the purpose and content of the report. To do this, you'll add elements from XHTML.

Combining Standard Vocabularies

So far you've worked only with the custom XML vocabularies that Gail has created for the Jackson Electronics assembly plant. The standard vocabularies that are shared throughout the world such as XHTML, RSS, or MathML, can also be combined within single documents. All of these standard vocabularies have unique URIs, some of which are listed in Figure 2-20.

Figure 2-20 **Namespace URIs for standard vocabularies**

Vocabulary	Namespace URI
CDF	http://www.microsoft.com/standards/channels.dtd
CML	http://www.xml-cml.org/dtd/cml1_0_1.dtd
MathML	http://www.w3.org/1998/Math/MathML
RSS 1.0	http://purl.org/rss/1.0/
SMIL	http://www.w3.org/2001/SMIL20/Language
SVG	http://www.w3.org/2000/svg
VoiceXML	http://www.w3.org/2001/vxml
XForms	http://www.w3.org/2002/xforms
XHTML	http://www.w3.org/1999/xhtml
XMLSchema	http://www.w3.org/2001/XMLSchema
XSLT	http://www.w3.org/1999/XSL/Transform

As XML continues to develop as the standard language for sharing markup data, Web browsers will extend and improve their ability to support documents that combine multiple vocabularies. At the moment, however, it's sometimes easiest to design XML documents that use multiple vocabularies for viewing on specialized browsers. For example, the W3C provides the Amaya Web browser, which can display documents combining elements from the MathML and XHTML vocabularies. Figure 2-21 demonstrates a single document that uses XHTML to display an h1 heading and two horizontal lines while also using elements from MathML to display the quadratic equation.

Figure 2-21 **A compound XHTML and MathML document in the Amaya browser**

```
<?xml version="1.0"?>
<html xmlns="http://www.w3.org/1999/xhtml"
      xmlns:ml="http://www.w3.org/1998/Math/MathML">
<head>
   <title>MathML with XHTML</title>
</head>
<body>
<h1>The Quadratic Equation</h1>
<hr />

<ml:mrow>
  <ml:mi>x</ml:mi>
  <ml:mo>=</ml:mo>
  <ml:mfrac>
    <ml:mrow>
      <ml:mrow>
        <ml:mo>-</ml:mo>
        <ml:mi>b</ml:mi>
      </ml:mrow>
      <ml:mo>&PlusMinus;</ml:mo>
      <ml:msqrt>
        <ml:mrow>
          <ml:msup>
            <ml:mi>b</ml:mi>
            <ml:mn>2</ml:mn>
          </ml:msup>
          <ml:mo>-</ml:mo>
          <ml:mrow>
            <ml:mn>4</ml:mn>
            <ml:mo>&InvisibleTimes;</ml:mo>
            <ml:mi>a</ml:mi>
            <ml:mo>&InvisibleTimes;</ml:mo>
            <ml:mi>c</ml:mi>
          </ml:mrow>
        </ml:mrow>
      </ml:msqrt>
    </ml:mrow>
    <ml:mrow>
      <ml:mn>2</ml:mn>
      <ml:mo>&InvisibleTimes;</ml:mo>
      <ml:mi>a</ml:mi>
    </ml:mrow>
  </ml:mfrac>
</ml:mrow>

<hr />
</body>
</html>
```

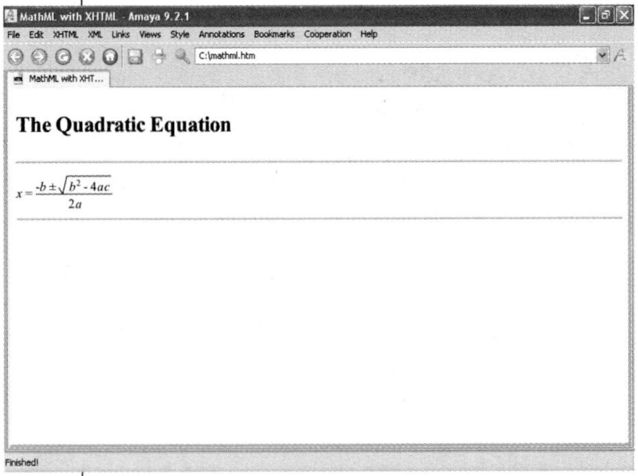

Other browsers like Jumbo can display compound documents that use XHTML and CML (Chemical Markup Language). These browsers all include built-in support and style sheets for the elements of those vocabularies. As you've seen, though, the elements of almost any XML document can be displayed in the current major browsers if you design style sheets to work with the elements of the XML vocabulary.

Combining XML and HTML

Gail has already entered the HTML code for the manufacturing report. She needs you to combine this document with the XML elements from the parts and model namespaces. Before you can create a compound document combining three different markup languages, however, you need to convert Gail's HTML file into an XHTML file. This can be done by adding an xml declaration at the top of the file and by setting the default namespace of the document to the XHTML vocabulary. As you saw in Figure 2-20, the URI of the XHTML namespace is http://www.w3.org/1999/xhtml.

To convert the HTML file to an XHTML file:

▶ 1. Use your text editor to open the **reptxt.htm** file from the tutorial.02x/tutorial folder. Enter *your name* and *the date* in the comment section at the top of the document. Save the file as **report.htm**.

▶ 2. Insert the following xml declaration as the very first line in the file (above the comment section):

```
<?xml version="1.0" encoding="UTF-8" standalone="yes" ?>
```

▶ 3. Add the following attribute to the opening <html> tag:

```
xmlns="http://www.w3.org/1999/xhtml"
```

Note that since the default namespace points to the URI for XHTML, every element in the document that lacks a namespace prefix is considered part of the XHTML vocabulary. This means you do not have to modify any of the element tags in Gail's document. Figure 2-22 shows the revised report.htm file.

Changing an HTML document to XHTML ◀ Figure 2-22

```
<?xml version="1.0" encoding="UTF-8" standalone="yes" ?>
<!--
    New Perspectives on XML
    Tutorial 2
    Tutorial Case

    Jackson Electronics Shipping Report
    Author:  Gail Oglund
    Date:    3/1/2008

    Filename:         report.xml
    Supporting Files: model.css, parts.css, pr205.jpg, report.css
-->

<html xmlns="http://www.w3.org/1999/xhtml">
<head>
    <title>Jackson Electronics Shipping Order</title>
    <link rel="stylesheet" href="report.css" type="text/css" />
</head>
```

Next you'll add the parts element to the report.htm file. Since this element comes from another namespace, you'll also add the namespace declaration to the <html> tag and insert a link element to link Gail's report to the parts.css style sheet.

To add the elements of the parts vocabulary:

▶ 1. Return to the **order.xml** file in your text editor.

▶ 2. Copy the parts element from the parts namespace, including all of the elements and contents it contains.

▶ 3. Return to the **report.htm** file in your text editor and paste the copied elements directly below the h2 heading "Parts List."

4. Add the following attribute to the opening <html> tag:

   ```
   xmlns:pa="http://jacksonelect.com/parts"
   ```

5. Below the link element that links the report.htm file to the report.css style sheet, insert the following link element:

   ```
   <link rel="stylesheet" href="parts.css" type="text/css" />
   ```

   Figure 2-23 shows the revised contents of the report.htm file.

Figure 2-23	Adding elements from the parts vocabulary

```
<html xmlns="http://www.w3.org/1999/xhtml"
      xmlns:pa="http://jacksonelect.com/parts">
<head>
   <title>Jackson Electronics Shipping Order</title>
   <link rel="stylesheet" href="report.css" type="text/css" />
   <link rel="stylesheet" href="parts.css" type="text/css" />
</head>

<body>
   <h1>JE Shipping Report</h1>
   <h2>Model Order</h2>

   <table border="1" cellpadding="5">
   <tr>
      <td rowspan="4"><img src="pr205.jpg" alt="" /></td>
      <th>Title</th>
      <td></td>
   </tr>
   <tr>
      <th>Description</th>
      <td></td>
   </tr>
   <tr>
      <th>Type</th>
      <td></td>
   </tr>
   <tr>
      <th>Items to be Built</th>
      <td></td>
   </tr>
   </table>

   <h2>Parts List</h2>

   <pa:parts>
      <pa:part id="chx201">
         <pa:title>Chassis and Roller Kit</pa:title>
         <pa:description>PR205 chassis and rollers</pa:description>
         <pa:instock>512</pa:instock>
      </pa:part>

      <pa:part id="fa100-5">
         <pa:title>Fuser Assembly</pa:title>
         <pa:description>Fuser assembly/JE series</pa:description>
         <pa:instock>1253</pa:instock>
      </pa:part>

      <pa:part id="eng005-2">
         <pa:title>Engine Kit</pa:title>
         <pa:description>Printer engine kit/JE series</pa:description>
         <pa:instock>3895</pa:instock>
      </pa:part>

      <pa:part id="cbx-450v4">
         <pa:title>Controller board</pa:title>
         <pa:description>PR205 printer controller board</pa:description>
         <pa:instock>483</pa:instock>
      </pa:part>

      <pa:part id="tn01-53">
         <pa:title>Toner Kit</pa:title>
         <pa:description>PR205 toner kit (b,m,c,y)</pa:description>
         <pa:instock>812</pa:instock>
      </pa:part>
   </pa:parts>

</body>
</html>
```

6. Save your changes and open **report.htm** in your Web browser.

   As shown in Figure 2-24, the Web page should show a combination of XHTML elements and content from the parts vocabulary.

JE Shipping Report

Model Order

	Title
	Description
	Type
	Items to be Built

Parts List

- Chassis and Roller Kit
- PR205 chassis and rollers
- 512

- Fuser Assembly
- Fuser assembly/JE series
- 1253

- Engine Kit
- Printer engine kit/JE series
- 3895

- Controller board
- PR205 printer controller board
- 483

- Toner Kit
- PR205 toner kit (b,m,c,y)
- 812

Trouble? If you are running the Opera browser, the title element in the parts list will not appear as a bulleted item.

Gail wants descriptive text added to each of the bulleted items in the parts list. She's already created a style for descriptive text enclosed within a span element. She wants you to add the appropriate span elements to each of the items in the parts list.

To describe the items in the parts list:

▶ **1.** Return to the **report.htm** file in your text editor.

▶ **2.** Scroll down to the first title element in the parts namespace. Directly after the opening <pa:title> tag, insert the text

```
<span>Title</span>
```

▶ **3.** Directly after the opening <pa:description> tag in the next line, insert the text

```
<span>Description</span>
```

▶ **4.** Directly after the opening <pa:instock> tag in the following line, insert the text

```
<span>Parts in Stock</span>
```

5. Repeats steps 2 through 4 for the four remaining parts in the list. Figure 2-25 shows the newly inserted text.

| Figure 2-25 | Inserting descriptive XHTML elements |

```
<pa:parts>
   <pa:part id="chx201">
      <pa:title><span>Title</span>Chassis and Roller Kit</pa:title>
      <pa:description><span>Description</span>PR205 chassis and rollers</pa:description>
      <pa:instock><span>Parts in Stock</span>512</pa:instock>
   </pa:part>

   <pa:part id="fa100-5">
      <pa:title><span>Title</span>Fuser Assembly</pa:title>
      <pa:description><span>Description</span>Fuser assembly/JE series</pa:description>
      <pa:instock><span>Parts in Stock</span>1253</pa:instock>
   </pa:part>

   <pa:part id="eng005-2">
      <pa:title><span>Title</span>Engine Kit</pa:title>
      <pa:description><span>Description</span>Printer engine kit/JE series</pa:description>
      <pa:instock><span>Parts in Stock</span>3895</pa:instock>
   </pa:part>

   <pa:part id="cbx-450V4">
      <pa:title><span>Title</span>Controller board</pa:title>
      <pa:description><span>Description</span>PR205 printer controller board</pa:description>
      <pa:instock><span>Parts in Stock</span>483</pa:instock>
   </pa:part>

   <pa:part id="tn01-53">
      <pa:title><span>Title</span>Toner Kit</pa:title>
      <pa:description><span>Description</span>PR205 toner kit (b,m,c,y)</pa:description>
      <pa:instock><span>Parts in Stock</span>812</pa:instock>
   </pa:part>
</pa:parts>
```

6. Save your changes and reload **report.htm** in your Web browser. As shown in Figure 2-26, descriptive text should now appear next to each item in the parts list.

| Figure 2-26 | Descriptive text in the parts list |

Parts List

- o <u>Title</u> Chassis and Roller Kit
- o <u>Description</u> PR205 chassis and rollers
- o <u>Parts in Stock</u> 512

- o <u>Title</u> Fuser Assembly
- o <u>Description</u> Fuser assembly/JE series
- o <u>Parts in Stock</u> 1253

- o <u>Title</u> Engine Kit
- o <u>Description</u> Printer engine kit/JE series
- o <u>Parts in Stock</u> 3895

- o <u>Title</u> Controller board
- o <u>Description</u> PR205 printer controller board
- o <u>Parts in Stock</u> 483

- o <u>Title</u> Toner Kit
- o <u>Description</u> PR205 toner kit (b,m,c,y)
- o <u>Parts in Stock</u> 812

Finally, you'll add information from the model elements to Gail's report. Once again, you'll have to insert a namespace declaration for these elements and add a link to the model.css style sheet.

To add elements from the models vocabulary:

► **1.** Return to the **report.htm** file in your text editor and add the following namespace declaration to the opening <html> tag:

```
xmlns:mod="http://jacksonelect.com/models"
```

► **2.** Add the following link to the document's head:

```
<link rel="stylesheet" href="model.css" type="text/css" />
```

► **3.** In the table cell directly after the Title table heading, insert the element

```
<mod:title>Laser4C (PR205)</mod:title>
```

► **4.** In the table cell directly after the Description table heading, insert the element

```
<mod:description>Entry level color laser printer</mod:description>
```

► **5.** In the table cell directly after the Type table heading, insert the element

```
<mod:type>color laser</mod:type>
```

► **6.** In the table cell directly after the "Items to be Built" table heading, insert the element

```
<mod:ordered>320</mod:ordered>
```

Figure 2-27 shows the newly added elements in the report.htm file.

Adding elements from the model vocabulary ◄ Figure 2-27

```
<html xmlns="http://www.w3.org/1999/xhtml"
      xmlns:pa="http://jacksonelect.com/parts"
      xmlns:mod="http://jacksonelect.com/models">
<head>
    <title>Jackson Electronics Shipping Order</title>
    <link rel="stylesheet" href="report.css" type="text/css" />
    <link rel="stylesheet" href="parts.css" type="text/css" />
    <link rel="stylesheet" href="model.css" type="text/css" />
</head>

<body>
    <h1>JE Shipping Report</h1>
    <h2>Model Order</h2>

    <table border="1" cellpadding="5">
    <tr>
        <td rowspan="4"><img src="pr205.jpg" alt="" /></td>
        <th>Title</th>
        <td><mod:title>Laser4C (PR205)</mod:title></td>
    </tr>
    <tr>
        <th>Description</th>
        <td><mod:description>Entry level color laser printer</mod:description></td>
    </tr>
    <tr>
        <th>Type</th>
        <td><mod:type>color laser</mod:type></td>
    </tr>
    <tr>
        <th>Items to be Built</th>
        <td><mod:ordered>320</mod:ordered></td>
    </tr>
    </table>
```

► **7.** Close the file, saving your changes.

► **8.** Reopen **report.htm** in your Web browser. Figure 2-28 shows the completed compound document.

Trouble? If you are using the Opera browser, your Web page will look slightly different than that shown in Figure 2-28.

Figure 2-28 | Completed compound report page

9. Close your Web browser.

You show the completed Web page to Gail, and she says it's exactly what she had in mind. She'll bring the completed documents to the programming staff so that they can work on automating the process. In the future, she hopes to have software in place that will automatically pull model and parts data from their source files and combine those elements with elements of the XHTML language; for now, this finished document is a good first step. She'll get back to you if she has future projects or questions about working with compound documents.

Review

Session 2.2 Quick Check

1. What rule do you add to a CSS style sheet to declare a namespace with the URI "http://ns.doc.book" and the prefix "book"?
2. What rule do you add to a CSS style sheet to make the namespace in Question 1 the default namespace for all selectors in the style sheet?
3. Using the namespace rule in Question 1, how would you modify the selector for the author element to indicate that it belongs to the book namespace?

4. How would you modify the selector in Question 3 to work with the Internet Explorer browser?

5. A document written in the SVG vocabulary has a root element named svg. How would you modify this element to indicate that the default namespace for the document is the SVG namespace?

6. You want to include elements from MathML and SVG in an XHTML document. How would you modify the root element, html, to indicate the presence of these three XML vocabularies? Assume that the default namespace is XHTML, and that elements from the MathML namespace have the prefix "MM" and elements from the SVG namespace have the prefix "SVG".

7. RSS is an XML vocabulary used for transferring syndicated news items. One RSS document has the following content:

```
<?xml version="1.0"?>
<rss version="2.0">
    <channel>
        <title>Jobless Rate Drops</title>
        <link>http://www.dol.gov/</link>
        <description>Unemployment dips to 4.9%</description>
        <language>en-us</language>
        <pubDate>Feb 3, 2008 04:00:00 GMT</pubDate>
    </channel>
</rss>
```

How would you modify this code to create a compound document that contains the following img element?

```
<img src="unempchart.jpg" alt="Unemployment Chart" />
```

Insert the img element directly below the pubDate element and indicate that the element belongs to the XHTML namespace by using "xhtml" as the namespace prefix. Be sure to add the XHTML namespace declaration to the root element of this document.

Review

Tutorial Summary

In this tutorial you learned how to create compound documents that combine elements and attributes from several XML vocabularies. In the first session, you learned how combining vocabularies in a single document can result in name collision. To solve the problem of name collision, you saw how to declare and apply namespaces to elements and attributes within a document. You also learned how namespaces can be associated with URIs to provide a unique identification for each vocabulary in a document. In the second session, you learned how to modify CSS style sheets to accommodate namespaces. The second session also showed you how to create an XHTML document that combines features from XHTML and other XML vocabularies.

Key Terms

compound document	qname	unqualified name
default namespace	qualified name	URI
local name	Uniform Resource	URL
local part	Identifier	URN
name collision	Uniform Resource	
namespace	Locator	
namespace prefix	Uniform Resource Name	

Practice

Practice the skills you learned in the tutorial using the same case scenario

Review Assignments

Data files needed for this Review Assignment: files.xml, filestxt.css, je.css, logo.jpg, pr205.jpg, pr205txt.htm, printer.xml, printtxt.css, temp.htm

Gail has talked to Jeff Drake about your work in creating compound documents involving several XML vocabularies. He has a problem similar to Gail's with his work on the Jackson Electronics Web site. The company has created several XML vocabularies for the Web site. One vocabulary contains descriptive information about the company's products. Another contains a list of downloadable files for updating drivers, software, and product firmware. Jeff wants to combine information from the two vocabularies into a single Web page along with elements from XHTML. Figure 2-29 shows a preview of the completed Web page.

Figure 2-29

Product

JE Laser4C

With a price appropriate for the home-office budget, the Jackson Electronics Laser4C is color laserjet printer suited for a high-end business. You'll enjoy the compact design that fits anywhere on your desktop and with a first page print speed of less than 20 seconds (in full color!) you won't be caught waiting for your latest flyer or business report.

$399.95

- BW Print Speed: 8 ppm
- Color Print Speed: 8 ppm
- BW Print Resolution: 600 x 600 dpi
- Color Print Resolution: 600 x 600 dpi
- Connectivity: 1 USB, 1 Ethernet
- Dimensions: 16 x 17.8 x 14.6 in

File Downloads

Name	Date	Size	Rev	File
Laser4C Driver	13 Feb 2008	13 MB	2.1	jelaser4crev21.exe
Laser4C Printing System	21 Nov 2007	82 MB	4.3	jeprintsys43.exe
Laser4C Plug and Play Bundle	28 Sep 2007	13 MB	5.6	jepnp56.exe
Laser4C Firmware Update	21 Feb 2008	1.2 MB	20080221	jelaserfw6.exe

Jeff has already created much of the Web page as well as the style sheets for the different elements in the three vocabularies. He needs you to edit the style sheets so that they support namespaces, and he would like you to combine the elements in a single compound document.

To complete this task:

1. Using your text editor, open the **printtxt.css** style sheet located in the tutorial.02x/ review folder. Enter *your name* and *the date* in the comment section at the top of the file and save the file as **printer.css**.

2. Below the initial comment section, insert a rule creating the printer namespace with the prefix prnt and the URI http://jacksonelect.com/printers. Edit all of the selectors in the style sheet so they belong to this namespace. Copy the style declarations and paste them at the bottom of the file. Change the selector names to use the escape style syntax employed by Internet Explorer. Close the file, saving your changes.

3. Open the **filestxt.css** style sheet in your text editor. Enter **your name** and **the date** and save the file as **files.css**. Insert a rule declaring the download namespace. The prefix of the namespace should be dwnld and the URI should be http://jacksonelect.com/files. Make all the selectors in the style sheet belong to this namespace using both the namespace style and the escape style. Close the file, saving your changes.

4. Open the **pr205txt.htm** file in your text editor, entering **your name** and **the date** in the comment section. Save the file as **pr205.htm**.

5. Change the document into an XHTML file by inserting an xml declaration at the top of the file.

6. Add attributes to the root element, html, making the XHTML namespace the default namespace for elements in the document. Add namespaces for the printer and download namespaces using the same prefixes and URIs you used in the printer.css and files.css style sheets.

7. Below the h1 Product heading, copy and paste the name, description, and price elements from the printer.xml document. Place those three elements in the printer namespace.

8. Directly above the h1 File Downloads heading, copy and paste the specs and item elements from the printer.xml file. Once again, place those newly pasted elements in the printer namespace.

9. Directly above the closing </body> tag, copy and paste the elements from the files.xml document. Place those elements in the download namespace.

10. Enclose the contents of each item element from the download namespace within an <a> tag, with the href attribute set to the file temp.htm.

11. Add link elements to the head section of the file, with links to the printer.css and files.css style sheets.

12. Close the file, saving your changes.

13. Open **pr205.htm** in your Web browser. Verify that the layout of the page resembles that shown in Figure 2-29 and that the links in the File Downloads section are pointed at the temp.htm file.

14. Submit the completed assignment to your instructor.

Apply

Use the skills you earned in this tutorial o create a contribution eport for a political ction committee

Case Problem 1

Data files needed for this Case Problem: agents.xml, agtxt.css, contrib.xml, conttxt.css, epac.css, logo.jpg, reptxt.htm

EPAC-MO   EPAC-MO is an environmental political action committee located in central Missouri. The committee is currently in the midst of a fundraising effort that involves several canvassers traveling to the nearby towns of Cutler and Davidton to collect donations. Sudha Bhatia is managing the reports for the committee's intranet. She has placed some of the information in XML documents. She's developed one XML vocabulary that lists the employees or agents of the organization that collect donations, and another XML vocabulary for the actual donations. She would like to create a compound document that lists the donations by each canvasser. Figure 2-30 shows the structure of the compound document you'll create for Sudha.

Figure 2-30

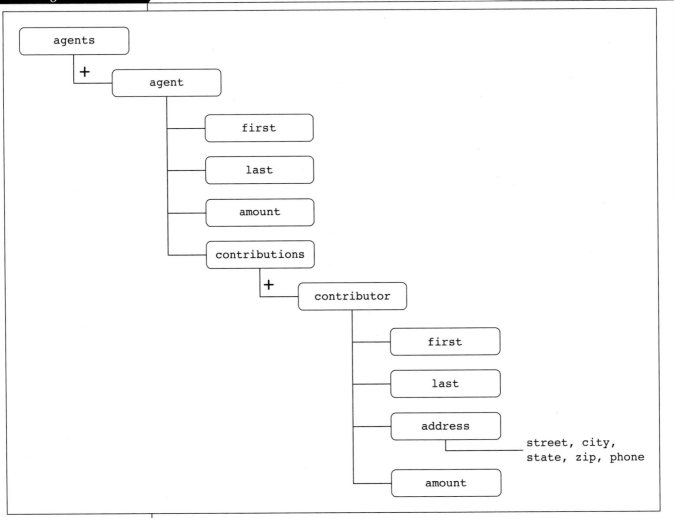

She wants the compound document placed within a Web page with different style sheets applied to the different vocabularies used in the page. Figure 2-31 shows a preview of the completed Web page.

Figure 2-31

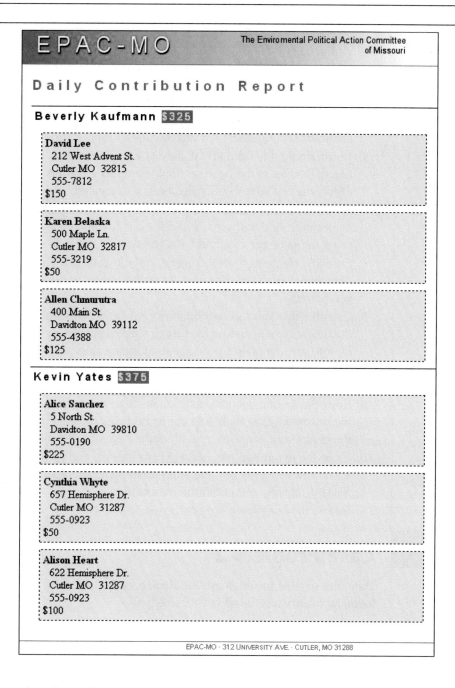

To complete this task:

1. Using your text editor, open the **agtxt.css** style sheet located in the tutorial.02x/ case1 folder. Enter *your name* and *the date* in the comment section, and then save the file as **agents.css**.

2. This file contains the styles used for the data on the canvassers employed by EPAC-MO. Below the initial comment section, insert a rule creating the agents namespace with the prefix ag and the URI http://www.epacmo.org/agents. Edit both of the selectors in the style sheet to belong to the agents namespace using both the namespace and the escape style syntax for each selector. Close the file, saving your changes.

3. Open the **conttxt.css** file using your text editor. Insert *your name* and *the date* in the comment section, and then save the file as **contrib.css**. This file contains the styles for the contributor data. Add a namespace rule to the style sheet creating the contributor namespace with the prefix cont and the URI http://www.epacmo.org/contrib. Apply this namespace to the selectors in the style sheet using both syntaxes. Close the file, saving your changes.

4. Open the **reptxt.htm** file with your text editor. Enter *your name* and *the date* in the comment section, and then save the file as **report.htm**.

5. Transform the file from HTML to XHTML by adding an xml declaration to the first line of the file. In the head section, insert link elements linking the Web page to the agents.css and contrib.css style sheets you created.

6. Set the default namespace of the elements in the document to the XHTML namespace. Add namespace declarations for the agents and contrib namespaces using the same prefixes and URIs you used in the style sheets.

7. Copy the elements from the agents.xml file and paste them into the report.htm file directly below the h1 heading. Apply the agents namespace to each of the elements you pasted.

8. Copy the first agent's contributions from the contrib.xml file and paste them into the document directly below the first closing </agent> tag. (*Hint*: The first agent's contributions are identified by the agent attribute value "a01". Use the tree structure displayed in Figure 2-30 as your guide.) Apply the contributor namespace to all of the newly pasted elements.

9. Copy the second agent's contributions from the contrib.xml file and paste them into the document directly below the second closing </agent> tag. Once again, apply the contributor namespace to all of the newly pasted elements.

10. Close the report.htm file, saving your changes, and then open the document in your Web browser. Verify that the appropriate styles are applied to the elements from the XHTML, agents, and contributor vocabularies.

11. Submit the completed project to your instructor.

Challenge

Explore how to create a compound document containing elements from XHTML and MathML vocabularies

Case Problem 2

Data files needed for this Case Problem: back.jpg, eq1.xml, eq2.xml, eq3.xml, eq4.xml, logo.jpg, mathtxt.css, quadtxt.xml, side.jpg

MathWeb Professor Laureen Cole of Coastal University is creating a Web site called "MathWeb" to use for online tutorials on mathematical topics. Laureen has been reading about the XML vocabulary MathML and how it can used to display mathematical equations and information. She's asked you to create a compound XML document containing elements from XHTML and MathML. A preview of the page that you'll create is shown in Figure 2-32.

Figure 2-32

MathWeb

Basic Math
Pre-Algebra
Algebra
Geometry
Trigonometry
Statistics
Calculus
Advanced Math
Math Games
Puzzles
Math History

Solving the Quadratic Equation

A **quadratic equation** is a polynomial equation of the second degree, having the general form:

$$a x^2 + b x + c = 0$$

The letters a, b and c are called coefficients: a is the coefficient of x^2, b is the coefficient of x, and c is the constant coefficient. A quadratic equation has two complex roots (i.e., solutions for the unknown term x). In some cases, these roots can have the same value. The roots can also belong to the realm of **complex numbers**. The values of the roots can be computed using the **quadratic formula** as shown below:

$$x = \frac{-b \pm \sqrt{b^2 - 4 a c}}{2 a}$$

For example, the roots of the quadratic equation

$$2 x^2 - 14 x + 20 = 0$$

can be determined by first substituting 2 for a, -14 for b, and 20 for c

$$x = \frac{14 \pm \sqrt{(-14)^2 - 4\,(2)\,(20)}}{2\,(2)}$$

and then solving the expression, which gives the roots of the equation as either $x = 5$ or $x = 2$.

Created using MathML and XHTML

Laureen has already created the content for the mathematical equations that she wants on her Web site. She wants your help in completing the Web page.

To complete this task:

Explore

1. Using your text editor, open **quadtxt.xml** from the tutorial.02x/case2 folder. Enter *your name* and *the date* in the comment section at the top of the file, and then save the document as **quad.xml**.
2. Directly below the comment section, insert a processing instruction that links this document to the math.css style sheet.
3. Within the root element, html, insert two namespace declarations for the XHTML and MathML namespaces. Make XHTML the default namespace of the document. Use the prefix "m" for all elements belonging to the MathML namespace.
4. Scroll down to the paragraph element with the id "eq1". Within this paragraph, paste the MathML elements from the eq1.xml file. Apply the MathML namespace to these pasted elements.
5. Repeat Step 4 for the paragraphs with the ids eq2 through eq4, pasting the elements from the eq2.xml through eq4.xml files. In each case, apply the MathML namespace to the pasted elements.

6. Close the file, saving your changes.

7. Open the **mathtxt.css** file in your text editor. Enter *your name* and *the date* in the comment section, and then save the file as **math.css**.

8. Directly below the comment section, insert a rule declaring the MathML namespace using the same prefix and URI you used in the quad.xml file.

9. At the bottom of the style sheet, insert style declarations to display any element named mrow from the MathML namespace in blue. Use both syntax methods to apply this style.

10. Close the style sheet, saving your changes.

Explore

11. Open the **quad.xml** file in your Web browser. Currently only the Amaya, Firefox, and Netscape browsers support MathML (if you are using Firefox or Netscape, you may be prompted to download and install special MathML fonts). You can download the Amaya browser for free from the W3C Web site. Verify that the MathML equations appear as shown in Figure 2-32. If you are using a browser that does not support MathML, verify that the XML document opens without a syntax error being reported.

12. Submit the completed project to your instructor.

Challenge

Explore how to create a compound document combining XHTML and RSS

Case Problem 3

Data files needed for this Case Problem: home.htm, hometxt.css, links.jpg, newstxt.css, sblogger.jpg, sblogtxt.xml

Sblogger   Steve Lavent runs a sports blog called Sblogger with links to sports sites, online chats, and Steve's own unique commentary on the daily events in the world of sports. Steve would like to start displaying the current headlines on his home page using RSS. **RSS** stands for **Really Simple Syndication** and is an XML vocabulary designed to share headlines and other Web content. Each RSS news feed is placed within a channel element, with individual stories or headlines placed within item elements. Each item element contains a title element and a description element to describe the news story, and often will contain a link element to link to the story's source. An RSS file also contains information about the administrator of the RSS news feed. An RSS news feed can be constantly updated, providing Web sites that subscribe to or retrieve the news feed with the most up-to-date news information from the Web.

Steve would like the home page of his Web site to be an RSS news document with any HTML elements added to the RSS document as a "wrapper" around the news headlines. Eventually he'll automate this process using scripts on his Web server, but he would like your help in designing a sample home page that combines XHTML and RSS. A preview of the Sblogger home page is shown in Figure 2-33.

Figure 2-33

SBLOGGER
Sports Blogging with a Difference

News Sites

ESPN
Sportsline
Sports Illustrated
CNN
MSNBC
Fox Sports

Columnists

Thomas Bacon
Steve Carls
Debbie Eggert
Frank Franks
Bob Mitchell
Sean Smith
Tom Upham
Mary Yancy

Blogs

Captain X
Die Yankees
Die BoSoxers
Packer Heaven
FBall Blog
Couch Potato
Sports Roundup
Fat, Drunk, and ...

Archives

January
February
March
April
May
June
July

Check that Pen!

ESPN is reporting that Houston running back JT Olson has come to terms with team, signing a three-year deal for $12 million. "I'm really happy with the contract," claims JT, "and I'm looking forward to holding out next year for a new contract after winning the rushing title." Yo Texas, check JT's pen to make sure it wasn't filled with disappearing ink!

A Cheesy Monument

Green Bay native Jeff Miller loves Packer QB Todd Rodgers. And he loves the Packers. And he loves cheese. So what could be more natural than carving a life-size statue of his beloved player in a huge block of gouda? Speaking of natural, Jeff's wife starting to complain about the natural odor of the monument. "I suppose I'll have to give it up," sighs Jeff. For his next creation, Jeff can do the entire porous GB defense ... in swiss cheese; or he can simply do a statue of beleagured GB defense back Chris Conners in toast.

Jenkins on Ice

Retired b-baller Dennis Jenkins announced today that he has signed a contract with "Long Sleep" to have his body frozen before death, to be revived only when medical science has discovered a cure to the aging process. "Lots of guys get frozen for cancer and stuff," explains the always-entertaining Jenkins, "I just want to return once they can give me back my eternal youth.[sic]" Perhaps Jenkins is also hoping medical science can cure his free-throw shooting - 47% and falling during his last year in the league.

A reader tells us that Jenkins may not be aware that part of the process of "Long Sleep" is to remove the head, keeping only the brain to be revived. This would be a problem for Jenkins since he would be left with his least-valuable asset.

Posted: 8/10/2008 @11:39 am Comments (39) Trackback (1)

Current Headlines

Carson leads PGA
Brett Carson took a three stroke lead into the final round of the PGA Championship at Whistling Straits with a birdie on the final hole.

Groveney Signs Deal
New York signed leading defenseman Steve Groveny to a 2-year contract on Thursday.

Olson Out for Two Weeks
Kansas City QB Drew Olson will miss two weeks of practice due to a sprained knee, team officials announced this morning.

Soccer Season Delayed
The start of Spain's soccer season will be delayed for two weeks because of financial problems and fallout from a league-wide drug scandal.

Gregg Called Up
Steve Gregg was recalled to the majors after allowing two hits in six innings in his third start for Triple-A Akron.

Steve has already created the style sheets, RSS code, and HTML elements for the Web page. He needs you to combine all of these elements in a single XML file.

To complete this task:

1. Use your text editor to open **sblogtxt.xml** from the tutorial.02x/case3 folder. Enter *your name* and *the date* in the comment section, and then save the file as **sblogger.xml**.

2. Directly below the comment section, insert two processing instructions to link the file to the home.css and news.css style sheets.

3. Within the root element, rss, declare the XHTML namespace using "html" as the namespace prefix.

4. Below the opening <rss> tag, insert the opening <html> tag. Place this element in the XHTML namespace.

5. Go to the home.htm file in your text editor and copy the elements from the file starting with the opening <head> tag through the opening <div> tag for the news feed section. Paste these elements into the sblogger.xml document directly above the opening <channel> tag.

Explore

6. Apply the XHTML namespace to all of the pasted HTML elements.

7. Directly below the closing </channel> tag, insert the closing </div>, </body>, and </html> tags. Place these three elements in the XHTML namespace.

8. Close the file, saving your changes.

9. Use your text editor to open the **hometxt.css** style sheet. Enter *your name* and *the date* in the comment section, and then save the file as **home.css**.

10. Directly below the comment section, insert a rule declaring the XHTML namespace using the same namespace prefix you used in the sblogger.xml file.

11. Place all of the selectors in the style sheet in the XHTML namespace using both forms.

12. Close the file, saving your changes.

13. Open the **newstxt.css** style sheet in your text editor. Enter *your name* and *the date* in the comment section, and then save the file as **news.css**.

Explore
14. Directly below the comment section, declare all four of the RSS namespaces declared in the sblogger.xml document. Use the same namespace prefixes.

Explore
15. Add style declarations in both formats to hide all of the elements from the sy and dc namespaces (*Hint*: Use the display: none style.)

16. Close the file, saving your changes.

17. Open **sblogger.xml** in your Web browser. Verify that the XHTML elements are properly formatted and that the headings from the RSS news feed appear in a box on the right margin of the page, as shown in Figure 2-33. Note that if you open the Web page in the Macintosh Safari browser, you may not see the document shown in Figure 2-33.

18. Submit your completed project to your instructor.

Create

Test your knowledge of compound documents by creating a real estate listing combining several XML vocabularies

Case Problem 4

Data files needed for this Case Problem: agents.xml, agtxt.css, house.css, housetxt.htm, listings.xml, listtxt.css, logo.jpg

MidWest Homes   Lisa Riccio manages the Web site for MidWest Homes, one of the many realtors in southern Wisconsin. Recently the company has begun storing information in XML documents. The company has developed an XML vocabulary for property listings and another vocabulary that describes real estate agents who work for the company. Lisa wants to combine information from these two vocabularies into a single Web page that displays new listings by the selling agent. Figure 2-34 shows how she wants elements from the two vocabularies combined.

Figure 2-34

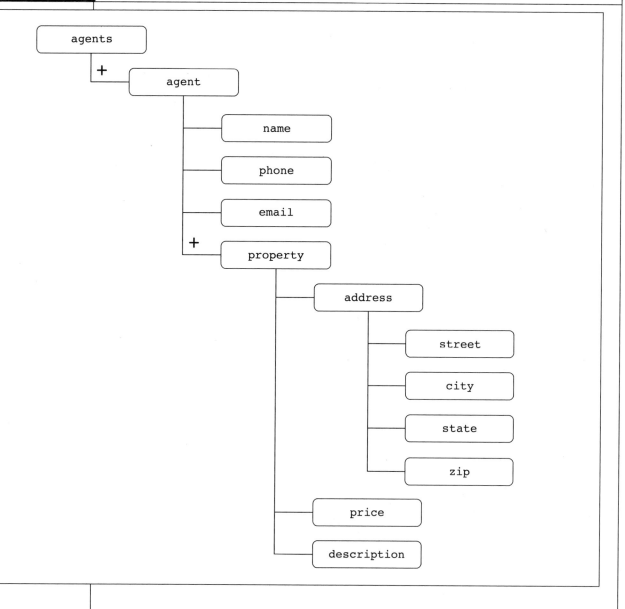

Lisa has already created style sheets for the Web page and the two XML vocabularies. She needs you to combine all of these features into a single document. Figure 2-35 shows a preview of the completed Web page for the first selling agent's listing.

Figure 2-35

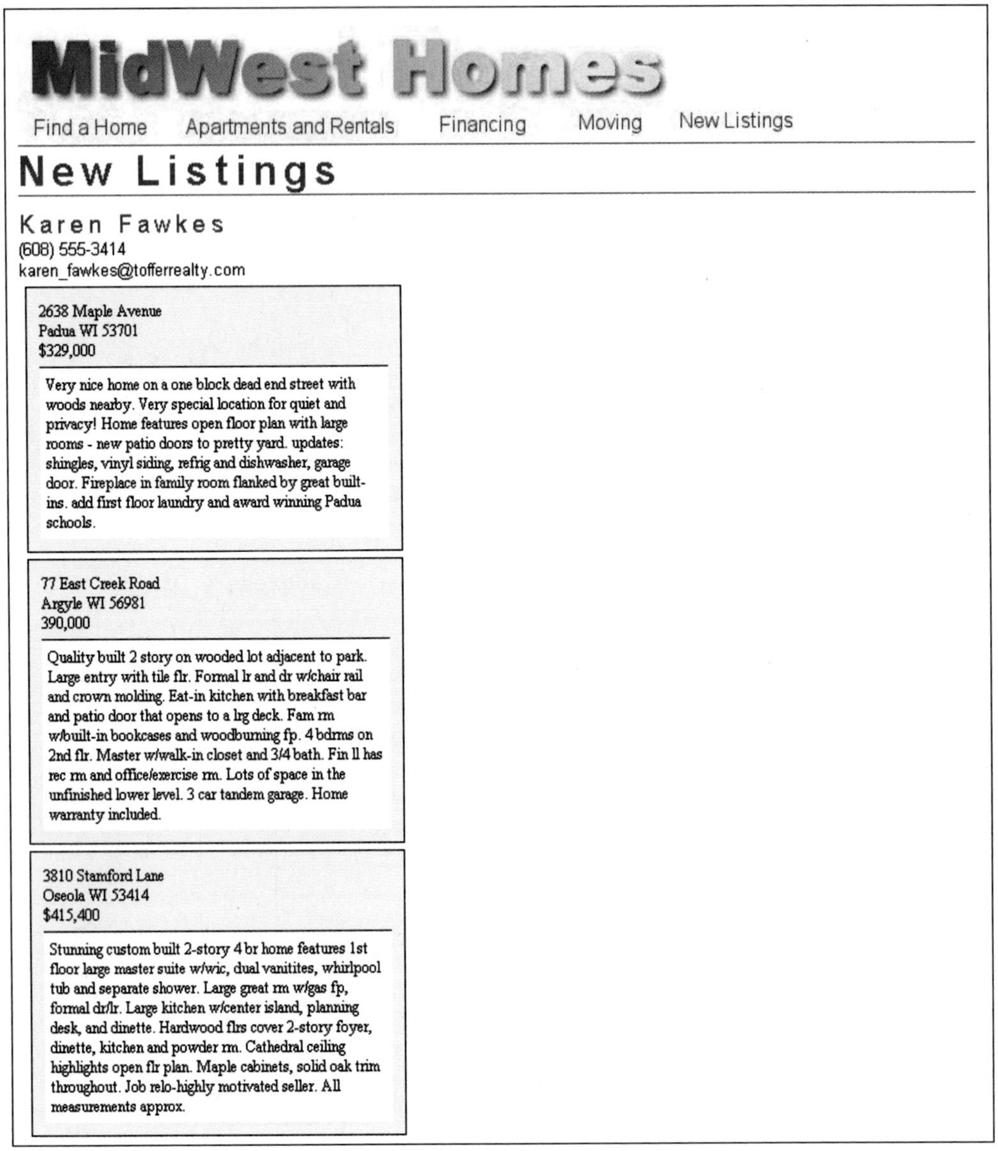

MidWest Homes

Find a Home   Apartments and Rentals   Financing   Moving   New Listings

New Listings

Karen Fawkes
(608) 555-3414
karen_fawkes@tofferrealty.com

2638 Maple Avenue
Padua WI 53701
$329,000

Very nice home on a one block dead end street with woods nearby. Very special location for quiet and privacy! Home features open floor plan with large rooms - new patio doors to pretty yard. updates: shingles, vinyl siding, refrig and dishwasher, garage door. Fireplace in family room flanked by great built-ins. add first floor laundry and award winning Padua schools.

77 East Creek Road
Argyle WI 56981
390,000

Quality built 2 story on wooded lot adjacent to park. Large entry with tile flr. Formal lr and dr w/chair rail and crown molding. Eat-in kitchen with breakfast bar and patio door that opens to a lrg deck. Fam rm w/built-in bookcases and woodburning fp. 4 bdrms on 2nd flr. Master w/walk-in closet and 3/4 bath. Fin ll has rec rm and office/exercise rm. Lots of space in the unfinished lower level. 3 car tandem garage. Home warranty included.

3810 Stamford Lane
Oseola WI 53414
$415,400

Stunning custom built 2-story 4 br home features 1st floor large master suite w/wic, dual vanitites, whirlpool tub and separate shower. Large great rm w/gas fp, formal dr/lr. Large kitchen w/center island, planning desk, and dinette. Hardwood flrs cover 2-story foyer, dinette, kitchen and powder rm. Cathedral ceiling highlights open flr plan. Maple cabinets, solid oak trim throughout. Job relo-highly motivated seller. All measurements approx.

To complete this task:

1. Use your text editor to open the **agtxt.css**, **housetxt.htm**, and **listtxt.css** files from the tutorial.02x/case4 folder. Enter *your name* and *the date* in the comment section of each of these files, and then save them as **agents.css**, **house.htm**, and **listings.css** respectively.

2. Change the house.htm file into an XML document by adding an XML declaration to the top of the file and adding namespaces to the html element for the XHTML, agents, and listings namespaces. Set XHTML as the default namespace. Use a prefix of ag for the agents namespace and a URI of http://www.midwesthomes.com/agents. Use a prefix of list and a URI of http://www.midwesthomes.com/listings for the listings namespace.

3. Within the head section of the HTML file, insert links to the agents.css and listings.css style sheets.

4. Within the main div element, insert the elements from the agents.xml file. Place these elements in the agents namespace.

5. Below each closing </agent> tag, insert the properties associated with that agent from the listings.xml file. Place the listing elements in the listings namespace.

6. Close the house.htm file, saving your changes.

7. Within the agents.css file, place the style declarations in the agents namespace, using both formats. Close the file, saving your changes.

8. Within the listings.css file, place the style declarations in the listings namespace, using both formats. Close the file, saving your changes.

9. Open house.htm in your Web browser, verifying that the styles for the XHTML, agents, and listings vocabularies have been properly applied.

10. Submit the completed project to your instructor.

Review

Quick Check Answers

Session 2.1

1. A names collision occurs when two elements from different XML vocabularies share the same name in a compound document.

2. A namespace is a defined collection of element and attribute names. By placing XML vocabularies in different namespaces, elements from the different vocabularies can share the same name without confusion.

3. xmlns:book="http://ns.doc.book"

4. <book:author>David Stevens</book:author>

5. xmlns="http://ns.doc.book"

6. <book book:isbn="0-1969-7">Blue Moon</book>

Session 2.2

1. @namespace book url(http://ns.doc.book);

2. @namespace url(http://ns.doc.book);

3. book|author

4. book\:author

5. <svg xmlns="http://www.w3.org/2000/svg">

6. <html xmlns="http://www.w3.org/1999/xhtml"
   xmlns:MM="http://www.w3.org/1998/Math/MathML"
   xmlns:SVG="http://www.w3.org/2000/svg">

7.
```
<?xml version="1.0"?>
<rss version="2.0"
xmlns:xhtml="http://www.w3.org/1999/xhtml">
<channel>
      <title>Jobless Rate Drops</title>
      <link>http://www.dol.gov/</link>
      <description>Unemployment dips to 4.9%</description>
      <language>en-us</language>
      <pubDate>Feb 3, 2008 04:00:00 GMT</pubDate>
      <xhtml:img src="unempchart.jpg" alt="Unemployment Chart" />
   </channel>
</rss>
```

Objectives

Validating an XML Document

Working with Document Type Definitions

Case

Pixal Digital Products

Pixal Digital Products sells imaging hardware and software such as scanners, digital cameras, copiers, and digital tablets to individual consumers and businesses. Kristin Laughlin is the customer service manager at Pixal, and part of her job is to record information on Pixal's customers, including the individual orders they make.

Kristin is starting to use XML to record this information and has already created a sample XML document containing information on customers and their orders. Kristin knows that her document needs to be well formed, following the rules of XML syntax exactly, but she would also like her document to follow certain rules regarding content. For example, data on each customer must include the customer's name, phone number, and address. Each customer order must contain a complete list of the items purchased, including the date they were ordered. Kristin has asked you to help her create an XML document that adheres to both the rules of XML and the rules she has set up for the document's content and structure.

Student Data Files

▼tutorial.03x

▽ **tutorial folder**

    codestxt.dtd

    ordertxt.xml

▽ **review folder**

    hwlisttxt.xml

    hwtxt.dtd

    pixaltxt.xml

    swlisttxt.xml

    swtxt.dtd

▽ **case1 folder**

    edltxt.xml

    teamstxt.dtd

Student Data Files	▼**tutorial.03x continued**

▽ case2 folder	▽ case3 folder	▽ case4 folder
arttxt.dtd	modtxt.dtd	lhouse.dtd
headtxt.xml	modtxt.xml	listtxt.xml
imgtxt.dtd	parttxt.dtd	members.txt
newstxt.dtd	parttxt.xml	
wnstxt.xml	waretxt.xml	

Session 3.1

Creating a Valid Document

You meet with Kristin to discuss the information she's collecting on Pixal's customers. To keep things to a manageable size, Kristin has limited her document to a subset of only three customers. Figure 3-1 shows a table of the information she's entered for those customers.

Figure 3-1 ▶ **Customer orders table**

Customer		Orders		Item	Qty.	Price
Name:	Mr. David Lynn	orderID:	or10311	DCT5Z	1	559.95
custID:	cust201	Date:	8/1/2008	SM128	1	199.95
Type:	home			RCL	2	29.95
Address:	211 Fox Street	orderID:	or11424	BCE4L	1	59.95
	Greenville, NH 80021	Date:	9/14/2008			
Phone:	(315) 555-1812					
E-mail:	dlynn@nhs.net					
Name:	Mrs. Jean Kaufmann	orderID:	or10899	WBC	1	59.99
custID:	cust202	Date:	8/11/2008	RCA	2	5.95
Type:						
Address:	411 East Oak Avenue					
	Cashton, MI 20401					
Phone:	(611) 555-4033					
E-mail:	JKaufmann@cshweb.com					
Name:	Adservices	orderID:	or11201	SCL4C	3	179.99
custID:	cust203	Date:	9/15/2008			
Type:	business					
Address:	55 Washburn Lane					
	Creighton, UT 98712					
Phone:	(811) 555-2987					
E-mail:						

For each customer, Kristin has recorded the customer's name, ID, type (home or business), address, phone number, and e-mail address. Each customer has placed one or more separate orders. For each order, Kristin has recorded the order's ID number and date. Finally, within each order, she has entered the items purchased and the quantity and price of each item. Kristin has already placed this information in an XML document. Open this file now.

To open Kristin's document:

▸ **1.** Use your text editor to open **ordertxt.xml** from the tutorial.03x/tutorial folder. Enter *your name* and *the date* in the comment section of the file and save the file as **orders.xml**.

Figure 3-2 displays the contents of the orders.xml document for the first customer.

The first customer in the orders.xml document ◂ Figure 3-2

```
<customers>
    <customer custID="cust201" custType="home">
        <name title="Mr.">David Lynn</name>
        <address>
            <![CDATA[
            211 Fox Street
            Greenville, NH 80021
            ]]>
        </address>
        <phone>(315) 555-1812</phone>
        <email>dlynn@nhs.net</email>
        <orders>
            <order orderID="or10311" orderBy="cust201">
                <orderDate>8/1/2008</orderDate>
                <items>
                    <item itemPrice="599.95">DCT5Z</item>
                    <item itemPrice="199.95">SM128</item>
                    <item itemPrice="29.95" itemQty="2">RCL</item>
                </items>
            </order>
            <order orderID="or11424" orderBy="cust201">
                <orderDate>9/14/2008</orderDate>
                <items>
                    <item itemPrice="59.95">BCE4L</item>
                </items>
            </order>
        </orders>
    </customer>
</customers>
```

▸ **2.** Take some time to examine the contents of Kristin's document. In particular, compare the elements entered in the document with the table in Figure 3-1.

Kristin tells you that some elements in her document, like the name and phone elements, should appear only once for each customer, whereas elements like the order and item elements can appear multiple times. The email element is optional: two customers have an e-mail address and one does not. Some of the attributes are also optional: there is no need for the title attribute when the customer is a company, nor has Kristin included an itemQty attribute when the number of items ordered is one.

Kristin has created the diagram shown in Figure 3-3 to better illustrate the structure of the elements and attributes in her document. Recall from Figure 1-5 in Tutorial 1 that the + symbol in front of an element indicates that at least one child element must be present in the document, and that the ? symbol indicates 0 or 1 children are present. Thus, from Kristin's diagram you can see that the customers, orders, and items elements must have at least one customer, order, or item child respectively, and that the email element is optional. Kristin has also indicated the presence of element attributes below each element name. Optional attributes are surrounded by square brackets. There are three optional attributes in the document: the custType attribute associated with the customer element, the title attribute associated with the name element, and the itemQty attribute associated with the item element.

Figure 3-3 | **The structure of the orders.xml document**

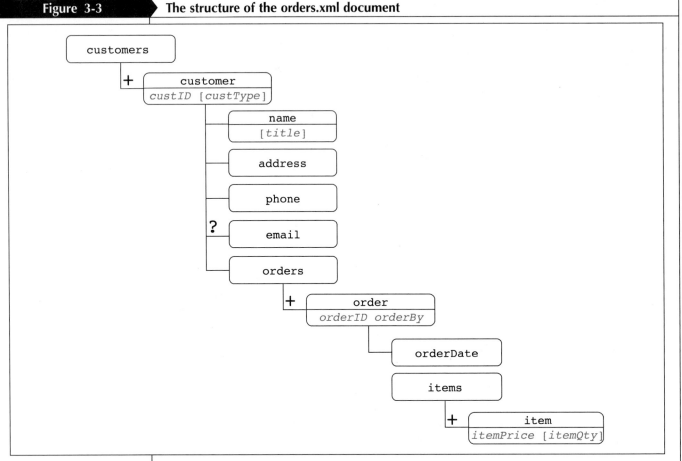

In order to keep accurate and manageable records, it's important that Kristin maintain this structure in her document. She wants to ensure that the customer information includes the address and phone number for each customer, the items the customer ordered, and the date the order was placed. In XML terms, this means that her document has to be not only well formed, but also valid.

Declaring a DTD

One way to create a valid document is to design a DTD for the document. As discussed in Tutorial 1, a **DTD** or **document type definition** is a collection of rules that define the content and structure of an XML document. Used in conjunction with an XML parser that supports data validation, a DTD can be used to

- ensure that all required elements are present in a document
- prevent undefined elements from being used in a document
- enforce a specific data structure on a document
- specify the use of element attributes and define their permissible values
- define default values for attributes
- describe how parsers should access non-XML or nontextual content

A DTD is entered into the document in a statement called a **document type declaration** or **DOCTYPE declaration**. The DOCTYPE declaration has to be added to the document prolog, after the XML declaration and before the document's root element. There can be only one DOCTYPE declaration in an XML document.

Although there can also be only one DOCTYPE declaration, you can divide the DTD into two parts: an internal subset and an external subset. The **internal subset** is a set of declarations placed within the XML document. The form of an internal subset is:

```
<!DOCTYPE root

[
    declarations
]>
```

where `root` is the name of the document's root element and `declarations` is the statements and rules that comprise the DTD. If the name of the `root` attribute doesn't match the name of the document's root element, XML parsers report an error and stop processing the document. For Kristin's orders.xml document, the root element is customers, so an internal subset would appear as

```
<!DOCTYPE customers

[
    declarations
]>
```

In an **external subset**, the declarations are placed in an external file that is accessed from the XML document. External subsets have two types of locations: system and public. For a system DTD, a **system identifier** allows you to specify the location of an external subset. The DOCTYPE declaration has the form

```
<!DOCTYPE root SYSTEM "uri">
```

where `root` is once again the document's root element and `uri` is the URI of the external file. For example, if Kristin places the DTD for her orders document in an external file named rules.dtd, she can access it using the following DOCTYPE declaration:

```
<!DOCTYPE customers SYSTEM "rules.dtd">
```

In some cases, the DTD for an XML vocabulary is placed in several locations, or the DTD is built into the XML parser itself. For these situations, the DTD can be processed as a public location. A **public identifier** is added to the DOCTYPE declaration to provide the public name of the DTD. The syntax of the DOCTYPE declaration using a public identifier is

```
<!DOCTYPE root PUBLIC "id" "uri">
```

where `root` is the document's root element, `id` is the public identifier, and `uri` is the system location of the DTD (included in case the XML parser cannot process the public identifier). In one sense, the public identifier acts like the namespace URI, in that it doesn't specify a physical location for the DTD but instead provides the DTD a unique name that can be recognized by an XML parser. For example, XHTML documents that conform strictly to standards employ the following DOCTYPE declaration:

```
<!DOCTYPE html PUBLIC "-//W3C//DTD XHTML 1.0 Strict//EN"
"http://www.w3.org/TR/xhtml1/DTD/xhtml1-strict.dtd">
```

The public identifier is "-//W3C//DTD XHTML 1.0 Strict//EN", a string of characters that Web browsers recognize as the identifier for the XHTML strict DTD. When a Web browser reads the file, it may have built-in code that corresponds to this DTD or it may have a specific location of its own from which it retrieves the DTD. Caching the DTD locally speeds up the processing time for the Web browser and frees the browser from having to download the DTD from a Web site. If the DTD is not built into the browser or XML parser, it can still access the DTD from the URL http://www.w3.org/TR/xhtml1/DTD/ xhtml1-strict.dtd. Thus, the system identifier acts as a backup to the public identifier. Most standard XML vocabularies like XHTML and RSS have public identifiers. However, for a customized XML vocabulary like the one Kristin has created for Pixal Products, there is usually no public identifier (unless Pixal has developed a customized XML parser to read its internal documents). In this case, Kristin can use an external file with a system identifier.

Given that there are two ways of accessing DTDs, you might wonder whether it is better to use an internal or external DTD. There are advantages to both approaches. By placing the DTD within the document, you have placed all of your code in one place and can more easily compare the DTD to the document's content without having to switch between files. However, an internal DTD cannot be shared among many documents written by different authors. An external DTD, on the other hand, can be used as a common DTD among many documents, forcing them to use the same elements, attributes, and document structure. Another approach is to combine both internal and external DTDs in either of the following forms:

```
<!DOCTYPE root SYSTEM "URI"
[
   declarations
]>
```

or

```
<!DOCTYPE root PUBLIC "id" "URI"
[
   declarations
]>
```

If a document contains both an internal and external subset, the internal subset has precedence over the external subset when there is conflict between the two. This is useful when an external subset is shared among several documents. The external subset would define some basic rules for all of the documents, and the internal subset would define those rules that are specific to each document (see Figure 3-4). In this way, internal and external DTDs work the same way as embedded and external style sheets. An XML environment composed of several documents and vocabularies might use both internal and external DTDs.

Using internal and external DTDs ◄ Figure 3-4

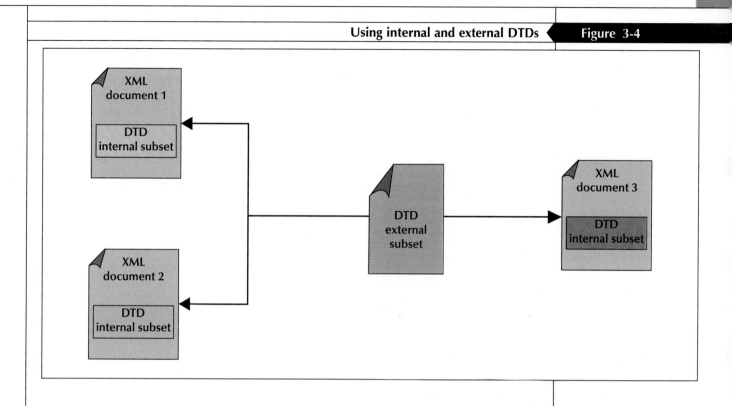

Declaring a DTD

- To declare an internal DTD subset, use the syntax
  ```
  <!DOCTYPE root
  [
  declarations
  ]>
  ```
  where `root` is the name of the document's root element, and `declarations` are the statements that comprise the DTD.
- To declare an external DTD subset with a system location, use
  ```
  <!DOCTYPE root SYSTEM "uri">
  ```
  where `uri` is the URI of the external DTD file.
- To declare an external DTD subset with a public location, use
  ```
  <!DOCTYPE root PUBLIC "id" "uri">
  ```
  where `id` is the public identifier of the DTD.

Writing the Document Type Declaration

Kristin decides to place the DTD directly in her XML document so she can easily compare the DTD to the document content.

To insert the DOCTYPE declaration:

1. Directly above the opening <customers> tag, insert the following DOCTYPE declaration (see Figure 3-5):

```
<!DOCTYPE customers
[

]>
```

Figure 3-5 ▶ **Inserting the DOCTYPE declaration**

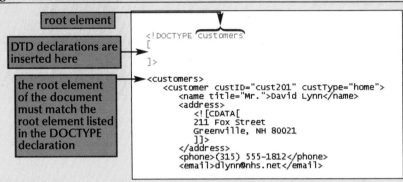

2. Save your changes to the file.

Now that you've created the document type declaration, you're ready to define the structure of Kristin's document.

Declaring Document Elements

In a valid document, every element must be declared in the DTD. An **element type declaration**, or **element declaration**, specifies an element's name and indicates what kind of content the element can contain. It can even specify the order in which elements appear in the document. The syntax of an element declaration is

```
<!ELEMENT element content-model>
```

where *element* is the name of the element. The element name is case sensitive, so if the element name is PRODUCTS, it must be entered as PRODUCTS (not Products or products) in the element declaration. Remember that element names cannot contain any spaces or reserved symbols such as "<" or ">".

The *content-model* variable specifies what type of content the element contains. Generally, elements contain parsed character data or child elements. For example, in Kristin's document, the phone element contains a text string that holds the customer's phone number. On the other hand, the customer element contains five elements (name, address, phone, email, and orders). Within a DTD you can specify the type of content an element can contain. There are five possible values for *content-model*:

- ANY—There are no restrictions on the element's content.
- EMPTY—The element cannot store any content.
- #PCDATA—The element can contain only parsed character data.
- *Elements*—The element can contain only child elements.
- *Mixed*—The element can contain both parsed character data and child elements.

Next, investigate each of these types in more detail.

ANY Content

The most general type of content model is ANY, which allows an element to store any type of content. The syntax to allow any element content is

```
<!ELEMENT element ANY>
```

For example, the declaration

```
<!ELEMENT products ANY>
```

in the DTD would allow the products element to contain any type of content. Thus, any of the following would satisfy this element declaration:

```
<products>SLR100 Digital Camera</products>
<products />
<products>
    <name>SLR100</name>
    <type>Digital Camera</type>
</products>
```

Allowing an element to contain any type of content has limited use in document validation. After all, the idea behind validation is to enforce a particular set of rules on elements and their content, and thus allowing any content defeats the purpose of a rule.

EMPTY Content

The EMPTY content model is reserved for elements that store no content. The syntax for an empty element declaration is

```
<!ELEMENT element EMPTY>
```

Therefore the element declaration

```
<!ELEMENT img EMPTY>
```

would require the img element to be entered as an empty element:

```
<img />
```

Attempting to add content to an empty element would result in XML parsers rejecting the document as invalid.

Parsed Character Data

Elements that can store parsed character data are declared as follows:

```
<!ELEMENT element (#PCDATA)>
```

For example, the declaration

```
<!ELEMENT name (#PCDATA)>
```

would permit the following element in an XML document:

```
<name>Lea Ziegler</name>
```

Element content declared as pcdata does not allow for child elements. Therefore, the content

```
<name>
   <first>Lea</first>
   <last>Ziegler</last>
</name>
```

would not be considered valid because child elements are not considered parsed character data.

The name, address, phone, email, orderDate, and item elements in Kristin's document contain only parsed character data. She would like you to add declarations for these elements to the DTD.

To declare elements containing parsed character data:

▶ **1.** Within the DOCTYPE declaration, insert the following element declarations (see Figure 3-6):

```
<!ELEMENT name (#PCDATA)>
<!ELEMENT address (#PCDATA)>
<!ELEMENT phone (#PCDATA)>
<!ELEMENT email (#PCDATA)>
<!ELEMENT orderDate (#PCDATA)>
<!ELEMENT item (#PCDATA)>
```

| Figure 3-6 | **Inserting element declarations** |

```
<!DOCTYPE customers
[
   <!ELEMENT name (#PCDATA)>
   <!ELEMENT address (#PCDATA)>
   <!ELEMENT phone (#PCDATA)>
   <!ELEMENT email (#PCDATA)>
   <!ELEMENT orderDate (#PCDATA)>
   <!ELEMENT item (#PCDATA)>
]>
```

elements can contain only parsed character data

▶ **2.** Save your changes to the file.

| Reference Window | **Specifying Element Content** |

- To declare that an element may contain any type of content insert the declaration
  `<!ELEMENT element ANY>`
  where `element` is the element name.
- To declare an empty element containing no content whatsoever, use
  `<!ELEMENT element EMPTY>`
- To declare that an element may contain only parsed character data, use
  `<!ELEMENT element (#PCDATA)>`

Working with Child Elements

Since XML documents follow a hierarchical tree structure, you must also declare the child elements of any parent. The syntax of the declaration for child elements is

`<!ELEMENT element (children)>`

where *element* is the parent element and *children* is a listing of its child elements. The simplest form for the listing consists of a single child element associated with a parent. For example, the declaration

```
<!ELEMENT customer (phone)>
```

indicates that the customer element can contain only a single child element, named phone. The following document would be invalid under this element declaration because the customer element is shown with two child elements: name and phone:

```
<customer>
    <name>Lea Ziegler</name>
    <phone>555-2819</phone>
</customer>
```

For content that involves multiple child elements, you can specify the elements in either a sequence or a choice of elements.

Specifying an Element Sequence

A **sequence** is a list of elements that follow a defined order. The syntax to specify child elements in a sequence is

```
<!ELEMENT element (child1, child2, ...)>
```

where *child1*, *child2*, etc., represents the sequence of child elements within the parent. The order of the child elements in an XML document must match the order defined in the element declaration. For example, the following element declaration defines a sequence of three child elements for each customer:

```
<!ELEMENT customer (name, phone, email)>
```

Under this declaration, the following document is valid:

```
<customer>
    <name>Lea Ziegler</name>
    <phone>(813) 555-8931</phone>
    <email>LZiegler@tempmail.net</email>
</customer>
```

However, even though the elements and their content are identical in the following document, the document is not valid because the sequence doesn't match the defined order:

```
<customer>
    <name>Lea Ziegler</name>
    <email>LZiegler@tempmail.net</email>
    <phone>(813) 555-8931</phone>
</customer>
```

Specifying an Element Choice

The other way of listing child elements, **choice**, presents a set of possible child elements. The syntax of the choice model is

```
<!ELEMENT element (child1 | child2 | ...)>
```

where *child1*, *child2*, etc., are the possible child elements of the parent. For example, the following declaration allows the customer element to contain either the name or the company element:

```
<!ELEMENT customer (name | company)>
```

Therefore, either of the following documents is valid:

```
<customer>
   <name>Lea Ziegler</name>
</customer>
```

or

```
<customer>
   <company>VTech Productions</company>
</customer>
```

However, under this declaration a document cannot include both the name and company elements, because the choice model allows only one of the child elements listed.

You can combine the choice and sequence models and use them together. The following declaration indicates that the customer element must have three child elements:

```
<!ELEMENT customer ((name | company), phone, email)>
```

The first must be either name or company, and the next two must be phone and email, in that order. With this declaration, either of the following sample documents is valid:

```
<customer>
   <name>Lea Ziegler</name>
   <phone>(813) 555-8931</phone>
   <email>LZiegler@tempmail.net</email>
</customer>
```

or

```
<customer>
   <company>VTech Productions</company>
   <phone>(813) 555-8931</phone>
   <email>LZiegler@tempmail.net</email>
</customer>
```

Reference Window

Specifying Child Elements

- To declare the order of child elements, use the declaration
  `<!ELEMENT element (child1, child2, ...)>`
  where *child1*, *child2*, ... is the order in which the child elements must appear within the parent element.
- To allow for a choice of child elements, use `<!ELEMENT element (child1 | child2 | ...)>`
  where *child1*, *child2*, ... are the possible children of the parent element.

Modifying Symbols

So far, all of the content models you've seen have limited the number of child elements to one. If you need to specify duplicates of the same element, you repeat the element name in the list. For example, the following element declaration indicates that the customer element must contain two phone elements:

```
<!ELEMENT customer (phone, phone)>
```

It's rare, however, that you will specify the exact number of duplicate elements. Instead, DTDs use more general numbering with a **modifying symbol** that specifies the number of occurrences of each element. There are three modifying symbols: the question mark (?), the plus sign (+), and the asterisk (*). As you may recall, these are the same modifying symbols you saw in Tutorial 1 when creating a tree diagram for an XML document. As before, the ? symbol indicates that an element occurs zero or one time, the + symbol indicates that an element occurs at least once, and the * symbol indicates that an element occurs 0 times or more. There are no other modifying symbols, so if you want to specify an exact number, such as the two phone elements discussed above, you have to repeat the element names.

In Kristin's document, the customers element must contain at least one element named customer. The element declaration for this is

```
<!ELEMENT customers (customer+)>
```

Note that a modifying symbol is placed directly after the element it modifies. You can also include modifying symbols in element sequences. For example, in Kristin's document, each customer element contains the name, address, phone, and email elements, but the email element is optional, occurring either 0 or 1 time. The element declaration for this would therefore be

```
<!ELEMENT customer (name, address, phone, email?)>
```

The three modifying symbols can also modify entire element sequences or choices. You do this by placing the character immediately following the closing parenthesis of the sequence or choice. When applied to a sequence, the modifying symbol is used to repeat the sequence. For example, the declaration

```
<!ELEMENT order (orderDate, items)+>
```

indicates that the child element sequence (orderDate, items) can be repeated one or more times within each order element. Of course, each time the sequence is repeated, the orderDate element must appear first, followed by the items element.

When applied to a choice model, the modifying symbols allow for multiple combinations of each child element. The declaration

```
<!ELEMENT customer (name | company)+>
```

allows any of the following lists of child elements:

```
name
company
name, company
name, name, company
name, company, company
```

and so forth. The only requirement is that the combined total of name and company elements be greater than zero.

| Reference Window | **Applying Modifying Symbols** |

- To specify that an element can appear 0 or 1 time, use
  `item?`
  where `item` is an element name or the list or sequence of elements.
- To specify one or more occurrences of an item, use
  `item+`
- To specify zero or more occurrences of an item, use
  `item*`

Now that you've seen how to specify the occurrences of child elements, you can add these declarations to the DTD for Kristin's document. The order of the declarations is not important, but it's useful to insert the declarations in the order in which the elements appear in the document. You can also insert blank lines between groups of declarations to make the code easier to read.

To declare child elements:

1. The root customers element must contain at least one customer element. Therefore, insert the following element declaration at the top of the list of declarations in the DTD:

   `<!ELEMENT customers (customer+)>`

2. The customer element must contain the name, address, phone, an optional email address, and an orders element. So, below the customers declaration, insert a blank line and then the declaration:

   `<!ELEMENT customer (name, address, phone, email?, orders)>`

3. The orders element must contain at least one order. Add the following declaration below the declaration for the email element.

   `<!ELEMENT orders (order+)>`

4. Each order contains the orderDate element and a list of items that were ordered. Below the orders declaration, insert a blank line and the following declaration:

   `<!ELEMENT order (orderDate, items)>`

5. Each items element must contain at least one item. Insert the following declaration below the orderDate declaration, and then insert another blank line.

   `<!ELEMENT items (item+)>`

   Figure 3-7 shows the complete element declaration in the DTD.

| Figure 3-7 | **Declaring child elements** |

```
<!DOCTYPE customers
[
  <!ELEMENT customers (customer+)>

  <!ELEMENT customer (name, address, phone, email?, orders)>
  <!ELEMENT name (#PCDATA)>
  <!ELEMENT address (#PCDATA)>
  <!ELEMENT phone (#PCDATA)>
  <!ELEMENT email (#PCDATA)>
  <!ELEMENT orders (order+)>

  <!ELEMENT order (orderDate, items)>
  <!ELEMENT orderDate (#PCDATA)>
  <!ELEMENT items (item+)>

  <!ELEMENT item (#PCDATA)>
]>
```

6. Save your changes to the file. If you plan on taking a break before the next session, you may also close the document.

To see how these element declarations represent the structure of the document, you can compare Figure 3-7 with the tree diagram shown earlier in Figure 3-3.

Working with Mixed Content

The final type of element content is **mixed content**, which allows an element to contain both parsed character data and child elements. The syntax for declaring mixed content is

```
<!ELEMENT element (#PCDATA | child1 | child2 | ...)*>
```

This form applies the * modifying symbol to a choice of parsed character data or child elements. Because the * symbol is used with a choice list, the element can contain anynumber of occurrences of child elements or pcdata, or it can contain no content at all. For example, the declaration

```
<!ELEMENT title (#PCDATA | subtitle)*>
```

allows the title element to contain any of the following:

```
<title>The Importance of Being Earnest</title>
<title>The Importance of Being Earnest
   <subtitle>A Trivial Comedy for Serious People</subtitle>
</title>

<title>The Importance of Being Earnest
   <subtitle>A Trivial Comedy for Serious People</subtitle>
   <subtitle>by Oscar Wilde</subtitle>
</title>
```

While very flexible, elements with mixed content do not add much defined structure to a document. You can specify only the names of the child elements, and you cannot constrain the order in which those child elements appear or control the number of occurrences for each element. An element might contain only pcdata or it might contain any number of child elements in any order. For this reason, it is best not to work with mixed content if you want a tightly structured document (which, after all, is one of the reasons for creating a DTD). Since Kristin's document contains no mixed content, you will not have to add this kind of declaration to the DTD.

At this point you've successfully defined a structure for the elements in the orders.xml file, but you haven't defined the attributes associated with those elements. You'll add attribute declarations in the next session.

Session 3.1 Quick Check

Review

1. What code would you enter to connect your document to a DTD stored in the file books.dtd (assume that the name of the root element is Inventory)?
2. What declaration would you enter to allow the book element to contain any content?
3. What declaration would you enter to specify that the video element is empty?
4. What declaration would you enter to indicate that the book element can contain only parsed character data?
5. What declaration would you enter to indicate that the book element contains only a single child element named author?

6. What declaration would you enter to indicate that the book element can contain one or more child elements named author?

7. What declaration would you enter to allow the book element to contain a choice of mixed content, including parsed character data or child elements named author or title?

Session 3.2

Declaring Attributes

In the last session, you defined the structure of Kristin's document by declaring all of the elements in her document and indicating what type of content each element could contain. However, for Kristin's document to be valid, you must also declare all of the attributes associated with those elements.

Figure 3-8 describes all of the attributes that Kristin intends to use in her document, indicating whether each attribute is required and what, if any, default values are assumed for each attribute.

| Figure 3-8 | Attributes used in orders.xml |

Element	Attributes	Description	Required?	Default Value(s)
customer	custID	Customer ID number	Yes	none
	custType	Customer type	No	"home" or "business"
name	title	Title associated with the customer's name	No	"Mr.", "Mrs.", or "Ms."
order	orderID	Order ID number	Yes	none
	orderBy	ID of the customer making the order	Yes	none
item	itemPrice	Item price	Yes	none
	itemQty	Quantity of the item ordered	No	"1"

To enforce these attribution properties on Kristin's document, you must add an **attribute-list declaration** to the document's DTD. The attribute-list declaration accomplishes the following:

- lists the names of all of the attributes associated with a specific element
- specifies the data type of each attribute
- indicates whether each attribute is required or optional
- provides a default value for each attribute, if necessary

The syntax for declaring a list of attributes is

```
<!ATTLIST element attribute1 type1 default1
                  attribute2 type2 default2
                  attribute3 type3 default3 ... >
```

where *element* is the name of the element associated with the attributes, *attribute* is the name of an attribute, *type* is the attribute's data type, and *default* indicates whether the attribute is required and whether it has a default value.

In practice, declarations for elements with multiple attributes are often easier to interpret if the attributes are declared separately rather than in one long declaration. An equivalent form in the DTD would be as follows:

```
<!ATTLIST element attribute1 type1 default1>
<!ATTLIST element attribute2 type2 default2>
<!ATTLIST element attribute3 type3 default3>
...
```

XML parsers combine the different statements into a single attribute declaration. If a processor encounters more than one declaration for the same attribute, it ignores the second statement. Attribute-list declarations can be located anywhere within the document type declaration, although it is often easiest to work with attribute declarations that are located adjacent to the declaration for the element with which they're associated.

Declaring Attributes in a DTD

- To declare a list of attributes associated with an element, enter the declaration

```
<!ATTLIST element attribute1 type1 default1
                  attribute2 type2 default2
                  attribute3 type3 default3 ...>
```

or

```
<!ATTLIST element attribute1 type1 default1>
<!ATTLIST element attribute2 type2 default2>
<!ATTLIST element attribute3 type3 default3>
...
```

where `element` is the element associated with the attributes, `attribute` is the name of an attribute, `type` is the attribute's data type, and `default` indicates whether the attribute is required and whether it has a default value.

As a first step, you'll declare the names of the attributes and the elements they're associated with for the orders.xml document. (Since you're not yet going to include the data type and default values for the attributes, these are not complete attribute declarations and would be rejected by any XML parser.)

To declare the attributes in the orders.xml document:

1. If necessary, reopen the **orders.xml** document in your text editor.

2. Below the customer declaration, insert the following two attribute declarations:

```
<!ATTLIST customer custID>
<!ATTLIST customer custType>
```

3. Below the declaration for the name element, insert

```
<!ATTLIST name title>
```

4. Below the declaration for the order element, insert the following two declarations:

```
<!ATTLIST order orderID>
<!ATTLIST order orderBy>
```

5. Below the declaration for the item element, insert

```
<!ATTLIST item itemPrice>
<!ATTLIST item itemQty>
```

You may wish to separate different groups of elements in the DTD for clarity. Figure 3-9 shows the newly inserted text with attribute declarations separated from the element declarations.

Figure 3-9 ▶ **Declaring attribute names**

```
<!DOCTYPE customers
[
    <!ELEMENT customers (customer+)>

    <!ELEMENT customer (name, address, phone, email?, orders)>
    <!ATTLIST customer custID>
    <!ATTLIST customer custType>

    <!ELEMENT name (#PCDATA)>
    <!ATTLIST name title>

    <!ELEMENT address (#PCDATA)>
    <!ELEMENT phone (#PCDATA)>
    <!ELEMENT email (#PCDATA)>
    <!ELEMENT orders (order+)>

    <!ELEMENT order (orderDate, items)>
    <!ATTLIST order orderID>
    <!ATTLIST order orderBy>

    <!ELEMENT orderDate (#PCDATA)>
    <!ELEMENT items (item+)>

    <!ELEMENT item (#PCDATA)>
    <!ATTLIST item itemPrice>
    <!ATTLIST item itemQty>
]>
```

The next step in writing these attribute declarations is to specify the data type for each attribute.

Working with Attribute Types

Attribute values can consist only of character data, but you can control the format of those characters. As shown in Figure 3-10, attribute values can be placed into several different categories. Each category gives you a varying degree of control over the attribute's content. You'll investigate each of these categories in greater detail, starting with character data.

Figure 3-10 ▶ **Attribute types**

Attribute Value	Description
CDATA	Character data
enumerated list	A list of possible attribute values
ID	A unique text string
IDREF	A reference to an ID value
IDREFS	A list of ID values separated by white space
ENTITY	A reference to an external unparsed entity
ENTITIES	A list of entities separated by white space
NMTOKEN	An accepted XML name
NMTOKENS	A list of XML names separated by white space

CDATA

Character data, or CDATA, is the simplest form for attribute text. Specifying character data allows an attribute to contain almost any data except those characters reserved by XML for other purposes (such as the <, >, and & characters). To declare an attribute value as character data, you add the CDATA data type to the attribute declaration with the following syntax:

```
<!ATTLIST element attribute CDATA default>
```

For example, the price of each item in Kristin's document is expressed in character data. To indicate this in the DTD, you would enter the following declaration:

```
<!ATTLIST item itemPrice CDATA ...>
```

Any of the following attribute values are allowed under this declaration:

```
<item itemPrice="29.95"> ... </item>
<item itemPrice="$29.95"> ... </item>
<item itemPrice="£29.95"> ... </item>
```

Note that the £ symbol in this example is treated as character data.

In Kristin's document, two attributes contain character data: itemPrice and itemQty. Add this information to their attribute declarations.

To specify that an attribute contains character data:

1. Within the attribute declarations for itemPrice and itemQty, insert the type **CDATA** as shown in Figure 3-11.

Specifying character data attribute values | Figure 3-11

```
<!DOCTYPE customers
[
    <!ELEMENT customers (customer+)>

    <!ELEMENT customer (name, address, phone, email?, orders)>
    <!ATTLIST customer custID>
    <!ATTLIST customer custType>

    <!ELEMENT name (#PCDATA)>
    <!ATTLIST name title>

    <!ELEMENT address (#PCDATA)>
    <!ELEMENT phone (#PCDATA)>
    <!ELEMENT email (#PCDATA)>
    <!ELEMENT orders (order+)>

    <!ELEMENT order (orderDate, items)>
    <!ATTLIST order orderID>
    <!ATTLIST order orderBy>

    <!ELEMENT orderDate (#PCDATA)>
    <!ELEMENT items (item+)>

    <!ELEMENT item (#PCDATA)>
    <!ATTLIST item itemPrice CDATA>
    <!ATTLIST item itemQty CDATA>
]>
```

2. Save your changes to the document.

It may seem strange that values of the itemQty attribute are expressed in character data. It makes more sense to declare that itemQty values must be integers or numbers, but no such data type exists for DTDs. To indicate that an attribute value must be an integer or number, you must use schemas—a topic you'll learn about in the next tutorial.

Enumerated Types

The CDATA data type allows for almost any string of characters, but in some cases you'll want to restrict the attribute to a set of possible values. For example, Kristin uses the custType attribute to indicate whether a customer is making purchases for business or home use. She needs to restrict the value of the custType attribute to either "home" or "business". Attributes that are limited to a set of possible values are known as **enumerated types**. The general form of an attribute declaration that uses an enumerated type is

```
<!ATTLIST element attribute (value1 | value2 | value3 | ...) default>
```

where `value1`, `value2`, etc., are allowed values for the specified attribute. Thus, to limit the value of the custType attribute to either "home" or "business", Kristin can include the following type in her declaration:

```
<!ATTLIST customer custType (home | business) ...>
```

Under this declaration, any custType attribute whose value is not "home" or "business" causes parsers to reject the document as invalid. Kristin wants you to add this enumerated type to the DTD.

To declare an enumerated data type:

1. Within the custType attribute declaration, insert the data type **(home | business)**

   Kristin also wants to limit the values of the title attribute to Mr., Mrs., or Ms.

2. Within the title attribute declaration, insert the data type **(Mr. | Mrs. | Ms.)**

   Figure 3-12 shows the revised DTD.

Figure 3-12 ▶ | **Specifying enumerated attribute values**

```
<!DOCTYPE customers
[
    <!ELEMENT customers (customer+)>

    <!ELEMENT customer (name, address, phone, email?, orders)>
    <!ATTLIST customer custID>
    <!ATTLIST customer custType (home | business)>

    <!ELEMENT name (#PCDATA)>
    <!ATTLIST name title (Mr. | Mrs. | Ms.)>

    <!ELEMENT address (#PCDATA)>
    <!ELEMENT phone (#PCDATA)>
    <!ELEMENT email (#PCDATA)>
    <!ELEMENT orders (order+)>

    <!ELEMENT order (orderDate, items)>
    <!ATTLIST order orderID>
    <!ATTLIST order orderBy>

    <!ELEMENT orderDate (#PCDATA)>
    <!ELEMENT items (item+)>

    <!ELEMENT item (#PCDATA)>
    <!ATTLIST item itemPrice CDATA>
    <!ATTLIST item itemQty CDATA>
]>
```

Another type of enumerated attribute is a notation. A **notation** associates the value of an attribute with a <!NOTATION> declaration that is inserted elsewhere in the DTD. Notations are used when an attribute value refers to a file containing nontextual data, like a graphic image or a video clip. You'll learn more about notations and how to work with nontextual data in the next session.

Tokenized Types

Tokenized types are character strings that follow certain rules (known as **tokens**) for format and content. DTDs support four kinds of tokens: IDs, ID references, name tokens, and entities.

An **ID token** is used when an attribute value must be unique within a document. In Kristin's document, the customer element contains the custID attribute, storing a unique ID for each customer. In order to prevent users from entering the same custID value for different customers, Kristin can define the attribute type for the CustID attribute as follows:

```
<!ATTLIST customer custID ID ...>
```

Under this declaration, the following elements are valid:

```
<customer custID="Cust021"> ... </customer>
<customer custID="Cust022"> ... </customer>
```

However, the following elements would not be valid because the same custID value is used more than once:

```
<customer custID="Cust021"> ... </customer>
<customer custID="Cust021"> ... </customer>
```

Once an ID value has been declared in a document, other attribute values can reference to it using the IDREF token. An attribute declared as an **IDREF token** must have a value equal to the value of an ID attribute located somewhere in the same document. This enables an XML document to contain cross-references between one element and another. The attribute declaration for an id reference is

```
<!ATTLIST element attribute IDREF default>
```

For example, the order element in Kristin's document has an attribute named orderBy, which contains the ID of the customer who made the order. Since this is an ID reference, Kristin can ensure that the orderBy value refers to an actual customer using the declaration

```
<!ATTLIST order orderBy IDREF ...>
```

When an XML parser encounters this attribute, it searches the XML document for an ID value that matches the value of the orderBy attribute. If it doesn't find one, it rejects the document as invalid. Note that you cannot specify that an XML parser limit its search to only particular elements or attributes. Any ID attribute in any element is a candidate for an ID reference.

Attributes can contain multiple IDs and IDREFs, placed in lists, with each entry separated by white space. To declare a list of IDs or IDREFS, you submit the following attribute declarations:

```
<!ATTLIST element attribute IDS default>
```

or

```
<!ATTLIST element attribute IDREFS default>
```

Kristin might want to do this if she were to list all of the orders made by a certain customer as an attribute, as in the following sample code:

```
<customer orders="OR3413 OR3910 OR5310"> ... </customer>
...
<order orderID="OR3413"> ... </order>
<order orderID="OR3910"> ... </order>
<order orderID="OR5310"> ... </order>
```

In this case, the attribute types of the Orders and OrderID attributes are defined as follows:

```
<!ATTLIST customer orders IDREFS ...>
```

```
<!ATTLIST order orderID ID ...>
```

As with the IDREF token, all of the IDs listed in an IDREFS token must be found in an ID attribute located somewhere in the file, or parsers will reject the document as invalid. In the orders.xml document, the custID and orderID attributes contain ID values, while the orderBy attribute contains an IDREF. Kristin would like you to add this information to the DTD.

To declare IDs and IDREFs:

1. Within the custID and orderID attribute declarations, insert the data type **ID**.

2. Within the orderBy attribute declaration, insert the data type **IDREF** (see Figure 3-13).

Figure 3-13	Specifying attribute IDs and IDREFs

```
<!DOCTYPE customers
[
    <!ELEMENT customers (customer+)>

    <!ELEMENT customer (name, address, phone, email?, orders)>
    <!ATTLIST customer custID ID>
    <!ATTLIST customer custType (home | business)>

    <!ELEMENT name (#PCDATA)>
    <!ATTLIST name title (Mr. | Mrs. | Ms.)>

    <!ELEMENT address (#PCDATA)>
    <!ELEMENT phone (#PCDATA)>
    <!ELEMENT email (#PCDATA)>
    <!ELEMENT orders (order+)>

    <!ELEMENT order (orderDate, items)>
    <!ATTLIST order orderID ID>
    <!ATTLIST order orderBy IDREF>

    <!ELEMENT orderDate (#PCDATA)>
    <!ELEMENT items (item+)>

    <!ELEMENT item (#PCDATA)>
    <!ATTLIST item itemPrice CDATA>
    <!ATTLIST item itemQty CDATA>
]>
```

The **NMTOKEN** (or **name token**) data type is used with character data whose values must be valid XML names. This means that NMTOKEN data types can contain letters, numbers, and the punctuation symbols underscore (_), hyphen (-), period (.), and colon (:). A name token can't contain white space, however. This constraint makes name tokens less flexible than character data, which can contain white space characters. If Kristin wants to make sure that an attribute value is always a valid XML name, she can use the NMTOKEN type instead of the CDATA type. An attribute that contains a list of name tokens, each separated by a blank space, can be defined using the **NMTOKENS** data type.

The final tokenized attribute type is an entity. You'll learn more about entities in the next session.

Reference Window

Declaring Attribute Types

- To indicate that an attribute contains character data, use
    `attribute CDATA`
  where `attribute` is the name of the attribute.
- To constrain an attribute value to a list of possible values, use
    `attribute (value1 | value2 | value3 | ...)`
  where `value1`, `value2`, etc., are allowed values for the attribute.
- To declare an attribute as a tokenized type, use
    `attribute token`
  where `token` indicates the type of token in use. DTDs support the following token types: ID, IDREF, IDREFS, NMTOKEN, NMTOKENS, ENTITY, and ENTITIES.

Working with Attribute Defaults

The final part of an attribute declaration is the attribute default. There are four possible values: #REQUIRED, #IMPLIED, a *default* value, and a *fixed default* value. Figure 3-14 describes each of these attribute defaults.

Attribute defaults ◄ Figure 3-14

Attribute Default	Description
#REQUIRED	The attribute must appear with every occurrence of the element.
#IMPLIED	The attribute is optional.
"*default*"	The attribute is optional. If an attribute value is not specified, a validating XML parser will supply the *default* value.
#FIXED *default*	The attribute is optional. If an attribute value is specified, it must match the *default* value.

Earlier, in Figure 3-8, Kristin outlined the properties for the attributes in her document. Note that a customer ID is required for every customer. Kristin can indicate this in the DTD by adding the #REQUIRED value to the attribute declaration:

```
<!ATTLIST customer custID ID #REQUIRED>
```

On the other hand, Kristin cannot always determine whether a customer represents a home or business, so she uses the #IMPLIED value for the custType attribute to indicate that use of this attribute is optional. The complete attribute declaration is

```
<!ATTLIST customer custType (home | business) #IMPLIED>
```

If an XML parser encounters a customer element without a custType attribute, it doesn't invalidate the document, but instead assumes a blank value for the attribute.

Another attribute from Kristin's document is the itemQty attribute, which indicates the quantity of each item on the order. The itemQty attribute is optional, but unlike the custType attribute, which gets a blank value if omitted, Kristin wants XML parsers to assume a value of "1" for this attribute if it's missing. The complete attribute declaration is as follows:

```
<!ATTLIST item itemQty CDATA "1">
```

The last type of attribute default is #FIXED *default*, which fixes the attribute to a specified *default* value. If you omit the attribute from the element, an XML parser supplies the default value; if you include the attribute, the attribute value must be equal to *default* or the document is invalid. You can't use the #FIXED form with an ID attribute, however, because ID attributes must have unique values.

Now that you've seen how to work with attribute defaults, you can complete the attribute declarations by adding the default specifications.

To specify the attribute default specifications:

▶ 1. Add **#REQUIRED** to the custID, orderID, orderBy, and itemPrice attribute declarations to indicate that these are required attributes.

▶ 2. Add **#IMPLIED** to the custType and title attributes to indicate that these are optional attributes.

▶ 3. Add **"1"** to the itemQty attribute to indicate that this is the default value of the attribute if no attribute value is entered in the document.

Figure 3-15 shows the final form of the attribute declarations in the DTD.

| Figure 3-15 | Specifying attribute defaults |

```
<!DOCTYPE customers
[
    <!ELEMENT customers (customer+)>

    <!ELEMENT customer (name, address, phone, email?, orders)>
    <!ATTLIST customer custID ID #REQUIRED>
    <!ATTLIST customer custType (home | business) #IMPLIED>

    <!ELEMENT name (#PCDATA)>
    <!ATTLIST name title (Mr. | Mrs. | Ms.) #IMPLIED>

    <!ELEMENT address (#PCDATA)>
    <!ELEMENT phone (#PCDATA)>
    <!ELEMENT email (#PCDATA)>
    <!ELEMENT orders (order+)>

    <!ELEMENT order (orderDate, items)>
    <!ATTLIST order orderID ID #REQUIRED>
    <!ATTLIST order orderBy IDREF #REQUIRED>

    <!ELEMENT orderDate (#PCDATA)>
    <!ELEMENT items (item+)>

    <!ELEMENT item (#PCDATA)>
    <!ATTLIST item itemPrice CDATA #REQUIRED>
    <!ATTLIST item itemQty CDATA "1">
]>
```

▶ 4. Save your changes to the document.

| Reference Window | **Specifying an Attribute Default** |

• Within an attribute declaration, insert the following attribute defaults:
#REQUIRED for an attribute that must appear with every occurrence of the element
#IMPLIED for an optional attribute
"*default*" for an optional attribute that has a *default* value when omitted
#FIXED "*default*" for an optional attribute that must be fixed to the *default* value

Now that you've created a DTD that declares all of the elements and attributes in the document, how do you know that all of your hard work has resulted in a valid XML document? It's possible that you've forgotten to declare an element or attribute, or you may have made a simple typing mistake. How do you test for validity?

Validating a Document with XMLSpy

To test for validity, an XML parser must be able to compare your XML document with the rules you set up in the DTD. The Web is an excellent source for validating parsers. This book uses XMLSpy to perform document validation. Instructions for installing XMLSpy are included in Appendix A; it should be installed before you perform the steps below. If you have any problems with the software, contact your instructor or technical support person. Your instructor might also choose a different validating parser to complete the assignments in this book. If so, contact your instructor for information on working with that software. If you are interested in using <Oxygen/> to work through the steps, alternative steps are available in this book's Student Online Companion.

To start XMLSpy:

1. Click the **Start** button on your Taskbar, point to **All Programs**, point to **Altova XMLSpy Home Edition**, and click **Altova XMLSpy** from the menu.

   Trouble? Your system may be configured with the XMLSpy program located in a different folder or menu. Contact your instructor if you are having problems locating or starting the program.

   Trouble? If XMLSpy displays a dialog box listing advanced features that you can install, click the Cancel button to go on to the main XMLSpy window.

2. In the XMLSpy window, click **File** on the menu bar, and then click **Open**.

3. Select the **orders.xml** file located in the tutorial.03x/tutorial folder and click the **Open** button. Figure 3-16 shows the contents of the document as viewed in XMLSpy.

XMLSpy opening window | Figure 3-16

The XMLSpy window is divided into three sections. On the left is the Info window, which provides information about the document currently being edited. The Main window displays the contents of the XML window in one of four formats: Text View, Schema/WSDL View, Authentic View, and Browser View (to use Browser View, you must have Internet Explorer 5.0 or higher installed on your system). The rightmost section of the screen displays the Entry Helper windows. The contents of these windows change based on the type of document being viewed. For an XML document, these windows display a list of the elements, attributes, and entities used in the document. You can learn more about parts of the XMLSpy window by reading Appendix A.

Next, Kristin would like you to test her orders document for both well-formedness and validity.

To validate orders.xml:

▶ **1.** Click the **Validate Document** button 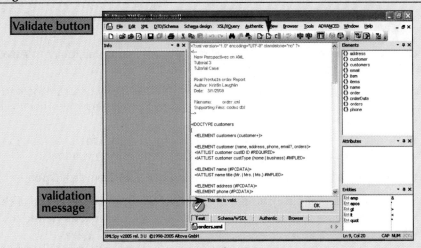 on the XMLSpy toolbar (or press the **F8** key on your keyboard).

If you have not made any mistakes in entering code for the DTD, XMLSpy reports that the document is valid (see Figure 3-17).

Figure 3-17	▶ Validating the orders.xml document

Trouble? If XMLSpy reports an error, note the error and then close XMLSpy. Compare the code in your DTD against that shown earlier in Figure 3-15, and then fix any mistakes in your text editor, saving the file when you're done. Restart XMLSpy and reopen your revised document.

▶ **2.** Click the **OK** button to close the validation message.

Though the file is valid, it is a good learning experience to place a few intentional errors into your XML code to see how validation errors are reported. You decide to change the name in the element declaration from email to mail. Since there is no longer a declaration for the email element, the first time XMLSpy encounters this undeclared element, it should report a validation error. You can edit the contents of orders.xml directly in the Main window.

To make orders.xml invalid:

▶ **1.** Locate the element declaration for the email element near the top of the document. Select the name "email" and change the name in the element declaration to **mail**.

▶ **2.** Click the **Validate Document** button (or press **F8**) to validate the file.

▶ **3.** XMLSpy reports that the file is not valid because the email element has not been declared. It also highlights the validation error in the document. See Figure 3-18.

element name changed from email to mail

location of validation error

document is not valid

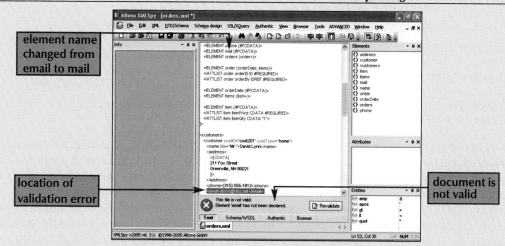

4. Change "mail" back to **email** in the element declaration to remove the error.

5. Click the **Revalidate** button next to the validation error message.

   XMLSpy reports that the file is once again valid.

6. Click the **OK** button to close the validation message.

   Trouble? If you still get an error message, examine the reason for the error and then make the necessary corrections.

   After confirming that orders.xml is a valid XML document, close XMLSpy. You should not have to save any changes you made during this session.

7. Click **File** and then click **Exit**. Click the **No** button to exit the document without permanently saving any of your changes.

Working with Namespaces and DTDs

Kristin is pleased with your work on validating her document. In the future, she might consider placing the order and customer information in separate files, combining them only in compound documents using namespaces. She wonders how a DTD would work with a namespace.

The brief answer is "not very well." DTDs are not namespace-aware, so you can't declare a namespace and apply it to a DTD in the same way that you can use an @namespace rule with a CSS style sheet. However, you can work with qualified names and namespace prefixes to achieve almost the same effect. For example, if the phone element is placed in the customers namespace using the "cust" prefix

```
<cust:phone>(315) 555-1812</cust:phone>
```

then the element declaration in the DTD would need to include the cust prefix

```
<!ELEMENT cust:phone (#PCDATA)>
```

In essence, the DTD treats a qualified name as a complete element name with the namespace prefix, colon, and local name as a single entity. It doesn't recognize the namespace prefix as significant. Any namespace declarations in a document must also be included in the DTD for the document to be valid. This is usually done using a fixed data type for the namespace's URI. For example, if the root element in a document declares the customers namespace using the attribute value

```
<cust:customers xmlns:cust="http://www.pixal.com/customers">
...
</cust:customers>
```

then the DTD should include the following attribute declaration:

```
<!ATTLIST cust:customers xmlns:cust CDATA #FIXED "http://www.pixal.com/
customers">
```

The drawback to mixing namespaces and DTDs is that you must know ahead of time the namespace prefix used in an XML document, and the DTD must be written to conform to that namespace. This makes it difficult to perform validation on a wide variety of documents that might employ any number of possible namespace prefixes. Moreover, for a given DTD, there is no way of knowing what namespace a prefix in the DTD points to, since DTDs do not include a mechanism for matching a prefix to a namespace URI. It is also difficult to validate a compound document using standard vocabularies like XHTML, because you cannot easily modify the standard DTDs to accommodate the namespaces in your document.

If combining validation and namespaces is an important issue, a better solution may be to use schemas, which are a validation tool that does support namespaces. You'll look at creating and applying schemas in the next tutorial.

You've completed your work in defining the content and structure of Kristin's document in a DTD. In the next session, you'll learn how to work with entities and nontextual content in your DTD, and you'll learn about the DTDs associated with some of the standard XML vocabularies.

Session 3.2 Quick Check

1. What attribute declaration would you enter to create an optional text string for the title attribute within the book element?
2. The play element has a required attribute named type, which can have one of four possible values: Romance, Tragedy, History, and Comedy. Enter the appropriate attribute declaration.
3. What is the main difference between an attribute with the CDATA type and one with the NMTOKEN type?
4. The book element has a required ID attribute named ISBN. Enter the appropriate attribute declaration.
5. An author element has an optional attribute named booksBy, which contains the ISBN numbers of the books the author has written. If ISBN is an ID attribute for another element in the document, what declaration would you use for the booksBy attribute?
6. The book element has an optional attribute named inStock that can have the value "yes" or "no". The default value is "yes". What is the declaration for the inStock attribute?

Session 3.3

Introducing Entities

In the orders.xml document, Kristin has inserted product codes for the different items ordered by customers. For example, the first customer in the file, Mr. David Lynn, ordered three items with the product codes DCT5Z, SM128, and RCL. Kristin would like some way of automatically replacing these codes with the longer product descriptions. Figure 3-19 shows the product codes and descriptions for all of the items found in the orders. xml file.

Product codes and descriptions ◄ **Figure 3-19**

Product Code	Description
DCT5Z	Tapan 5 megapixel digital camera with optical zoom
SM128	128 megabyte SmartMedia card
RCL	Rechargeable lithium-ion battery
BCE4L	Four-port lithium battery charger
WBC500	WebNow Webcam 500
RCA	Rechargeable alkaline battery
SCL4C	Linton Flatbed Scanner 4C

In the first tutorial, you worked with entities to insert special character strings into an XML document. Five built-in entity references are particularly helpful in XML:

- **&** for the & character
- **<** for the < character
- **>** for the > character
- **'** for the ' character
- **"** for the " character

You can also create these characters using character references, in which numbers from the ISO/IEC character set are substituted for the entity names. When an XML parser encounters these character or entity references, it parses the code and displays the corresponding character symbol. These standard character and entity references are built into the language of XML. Using DTDs, you can create your own customized set of entities corresponding to text strings like Kristin's product descriptions, files, or nontextual content that you want inserted into an XML document.

Working with General Entities

To create your own customized entity, you add a general entity to a document's DTD. A **general entity** is an entity that references content to be used within an XML document. That content can be either parsed or unparsed. A **parsed entity** references text that can be readily interpreted or parsed by an application reading the XML document. Parsed entities can reference characters, words, phrases, paragraphs, or entire documents. The only requirement is that the text be well formed. An entity that references content that is either nontextual or which cannot be interpreted by an XML parser is an **unparsed entity**. An entity that references a graphic image would be an unparsed entity. The content can be placed either within the DTD or in an external file. **Internal entities** include their content in the DTD. **External entities** draw their content from external files. Since there are different types of general entities, there are different types of entity declarations. You'll start by examining how to create a parsed entity for character data. Later in this session, you'll examine how to work with noncharacter data in unparsed entities.

Parsed Entities

To create an internal parsed entity, you add the following declaration to the DTD:

```
<!ENTITY entity "value">
```

where `entity` is the name you've assigned to the entity and `value` is the entity's value. The entity name follows the same rules that apply to all XML names: there can be no blank spaces in the name, and the name must begin with either a letter or an underscore. The entity value itself must be well-formed XML text. This can be a simple text string, or it can be well-formed XML code. For example, to store the product description for the Tapan digital camera, you could use the following entity:

```
<!ENTITY DCT5Z "Tapan Digital Camera 5 Mpx - zoom">
```

If you wanted to include markup tags around this product description, you might insert the following declaration:

```
<!ENTITY DCT5Z "<desc>Tapan Digital Camera 5 Mpx - zoom</desc>">
```

Any text is allowed for an entity's value, as long as it corresponds to well-formed XML. The entity declaration

```
<!ENTITY DCT5Z "<desc>Tapan Digital Camera 5 Mpx - zoom">
```

would not be valid because it lacks the closing </desc> tag in the entity's value. Entity values must be well formed within themselves without reference to other entities or document content. You couldn't, for example, place the closing </desc> tag in another entity declaration or within the XML document itself.

For longer text strings, it is preferable to place the content in an external file. To create an external parsed entity, you use the declaration

```
<!ENTITY entity SYSTEM "uri">
```

where `entity` is once again the entity's name and `uri` is the URI of the external file containing the entity's content. The following entity declaration references the content of the description.xml file:

```
<!ENTITY DCT5Z SYSTEM "description.xml">
```

The description.xml file must contain well-formed XML content. However, it should not contain an xml declaration. Since XML documents can contain only one xml declaration, placing a second one in a document via an external entity results in an error.

An external entity can also reference a public location using the declaration

```
<!ENTITY entity PUBLIC "id" "uri">
```

where `id` is the public identifier and `uri` is the system location of the external file (included in case the XML parser doesn't recognize the public identifier). A public location for an external entity might look like the following:

```
<!ENTITY DCT5Z PUBLIC "-//PIXAL//DCT5Z INFO" "description.xml">
```

In this case, the public identifier "-//PIXAL//DCT5Z INFO" is used by an XML parser to load the external content. If that id is not recognized, the parser falls back to the system location of the description.xml file. In this way, external entities behave like the external references for DOCTYPE declarations discussed earlier in Session 3.1.

Declaring General Parsed Entities

- To declare a parsed internal entity, add the following declaration to the DTD:
    ```
    <!ENTITY entity "value">
    ```
  where *entity* is the entity's name and *value* is the entity's value.
- To declare a parsed external entity, use the declaration
    ```
    <!ENTITY entity SYSTEM "uri">
    ```
  where *uri* is the URI of the external file containing the entity value. You can also set up a public external entity with the declaration
    ```
    <!ENTITY entity PUBLIC "id" "uri">
    ```
  where *id* is the public identifier for the external file.

Referencing a General Entity

Once a general entity has been declared in a DTD, it can be referenced anywhere within the body of the XML document. The syntax for referencing a general entity is

```
&entity;
```

where *entity* is the entity's name as declared in the DTD. For example, if the DCT5Z entity is declared in the DTD as

```
<!ENTITY DCT5Z "Tapan Digital Camera 5 Mpx - zoom">
```

you can insert the entity's value into the XML document with the reference

```
<item>&DCT5Z;</item>
```

When an XML parser encounters this general entity, it expands the entity's value into the XML document, resulting in the following content:

```
<item>Tapan Digital Camera 5 Mpx - zoom</item>
```

The fact that the entity's value is expanded into the code of the XML document is one reason why entity values must correspond to well-formed XML code. Note that because of the way entities are parsed, you cannot include the & symbol as part of an entity's value. XML parsers interpret the & symbol as a reference to another entity and attempt to resolve the reference. If you need to include the & symbol, you should use the built-in entity reference &. You also cannot use the % symbol in an entity's value because, as you'll learn later, this is the symbol used for inserting parameter entities.

Referencing a General Entity

- To reference a general entity within an XML document, enter the code
    ```
    &entity;
    ```
  where *entity* is the entity name declared in the DTD associated with the XML document.

Kristin asks that you declare parsed entities for the product codes in the orders.xml document. Since these product codes are also used in the other XML documents she's working on, she would like the declarations placed in an external DTD file named codes.dtd.

To create the entity declarations:

▶ **1.** Use your text editor to open the **codestxt.dtd** file from the tutorial.03x/tutorial folder. Enter *your name* and *the date* in the comment section at the top of file.

▶ **2.** Add the following entity declarations below the comment section (see Figure 3-20):

```
<!ENTITY DCT5Z "Tapan Digital Camera 5 Mpx - zoom">
<!ENTITY SM128 "SmartMedia 128MB Card">
<!ENTITY RCL "Rechargeable Lithium Ion Battery">
<!ENTITY BCE4L "Battery Charger 4pt Lithium">
<!ENTITY WBC500 "WebNow Webcam 500">
<!ENTITY RCA "Rechargeable Alkaline Battery">
<!ENTITY SCL4C "Linton Flatbed Scanner 4C">
```

Figure 3-20 ▶ **Creating general entities**

```
<!ENTITY DCT5Z "Tapan Digital Camera 5 Mpx - zoom">
<!ENTITY SM128 "SmartMedia 128MB Card">
<!ENTITY RCL "Rechargeable Lithium Ion Battery">
<!ENTITY BCE4L "Battery Charger 4pt Lithium">
<!ENTITY WBC500 "WebNow Webcam 500">
<!ENTITY RCA "Rechargeable Alkaline Battery">
<!ENTITY SCL4C "Linton Flatbed Scanner 4C">
```

▶ **3.** Save the file as **codes.dtd**.

Because you placed these entity declarations in an external DTD file, you need some way of linking the orders.xml document to that DTD. One way would be to revise the DOCTYPE declaration to include the codes.dtd file along with the internal declarations you've already created; another option is to use a parameter entity.

Working with Parameter Entities

Just as you use general entities when you want to insert content into an XML document, you use a **parameter entity** when you want to insert content into a DTD itself. With parameter entities, a DTD can be broken into smaller chunks, or **modules**, placed in different files. Imagine a team of programmers working on a DTD for a large XML vocabulary like XHTML, containing hundreds of elements and attributes. Rather than placing all of the declarations within a single file, individual programmers could work on sections suited to their expertise. Parameter entities also allow XML programmers to reuse large blocks of DTD code without retyping the same code multiple times. The declaration to create a parameter entity is similar to the declaration for a general entity, with the syntax

```
<!ENTITY % entity "value">
```

where *entity* is the name of the parameter entity and *value* is the text of the entity's value. Like general entities, parameter entities can also reference external content in either system or public locations. The declarations for external parameter entities are:

```
<!ENTITY % entity SYSTEM "uri">
```

or

```
<!ENTITY % entity PUBLIC "id" "uri">
```

where `id` is the public identifier for the parameter entity and `uri` is the location of the external file containing DTD content. For example, the following code shows an internal parameter entity for a collection of elements and attributes:

```
<!ENTITY % books
    "<!ELEMENT Book (Title, Author)>
    <!ATTLIST Book Pages CDATA #REQUIRED>
    <!ELEMENT Title (#PCDATA)>
    <!ELEMENT Author (#PCDATA)>"
>
```

If you place these elements and attributes in an external DTD file named "books.dtd", you could declare the following external parameter entity to access the content of that document:

```
<!ENTITY % books SYSTEM "books.dtd">
```

Once a parameter has been declared, you can add a reference to it within the DTD using the statement

```
%entity;
```

where `entity` is the name assigned to the parameter entity. Parameter entity references can be placed only where a declaration would normally occur, such as within an internal or external DTD. You *cannot* insert a parameter entity reference within the content of an XML document. For example, to reference the books parameter entity described above, you would enter the following line into your DTD:

```
%books;
```

Figure 3-21 shows how parameter entities can be used to combine DTDs from multiple files into a single DTD.

| Figure 3-21 | Combining DTDs with parameter entities |

books.dtd

```
<!ELEMENT Book (Title, Author)>
<!ATTLIST Book Pages CDATA #REQUIRED>
<!ELEMENT Title (#PCDATA)>
<!ELEMENT Author (#PCDATA)>
```

magazines.dtd

```
<!ELEMENT Magazine (Name)>
<!ATTLIST Magazine Publisher CDATA #REQUIRED>
<!ELEMENT Name (#PCDATA)>
```

```
<!ENTITY % books SYSTEM "books.dtd">
<!ENTITY % mags SYSTEM "magazines.dtd">

%books;
%mags;
```

```
<!ENTITY % books SYSTEM "books.dtd">
<!ENTITY % mags SYSTEM "magazines.dtd">

<!ELEMENT Book (Title, Author)>
<!ATTLIST Book Pages CDATA #REQUIRED>
<!ELEMENT Title (#PCDATA)>
<!ELEMENT Author (#PCDATA)>
<!ELEMENT Magazine (Name)>
<!ATTLIST Magazine Publisher CDATA #REQUIRED>
<!ELEMENT Name (#PCDATA)>
```

XML parser expands the parameter entity references into the DTD

Reference Window | **Declaring and Referencing a Parameter Entity**

- To declare an internal parameter entity, add the following line to the DTD:
     `<!ENTITY % entity "value">`
  where `entity` is the entity's name and `value` is the entity value.
- To declare an external parameter entity, use the following system location:
     `<!ENTITY % entity SYSTEM "uri">`
  where `uri` is the URI of the system file. For a public location, use
     `<!ENTITY % entity PUBLIC "id" "uri">`
  where `id` is the public identifier.
- To reference a parameter entity, add the following line to the DTD:
     `%entity;`
  where `entity` is the name of the parameter entity.

Now that you've seen how to create and apply a parameter entity, Kristin wants you to add one to the DTD within the orders.xml file to load the contents of the codes.dtd file you just created. You'll name the parameter entity itemCodes.

To insert a parameter entity:

▶ **1.** If necessary, reopen the **orders.xml** file in your text editor.

▶ **2.** Add the following entity declaration to the internal DTD:

```
<!ENTITY % itemCodes SYSTEM "codes.dtd">
```

Now add a reference to the parameter entity.

▶ **3.** Insert the following reference:

```
%itemCodes;
```

Figure 3-22 shows the completed DTD.

Accessing the codes.dtd file ◀ Figure 3-22

```
<!DOCTYPE customers
[
    <!ELEMENT customers (customer+)>

    <!ELEMENT customer (name, address, phone, email?, orders)>
    <!ATTLIST customer custID ID #REQUIRED>
    <!ATTLIST customer custType (home | business) #IMPLIED>

    <!ELEMENT name (#PCDATA)>
    <!ATTLIST name title (Mr. | Mrs. | Ms.) #IMPLIED>

    <!ELEMENT address (#PCDATA)>
    <!ELEMENT phone (#PCDATA)>
    <!ELEMENT email (#PCDATA)>
    <!ELEMENT orders (order+)>

    <!ELEMENT order (orderDate, items)>
    <!ATTLIST order orderID ID #REQUIRED>
    <!ATTLIST order orderBy IDREF #REQUIRED>

    <!ELEMENT orderDate (#PCDATA)>
    <!ELEMENT items (item+)>

    <!ELEMENT item (#PCDATA)>
    <!ATTLIST item itemPrice CDATA #REQUIRED>
    <!ATTLIST item itemQty CDATA "1">

    <!ENTITY % itemCodes SYSTEM "codes.dtd">
    %itemCodes;
]>
```

▶ **4.** Save your changes to the file.

With the parameter entity added to the DTD to access the contents of the codes.dtd file, you can now insert entity references in the body of the XML document, replacing Kristin's product codes.

To add entity references:

▶ **1.** Return to the **orders.xml** file in your text editor.

▶ **2.** Locate the first product code for the first customer item and change DCT5Z to **&DCT5Z;**

▶ **3.** Locate the second product code and change SM128 to **&SM128;**.

▶ **4.** Continue through the rest of document and change the five remaining product codes to entity references by inserting an ampersand (&) before the product code and a semi-colon after the product code. Figure 3-23 shows the revised orders.xml file with the modified item values highlighted in red.

Figure 3-23 | Inserting general entities

```
<customers>
    <customer custID="cust201" custType="home">
        <name title="Mr.">David Lynn</name>
        <address>
            <![CDATA[
            211 Fox Street
            Greenville, NH 80021
            ]]>
        </address>
        <phone>(315) 555-1812</phone>
        <email>dlynn@nhs.net</email>
        <orders>
            <order orderID="or10311" orderBy="cust201">
                <orderDate>8/1/2008</orderDate>
                <items>
                    <item itemPrice="599.95">&DCT5Z;</item>
                    <item itemPrice="199.95">&SM128;</item>
                    <item itemPrice="29.95" itemQty="2">&RCL;</item>
                </items>
            </order>
            <order orderID="or11424" orderBy="cust201">
                <orderDate>9/14/2008</orderDate>
                <items>
                    <item itemPrice="59.95">&BCE4L;</item>
                </items>
            </order>
        </orders>
    </customer>

    <customer custID="cust202">
        <name title="Mrs.">Jean Kaufmann</name>
        <address>
            <![CDATA[
            411 East Oak Avenue
            Cashton, MI  20401
            ]]>
        </address>
        <phone>(611) 555-4033</phone>
        <email>JKaufmann@cshweb.com</email>
        <orders>
            <order orderID="or10899" orderBy="cust202">
                <orderDate>8/11/2008</orderDate>
                <items>
                    <item itemPrice="59.99">&WBC500;</item>
                    <item itemPrice="5.95" itemQty="2">&RCA;</item>
                </items>
            </order>
        </orders>
    </customer>

    <customer custID="cust203" custType="business">
        <name>AdServices</name>
        <address>
            <![CDATA[
            55 Washburn Lane
            Creighton, UT  98712
            ]]>
        </address>
        <phone>(811) 555-2987</phone>
        <orders>
            <order orderID="or11201" orderBy="cust203">
                <orderDate>9/15/2008</orderDate>
                <items>
                    <item itemPrice="179.99" itemQty="3">&SCL4C;</item>
                </items>
            </order>
        </orders>
    </customer>
</customers>
```

With the entity references added to Kristin's document, you can check whether their values are resolved in your Web browser. Unfortunately, at the time of this writing only Internet Explorer can resolve content placed in external entities and DTDs. The built-in XML parsers in browsers such as Netscape and Firefox do not allow for this.

To view the entity values:

1. Save your changes to **orders.xml**.

2. Open **orders.xml** in Internet Explorer. As shown in Figure 3-24, the contents of the file, viewed in Internet Explorer's outline format, display the values of each of the seven product codes.

Entity references and values   Figure 3-24

```
<customers>
    <customer custID="cust201" custType="home">
        <name title="Mr.">David Lynn</name>
        <address>
            <![CDATA[
            211 Fox Street
            Greenville, NH 80021
            ]]>
        </address>
        <phone>(315) 555-1812</phone>
        <email>dlynn@nhs.net</email>
        <orders>
            <order orderID="or10311" orderBy="cust201">
                <orderDate>8/1/2008</orderDate>
                <items>
                    <item itemPrice="599.95">&OCT5Z;</item>
                    <item itemPrice="199.95">&SM128;</item>
                    <item itemPrice="29.95" itemQty="2">&RCL;</item>
                </items>
            </order>
            <order orderID="or11424" orderBy="cust201">
                <orderDate>9/14/2008</orderDate>
                <items>
                    <item itemPrice="59.95">&BCE4L;</item>
                </items>
            </order>
        </orders>
    </customer>
</customers>
```

XML code

```
- <customers>
    - <customer custID="cust201" custType="home">
        <name title="Mr.">David Lynn</name>
      - <address>
            <![CDATA[          211 Fox Street
                    Greenville, NH 80021
                    ]]>
        </address>
        <phone>(315) 555-1812</phone>
        <email>dlynn@nhs.net</email>
      - <orders>
          - <order orderID="or10311" orderBy="cust201">
                <orderDate>8/1/2008</orderDate>
              - <items>
                    <item itemPrice="599.95" itemQty="1">Tapan Digital Camera 5 Mpx - zoom</item>
                    <item itemPrice="199.95" itemQty="1">SmartMedia 128MB Card</item>
                    <item itemPrice="29.95" itemQty="2">Rechargeable Lithium Ion Battery</item>
                </items>
            </order>
          - <order orderID="or11424" orderBy="cust201">
                <orderDate>9/14/2008</orderDate>
              - <items>
                    <item itemPrice="59.95" itemQty="1">Battery Charger 4pt Lithium</item>
                </items>
            </order>
        </orders>
    </customer>
</customers>
```

XML code with expanded entity values

Trouble? If you open the file with a browser other than Internet Explorer, you may not see the entity values resolved in the rendered page. Netscape and Firefox report a parsing error due to an undefined entity. You'll fix this problem shortly.

Current browsers do not universally support external entities and DTDs. In particular, both Netscape and Firefox use a built-in XML parser called Expat, which does not support resolution of external entities. The reason is that if an entity declaration is placed in a file on a remote Web server, the XML parser has to establish a TCP/IP connection with the remote file, which might not always be possible. Thus, to ensure that an XML document can be properly read and rendered, Expat requires entities to be part of the internal DTD. This situation might be resolved in future releases of these browsers, so Kristin does not want you to completely remove the code you entered. However, to remove the error message within these browsers, you can copy the entity declarations from the codes.dtd file and paste them into the internal DTD.

To copy and paste the general entities:

1. Return to the **codes.dtd** file in your text editor and copy the seven entity declarations.

2. Go to the **orders.xml** file in your text editor and, at the top of the DTD, paste the entity declarations as shown in Figure 3-25.

| Figure 3-25 | Adding entities to the internal DTD |

```
<!DOCTYPE customers
[
    <!ENTITY DCT5Z "Tapan Digital Camera 5 Mpx - zoom">
    <!ENTITY SM128 "SmartMedia 128MB Card">
    <!ENTITY RCL "Rechargeable Lithium Ion Battery">
    <!ENTITY BCE4L "Battery Charger 4pt Lithium">
    <!ENTITY WBC500 "WebNow Webcam 500">
    <!ENTITY RCA "Rechargeable Alkaline Battery">
    <!ENTITY SCL4C "Linton Flatbed Scanner 4C">

    <!ELEMENT customers (customer+)>

    <!ELEMENT customer (name, address, phone, email?, orders)>
    <!ATTLIST customer custID ID #REQUIRED>
    <!ATTLIST customer custType (home | business) #IMPLIED>

    <!ELEMENT name (#PCDATA)>
    <!ATTLIST name title (Mr. | Mrs. | Ms.) #IMPLIED>

    <!ELEMENT address (#PCDATA)>
    <!ELEMENT phone (#PCDATA)>
    <!ELEMENT email (#PCDATA)>
    <!ELEMENT orders (order+)>

    <!ELEMENT order (orderDate, items)>
    <!ATTLIST order orderID ID #REQUIRED>
    <!ATTLIST order orderBy IDREF #REQUIRED>

    <!ELEMENT orderDate (#PCDATA)>
    <!ELEMENT items (item+)>

    <!ELEMENT item (#PCDATA)>
    <!ATTLIST item itemPrice CDATA #REQUIRED>
    <!ATTLIST item itemQty CDATA "1">

    <!ENTITY % itemCodes SYSTEM "codes.dtd">
    %itemCodes;
]>
```

3. Save **orders.xml**, then reload the file in a Netscape or Firefox browser and verify that the browser now displays the extended descriptions associated with each product code.

Inserting Comments

Kristin is pleased that you were able to fix the problem with the Netscape and Firefox browsers. She's now concerned that the code in the DTD might be confusing to other programmers, and suggests that you add a few lines of comments. Comments in a DTD follow the same syntax as comments in XML. The specific form of a DTD comment is

```
<!--
    comment
-->
```

where *comment* is the text of the DTD comment. White space is ignored within a comment, so you can spread comment text over several lines without affecting DTD code.

To add comments to the DTD:

1. Return to **orders.xml** in your text editor.

2. Above the first general entity (for the DCT5Z product code), insert the following comment line:

    ```
    <!-- Product code descriptions inserted as general entities -->
    ```

3. Above the first parameter entity linking the DTD to the codes.dtd file, insert the comment

```
<!-- codes.dtd contains a list of product codes (IE browser only)
-->
```

Figure 3-26 shows the final form of the DTD for the orders.xml file

Adding DTD comments | Figure 3-26

```
<!DOCTYPE customers
[
    <!-- Product code descriptions inserted as general entities -->
    <!ENTITY DCT5Z "Tapan Digital Camera 5 Mpx - zoom">
    <!ENTITY SM128 "SmartMedia 128MB Card">
    <!ENTITY RCL "Rechargeable Lithium Ion Battery">
    <!ENTITY BCE4L "Battery Charger 4pt Lithium">
    <!ENTITY WBC500 "WebNow Webcam 500">
    <!ENTITY RCA "Rechargeable Alkaline Battery">
    <!ENTITY SCL4C "Linton Flatbed Scanner 4C">

    <!ELEMENT customers (customer+)>

    <!ELEMENT customer (name, address, phone, email?, orders)>
    <!ATTLIST customer custID ID #REQUIRED>
    <!ATTLIST customer custType (home | business) #IMPLIED>

    <!ELEMENT name (#PCDATA)>
    <!ATTLIST name title (Mr. | Mrs. | Ms.) #IMPLIED>

    <!ELEMENT address (#PCDATA)>
    <!ELEMENT phone (#PCDATA)>
    <!ELEMENT email (#PCDATA)>
    <!ELEMENT orders (order+)>

    <!ELEMENT order (orderDate, items)>
    <!ATTLIST order orderID ID #REQUIRED>
    <!ATTLIST order orderBy IDREF #REQUIRED>

    <!ELEMENT orderDate (#PCDATA)>
    <!ELEMENT items (item+)>

    <!ELEMENT item (#PCDATA)>
    <!ATTLIST item itemPrice CDATA #REQUIRED>
    <!ATTLIST item itemQty CDATA "1">

    <!-- codes.dtd contains a list of product codes (IE browser only) -->
    <!ENTITY % itemCodes SYSTEM "codes.dtd">
    %itemCodes;
]>
```

4. Close the **orders.xml** file, saving your changes. You may also close any other open files or programs from this project.

Creating Conditional Sections

When you're creating a new DTD, it's useful to be able to try out different combinations of declarations. You can do this by using a **conditional section**, which XML parsers process conditionally. Rather than rewriting a DTD each time you make a change, a conditional section enables you to divide the DTD into two sections. One section contains declarations that are interpreted by parsers, and the other contains declarations that parsers ignore. As you experiment with the structure of your DTD, you can move declarations from one section to the other without losing the code.

The syntax for creating a conditional section is

```
<![keyword[
    declarations
]]>
```

where *keyword* is either INCLUDE (for a section of declarations that you want parsers to interpret) or IGNORE (for the declarations that you want parsers to pass over). For example, the following code creates two sections of declarations:

```
<![IGNORE[
    <!ELEMENT Magazine (Name)>
```

```
        <!ATTLIST Magazine Publisher CDATA #REQUIRED>
        <!ELEMENT Name (#PCDATA)>
]]>
<![INCLUDE[
    <!ELEMENT Book (Title, Author)>
    <!ATTLIST Book Pages CDATA #REQUIRED>
    <!ELEMENT Title (#PCDATA)>
    <!ELEMENT Author (#PCDATA)>
]]>
```

Parsers process the declarations involving the Book element, but ignore the declarations involving the Magazine element.

One effective way of creating IGNORE sections is to create a parameter entity that defines whether those sections should be included or not, and to use the value of the entity as the keyword for the conditional section. For example, the following UseFull-DTD entity has a value of IGNORE, which causes the conditional section that follows it to be ignored by the XML parser:

```
<!ENTITY % UseFullDTD "IGNORE">
<![ %UseFullDTD; [
    <!ELEMENT Magazine (Name)>
    <!ATTLIST Magazine Publisher CDATA #REQUIRED>
    <!ELEMENT Name (#PCDATA)>
]]>
```

By changing the value of the UseFullDTD from IGNORE to INCLUDE, you can add any conditional section that uses this entity reference to the document's DTD. Thus, you can switch multiple sections in the DTD off and on by editing a single line in the file. This is most useful when several conditional sections are scattered throughout a very long DTD. Rather than locating and changing each of the conditional sections, you can switch the sections on and off by changing the parameter entity's value.

Conditional sections can be applied only to external DTDs. Thus, while they may be useful in other contexts, you cannot apply them to the DTD in Kristin's document.

Working with Unparsed Data

In this session, you have looked at creating entities for character data. For a DTD to be able to validate either binary data, such as images or video clips, or character data that is not well formed, you need to work with unparsed entities as well. Because an XML parser cannot work with this type of data directly, a DTD needs to include instructions for how to treat the unparsed entity.

The first step is to declare a notation which identifies the data type of the unparsed data. A notation must supply a name for the data type and provide clues about how XML parsers should treat the data. Since notations refer to external content (they are, by definition, not well-formed XML), you must specify an external location. One option is to use a system location, which you specify with the code

```
<!NOTATION notation SYSTEM "uri">
```

where *notation* is the notation's name and *uri* is a system location that tells XML parsers how to work with the data. The other option is to specify a public location, using the declaration

```
<!NOTATION notation PUBLIC "id" "uri">
```

where *id* is, as usual, a public identifier recognized by XML parsers. The URI for the resource can be either a program that can work with the unparsed data, or the actual data type. For example, if Kristin wanted to include references in her XML document to graphic image files stored in the JPEG format, she could enter the following notation in the document's DTD:

```
<!NOTATION jpeg SYSTEM "paint.exe">
```

Since an XML parser doesn't know how to handle graphic data, this notation associates the paint.exe program with the jpeg data type. If you don't want to specify a particular program, you could instead indicate the data type by using the mime-type value with the notation

```
<!NOTATION jpeg SYSTEM "image/jpeg">
```

In this case, an XML parser associates the jpeg notation with the image/jpeg data type as long as the operating system already knows how to handle jpeg files. Once a notation is declared, you can create an unparsed entity that references specific items that use that notation. The syntax of the declaration for an unparsed entity is

```
<!ENTITY entity SYSTEM "uri" NDATA notation>
```

where *uri* is the URI of the unparsed data and *notation* is the name of the notation that defines the data type for the XML parser. Once again, you can also provide a public location for the unparsed data if an XML parser supports it, using the form

```
<!ENTITY entity PUBLIC "id" "uri" NDATA notation>
```

For example, the following declaration creates an unparsed entity named DCT5ZIMG that references the graphic image file dct5z.jpg:

```
<!ENTITY DCT5ZIMG SYSTEM "dct5z.jpg" NDATA jpeg>
```

Entities can be associated with attribute values by using the ENTITY data type in the attribute declaration. If Kristin wanted to add an image attribute to every item element in her document, she could insert the following attribute declaration in the DTD:

```
<!ATTLIST item image ENTITY #REQUIRED>
```

With this declaration added, Kristin could then add the image attribute to her XML document, using the DCT5ZIMG entity as the attribute's value:

```
<item image="DCT5ZIMG">DCT5Z</item>
```

It's important to understand precisely what this code does and does not accomplish: it tells XML parsers what kind of data is represented by the DCT5ZIMG entity, and it provides information on how to interpret the data stored in the dct5z.jpg file, but it does not tell parsers anything beyond that. Whether a program reading the XML document opens a device to display the image file depends solely on the program. Remember that XML's purpose is to create structured documents, but not necessarily to tell programs how to render the data in a document. If a validating XML parser reads this code, it probably wouldn't try to read the graphic image file, but it might check that the file is there. By doing so, the parser would confirm that the document is complete in its content and in all of its references to unparsed data.

Current Web browsers do not support mechanisms for validating and rendering unparsed data declared in the DTDs of XML documents, so you will not add this feature to the orders.xml file.

Declaring an Unparsed Entity

- To declare an unparsed entity, you must first declare a notation for the data type used in the entity. The syntax for declaring a notation is

  `<!NOTATION notation SYSTEM "uri">`

  where *notation* is the name of the notation and *uri* is a system location that defines the data type or a program that can work with the data type. To specify a public location for the notation use

  `<!NOTATION notation PUBLIC "id" "uri">`

  where *id* is a public identifier for the data type associated with the notation.
- To associate a notation with an unparsed entity, use the declaration

  `<!ENTITY entity SYSTEM "uri" NDATA notation>`

  where *entity* is the name of the enity, *uri* is the system location of a file containing the unparsed data, and *notation* is the name of the notation that defines the data type. For a public location of the unparsed entity, use

  `<!ENTITY entity PUBLIC "id" "uri" NDATA notation>`

Validating Standard Vocabularies

All of your work in this tutorial has involved the custom XML vocabulary developed by Kristin for Pixal Products. Most of the standard XML vocabularies in popular use have existing DTDs associated with them. To validate a document used with a standard vocabulary, you usually have to access an external DTD located on a Web server. Figure 3-27 lists the DOCTYPE declarations for some popular XML vocabularies.

Figure 3-27 ▶ **DOCTYPE declarations for standard vocabularies**

Vocabulary	DOCTYPE
XHTML 1.0 strict	`<!DOCTYPE html PUBLIC "-//W3C//DTD XHTML 1.0 Strict//EN" "http://www.w3.org/TR/xhtml1/DTD/xhtml1-strict.dtd">`
XHTML 1.0 transitional	`<!DOCTYPE html PUBLIC "-//W3C//DTD XHTML 1.0 Transitional//EN" "http://www.w3.org/TR/xhtml1/DTD/xhtml1-transitional.dtd">`
XHTML 1.0 frameset	`<!DOCTYPE html PUBLIC "-//W3C//DTD XHTML 1.0 Frameset//EN" "http://www.w3.org/TR/xhtml1/DTD/xhtml1-frameset.dtd">`
XHTML 1.1	`<!DOCTYPE html PUBLIC "-//W3C//DTD XHTML 1.1//EN" "http://www.w3.org/TR/xhtml11/DTD/xhtml11.dtd">`
MathML 1.01	`<!DOCTYPE math SYSTEM "http://www.w3.org/Math/DTD/mathml1/mathml.dtd">`
MathML 2.0	`<!DOCTYPE math PUBLIC "-//W3C//DTD MathML 2.0//EN" "http://www.w3.org/TR/MathML2/dtd/mathml2.dtd">`
SVG 1.1 basic	`<!DOCTYPE svg PUBLIC "-//W3C//DTD SVG 1.1 Basic//EN" "http://www.w3.org/Graphics/SVG/1.1/DTD/svg11-basic.dtd">`
SVG 1.1 full	`<!DOCTYPE svg PUBLIC "-//W3C//DTD SVG 1.1//EN" "http://www.w3.org/Graphics/SVG/1.1/DTD/svg11.dtd">`
SMIL 1.0	`<!DOCTYPE smil PUBLIC "-//W3C//DTD SMIL 1.0//EN" "http://www.w3.org/TR/REC-smil/SMIL10.dtd">`
SMIL 2.0	`<!DOCTYPE SMIL PUBLIC "-//W3C//DTD SMIL 2.0//EN" "http://www.w3.org/TR/REC-smil/2000/SMIL20.dtd">`
VoiceXML 2.1	`<!DOCTYPE vxml PUBLIC "-//W3C//DTD VOICEXML 2.1//EN" "http://www.w3.org/TR/voicexml21/vxml.dtd">`

For example, to validate an XHTML document against the XHTML 1.0 strict standard, you would add the following code to the start of the document:

```
<?xml version="1.0" encoding="UTF-8" standalone="no" ?>
<!DOCTYPE html PUBLIC "-//W3C//DTD XHTML 1.0 Strict//EN"
  "http://www.w3.org/TR/xhtml1/DTD/xhtml1-strict.dtd">
<html>
 ...
</html>
```

The W3C provides an online validator at http://validator.w3.org/ that you can use to validate HTML, XHTML, MathML, and SVG. The validator works with files either placed on the Web or uploaded via a Web form. You can also use programs like XMLSpy to validate your files based on standard vocabularies.

Most standard vocabularies make their DTDs available online for inspection. Studying the DTDs of other XML vocabularies is a great way to learn how to design your own. Figure 3-28 shows the part of the DTD for XHTML 1.0 that sets the syntax rules for the br (line break) element. The DTD includes substantial use of parameter entities to allow the same set of attributes to be shared among the many elements of XHTML. For example, the coreattrs parameter entity contains a list of core attributes used by most XHTML elements. The StyleSheet and Text parameter entities contain code that sets the data type for style sheets and title attributes. From the DTD you can quickly see that the four core attributes of XHTML are the id, class, style, and title attributes, and while they are available to almost all elements in the XHTML language, they are not required attributes. The specifications for the br element are fairly simple. Other elements of the XHTML language have more complicated and far-ranging rules.

| The XHTML 1.0 strict DTD for the br element | Figure 3-28 |

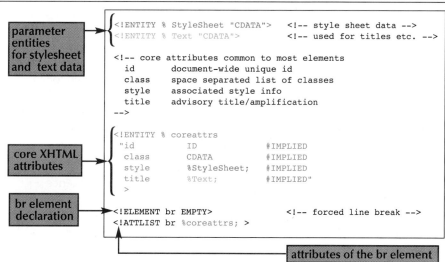

```
<!ENTITY % StyleSheet "CDATA">      <!-- style sheet data -->
<!ENTITY % Text "CDATA">            <!-- used for titles etc. -->

<!-- core attributes common to most elements
  id         document-wide unique id
  class      space separated list of classes
  style      associated style info
  title      advisory title/amplification
-->

<!ENTITY % coreattrs
 "id          ID              #IMPLIED
  class       CDATA           #IMPLIED
  style       %StyleSheet;    #IMPLIED
  title       %Text;          #IMPLIED"
  >

<!ELEMENT br EMPTY>                  <!-- forced line break -->
<!ATTLIST br %coreattrs; >
```

- parameter entities for stylesheet and text data
- core XHTML attributes
- br element declaration
- attributes of the br element

You've completed your work on Kristin's document. She will use the DTD you developed to ensure that any new data added to the orders.xml document conforms to the standards you set up. She has other XML documents for which she may want you to develop DTDs in the future.

Session 3.3 Quick Check

Review

1. What is the difference between a general entity and a parameter entity?
2. What is the difference between a parsed entity and an unparsed entity?
3. What declaration would you enter to store the text string "<Title>Hamlet</Title>" as a general entity named "Play"? What command would you enter to reference this entity in a document?

4. What declaration would you enter to store the contents of the plays.xml file as a general entity named Plays?
5. What code would you enter to store the contents of the plays.dtd file as a parameter entity named Works?
6. What is a notation?
7. How would you reference the image file shakespeare.gif in an unparsed entity named Portrait? Assume that this entity is using a notation named GIF.

Review

Tutorial Summary

In this tutorial you learned how to create well-formed and valid documents using DTDs. The first session reviewed the basic principles of document validation, showing how to declare a document type definition. The session examined two types of DTDs, internal and external, and explained the benefits of both types. The rest of the session showed how to set syntax rules for elements, specifying the element content and the structure of any child elements. The second session focused on working with attributes. The session covered the various attribute types and the DTD declarations for setting rules for attribute values. The second session then explored how to validate an XML document using the XML Spy program. The session concluded with a look at the challenges that namespaces provide for data validation. The third session focused on entities. It looked at the different types of entities and explored how to insert entity references into an XML document. The session also examined how to use parameter entities to combine different DTDs into a single file and how to create references to noncharacter data. The tutorial concluded with a brief look at how DTDs are used with standard XML vocabularies such as XHTML.

Key Terms

choice	enumerated types	name token
conditional section	external entity	NMTOKEN
DOCTYPE declaration	external subset	notation
document type	general entity	parameter entity
declaration	ID token	parsed entity
document type	IDREF token	public identifier
definition	internal entity	sequence
DTD	internal subset	system identifier
element type declaration	mixed content	tokenized types
ENTITY token	modifying symbol	unparsed entity
ENTITIES token	module	

Note: In the problems that follow, some of the XML documents have intentional errors. Part of your job is to find and correct those errors using the validation report from the DTDs you create.

Practice

Practice the skills you learned in the tutorial using the same case scenario

Review Assignments

Data files needed for this Review Assignment: hwlisttxt.xml, hwtxt.dtd, pixaltxt.xml, swlisttxt.xml, swtxt.dtd

Kristin has two additional documents on which she needs your help. One document lists some of Pixal's software products, and the other describes a few of its hardware offerings. Figure 3-29 shows the tree structures of the two XML vocabularies.

Figure 3-29

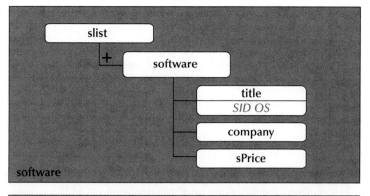

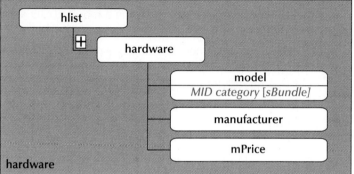

The software vocabulary contains a root element named slist, with multiple occurrences of a software element containing information on individual software products. The software element contains three child elements: title, company, and sPrice. The title element stores the name of the software title and supports two attributes: SID, an ID number of the software title, and OS, the operating system supported by the software title. The company and sPrice elements store the software company and the price of the software title.

The hardware vocabulary contains a root element named hlist containing multiple hardware elements. Each hardware element contains three child elements: model, manufacturer, and mPrice. The model element stores the name of the hardware item and includes the following attributes: MID (the model ID number), category, and an optional attribute, sBundle, which identifies a software title bundled with the hardware item. The manufacturer and mPrice elements indicate the hardware manufacturer and price of the item.

From these two documents, Kristin wants to create a master document containing a list of both software and hardware offerings. As you did with Kristin's orders document, it is important to enforce a document structure to ensure that information recorded in these documents is valid. Therefore, part of your task will be to combine the DTDs from the software and hardware vocabularies into a single DTD for the compound document. None of the element names overlap, so you do not need to use namespaces in this document.

To complete this task:

1. Using your text editor, open the following files from the tutorial.03x/review folder: hwlisttxt.xml, hwtxt.dtd, pixaltxt.xml, swlisttxt.xml, and swtxt.dtd. Enter *your name* and *the date* in the comment section of each file and save them as **hwlist.xml**, **hw.dtd**, **pixal.xml**, **swlist.xml**, and **sw.dtd** respectively.

2. Take some time to review the content of the swlist.xml file, which contains the list of software products. Then, within the **sw.dtd** file, declare the following elements:
   - The slist element containing at least one occurrence of the child element software
   - The software element containing three child elements, in the sequence title, company, sPrice
   - The title, company, and sPrice elements, each containing parsed character data

3. Add the following attribute declarations to the software dtd:
   - The title element containing a required SID attribute, with the value equal to an ID token.
   - The title element containing a required OS attribute with a value equal to one of the following text strings: Macintosh, Windows, UNIX, or Other.

4. Close the **sw.dtd** file, saving your changes.

5. Review the contents of the hwlist.xml file and then declare the following elements in the **hw.dtd** file:
   - The hlist element, containing at least one occurrence of the child element hardware
   - The hardware element, containing three child elements in the sequence model, manufacturer, mPrice
   - The model, manufacturer, and mPrice elements, each containing parsed character data

6. Add the following attribute declarations to the hardware DTD:
   - The model element containing a required MID attribute with a value equal to an ID token.
   - The model element containing a required category attribute limited to one of the following values: Camera, Scanner, or Tablet.
   - The model element containing an optional sBundle attribute with a value equal to an ID reference token.

7. Close the **hw.dtd** file, saving your changes.

8. Go to **pixal.xml** in your text editor and insert an internal DTD for the root element, product_list, directly after the comment section and before the opening <product_list> tag.

9. Within the internal DTD, declare the following items:
   - The product_list element, containing the child element sequence hlist, slist
   - An external general entity named hw_list, referencing the hwlist.xml file
   - An external general entity named sw_list, referencing the swlist.xml file
   - An external parameter entity named hw_dtd, referencing the hw.dtd file
   - An external parameter entity named sw_dtd, referencing the sw.dtd file

10. Below the entity declarations within the DTD, insert references to the hw_dtd and sw_dtd parameters. Add the DTD comments "hardware list DTD" and "software list DTD" to the corresponding lines of code.

11. Within the product_list element, insert references for the hw_list and sw_list entities.

12. Save your changes to the pixal.xml file.

13. Use XMLSpy or another validating parser to validate the pixal.xml file. There should be one well-formedness error in the hwlist.xml file and one validation error in each of the hwlist.xml and swlist.xml files. Fix these errors as indicated in the hwlist.xml and swlist.xml files.

14. If you have access to the Internet Explorer browser, open pixal.xml in it and verify that the contents of the hwlist.xml and swlist.xml files appear in the document.

15. Submit your completed and valid project to your instructor.

Apply

Use the skills you earned in this tutorial o validate a document of sports data

Case Problem 1

Data files needed for this Case Problem: edltxt.xml, teamstxt.dtd

Professional Basketball Association   Kurt Vaughn works for the Professional Basketball Association (PBA) and is responsible for coordinating information and statistics for the PBA's many developmental leagues. Part of Kurt's job is to maintain a document that lists the starting lineup for each team as well as providing statistics on individual players. Kurt has asked for your help in creating XML documents that maintain a consistent document structure. He has created a sample document describing six teams from the Eastern Developmental League (EDL). The document lists the five starting players on each team, including the following statistics about each player: PPG (points per game), RPG (rebounds per game), and Assists (assists per game). Figure 3-30 shows a tree diagram of the vocabulary. Note that the PPG, RPG, and Assists attributes are all optional.

Figure 3-30

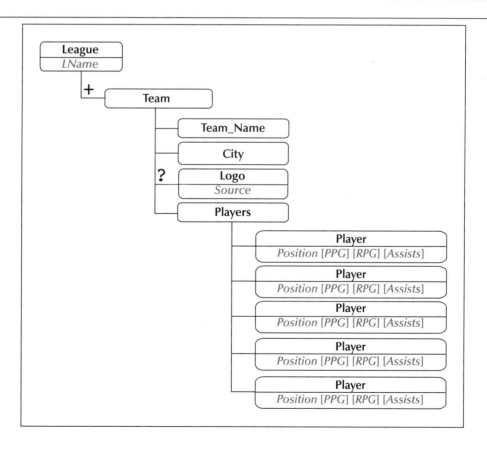

The document also contains an element that stores information about graphic files of team logos. The logo element is optional. Any DTD that you create for this document will also need to work with the unparsed data contained in these graphic files.

To complete this task:

1. Using your text editor, open **edltxt.xml** and **teamstxt.dtd** from the tutorial.03x/case1 folder. Enter *your name* and *the date* in the comment section of each file and save them as **edl.xml** and **teams.dtd** respectively.

2. Review the contents of the edl.xml file and then, within the teams.dtd file, declare the following elements:
   - The League element, containing at least one occurrence of the child element Team
   - The Team element, containing child elements in the sequence Team_Name, City, Logo (optional), and Players
   - The Team_Name and City elements, containing parsed character data
   - The Logo element as an empty element
   - The Players element, containing five child elements, each named Player
   - The Player element, containing parsed character data

3. Declare the following required attributes in the DTD:
   - The League element should contain a single attribute named LName containing character data.
   - The Logo element should contain an entity attribute named Source.
   - The Player element should contain an attribute named Position with values limited to: Center, Forward, or Guard.
   - The Player element should also contain three optional attributes named PPG, RPG, and Assists, all containing character data.

4. Declare a notation named BMP with a system location equal to "image/bmp".

5. Close the teams.dtd file, saving your changes.

6. Go to the edl.xml file in your text editor. Directly after the comment section, insert a DOCTYPE declaration that references the system location teams.dtd.

7. Add an internal subset to the DTD and, within the subset, create three unparsed entities. Each entity should reference the BMP notation. The first entity should be named "Tigers" and should reference the Tigers.bmp file. The second entity, named "Raiders," should reference the Raiders.bmp file. Finally, the third entity should be named "Storm" and should reference the Storm.bmp file.

8. Save your changes to the edl.xml file.

9. Test the edl.xml file using XMLSpy or another validating parser. Correct any reported errors to make the document valid. If you have access to a different XML parser, you may use that as well.

10. Submit the completed and validated project to your instructor.

Apply

Use the skills you learned in this tutorial to validate a news feed document

Case Problem 2

Data files needed for this Case Problem: arttxt.dtd, headtxt.xml, imgtxt.dtd, newstxt.dtd, wnstxt.xml

Web News Service, Inc. Alan Li works for the Web News Service, Inc. (WNS), a Web site for current and archived news stories. WNS publishes stories about national and international events, sports, entertainment, and leisure. The company is investigating setting up an XML vocabulary for this information and has asked Alan to develop a prototype. Alan envisions an XML document, headlines.xml, containing a listing of the current news headlines. Each headline would be accompanied by a synopsis, a reference to a Web page containing the news article, and in some cases, references to image files that accompany the report. A DTD for the headlines.xml content would be placed in an external file named news.dtd. Entity references for the Web page articles and image files would be placed in external DTDs named articles.dtd and images.dtd. The headlines.xml file and DTDs would then be linked to a central XML document named wns.xml. Figure 3-31 shows a schematic of the file structure envisioned by Alan.

Figure 3-31

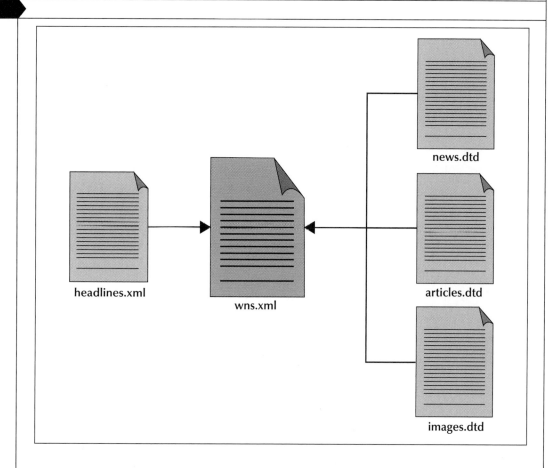

Figure 3-32 shows the tree structure of the elements and attributes for the stories and articles placed in the wns.xml file. Note that the news_feed element must contain at least one story element and that story elements can contain any number of image elements. Also note that a news story may or may not contain a journalist's byline.

Figure 3-32

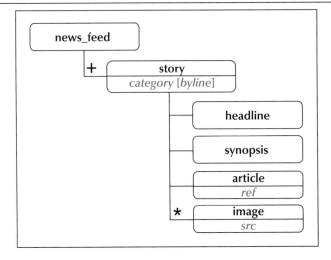

To complete this task:

1. Using your text editor, open the following files from the tutorial.03x/case2 folder: **arttxt.dtd**, **headtxt.xml**, **imgtxt.dtd**, **newstxt.dtd**, and **wnstxt.xml**. Enter *your name* and *the date* in the comment section of each file and save them as **articles.dtd**, **headlines.xml**, **images.dtd**, **news.dtd**, and **wns.xml** respectively.

2. Go to the articles.dtd file in your text editor and add the following declarations to the document:
   - A notation named HTM with the system location "text/html"
   - An unparsed entity named news801 pointing to the file "article801.html" using the notation HTM
   - Four more unparsed entities named news802 through news805 pointing to the files "article802.html" through "article805.html" and using the HTM notation

3. Close the file, saving your changes.

4. Go to the images.dtd file in your text editor and add the following declarations:
   - A notation named JPG with the system location "image/jpg"
   - An unparsed entity named img2071 pointing to the file "img2071.jpg" using the notation JPG
   - Four more unparsed entities named img2072 through img2075 pointing to the files "img2072.jpg " through "img2075.jpg" and using the JPG notation

5. Close the file, saving your changes.

6. Go to the news.dtd file and create the following element declarations:
   - An element named story containing the following sequence of child elements: headline, synopsis, article, and image (which can appear any number of times)
   - An element named headline containing parsed character data
   - Empty elements named article and image

7. Add the following attribute declarations:
   - The story element contains a required category attribute limited to the values national, international, sports, entertainment, leisure, and weather.
   - The story element also contains an optional attribute named byline containing character data.
   - The article element contains an entity attribute named ref.
   - The image element contains an entity attribute named src.

8. Close the news.dtd file, saving your changes.

9. Go the wns.xml file in your text editor. Directly below the comment section, insert an internal DTD with news_feed as the root element.

10. Declare the news_feed element containing one or more child elements named story.

11. Insert parameter entities named articles, images, and news pointing to the articles. dtd, images.dtd, and news.dtd files.

12. Below the parameter entity declarations, insert references to the articles, images, and news entities.

13. Insert an external parsed entity named headlines that points to the headlines.xml file.

14. Within the news_feed element, insert a reference to the headlines entity.

15. Close the file, saving your changes.

16. Validate the wns.xml file using XMLSpy or another validating parser. Correct any errors you discover, including errors in the headlines.xml file.

17. If you have the Internet Explorer browser, use it to view the contents of the wns.xml file. Verify that the contents of the headlines.xml file are displayed by the browser.

18. Submit your completed and validated project to your instructor.

Challenge

xplore how to use oth DTDs and amespaces in a compound document

Case Problem 3

Data files needed for this Case Problem: modtxt.dtd, modtxt.xml, parttxt.dtd, parttxt. xml, waretxt.xml

Jackson Electronics   Gail Oglund processes orders for an assembly plant for Jackson Electronics. As part of her job, she has created several XML vocabularies dealing with model orders and the parts available to assemble them. She wants to create a compound document combining information from the models and parts vocabularies. She would also like to validate any data entered into her documents, so she has come to you for help in developing DTDs. Since she is creating compound documents that combine elements from the models and parts namespaces, she needs her DTDs to work with namespaces. Figure 3-33 shows the tree structure of the compound document.

Figure 3-33

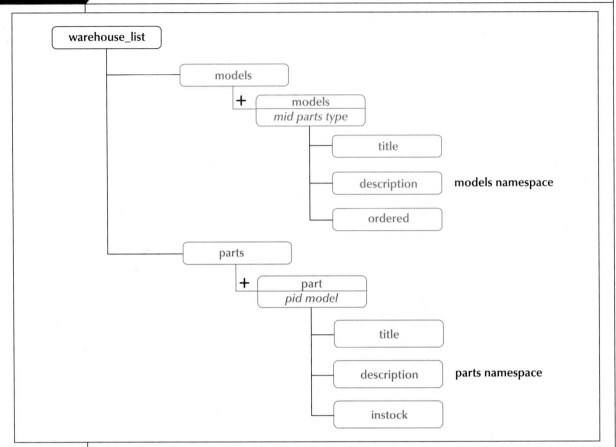

Gail wants you to create separate DTDs for the models and parts namespaces and then use entities to read the information from different XML documents into a master compound document. Figure 3-34 shows a schematic of the file relationships in Gail's proposed project.

Figure 3-34

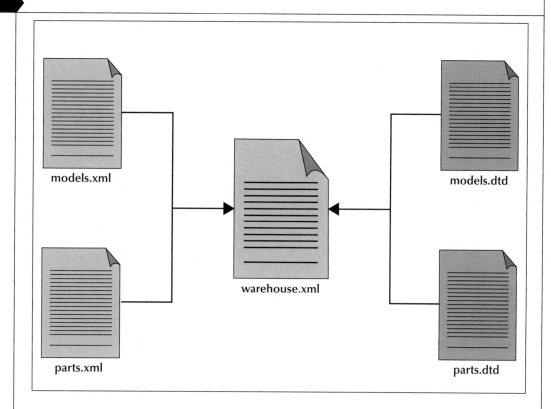

models.xml

warehouse.xml

parts.xml

models.dtd

parts.dtd

To complete this task:

1. Using your text editor, open the following files from the tutorial.03x/case3 folder: **modtxt.dtd**, **modtxt.xml**, **parttxt.dtd**, **parttxt.xml**, and **waretxt.xml**. Enter *your name* and *the date* in the comment section of each file and save them as **models.dtd**, **models.xml**, **parts.dtd**, **parts.xml**, and **warehouse.xml** respectively.

2. Go to the models.dtd file in your text editor and add the following element declarations:
   - The models element, containing at least one child element named model
   - The model element, containing the following sequence of child elements: title, description, and ordered
   - The title, description, and ordered elements, containing parsed character data

3. Add the following attribute declarations to the model element:
   - An ID attribute named mid
   - An attribute named parts containing a list of ID references
   - An attribute named type whose value is limited to scanner, color_laser, bw_laser, inkjet, and camera

Explore

4. Add the namespace prefix "m" to all element names in the DTD, and then close the models.dtd file, saving your changes.

5. Go to the parts.dtd file in your text editor and add the following element declarations:
   - The parts element, containing at least one child element named part
   - The part element, containing the following sequence of child elements: title, description, and instock
   - The title, description, and instock elements, containing parsed character data

6. Add the following attribute declarations:
   - The part element contains an ID attribute named pid.
   - The part element should also include a model attribute containing a list of ID references.
7. Place all of the element names in the DTD in a namespace with the prefix "p" and then close parts.dtd, saving your changes.
8. Open the warehouse.xml file in your text editor. Declare the following namespaces in the root element, warehouse_list:
   - The models namespace with the prefix "m" and the URI "http://jacksonelect.com/models"
   - The parts namespace with the prefix "p" and the URI "http://jacksonelect.com/parts"

Explore

9. Between the comment section and the opening <warehouse_list> tag, insert an internal DTD subset with the following declarations:
   - The warehouse_list element containing the two child elements: m:models and p:parts
   - A fixed attribute of the warehouse_list element named xmlns:m and equal to the URI of the models namespace
   - Another fixed attribute of the warehouse_list element named xmlns:p and equal to the URI of the parts namespace
   - A parameter entity named models_dtd with a system location equal to the models.dtd file
   - A parameter entity named parts_dtd with a system location equal to the parts.dtd file
   - An external entity named models_list with a system location pointing to the models.xml file
   - An external entity named parts_list with a system location pointing to the parts.xml file
10. At the end of the internal DTD subset, insert references to the models_dtd and parts_dtd parameters.
11. Within the warehouse_list element, insert references to the models_list and parts_list entities.
12. Close the warehouse.xml file, saving your changes.
13. Go to the models.xml file in your text editor and add the "m" namespace prefix to all the element names in the document. Close the file, saving your changes.
14. Go to the parts.xml file in your text editor and add the "p" namespace prefix to all the element names. Close the file, saving your changes.

Explore

15. Validate the warehouse.xml file using XMLSpy or another validating parser. Correct any errors you discover. Note the parts.xml and models.xml files will contain a couple of errors. (*Hint*: Remember that all the ID references must point to actual IDs found in the compound document, and the ID names must match both upper- and lowercase letters.)
16. Submit your completed and validated project to your instructor.

Create

Test your knowledge of DTDs by creating a DTD for a contribution list

Case Problem 4

Data files needed for this Case Problem: lhouse.dtd, listtxt.xml, members.txt

The Lighthouse Charitable Trust Sela Voight is the Membership Coordinator for The Lighthouse, a charitable organization located in central Kentucky. One of her responsibilities is to maintain a membership list of people in the community who have contributed to The Lighthouse. Members can belong to one of three categories: Platinum, Gold, and Premium. The categories assist Sela in defining her fundraising goals and strategies to reach those goals.

Currently, most of the data that Sela has compiled resides in text files. To be a more effective fundraiser, she wants to convert this data into an XML document and ensure that the resulting document follows some specific guidelines.

To complete this task:

1. Use your text editor to open the **listtxt.xml** file from the tutorial.03x/case4 folder in your text editor. Insert ***your name*** and ***the date*** in the comment section, and save the file as **list.xml**.

2. Using the data stored in the members.txt file for the document content, create a document structure in the list.xml file. The appearance of the document is up to you, but it should include the following features:
   - A root element named list should contain several member elements.
   - Each member element should contain the following child elements, which should appear no more than once within the member element: name, address, phone, email (optional), contribution, and notes (optional).
   - The member element contains an attribute named level that identifies the donor level: Platinum, Gold, or Premium. This is a required attribute for each member.

3. Use your text editor to open the **lhouse.dtd** file and insert ***your name*** and ***the date*** in the comment section. Use the structure you created in the list.xml file as a model for this external DTD subset. Close the file, saving your changes.

4. Apply the lhouse DTD to the contents of the list.xml file. Close the list.xml file, saving your changes.

5. Test the list.xml file and verify its validity.

6. Submit your completed and validated project to your instructor.

Review

Quick Check Answers

Session 3.1

1. <!DOCTYPE Inventory SYSTEM "books.dtd">
2. <!ELEMENT book ANY>
3. <!ELEMENT video EMPTY>
4. <!ELEMENT book (#PCDATA)>
5. <!ELEMENT book (author)>
6. <!ELEMENT book (author+)>
   <!ELEMENT book (author)+>
7. <!ELEMENT book (#PCDATA | author | title)*>

Session 3.2

1. <!ATTLIST book title CDATA #IMPLIED>
2. <!ATTLIST play type (Romance | Tragedy | History | Comedy) #REQUIRED>
3. NMTOKEN types cannot contain blank spaces.
4. <!ATTLIST book ISBN ID #REQUIRED>
5. <!ATTLIST author booksBy IDREF #IMPLIED>
6. <!ATTLIST book inStock (yes | no) "yes">

Session 3.3

1. General entities are used only with the contents of an XML document. Parameter entities are used only with the contents of a DTD.
2. Parsed entities consist entirely of well-formed XML content. Unparsed entities are constructed from nonXML data, including nontextual data.
3. <!ENTITY Play "<Title>Hamlet</Title>">
   &Play;
4. <!ENTITY Plays SYSTEM "plays.xml">
5. <!ENTITY % Works SYSTEM "plays.dtd">
6. A notation is a resource that an XML parser uses to handle or identify unparsed data.
7. <!ENTITY Portrait SYSTEM "shakespeare.gif" NDATA GIF>

Objectives

Working with Schemas

Validating Documents with XML Schema

Case

University Hospital Clinical Cancer Center

Allison Grant is a project coordinator at the Clinical Cancer Center (CCC) of University Hospital where she manages the center's various ongoing research projects. Allison would like to use XML to create structured documents containing information on the different studies and the patients enrolled in those studies. Eventually the XML documents can be used as a data resource for the center's intranet, allowing investigators to view project and patient data online. Allison is new to XML and has sought out your help on a couple of issues.

Accuracy is important to the CCC. Allison needs to know that the data she enters is error free. Some of the studies are limited to patients of a certain age, medical condition, or gender, and Allison has to be able to confirm that the patient data in her XML documents matches the criteria for the studies. Allison also needs to create compound documents from the various XML vocabularies she's created. For example, she may need to create a document that combines patient information with information on the study itself.

Allison knows that DTDs cannot fulfill her needs. DTDs have a limited range of data types and provide no way to deal with numeric data. She's also aware that DTDs and namespaces do not mix well. However, Allison has heard that schemas can work with a wide range of data types and do a better job than DTDs in supporting namespaces and compound documents. She's asked your help in developing schemas for the XML documents that she's already created.

Student Data Files

Session 4.1

Introducing XML Schema

You and Allison meet at the hospital to discuss her work for the Clinical Cancer Center. She has brought along a file named patients.xml, which contains a list of patients participating in a study examining the effects of the drug Tamoxifen on breast cancer. Open this file now.

To open the patient list:

1. Use your text editor to open **pattxt.xml** from the tutorial.04x/tutorial folder. Enter *your name* and *the date* in the comment section at the top of file and save the file as **patients.xml**.

   Figure 4-1 displays the contents of the patients.xml document.

Contents of the patients.xml document | Figure 4-1

```xml
<patients>
    <patient patID="MR890-041-02" onStudy="TBC-080-5">
        <lastName>Dibbs</lastName>
        <firstName>Cynthia</firstName>
        <dateOfBirth>1945-05-22</dateOfBirth>
        <age>62</age>
        <stage>II</stage>
        <performance scale="Karnofsky">0.81</performance>
    </patient>
    <patient patID="MR771-121-10" onStudy="TBC-080-5">
        <lastName>Wilkes</lastName>
        <firstName>Karen</firstName>
        <dateOfBirth>1959-02-24</dateOfBirth>
        <age>48</age>
        <stage>II</stage>
        <comment>Dropped out of study.</comment>
        <performance scale="Karnofsky">0.84</performance>
    </patient>
    <patient patID="MR701-891-05" onStudy="TBC-080-5">
        <lastName>Sanchez</lastName>
        <firstName>Olivia</firstName>
        <dateOfBirth>1958-08-14</dateOfBirth>
        <age>49 years old</age>
        <stage>II</stage>
        <comment>Possibly stage I/II</comment>
        <comment>Karnofsky performance rating unavailable.</comment>
        <performance scale="Bell">0.89</performance>
    </patient>
    <patient patID="MR805-891-08" onStudy="TBC-080-5">
        <lastName>Russell</lastName>
        <firstName>Alice</firstName>
        <dateOfBirth>1952-9-14</dateOfBirth>
        <age>55</age>
        <stage>II</stage>
        <performance scale="Karnofsky">1.76</performance>
    </patient>
    <patient patID="mr815-741-03" onStudy="tbc-080-5">
        <lastName>Browne</lastName>
        <firstName>Brenda</firstName>
        <dateOfBirth>1964-04-25</dateOfBirth>
        <age>39</age>
        <stage>I</stage>
        <performance scale="Karnosfky">0.88</performance>
    </patient>
</patients>
```

2. Take some time to examine the contents of the document, paying close attention to the order of the elements and the values of the elements and attributes.

Figure 4-2 shows the tree structure of the XML vocabulary used in the document.

Figure 4-2 | **Structure of the patients vocabulary**

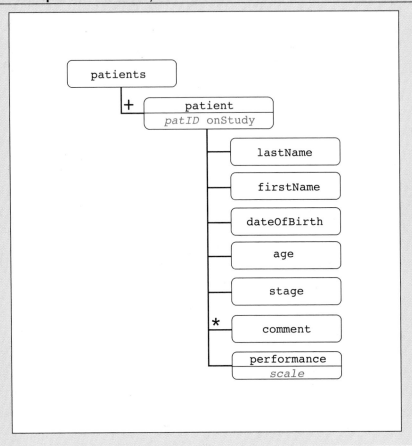

For each patient element in the document, Allison has inserted two attributes, patID and onStudy. The first contains the patient's medical record number and the second contains the ID of the study in which the patient is enrolled. She's collected each patient's first and last name, date of birth, age, breast cancer stage, and health performance score. Allison has also allowed each patient element to contain multiple comment elements for any additional information that a study's investigator may want to add.

The patients.xml file contains the initial patients entered into the Tamoxifen study, but it will eventually contain more entries. As more patients are added, Allison wants to ensure that the new data obeys the study's eligibility guidelines. For example, patients must be at least 21 years of age in order to give informed consent. Every patient has to have a valid medical record number. For the Tamoxifen study, patients must be diagnosed with either Stage I or Stage II cancer. You and Allison discuss whether a DTD can meet her needs.

The Limits of DTDs

DTDs are commonly used for validation largely because of XML's origins as an offshoot of SGML. SGML was originally designed for text-based documents, such as reports and technical manuals. As long as data content is limited to simple text, DTDs work well for validation. However, today XML is being used for a wider range of document types, and several limitations have prompted XML developers to explore alternatives to DTDs.

One complaint about DTDs is their lack of data types. For example, Allison can declare an age element in her DTD, but she cannot specify that the age element may contain only numbers, or that numbers must fall within a specified range of values. She can declare a dateOfBirth element, but the DTD won't have the tools to force the element to contain only dates. DTDs simply do not provide the control over data that Allison requires. DTDs also do not recognize namespaces, so they are not well suited to an environment in which a compound document contains data collected from dozens of XML vocabularies. This is a concern for Allison because the CCC is working on several XML vocabularies supporting a wide range of information.

Finally, DTDs employ a syntax called **Extended Backus Naur Form** (**EBNF**), which is different from the syntax used for XML. This means that the document's author must be able to work not only with the syntax of XML, but with EBNF as well. This adds overhead costs that Allison wants to avoid. Because XML stands for *Extensible* Markup Language, why not use XML to create a markup language that can validate other XML documents? This is the idea behind schemas.

Schemas and DTDs

A **schema** is an XML document that can validate the content and structure of other XML documents. To avoid confusion, the XML document to be validated is called the **instance document** because it represents a specific instance of the structure defined in the schema. Schemas have a number of advantages over DTDs. XML parsers need to understand only XML, and thus all of the tools used to create an instance document can also be applied to designing the schema. Schemas also support more data types, including data types for numbers and dates; and they also allow users to design custom data types for special needs. Additionally, schemas are more flexible than DTDs in dealing with mixed content, and they provide support for namespaces, making it easier to validate compound documents. Figure 4-3 summarizes some of the more important differences between schemas and DTDs.

Schemas vs. DTDs ◄ **Figure 4-3**

Feature	Schemas	DTDs
Document language	XML	Extended Backus Naur Form (EBNF)
Standards	multiple standards	one standard
Supported data types	44	10
Customized data types	yes	no
Mixed content	easy to develop	difficult to develop
Namespaces	completely supported	only namespace prefixes are supported
Entities	no	yes

So if schemas are so useful, why do you need DTDs at all? First of all, DTDs represent an older standard for XML documents and are, therefore, more widely supported. It will still be a few years before schemas entirely replace DTDs for document validation. DTDs can also do a few things that schemas cannot, such as create entities. Schemas and DTDs should be viewed as complementary approaches to data validation, not competing approaches. It's not unusual for an XML document to use both a schema and a DTD.

Schema Vocabularies

Unlike DTDs, schemas do not use a single form. Instead, several schema vocabularies have been created by various developers. Figure 4-4 lists a few of the schema vocabularies.

| Figure 4-4 | Schema vocabularies |

Schema	Description
XML Schema	The most widely used schema standard, XML Schema is developed and maintained by the W3C and is designed to handle a broad range of document structures. It is also referred to as XSD.
Document Definition Markup Language (DDML)	One of the original schema languages, DDML (originally known as XSchema) was created to replicate all DTD functionality in a schema. DDML does not support any data types beyond what could be found in DTDs.
XML Data	One of the original schema languages, XML Data was developed by Microsoft to replace DTDs.
XML Data Reduced (XDR)	XDR is a subset of the XML Data schema, primarily used prior to the release of XML Schema.
Regular Language for XML (RELAX)	A simple alternative to the W3C's XML schema standard, RELAX provides much of the same functionality as DTDs, with additional support for namespaces and data types. RELAX does not support entities or notations.
Tree Regular Expressions (TREX)	A TREX schema specifies a pattern for an XML document's structure and content, and thus identifies a class of XML documents that match the pattern. TREX has been merged with RELAX into RELAX NG.
RELAX NG (Regular Language for XML Next Generation)	RELAX NG is the current version of RELAX, combining the features of RELAX and TREX.
Schematron	The Schematron schema represents documents using a tree pattern, allowing support for document structures that might be difficult to represent in traditional schema languages.

Note that support for a particular schema depends solely on the XML parser being used for validation. Before applying any of the schemas listed in Figure 4-4, you have to verify the level of support offered by your application for that particular schema. XML Schema, developed by the W3C in March of 2001, is the most widely adopted schema standard. The focus of this tutorial is primarily on XML Schema, though many of the concepts involved with XML Schema can be applied to the other schema vocabularies as well. You can convert DTD files to XML Schema files using the dtd2xs converter, available at http://www.w3.org/XML/Schema.

Starting a Schema File

DTDs can be divided into internal and external subsets but a schema is always placed in a separate XML document. A file written in XML Schema typically ends with the ".xsd" file extension. Allison has provided a blank XML Schema file for you. Open it now.

To start work on the schema file:

1. Use your text editor to open **pschemtxt.xsd** from the tutorial.04x/tutorial folder. Enter **your name** and **the date** in the comment section.

2. Save the file as **pschema.xsd**.

The root element in any XML Schema document is the schema element. In order for a parser to recognize that the document is written in the XML Schema vocabulary, the schema element must include a declaration for the XML Schema namespace using the URI http://www.w3.org/2001/XMLSchema. Thus, the general structure of an XML Schema file is

```
<schema xmlns="http://www.w3.org/2001/XMLSchema">
   schema content
</schema>
```

where *schema content* is the list of elements and attributes that define the structure of the instance document. By convention, the namespace prefix xsd or xs is assigned to the XML Schema namespace in order to identify elements and attributes that belong to the XML Schema vocabulary. Keeping well-defined namespaces in an XML Schema document becomes very important when you start creating schemas for compound documents involving several namespaces. The usual form of an XML Schema document is therefore

```
<xs:schema xmlns:xs="http://www.w3.org/2001/XMLSchema">
   schema content
</xs:schema>
```

This tutorial assumes a namespace prefix of xs in discussing the elements and attributes of the XML Schema language; however, you may choose to use a different prefix in your own XML Schema documents. You may alternatively set XML Schema as the document's default namespace and thus not need any prefix. The only requirement is that you be consistent in applying (or not applying) the namespace prefix.

Add the root schema element to the pschema.xsd file now.

To insert the schema element in the pschema.xsd file:

1. Directly below the comment section, insert the following code (see Figure 4-5):

```
<xs:schema xmlns:xs="http://www.w3.org/2001/XMLSchema">
</xs:schema>
```

Inserting the XML Schema root element — Figure 4-5

2. Save your changes to the file.

Reference Window

Creating a Schema

- Create an XML document with the file extension ".xsd", and add the following structure to the XML document:

  ```
  <schema xmlns="http://www.w3.org/2001/XMLSchema">

     schema content

  </schema>
  ```
  where *schema content* is the elements and attributes of the schema.
- You can also apply a namespace prefix to the elements and attributes of the schema. It is customary to use a namespace prefix of xs or xsd. Using the xs prefix, the structure of the schema would be

  ```
  <xs:schema xmlns:xs="http://www.w3.org/2001/XMLSchema">

     schema content

  </xs:schema>
  ```
  where *schema content* is the elements and attributes of the schema.

Understanding Simple and Complex Types

XML Schema supports two types of content: simple and complex. A **simple type** contains a single value, such as the value of an attribute or the textual content of an element. A **complex type** contains one or more values placed within a defined structure. Examples of complex types include empty elements that contain attributes or elements that contain child elements. Figure 4-6 shows examples of simple and complex types that you might find in an instance document.

Figure 4-6 | Simple and complex types

Simple Types	Complex Types
An element containing only text	**An empty element containing attributes**
`<subject>Cynthia Dibbs</subject>`	`<subject name="Cynthia Dibbs" age="62" />`
An attribute	**An element containing text and an attribute**
`age="62"`	`<subject age="62">Cynthia Dibbs</subject>`
	An element containing child elements

	`<subject>`
	`   <name>Cynthia Dibbs</name>`
	`   <age>62</age>`
	`</subject>`

	An element containing child elements and an attribute

	`<subject age="62">`
	`   <name>Cynthia Dibbs</name>`
	`</subject>`

Figure 4-7 shows a list of the simple and complex types in the patients.xml file.

List of simple and complex types in the patients.xml document ◀ Figure 4-7

Item	Content	Content Type
patients	element	complex
patient	element	complex
patID	attribute	simple
onStudy	attribute	simple
lastName	element	simple
firstName	element	simple
dateOfBirth	element	simple
age	element	simple
stage	element	simple
comment	element	simple
performance	element	complex
scale	attribute	simple

Note that all of the attributes in the document are, by default, simple types. The patients, patient, and performance elements are complex types, since they contain either child elements or attributes. The lastName, firstName, dateOfBirth, age, stage, and comment elements are all simple types. In XML Schema, the code to define simple types differs markedly from complex types. You decide to start the schema by creating definitions for all of the simple type elements in Allison's document.

Working with Simple Type Elements

Simple type elements are defined within an XML Schema document using the empty element

```
<xs:element name="name" type="type" />
```

where *name* is the name of the element in the instance document and *type* is the type of data stored in the element. XML Schema supports a collection of built-in data types and also allows programmers to define their own. If you use one of the built-in data types, you have to indicate that it belongs to the XML Schema namespace, since it is a feature of the XML Schema language. The code to use a built-in data type is therefore

```
<xs:element name="name" type="xs:type" />
```

where *type* is now a particular data type used by XML Schema. If you use a different namespace prefix or declare XML Schema as the default namespace for the document, the prefix will be different.

Perhaps the most commonly used data type in XML Schema is string, which allows an element to contain any text string. For example, in the patients.xml file, the lastName element contains the text of the patient's last name. Thus, to indicate that this element contains string data, you would add the following element to the XML Schema file:

```
<xs:element name="lastName" type="xs:string" />
```

Add this declaration for the simple type elements in Allison's document. For now, use the string data type for each element. You'll revise this in the next session, when you examine the wide variety of data types supported by XML Schema.

To add simple type elements to the schema:

1. Within the schema root element, insert the following simple type elements (see Figure 4-8):

```
<xs:element name="lastName" type="xs:string" />
<xs:element name="firstName" type="xs:string" />
<xs:element name="dateOfBirth" type="xs:string" />
<xs:element name="age" type="xs:string" />
<xs:element name="stage" type="xs:string" />
<xs:element name="comment" type="xs:string" />
```

Figure 4-8	Declaring simple type elements

```
<xs:schema xmlns:xs="http://www.w3.org/2001/XMLSchema">

    <xs:element name="lastName" type="xs:string" />
    <xs:element name="firstName" type="xs:string" />
    <xs:element name="dateOfBirth" type="xs:string" />    simple type
    <xs:element name="age" type="xs:string" />            elements
    <xs:element name="stage" type="xs:string" />
    <xs:element name="comment" type="xs:string" />

</xs:schema>
```

2. Save your changes to the file.

Creating a Simple Type Element

- To define a simple type element, use the syntax
  ```
  <xs:element name="name" type="type" />
  ```
  where *name* is the element name in the instance document and *type* is the data type. To use a built-in data type, you must place the *type* value in the XML Schema namespace:
  ```
  <xs:element name="name" type="xs:type" />
  ```

Declaring an Attribute

An attribute is another example of a simple type. The syntax to define an attribute is

```
<xs:attribute name="name" type="type" default="default"
fixed="fixed" />
```

where *name* is the name of the attribute, *type* is the data type, *default* is the attribute's default value, and *fixed* is a fixed value for the attribute. Attributes use the same collection of data types that simple type elements do. For example, the following code declares the Gender attribute and indicates that it contains a text string with a default value of "female":

```
<xs:attribute name="Gender" type="xs:string" default="female" />
```

The default and fixed attributes are optional. You use them when you want to specify a default attribute value (applied when no attribute value is entered in the instance document) or when you want to fix an attribute to a specific value.

The patients.xml file has three attributes: patID, onStudy, and scale. None of these attributes has a default or fixed value. Add the attribute declarations to the schema file below the element declarations you just created.

To declare attributes in the schema:

▶ **1.** Add the following attribute declarations to the schema, as shown in Figure 4-9:

```
<xs:attribute name="patID" type="xs:string" />
<xs:attribute name="onStudy" type="xs:string" />
<xs:attribute name="scale" type="xs:string" />
```

Declaring attributes ◀ Figure 4-9

```
<xs:schema xmlns:xs="http://www.w3.org/2001/XMLSchema">

    <xs:element name="lastName" type="xs:string" />
    <xs:element name="firstName" type="xs:string" />
    <xs:element name="dateOfBirth" type="xs:string" />
    <xs:element name="age" type="xs:string" />
    <xs:element name="stage" type="xs:string" />
    <xs:element name="comment" type="xs:string" />

    <xs:attribute name="patID" type="xs:string" />      ⎫
    <xs:attribute name="onStudy" type="xs:string" />    ⎬ ← attribute declarations
    <xs:attribute name="scale" type="xs:string" />      ⎭

</xs:schema>
```

▶ **2.** Save your changes to the file.

Declaring an Attribute

Reference Window

• To declare an attribute, use the syntax
```
<xs:attribute name="name" type="type" default="default"
fixed="fixed" />
```
where *name* is the element name in the instance document and *type* is the data type of the element. For built-in data types, you must place *type* in the XML Schema namespace:
```
<xs:attribute name="name" type="xs:type" default="default"
fixed="fixed" />
```

Associating Attributes and Elements

You've defined the three attributes, but they are not yet associated with any elements in Allison's document. To do that, you have to first define the elements containing each of these attributes. Since those elements contain attributes, they are complex type elements. The basic structure for defining a complex type element with XML Schema is

```
<xs:element name="name">
    <xs:complexType>
        declarations
    </xs:complexType>
</xs:element>
```

where *name* is the name of the element and *declarations* is schema commands specific to the type of complex element being defined. As shown earlier in Figure 4-6, four complex type elements that usually appear in an instance document are the following:

• The element is an empty element and contains only attributes.
• The element contains textual content and attributes but no child elements.
• The element contains child elements but not attributes.
• The element contains both child elements and attributes.

XML Schema applies a different code structure to each of these four possibilities. Start by looking at the case in which an empty element contains one or more attributes.

Empty Elements and Attributes

The code to declare the attributes of an empty element is

```
<xs:element name="name">
    <xs:complexType>
        attributes
    </xs:complexType>
</xs:element>
```

where *attributes* is the set of declarations that define the attributes associated with the element. For example, the empty element

```
<subject name="Cynthia Dibbs" age="62" />
```

has two attributes: name and age. The code for this complex type element has the following structure:

```
<xs:element name="subject">
    <xs:complexType>
        <xs:attribute name="name" type="xs:string" />
        <xs:attribute name="age" type="xs:string" />
    </xs:complexType>
</xs:element>
```

The order of the attribute declarations is unimportant. XML Schema allows attributes to be entered in any order within a complex type element.

Simple Content and Attributes

If an element is not empty and contains textual content (but no child elements), the structure of the complex type element is slightly different. In these cases, you must include a declaration indicating that the complex type contains simple content, and you must include a collection of one or more attributes. The code structure is

```
<xs:element name="name">
    <xs:complexType>
        <xs:simpleContent>
            <xs:extension base="type">
                attributes
            </xs:extension>
        </xs:simpleContent>
    </xs:complexType>
</xs:element>
```

where *type* is the data type of the element's content and *attributes* is a list of the attributes associated with the element. The purpose of the <simpleContent> tag in this code is to indicate that the element contains simple content—that is, text with no child elements. However, since the element also contains attributes, you have to extend the content model to include attributes through the use of the <extension> tag. The simple-Content and extension elements are important tools used by XML Schema to derive new data types and design complex content models. In this case, you are using them to define complex element types that contain text and attributes.

One such element in the patients.xml file is the performance element. The following is a sample of the type of content stored in this element:

```
<performance scale="Karnofsky">0.81</performance>
```

The code to associate the scale attribute with the performance element would therefore be

```
<xs:element name="performance">
   <xs:complexType>
      <xs:simpleContent>
         <xs:extension base="xs:string">
            <xs:attribute name="scale" type="xs:string" />
         </xs:extension>
      </xs:simpleContent>
   </xs:complexType>
</xs:element>
```

Specifying the Use of an Attribute

An attribute may or may not be required with a particular element. To indicate whether an attribute is required, you add the use attribute to the element declaration or reference. The use attribute has the following values:

- **required**—The attribute must always appear with the element
- **optional**—The use of the attribute is optional with the element
- **prohibited**—The attribute cannot be used with the element

For example, in Allison's document the scale attribute is required with every performance element. To force the instance document to follow this rule, you add the use attribute to the element declaration:

```
<xs:attribute name="scale" type="xs:string" use="required" />
```

If you neglect to add the use attribute to an element declaration, the parser assumes that the attribute is optional.

Referencing an Element or Attribute

You've already declared the scale attribute in your schema document. You could revise your code to nest that attribute declaration within the declaration for the performance element; however XML Schema allows for a great deal of flexibility in designing complex types. Rather than nesting the attribute declaration within the element, you can create a reference to it. The code to create a reference to an element or attribute declaration is

```
<xs:element ref="elemName" />
<xs:attribute ref="attName" />
```

where *elemName* is the name used in an element declaration and *attName* is the name used in an attribute declaration. To reference the scale attribute from within the performance element, the code would looks as follows:

```
<xs:attribute name="scale" type="xs:string" />
<xs:element name="performance">
   <xs:complexType>
      <xs:simpleContent>
         <xs:extension base="xs:string">
            <xs:attribute ref="scale" use="required" />
         </xs:extension>
      </xs:simpleContent>
   </xs:complexType>
</xs:element>
```

Notice that the use attribute in this code is added to the attribute reference, not to the declaration. The value of the use attribute must always be nested in this fashion, since it indicates how the attribute is used with the element. After all, an attribute might be required for one element and optional for another.

The issue of whether to nest a declaration or create a reference to it is an important one. Where an element or attribute is declared determines how it can be used in the schema. Declarations that are placed as children of the root schema element have **global scope** and can be referenced throughout the schema file. Thus, rather than repeating the same attribute declaration, you can declare it once and reference it throughout the schema. On the other hand, a declaration that is nested within a complex type has **local scope** and is available only to that complex type. This avoids the confusion of an attribute or element being reused in different contexts throughout the schema. You'll explore the issues surrounding local and global scope in greater detail in Session 4.3.

The element and attribute declarations you've already added to the schema file all have global scope. You decide to add a reference to the scale attribute and use it in the declaration for the performance element.

To define the performance element:

▶ **1.** Below the declaration for the scale attribute, add the following complex type declaration (see Figure 4-10):

```
<xs:element name="performance">
   <xs:complexType>
      <xs:simpleContent>
         <xs:extension base="xs:string">
            <xs:attribute ref="scale" use="required" />
         </xs:extension>
      </xs:simpleContent>
   </xs:complexType>
</xs:element>
```

| Figure 4-10 | Declaring an element containing text and attributes |

```
<xs:attribute name="patID" type="xs:string" />
<xs:attribute name="onStudy" type="xs:string" />
<xs:attribute name="scale" type="xs:string" />

<xs:element name="performance">
   <xs:complexType>
      <xs:simpleContent>
         <xs:extension base="xs:string">
            <xs:attribute ref="scale" use="required" />
         </xs:extension>
      </xs:simpleContent>
   </xs:complexType>
</xs:element>

</xs:schema>
```

global attribute declaration

attribute is required

attribute declaration reference

▶ **2.** Save your changes to the file.

Defining Attributes and Elements

- To define an empty element containing one or more attributes, use the syntax
  ```
  <xs:element name="name">
    <xs:complexType>
          attributes
    </xs:complexType>
  </xs:element>
  ```
  where *name* is the element name and `attributes` is a list of attributes.
- To define an element containing attributes and simple text content, use the syntax
  ```
  <xs:element name="name">
    <xs:complexType>
        <xs:simpleContent>
            <xs:extension base="type">
                attributes
            </xs:extension>
        </xs:simpleContent>
    </xs:complexType>
  </xs:element>
  ```
  where *type* is the data type of the text content of the element.

Working with Child Elements

Another kind of complex type element contains child elements, but no attributes. To define these child elements, use the code structure

```
<xs:element name="name">
   <xs:complexType>
      <xs:compositor>
          elements
      </xs:compositor>
   </xs:complexType>
</xs:element>
```

where `elements` is the list of simple type element declarations for each child element, and `compositor` defines how the child elements are organized.

Using Compositors

XML Schema supports the following compositors:

- **sequence** defines a specific order for the child elements
- **choice** allows any *one* of the child elements to appear in the instance document
- **all** allows any of the child elements to appear in any order in the instance document; however, they must appear either only once or not all.

For example, the following complex type assigns four child elements—street, city, state, and country—to the address element. Because the complex type uses the sequence compositor, the document will be invalid if the address element doesn't contain all of these child elements in the specified order.

```
<element name="address">
   <xs:complexType>
      <xs:sequence>
         <xs:element name="street" type="xs:string"/>
         <xs:element name="city" type="xs:string"/>
         <xs:element name="state" type="xs:string"/>
         <xs:element name="country" type="xs:string"/>
      </xs:sequence>
```

```
        </xs:complexType>
    </xs:element>
```

The following declaration allows XML authors to choose between parent and guardian as the child element of the sponsor element. Because the complex type uses the choice compositor, the sponsor element can contain either element, but not both.

```
<xs:element name="sponsor">
    <xs:complexType>
        <xs:choice>
            <xs:element name="parent" type="xs:string"/>
            <xs:element name="guardian" type="xs:string"/>
        </xs:choice>
    </xs:complexType>
</xs:element>
```

Finally, the following code uses the all compositor to allow the Family element to contain an element named "Father" and/or an element named "Mother," in no particular order:

```
<xs:element name="Family">
    <xs:complexType>
        <xs:all>
            <xs:element name="Father" type="xs:string"/>
            <xs:element name="Mother" type="xs:string"/>
        </xs:all>
    </xs:complexType>
</xs:element>
```

Compositors can be nested and combined with each other. The following code uses choice compositors to allow the Account element to contain either the Person or Company element followed by either the Cash or Credit element:

```
<xs:element name="Account">
    <xs:complexType>
        <xs:sequence>
            <xs:choice>
                <xs:element name="Person" type="xs:string"/>
                <xs:element name="Company" type="xs:string"/>
            </xs:choice>
            <xs:choice>
                <xs:element name="Cash" type="xs:string"/>
                <xs:element name="Credit" type="xs:string"/>
            </xs:choice>
        </xs:sequence>
    </xs:complexType>
</xs:element>
```

The only restriction with combining compositors occurs when using the all compositor: a complex type element can contain only one all compositor, and the all compositor must appear as the first child of the complex type element. You cannot combine the all compositor with either the choice or sequence compositors.

Specifying the Occurrences of an Item

In the previous code samples, it was assumed that each element in the list appeared once and only once. This will not always be the case. To specify the number of times each element appears in the instance document, you can use the minOccurs and maxOccurs attributes.

For example, the following element declaration specifies that the patient element appears one to three times in the instance document:

```
<xs:element name="patient" type="xs:string" minOccurs="1"
maxOccurs="3"/>
```

Any time the minOccurs attribute is set to 0, the declared item is optional. The maxOccurs attribute can be any positive value, or it can have a value of "unbounded" for unlimited occurrences of the child element. If a value is specified for the minOccurs attribute, but the maxOccurs attribute is missing, the value of the maxOccurs attribute is assumed to be equal to the value of the minOccurs attribute. Finally, if both attributes are missing, their values are assumed to be 1. Like the use value for attribute declarations, the minOccurs and maxOccurs values must be set locally within a complex type element.

The minOccurs and maxOccurs attributes can also be used with compositors to repeat entire sequences of items. In the following code, the sequence of three child elements (FirstName, MiddleName, LastName) can be repeated countless times within the Customer element:

```
<xs:element name="Customer">
   <xs:complexType>
      <xs:sequence minOccurs="1" maxOccurs="unbounded">
         <xs:element name="FirstName" type="xs:string"/>
         <xs:element name="MiddleName" type="xs:string"/>
         <xs:element name="LastName" type="xs:string"/>
      </xs:sequence>
   </xs:complexType>
</xs:element>
```

The patients.xml file contains a root element named patients that contains a child element named patient. The patient element must occur at least once, but its upper limit is unbounded.

To define the patients element:

1. Insert the following code below the opening schema element (see Figure 4-11):

```
<xs:element name="patients">
   <xs:complexType>
      <xs:sequence>
         <xs:element ref="patient" minOccurs="1" maxOccurs=
"unbounded" />
      </xs:sequence>
   </xs:complexType>
</xs:element>
```

Declaring an element containing child elements   **Figure 4-11**

```
<xs:schema xmlns:xs="http://www.w3.org/2001/XMLSchema">

   <xs:element name="patients">
      <xs:complexType>
         <xs:sequence>
            <xs:element ref="patient" minOccurs="1" maxOccurs="unbounded" />
         </xs:sequence>
      </xs:complexType>
   </xs:element>
```

the patient element must occur at least once, but its upper limit is unbounded

2. Save your changes.

It doesn't matter where you place the declaration for the patients element. Placing it at the beginning of the schema allows the order of the declarations to follow the order of the elements in Allison's document. Also note that you use the ref attribute to reference the patient element declaration. You'll add the declaration for this element next.

Working with Child Elements and Attributes

The patient element contains two attributes (patID and onStudy) and seven child elements (lastName, firstName, dateOfBirth, age, stage, comment, and performance.) The code for a complex type element that contains both attributes and child elements is

```
<xs:element name="name">
   <xs:complexType>
      <xs:compositor>
          elements
      </xs:compositor>
   </xs:complexType>
   attributes
</xs:element>
```

Note that this code structure is the same as the one you used for the child elements, with a list of attributes added. The declaration for the patient element would therefore be

```
<xs:element name="patient">
  <xs:complexType>
    <xs:sequence>
      <xs:element ref="lastName"/>
      <xs:element ref="firstName"/>
      <xs:element ref="dateOfBirth"/>
      <xs:element ref="age"/>
      <xs:element ref="stage"/>
      <xs:element ref="comment" minOccurs="0" maxOccurs="unbounded"/>
      <xs:element ref="performance"/>
    </xs:sequence>
    <xs:attribute ref="patID" use="required"/>
    <xs:attribute ref="onStudy" use="required"/>
  </xs:complexType>
</xs:element>
```

Since you've already defined the elements and declarations, you only have to add references to them. Note that the comment element is optional, but can occur an unlimited number of times. Also note that the patID and onStudy attributes are both required with the patient element. Add this code to the pschema.xsd file.

To define the patient element:

1. Insert the following code below the patients complex type (see Figure 4-12):

```
<xs:element name="patient">
  <xs:complexType>
    <xs:sequence>
      <xs:element ref="lastName"/>
      <xs:element ref="firstName"/>
      <xs:element ref="dateOfBirth"/>
      <xs:element ref="age"/>
      <xs:element ref="stage"/>
      <xs:element ref="comment" minOccurs="0" maxOccurs
="unbounded"/>
      <xs:element ref="performance"/>
    </xs:sequence>
```

```
        <xs:attribute ref="patID" use="required"/>
        <xs:attribute ref="onStudy" use="required"/>
    </xs:complexType>
</xs:element>
```

Complete schema for the patient data Figure 4-12

```
<xs:schema xmlns:xs="http://www.w3.org/2001/XMLSchema">

    <xs:element name="patients">
        <xs:complexType>
            <xs:sequence>
                <xs:element ref="patient" minOccurs="1" maxOccurs="unbounded" />
            </xs:sequence>
        </xs:complexType>
    </xs:element>

    <xs:element name="patient">
        <xs:complexType>
            <xs:sequence>
                <xs:element ref="lastName"/>
                <xs:element ref="firstName"/>
                <xs:element ref="dateOfBirth"/>
                <xs:element ref="age"/>
                <xs:element ref="stage"/>
                <xs:element ref="comment" minOccurs="0" maxOccurs="unbounded"/>
                <xs:element ref="performance"/>
            </xs:sequence>
            <xs:attribute ref="patID" use="required"/>
            <xs:attribute ref="onStudy" use="required"/>
        </xs:complexType>
    </xs:element>

    <xs:element name="lastName" type="xs:string" />
    <xs:element name="firstName" type="xs:string" />
    <xs:element name="dateOfBirth" type="xs:string" />
    <xs:element name="age" type="xs:string" />
    <xs:element name="stage" type="xs:string" />
    <xs:element name="comment" type="xs:string" />

    <xs:attribute name="patID" type="xs:string" />
    <xs:attribute name="onStudy" type="xs:string" />
    <xs:attribute name="scale" type="xs:string" />

    <xs:element name="performance">
        <xs:complexType>
            <xs:simpleContent>
                <xs:extension base="xs:string">
                    <xs:attribute ref="scale" use="required" />
                </xs:extension>
            </xs:simpleContent>
        </xs:complexType>
    </xs:element>

</xs:schema>
```

patient element definition

2. Take some time to review the entire code in your schema file against that shown in Figure 4-12. When you are satisfied that you have duplicated the code exactly, close the pschema.xsd file, saving your changes.

Defining Child Elements

- To define an element containing only child elements, use the syntax
  ```
  <xs:element name="name">
     <xs:complexType>
        <xs:compositor>
           elements
        </xs:compositor>
     </xs:complexType>
  </xs:element>
  ```
  where *name* is the element name, *elements* is a list of the child elements, and *compositor* is sequence, choice, or all.
- To define an element containing attributes and child elements, use the syntax
  ```
  <xs:element name="name">
     <xs:complexType>
        <xs:compositor>
           elements
        </xs:compositor>
     </xs:complexType>
     attributes
  </xs:element>
  ```
  where *attributes* is a list of the attributes associated with the element.

Specifying Mixed Content

As was discussed in Tutorial 3, one of the limitations of using DTDs is their inability to define mixed content, which is an element that contains both text and child elements. You can specify the child elements with a DTD, but you cannot constrain their order or number. XML Schema gives you more control over mixed content. To specify that an element contains both text and child elements, add the mixed attribute to the <complexType> tag. When the mixed attribute is set to the value "true," XML Schema assumes that the element contains both text and child elements. The structure of the child elements can then be defined with the conventional method. For example, the XML content

```
<Summary>
   Patient <Name>Cynthia Davis</Name> was enrolled in
   the <Study>Tamoxifen Study</Study> on 8/15/2003.
</Summary>
```

can be declared in the schema file using the following complex type:

```
<element name="Summary">
   <complexType mixed="true">
      <sequence>
         <element name="Name" type="string"/>
         <element name="Study" type="string"/>
      </sequence>
   </complexType>
</element>
```

Note that XML Schema allows content text to appear before, between, and after any of the child elements.

Applying a Schema

Now that you've created a schema for the patients.xml document, you are ready to test whether the document that Allison gave you is valid according to her rules. To attach a schema to the document, you must do the following:

1. Declare a namespace for XML Schema in the instance document.
2. Indicate the location of the schema file.

To declare the XML Schema namespace in the instance document, you add the following attribute to the document's root element:

```
xmlns:xsi="http://www.w3.org/2001/XMLSchema-instance"
```

The namespace prefix xsi is commonly used for XML Schema instances, though you may specify a different prefix in your documents. The code to specify the location of the schema file depends on whether the instance document has been placed in a namespace. If there is no namespace for the contents of the instance document, add the following attribute to the root element:

```
xsi:noNamespaceSchemaLocation="schema"
```

where *schema* is the location and name of the schema file. Notice that this attribute has to be placed in the XML Schema instance namespace.

Specifying a schema in an XML document is treated only as a hint by validating parsers, and some parsers ignore specified schemas. For example, an XHTML editor may have a built-in XHTML schema that it uses in place of any schema you might specify for a document. In commerce programs, parsers are often written to accept validation only from approved schemas, and do not allow document authors to specify their own. This is done to prevent improper financial documents from being fraudulently submitted to a server attached to an unsupported schema.

Currently Allison's document does not employ a namespace, so you'll add the following attribute to the root patients element:

```
xsi:noNamespaceSchemaLocation="pschema.xsd"
```

You'll explore how to apply schemas to instance documents with namespaces in Session 4.3.

To apply a schema to the patients document:

▶ **1.** Return to the patients.xml file in your text editor.

▶ **2.** Within the patients element, add the following attributes (see Figure 4-13):

```
xmlns:xsi="http://www.w3.org/2001/XMLSchema-instance"
xsi:noNamespaceSchemaLocation="pschema.xsd"
```

Applying a schema to a document without a namespace ◀ **Figure 4-13**

XML Schema instance namespace

```
<patients xmlns:xsi="http://www.w3.org/2001/XMLSchema-instance"
          xsi:noNamespaceSchemaLocation="pschema.xsd">
    <patient patID="MR890-041-02" onStudy="TBC-080-5">
        <lastName>Dibbs</lastName>
        <firstName>Cynthia</firstName>
        <dateOfBirth>1945-05-22</dateOfBirth>
        <age>62</age>
        <stage>II</stage>
        <performance scale="Karnofsky">0.81</performance>
    </patient>
```

location of the schema document

3. Close the file, saving your changes.

Applying a Schema to a Document without a Namespace

- To apply a schema to a document without a namespace, add the following attributes to the instance document's root element:

  ```
  xmlns:xsi="http://www.w3.org/2001/XMLSchema-instance"
  xsi:noNamespaceSchemaLocation="schema"
  ```
  where *schema* is the location and name of the schema file.

Now you can validate Allison's document against the structure you defined in the pschema.xsd file. To validate the document, you need a validating parser like XMLSpy.

To validate the patients document:

1. Start **XMLSpy** on your computer.

2. Open the **patients.xml** file from the tutorial.04x/tutorial folder.

3. Click the **Validate button** on the toolbar or press the **F8** key.

As shown in Figure 4-14, XMLSpy should report that the file is valid.

Figure 4-14 ▶ **Validating the patients.xml file**

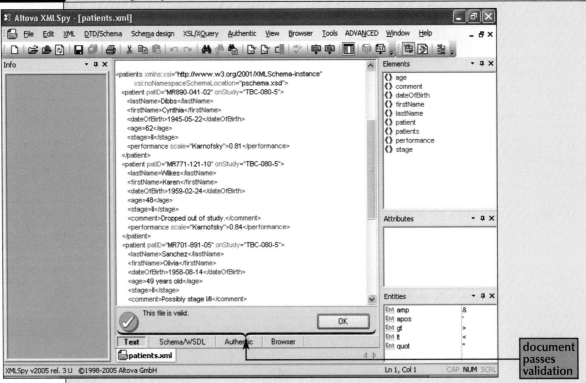

4. If you intend to take a break before the next session, close any open files.

Trouble? If you receive an error message when the patient.xml file is initially loaded or when you validate the file, close XMLSpy and then reopen the patients. xml and pschema.xsd files in your text editor. Carefully examine the code for errors. Common mistakes include forgetting to insert the namespace prefix before XML Schema attribute and element names, mismatching the upper- and lower-case letters, and forgetting to add closing tags to the two-sided elements.

You've concluded your initial work in creating a schema for Allison's patient data. You have not implemented all of the rules that Allison instructed; you'll do that in the next session as you learn about data types and how to apply them.

Session 4.1 Quick Check

Review

1. What is a schema? What is an instance document?
2. How do schemas differ from DTDs?
3. What is a simple type? What is a complex type?
4. How do you declare a simple type element named Weight containing string data?
5. How do you declare a complex type element named Contact containing the child elements Mail and/or Phone? (Assume that the Mail and Phone elements are simple type elements containing text strings.)
6. The Book element contains simple text and a Title attribute. What code would you enter into your schema file to define this complex type element?
7. What code would you enter into a schema to create a reference to an attribute named patientID?
8. What attribute would you add to the root element of an instance document to attach it to a schema file named Schema1.xsd? Assume that no namespace has been assigned to the schema file and that you are using the XML Schema vocabulary.

Session 4.2

Working with XML Schema Data Types

Allison is pleased with the initial work you've done designing a schema for the patients document. However, she needs to have more control over data entry. Currently the schema uses the string data type for all element and attribute content, thereby allowing users to enter any text string into those items. She wants to ensure that dates are entered in the proper form, that only positive integers are entered for the patient ages, and that the patient and study IDs follow a prescribed pattern. You can do all of these using XML Schema's data types.

XML Schema supports two general categories of data types: built-in and user-derived. A **built-in data type** is part of the XML Schema language and is available to all XML Schema authors. A **user-derived data type** is created by a schema author for specific data values in an instance document. As you saw in the last session, built-in data types need to be placed in the XML Schema namespace.

XML Schema divides its built-in data types into two classes: primitive and derived. A **primitive data type**, or **base type**, is one of 19 fundamental data types that are not defined in terms of other types. A **derived data type** is a collection of 25 data types that the XML Schema developers created based on the 19 primitive types. Figure 4-15 provides a schematic diagram of all 44 built-in data types.

Figure 4-15 ► **XML Schema built-in data types**

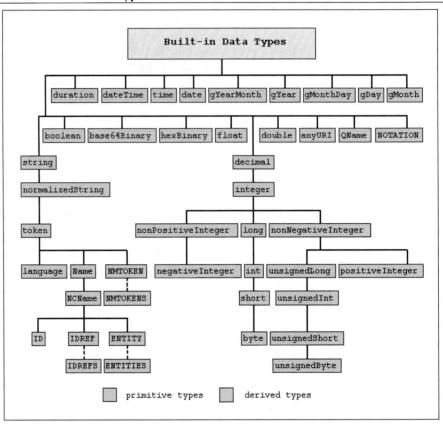

Derived data types share many of the same characteristics as the primitive data types they are derived from, but with a restriction or a modification added to create a new data type. To see how this is done, you'll start by examining the string data types.

String Data Types

In the last session, you used only the primitive string type, allowing almost any text string in the elements and attributes of Allison's document. The string data type is the most general of XML Schema's built-in data types, and for that reason it's not very useful if you need to exert more control over element and attribute values in an instance document. XML Schema provides several derived data types that enable you to restrict text strings. Figure 4-16 describes some of these types.

String data types ◄ Figure 4-16

Data Type	Description
xs:string	A text string containing all legal characters from the ISO/IEC character set, including all white space characters
xs:normalizedString	A text string in which all white space characters are replaced with blank spaces
xs:token	A text string in which blank spaces are replaced with a single blank space; opening and closing spaces are removed
xs:NMTOKEN	A text string containing valid XML names with no white space
xs:NMTOKENS	A list of NMTOKEN data values separated by white space
xs:Name	A text string similar to the NMTOKEN data type except that names must begin with a letter or the character ":" or "-"
xs:NCName	A "noncolonized name," derived from the Name data type but restricting the use of colons anywhere in the name
xs:ID	A unique ID name found nowhere else in the instance document
xs:IDREF	A reference to an ID value found in the instance document
xs:IDREFS	A list of ID references separated by white space
xs:ENTITY	A value matching an unparsed entity defined in a DTD
xs:ENTITIES	A list of entity values matching an unparsed entity defined in a DTD

Some of the other data types in the list should be familiar from the previous tutorial. For example, the ID type allows text strings containing unique ID values, and the IDREF and IDREFS data types allow only text strings that contain references to ID values located in the instance document. Thus, with these data types, the content of a text string is restricted to unique values or references.

Each patient in Allison's document has a unique medical reference number that identifies the patient to the investigator. You decide to apply the ID data type to values of this attribute.

To apply the ID data type:

1. If necessary, reopen the **pschema.xsd** file in your text editor.

2. Scroll down the document and locate the declaration for the patID attribute.

3. Change the type value from "xs:string" to "**xs:ID**" (see Figure 4-17).

   Remember that because the ID data type is built into XML Schema, you have to add the xs prefix to place it in the XML Schema namespace.

Applying the ID data type ◄ Figure 4-17

```
<xs:attribute name="patID" type="xs:ID" />
<xs:attribute name="onStudy" type="xs:string" />
<xs:attribute name="scale" type="xs:string" />
```

Numeric Data Types

Unlike DTDs, schemas do allow numeric data types. Most numeric types are derived from four primitive data types: decimal, double, float, and boolean. Figure 4-18 describes some of the numeric data types supported by XML Schema.

Figure 4-18 ▶ **Numeric data types**

Data Type	Description
xs:decimal	A decimal number in which the decimal separator is always a dot (.) with a leading + or - character allowed; no non-numeric characters are allowed, nor is exponential notation.
xs:integer	An integer
xs:nonPositiveInteger	An integer less than or equal to zero
xs:negativeInteger	An integer less than zero
xs:nonNegativeInteger	An integer greater than or equal to zero
xs:positiveInteger	An integer greater than zero
xs:float	A floating point number allowing decimal values and values in scientific notation; infinite values can be represented by -INF and INF, non-numeric values can be represented by NaN.
xs:double	A double precision floating point number
xs:boolean	A Boolean value that has the value true, false, 0, or 1

Allison has entered the ages of all of the patients in the Tamoxifen study, and she would like you to validate that the ages have been entered as positive integers. She has also recorded a numeric score for each patient's performance on a medical evaluation test. The score varies from 0 to 1. She would like the data type for the performance element to be decimal. Note that, unlike DTDs, schemas use the same data types for both elements and attributes.

To apply the positiveInteger and decimal data types:

▶ 1. Change the data type for the age element from "xs:string" to "**xs: positiveInteger**".

▶ 2. Change the base value of the performance element from "xs:string" to "**xs: decimal**".

Figure 4-19 shows the revised code.

Figure 4-19 ▶ **Applying numeric data types**

```
<xs:element name="lastName" type="xs:string" />
<xs:element name="firstName" type="xs:string" />
<xs:element name="dateOfBirth" type="xs:string" />
<xs:element name="age" type="xs:positiveInteger" />
<xs:element name="stage" type="xs:string" />
<xs:element name="comment" type="xs:string" />

<xs:attribute name="patID" type="xs:ID" />
<xs:attribute name="onStudy" type="xs:string" />
<xs:attribute name="scale" type="xs:string" />

<xs:element name="performance">
  <xs:complexType>
    <xs:simpleContent>
      <xs:extension base="xs:decimal">
        <xs:attribute ref="scale" use="required" />
      </xs:extension>
    </xs:simpleContent>
  </xs:complexType>
</xs:element>
```

Because performance is a complex type element containing text and attributes, you add the data type to the base attribute in the simpleContent element.

Dates and Times

XML Schema provides several data types for dates and times and durations. However, XML Schema does not allow for any flexibility in the date and time format. Date values must be entered in the format

yyyy-mm-dd

where yyyy is the four-digit year value, mm is the two-digit month value, and dd is the two-digit day value. Month values range from "01" to "12", while day values range from "01" to "31" (depending on the month). Thus, the date value

2008-01-08

would be valid under XML Schema, but the date

2008-1-8

would not, since its month and day values are not two digits. To support a date format such as 1/8/2008 or Jan. 8, 2008, you need to create a user-defined data type that matches the date pattern you want to use.

Times in XML Schema must be entered using 24-hour (or military) time. The format is

hh:mm:ss

where hh is the hour value ranging from "0" to "23", and mm and ss are the minutes and seconds values ranging from "00" to "59". There is no data type for expressing time in the 12-hour AM/PM format, but you can create a custom data type for that time pattern. In the time format, each time value (hours, minutes, and seconds) must be specified. Thus, the time value

15:45

would be invalid since it does not specify a value for seconds. Figure 4-20 summarizes the different date and time formats supported by XML Schema.

Date and time data types　　**Figure 4-20**

Data Type	Description
xs:datetime	A date and time entered in the format *yyyy-mm-ddThh:mm:ss* where *yyyy* is the four-digit year, *mm* is the two-digit month, *dd* is the two-digit day, *T* is the time zone, *hh* is the two-digit hour, *mm* is the two-digit minute, and *ss* is the two-digit second
xs:date	A date entered in the format *yyyy-mm-dd*
xs:time	A time entered in the format *hh:mm:ss*
xs:gYearMonthDay	A date based on the Gregorian calendar entered in the format *yyyy-mm-dd* (equivalent to xs:date)
xs:gYearMonth	A date entered in the format *yyyy-mm* (no day is specified)
xs:gYear	A year entered in the format *yyyy*
xs:gMonthDay	A month and day entered in the format *--mm-dd*
xs:gMonth	A month entered in the format *--mm*
xs:gDay	A day entered in the format *---dd*
xs:duration	A time duration entered in the format *PyYmMdDhHmMsS* where *y, m, d, h, m,* and *s* are the duration values in years, months, days, hours, minutes, and seconds; an optional negative sign is also permitted to indicate a negative time duration

Allison has recorded the date of birth of each patient in her XML document and has entered the value into the dateOfBirth element. Apply the date data type to values of this element.

To apply the date data type:

1. Locate the declaration for the dateOfBirth element and change the data type to **xs:date**, as shown in Figure 4-21.

Figure 4-21	Applying a date data type

```
<xs:element name="lastName" type="xs:string" />
<xs:element name="firstName" type="xs:string" />
<xs:element name="dateOfBirth" type="xs:date" />
<xs:element name="age" type="xs:positiveInteger" />
<xs:element name="stage" type="xs:string" />
<xs:element name="comment" type="xs:string" />
```

2. Save your changes to the document.

Reference Window

Applying Built-in XML Schema Data Types:

- For any string content, use the data type xs:string.
- For ID values, use xs:ID.
- For references to an ID value, use xs:IDREF.
- For decimal values, use xs:decimal.
- For integer values, use xs:integer.
- For positive integers, use xs:positiveInteger.
- For dates in the format *yyyy-mm-dd* use xs:date.
- For time in the format *hh:mm:ss*, use xs:time.

With the new data types entered, you decide to validate the contents of the patients.xml file.

To validate the patients.xml file:

1. Open or reload the **patients.xml** file using XMLSpy or another parser that validates documents against schemas.

2. If necessary, click the **Validate button** on the toolbar or press the **F8** key.

As shown in Figure 4-22, XMLSpy encounters a validation error. The age for one of the patients has been entered as "49 years old" rather than the integer value "49". Fix this problem and revalidate the file.

Catching an invalid age

Figure 4-22

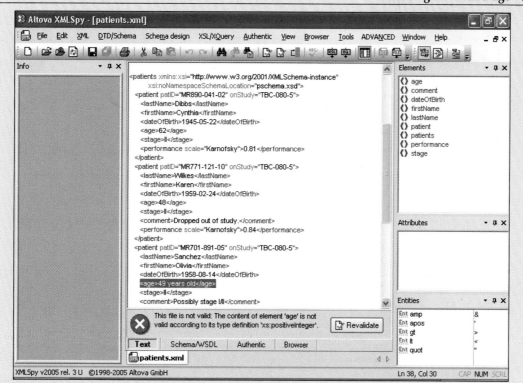

3. Open the **patients.xml** file in your text editor and change the age value for the patient from "49 years old" to **49**. Save your changes to the file, then return to XMLSpy.

   Trouble? You can also make changes to the file from within the editor window in XMLSpy. If you edit the file in XMLSpy, be sure to save your changes when you exit the program. Note that editing the document in XMLSpy may cause the layout of the elements in the document to change slightly.

4. XMLSpy notifies you that the file has been changed outside of the program. Click the **Yes** button to reload the file and revalidate its contents.

   The next validation error appears as shown in Figure 4-23. In this error, the date of birth has been entered in an improper format: 1952-9-14 rather than 1952-09-14.

| Figure 4-23 | Catching an invalid date |

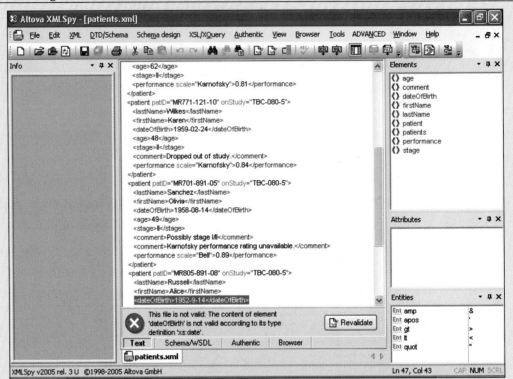

5. Return to the patients.xml file in your text editor and change the date of birth from 1952-9-14 to **1952-09-14**. Save your changes to the file and reload the document in XMLSpy.

6. Click the **Validate button** or press the **F8** key to confirm that XMLSpy validates the data of the patients.xml file based on the schema you created.

7. Close XMLSpy. If you chose above to edit the patients.xml document from within the program, save your changes.

Deriving New Data Types

In addition to the built-in data types, you also need to create some new data types to fully validate Allison's document. Allison has laid out the following rules for the elements and attributes in her document:

- Patients must be at least 21 years of age.
- The stage of the breast cancer must be I or II.
- The performance score must fall between 0 and 1.
- The value of the performance scale attribute must be either "Bell" or "Karnofsky".

While there are no built-in data types for these rules, you can derive your own data types based on XML Schema's built-in types. New data types are considered simple types because they contain values like attributes and simple type elements. Thus, to create a new data type, you create a new simple type using the code

```
<xs:simpleType name="name">
    Rules
</xs:simpleType>
```

where *name* is the name of the user-defined data type and *rules* is the list of statements that define the properties of the data type. The base type can be one of the built-in XML Schema data types, or it can be another customized data type. Three components are involved in deriving a new data type:

- **value space**—the set of values that correspond to the data type; for example, a positiveInteger data type consists of the numbers 1, 2, 3, etc., but does not contain zero, negative integers, fractions, or text strings.
- **lexical space**—the set of textual representations of the value space; for example, the floating data type supports the value 42, which can be represented in several ways (such as 42, 42.0, or 4.2E01).
- **facets**—the properties that distinguish one data type from another; facets can include such properties as text string length or a range of allowable values; XML Schema uses one such facet to distinguish the integer data type from the positiveInteger data type by constraining integers to the realm of positive numbers

New data types are derived by manipulating the characteristics of these three components. User-derived data types fall into three general categories: list, union, and restriction. Start by examining how to create a list data type.

Deriving a List Data Type

A **list data type** is a list of values separated by white space, in which each item in the list is derived from an established data type. You've already seen a couple of examples of built-in lists, including the xs:ENTITIES and xs:IDREFS lists. In these cases, the data types are derived from the xs:ENTITY and xs:IDREF types. The syntax for deriving a customized list data type is

```
<xs:simpleType name="name">
   <xs:list itemType="type" />
</xs:simpleType>
```

where *name* is the name assigned to the list data type and *type* is the data type from which each item in the list is derived. The clinical studies at the University Hospital often involve recording patients' weekly white blood cell counts. An element containing this information might appear as follows:

```
<wbc>15.1 15.8 12.0 9.3 7.1 5.2 4.3 3.4</wbc>
```

A list data type must always use white space as the delimiter. You cannot use commas or other non-white space characters. To create a data type for this information, you could add the following simple type to the schema:

```
<xs:simpleType name="wbcList">
   <xs:list itemType="xs:decimal" />
</xs:simpleType>
```

In this case, you have a simple type named wbcList that contains a list of decimal values. To apply this new data type to the wbc element, you add the data type to the element declaration:

```
<xs:element name="wbc" type="wbcList" />
```

Notice that the type value does not have the xs prefix, because wbcList is not part of the XML Schema namespace.

Deriving a Union Data Type

A **union data type** is composed of the value and/or lexical spaces from any number of base types. Each of the base types is known as a **member type**. When a union data type is validated, the validating parser examines each member type in the order in which it is defined in the schema. The syntax for deriving a union data type is

```
<xs:simpleType name="name">
   <xs:union memberTypes="type1 type2 type3 ..." />
</xs:simpleType>
```

where *type1*, *type2*, *type3*, etc., are the member types that comprise the union. XML Schema also allows unions to be created from nested simple types. The syntax is

```
<xs:simpleType name="name">
   <xs:union>
      <xs:simpleType>
         rules1
      </xs:simpleType>
      <xs:simpleType>
         rules2
      </xs:simpleType>
   </xs:union>
</xs:simpleType>
```

where *rules1*, *rules2*, etc. are the rules for creating different user-derived data types within the union. When compiling data on white blood cell counts, Allison may have precise counts as well as more narrative levels—such as high, normal, or low—to record in her research. As a result of this variety, the WBC element might look as follows:

```
<wbc>15.9 high 14.2 9.8 normal low 5.3</wbc>
```

To validate this element containing a mixture of numeric and descriptive measures, she could create the following derived data type:

```
<xs:simpleType name="wbcType">
   <xs:union memberTypes="xs:decimal xs:string"/>
</xs:simpleType>
```

Next, she could use this data type to derive a list type based on the union data type:

```
<xs:simpleType name="wbcList">
   <xs:list itemType="wbcType"/>
</xs:simpleType>
```

Union data types are often used for multilingual documents in which the data content is expressed in different languages, but must be validated based on a single schema.

Deriving a Restricted Data Type

The final kind of derived data type is a **restricted data type**, in which a restriction is placed on the facets of the base type. For example, an integer data type could be constrained to fall within a range of values. XML Schema provides twelve constraining facets that can be used to derive new data types. These are explained in Figure 4-24.

Facet	Description
enumeration	Constrains the data type to a specified list of values
length	Specifies the length of the data type in characters (for text strings) or items (for lists)
maxLength	Specifies the maximum length of the data type in characters (for text strings) or items (for lists)
minLength	Specifies the minimum length of the data type in characters (for text strings) or items (for lists)
pattern	Constrains the lexical space of the data type to follow a specific character pattern
whiteSpace	Controls the use of blanks in the lexical space of the data type; the whiteSpace facet has three values: preserve (preserve all white space) replace (replace all tabs, carriage returns, and line feed characters with blank spaces) collapse (collapse all consecutive occurrences of white space to a single blank space, remove any leading or trailing white space)
maxExclusive	Constrains the data type to be less than a maximum value
maxInclusive	Constrains the data type to be less than or equal to a maximum value
minExclusive	Constrains the data type to be greater than a minimum value
minInclusive	Constrains the data type to be greater than or equal to a minimum value
fractionDigits	Specifies the maximum number of decimal places to the right of the decimal point in the data type's value
totalDigits	Specifies the maximum number of decimals in the data type's value

Constraining facets are applied to a base type using the syntax

```
<xs:simpleType name="name">
   <xs:restriction base="type">
      <xs:facet1 value="value1" />
      <xs:facet2 value="value2" />
   </xs:restriction>
</xs:simpleType>
```

where `type` is the data type of the base type; `facet1`, `facet2`, etc., are constraining facets; and `value1`, `value2`, etc., are values for each constraining facet. In Allison's document, the age of each patient must be at least 21. The restricted data type would therefore be

```
<xs:simpleType name="ageType">
   <xs:restriction base="xs:integer">
      <xs:minInclusive value="21"/>
   </xs:restriction>
</xs:simpleType>
```

Add this data type to the schema and apply it to the age element.

To create the ageType data type:

▶ **1.** Return to the pschema.xsd file in your text editor.

▶ **2.** Below the declaration for the performance element, insert the following code:

```
<xs:simpleType name="ageType">
   <xs:restriction base="xs:integer">
      <xs:minInclusive value="21"/>
   </xs:restriction>
</xs:simpleType>
```

3. Change the data type for the age element from "xs:positiveInteger" to **"ageType"**. Figure 4-25 shows the revised code in the schema.

Figure 4-25 **Creating the ageType data type**

```
<xs:element name="lastName" type="xs:string" />
<xs:element name="firstName" type="xs:string" />
<xs:element name="dateofBirth" type="xs:date" />
<xs:element name="age" type="ageType" />
<xs:element name="stage" type="xs:string" />
<xs:element name="comment" type="xs:string" />

<xs:attribute name="patID" type="xs:ID" />
<xs:attribute name="onStudy" type="xs:string" />
<xs:attribute name="scale" type="xs:string" />

<xs:element name="performance">
    <xs:complexType>
        <xs:simpleContent>
            <xs:extension base="xs:decimal">
                <xs:attribute ref="scale" use="required" />
            </xs:extension>
        </xs:simpleContent>
    </xs:complexType>
</xs:element>

<xs:simpleType name="ageType">
    <xs:restriction base="xs:integer">
        <xs:minInclusive value="21"/>
    </xs:restriction>
</xs:simpleType>
```

Facets can also be used to define a lower and upper range for data. In Allison's data, performance scores are recorded on a 0 to 1 scale, with 0 and 1 excluded as possible values. To create a data type for this interval, you use the minExclusive and maxExclusive facets, setting the value of the minExclusive facet to 0 and the value of the maxExclusive facet to 1. Use these two facets to create a data type named perfType for the performance score.

To create the perfType data type:

1. Below the ageType simple type, insert:

```
<xs:simpleType name="perfType">
   <xs:restriction base="xs:decimal">
      <xs:minExclusive value="0" />
      <xs:maxExclusive value="1" />
   </xs:restriction>
</xs:simpleType>
```

2. Change the base type in the performance element from "xs:decimal" to **"perfType"**. See Figure 4-26.

Creating the perfType data type Figure 4-26

```
<xs:element name="performance">
   <xs:complexType>
      <xs:simpleContent>
         <xs:extension base="perfType">
            <xs:attribute ref="scale" use="required" />
         </xs:extension>
      </xs:simpleContent>
   </xs:complexType>
</xs:element>

<xs:simpleType name="ageType">
   <xs:restriction base="xs:integer">
      <xs:minInclusive value="21"/>
   </xs:restriction>
</xs:simpleType>

<xs:simpleType name="perfType">
   <xs:restriction base="xs:decimal">
      <xs:minExclusive value="0" />
      <xs:maxExclusive value="1" />
   </xs:restriction>
</xs:simpleType>
```

When data values belong to a set of values rather than a range, you can create a list of possible values using the enumerate element. Allison wants the stage element to contain either "I" for Stage I cancer patients or "II" for Stage II patients. To restrict the element to only these two possibilities, she would create the following simple type:

```
<xs:simpleType name="stageType">
   <xs:restriction base="xs:string">
      <xs:enumeration value="I" />
      <xs:enumeration value="II" />
   </xs:restriction>
</xs:simpleType>
```

Allison also needs a similar structure to restrict the value of the scale attribute to either "Bell" or "Karnofsky". Add both of these enumerated types to the schema.

To create the stageType and scaleType data types:

1. Below the ageType simple type, insert:

   ```
   <xs:simpleType name="stageType">
      <xs:restriction base="xs:string">
         <xs:enumeration value="I" />
         <xs:enumeration value="II" />
      </xs:restriction>
   </xs:simpleType>
   ```

2. Next insert the code for the scaleType data type:

   ```
   <xs:simpleType name="scaleType">
      <xs:restriction base="xs:string">
         <xs:enumeration value="Bell" />
         <xs:enumeration value="Karnofsky" />
      </xs:restriction>
   </xs:simpleType>
   ```

3. Change the data type of the stage element from "xs:string" to **"stageType"**.

4. Change the data type of the scale attribute from "xs:string" to **"scaleType"**.

   Figure 4-27 highlights the revised code.

Figure 4-27   **Creating the perfType data type**

```
<xs:element name="lastName" type="xs:string" />
<xs:element name="firstName" type="xs:string" />
<xs:element name="dateOfBirth" type="xs:date" />
<xs:element name="age" type="ageType" />
<xs:element name="stage" type="stageType" />
<xs:element name="comment" type="xs:string" />

<xs:attribute name="patID" type="xs:ID" />
<xs:attribute name="onStudy" type="xs:string" />
<xs:attribute name="scale" type="scaleType" />

<xs:element name="performance">
   <xs:complexType>
      <xs:simpleContent>
         <xs:extension base="perfType">
            <xs:attribute ref="scale" use="required" />
         </xs:extension>
      </xs:simpleContent>
   </xs:complexType>
</xs:element>

<xs:simpleType name="ageType">
   <xs:restriction base="xs:integer">
      <xs:minInclusive value="21"/>
   </xs:restriction>
</xs:simpleType>

<xs:simpleType name="stageType">
   <xs:restriction base="xs:string">
      <xs:enumeration value="I" />
      <xs:enumeration value="II" />
   </xs:restriction>
</xs:simpleType>

<xs:simpleType name="scaleType">
   <xs:restriction base="xs:string">
      <xs:enumeration value="Bell" />
      <xs:enumeration value="Karnofsky" />
   </xs:restriction>
</xs:simpleType>
```

5. Save your changes to the file.

Deriving New Data Types

- To derive a list data type, create the simple type

```
<xs:simpleType name="name">
    <xs:list itemType="type"/>
</xs:simpleType>
```

where *name* is the name of the list type and *type* is the data type of the values in the list.

- To derive a union data type, use the syntax

```
<xs:simpleType name="name">
    <xs:union memberTypes="type1 type2 type3 ..."/>
</xs:simpleType>
```

where *type1*, *type2*, *type3*, etc., are the member types that comprise the union. Alternatively, use the nested form

```
<xs:simpleType name="name">
    <xs:union>
        <xs:simpleType>
            rules1
        </xs:simpleType>
        <xs:simpleType>
            rules2
        </xs:simpleType>
    </xs:union>
</xs:simpleType>
```

where *rules1*, *rules2*, etc. are the rules of the simple types in the uion.

- To derive a restricted data type, use the syntax

```
<xs:simpleType name="name">
    <xs:restriction base="type">
        <xs:facet1 value="value1" />
        <xs:facet2 value="value2" />
    </xs:restriction>
</xs:simpleType>
```

where *facet1*, *facet2*, etc., are constraining facets, and *value1*, *value2*, etc., are values for the constraining facets.

Before editing this schema further, you should test the revised schema against the current contents of the patients.xml file.

To validate the custom data types in the patients.xml file:

1. Reload the **patients.xml** file in XMLSpy or another validating parser.

2. If necessary, click the **Validate button** on the toolbar or press the **F8** key.

   As shown in Figure 4-28, XMLSpy encounters a validation error due to the fact that a performance score greater than 1 has been entered for a patient. You talk to Allison and discover that the correct value is 0.76, not 1.76.

Figure 4-28 | **An invalid performance score value**

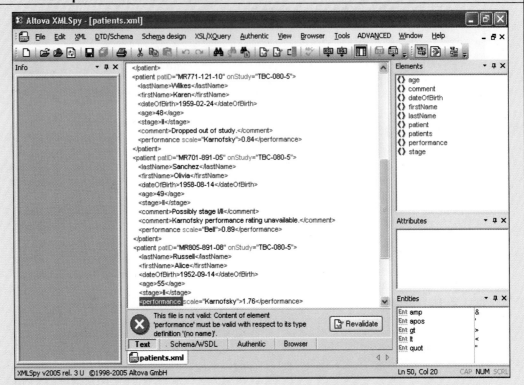

3. Go to the patients.xml file in your text editor and change the value from 1.76 to **0.76**. Save your changes and reload the document in XMLSpy. Validate the file again.

Figure 4-29 shows a second validation error in which the value of the scale attribute has been entered as "Karnosfky" rather than "Karnofsky".

An invalid performance scale ◀ Figure 4-29

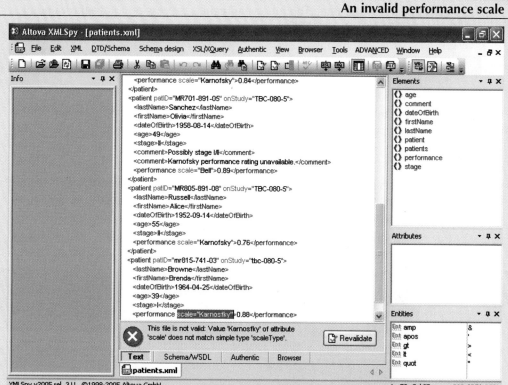

4. Correct this typo by once again going to the patients.xml file in your text editor and changing "Karnosfky" to "**Karnofsky**". Save your changes and revalidate the file in XMLSpy. At this point the file should pass the validation test.

Working with Character Patterns

Allison has two final restrictions to place on data values in the patients document:

• Each patient's medical record number must be entered in the form MR###-###-## where # is a digit from 0 to 9.

• The study name must follow the form *AAA-###-#* where *A* is a capital letter from A through Z and # is a digit from 0 to 9.

These rules involve the representation of the values, so you need to create a restriction based on the lexical space. One way of doing this is through a regular expression.

Regular Expressions

A **regular expression** is a text string that defines a character pattern. Regular expressions can be created to define patterns for phone numbers, postal address codes, e-mail addresses, and in the case of Allison's document, personal IDs. To apply a regular expression in a data type, you use the code

```
<xs:simpleType name="name">
   <xs:restriction base="type">
      <xs:pattern value="regex"/>
   </xs:restriction>
</xs:simpleType>
```

where *regex* is a regular expression pattern. The most basic pattern specifies the characters that must appear in valid data. The following regular expression forces the value of the data type to be the text string "ABC"; any other combination of letters, or the use of lowercase letters, would be invalid:

```
<xs:pattern value="ABC"/>
```

Instead of a pattern involving specific characters, you usually want a more general pattern involving **character types** that represent different kinds of characters. The general form of a character type is

```
\char
```

where *char* represents a specific character type. Character types can include digits, word characters, boundaries around words, and white space characters. Figure 4-30 describes the code for representing each of these character types.

Figure 4-30   **Regular expression character types**

Character Type	Description
\d	A digit from 0 to 9
\D	A nondigit character
\w	A word character (an upper- or lowercase letter, a digit, or an underscore (_)
\W	A no-word character
\b	A boundary around a word (a text string of word characters)
\B	The absence of a boundary around a word
\s	A white space character (a blank space, tab, new line, carriage return, or form feed)
\S	A non-white space character
.	Any character

For example, a digit in a regular expression is indicated using a \d. To create a regular expression representing three consecutive digits, you would use the pattern

```
<xs:pattern value="\d\d\d"/>
```

Note that a lowercase letter represents the character type, while an uppercase letter represents the opposite of the character type. Thus the pattern

```
<xs:pattern value="\D\D\D"/>
```

would match any sequence of three nondigit characters. For more general patterns, characters can also be grouped into lists called **character sets** that specify exactly what characters or range of characters are allowed in the pattern. The syntax of a character set is

```
[chars]
```

where *chars* is the set of characters in the character set. For example, the pattern

```
<xs:pattern value="[dog]"/>
```

matches the symbols "d", "o", or "g". Thus, the letters in "dog" or "god" are both matched by this pattern. Since characters can be sorted alphabetically or numerically, character sets can also be created for a range of characters. The general syntax is

```
[char1 - charN]
```

where *char1* is the first character in the range and *charN* is the last letter in the range. To create a range of lowercase letters, you would use the following pattern:

```
<xs:pattern value="[a-z]"/>
```

To match digits from 1 to 5, you would use

```
<xs:pattern value="1-5"/>
```

Figure 4-31 shows a list of the common character sets used in regular expressions.

Regular expression character lists ◄ **Figure 4-31**

Character Set	Description
[*chars*]	Match any character in the *chars* list
[^*chars*]	Do not match any character in *chars*
[*char1-charN*]	Match any character in the range *char1* through *charN*
[^*char1-charN*]	Do not match any character in the range *char1* through *charN*
[a-z]	Match any lowercase letter
[A-Z]	Match any uppercase letter
[a-zA-Z]	Match any letter
[0-9]	Match any digit from 0 to 9
[0-9a-zA-Z]	Match any digit or letter

The regular expressions you've looked at so far have involved individual characters. To specify the number of occurrences for a particular character or group of characters, a **quantifier** can be appended to a character type or set. Figure 4-32 lists the different quantifiers used in regular expressions. Some of these quantifiers should be familiar to you after your work with DTDs.

Regular expression quantifiers ◄ **Figure 4-32**

Quantifier	Description
*	Repeat 0 or more times
?	Repeat 0 or 1 time
+	Repeat 1 or more times
{*n*}	Repeat exactly *n* times
{*n*,}	Repeat at least *n* times
{*n,m*}	Repeat at least *n* times but no more than *m* times

As you saw earlier, to specify a pattern of three consecutive digits, you can use the regular expression \d\d\d. Alternatively, you can also employ the quantifier {3} using the following pattern:

```
<xs:pattern value="\d{3}" />
```

To validate a string of uppercase characters of any length, you use the * quantifier as follows:

```
<xs:pattern value="[A-Z]*"/>
```

The following pattern allows a character string of uppercase letters from zero to ten characters long:

```
<xs:pattern value="[A-Z]{0,10}"/>
```

By combining different character types, character sets, and quantifiers, you can create complicated regular expressions to match phone numbers, Social Security numbers, or even e-mail addresses and Web site URLs.

Deriving a Patterned Data Type

- To derive a data type based on a pattern, use the syntax:

```
<xs:simpleType name="name">
   <xs:restriction base="type">
      <xs:pattern value="regex"/>
   </xs:restriction>
</xs:simpleType>
```

  where *name* is the element name, *type* is the base type, and *regex* is a regular expression defining the character pattern.

Applying a Regular Expression

You've only scratched the surface of what regular expressions can do. The topic of regular expressions could fill an entire chapter by itself. However, you have covered enough to be able to solve Allison's request that all ID strings be in the format MR###-###-## where # is a digit from 0 to 9. The pattern for this expression is

```
<xs:pattern value="MR\d{3}-\d{3}-\d{2}"/>
```

Note that you use the character type \d to represent a single digit and the quantifiers {3} to and {2} to indicate that the digits must be repeated three and two times. Study IDs must follow the *AAA-###-#* pattern, where *A* is any uppercase letter and *#* is a digit. The regular expression for this pattern is

```
<xs:pattern value="[A-Z]{3}-\d{3}-\d"/>
```

This pattern uses the character set and quantifier [A-Z]{3} to represent any three uppercase letters. Create data types named mrType and studyType based on these patterns.

To create a data type based on a pattern:

1. Return to the pschema.xsd file in your text editor and insert the following code directly below the declaration for the scale attribute:

```
<xs:simpleType name="mrType">
   <xs:restriction base="xs:ID">
      <xs:pattern value="MR\d{3}-\d{3}-\d{2}" />
   </xs:restriction>
</xs:simpleType>
```

   Note that the base type is xs:ID, meaning that this data type still represents a unique ID value in the document.

2. Add the following code for the studyType data type:

```
<xs:simpleType name="studyType">
   <xs:restriction base="xs:string">
      <xs:pattern value="[A-Z]{3}-\d{3}-\d" />
   </xs:restriction>
</xs:simpleType>
```

3. Change the data type of the patID attribute from xs:ID to **"mrType"**.

4. Change the data type of the onStudy attribute from xs:string to **"studyType"**.

Figure 4-33 shows the revised code of the schema file.

Creating the mrType and studyType data types ◀ Figure 4-33

```
<xs:attribute name="patID" type="mrType" />
<xs:attribute name="onStudy" type="studyType" />
<xs:attribute name="scale" type="scaleType" />

<xs:simpleType name="mrType">
   <xs:restriction base="xs:ID">
      <xs:pattern value="MR\d{3}-\d{3}-\d{2}" />
   </xs:restriction>
</xs:simpleType>

<xs:simpleType name="studyType">
   <xs:restriction base="xs:string">
      <xs:pattern value="[A-Z]{3}-\d{3}-\d" />
   </xs:restriction>
</xs:simpleType>
```

5. Save your changes to the file.

Now validate Allison's document to ensure that all the medical record numbers and study ids match the patterns you've defined.

To validate the medical record numbers and the study ids:

1. Reload the **patients.xml** file in XMLSpy or another validating parser.

2. If necessary, click the **Validate button** on the toolbar or press the **F8** key.

XMLSpy encounters a validation error because the medical record number for the last patient has been entered as mr815-741-03 rather than MR815-741-03 (see Figure 4-34).

Figure 4-34 An invalid onStudy value

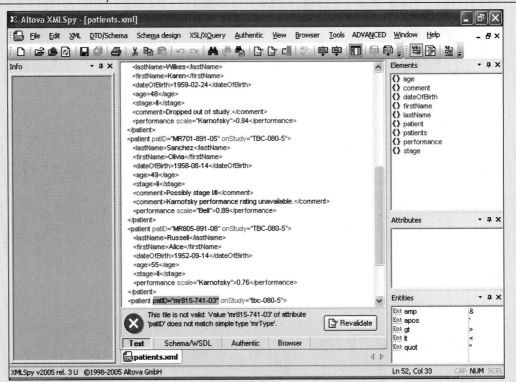

3. Go to the patients.xml file in your text editor and change value of the patID attribute from mr815-741-03 to **MR815-741-03**. Save your changes and reload the document in XMLSpy. Validate the file again.

Figure 4-35 shows a second validation error caused by entering the number as tbc-080-5 rather than TBC-080-5 a patient's record number has been entered as mr815-741-03 rather than MR815-741-03. Correct this problem.

An invalid medical record number

Figure 4-35

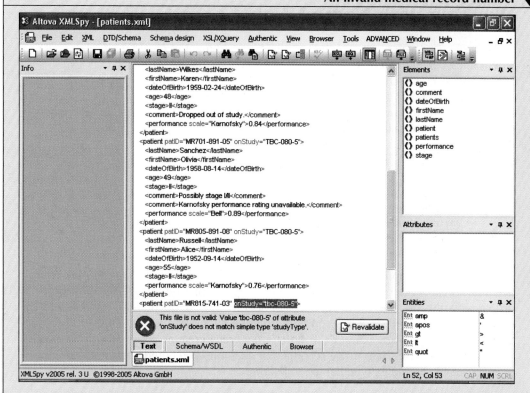

4. Once again, go to the patients.xml file in your text editor and change tbc-080-05 to **TBC-080-05**. Save your changes and revalidate the file in XMLSpy. The file should be valid based on the rules in the schema.

5. If you want to take a break before starting the next session, you may close any open files or programs now.

Derived data types are a powerful and versatile feature of XML Schema. You can create a schema containing an entire library of customized data types to supplement the built-in data types supplied by XML Schema. By attaching this schema to a namespace, you can access those data types from other schema documents. You'll explore how to use schemas and namespaces in the next session through creating schemas for compound documents.

Session 4.2 Quick Check

Review

1. Enter a declaration for a simple type element named Weight containing only decimal data.
2. Enter the declaration for the itemIDs attribute containing a list of ID references.
3. Declare a data type named VisitDates containing a list of dates.
4. Declare a data type named Status that contains either a decimal or a text string.
5. Declare a data type named Party limited to one of following: Democrat, Republican, or Independent.
6. Declare a data type named Percentage limited to decimal values falling between 0 and 1 (inclusive).
7. Declare a data type named SocSecurity containing a text string matching the pattern ###-##-#### where # is a digit from 0 to 9.

Session 4.3

Working with Named Types

In the last session you worked with the simpleType element to create customized data types. Since content can be either simple or complex, it is not surprising that XML Schema also allows schema authors to create customized complex types. The advantage of creating a complex type is that the complex structure can be reused in the document. For example, the following code declares an element named client containing the complex content of two child elements named firstName and lastName:

```
<xs:element name="client">
   <xs:complexType>
      <xs:sequence>
         <xs:element name="firstName" type="xs:string"/>
         <xs:element name="lastName" type="xs:string" />
      </xs:sequence>
   </xs:complexType>
</xs:element>
```

The complex type applied to the client element is called an **anonymous complex type** because no name attribute is used in the opening <complexType> tag. Because such firstName/lastName child elements occur frequently in XML documents, it would clearly be helpful if you could store this complex structure rather than retyping it over and over again. You can do this by naming the structure, thereby creating a **named complex type** that can be used elsewhere in the schema. For example, you could enter the following code to create a complex type named fullName:

```
<xs:complexType name="fullName">
   <xs:sequence>
      <xs:element name="firstName" type="xs:string"/>
      <xs:element name="lastName" type="xs:string" />
   </xs:sequence>
</xs:complexType>
```

This named complex type could then be applied to any complex type element using the type attribute (just as you used the type attribute to apply a customized data type). For example, to apply this same structure to complex type elements named client and salesperson, you could add the following code to the schema:

```
<xs:element name="client" type="fullName" />
<xs:element name="salesperson" type="fullName" />
```

Because they both use the complex type fullName, the client and the salesperson elements have the same complex structure: two child elements named firstName and lastName.

Named Model Groups

Named complex types are not the only structures you can create to be reused in your schemas. Another structure is a named model group. As the name suggests, a **named model group** is a collection, or group, of elements. The syntax for creating a model group is

```
<xs:group name="name">
   elements
</xs:group>
```

where *name* is the name of the model group, and *elements* is a collection of element declarations. The element declarations must be enclosed within a sequence, choice, or all compositor. The following code creates a model group named "fullName" that contains two elements:

```
<xs:group name="fullName">
   <xs:sequence>
      <xs:element name="firstName" type="xs:string" />
      <xs:element name="lastName" type="xs:string" />
   </xs:sequence>
</xs:group>
```

To apply a named model group to an element declaration, you use the ref attribute. For example, to reference the fullName model group from the client element, you would use the code

```
<xs:element name="client">
   <xs:complexType>
      <xs:group ref="fullName"/>
   </xs:complexType>
</xs:element>
```

As with named complex types, model groups are useful when a document contains element declarations or code that you want to repeat throughout the schema.

Working with Named Attribute Groups

Like elements, attributes can be grouped into collections called **named attribute groups**. This is particularly useful for attributes that you want to use with several different elements in a schema. The syntax for a named attribute group is

```
<xs:attributeGroup name="name">
   attributes
</xs:attributeGroup>
```

where *name* is the name of the attribute group and *attributes* is a collection of attributes assigned to the group. For example, one of Allison's documents might contain the following element to identify a physician:

```
<doctor DRID="DR251" dept="Pediatrics">
   Curt Hurley
</doctor>
```

Both the DRID and dept attributes may need to be used in other elements. To place both of these within an attribute group named DRInfo, you would use the following code:

```
<xs:attributeGroup name="DRInfo">
   <xs:attribute name="DRID" type="xs:string" use="required" />
   <xs:attribute name="dept" type="xs:string" use="required" />
</xs:attributeGroup>
```

To use the DRInfo attribute group with the Doctor element, you would create a reference within an attributeGroup tag as follows:

```
<xs:element name="doctor" type="deptData"/>
<xs:complexType name="deptData">
   <xs:simpleContent>
      <xs:extension base="string">
         <xs:attributeGroup ref="DRInfo"/>
      </xs:extension>
   </xs:simpleContent>
</xs:complexType>
```

Note that this code not only references an attribute group, but it also uses a named complex type to simplify the declaration of the Doctor element.

Structuring a Schema

The use of named types, element groups, and attribute groups becomes important in the overall design of a schema file. One important issue in schema design is determining which items are global and which items are local. You touched briefly on the topic of global and local scope in Session 4.1. Recall that an item has global scope when it is a child of the root schema element, and it has local scope when it is nested within another element. Items with global scope can be referenced and reused anywhere in a schema file, while an item with local scope can be referenced and used only within the item in which it is declared. As you'll see later, the issue of whether an element or attribute is declared globally or locally also has an impact on validating a document within a namespace. The distinction between global and local declarations leads to three basic schema designs: flat catalog, Russian doll, and Venetian blind.

The Flat Catalog Design

In a **flat catalog design**—sometimes referred to as a **salami slice design**—all declarations are made globally. The structure of the instance document is created by referencing these global element declarations at another point in the schema document. The pschema.xsd file you created for Allison is an example of a flat catalog. Figure 4-36 highlights the different parts of a flat catalog.

Figure 4-36 ▶ **A flat catalog design**

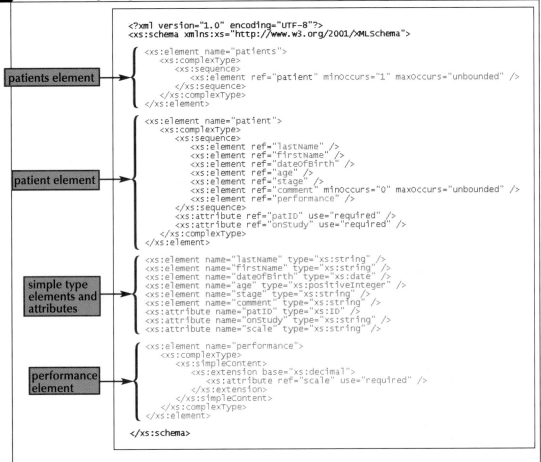

```
<?xml version="1.0" encoding="UTF-8"?>
<xs:schema xmlns:xs="http://www.w3.org/2001/XMLSchema">

  <xs:element name="patients">
    <xs:complexType>
      <xs:sequence>
        <xs:element ref="patient" minOccurs="1" maxOccurs="unbounded" />
      </xs:sequence>
    </xs:complexType>
  </xs:element>

  <xs:element name="patient">
    <xs:complexType>
      <xs:sequence>
        <xs:element ref="lastName" />
        <xs:element ref="firstName" />
        <xs:element ref="dateOfBirth" />
        <xs:element ref="age" />
        <xs:element ref="stage" />
        <xs:element ref="comment" minOccurs="0" maxOccurs="unbounded" />
        <xs:element ref="performance" />
      </xs:sequence>
      <xs:attribute ref="patID" use="required" />
      <xs:attribute ref="onStudy" use="required" />
    </xs:complexType>
  </xs:element>

  <xs:element name="lastName" type="xs:string" />
  <xs:element name="firstName" type="xs:string" />
  <xs:element name="dateOfBirth" type="xs:date" />
  <xs:element name="age" type="xs:positiveInteger" />
  <xs:element name="stage" type="xs:string" />
  <xs:element name="comment" type="xs:string" />
  <xs:attribute name="patID" type="xs:ID" />
  <xs:attribute name="onStudy" type="xs:string" />
  <xs:attribute name="scale" type="xs:string" />

  <xs:element name="performance">
    <xs:complexType>
      <xs:simpleContent>
        <xs:extension base="xs:decimal">
          <xs:attribute ref="scale" use="required" />
        </xs:extension>
      </xs:simpleContent>
    </xs:complexType>
  </xs:element>

</xs:schema>
```

patients element

patient element

simple type elements and attributes

performance element

Each element or attribute declaration in Figure 4-36 is a child of the schema element, with references used to associate each child element with its parent and each attribute with its containing element. One of the advantages of flat catalog designs is simplicity: a flat catalog design resembles the layout of a DTD. Flat catalogs also allow elements and attributes to be reused throughout the schema because everything is declared globally.

The Russian Doll Design

A **Russian doll design** has only one global element with everything else nested inside of it, much like Russian dolls nest one inside another. Figure 4-37 shows the schema from Figure 4-36 reorganized into a Russian doll design. The only declaration with global scope is for the patients element; all other declarations are made locally.

A Russian Doll design ◀ **Figure 4-37**

```xml
<?xml version="1.0" encoding="UTF-8"?>
<xs:schema xmlns:xs="http://www.w3.org/2001/XMLSchema">

  <xs:element name="patients">
    <xs:complexType>
      <xs:sequence>
        <xs:element name="patient" minOccurs="1" maxOccurs="unbounded">
          <xs:complexType>
            <xs:sequence>
              <xs:element name="lastName" type="xs:string" />
              <xs:element name="firstName" type="xs:string" />
              <xs:element name="dateOfBirth" type="xs:date" />
              <xs:element name="age" type="xs:positiveInteger" />
              <xs:element name="stage" type="xs:string" />
              <xs:element name="comment" type="xs:string" minOccurs="0" maxOccurs="unbounded" />
              <xs:element name="performance">
                <xs:complexType>
                  <xs:simpleContent>
                    <xs:extension base="xs:decimal">
                      <xs:attribute name="scale" type="xs:string" use="required" />
                    </xs:extension>
                  </xs:simpleContent>
                </xs:complexType>
              </xs:element>
            </xs:sequence>
            <xs:attribute name="patID" type="xs:ID" use="required" />
            <xs:attribute name="onStudy" type="xs:string" use="required" />
          </xs:complexType>
        </xs:element>
      </xs:sequence>
    </xs:complexType>
  </xs:element>

</xs:schema>
```

Russian doll designs mimic the nesting structure of the elements in the instance document. The root element of the instance document becomes the topmost element declaration in the schema. All child elements within the root element are similarly nested in the schema. A Russian doll design is much more compact than a flat catalog, but the multiple levels of nested elements can be confusing and difficult to work with. Also, because the element and attribute declarations are local (other than the single root element), they cannot be reused elsewhere in the schema.

The Venetian Blind Design

A **Venetian blind design** is similar to a flat catalog, except that instead of declaring elements and attributes globally, it creates named types and references those types within a single global element. Figure 4-38 shows the schema file laid out in a Venetian blind design. In this layout, the only globally declared element is the patients element; all other elements and attributes are placed within element or attribute groups or, in the case of the performance element, within a named complex type.

| Figure 4-38 | A Venetian blind design |

```xml
<?xml version="1.0" encoding="UTF-8"?>
<xs:schema xmlns:xs="http://www.w3.org/2001/XMLSchema">

    <xs:element name="patients">
        <xs:complexType>
            <xs:sequence>
                <xs:element name="patient" type="pType" minOccurs="1" maxOccurs="unbounded" />
            </xs:sequence>
        </xs:complexType>
    </xs:element>

    <xs:complexType name="pType">
        <xs:group ref="childElements" />
        <xs:attributeGroup ref="patientAtt" />
    </xs:complexType>

    <xs:group name="childElements">
        <xs:sequence>
            <xs:element name="lastName" type="xs:string" />
            <xs:element name="firstName" type="xs:string" />
            <xs:element name="dateOfBirth" type="xs:date" />
            <xs:element name="age" type="xs:positiveInteger" />
            <xs:element name="stage" type="xs:string" />
            <xs:element name="comment" type="xs:string" minOccurs="0" maxOccurs="unbounded" />
            <xs:element name="performance" type="perfType" />
        </xs:sequence>
    </xs:group>

    <xs:attributeGroup name="patientAtt">
        <xs:attribute name="patID" type="xs:ID" />
        <xs:attribute name="onStudy" type="xs:string" />
    </xs:attributeGroup>

    <xs:complexType name="perfType">
        <xs:simpleContent>
            <xs:extension base="xs:decimal">
                <xs:attribute name="scale" type="xs:string" use="required" />
            </xs:extension>
        </xs:simpleContent>
    </xs:complexType>

</xs:schema>
```

A Venetian blind design represents a compromise between flat catalogs and Russian dolls. While the various element and attribute groups and named types are declared globally (and thus can be reused throughout the schema), the declarations for the elements and attributes for the instance document are local and nested.

Which schema layout you use depends on several factors. If your schema has several lines of code that need to be repeated, you probably want to use a flat catalog or Venetian blind. If you're interested in a compact schema that mirrors the structure of the instance document, you should use a Russian doll design. Figure 4-39 summarizes some of the differences between the three layouts.

Feature	Russian Doll	Flat Catalog (Salami Slice)	Venetian Blind
Global and local declarations	The schema contains one single global element; all other declarations are local.	All declarations are global.	The schema contains one single global element; all other declarations are local.
Nesting of elements	Element declarations are nested within a single global element.	Element declarations are not nested.	Element declarations are nested within a single global element referencing named complex types, element groups, and attribute groups.
Reusability	Element declarations can only be used once.	Element declarations can be reused throughout the schema.	Named complex types, element groups, and attribute groups can be reused throughout the schema.
Interaction with namespaces	If a namespace is attached to the schema, only the root element needs to be qualified in the instance document.	If a namespace is attached to the schema, all elements need to be qualified in the instance document.	If a namespace is attached to the schema, only the root element needs to be qualified in the instance document.

Rather than continuing to work on the flat catalog design for the schema file, Allison has asked you to switch to a Venetian blind design. She thinks that the layout of the Venetian blind maintains the flexibility of a flat catalog, while providing a structure similar to the contents of her instance document. Making the change will also make it easier to apply a namespace to the schema and instance document, as you'll see shortly. Allison has already created a schema file in a Venetian blind layout for you.

To open the Venetian blind version of the schema:

▶ 1. Use your text editor to open the **patvbtxt.xsd** file from the tutorial.04x/tutorial folder. Enter *your name* and *the date* in the comment section of the file. Save the file as **patvb.xsd**.

▶ 2. Take some time to review the contents of the schema file, taking note of the use of named types, element groups, and attribute groups. Note that only the patients element is declared globally.

Placing a Schema in a Namespace

Allison has learned that several XML vocabularies have been developed for the research at the hospital. In order to avoid confusion with other vocabularies, Allison has reserved the URI http://uhosp.edu/patients/ns as the URI for the patients vocabulary. She now needs you to place the schema you developed and her patient data in this namespace.

Targeting a Namespace

To associate a schema with a namespace, you first declare the namespace and then make that namespace the target of the schema. To do this, you add the following attributes to the schema's root element:

```
prefix:xmlns="uri"
targetNamespace="uri"
```

where *prefix* is the prefix of the XML Schema namespace and *uri* is the URI of the target namespace. You do not have to specify a prefix if XML Schema is the default namespace of the schema file. Also note that, unlike with DTDs, namespace prefixes in the schema do not have to match the prefixes used in the instance document; only the URIs must match. This awareness of namespace URIs is one of the reasons that schemas are much easier to apply than DTDs for compound documents.

You'll use the patients vocabulary as the default namespace in Allison's schema file; thus, you do not have to qualify any customized object references or data types.

To apply the namespace to the schema:

1. Add the following attributes to the root schema element from the patvb.xsd file, as shown in Figure 4-40.

   ```
   xmlns="http://uhosp.edu/patients/ns"
   targetNamespace="http://uhosp.edu/patients/ns"
   ```

Figure 4-40 | Applying a namespace to a schema

```
<xs:schema xmlns:xs="http://www.w3.org/2001/XMLSchema"
           xmlns="http://uhosp.edu/patients/ns"
           targetNamespace="http://uhosp.edu/patients/ns">

    <xs:element name="patients">
        <xs:complexType>
            <xs:sequence>
                <xs:element name="patient" type="pType" minOccurs="1" maxOccurs="unbounded" />
            </xs:sequence>
        </xs:complexType>
    </xs:element>
```

2. Close the patvb.xsd file, saving your changes.

Any customized data types, named types, elements, element groups, or attributes are placed in the target namespace. This allows you to create customized schema objects and associate them directly with an XML vocabulary. If you choose to use the vocabulary's namespace as the default namespace for the schema, you do not have to qualify any references to those customized objects. On the other hand, if you apply a prefix to the namespace, references to those objects have to be qualified by that prefix. Figure 4-41 shows both possibilities: one in which references to objects from the XML Schema vocabulary are qualified, and the other in which XML Schema is the default namespace, but references to objects in the target namespace are qualified. Understanding exactly what objects are in what namespaces becomes important when you combine multiple vocabularies in a single schema.

Namespaces in a schema file ◄ Figure 4-41

```
<xs:schema xmlns:xs="http://www.w3.org/2001/XMLSchema"
           xmlns="http://uhosp.edu/patients/ns"
           targetNamespace="http://uhosp.edu/patients/ns">

  <xs:element name="patients">
    <xs:complexType>
      <xs:sequence>
        <xs:element name="patient" type="pType" minOccurs="1" maxOccurs="unbounded" />
      </xs:sequence>
    </xs:complexType>
  </xs:element>

  <xs:complexType name="pType">
    <xs:group ref="childElements" />
    <xs:attributeGroup ref="patientAtt" />
  </xs:complexType>

  <xs:group name="childElements">
    <xs:sequence>
      <xs:element name="lastName" type="xs:string" />
      <xs:element name="firstName" type="xs:string" />
      <xs:element name="dateOfBirth" type="xs:date" />
      <xs:element name="age" type="ageType" />
      <xs:element name="stage" type="stageType" />
      <xs:element name="comment" type="xs:string" minOccurs="0" maxOccurs="unbounded" />
      <xs:element name="performance" type="perfComplex" />
    </xs:sequence>
  </xs:group>
```

the XML Schema namespace is qualified

```
<schema xmlns="http://www.w3.org/2001/XMLSchema"
        xmlns:pat="http://uhosp.edu/patients/ns"
        targetNamespace="http://uhosp.edu/patients/ns">>

  <element name="patients">
    <complexType>
      <sequence>
        <element name="patient" type="pat:pType" minOccurs="1" maxOccurs="unbounded" />
      </sequence>
    </complexType>
  </element>

  <complexType name="pType">
    <group ref="pat:childElements" />
    <attributeGroup ref="pat:patientAtt" />
  </complexType>

  <group name="childElements">
    <sequence>
      <element name="lastName" type="string" />
      <element name="firstName" type="string" />
      <element name="dateOfBirth" type="date" />
      <element name="age" type="pat:ageType" />
      <element name="stage" type="pat:stageType" />
      <element name="comment" type="string" minOccurs="0" maxOccurs="unbounded" />
      <element name="performance" type="pat:perfComplex" />
    </sequence>
  </group>
```

the patients namespace is qualified

Targeting a Namespace

Reference Window

- To target a schema to a namespace, add the following attributes to the schema element:
    ```
    prefix:xmlns="uri"
    targetNamespace="uri"
    ```
  where *prefix* is the prefix of the XML Schema namespace and *uri* is the URI of the schema's target. If no *prefix* is specified, XML Schema is the default namespace of the schema file.

Applying the Namespace to the Instance Document

In Session 4.1, you validated the patients.xml document without a namespace, by adding the following attribute to the root element:

```
xsi:noNamespaceSchemaLocation="schema"
```

where *schema* is the location and name of the schema file. However, because you now have a namespace that is associated with the schema, you need to replace the above attribute with

```
xsi:schemaLocation="uri schema"
```

where *uri* is the URI of the target namespace and *schema* is once again the location and name of the schema file. If a document contains several target namespaces, each associated with its own schema, the locations can be entered in the following pairs:

```
xsi:schemaLocation="uri1 schema1 uri2 schema2 uri3 schema3 ..."
```

where *uri1*, *uri2*, etc., are the URIs of the different namespaces and *schema1*, *schema2*, etc., are the schemas associated with each namespace. Since the content of the patients document is associated with only one namespace, you will enter the following attribute to the root patient element:

```
xsi:schemaLocation="http://uhosp.edu/patients/ns patvb.xsd"
```

To apply the schema to the patients document:

1. Return to the **patients.xml** file in your text editor and save the file as **patients2.xml**.

2. Place the document in the patients namespace by adding the following declaration to the patients element:

   ```
   xmlns="http://uhosp.edu/patients/ns"
   ```

3. Remove the xsi:noNamespaceSchemaLocation attribute, replacing it with the following:

   ```
   xsi:schemaLocation="http://uhosp.edu/patients/ns patvb.xsd"
   ```

   Figure 4-42 shows the revised code of the file.

Figure 4-42 ▸ **Attaching a schema namespace to the instance document**

```
<patients xmlns:xsi="http://www.w3.org/2001/XMLSchema-instance"
          xmlns="http://uhosp.edu/patients/ns"
          xsi:schemaLocation="http://uhosp.edu/patients/ns patvb.xsd">
   <patient patID="MR890-041-02" onStudy="TBC-080-5">
      <lastName>Dibbs</lastName>
      <firstName>Cynthia</firstName>
      <dateOfBirth>1945-05-22</dateOfBirth>
      <age>62</age>
      <stage>II</stage>
      <performance scale="Karnofsky">0.81</performance>
   </patient>
```

Now validate the file in XMLSpy or another validating parser.

4. Save your changes to the file and open **patients2.xml** in XMLSpy. Validate the file.

The validation results are shown in Figure 4-43.

Validation error in the patients2 document ◀ Figure 4-43

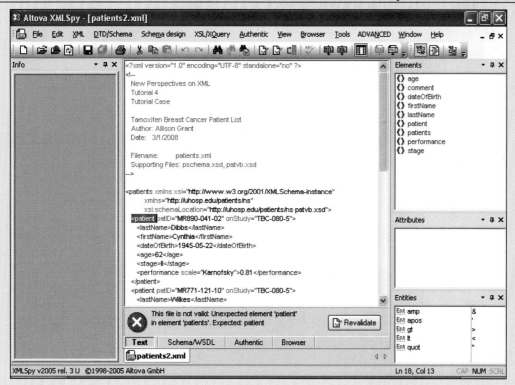

XMLSpy reports a rather cryptic error message: "Unexpected element 'patient' in element 'patients'. Expected: patient". What went wrong? Why did the document become invalid after adding support for namespaces?

Qualified and Unqualified Names

The error is due to the way that schemas handle global and local elements. In XML Schema, any element or attribute that is declared globally has to be entered as a qualified name in the instance document. The reason is that global elements and attributes are added to the target namespace, while local objects are not. Local objects are interpreted based on the namespace affiliation of the object in which they're nested. Because global objects are attached to the namespace, they have to be qualified in the instance document with a namespace prefix. The target namespace applies the document validation through the qualified elements in the instance document using them as the starting points for the validation process. You can't go down the hierarchy and validate only the local elements and attributes.

This fact may also impact your choice of schema designs. In a flat catalog, all elements and attributes are declared globally, so each element and attribute has to be qualified in the instance document. Since Venetian blind and Russian doll designs have a single global element, only the topmost element has to be qualified. By switching from the flat catalog to the Venetian blind layout, you avoided having to qualify every element and attribute name in the patients document (which is certainly a time-saver!). To verify that the patients2 document is valid, return to the document and add a namespace prefix to the patients namespace.

To qualify the patients element:

1. Return to the **patients2.xml** file in your text editor.

2. Change the namespace declaration to:

   `xmlns:pat="http://uhosp.edu/patients/ns"`

3. Add the **pat:** namespace prefix to both the opening and closing tags of the patients element (see Figure 4-44).

Figure 4-44	Qualifying the patients element

```
<pat:patients xmlns:xsi="http://www.w3.org/2001/XMLSchema-instance"
         xmlns:pat="http://uhosp.edu/patients/ns"
         xsi:schemaLocation="http://uhosp.edu/patients/ns patvb.xsd">
   <patient patID="MR890-041-02" onStudy="TBC-080-5">
      <lastName>Dibbs</lastName>
      <firstName>Cynthia</firstName>
      <dateOfBirth>1945-05-22</dateOfBirth>
      <age>62</age>
      <stage>II</stage>
      <performance scale="Karnofsky">0.81</performance>
   </patient>
```

```
   <patient patID="MR815-741-03" onStudy="TBC-080-5">
      <lastName>Browne</lastName>
      <firstName>Brenda</firstName>
      <dateOfBirth>1964-04-25</dateOfBirth>
      <age>39</age>
      <stage>I</stage>
      <performance scale="Karnofsky">0.88</performance>
   </patient>
</pat:patients>
```

Note that you don't have to qualify the child elements and attributes of the patients element, because they will inherit the namespace declaration by default.

4. Save your changes to the file and then reload the file in XMLSpy and revalidate the document. Verify that the document is now valid based on the rules of the schema.

Reference Window	**Applying a Schema to a Document with a Namespace**

- To apply a schema to a document with a namespace, add the following attributes to the instance document's root element:

   `xmlns:xsi="http://www.w3.org/2001/XMLSchema-instance"`
   `xsi:schemaLocation="uri schema"`

   where *uri* is the URI of the namespace and *schema* is the location and name of the schema file.

- All global elements and attributes from the schema must be qualified in the instance document.

On occasion, you may want more control over which elements and attributes have to be qualified in the instance document. Two attributes, elementFormDefault and attribute-FormDefault, can be added to the root schema element of the schema document to specify how XML Schema should handle qualification in the instance document. The syntax of these attributes is

```
<xs:schema
   elementFormDefault="qualify"
   attributeFormDefault="qualify"
>
```

where `qualify` is either "qualified" or "unqualified", specifying whether the elements and attributes of the instance document should be qualified or not. The default value of both of these attributes is "unqualified" except for global elements and attributes, which must always be qualified. To require all elements to be qualified but not all attributes (other than globally-declared attributes), you would enter the following code into the schema element:

```
<xs:schema
    elementFormDefault="qualified"
    attributeFormDefault="unqualified"
>
```

This is probably the most common setup for instance documents in which you want to explicitly associate each element with its namespace through a namespace prefix. You can also control qualification for individual elements or attributes by using the form attribute:

```
<xs:element name="name" form="qualify" />
<xs:attribute name="name" form="qualify" />
```

where `qualify` is once again either "qualified" or "unqualified". Thus, the element declaration

```
<xs:element name="patient" form="qualified" />
```

requires the patient element to be qualified in the instance document, whether it has been declared globally or locally in the schema.

Validating a Compound Document

Allison has been given an XML vocabulary that describes the different clinical studies occurring at the hospital. Figure 4-45 shows the structure of that vocabulary. At present, the study vocabulary contains only basic information about the clinical studies: it records the title and subtitle of the study and the name of the study's principal investigator (PI).

Structure of the study vocabulary ◀ Figure 4-45

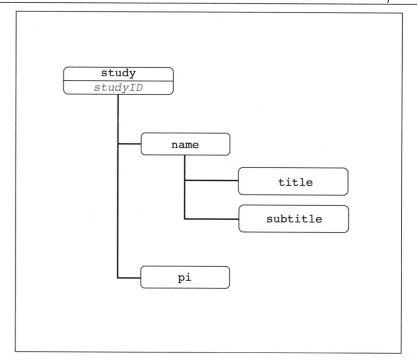

Allison has already created a schema for this vocabulary. Open her schema file now.

To view the schema file for the study vocabulary:

1. Use your text editor to open the **studtxt.xsd** file from the tutorial.04x/tutorial folder. Enter *your name* and *the date* in the comment section of the file. Save the file as **study.xsd**.

2. Take some time to study the contents and structure of the study schema shown in Figure 4-46.

| Figure 4-46 | The schema for the study vocabulary |

```xml
<xs:schema xmlns:xs="http://www.w3.org/2001/XMLSchema"
           xmlns="http://uhosp/studies/ns"
           targetNamespace="http://uhosp/studies/ns">

   <xs:element name="study">
      <xs:complexType>
         <xs:sequence>
            <xs:element name="name">
               <xs:complexType>
                  <xs:sequence>
                     <xs:element name="title" />
                     <xs:element name="subtitle" />
                  </xs:sequence>
               </xs:complexType>
            </xs:element>
            <xs:element name="pi" type="xs:string" />
         </xs:sequence>
         <xs:attribute name="studyID" type="xs:ID" />
      </xs:complexType>
   </xs:element>

</xs:schema>
```

Notice that this schema uses a Russian doll design, with study being the only element declared globally in the file. Allison has already entered the target namespace of this vocabulary using a URI of http://uhosp/studies/ns. Allison would like to create a compound document that combines study information for the Tamoxifen Breast Cancer study with a list of the patients enrolled in the study. Figure 4-47 shows the compound structure she has in mind.

A compound document combining the study and patients vocabularies | Figure 4-47

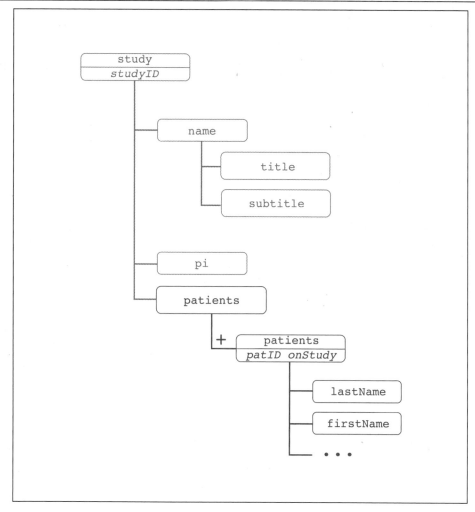

Allison has stored information on the Tamoxifen study in an XML document. She wants you to paste the patients data into this document.

To create the compound document:

1. Use your text editor to open the **tamoxtxt.xml** file from the tutorial.04x/tutorial folder. Enter *your name* and *the date* in the comment section of the file. Save the file as **tamoxifen.xml**.

   Allison has already attached the study.xsd schema file and study namespace to this document. The contents have already been validated based on the rules specified in the study.xsd file.

2. Go to the **patients2.xml** file in your text editor and copy the contents of the document from the opening patients tag to the closing tag. Do not copy any of the document prolog.

3. Paste the copied elements into the tamoxifen document between the pi element and the closing tag of the study element.

> **4.** You do not need to declare the XML Schema instance namespace in the patients element (since it is already declared in the study element), so remove this attribute from the patients element. Figure 4-48 shows the compound document containing elements from both the study and patients vocabularies.

Figure 4-48	Create the study and patients compound document

```
<std:study studyID="TBC-080-5"
           xmlns:xsi="http://www.w3.org/2001/XMLSchema-instance"
           xmlns:std="http://uhosp/studies/ns"
           xsi:schemaLocation="http://uhosp/studies/ns study.xsd">

    <name>
        <title>Tamoxifen Breast Cancer Study</title>
        <subtitle>Randomized Phase 3 Clinical Trial</subtitle>
    </name>
    <pi>Dr. Diane West</pi>

<pat:patients xmlns:pat="http://uhosp.edu/patients/ns"
              xsi:schemaLocation="http://uhosp.edu/patients/ns patvb.xsd">
    <patient patID="MR890-041-02" onStudy="TBC-080-5">
        <lastName>Dibbs</lastName>
        <firstName>Cynthia</firstName>
        <dateOfBirth>1945-05-22</dateOfBirth>
        <age>62</age>
        <stage>II</stage>
        <performance scale="Karnofsky">0.81</performance>
    </patient>
```

```
    <patient patID="MR815-741-03" onStudy="TBC-080-5">
        <lastName>Browne</lastName>
        <firstName>Brenda</firstName>
        <dateOfBirth>1964-04-25</dateOfBirth>
        <age>39</age>
        <stage>I</stage>
        <performance scale="Karnofsky">0.88</performance>
    </patient>
</pat:patients>

</std:study>
```

Including and Importing Schemas

The tamoxifen.xml file contains all of the information that Allison needs on the Tamoxifen Breast Cancer study. However, in its current state it cannot be validated. The problem is that the study element now contains a new child element named patients, pasted from the patients2 document. Thus, the schema for the study vocabulary needs to be modified to include this element. Rather than rewriting the entire schema, you can take advantage of the fact that XML Schema can work with multiple namespaces. This ability enables you to insert the schema definitions from the patients vocabulary into the study vocabulary.

XML Schema provides two ways of adding one schema file to another. One method is to include a schema file using the element

```
<xs:include schemaLocation="schema" />
```

where *schema* is the location and name of the schema file to be inserted. The include element performs a straight inclusion of the schema, and is used when both schemas describe the same target namespace. The effect is to merge the two schema files into a single schema. The included schema does not have to be a complete schema by itself; it may contain only a collection of custom data types that the schema author wants to access. One use of the include element is to access a library of schema elements that can be combined in a variety of different ways. In an environment in which large and complicated XML vocabularies are developed, different teams might work on different parts of the schema, using the include element to combine the different parts into a finished product.

When schemas come from different namespaces, they're combined using the import element, which has a similar syntax:

```
<xs:import namespace="uri" schemaLocation="schema" />
```

where `uri` is the URI of the namespace for the imported schema and `schema` is once again the location and name of the schema file. For example, to import the contents of the patients schema into Allison's study schema, you would add the following import element:

```
<xs:import namespace="http://uhosp.edu/patients/ns"
        schemaLocation="patvb.xsd" />
```

A schema file may contain any number of include and import elements. Each must be entered as a child of the root schema element. You need to import only the patvb.xsd schema into the study.xsd document.

To import the patvb.xsd schema:

1. Return to the **study.xsd** file in your text editor.

2. Directly below the opening tag of the schema element, insert the following import element (see Figure 4-49):

   ```
   <xs:import namespace="http://uhosp.edu/patients/ns"
           schemaLocation="patvb.xsd" />
   ```

Importing a schema   Figure 4-49

```
<xs:schema xmlns:xs="http://www.w3.org/2001/XMLSchema"
           xmlns="http://uhosp/studies/ns"
           targetNamespace="http://uhosp/studies/ns">

   <xs:import namespace="http://uhosp.edu/patients/ns"
           schemaLocation="patvb.xsd" />
```

Including and Importing Schemas

Reference Window

- To include a schema from the same namespace, add the following element as a child of the schema element:
  ```
  <xs:include schemaLocation="schema" />
  ```
  where `schema` is the name and location of the schema file.
- To import a schema from a different namespace, use the syntax
  ```
  <xs:import namespace="uri" schemaLocation="schema" />
  ```
  where `uri` is the URI of the imported schema's namespace and `schema` is the name and location of the schema file.

Referencing Objects from Other Schemas

Once a schema is imported, any objects it contains with global scope can be referenced. To reference an object from an imported schema, you must declare the namespace of the imported schema in the schema element. You can then reference the object using the ref attribute or the type attribute for customized simple and complex types. Allison wants the patients element to be placed directly after the pi element in this schema. Add the reference to that element to the schema document.

To reference the patients element:

1. Add the following namespace declaration to the root schema element:

   `xmlns:pat="http://uhosp.edu/patients/ns"`

2. Insert the following element reference directly below the pi element declaration. Note that the pat namespace prefix is used to place this reference in the patients namespace.

   `<xs:element ref="pat:patients" />`

   Figure 4-50 shows the revised schema code.

Figure 4-50   **Referencing the patients element from the patients namespace**

```
<xs:schema xmlns:xs="http://www.w3.org/2001/XMLSchema"
           xmlns="http://uhosp/studies/ns"
           targetNamespace="http://uhosp/studies/ns"
           xmlns:pat="http://uhosp.edu/patients/ns">

<xs:import namespace="http://uhosp.edu/patients/ns"
           schemaLocation="patvb.xsd" />

    <xs:element name="study">
        <xs:complexType>
            <xs:sequence>
                <xs:element name="name">
                    <xs:complexType>
                        <xs:sequence>
                            <xs:element name="title" />
                            <xs:element name="subtitle" />
                        </xs:sequence>
                    </xs:complexType>
                </xs:element>
                <xs:element name="pi" type="xs:string" />
                <xs:element ref="pat:patients" />
            </xs:sequence>
            <xs:attribute name="studyID" type="xs:ID" />
        </xs:complexType>
    </xs:element>

</xs:schema>
```

3. Close the study.xsd file, saving your changes.

4. Open the **tamoxifen.xml** file in XMLSpy or another validating parser.

5. Confirm that this compound document passes the validation test as it draws its rules for content and structure from the two schema files.

6. Close XMLSpy or your validating parser, along with any open files.

This example provides a glimpse of the power and flexibility of schemas in working with multiple vocabularies and namespaces. In more advanced applications, large schema structures can be created to validate equally complex XML environments involving hundreds of documents and vocabularies.

Allison is pleased with the work you've done in providing an environment for validating the data she is collecting for the hospital's ongoing cancer research. She'll apply what you've shown her about schemas for her future projects and get back to you with more questions and tasks.

Session 4.3 Quick Check

1. What is a named complex type? What is an anonymous complex type?
2. What code would you enter to create an element group named address containing elements named street, city, state, and zip? Assume that each of the elements is a string data type.
3. What is a flat catalog and how does it differ from a Russian doll design?
4. What attributes would you add to a schema element to place the schema in the target namespace http://jazzwarehouse.com/sales? Assume that the namespace is also the default namespace for the schema.
5. What attribute would you add to the topmost element in an instance document to attach it to a schema file named jazz.xsd with the namespace http://jazzwarehouse.com/sales?
6. If a namespace is used, what must you do for every element and attribute that is declared globally in the schema?
7. What attribute would you add to a schema element to force every element to be qualified in the instance document?
8. What element would you add to a schema to import the schema file jazz.xsd from the namespace http://jazzwarehouse.com/sales?
9. How does importing a schema differ from including a schema, with respect to the use of namespaces?

Tutorial Summary

This tutorial covered how to perform validation using XML Schema. The first session introduced the topic of schemas, discussing different schema vocabularies, and compared them to DTDs. The session continued with the creation of a basic schema that declared simple type elements, attributes, and a variety of complex type elements. The session concluded with a validation of an XML document based on that schema. The second session focused on the topic of data types. It began by exploring the wide variety of built-in XML Schema data types used for text strings, numeric values, and dates and times. The session then looked at how to create customized data types for lists and unions, and it examined restrictions on the value space, lexical space, and facets of a base data type. The session provided a brief introduction to regular expressions and demonstrated how to create a regular expression for an ID value. The third session looked at schema structures and compared three schema designs. The final session demonstrated how to merge schemas with namespaces and how to validate a compound document based on several XML vocabularies and associated schemas.

Key Terms

anonymous complex type	flat catalog design	regular expression
base type	global scope	restricted data type
built-in data type	instance document	Russian doll design
character set	lexical space	salami slice design
character type	list data type	schema
complex type	local scope	simple type
derived data type	member data type	union data type
EBNF	named attribute group	user-derived data type
Extended Backus Naur Form	named complex type	value space
facet	named model group	Venetian blind design
	primitive data type	
	quantifier	

Note: In the case problems that follow, some of the XML documents have intentional errors. Part of your job is to find and correct those errors using validation reports from the schemas you create.

Review Assignments

Data files needed for this Review Assignment: granttxt.xml, granttxt.xsd, slisttxt.xsd, studtxt.xml

Allison is very pleased with your work on the patient vocabulary. She has approached you with a new task. Each of the studies at the University Hospital's Clinical Cancer Center receives funding from a federal, state, local, or private agency grant. Allison has created an XML vocabulary containing information about the different grants that have been awarded to the center. She would like you to create a schema to validate grant information. In addition, Allison has also added more information to the studies XML vocabulary for information on individual research projects. Figure 4-51 shows the structures of the grant and studies vocabularies.

Figure 4-51

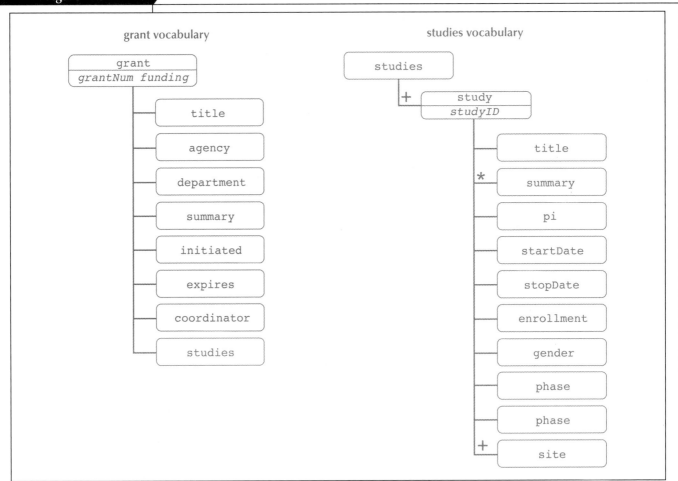

A description of the elements and attributes used in both vocabularies is shown in Figure 4-52.

Figure 4-52

Vocabulary	Element or Attribute	Description
grant	grant	The root element
	grantNum	ID number of the grant with the format *AAAAAA-####-##* where *A* is an uppercase letter and # is a digit
	funding	Funding agency (federal, state, local, or private)
	title	Grant title
	agency	Granting agency
	department	Hospital department
	summary	Summary of grant
	initiated expires	Date the grant starts and ends
	coordinator	Name of grant coordinator
studies	studies	The root element
	study	Element storing information on each study
	studyID	ID number of the study in the format CCC-###-## where # is a digit
	title	Study title
	summary	An optional summary describing the study
	pi	The study's principal investigator
	startDate stopDate	The date the study starts and ends
	enrollment	The number of patients enrolled in the study
	gender	The gender of patients in the study (female, male, or all)
	phase	The study phase (1, 2, or 3)
	site	The study site (there may be more than one)

Allison has already created a document containing information on one particular grant and another document containing a list of studies funded by that grant. She wants both documents validated based on schemas you create. Finally, she wants you to create and validate a compound document containing both grant and study information.

To complete this task:

1. Using your text editor, open the following files from the tutorial.04x/review folder: granttxt.xml, granttxt.xsd, slisttxt.xsd, and studtxt.xml. Enter *your name* and *the date* in the comment section of each file and save them as: **grant.xml**, **grant.xsd**, **slist.xsd** and **studies.xml** respectively.

2. Go to the **grant.xsd** file in your text editor. Add the root schema element to the document and declare the XML Schema namespace using the xs prefix. Set the default namespace of the document to the URI http://uhosp.edu/grant/ns and make this URI the target of the schema.

3. Create the following custom data types:
   - grantType, based on the ID data type and following the regular expression pattern "[A-Z]{6}-\d{4}-\d{2}"
   - fundingType based on the string data type and limited to the following values: federal, state, local, and private
4. Using a Russian doll design, declare the grant element with the following nested child elements: title, agency, department, summary, initiated, expires, and coordinator. All of the child elements should contain string data except the initiated and expires elements, which contain dates. The grant element should also support two attributes: grantNum and funding. The grantNum attribute contains grantType data. The funding attribute contains fundingType data.
5. Save your changes to the grant.xsd file.
6. Go to the **grant.xml** file in your text editor. Within the root element, declare the XML Schema instance namespace using the xsi namespace prefix. Declare the grant namespace using the URI http://uhosp.edu/grant/ns= and the prefix gr. Set the location of the schema to the grant namespace and the grant.xsd file.
7. Change the name of the grant element to a qualified name by adding the gr prefix to the opening and closing tags.
8. Save your changes to the grant.xml file and then validate the document using XML-Spy or another validating parser. Correct any validation errors you discover in the instance document.
9. Go to the **slist.xsd** file in your text editor. Insert the root schema element and declare the XML Schema namespace using the xs prefix. Set the default namespace and schema target to the URI http://uhosp.edu/studies/ns.
10. Create the following user-defined data types:
    - studyIDType, based on the ID data type and following the regular expression pattern "CCC-\d{3}-\d{2}"
    - genderType, based on the string data type and limited to the values: female, male, and all
    - phaseType, based on the positive integer data type and having a maximum value of 3 (inclusive)
11. Apply a Venetian blind layout to this schema. Start by creating an element group named studyElements containing the following sequence of elements: title, summary, pi, startDate, stopDate, enrollment, gender, phase, and site. The title, summary, pi, and site elements contain string data. The startDate and stopDate elements contain dates. The enrollment element contains a nonnegative integer. The gender and phase elements contain genderType and phaseType data, respectively. The summary element can occur 0 times. The site element must occur at least once, but its upper limit is unbounded. All other elements are assumed to occur only once.
12. Create a complex type named studyType. Within this complex type, insert a reference to the studyElements element group. Also declare the studyID attribute containing studyIDType data.
13. Declare the studies complex type element. Within this element, insert an element sequence containing the study element. The study element contains studyType data and must occur at least once.
14. Save your changes to the **slist.xsd** file and then go to the **studies.xml** file in your text editor. Declare the XML Schema instance namespace in the root element using the xsi prefix. Declare the studies namespace using the URI http://uhosp.edu/studies/ns and the prefix std. Set the location of the schema to the studies namespace and the slist.xsd file.

15. Qualify the name of the studies root element by adding the std namespace prefix.

16. Save your changes to the studies.xml file and then validate the document. Correct any errors the validator discovers in the instance document.

17. Create a schema for the compound document by returning to the **grant.xsd** file in your text editor. Within the root element, declare the studies namespace using the appropriate URI and the std namespace prefix.

18. Directly after the opening tag of the schema element, import the contents of the slist.xsd schema file specifying the studies namespace.

19. Directly after the declaration for the coordinator element, insert an element reference to the studies element located in the studies namespace. Save your changes to the grant.xsd file.

20. Return to the **studies.xml** document in your text editor and copy the document body including the opening and closing tags of the studies element.

21. Go to the **grant.xml** file in your text editor. Directly after the coordinator element, paste the copied contents of the studies.xml file. Remove the XML Schema instance namespace declaration from the studies element. Save your changes to the file.

22. Validate the contents of the grant.xml file, now containing elements from both the grant and studies namespaces.

23. Submit the complete and validated project to your instructor.

Apply

se the skills you
arned in this tutorial
validate a music
atalog

Case Problem 1

Data files needed for this Case Problem: jwtxt.xml, musictxt.xsd

The Jazz Warehouse Richard Brooks is working on an XML document to store the inventory of vintage albums sold by the Jazz Warehouse. Figure 4-53 shows the structure of the vocabulary employed in the document. A description of the elements and attributes used in the music catalog is shown in Figure 4-54.

Figure 4-53

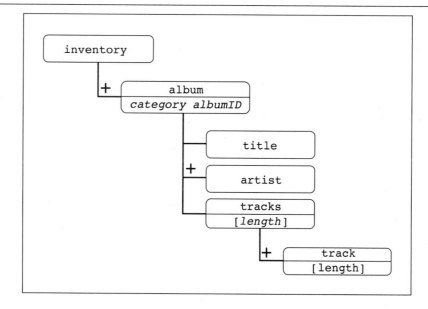

Figure 4-54

Element or Attribute	Description
inventory	The root element
album	Element storing information about each album
category	The album category (New Orleans, Swing, Bebop, Modern)
albumID	Album ID number in the form JW###### where # is a digit
title	The album title
artist	The album artist (there may be more than one)
tracks	Element storing information on the album tracks
length	An optional attribute storing the length (in *hours:minutes:seconds*) of an entire album or track
track	The name of an individual album track

Richard needs your help in creating a schema that will validate the data he's already entered and will enter in the future. In order to keep the code compact, you'll use a Russian doll design for the schema layout. Richard is not planning to use this schema with other XML documents, so you do not have to define a namespace for the vocabulary he created.

To complete this task:

1. Using your text editor, open jwtxt.xml and musictxt.xsd from the tutorial.04x/case1 folder. Enter *your name* and *the date* in the comment section of each file and save them as **jw.xml** and **music.xsd** respectively.
2. Go to the **music.xsd** file in your text editor and insert the root schema element. Declare the XML Schema namespace with xsd as the namespace prefix.
3. Define the following data types:
   - albumIDType, based on the ID data type and following the pattern JW######, where # is a digit
   - jazzType, based on the string data type and limited to: New Orleans, Swing, Bebop, and Modern
4. Declare the inventory complex element type and nest the album element within it. The album must occur at least once, but its upper limit is unbounded.
5. Within the album element, create a Russian doll layout, first nesting the child elements title, artist, and tracks, and the attributes category and albumID. The title and artist elements are both simple types containing string data. The artist element may occur multiple times, but must occur at least once. The category attribute is required and contains jazzType data. The albumID attribute is also required and contains albumIDType data.
6. The tracks element is a complex type element and contains at least one track element. The tracks element also contains an optional length attribute containing time data.
7. The track element is a complex type element contains a simple text string and the length attribute. The length attribute is optional and stores time data.
8. Close the music.xsd file, saving your changes.
9. Go to the **jw.xml** file in your text editor. Within the root inventory element, declare the XML Schema instance namespace. Use xsi as the namespace prefix. Attach the schema file music.xsd to this instance document. Do not place the schema or the instance document in a namespace.

10. Save your changes to the jw.xml file and then validate jw.xml in XMLSpy or another validating parser. Correct any data entry errors you find in the instance document.

11. Submit your complete and validated project to your instructor.

Case Problem 2

Data files needed for this Case Problem: canvtxt.xsd, clisttxt.xsd, contrib.xml, libtxt.xsd, reptxt.xml

EPAC-MO EPAC-MO is an environmental political action committee operating in central Missouri. Sudha Bhatia manages fundraising reports for the committee and has been using XML to record information on contributors and canvassers who collect donations. She's developed a vocabulary for the canvassers to record each canvasser's name, address, and total amount collected. She's also developed a vocabulary for contributions, recording each contributor's name, address, and total amount donated. Sudha wants your help in developing a schema to validate the information she puts in her documents. Since Sudha will create a compound document displaying information on both canvassers and contributions, she needs the schema to combine information from several namespaces. Figure 4-55 shows the tree structure for the vocabulary of the compound document.

Figure 4-55

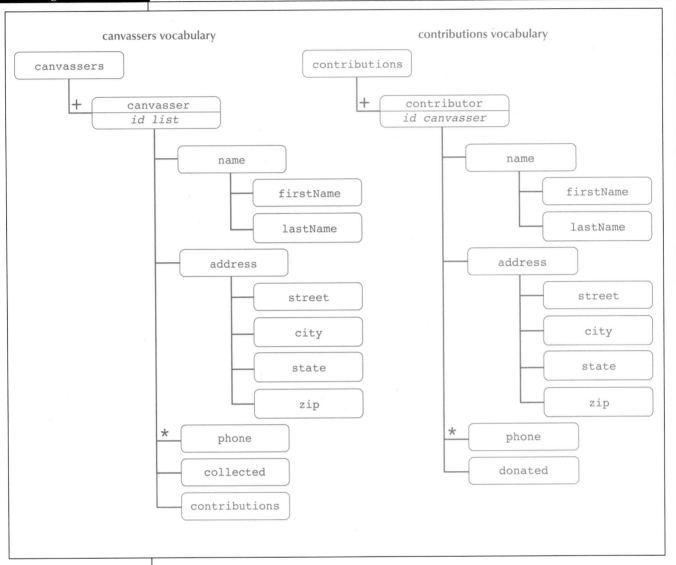

You notice that several simple and complex types, such as the name and address elements, are repeated in both vocabularies. Rather than repeating the definitions in both schemas, you decide to place the definitions for these common elements in a third schema containing a library of common data types. You'll import that schema into the schema files for both the canvasser and contributions vocabularies.

To complete this task:

1. Using your text editor, open canvtxt.xsd, clisttxt.xsd, libtxt.xsd, and reptxt.xml from the tutorial.04x/case2 folder. Enter *your name* and *the date* in the comment section of each file and save them as **canvlist.xsd**, **clist.xsd**, **lib.xsd**, and **report.xml** respectively.

2. Go to the **lib.xsd** file in your text editor. Within this schema you'll create a library of data types. Add the root schema element and insert the declaration for the XML Schema namespace using the xs prefix. Set the default namespace and target of the schema to the URI http://epacmo.org/library.

3. Create the following data types:
   - stateType, based on the string data type and limited to two uppercase letters
   - zipType, based on the integer data type and following the pattern d#### where d is a digit from 1 to 9 and # is any digit
   - phoneType, based on the string data type and following the pattern d##-#### where d is a digit from 1 to 9 and # is any digit

4. Create a complex type named nameType containing the following sequence of elements: firstName and lastName. Both elements should contain string data.

5. Create a complex type named addressType containing the following sequence of elements: street, city, state, and zip. The street and city elements contain string data. The state element contains stateType data. The zip element contains zipType data.

6. Close the lib.xsd file, saving your changes and go to the **clist.xsd** file in your text editor. Within this file you'll create the schema for the contributions vocabulary.

7. Insert the root schema element, declaring the XML Schema namespace with the xs prefix. Declare the library namespace using the URI http://epacmo.org/library and the prefix lib. Set the default namespace and the schema target to the URI http://epacmo.org/contributors.

8. Import the lib.xsd schema file using the URI of the library namespace.

9. Using a Russian doll design, insert the declaration for the complex type element contributions. The element contains the child element contributor, which occurs at least once in the instance document.

10. The contributor element is also a complex type element containing the child elements name, address, phone, and donated, and the attributes id and canvasser. The phone element may occur any number of times.

11. Set the data types of the elements and attributes of the contributor element as follows:
    - The name element contains nameType data (taken from the library namespace).
    - The address element contains addressType data (taken from the library namespace).
    - The phone element contains phoneType data (taken from the library namespace).
    - The donated element contains positive integer data.
    - The id attribute contains ID data.
    - The canvasser attribute contains an ID reference.

12. Close the clist.xsd file, saving your changes. Go to the **canvlist.xsd** file in your text editor. This file contains the schema for the canvasser vocabulary.

13. Insert the root schema element, declaring the XML Schema namespace with the xs prefix. Declare the library namespace using the lib prefix and the contributors namespace using the clist prefix. Set the default namespace and the schema target to the URI http://epacmo.org/canvassers.

14. Import the library and contributors schemas using the appropriate namespace URIs and schema locations (you will need to import elements).

15. Using a Russian doll design, declare the complex type element canvassers. The element has a single child element, canvasser, that occurs at least once. The canvasser element contains the child sequence: name, address, phone, collected, and a reference to the contributions element from the contributions namespace. The canvasser element also contains the id and list attributes. The phone element can occur any number of times.

16. As with the contributions schema, the name, address, and phone elements contain nameType, addressType, and phoneType data, respectively. The collected element contains positive integers. The id attribute contains ID data. The list attribute contains a list of ID references.

17. Close the file, saving your changes; and then go to the **report.xml** file in your text editor.

18. Within the root canvassers element, declare the XML Schema instance namespace using the prefix xsi. Declare the canvassers namespace using the prefix canvlist. Declare the contributions namespace using the prefix contlist. Attach schema from the canvlist.xsd file using the appropriate namespace.

19. Change the opening and closing tags of the canvassers element to a qualified name using the canvlist prefix. Change the opening and closing tags of the two contributions elements to qualified names using the contlist prefix.

20. Go to the **contrib.xml** file in your text editor. Copy and paste the contributor information for contributors c001, c002, and c004 within the first set of contributions tags in the report.xml file. Copy and paste the contributor information for contributors c003, c005, and c006 from the contrib.xml file to within the second set of contributions tags in the report.xml file.

21. Save your changes to the **report.xml** file and then validate the file. Correct any mistakes found in the document.

22. Submit the completed and validated project to your instructor.

Challenge

Explore how to combine DTDs and schemas to validate a compound document

Case Problem 3

Data files needed for this Case Problem: invtxt.xml, invtxt.xsd, modtxt.xml, modtxt.xsd, parttxt.xml, parttxt.xsd, typestxt.xsd

GrillRite Grills   James Castillo manages the inventory for GrillRite Grills, one of the leading manufacturers of grills in North America. He has been using XML to keep records of models to be assembled and the parts required to assemble them at the Grill-Rite Grills warehouse. James needs your help in developing a system to store valid inventory data. He envisions a collection of XML documents and schema files linked in the structure displayed in Figure 4-56.

Figure 4-56

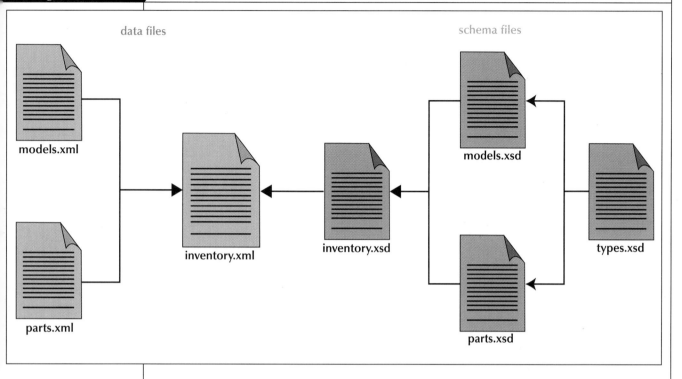

In his proposed structure, James wants to be able to insert model and parts information in separate documents which can then be read into an inventory report through the use of external entities. Validation will be done through a collection of schemas. One schema contains a library of customized data types that James uses for his documents. The models and parts schemas validate the models and parts data. Finally, the inventory schema accesses both the models and parts schemas to validate the inventory report.

James has already laid out the structure for the models and parts vocabularies. The structure of those two vocabularies is shown in Figure 4-57.

Figure 4-57

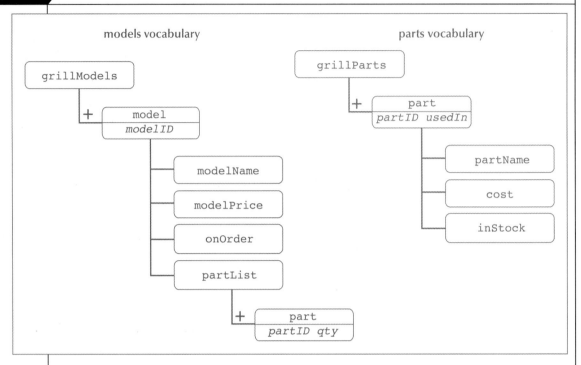

A description of the elements and attributes used in the models and parts vocabulary is given in Figure 4-58.

Figure 4-58

Vocabulary	Element or Attribute	Description
models	grillModels	The root element
	model	Element storing information about each model
	modelID	Attribute containing the model ID entered in the format *aaa###* where *a* is a lowercase letter and # is a digit
	modelName	The name of the model
	modelPrice	Price of the model
	onOrder	The number of models on order to be assembled
	partList	Element storing the list of parts required to assemble the model
	part	An empty element containing information about each part
	partID	Attribute containing a reference to the part ID
	qty	Attribute containing the quantity of each part to be assembled in the model
parts	grillParts	The root element
	part	Element storing information about each part
	partID	Attribute containing the part ID entered in the format *aaa###* where *a* is a lowercase letter and # is a digit
	usedIn	Attribute containing a list of ID references to the models that use the part
	partName	The name of the part
	cost	The cost of the part
	inStock	Number of each part in stock

Your task will be to finish the various XML document files and insert the linkages between the files to create a finished project. To do this you'll have to use a combination of DTDs and schemas.

To complete this task:

1. Using your text editor, open the following files from the tutorial.04x/case3 folder: invtxt.xml, invtxt.xsd, modtxt.xml, modtxt.xsd, parttxt.xml, parttxt.xsd, and typestxt.xsd. Enter **your name** and **the date** in the comment section of each file and as save them as **inventory.xml**, **inventory.xsd**, **models.xml**, **models.xsd**, **parts.xml**, **parts.xsd**, and **types.xsd** respectively.

2. Go to the **types.xsd** file and insert the root schema element, declaring the XML Schema namespace with the xs prefix. The URI of the default namespace and the schema target is http://grillrite.com/datatypes.

3. Create the following custom data types:
   - The itemID data type, based on the ID type and following the pattern *aaa###*, where *a* is a lowercase letter and # is a digit
   - The itemIDREF data type, based on the IDREF type and also following the pattern *aaa###*
   - The priceType data type, based on the string type and following the regular expression pattern "[$]\d+(\.\d{2})?"

4. Save your changes to the types.xsd file and go to the **parts.xml** file. Take some time to study the contents of this file and then declare the parts namespace in the grill-Parts element. The parts namespace URI is http://grillrite.com/parts and the namespace prefix is part. Qualify the opening and closing tags of the grillParts element. Close parts.xml, saving your changes.

5. Go to the **parts.xsd** file in your text editor. Add the root schema element, declaring the XML Schema namespace with the xs prefix. Declare the datatypes namespace using the lib prefix. Declare the parts namespace as the default namespace and make it the target of the schema.

6. Import the types.xsd file into the schema.

7. Declare the complex type element grillParts containing the part element. The part element should occur at least once in the instance document.

Explore

8. The part element contains the following child elements: partName, cost, and inStock; and the attributes partID and usedIn. The partName element contains string data, the cost element contains priceType data, and the inStock element contains nonnegative integers. The partID attribute contains itemID data and the usedIn attribute contains IDREFS data.

9. Save your changes to the parts.xsd file and go to the **models.xml** file. Review the contents of the file. Add a namespace declaration to the root grillModels element using the URI http://grillrite.com/models and the prefix mod. Qualify the opening and closing tags of the grillModels element. Save your changes to the file.

10. Go to the **models.xsd** file in your text editor. Add the schema element to the file, once again declaring the XML Schema namespace using the xs prefix. Declare the datatypes namespace using the lib prefix. Set the models namespace as the default namespace and target of the schema.

11. Import the types.xsd schema.

12. Using a Russian doll design, declare the complex type element grillModels. Nested within this element, declare the model element, allowing it to occur at least once. The model element contains the child elements modelName, modelPrice, onOrder, and partList, and the modelID attribute.

13. The modelName element contains string data. The modelPrice element contains priceType data, and the onOrder element contains nonnegative integers. The modelID attribute contains itemID data.

14. The partList element is a complex type element containing one or more part elements. Each part element is an empty element containing the partID and qty attributes. The partID attribute stores itemIDREF data. The qty attribute stores positive integers.

15. Save your changes to the models.xsd schema. Go to the **inventory.xsd** file in your text editor. Declare the XML Schema namespace in the root schema element using the xs prefix. Declare the models and parts namespaces using the namespace prefixes mod and parts respectively. Use the URI http://grillrite.com/inventory as the default namespace and target of the schema.

16. Import the models.xsd and parts.xsd schemas.

17. Declare a complex type element named inventory containing the element references grillModels from the models namespace, and grillParts from the parts namespace. Close the inventory.xsd file, saving your changes.

18. Go to the inventory .xml element. Copy and paste the content from the models.xml document within the inventory element.

19. Copy and paste the content from the parts.xml document within the inventory element directly below the models data.

20. Within the inventory element, declare the XML Schema instance namespace. Declare the inventory namespace using inv as the namespace prefix. Attach the inventory.xsd schema.

21. Qualify the opening and closing tags of the inventory element and then close the inventory.xml file, saving your changes.

Explore

22. Validate the inventory.xml file. Note that the validation errors will be discovered in the models.xml and parts.xml files. Correct any mistakes you find in those files.

23. Submit your completed and validated project to your instructor.

Case Problem 4

Create

Test your knowledge of schemas by creating a schema structure for an online store

Data files needed for this Case Problem: books.txt, movies.txt, music.txt

**MediaMart Online**   MediaMart is an online store that specializes in selling used videos, books, and movies. Terrance Dawes, who works for MediaMart, has been given the task of putting some of the store's product information into XML documents. He's not very experienced with XML and would like your help in making the transfer, as well as ensuring the integrity of his data. Terrance has put a small list of products into three text files named books.txt, movies.txt, and music.txt. Figure 4-59 describes the contents of the three files.

Figure 4-59

Media	Content
Books	The book name
	The author
	The genre (fiction or nonfiction)
	The format (hardcover or paperback)
	The sales price
Movies	The movie name
	The genre (comedy, drama, fantasy, children, musical, or family)
	A list of actors and actresses in the movie
	The sales price
	The year the movie was released
	The format (VHS or DVD)
Music	The name of the musical work
	The artist
	The genre (rock, classical, opera, jazz, blues, rap, or pop)
	The format (cassette or CD)
	The sales price

Your job will be to first create XML documents from the three text files that Terrance has given you. Then, create schemas to validate the contents of these files.

To complete this task:

1. Using the three text files, create three XML documents named **books.xml**, **movies. xml**, and **music.xml**. Each XML document should have a content section describing the purpose of the file, the file's author, and the date. The structure of the documents is left up to you, but it should contain all of the information from the text files organized in readable and easy-to-understand format.

2. Draw a tree structure of the vocabularies you created for the three files.

3. Based on your vocabularies, create three schema files named **books.xsd**, **movies.xsd**, and **music.xsd**. The design of the schemas is up to you, but the schemas should ensure the integrity of Terrance's data, following the guidelines laid out in Figure 4-59. Place the books schema in the namespace http://mediamart.com/books, the movies schema in the namespace http://mediamart.com/movies, and the music schema in the namespace http://mediamart.com/music.

4. Attach the schemas you created to their corresponding XML documents. Include any namespace information in the instance documents and qualify all globally declared elements and attributes. Validate each of the documents.

5. Create an XML document named **mmart.xml** that retrieves the contents of the books.xml, movies.xml, and music.xml files through the use of an external entity. Name the root element mediaProducts. Place the document in the namespace http://mediamart.com/products.

6. Create a schema for the mmart.xml document named **mmart.xsd**, importing the contents of the books.xsd, movies.xsd, and music.xsd schema files. Include all necessary namespace declarations.

7. Confirm your work on the compound document by validating the mmart.xml file.

8. Submit the completed and validated project to your instructor.

Review

Quick Check Answers

Session 4.1

1. A schema is an XML document that can validate the content and structure of other XML documents. An instance document is the XML document to be validated by a given schema.

2. Schemas support namespaces and work with combined documents better than DTDs. Schemas support more data types and allow the user to easily create customized data types.

3. A simple type element contains a single value, such as the value of an attribute or the textual content of an element. A complex type element contains structured content in the form of child elements and/or attributes.

4. `<xs:element name="Weight" type="xs:string" />`

5. ```
   <xs:element name="Contact">
      <xs:complexType>
        <xs:all>
           <xs:element name="Mail" type="xs:string" />
           <xs:element name="Phone" type="xs:string" />
        </xs:all>
      </xs:complexType>
   </xs:element>
   ```
6. ```
   <xs:element name="Book">
      <xs:complexType>
        <xs:simpleType>
           <xs:extension base="xs:string">
              <xs:attribute name="Title" type="xs:string" />
           </xs:extension>
        </xs:simpleType>
      </xs:complexType>
   </xs:element>
   ```
7. ```
   <xs:attribute ref="patientID" />
   ```
8. ```
   xmlns:xsi="http://www.w3.org/2001/XMLSchema-instance"
   xsi:noNamespaceSchemaLocation="Schema1.xsd"
   ```

Session 4.2

1. ```
   <xs:element name="Weight" type="xs:decimal" />
   ```
2. ```
   <xs:attribute name="itemIDs" type="xs:IDREFS" />
   ```
3. ```
   <xs:simpleType name="VisitDates">
      <xs:list itemType="xs:date" />
   </xs:simpleType>
   ```
4. ```
   <xs:simpleType name="Status">
      <xs:union memberTypes="xs:decimal xs:string" />
   </xs:simpleType>
   ```
5. ```
   <xs:simpleType name="Party">
      <xs:restriction base="xs:string">
        <xs:enumeration value="Democrat" />
        <xs:enumeration value="Republican" />
        <xs:enumeration value="Independent" />
      </xs:restriction>
   </xs:simpleType>
   ```
6. ```
   <xs:simpleType name="Percentage">
      <xs:restriction base="xs:decimal">
        <xs:minInclusive value="0" />
        <xs:maxInclusive value="1" />
      </xs:restriction>
   </xs:simpleType>
   ```
7. ```
   <xs:simpleType name="SocSecurity">
      <xs:restriction base="xs:stringl">
        <xs:pattern value="\d{3}-\d{2}-\d{4}" />
      </xs:restriction>
   </xs:simpleType>
   ```
   ```

Session 4.3

1. A named complex type is a complex type with a value assigned to the name attribute. An anonymous complex type has no name value.

2. ```
   <xs:group name="address">
       <xs:sequence>
           <xs:element name="street" type="xs:string" />
           <xs:element name="city" type="xs:string" />
           <xs:element name="state" type="xs:string" />
           <xs:element name="zip" type="xs:string" />
       </xs:sequence>
   </xs:group>
   ```

3. A flat catalog is a schema design in which all element and attribute declarations are global. In a Russian doll design, only one element is global and all of the rest of the elements and attributes are nested within that one global element.

4. xmlns="http://jazzwarehouse.com/sales"
   targetNamespace="http://jazzwarehouse.com/sales"

5. xsi:schemaLocation="http://jazzwarehouse.com/sales jazz.xsd"

6. You must qualify the global element and attributes with a namespace prefix.

7. elementFormDefault="qualified"

8. <xs:import namespace="http://jazzwarehouse.com/sales" schemaLocation= "jazz.xsd">

9. An included schema must belong to the same target namespace as the current schema. An imported schema belongs to a different namespace.
   ```

New Perspectives on

XML

Read This Before You Begin: Tutorials 5–10

To the Student

Data Files

To complete the Level II XML Tutorials (Tutorials 5–10), you need the starting student Data Files. Your instructor will either provide you with these Data Files or ask you to obtain them yourself.

The Level II XML Tutorials require the folders shown to complete the Tutorials, Review Assignments, and Case Problems. You will need to copy these folders from a file server, a standalone computer, or the Web to the drive and folder where you will be storing your Data Files.

Your instructor will tell you which computer, drive letter, and folder(s) contain the files you need. You can also download the files by going to www.course.com; see the inside back cover for more information on downloading the files, or ask your instructor or technical support person for assistance.

▼**XML**

    Tutorial.05x
    Tutorial.06x
    Tutorial.07x
    Tutorial.08x
    Tutorial.09x
    Tutorial.10x

Student Online Companion

The Student Online Companion can be found at www.course.com/carey. It contains additional information to supplement what you are learning in the text, as well as links to downloads and other tools.

To the Instructor

The Data Files are available on the Instructor Resources CD for this title. Follow the instructions in the Help file on the CD to install the programs to your network or standalone computer. See the "To the Student" section above for information on how to set up the Data Files that accompany this text.

You are granted a license to copy the Data Files to any computer or computer network used by students who have purchased this book.

System Requirements

If you are going to work through this book using your own computer, you need:

- **System Requirements** You will need a basic text editor, the current version of Internet Explorer for Windows or Firefox, and an XML editor to complete all of the tasks in this book. If you use another browser such as Safari for the Macintosh or Netscape, be aware that you might not be able to complete all of the assignments and cases. Browser compatibility issues are highlighted throughout the book to notify you of potential problems, but since new browser versions are constantly being released, it is possible that some of the browser issues noted in this book will have been resolved by more current releases. This book assumes that you will be using the free non-commercial version of Exchanger XML to validate and transform your XML documents. You may use another XML editor such as <oXygen />, saxon, or xt. The Student Online Companion for this book contains additional information on the <oXygen /> XML editor.

- **Data Files** You will not be able to complete the tutorials or exercises in this book using your own computer until you have the necessary starting Data Files.

Objectives

Session 5.1
- Understand the history and theory of CSS
- Write selectors for specific XML elements
- Set the display style for elements
- Size and position elements on a rendered page

Session 5.2
- Understand the different parts of the box model for block elements
- Set the margin and padding size of an element
- Define border styles for an element
- Apply and format background images

Session 5.3
- Create CSS styles for text and font formatting
- Apply styles to elements based on id values
- Apply styles to elements belonging to a common class
- Apply styles to pseudo-elements

Working with Cascading Style Sheets

Formatting Your XML Documents with CSS

Case

Tour Nation

Janet Schmidtt works in the Advertising Department of Tour Nation, a leading bicycle manufacturer. One of her responsibilities is to maintain an XML document that describes the various models offered by Tour Nation. Janet created a test document listing a few of the bikes in the Tour Nation catalog. The document includes a descriptive paragraph and list of features for each bicycle. As Janet learns more about XML, she plans to add more information and more bicycles to her document.

In its current form, the document is not very easy for other Tour Nation employees to read. Janet wants to format the document with an interesting and readable layout and make the document available on the Tour Nation intranet site. She knows that the Cascading Style Sheet (CSS) language is often used with HTML and XHTML files to create interesting page designs, but she doesn't know if it can be used with XML. She wants your help in applying a style sheet to her document. To do this, you'll have to learn more about CSS and how it interacts with XML.

Student Data Files

▼**tutorial.05x**

▽ **tutorial folder**
   biketxt.css
   biketxt.xml
   + 7 image files

▽ **review folder**
   bike2txt.css
   bike2txt.xml
   + 7 image files

▽ **case1 folder**
   nasdaqtxt.css
   nasdaqtxt.xml
   + 2 image files

▽ **case2 folder**
   elemtxt.xml
   pcharttxt.css

▽ **case3 folder**
   schedtxt.css
   schedtxt.xml

▽ **case4 folder**
   mealstxt.css
   mealstxt.xml

Session 5.1

Introducing CSS

You meet with Janet to discuss the document she's created, which describes some of the bike models sold by Tour Nation. A list of the elements contained in Janet's document is shown in Figure 5-1. Janet has created a compound document with the img element taken from the XHTML vocabulary. The img element is used to display both the Tour Nation logo and images of the different bike models. The rest of the elements in the document come from a vocabulary that Janet has created for Tour Nation.

Figure 5-1	Elements in the bike document

Element	Description
document	The root element
author	The author of the document
date	The date the document was last revised
title	The title of the document
subtitle	The subtitle of the document
models	A list of bikes sold by Tour Nation
model	A record for an individual bike model
name	The name of a bike model (the class attribute indicates the bike model category)
description	A bike model description
img	An HTML img element
features	A list of the features of a bike model
feature	A specific feature for a bike model
fName	The name of a feature

Figure 5-2 shows the structure of Janet's document. The root element is named document and contains the author, date, title, subtitle, and models elements. The models element contains information on one or more bike models. For each bike model, a features element contains one or more features of the bike. Each bike belongs to a class of bike models (city, road, or combo) with the class attribute added to the name element in the document.

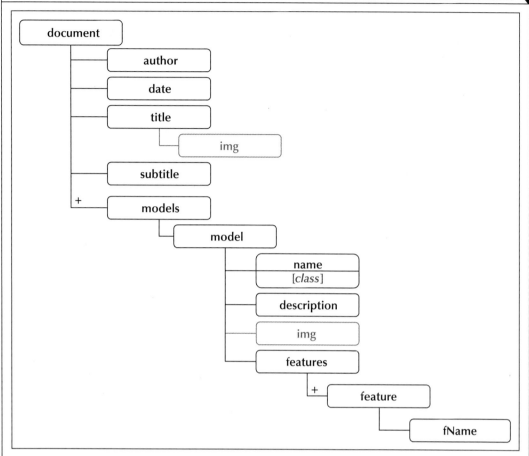

Before going further with Janet's project, you ask for a copy of her document so that you can view the actual data yourself. Open that document now.

To open the bicycle document:

► **1.** Use your text editor to open **biketxt.xml** from the tutorial.05x/tutorial folder. Enter *your name* and *the date* in the comment section at the top of the file, and save the file as **bike.xml**.

Figure 5-3 displays the contents of the first model in the bike.xml file. Note that Janet has already declared the XHTML namespace and used the namespace prefix "html" to place the img element within that namespace.

Figure 5-3

Model information in the bike.xml file

```
<document xmlns:html="http://www.w3.org/1999/xhtml">
   <author>Janet Schmidtt</author>
   <date>8/17/2007</date>
   <title><html:img src="tnation.jpg" alt="Tour Nation" /></title>
   <subtitle>Bike Models</subtitle>

   <models>
      <model>
         <name class="city">City Cruiser 100</name>
         <description>
            The City Cruiser 100 is designed to give you the perfect blend of
            comfort and performance, taking away the bumps and bruises of city
            roads. Our patented aluminum frame process provides a comfortable frame
            that is light, durable, and shock absorbing. The City Cruiser 100 includes
            several comfort features, like a suspension seat post, spring saddle, and
            adjustable high-rise seat stem. The City Cruiser 100 also includes
            semi-smooth tires that roll on the pavement, giving the rider plenty of
            traction while soaking up the bumps.
         </description>
         <html:img src="c100.jpg" alt="" />
         <features>
            <feature><fName>sizes: </fName>(L) 16.5", (XL) 18.5", (XXL) 21"</feature>
            <feature><fName>frame: </fName>Prime Aluminum Comfort Specific</feature>
            <feature><fName>fork: </fName>Trek high tensile steel ATB</feature>
            <feature><fName>wheels: </fName>Matrix 550 rims</feature>
            <feature><fName>tires: </fName>Bontrager Comfort, 26x1.95" f/r </feature>
            <feature><fName>shifters: </fName>SRAM 5.0 Royale</feature>
            <feature><fName>front derailleur: </fName>Lancaster C051</feature>
            <feature><fName>rear derailleur: </fName>SRAM ESP 4.0</feature>
            <feature><fName>crankset: </fName>SunRace FCM36 48/38/28</feature>
         </features>
      </model>
```

2. Take some time to examine the rest of the file, paying attention to the structure and content of the document.

Next, view the contents of this document in your Web browser.

3. Start your Web browser, and use it to open the bike.xml file. Figure 5-4 shows the current appearance of the document in the Internet Explorer browser. Other browsers may show a different view of the document.

Figure 5-4

Default display in the Internet Explorer browser

```
- <document xmlns:html="http://www.w3.org/1999/xhtml">
     <author>Janet Schmidtt</author>
     <date>8/17/2007</date>
  - <title>
       <html:img src="tnation.jpg" alt="Tour Nation" />
    </title>
     <subtitle>Bike Models</subtitle>
  - <models>
    - <model>
         <name class="city">City Cruiser 100</name>
         <description>The City Cruiser 100 is designed to give you the perfect blend of comfort
            and performance, taking away the bumps and bruises of city roads. Our patented
            aluminum frame process provides a comfortable frame that is light, durable, and
            shock absorbing. The City Cruiser 100 includes several comfort features, like a
            suspension seat post, spring saddle, and adjustable high-rise seat stem. The City
            Cruiser 100 also includes semi-smooth tires that roll on the pavement, giving the rider
            plenty of traction while soaking up the bumps.</description>
         <html:img src="c100.jpg" alt="" />
       - <features>
         - <feature>
              <fName>sizes:</fName>
              (L) 16.5", (XL) 18.5", (XXL) 21"
           </feature>
```

Your Web browser applies a default style and layout to any XML document it opens. In the case of the Internet Explorer browser, the document appears as an expandable/ collapsible outline. However, Janet wants the document to appear in a form that is more accessible to the employees at Tour Nation. Figure 5-5 shows the layout she has in mind for the contents of the bike.xml file.

Janet's proposed style for the bike document   Figure 5-5

To create the layout that Janet has proposed, you'll apply a style sheet of your own creation to the bike document. Before exploring how to do that, you'll first look at how style sheet languages developed.

The History of CSS

The primary purpose of a markup language such as XML is to create structured documents but not necessarily to describe how such documents should be rendered. Indeed, markup files should be accessible to a wide variety of devices and output media. The original vision of the HTML markup language did not specify how HTML elements appear, leaving those issues to the browsers rendering Web pages. However, as HTML developed and the Web expanded worldwide, Web page authors demanded elements and attributes that would give them many of the same formatting tools found in word-processing programs. After all, for most Web pages, appearance was just as important as content. This demand resulted in the introduction of several HTML attributes and elements describing how browsers should render a document. However, this development was not true to the original vision of a markup language, and as a result many of these HTML elements have now been deprecated in favor of style sheets. When XML was developed, it did not include any formatting elements or attributes, but instead was created to be compatible with the same style sheet language used with HTML.

A **style sheet** is a collection of properties called **styles** that describe how elements within a document should be rendered by the device presenting the document. The advantage of style sheets is that they separate document content from document presentation. Thus, by applying different style sheets, the same document can be rendered on different types of devices—from computer monitors to printers to speech-synthesized browsers—without having to alter the content or structure of the original document.

Although several style sheet languages exist, by far the most commonly used on the Web is the **Cascading Style Sheets** language, also known as **CSS**. As with XML, the specifications for CSS are maintained by the World Wide Web Consortium, and, similar to those languages, several versions of CSS exist with varying levels of browser support. The first version of CSS, called **CSS1**, was introduced in 1996 but was not fully implemented in the browser market for another three years. CSS1 introduced styles for the following document features:

- *Fonts*: Setting font size, type, and other properties
- *Text*: Controlling text alignment and applying decorative elements such as underlining, italics, and capitalization
- *Color*: Specifying background and foreground colors of different page elements
- *Backgrounds*: Setting and tiling background images for page elements
- *Block-level elements*: Controlling margins and borders around blocks, setting the padding space within a block, and floating block-level elements on a page

The second version of CSS, **CSS2**, was introduced in 1998. It expanded the language to support styles for the following features:

- *Positioning*: Placing elements at specific coordinates on a page
- *Visual formatting*: Clipping and hiding element content
- *Media types*: Creating styles for different output devices, including printed media and aural devices
- *Interfaces*: Controlling the appearance and behavior of system features such as scrollbars and mouse cursors

At present, browser support for CSS2 is mixed. Most of the styles for positioning and visual formatting are supported, but many of the other CSS2 styles are not. An update to CSS2, **CSS2.1**, was introduced by the W3C in April 2002. Although the update did not add any new features to the language, it cleaned up some minor errors that were introduced in the original specification.

Even though browsers are still trying to catch up to all the features of CSS2, the W3C has pressed forward with the next version, **CSS3**. Still in development as of this writing, CSS3 is being designed in individual modules. This approach should make it easier for software developers to design applications that support only those features of CSS that are relevant to their products. For example, an aural browser might not need to support the CSS styles associated with printed media, so the developers of this type of browser can concentrate only on the CSS3 modules that deal with aural properties. This setup promises to make browser development easier and the resulting browser products more compact in size and therefore more efficient. This is an especially important consideration in trying to fit a browser into a small handheld device such as a PDA or cell phone. CSS3 will also expand the range of styles supported by the language, including the following:

- *User interfaces*: Adding dynamic and interactive features
- *Accessibility*: Supporting users with disabilities and other special needs
- *Columnar layout*: Giving document authors more page layout options
- *International features*: Providing support for a wide variety of languages and typefaces
- *Mobile devices*: Supporting the device requirements of PDAs and cell phones
- *Scalable vector graphics*: Making it easier for document authors to add graphic elements to their pages

The applicability of these features depends on the support of the market. Because CSS2 is still not completely supported, it is unclear how long it will take after the W3C releases the final specification for CSS3 styles before they are adopted in browsers and other information devices. Document authors need to be aware of compatibility issues between different versions of CSS and the level of support offered by various browsers. In Janet's case, her work is seen only on Tour Nation's intranet. The company has settled on the most recent versions of the major browsers. You tell Janet that if she intends to make her document available to a wider audience, she must test the appearance of her document on a variety of browsers and operating systems.

Attaching a Style Sheet

To replace the default style for XML documents in your users' browsers with one of your own making, you have to create and attach a CSS style sheet to a document that you create. As you saw in Tutorial 1, this can be done by adding the following processing instruction to the document's head:

```
<?xml-stylesheet  type="text/css"  href="url"  ?>
```

where `url` is the URL of the file containing the style sheet. You can include multiple processing instructions in a single XML document to attach several style sheets to the same document. Janet plans to store her style sheet in a file named bike.css. Create that document now and add a processing instruction to the bike.xml file for it.

To create and attach a style sheet:

1. Use your text editor to open **biketxt.css** from the tutorial.05x/tutorial folder. Enter *your name* and *the date* in the comment section at the top of file, and save the file as **bike.css**.

2. Return to the **bike.xml** file in your text editor, and insert the following processing instruction directly above the opening <document> tag (see Figure 5-6):

```
<?xml-stylesheet type="text/css" href="bike.css" ?>
```

Figure 5-6 **Attaching the bike.css style sheet**

```
<?xml-stylesheet type="text/css" href="bike.css" ?>
<document xmlns:html="http://www.w3.org/1999/xhtml">
   <author>Janet Schmidtt</author>
   <date>8/17/2007</date>
   <title><html:img src="tnation.jpg" alt="Tour Nation" /></title>
   <subtitle>Bike Models</subtitle>
```

3. Close the file, saving your changes.
4. Reload bike.xml in your Web browser. Figure 5-7 shows the appearance of the bike.xml document.

Figure 5-7 **Bike document without any defined styles**

Janet Schmidtt 8/17/2007

Tour Nation

Bike Models City Cruiser 100 The City Cruiser 100 is designed to give you the perfect blend of comfort and performance, taking away the bumps and bruises of city roads. Our patented aluminum frame process provides a comfortable frame that is light, durable, and shock absorbing. The City Cruiser 100 includes several comfort features, like a suspension seat post, spring saddle, and adjustable high-rise seat stem. The City Cruiser 100 also includes semi-smooth tires that roll on the pavement, giving the rider plenty of traction while soaking up the bumps. sizes: (L) 16.5", (XL) 18.5", (XXL) 21" frame: Prime Aluminum Comfort Specific fork: Trek high tensile steel ATB wheels: Matrix 550 rims tires: Bontrager Comfort, 26x1.95" f/r shifters: SRAM 5.0 Royale front derailleur: Lancaster C051 rear derailleur: SRAM ESP 4.0 crankset: SunRace FCM36 48/38/28 City Cruiser 200 For those looking for a superior city bike at a reasonable price, the City Cruiser 200 is the answer. As with all City Cruiser models the 200 provides unparalleled performance and comfort. Tour Nation's patented aluminum frame is light, durable, and shock absorbing. The City Cruiser 200 provides a wider gear range than other models in this class, giving you just the right gear for pedaling on any incline. The 200's design puts you in an upright, relaxed riding position that makes pedaling easier and more enjoyable. As with all City Cruiser models, the 200 also includes semi-smooth tires to soak

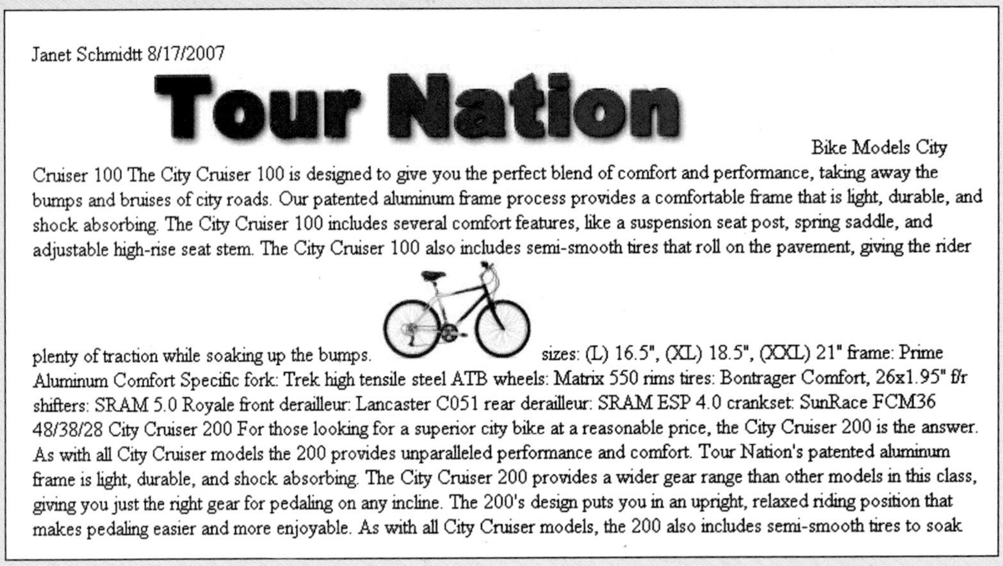

As no styles are defined in the bike.css file, the browser shows only the content of the bike.xml document, without any formatting. Note that the img elements defined in the XHTML namespace appear as inline images in the rendered document. Now that you've created and attached the bike.css style sheet to the bike.xml document, you can begin defining the styles and layout that Janet wants applied. The first step is to identify those elements of the XML document to which you want to apply styles.

Working with Selectors

The syntax of CSS is relatively simple and easy to follow. Each line of the CSS file attaches a collection of styles to an element or group of elements called a **selector**. The general syntax is

```
selector {style1:value1; style2:value2;  ...  }
```

where `selector` is the items in the document that receive the style; `style1`, `style2`, etc., are CSS style attributes; and `value1`, `value2`, etc., are the values applied to those styles. For example, the following CSS style sets the font color of the name element to red:

```
name {color:red}
```

By default, styles are passed from parent elements to their descendant elements. For example, if you set the font color of the model element to red using the style declaration

```
model {color:red}
```

then the font color for the descendant elements of the model element (name, description, features, etc.) is also red.

You'll learn more about the different styles later in this tutorial. For now, examine the syntax used to specify a selector.

Working with Selectors

Reference Window

- To apply a set of style rules to items in an XML document, use the syntax
    `selector {style1:value1; style2:value2; ... }`
  where `selector` is the items in the document that receive the style; `attribute1`, `attribute2`, etc., are CSS style attributes; and `value1`, `value2`, etc., are the values applied to those styles.
- To apply the same style rules to all elements in a document, use the declaration
    `* {style1:value1; style2:value2; ... }`
- To apply the same style rules to a group of elements, use the declaration
    `element1, element2, ... {style1:value1; style2: value2; ... }`
  where `element1`, `element2`, ... and so forth are element names from the XML document.
- To apply styles to the child of a parent element, use the declaration
    `parent > child {style1:value1; style2:value2; ... }`
  where `parent` and `child` are the names of the parent and child elements.

The most common selector is simply the name of an element in an XML document. In the previous code, the font color red is applied only to the contents of the name element and its descendant elements. To apply a red font color to all the elements in the document, you can use the wildcard symbol, *, as in the following style declaration:

```
* {color:red}
```

To apply a style to a group of elements, you separate the element names by commas. For example, the style

```
author, date, title, subtitle {color:red}
```

specifies the font color for only the author, date, title, and subtitle elements. If the element names belong to a namespace, you must declare the namespace and add the namespace prefix using the techniques described in Tutorial 2.

You can also define selectors based on the content of an element, the element's location in the structure of the XML document, or the values contained in attributes associated with the element. Figure 5-8 describes the different forms a selector can take.

Figure 5-8	CSS selector forms

Selector	Description	Example
*	Applies the style to every element in the document	* {color:red}
e	Applies the style to the element e	name {color:red}
e1, e2, ...	Applies the style to each of the named elements	title, subtitle {color:red}
e f	Matches any element f that is a descendant of the element e	models description {color:red}
e > f	Matches any element f that is a direct child of an element e	model > name {color:red}
e + f	Matches any element f that is immediately preceded by a sibling element e	title + subtitle {color:red}
[att]	Matches an element containing the attribute att	name[category] {color:red}
[att="val"]	Matches an element whose att attribute value equals val	name[category="city"] {color:red}
[att~="val"]	Matches an element whose att attribute value is a space-separated list of words, one which is exactly val	name[category~="c"] {color:red}
[att|="val"]	Matches an element whose att attribute value is a hyphen-separated list of words beginning with val	name[category|="c"] {color:red}
[att^="val"]	Matches an element whose att attribute value begins with val (CSS3)	name[category^="c"] {color:red}
[att$="val"]	Matches an element whose att attribute value ends with val (CSS3)	name[category$="y"] {color:red}
[att*="val"]	Matches an element whose att attribute value contains val (CSS3)	name[category*="it"] {color:red}

For example, if a document has two title elements, the style sheet can distinguish one from the other by indicating its relation to a parent element, as in the following style declaration:

```
document > title {color:red}
```

In this case, only the title element whose parent element is document has a red font color; title elements located elsewhere in the document hierarchy do not have this style. Unfortunately, most of the selector forms described in Figure 5-8, while a part of CSS, are not well supported by browsers working in conjunction with XML. At this time, only the following selectors are reliably supported by all browsers:

- *
- *element*
- *element1, element2, ...*
- *parent descendant*

However, new browser versions regularly expand their support for selectors, and in time the complete list of CSS selectors should be supported by all browsers.

Setting the Display Style

As you examine Janet's proposed layout from Figure 5-5, you notice that she places much of the information into distinct sections called **blocks** or **block elements**. For example, one block contains a bulleted list of bike features; another block contains a descriptive paragraph for each bike model. However, if no style is specified for an element, browsers display the content of each element as an **inline element**, so that the document's content appears as one continuous string in line with other document content within the block element. You can set the appearance of an element by using a display style, with the following CSS style:

```
display: type
```

where `type` is one of the CSS displays styles described in Figure 5-9.

CSS display styles   Figure 5-9

Display	Description
block	Display as a block-level element
inline	Display as an inline element
inline-block	Display as an inline element with some of the properties of a block (much like an inline image or a frame)
inherit	Inherit the display property of the element's parent
list-item	Display as a list item
none	Do not display the element
run-in	Display as either an inline or a block-level element, depending on the context
table	Display as a block-level table
inline-table	Display as an inline table
table-caption	Treat as a table caption
table-cell	Treat as a table cell
table-column	Treat as a table column
table-column-group	Treat as a group of table columns
table-footer-group	Treat as a group of table footer rows
table-header-group	Treat as a group of table header rows
table-row	Treat as a table row
table-row-group	Treat as a group of table rows

For example, to display the name element in its own block, separated from other elements in the document, you use the style

```
name {display: block}
```

At the time of this writing, only the block, inline, inherit, list-item, and none display styles are supported by all browsers. You should use the other display styles with caution.

Hiding Elements

You can also use CSS to prevent elements from being displayed on a rendered Web page. This is useful in situations where you want an element to be displayed in a particular output medium (such as the computer screen) but not displayed in another medium (such as printed output). There are two ways of hiding an element. One is to set the value of the display style to "none", as in the following style declaration:

```
author {display: none}
```

This turns off the display of the author element. Alternatively, you can use the visibility style, which has the syntax

```
visibility: type
```

where *type* is visible, hidden, collapse, or inherit (the default). A value of "visible" makes an element visible; the "hidden" value hides the element; a value of "collapse" can be used within a table to prevent a row or column from being displayed; and the "inherit" value causes an element to inherit the visibility style from its parent. Unlike the display style, the visibility style hides an element, but does not remove it from the flow of elements in a page. As shown in Figure 5-10, setting the display style to none not only hides an element, but also removes it from the page flow.

Figure 5-10 ▶ **Comparing the display and visibility styles**

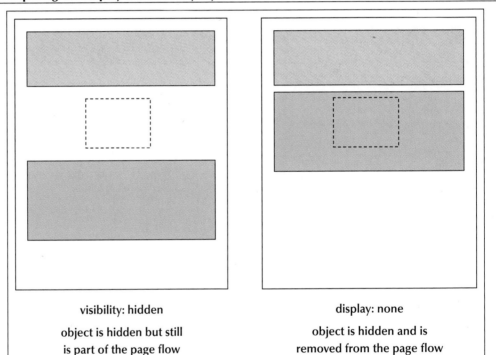

visibility: hidden	display: none
object is hidden but still is part of the page flow	object is hidden and is removed from the page flow

The display: none style is more appropriate for hiding elements in most cases. Use of the visibility: hidden style is usually reserved for scripts in which an element is alternatively hidden and made visible in order to create an animated effect.

You decide to format Janet's document so that all elements in the document appear as blocks, except the author element, which you'll hide; the feature element, which you'll set up as a list item; and the fName element, which you'll display inline.

Setting the Display Style

- To display an element's content inline with the contents of other elements in the document, use the style
  ```
  display: inline
  ```
- To display an element's content in a block, use the style
  ```
  display: block
  ```
- To hide an element's content on the page, use the style
  ```
  display: none
  ```

To set the display styles:

1. Return to **bike.css** in your text editor.

2. At the bottom of the document, enter the following display styles (see Figure 5-11):

   ```
   *          {display: block}
   author     {display: none}
   feature    {display: list-item}
   fName      {display: inline}
   ```

Setting the display styles   **Figure 5-11**

```
*          {display: block}
author     {display: none}
feature    {display: list-item}
fName      {display: inline}
```

3. Save your changes to the file, and reload **bike.xml** in your Web browser. Figure 5-12 shows the revised layout of the page.

Elements displayed in blocks, lists, and inline styles   **Figure 5-12**

8/17/2007

Tour Nation

Bike Models
City Cruiser 100
The City Cruiser 100 is designed to give you the perfect blend of comfort and performance, taking away the bumps and bruises of city roads. Our patented aluminum frame process provides a comfortable frame that is light, durable, and shock absorbing. The City Cruiser 100 includes several comfort features, like a suspension seat post, spring saddle, and adjustable high-rise seat stem. The City Cruiser 100 also includes semi-smooth tires that roll on the pavement, giving the rider plenty of traction while soaking up the bumps.

sizes: (L) 16.5", (XL) 18.5", (XXL) 21"
frame: Prime Aluminum Comfort Specific
fork: Trek high tensile steel ATB
wheels: Matrix 550 rims
tires: Bontrager Comfort, 26x1.95" f/r
shifters: SRAM 5.0 Royale
front derailleur: Lancaster C051
rear derailleur: SRAM ESP 4.0
crankset: SunRace FCM36 48/38/28

This style sheet illustrates an important point regarding style precedence. When two styles can be applied to the same element, the style appearing later in the document overrides earlier styles. Thus, the style sheet initially defines every element in the document as a block element but then overrules this style for the author, feature, and fName elements using the additional styles that occur later in the style sheet.

The author's name now no longer appears on the Web page, and the contents of the fName attribute (sizes, frame, fork, etc.) appear inline with the associated text for those features. However, the features lists, while formatted with the list-item style, do not look any different than the other block-level elements in the document. Your next task is to format the features lists so that they appear as bulleted lists.

Formatting Lists

CSS allows you to determine the type of marker associated with each list item and control the placement of the list markers. To specify the list marker use the style

```
list-style-type: type
```

where *type* defines the marker that appears with each list-item. Figure 5-13 describes the different type values supported by CSS.

Figure 5-13 | **List style types**

list-style-type	Marker
disc	•
circle	○
square	■
decimal	1, 2, 3, 4, ...
lower-alpha	a, b, c, d, ...
upper-alpha	A, B, C, D, ...
lower-roman	i, ii, iii, iv, ...
upper-roman	I, II, III, IV, ...
none	

If none of the CSS list markers meet your needs, you can substitute your own using the style

```
list-style-image: url(url)
```

where *url* is the URL of an image file containing the marker image.

Finally, the placement of the marker can be set using the style

```
list-style-position: position
```

where *position* is either inside or outside. If the marker is placed inside, any wrapped text in the list lines up with the placement of the marker. If the marker is placed outside, the list item text is wrapped next to the marker. Figure 5-14 illustrates the difference between two for a given list.

Marker positions Figure 5-14

◇ sizes: (L) 16.5", (XL) 18.5", (XXL) 21"	◇ sizes: (L) 16.5", (XL) 18.5", (XXL) 21"
◇ frame: Prime Aluminum Comfort Specific	◇ frame: Prime Aluminum Comfort Specific
◇ fork: Trek high tensile steel ATB	◇ fork: Trek high tensile steel ATB
◇ wheels: Matrix 550 rims	◇ wheels: Matrix 550 rims
◇ tires: Bontrager Comfort, 26x1.95" f/r	◇ tires: Bontrager Comfort, 26x1.95" f/r
◇ shifters: SRAM 5.0 Royale	◇ shifters: SRAM 5.0 Royale
◇ front derailleur: Lancaster C051	◇ front derailleur: Lancaster C051
list-style-position: outside	list-style-position: inside

The three CSS styles for lists can be combined into the following single style:

```
list-style: type position url(url)
```

If you don't suggest an image file for the list marker, browsers use the marker specified with the *type* parameter. Janet suggests that you display each of the items in the feature list using a square list marker placed inside of the list item text.

To format the features list:

1. Return to **bike.css** in your text editor.

2. Within the style declaration for the feature element, insert the following styles (see Figure 5-15). Note that you have to separate one style from another with a semicolon.

   ```
   ; list-style: square inside
   ```

Setting the list style type and position Figure 5-15

```
*          {display: block}
author     {display: none}
feature    {display: list-item; list-style: square inside}
fName      {display: inline}
```

3. Save your changes to bike.css, and then refresh **bike.xml** in your browser. The features list now appears with a square bullet, as shown in Figure 5-16.

Features list with square markers Figure 5-16

- sizes: (L) 16.5", (XL) 18.5", (XXL) 21"
- frame: Prime Aluminum Comfort Specific
- fork: Trek high tensile steel ATB
- wheels: Matrix 550 rims
- tires: Bontrager Comfort, 26x1.95" f/r
- shifters: SRAM 5.0 Royale
- front derailleur: Lancaster C051
- rear derailleur: SRAM ESP 4.0
- crankset: SunRace FCM36 48/38/28

Creating a List

- To display an element as an item in a list, use the style
  ```
  display: list-item
  ```
- To control the appearance of the markers in a list, use the style
  ```
  list-style: type position url(url)
  ```
  where *type* is the type of marker that appears with each list-item, *position* indicates the position of the markers relative to the list text, and *url* is the URL of an image file to be used in the list. The type style can have the values disc, circle, square, decimal, lower-alpha, upper-alpha, lower-roman, and upper-roman. The position style can have the values inside and outside.

Lists are a special class of block elements. In the following tasks, you'll work with general properties that apply to all blocks.

Sizing Block Elements

One of the features of block elements is the ability to resize them and place them at particular locations on the Web page. As you refer to Janet's proposed layout, shown in Figure 5-5, you notice that she wants the date placed in the upper-right corner of the page, and she wants the description element reduced in width and placed in the right margin of each model block. Before you can start moving these elements around, you must study the methods used to resize them.

Setting an Element's Width

To set the width of a block element, use the style

```
width: value
```

where *value* is expressed as a percentage of the width of the parent element, or in absolute units. CSS supports the following **absolute units** of measurement:

- millimeter (mm)
- centimeter (cm)
- inch (in)
- point (pt)
- pica (pc)
- pixel (px)

Thus, to set the width of the model element to 4 pixels, you use the style

```
model {width: 4px}
```

If you don't specify a width for a block element, its width is the same as the width of the parent element that contains it.

Janet wants to set the exact width of the major elements in the document. She asks you to set the width of the root document element to 720 pixels, the width of the description element to 400 pixels, and the width of the features elements to 250 pixels. The other block elements in the document are, by default, set to the widths of their parent elements.

To set element widths in the document:

1. Return to **bike.css** in your text editor.

2. Insert the following line of code below the line that sets the default display style to block:

```
document {width: 720px}
```

3. Above the style for the feature element, insert the following styles:

```
description {width: 400px}
features    {width: 250px}
```

Figure 5-17 shows the revised style code.

Setting the element widths ◄ **Figure 5-17**

```
*           {display: block}
document    {width: 720px}
author      {display: none}
description {width: 400px}
features    {width: 250px}
feature     {display: list-item; list-style: square inside}
fName       {display: inline}
```

4. Save your changes to the bike.css file.

Setting an Element's Height

To set the height of an element, use the style

```
height: value
```

where `value` is the height of the element, specified either as a percentage of the parent element or in absolute units. If you do not specify a height, browsers expand the height of the block until all the element content is visible.

Handling Content Overflow

If you specify a height for an element, you run the risk of not being able to fit the content into a defined space. In this case, you can control how browsers handle extra content by using the style

```
overflow: type
```

where `type` is either visible (the default), hidden, scroll, or auto. A value of "visible" instructs browsers to increase the height of the element to fit the extra content. A value of "hidden" hides the extra content. Both the "scroll" and "auto" values instruct browsers to display scroll bars to view the extra content. The "auto" option adds scroll bars only when needed, while the "scroll" option adds scroll bars whether they are needed or not (see Figure 5-18).

Figure 5-18 ▶ **Setting the overflow style values**

The City Cruiser 100 is designed to give you the perfect blend of comfort and performance, taking away the bumps and bruises of city roads. Our patented aluminum frame process provides a comfortable frame that is light, durable, and shock absorbing. The City Cruiser 100 includes several comfort features, like a suspension seat post, spring saddle, and adjustable high-rise seat stem. The City Cruiser 100 also includes semi-smooth tires that roll on the pavement, giving the rider plenty of traction while soaking up the bumps.

`overflow: visible`

The City Cruiser 100 is designed to give you the perfect blend of comfort and performance, taking away the bumps and bruises of city roads. Our patented aluminum frame process provides a comfortable frame that is light, durable, and shock absorbing. The City Cruiser 100 includes several comfort features, like a suspension seat post, spring saddle, and adjustable high-rise seat stem. The City Cruiser 100 also includes semi-smooth tires that

`overflow: hidden`

The City Cruiser 100 is designed to give you the perfect blend of comfort and performance, taking away the bumps and bruises of city roads. Our patented aluminum frame process provides a comfortable frame that is light, durable, and shock absorbing. The City Cruiser 100 includes several comfort features, like a suspension seat post, spring saddle, and

`overflow: scroll`

The City Cruiser 100 is designed to give you the perfect blend of comfort and performance, taking away the bumps and bruises of city roads. Our patented aluminum frame process provides a comfortable frame that is light, durable, and shock absorbing. The City Cruiser 100 includes several comfort features, like a suspension seat post, spring saddle, and adjustable high-rise seat stem. The City Cruiser 100 also

`overflow: auto`

Related to the overflow style is the clip style. The clip style allows a Web designer to define a rectangular area through which the contents of an element can be viewed. Any content that falls outside of the clip area is hidden. The syntax for the clip style is

`clip: rect(top, right, bottom, left)`

where *top*, *right*, *bottom*, and *left* define the coordinates of the rectangular region. For example, a clip value of rect (25px, 250px, 200px, 15px) defines a clip region whose top and bottom edges are 25 and 200 pixels from the top of the element, and whose right and left edges are 250 and 15 pixels from the left edge of the element (see Figure 5-19).

Figure 5-19 ▶ **Clipping an element's content**

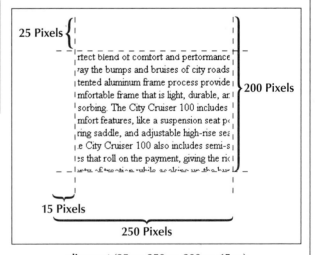

The City Cruiser 100 is designed to give you the perfect blend of comfort and performance, taking away the bumps and bruises of city roads. Our patented aluminum frame process provides a comfortable frame that is light, durable, and shock absorbing. The City Cruiser 100 includes several comfort features, like a suspension seat post, spring saddle, and adjustable high-rise seat stem. The City Cruiser 100 also includes semi-smooth tires that roll on the payment, giving the rider plenty of traction while soaking up the bumps.

full element content

25 Pixels

200 Pixels

15 Pixels

250 Pixels

clip: rect (25px, 250px, 200px, 15px)

The top, right, bottom, and left values can also be set to "auto," which shifts the specified edge of the clipping region to the edge of the element. For example, a clip value of rect (10px, auto, 125px, 75px) creates a clipping rectangle whose right edge matches the right edge of the element, while the rest of the edges are clipped.

The clip style can be used only with absolute positioning (a topic you'll learn about shortly). Janet does not need to use the height, overflow, or clip styles with her document.

Positioning Elements

Now that you've learned how to resize a block-level element, you can focus on placing an element in a specific location on a page. To position an element with CSS, use the style

```
position: type; top:value; right:value; bottom:value; left:value
```

where *type* indicates the type of positioning applied to the element, and the *top*, *right*, *bottom*, and *left* styles indicate the coordinates of the top, right, bottom, and left edges of the element.

Coordinates can be expressed as absolute units or as a percentage of the parent element. For example, to center the upper-left corner of an element within its parent, use the style

```
top: 50%; left: 50%
```

Assuming that an element has a fixed size, only the location of the element's top or bottom edge in the vertical direction and left or right edge in the horizontal direction must be specified. The most common practice by page designers is to specify only the top and left styles.

There are four possible values for the position type: absolute, relative, fixed, and static.

An **absolute position** places an element at defined coordinates within its parent element. In most cases, the parent element is the document window itself, so the absolute position coordinates refer to the coordinates within the window.

The coordinates are specified with respect to the upper-left corner of the parent element. A positive top value places the object down from the top edge; a negative value moves the object above the top edge of the parent. Similarly, a positive left value moves the element to the right of the left edge, while a negative value moves the element to the left of the parent. If you specify only one of the coordinates, such as the top coordinate, the remaining coordinate is assumed to be in the default position. For example, the style

```
position: absolute; left: 400px;
```

places the element 400 pixels to the right of the left edge of the parent element, but the top coordinate keeps its default value.

Figure 5-20 shows an object placed 100 pixels to the right and 150 pixels down from the upper-left corner of its parent. The style to move this element is

```
position: absolute; left: 100px; top: 150px
```

Figure 5-20 ▶ Absolute positioning

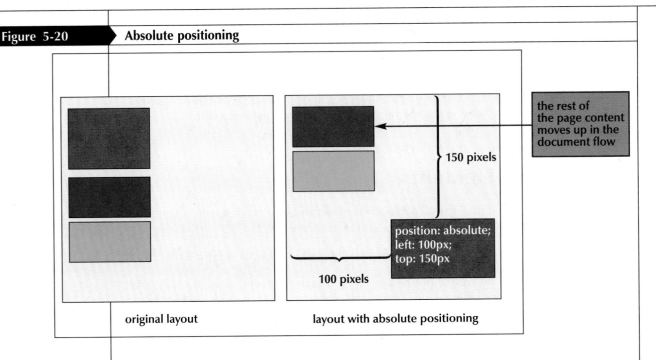

Absolute positioning essentially takes an element out of the normal flow in the document layout. Other elements in the document move up in the flow of the document layout, occupying the space that would have been taken by the absolutely positioned object.

An alternative approach is to offset an element using a **relative position**. This approach moves the element a specific distance from where it would have been placed in the layout. For example, the element shown in Figure 5-21 is offset 50 pixels to the right and 75 pixels down from the original location on the page. The style to shift the element from its default position is

```
position: relative; left: 50px; top: 75px
```

Figure 5-21 ▶ Relative positioning

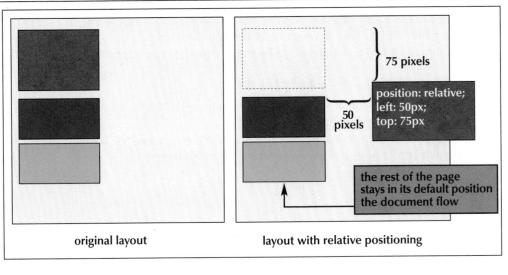

Unlike absolute positioning, relative positioning does not affect the placement of subsequent elements on the page. Other elements are placed at their default locations just as if no relative positioning had taken place. Relative positioning affects only the element being moved.

A **fixed position** places an element at a fixed location in the display window. The element remains in this location and does not scroll with other elements on the page. A **static position** places an object in its natural position in the flow of the document, as determined by the browser. In this case, you are allowing the browser, or whatever application is rendering the document, to determine the element's location. Therefore, you do not specify a top, right, bottom, or left value when using static positioning. This is the same as using no positioning styles at all.

Reference Window

Positioning an Element

- To place an element at defined coordinates within its parent element (usually the display window), use the style

  ```
  position: absolute; top: value; left: value;
  ```
  where the top and left styles define the coordinate of the upper-left corner of the element.
- To offset an element from its default location within its parent element, use the style

  ```
  position: relative; top: value; left: value;
  ```
  where the top and left styles define the distance down and to the left from the element's default location.

Janet wants the contents of the date element to be placed in the upper-right portion of the page. You decide to position the element there using absolute positioning, placing it 660 pixels from the left and 0 pixels down from the edge of the display window.

To position the date element:

1. Below the style declaration for the author element, insert the following style declaration, as shown in Figure 5-22:

   ```
   date {position: absolute; top: 0px; left: 660px}
   ```

Placing the date element ◄ **Figure 5-22**

```
*              {display: block}
document       {width: 720px}
author         {display: none}
date           {position: absolute; top: 0px; left: 660px}
description     {width: 400px}
features       {width: 250px}
feature        {display: list-item; list-style: square inside}
fName          {display: inline}
```

2. Save your changes to the file.

3. Reload **bike.xml** in your Web browser, and verify that the date element is now positioned at the upper-right corner of the screen at the coordinates (660, 0).

Floating an Element

Another way to position an element is to float it. When a browser renders a document, the default behavior is to display one block-level element after another on the page. **Floating** an element places it along the left or right margin of the page, allowing subsequent blocks to flow around it. The style to float an element is

```
float: margin
```

where *margin* is either left or right. Figure 5-23 shows an example of a resized block-level element that is floating on the right margin of the page.

Figure 5-23　**Floating an element**

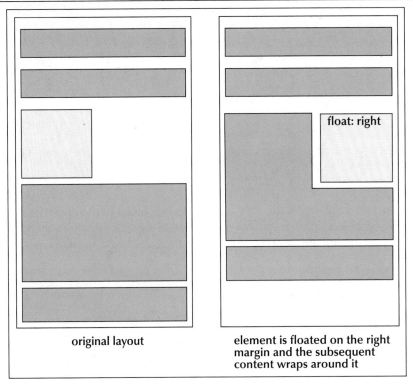

original layout

element is floated on the right margin and the subsequent content wraps around it

You can prevent an element from wrapping around a floating element using the style

```
clear: margin
```

where *margin* is either left, right, or both. For example, if the value of the clear style is set to "right," an element is not rendered on the page until the right margin is clear of all floating elements. A clear value of "both" requires both margins to be clear. Figure 5-24 illustrates the flow of block-level elements when both the float and clear styles are used.

The clear style Figure 5-24

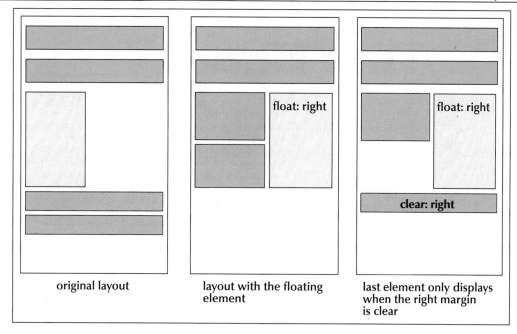

original layout

layout with the floating element

last element only displays when the right margin is clear

Janet wants the description element to float along the right margin of the document element with the features list and the model image flowing past to the left of the description.

To float the description element:

1. Return to the **bike.css** file in your text editor.

2. Within the style declaration for the description element, insert the following style (be sure to separate this style from the preceding style using a semicolon). Figure 5-25 shows the revised file.

   ```
   float: right
   ```

Setting the float style Figure 5-25

```
*            {display: block}
document     {width: 720px}
author       {display: none}
date         {position: absolute; top: 0px; left: 660px}
description  {width: 400px; float: right}
features     {width: 250px}
feature      {display: list-item; list-style: square inside}
fName        {display: inline}
```

3. Save your changes to the file. If you want to take a break before starting the next session, you may close the style sheet file.

4. Reload **bike.xml** in your Web browser. Figure 5-26 shows the revised layout of the document.

Figure 5-26   **Revised document layout**

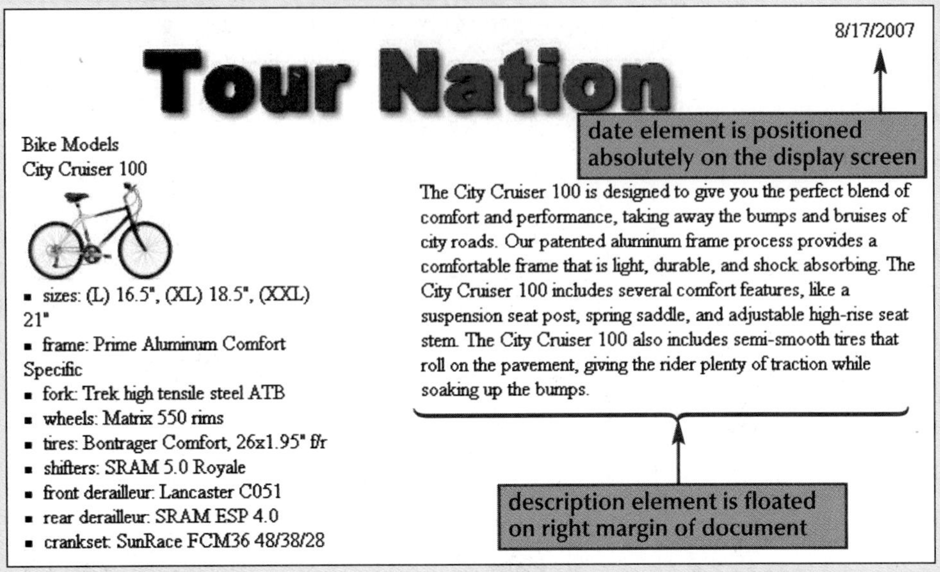

date element is positioned absolutely on the display screen

description element is floated on right margin of document

5. If you plan to take a break after this session, you may close your Web browser.

Reference Window

Floating an Element

- To place an element along its parent element's left or right margin and flow any content that follows around the element, use the style
    ```
    float: margin
    ```
  where *margin* is either left or right.
- To prevent an element from wrapping around a floating element, use the style
    ```
    clear: margin;
    ```
  where *margin* is left, right, or both.

Stacking Elements

The ability to move elements to different locations on a page can lead to overlapping elements. By default, elements that are defined later in an XML document are placed on top of earlier elements. To specify a different stacking order, use the style

```
z-index: value
```

where *value* is a positive or negative integer, or the value "auto". Elements are stacked based on their z-index values, with the highest z-index values placed on top. A value of "auto" uses the default stacking order. Figure 5-27 shows the effect of the z-index style on the stacking of several different elements.

Stacking elements ◄ **Figure 5-27**

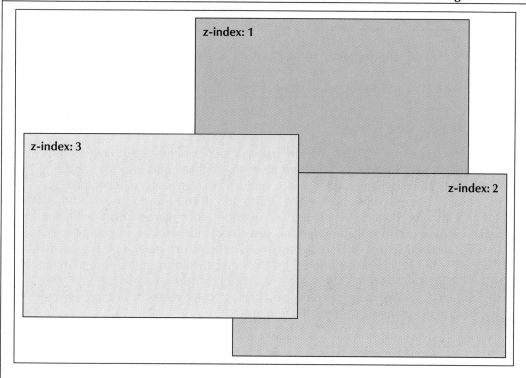

Note that the z-index style is applied only when elements share the same parent; it has no effect on elements with different parents.

At this point, you've finished your work on the page layout. In the next session, you'll learn how to use CSS to modify the appearance of a page by working with fonts, background colors, borders, and margins.

Session 5.1 Quick Check

Review

1. What command would you use in an XML document to attach the document to a style sheet named "styles.css"?
2. What style declaration would you use to apply the color red to the document element?
3. What selector would you use to select the model element that is a direct descendant (child) of the models element?
4. What style declaration would you use to display the cName element as an inline item?
5. What style declaration would you use to display the notes element as an open-circle bulleted list, with the bullet marker outside of the list text?
6. How would you set the width of the notes element to 300 pixels?
7. What style would you use to place the notes element at 10 pixels down and 50 pixels to the right of its default position using absolute positioning?
8. How would you align the notes element with the left margin of its parent element?

Working with Color Styles

Janet has reviewed your work from the last session, and she is pleased that you were able to use CSS to control the layout of the page. At this point in the project, she wants you to make the page more readable and interesting by adding some color.

Applying a Font Color

Color can be expressed in CSS by a color name or a color value. **Color names** are descriptive names given to colors and are easier to use than color values. However, CSS supports only 16 color names: aqua, black, blue, fuchsia, gray, green, lime, maroon, navy, olive, purple, red, silver, teal, white, and yellow. If you wanted to use a color name not in this list, you could use one of the 142 extended color names supported by the Internet Explorer and Mozilla browsers; however, because these are not part of the CSS standard, it is possible that other browsers would not correctly interpret these extended color names. You can find the complete list of extended color names at several different sites on the Web.

For access to a wider range of colors, you can use **color values**. CSS expresses color values as a triplet of numbers, using the format

```
rgb(red, green, blue)
```

where `red`, `green`, and `blue` are numeric values indicating the intensity of the primary colors red, green, and blue. The value of each component ranges from 0 (lowest intensity) to 255 (highest intensity). As you would expect, the color red has the color value rgb(255, 0, 0), green has the value rgb(0, 255, 0), and blue has the value rgb(0, 0, 255). White, being a mixture of all three primary colors at their highest intensity, has a color value of rgb(255, 255, 255), and black, the absence of the three primary colors, has a color value of rgb(0, 0, 0). Other colors are mixtures of the three primary colors. For example, the color teal is a mixture of green and blue at moderate intensity and therefore has a color value of rgb(0, 128, 128). Over 16 million colors, more colors than the human eye can distinguish, can be represented by the color value system. If you're not sure of a color's value, you can usually find this information in the color dialog boxes of most graphic design and image-editing applications.

Color values can also be expressed as percentages as follows:

```
rgb(red%, green%, blue%)
```

where `red%`, `green%`, and `blue%` specify the percentages of red, green, and blue in the desired color. For example, the color white is defined as rgb(100%, 100%, 100%), and the color teal is defined as rgb(0, 50%, 50%) under this system.

Finally, color values are also often expressed in hexadecimal format using the syntax

```
#rrggbb
```

where `rr`, `gg`, and `bb` are the hexadecimal representations of the color values. The color white, for example, has a hexadecimal representation of #FFFFFF.

Once you determine how to set the color, you use the following style to set the font color:

```
color: color
```

where `color` is either a color name or a color value.

Janet wants the features list entries for each bike displayed in a blue font, but with the name of each feature (sizes, frame, fork, and so forth) displayed in a red font. Add these color styles to bike.css.

To set the font color:

1. If necessary, reopen **bike.css** in your text editor.

2. In the style declaration for the features element, enter the style:

```
color: blue
```

3. In the style declaration for the fName element, enter the style:

```
color: red
```

Figure 5-28 shows the revised file. Be sure to separate the styles you add in Steps 2 and 3 from the others using a semicolon.

Setting the font color ◂ **Figure 5-28**

```
*            {display: block}
document     {width: 720px}
author       {display: none}
date         {position: absolute; top: 0px; left: 660px}
description  {width: 400px; float:right}
features     {width: 250px; color: blue}
feature      {display: list-item; list-style: square inside}
fName        {display: inline; color: red}
```

4. Save your changes to the style sheet.

5. Reopen **bike.xml** in your Web browser, and verify that the feature names appear in red and the feature text appears in blue, as shown in Figure 5-29.

Font colors in the features list ◂ **Figure 5-29**

City Cruiser 100

- sizes: (L) 16.5", (XL) 18.5", (XXL) 21"
- frame: Prime Aluminum Comfort Specific
- fork: Trek high tensile steel ATB
- wheels: Matrix 550 rims
- tires: Bontrager Comfort, 26x1.95" f/r
- shifters: SRAM 5.0 Royale
- front derailleur: Lancaster C051
- rear derailleur: SRAM ESP 4.0
- crankset: SunRace FCM36 48/38/28

Working with Color

- To set the font color of an element, use the style
  ```
  color: color
  ```
  where *color* is a color name or a color value.
- To set the background color of an element, use the style
  ```
  background-color: color
  ```

Applying a Background Color

The background of an element can also appear in a color using the style

```
background-color: color
```

where *color* is either a color name or a color value. Janet wants you to change the background color of the features list to ivory.

To set the background color:

1. Return to the **bike.css** file in your text editor.

2. Add the following style to the features element (see Figure 5-30):

   ```
   background-color: ivory
   ```

Figure 5-30 | **Setting the background color**

```
*                  {display: block}
document           {width: 720px}
author             {display: none}
date               {position: absolute; top: 0px; left: 660px}
description         {width: 400px; float:right}
features           {width: 250px; color: blue; background-color: ivory}
feature            {display: list-item; list-style: square inside}
fName              {display: inline; color: red}
```

3. Save your changes to the file, and reload **bike.xml** in your Web browser. Figure 5-31 shows the features list with the ivory background.

Figure 5-31 | **Ivory background color in the features list**

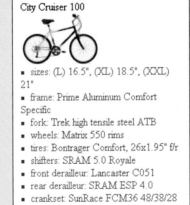

City Cruiser 100

- sizes: (L) 16.5", (XL) 18.5", (XXL) 21"
- frame: Prime Aluminum Comfort Specific
- fork: Trek high tensile steel ATB
- wheels: Matrix 550 rims
- tires: Bontrager Comfort, 26x1.95" f/r
- shifters: SRAM 5.0 Royale
- front derailleur: Lancaster C051
- rear derailleur: SRAM ESP 4.0
- crankset: SunRace FCM36 48/38/28

Janet likes the text and background colors you added to the document. To enhance the document further, she wants to see more space between information on the different bike models. To add this space, you'll work with some additional styles of block-level elements.

Working with Borders, Margins, and Padding

For each block element, CSS defines a **box model** that identifies the different parts of the block. The box model comprises four parts (see Figure 5-32):

- The *margin* between the block element and other elements
- The *border* of the block
- The *padding* between the element's content and the border
- The *element content*

Parts of block elements in the box model ◄ Figure 5-32

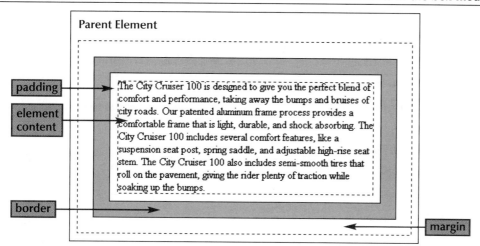

Janet wants you to increase the size of the name element's top margin in order to offset one bike model from another on the Web page.

Working with Margins

CSS supports four styles that can be used to control the margin size of a block-level element. These styles are

```
margin-top: value
margin-right: value
margin-bottom: value
margin-left: value
```

where `value` is the size of the margin expressed in absolute units or as a percentage of the width of the parent element. You can also use a value of auto, which instructs the browser to determine the margin size. For example, to create margins of 10 pixels on each side and 5 pixels above and below the title element, you would use the following style declaration:

```
title {margin-top: 5px; margin-right: 10px; margin-bottom: 5px;
margin-left: 10px}
```

Margin sizes can also be negative to crowd or overlap elements on a page.

The four margin styles can be combined into the single style

```
margin: top right bottom left
```

where *top*, *right*, *bottom*, and *left* are the sizes of the corresponding margins. Thus, to set the margins of the title element using a single style, you could enter the following:

```
title {margin: 5px 10px 5px 10px}
```

If you include only three values in the combined style they are assigned to the top, right, and bottom margins, and browsers match the size of the left and right margins. If only two values are specified, they are applied to the top and right margins, with the bottom and left margins matching those two values. If only one value is entered, browsers apply that size to all four margins. Thus, the following style declaration is a more compact way of setting the top and bottom margins to 5 pixels and the left and right margins to 10 pixels:

```
title {margin: 5px 10px}
```

You decide to set the size of the margin around the model element to 10 pixels in order to increase the space between one model description and another.

To set the size of the margin around the model element:

1. Return to the **bike.css** file in your text editor.

2. Below the style declaration for the date element insert the following style declaration for the model element (see Figure 5-33):

   ```
   model {margin: 10px}
   ```

Figure 5-33	Setting the margin size around the model element

```
*              {display: block}
document       {width: 720px}
author         {display: none}
date           {position: absolute; top: 0px; left: 660px}
model          {margin: 10px}
description {width: 400px; float: right}
features       {width: 250px; color: blue; background-color: ivory}
feature        {display: list-item; list-style: square inside}
fName          {display: inline; color: red}
```

3. Save your changes to the file, and reload **bike.xml** in your browser. Verify that the space between bike models is increased.

Working with Borders

You can create a border around any element, and define the thickness, color, and style for a border. Styles can be applied to individual borders, or to all four borders at once. Figure 5-34 describes the various CSS border styles.

Border styles ◀ Figure 5-34

Border style	Description	Notes
border-top-width: *value*	Width of the top border	Where *value* is the size of the border in absolute units, as a percentage of the width of the parent element, or defined with the keywords "thin," "medium," or "thick"
border-right-width: *value*	Width of the right border	
border-bottom-width: *value*	Width of the bottom border	
border-left-width: *value*	Width of the left border	
border-width: *top right bottom left*	Width of any or all of the borders	
border-top-color: *color*	Color of the top border	Where *color* is a color name or a color value
border-right-color: *color*	Color of the right border	
border-bottom-color: *color*	Color of the bottom border	
border-left-color: *color*	Color of the left border	
border-color: *top right bottom left*	Color of any or all of the borders	
border-top-style: *style*	Style of the top border	Where *style* is one of the nine defined border styles
border-right-style: *style*	Style of the right border	
border-bottom-style: *style*	Style of the bottom border	
border-left-style: *style*	Style of the left border	
border-style: *top right bottom left*	Style of any or all of the borders	

Border widths can be expressed using units of length, or with the keywords "thin," "medium," or "thick." The border color is defined using a color name or value. For the border style, CSS supports the nine different styles described in Figure 5-35.

Border style types ◀ Figure 5-35

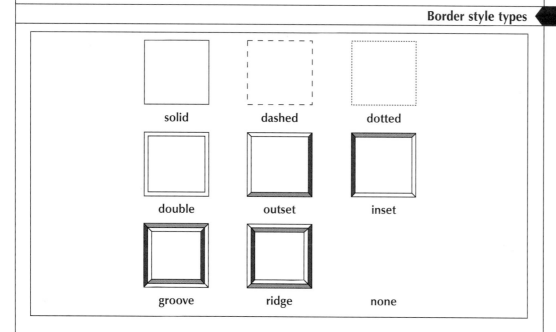

For example, to place a double border around the model element, you would use the style declaration

```
model {border-style: double}
```

All the border styles can be combined into a single-style declaration using

```
border: width style color
```

Thus, to create a 5-pixel blue, dotted border around the model element, you could use the style declaration

```
model {border-width: 5px; border-style: dotted; border-color: blue}
```

or

```
model {border: 5px dotted blue}
```

To work with individual borders, you can identify which border you want to format using the styles

```
border-top: width style color
border-right: width style color
border-bottom: width style color
border-left: width style color
```

Janet wants you to add the following borders to her document:

- A 2-pixel solid purple border below the title element
- A 7-pixel outset border around the model element displayed in the color value rgb(255, 128, 255)
- A 1-pixel solid black border below the name element
- A 2-pixel sold purple border around the features element

To add these borders to the bike style sheet:

1. Return to the **bike.css** file in your text editor.

2. Below the style declaration for the date element, insert the following style declaration:

   ```
   title {border-bottom: 2px solid purple}
   ```

3. Add the following style to the model element (be sure to separate this style from the margin style with a semicolon):

   ```
   border: 7px outset rgb(255,128,255)
   ```

4. Below the model styles, add the following style declaration for the name element:

   ```
   name {border-bottom: 1px solid black}
   ```

5. Finally, add the following border style to the features element (be sure to separate the border style from the background-color style with a semicolon):

   ```
   border: 2px solid purple
   ```

   Figure 5-36 highlights the newly added styles.

```
*               {display: block}
document        {width: 720px}
author          {display: none}
date            {position: absolute; top: 0px; left: 660px}
title           {border-bottom: 2px solid purple}
model           {margin: 10px; border: 7px outset rgb(255,128,255)}
name            {border-bottom: 1px solid black}
description     {width: 400px; float: right}
features        {width: 250px; color: blue; background-color: ivory; border: 2px solid purple}
feature         {display: list-item; list-style: square inside}
fName           {display: inline; color: red}
```

▶ **6.** Save your changes to the file, and reload **bike.xml** in your Web browser. Figure 5-37 shows the borders added around the elements of the document.

8/17/2007

Tour Nation

Bike Models

City Cruiser 100

- sizes: (L) 16.5", (XL) 18.5", (XXL) 21"
- frame: Prime Aluminum Comfort Specific
- fork: Trek high tensile steel ATB
- wheels: Matrix 550 rims
- tires: Bontrager Comfort, 26x1.95" f/r
- shifters: SRAM 5.0 Royale
- front derailleur: Lancaster C051
- rear derailleur: SRAM ESP 4.0
- crankset: SunRace FCM36 48/38/28

The City Cruiser 100 is designed to give you the perfect blend of comfort and performance, taking away the bumps and bruises of city roads. Our patented aluminum frame process provides a comfortable frame that is light, durable, and shock absorbing. The City Cruiser 100 includes several comfort features, like a suspension seat post, spring saddle, and adjustable high-rise seat stem. The City Cruiser 100 also includes semi-smooth tires that roll on the pavement, giving the rider plenty of traction while soaking up the bumps.

Janet likes the effect of adding borders to the different elements on the page but feels that some of the text is too close to the borders, making the text difficult to read. She wants you to correct this situation.

Working with Padding

To increase the space between an element's content and its border, you increase the size of the padding for the block. This is done using any of the following styles:

```
padding-top: value
padding-right: value
padding-bottom: value
padding-left: value
padding: top right bottom left
```

where the padding values can be expressed either in absolute units or as a percentage of the width of the block-level element. As with the combined margin style discussed earlier, you can enter less than four of the top, right, bottom, or left values, and the browser matches the opposite sides. For example, to set the padding of all sides to 5 pixels, you would use the style

```
padding: 5px
```

You decide to set the padding of the following elements in the rendered page:

- The model element with 7 pixels of padding
- The features element with 5 pixels of padding

To set the padding size:

1. Return to the **bike.css** file in your text editor, and add the following style to the model element:

   padding: 7px

2. Add the following style to the features element:

   padding: 5px

   Be sure to separate the styles with a semicolon. Figure 5-38 shows the revised styles in the bike.css style sheet.

Figure 5-38 | Setting the padding size

```
*              {display: block}
document       {width: 720px}
author         {display: none}
date           {position: absolute; top: 0px; left: 660px}
title          {border-bottom: 2px solid purple}
model          {margin: 10px; border: 7px outset rgb(255,128,255); padding: 7px}
name           {border-bottom: 1px solid black}
description    {width: 400px; float: right}
features       {width: 250px; color: blue; background-color: ivory; border: 2px solid purple;
                padding: 5px}
feature        {display: list-item; list-style: square inside}
fName          {display: inline; color: red}
```

3. Save your changes, and reload **bike.xml** in your Web browser. Verify that there is now more space between the content and the borders in the model and features elements.

Adding Background Images

There are two ways to add graphic images to a rendered XML document. One is to create a compound document combining elements from the XML vocabulary with inline images from the XHTML vocabulary. Janet has already done this by adding inline images for the company logo and the various bike models. Another way is to add a background image to an element.

Almost any element can appear with a background image, and four properties can be set with a background image:

- The source of the image file
- The placement of the image in the background of the element
- How the image is repeated across the background of the element
- Whether the background image scrolls with the element or remains fixed

To specify the source of a background image file, use the style

```
background-image: url(url)
```

where `url` is the location of the image file. By default, background images are **tiled**, or repeated, both horizontally and vertically until they occupy the entire background space of the element. You can control how browsers tile an image using the style

```
background-repeat: type
```

where `type` equals repeat, repeat-x, repeat-y, or no-repeat. The default value of repeat tiles an image both horizontally and vertically. The values repeat-x and repeat-y tile an image horizontally or vertically, respectively. A value of no-repeat displays an image once with no tiling.

Background images are placed in the upper-left corner of the element space by default, and then repeated from there if tiling is in effect. You can place a background image in a different location using the style

```
background-position: horizontal vertical
```

where `horizontal` and `vertical` are the horizontal and vertical coordinates of the upper-left corner of the image. Placing a background image operates the same way as placing a block-level element inside of its parent. For example, the style

```
background-position: 30px 50px
```

places the background image 30 pixels to the right and 50 pixels down from the upper-left corner of the element space. If you specify one value, a browser applies the value to both the horizontal and vertical coordinates.

For a more general description of the image position, you can use a combination of six keywords: left, center, right (for the horizontal position); and top, center, bottom (for the vertical position). You can also define the position of the image as a percentage of the width and height of the element. For example, the style

```
background-position: 50% 50%
```

places the background image at the center of the element.

By default, background images scroll with the element as the page scrolls through the browser display window. You can change this behavior using the style

```
background-attachment: attach
```

where `attach` is either scroll (the default) to scroll the image with the page, or fixed to place the image at a fixed location in the display window. Fixed background images are often used to create the illusion of a **watermark**, which is a translucent graphic impressed into the very fabric of paper, often used in specialized stationery.

Setting a Background Image

- To add a background image to an element, use the style
  ```
  background-image: url(url)
  ```
  where `url` is the location of the graphic image file to be used as the background image.
- To control how the image is tiled over the element's background, use the style
  ```
  background-repeat: type
  ```
  where `type` is repeat, repeat-x, repeat-y, or none.
- To place the image in a specific location in the element's background, use
  ```
  background-position: horizontal vertical
  ```
  where `horizontal` and `vertical` are coordinates that can be expressed as the horizontal and vertical distance from the upper-left corner of the background, using either length, percentages, or one of the following keywords: top, center, bottom, right, or left.
- To specify whether the image scrolls with the background, use
  ```
  background-attachment: type
  ```
  where `type` is scroll, allowing the image to scroll along with the background, or fixed, preventing the image from scrolling.
- To combine all background-image styles into a single style, use
  ```
  background: color image repeat attachment position
  ```
  where `color` is the color of the element background, `image` is the URL of the background image file, `repeat` specifies how the image is tiled in the background, `attachment` specifies whether the image scrolls with the page, and `position` provides the coordinates of the background image.

Like the border style, all the various background-image styles can be combined into a single style:

```
background: color image repeat attachment position
```

where `color` is the color of the element background, `image` is the URL of the background image file, `repeat` specifies how the image is tiled in the background, `attachment` specifies whether the image scrolls with the page, and `position` provides the coordinates of the background image. For example, the declaration

```
name {background: yellow url(paper.gif) no-repeat fixed center center}
```

applies a nontiled background image fixed on a yellow background, which uses the image file paper.gif. You do not have to enter all the values of the background style, but the ones you do enter must follow the specified order.

Janet wants to display the name of each bike model with a background image taken from the back.jpg file. You do not have to specify any values for the background image's position, attachment, or method of tiling. To make the foreground text more legible, you decide to change the font color of the bike name to white.

To add a background image to the name element:

1. Return to the **bike.css** file in your text editor, and add the following styles to the name element (see Figure 5-39):

   ```
   color: white; background-image: url(back.jpg)
   ```

Inserting a background image — Figure 5-39

```
*              {display: block}
document       {width: 720px}
author         {display: none}
date           {position: absolute; top: 0px; left: 660px}
title          {border-bottom: 2px solid purple}
model          {margin: 10px; border: 7px outset rgb(255,128,255); padding: 7px}
name           {border-bottom: 1px solid black; color: white; background-image: url(back.jpg)}
description    {width: 400px; float: right}
features       {width: 250px; color: blue; background-color: ivory; border: 2px solid purple;
                padding: 5px}
feature        {display: list-item; list-style: square inside}
fName          {display: inline; color: red}
```

2. Save your changes to the file. If you want to take a break before starting the next session, you may close the style sheet file.

3. Reload **bike.xml** in your Web browser. Figure 5-40 shows the revised document layout including the image tiled in the background of the name element.

Background image behind the name element — Figure 5-40

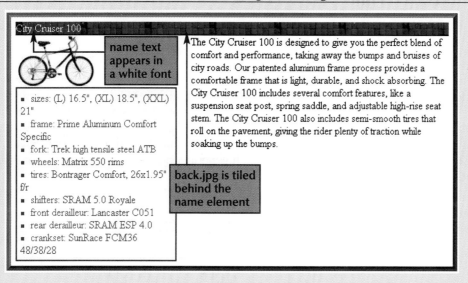

name text appears in a white font

back.jpg is tiled behind the name element

4. If you want to take a break before starting the next session, you may close your Web browser now.

You show Janet the current state of the document layout. She's pleased with your work in adding border, margin, and background image styles to the page. In the next session, you'll look at styles that control how the text in a document is formatted.

Session 5.2 Quick Check

Review

1. What style would you use to change the background color of the summary element to the color value (255, 192, 255)?

2. What style would you use to set the left and right margins for an element to 3 pixels?

3. What style would you use to define a dashed red border that is 5 pixels wide for the Summary element?

4. How would you increase the padding for the Summary element to 10 pixels?

5. How would you display the Document element using the image file paper.gif as a background image?

6. How would you tile the paper.gif image file only in the vertical direction?
7. How would you fix the paper.gif image file in the display window so that it doesn't scroll with the rest of the page?

Session 5.3

Setting Font and Text Styles

Janet now wants you to modify the document style to make the text more pleasing and easier to read. Browsers apply a set of default text styles to the content of XML elements. In many Web browsers, the text is displayed in a 12-point Times New Roman font. Janet wants you to apply different fonts and font sizes to her text to make the page more readable and interesting.

Choosing a Font

To change the font of an element's text, use the style

```
font-family: fonts
```

where *fonts* is a list of possible fonts separated by commas. CSS works with two types of fonts: specific and generic. A **specific font** is one that is installed on a user's computer, such as Times New Roman, Arial, or Helvetica. A **generic font** is a general description of a font, allowing a user's operating system to determine which installed font best matches the description. CSS supports five generic fonts: serif, sans-serif, monospace, cursive, and fantasy. Figure 5-41 shows examples of each generic font. Each type can encompass a wide range of designs.

Figure 5-41 | **Generic fonts**

	Font Samples		
serif	defg	defg	defg
sans-serif	defg	defg	defg
monospace	defg	defg	defg
cursive	defg	defg	defg
fantasy	defg	defg	DEFG

Choosing a Font

- To select a font for an element, use the style
    font-family: *fonts* ...
  where *fonts* is a comma-separated list of font names, starting with the most specific and desirable fonts and ending with a generic font name.

When you use a generic font, you cannot be sure which font any Web browser will use to display your text. For this reason, it is generally a good idea to use specific fonts; they give you a more accurate idea of what your audience sees. To do this effectively, you can provide Web browsers with a choice of several fonts. Browsers that don't have access to the font you specify as your first choice may have your second or third choices available. As a backup, specify a generic font as your last choice. For example, the following style provides browsers with a list of sans-serif fonts to use with the name element:

```
name {font-family: Arial, Helvetica, sans-serif}
```

A browser first attempts to display the name element in an Arial font; if that is not available, it tries Helvetica; and finally if neither of the specific fonts is found, it uses whatever generic sans-serif font is available. Janet wants you to specify the use of a sans-serif font for the subtitle, name, and features elements.

To set the font family:

1. If necessary, reopen the **bike.css** file in your text editor.

2. Insert the following declaration below the title element:

   subtitle {font-family: Arial, Helvetica, sans-serif}

3. Add the following style to the name and features elements (be sure to separate the new style from other styles with a semicolon):

   font-family: Arial, Helvetica, sans-serif

   Figure 5-42 shows the revised text in the style sheet.

Setting the font family **Figure 5-42**

```
*            {display: block}
document     {width: 720px}
author       {display: none}
date         {position: absolute; top: 0px; left: 660px}
title        {border-bottom: 2px solid purple}
subtitle     {font-family: Arial, Helvetica, sans-serif}
model        {margin: 10px; border: 7px outset rgb(255,128,255); padding: 7px}
name         {border-bottom: 1px solid black; color: white; background-image: url(back.jpg);
              font-family: Arial, Helvetica, sans-serif}
description  {width: 400px; float: right}
features     {width: 250px; color: blue; background-color: ivory; border: 2px solid purple;
              padding: 5px; font-family: Arial, Helvetica, sans-serif}
feature      {display: list-item; list-style: square inside}
fName        {display: inline; color: red}
```

4. Save your changes to the file, and reload **bike.xml** in your Web browser. Figure 5-43 shows the revised font used in the rendered document.

Figure 5-43 **Displaying text in a sans-serif font**

8/17/2007

Tour Nation

Bike Models

City Cruiser 100

- sizes: (L) 16.5", (XL) 18.5", (XXL) 21"
- frame: Prime Aluminum Comfort Specific
- fork: Trek high tensile steel ATB
- wheels: Matrix 550 rims
- tires: Bontrager Comfort, 26x1.95" f/r
- shifters: SRAM 5.0 Royale
- front derailleur: Lancaster C051
- rear derailleur: SRAM ESP 4.0
- crankset: SunRace FCM36 48/38/28

The City Cruiser 100 is designed to give you the perfect blend of comfort and performance, taking away the bumps and bruises of city roads. Our patented aluminum frame process provides a comfortable frame that is light, durable, and shock absorbing. The City Cruiser 100 includes several comfort features, like a suspension seat post, spring saddle, and adjustable high-rise seat stem. The City Cruiser 100 also includes semi-smooth tires that roll on the pavement, giving the rider plenty of traction while soaking up the bumps.

Note that an element inherits the font family of its parent. For example, because the feature element is a child of the features element in bike.xml, it uses the same font family unless the style sheet specifies otherwise.

Managing Font Sizes

Janet feels that the features list would look better if the font size were decreased, while the subtitle and the name of the bike model would look better with a larger font size. The style to set the font size of an element is

```
font-size: value
```

where `value` is the size of the font. Font sizes can be expressed as

- A unit of length
- A keyword description
- A percentage of the size of the element
- A size relative to the default font size of the element

If you choose to express the font size as a unit of length, you can use an **absolute unit** such as millimeters (mm), centimeters (cm), points (pt), and so forth, or you can use a relative unit. A **relative unit** expresses the font size relative to the size of a standard character. CSS recognizes two standard characters for defining relative units: em and ex. The **em unit** is equal to the width of the capital letter "M" in a browser's default font size. The **ex unit** is equal to the height of the lowercase letter "x" in the default font (see Figure 5-44).

The em and ex units

Figure 5-44

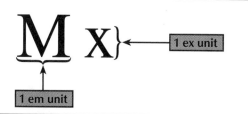

Setting the Font Size

• To specify the font size of an element, use the style

    font-size: value

where value can either be a unit of length (specified as mm, cm, in, pt, pc, em, or ex), a keyword (xx-small, x-small, small, medium, large, x-large, xx-large), a percentage of the font size of the parent element, or a keyword describing the size relative to the font size of the parent element (larger or smaller).

For example, to set the font size of the name element at twice the "normal" size, use the style

```
name {font-size: 2em}
```

You can use relative units to make a page **scalable**, allowing the page to be rendered the same way no matter how a particular browser is configured. For example, one user may have a large monitor and have set the default font size for body text to 18pt. Another user may have a smaller monitor and have set the default font size to 12pt. You want your heading text to be about 50% larger than the body text for either user. You can't specify the default font size for each user's browser, but if you use a value of 1.5em for the heading, it is sized appropriately on either monitor. Note that you can achieve the same effect by expressing a font size as a percentage of an element's default font size. For example, the style

```
font-size: 150%
```

causes a heading to appear 50% larger than the default size. Because of the advantages of scalability, Web designers often opt for the em unit over an absolute unit such as point size (even though point size is the most commonly used unit in desktop publishing).

Finally, you can express font sizes using seven descriptive keywords: xx-small, x-small, small, medium, large, x-large, or xx-large. Each browser is configured to display text at a particular size for each of these keywords, thus enabling you to achieve some uniformity across browsers. You can also use the keywords "larger" and "smaller" to relate the font size of an element to the font size of its parent element. For example, the following style declarations make the font size of the name element one step larger than the font size for the document element. The exact difference in the font size is left to each browser to determine.

```
document {font-size: 12pt}
name {font-size: larger}
```

After reviewing this material, Janet asks you to set the font size of the document element to 12 points and to set the sizes of other elements to

- date: 8pt
- subtitle: 14pt
- name: 14pt
- features: 8pt

Note that because the document element is the root element of bike.xml, setting the font size to 12 points makes all elements in the file 12 points, unless otherwise specified.

To set the font sizes of the elements:

▶ 1. Return to the **bike.css** file in your text editor, and add the following style to the document element:

```
font-size: 12pt
```

▶ 2. Add the following font-size style to the date and features elements:

```
font-size: 8pt
```

▶ 3. Finally, set the font size of the subtitle, and name elements to 14 points using the following style:

```
font-size: 14pt
```

Figure 5-45 shows the revised style code. Note that each of the new styles is separated from the others with a semicolon.

Figure 5-45	Setting the font size

```
*             {display: block}
document      {width: 720px; font-size: 12pt}
author        {display: none}
date          {position: absolute; top: 0px; left: 660px; font-size: 8pt}
title         {border-bottom: 2px solid purple}
subtitle      {font-family: Arial, Helvetica, sans-serif; font-size: 14pt}
model         {margin: 10px; border: 7px outset rgb(255,128,255); padding: 7px}
name          {border-bottom: 1px solid black; color: white; background-image: url(back.jpg);
               font-family: Arial, Helvetica, sans-serif; font-size: 14pt}
description   {width: 400px; float: right}
features      {width: 250px; color: blue; background-color: ivory; border: 2px solid purple;
               padding: 5px; font-family: Arial, Helvetica, sans-serif; font-size: 8pt}
feature       {display: list-item; list-style: square inside}
fName         {display: inline; color: red}
```

▶ 4. Save your changes to the style sheet, and reload **bike.xml** in your Web browser. Figure 5-46 shows the revised layout of the page incorporating the new font sizes.

Revised font sizes **Figure 5-46**

8/17/2007

Tour Nation

Bike Models

City Cruiser 100

- sizes: (L) 16.5", (XL) 18.5", (XXL) 21"
- frame: Prime Aluminum Comfort Specific
- fork: Trek high tensile steel ATB
- wheels: Matrix 550 rims
- tires: Bontrager Comfort, 26x1.95" f/r
- shifters: SRAM 5.0 Royale
- front derailleur: Lancaster C051
- rear derailleur: SRAM ESP 4.0
- crankset: SunRace FCM36 48/38/28

The City Cruiser 100 is designed to give you the perfect blend of comfort and performance, taking away the bumps and bruises of city roads. Our patented aluminum frame process provides a comfortable frame that is light, durable, and shock absorbing. The City Cruiser 100 includes several comfort features, like a suspension seat post, spring saddle, and adjustable high-rise seat stem. The City Cruiser 100 also includes semi-smooth tires that roll on the pavement, giving the rider plenty of traction while soaking up the bumps.

Setting Font Styles and Weights

Another way of modifying the appearance of text in a rendered document is to modify the text style. Italics are an example of a style or format applied to a font's appearance, making the text appear slanted in order to give it emphasis and interest. To change the font style used by an element, apply the style

```
font-style: type
```

where `type` is normal, italic, or oblique. The italic and oblique styles are similar in appearance, though there are subtle differences depending on the font.

You can also modify the appearance of text by setting the weight of the font. A bold-faced font appears heavier and thicker than a normal-weight font. To set the weight of text font, use the style

```
font-weight: weight
```

where `weight` is the level of bold formatting applied to the font. Font weights can be expressed as a value that ranges from 100 to 900, in increments of 100. Although this scale makes theoretical sense, most fonts do not support nine different font weights. For practical purposes, assume that a weight of 400 displays normal text, 700 displays bold text, and 900 displays extra bold text. You can also use the keywords "normal" and "bold" in place of a weight value, or you can express the font weight relative to the parent element by using the keywords "bolder" or "lighter."

Janet would like the subtitle to appear in italics and the model names to appear in a boldfaced font. Add these styles to the bike.css style sheet:

To apply italic and boldface styles to a font:

1. Return to the **bike.css** file in your text editor.

2. Add the following style to the subtitle element:

```
font-style: italic
```

3. Display the model names in a boldfaced font by adding the following style to the name element:

```
font-weight: bold
```

Figure 5-47 highlights the revised style code.

Figure 5-47 | **Setting the font style and weight**

```
*              {display: block}
document       {width: 720px; font-size: 12pt}
author         {display: none}
date           {position: absolute; top: 0px; left: 660px; font-size: 8pt}
title          {border-bottom: 2px solid purple}
subtitle       {font-family: Arial, Helvetica, sans-serif; font-size: 14pt; font-style: italic}
model          {margin: 10px; border: 7px outset rgb(255,128,255); padding: 7px}
name           {border-bottom: 1px solid black; color: white; background-image: url(back.jpg);
                font-family: Arial, Helvetica, sans-serif; font-size: 14pt; font-weight: bold}
description    {width: 400px; float: right}
features       {width: 250px; color: blue; background-color: ivory; border: 2px solid purple;
                padding: 5px; font-family: Arial, Helvetica, sans-serif; font-size: 8pt}
feature        {display: list-item; list-style: square inside}
fName          {display: inline; color: red}
```

4. Save your changes to the file, and reload **bike.xml** in your browser. Verify that the subtitle is italicized and the model names appear in a boldfaced font.

Reference Window | **Setting Font Style and Weight**

- To specify an appearance for an element's font, use the style
    font-style: *type*
  where *type* is either normal, italic, or oblique.
- To specify a font's weight, use
    font-weight: *value*
  where *value* is either a number ranging from 100 (lightest) to 900 (heaviest) in intervals of 100, a keyword describing the font's weight (normal or bold), or a keyword that describes the weight relative to the weight of the parent element's font (lighter or bolder).

Aligning Content Horizontally and Vertically

After examining the page you created, Janet decides that the title and subtitle would look better and have more impact if centered on the page. In addition, she wants to see the description for each bicycle justified to the left and right margins of the block that contains it.

CSS provides two styles for aligning an element with its surrounding content. To modify the horizontal alignment for an element's text, use the style

```
text-align: alignment
```

where *alignment* is left, center, right, or justify. The default alignment is left. This style can be used for any type of content, including text and inline images. Use this style to center the title and subtitle elements and to apply full justification to the description of each bike model.

To align element content in the bike document:

▶ 1. Return to the **bike.css** file in your text editor, and add the following style to the title and subtitle elements:

```
text-align: center
```

▶ 2. Add the following alignment style to the description element (see Figure 5-48):

```
text-align: justify
```

Aligning element text ◀ Figure 5-48

```
*            {display: block}
document     {width: 720px; font-size: 12pt}
author       {display: none}
date         {position: absolute; top: 0px; left: 660px; font-size: 8pt}
title        {border-bottom: 2px solid purple; text-align: center}
subtitle     {font-family: Arial, Helvetica, sans-serif; font-size: 14pt; font-style: italic;
              text-align: center}
model        {margin: 10px; border: 7px outset rgb(255,128,255); padding: 7px}
name         {border-bottom: 1px solid black; color: white; background-image: url(back.jpg);
              font-family: Arial, Helvetica, sans-serif; font-size: 14pt; font-weight: bold}
description  {width: 400px; float: right; text-align: justify}
features     {width: 250px; color: blue; background-color: ivory; border: 2px solid purple;
              padding: 5px; font-family: Arial, Helvetica, sans-serif; font-size: 8pt}
feature      {display: list-item; list-style: square inside}
fName        {display: inline; color: red}
```

▶ 3. Save your changes to the style sheet, and reload **bike.xml** in your browser. Figure 5-49 shows the revised layout of the page.

Revised page layout ◀ Figure 5-49

title and subtitle are centered in the document →

Tour Nation

Bike Models

City Cruiser 100

- sizes: (L) 16.5", (XL) 18.5", (XXL) 21"
- frame: Prime Aluminum Comfort Specific
- fork: Trek high tensile steel ATB
- wheels: Matrix 550 rims
- tires: Bontrager Comfort, 26x1.95" f/r
- shifters: SRAM 5.0 Royale
- front derailleur: Lancaster C051
- rear derailleur: SRAM ESP 4.0
- crankset: SunRace FCM36 48/38/28

The City Cruiser 100 is designed to give you the perfect blend of comfort and performance, taking away the bumps and bruises of city roads. Our patented aluminum frame process provides a comfortable frame that is light, durable, and shock absorbing. The City Cruiser 100 includes several comfort features, like a suspension seat post, spring saddle, and adjustable high-rise seat stem. The City Cruiser 100 also includes semi-smooth tires that roll on the pavement, giving the rider plenty of traction while soaking up the bumps.

description text appears with full justification

Reference Window **Aligning Content Horizontally and Vertically**

- To align content horizontally, use the style
    text-align: *alignment*
  where *alignment* is either left, center, right, or justify.
- To align content vertically relative to the baseline of the parent element, use
    vertical-align: *alignment*
  where *alignment* is baseline, bottom, middle, sub, super, text-bottom, text-top, or top, or is expressed as a distance or percentage that the element is raised or lowered relative to the height of the parent element.

For inline elements, CSS also allows you to vertically align the content of an element with the surrounding content of the parent element. The style for controlling vertical alignment for the content of an element is

    vertical-align: *alignment*

where *alignment* is one of the style keyword values described in Figure 5-50.

Figure 5-50 **Vertical alignment options**

Vertical Alignment	Description
baseline	Aligns the element with the bottom of lowercase letters in surrounding text (the default)
bottom	Aligns the bottom of the element with the bottom of the lowest element in surrounding content
middle	Aligns the middle of the element with the middle of the surrounding content
sub	Subscripts the element
super	Superscripts the element
text-bottom	Aligns the bottom of the element with the bottom of the font of the surrounding content
text-top	Aligns the top of the element with the top of the font of the surrounding content
top	Aligns the top of the element with the top of the tallest object in the surrounding content

Instead of using keywords, you can enter a distance or percentage to raise an element relative to the surrounding content. A positive value or percentage raises the element above the surrounding content, and a negative value lowers the element. For example, the style

    vertical-align: 50%

raises the element by half of the line height of the parent element, while the style

    vertical-align: -50%

drops the element half a line below the baseline of the parent element.

Controlling Spacing and Indentation

CSS supports styles that allow you to perform some basic typographic tasks, such as setting the **kerning** (the amount of space between letters) and **tracking** (the amount of space between words). The styles to control an element's kerning and tracking are

```
letter-spacing: value
word-spacing: value
```

where *value* is the size of the space between individual letters or words. You specify these sizes with the same units that you use for font sizing. As with font sizes, the default unit of length for kerning and tracking is the pixel (px). The default kerning and tracking values are 0 pixels each. A positive value increases letter and word spacing. A negative value reduces the space between letters and words.

Another typographic feature that you can set is **leading**, which is the space between lines of text. The style to set the leading for the text within an element is

```
line-height: value
```

where *value* is either a specific length, a percentage of the font size, or a number representing the ratio of the line height to the font size. The standard ratio is 1.2, which means that the line height is typically 1.2 times the font size. If Janet wanted the text of the description element to be double-spaced, she would use the following style:

```
description {line-height: 2}
```

The final way to control the spacing of your text is to set the indentation used in the first line. The style is

```
text-indent: value
```

where *value* is the size of the indentation in either absolute or relative units, or as a percentage of the width of the element. For example, an indentation value of 5% indents the first line by 5% of the width of the element. Additionally, the length and percentage values can be negative, extending the first line to the left of the paragraph to create a **hanging indent**.

Setting Text Spacing

Reference Window

- To set the space between letters (kerning), use the style
    ```
    letter-spacing: value
    ```
  where *value* is the space between individual letters. The default is 0 pixels.
- To set the space between words (tracking), use
    ```
    word-spacing: value
    ```
  where *value* is the space between individual words. The default is 0 pixels.
- To set the space between lines of text (leading), use
    ```
    line-height: value
    ```
  where *value* is the space between lines, expressed as a percentage of the font size or as the ratio of the line height to the font size. The default is a ratio of 1.2:1.
- To set the width of the indentation of the first line, use
    ```
    text-indent: value
    ```
  where *value* is the length of the indentation expressed either as a length or as a percentage of the width of the block element. The default is 0 pixels.

To make the model name text more readable, you decide to increase the kerning (space between letters) to 10 pixels. This will make the text feel less compressed. You will also increase the size of the text indent to 10 pixels.

To set the text spacing in the model name element:

▶ 1. Return to the **bike.css** file in your text editor, and add the following styles to the name element (see Figure 5-51):

```
letter-spacing: 10px; text-indent: 10px
```

Figure 5-51	Setting the text spacing for the name element

```
name        {border-bottom: 1px solid black; color: white; background-image: url(back.jpg);
             font-family: Arial, Helvetica, sans-serif; font-size: 14pt; font-weight: bold;
             letter-spacing: 10px; text-indent: 10px }
```

▶ 2. Save your changes to the file, and reload **bike.xml** in your browser. Figure 5-52 shows the revised appearance of the model name element.

Figure 5-52	Text spacing in the model name

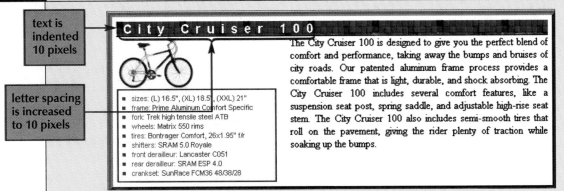

text is indented 10 pixels

letter spacing is increased to 10 pixels

Trouble? Under certain Mozilla browsers, such as Netscape and Firefox, the text of the model name "City Cruiser 200" may wrap onto a second line. To remove this line wrap, click the Reload button on your browser.

Working with Special Text Styles

CSS provides three styles that can be used to apply special effects to your text. To add lines above, below, or through your text use the style

```
text-decoration: type
```

where *type* equals none, underline, overline, or line-through. Note that the text-decoration style cannot be applied to nontextual elements such as inline images. You can apply several decorative features to the same element. For example, the following style adds a line above and below the name element:

```
name {text-decoration: underline overline}
```

To change the case of an element, use the style

```
text-transform: type
```

where *type* is capitalize, uppercase, lowercase, or none (to make no changes to the text case). To display the model names in uppercase letters (regardless of how the model name text is entered in the XML document), you would apply the style

```
name {text-transform: uppercase}
```

Finally, you can display the element in small capital letters using the style

```
font-variant: small-caps
```

Small caps are often used in legal documents, such as software agreements, where the capital letters indicate the importance of a phrase or point, but the text is made small so as not to detract from other elements in the document. Earlier, when you were designing the style for the features list for the bike document, you decreased the font size. Janet suggests that you make the name of each feature easier to read by displaying the feature names in a small caps style. Add this style to the bike.css style sheet.

To display feature names in a small caps style:

▶ **1.** Return to the **bike.css** file in your text editor, and add the following style to the fName element (see Figure 5-53):

```
font-variant: small-caps
```

Using the font-variant style ◀ **Figure 5-53**

```
feature      {display: list-item; list-style: square inside}
fName        {display: inline; color: red; font-variant: small-caps}
```

▶ **2.** Save your changes to the style sheet, and reload **bike.xml** in your browser. Figure 5-54 shows the revised appearance of the features list.

Displaying feature names in small caps ◀ **Figure 5-54**

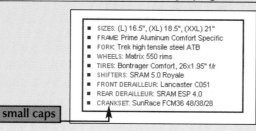

small caps

- SIZES: (L) 16.5", (XL) 18.5", (XXL) 21"
- FRAME: Prime Aluminum Comfort Specific
- FORK: Trek high tensile steel ATB
- WHEELS: Matrix 550 rims
- TIRES: Bontrager Comfort, 26x1.95" f/r
- SHIFTERS: SRAM 5.0 Royale
- FRONT DERAILLEUR: Lancaster C051
- REAR DERAILLEUR: SRAM ESP 4.0
- CRANKSET: SunRace FCM36 48/38/28

| **Decorating Text**

- To decorate an element's text, use the style
    text-decoration: *type*
  where *type* is blink, line-through, overline, underline, or none.
- To change the case of a text font, use
    text-transform: *type*
  where *type* is capitalize, lowercase, uppercase, or none.
- To display a variant of a font in small caps, use
    text-transform: small-caps

Using the Font Style

You can combine many of the text and font styles discussed here into the following single style:

```
font: font-style font-weight font-variant font-size/line-height
      font-family
```

where *font-style*, *font-weight*, and so forth are the values for the font and text styles. The font style provides an efficient way to define multiple style attributes. The *font-style*, *font-weight*, and *font-variant* styles can be entered in any order (and you do not have to include all three). The *font-size* attribute must follow these style attributes if they are included. The following style declarations demonstrate two different approaches that yield the same result when applied to the name element:

```
name {font-style: italic; font-variant: small-caps;
      font-weight: bold; font-size: 3em; line-height: 0.8em;
      font-family: Times Roman}
name {font: italic bold small-caps 3em/0.8em Times Roman}
```

Note that you can set the line height value only if you've also set the font size.

Using IDs and Classes

Tour Nation groups its bikes into three classes: city, road, and combo, used for city riding, road tours, and combinations of the two. Janet thinks it would be helpful if there were some way of visually separating one class of bike from another in the rendered document. She suggests that you display the names of all city bikes with a yellow font, combo bikes in a light green font, and road bikes in the white font you've been already using in the style sheet.

If you're familiar with HTML, you know that the id and class attributes are features of HTML used to distinguish one HTML tag from another. The **id attribute** identifies a unique element tag in an HTML document, while the **class attribute** identifies element tags belonging to the same group or class. In HTML, you enter the id and class attributes using the syntax

```
<elem id="id"> ... </elem>

<elem class="class"> ... </elem>
```

where *elem* is the name of an HTML element, *id* is the id assigned to that element tag, and *class* is the class to which the element tag belongs. For example, you can add id and class attributes to the opening tag of the h1 elements as follows:

```
<h1 id="c100" class="city"> ... </h1>
<h1 id="c200" class="city"> ... </h1>
<h1 id="combo750" class="combo"> ... </h1>
<h1 id="tour250" class="road"> ... </h1>
<h1 id="tri200" class="road"> ... </h1>
```

Note that the id attribute must be different for each tag, but multiple tags can share the same class value.

CSS allows designers to create styles based on the id and class names of tags from an HTML file. The syntax for applying a style to a particular id element is

```
#id {styles}
```

where *id* is the name used in the id attribute in an HTML tag and *styles* is a list of styles associated with that particular element tag. Creating a style for an id attribute with the value "c100" would look as follows:

```
#c100 {styles}
```

The syntax for applying a style to a particular class of HTML elements is

```
.class {styles}
```

where *class* is the name used for the class attribute in those HTML tags. If different types of elements belong to the same class, you can distinguish one element class from another using the selector form

```
elem.class {styles}
```

where *elem* is the name of the element. Thus, to create a style for elements belonging to the "city" class, you would use the selector form

```
.city {styles}
```

To apply the styles only to h1 elements belonging to the city class, you would enter

```
h1.city {styles}
```

When you move from HTML to XML, you find that support for the id and class attributes is dependent on a user's browser. Both Internet Explorer and Opera support the use of id and class attributes in an XML document, and you can write a CSS style sheet to apply styles to those ids and classes. For example, to apply styles to all name elements belonging to the city class, you would enter the following selector in the CSS style sheet:

```
name.city {styles}
```

In the same way, a model element that has the id value "c100" can be identified with the selector

```
#c100 {styles}
```

However, this is not the case in Mozilla browsers such as Firefox and Netscape. These browsers do not recognize the id and class attributes as being special attribute names. To apply a style to an element with a particular id, you must first attach a DTD to the document identifying the attribute as an ID attribute. Once that is done, you can apply the id selector from the CSS style sheet. Thus, if an XML document's DTD contained the declaration

```
<!ATTLIST model modelID ID #REQUIRED>
```

you could apply a style to the XML tag

```
<model modelID="c100"> ... </model>
```

using

```
#c100 {styles}
```

Because XML includes no native support for the class attribute, you cannot write CSS styles for classes of elements in an XML document unless you're using Internet Explorer or Opera. Instead, you should use the attribute selectors described earlier in Figure 5-8. For example, to create a style for name elements containing a class attribute with values equal to "city" you would enter the following selector:

```
name[class="city"] {styles}
```

The selector for any element belonging to the city class would be

```
[class="city"] {styles}
```

This approach does not work for Internet Explorer or Opera at the time of this writing, because these browsers do not currently support the attribute selector form. This will change in future releases of these browsers.

To modify the bike.css style sheet to display different font colors for bike names from different classes, you must enter style declarations using both selector forms. Thus, to display city bike names in a yellow font and combo bike names in a light green font, you need to add the following styles to the style sheet:

```
name.city              {color: yellow}
name[class="city"]     {color: yellow}
name.combo             {color: lightgreen}
name[class="combo"]    {color: lightgreen}
```

Modify the bike.css style sheet now, adding these declarations.

To create styles for different classes of bikes:

1. Return to the **bike.css** file in your text editor, and add the following style declarations at the bottom of the file (see Figure 5-55):

```
name.city              {color: yellow}
name[class="city"]     {color: yellow}
name.combo             {color: lightgreen}
name[class="combo"]    {color: lightgreen}
```

| Figure 5-55 | Applying a style to a class of elements |

```
feature    {display: list-item; list-style: square inside}
fName      {display: inline; color: red; font-variant: small-caps}

name.city              {color: yellow}
name[class="city"]     {color: yellow}

name.combo             {color: lightgreen}
name[class="combo"]    {color: lightgreen}
```

2. Save your changes to the style sheet, and reload the document in your Web browser. Verify that the first two model names appear in yellow, the third model name appears in a light green font color, and the last two bike names appear in white by default (see Figure 5-56).

Model names from different classes ◀ Figure 5-56

class = "city"

City Cruiser 200

- SIZES: (L) 16.5", (XL) 18.5", (XXL) 21"
- FRAME Prime Aluminum Comfort Specific.
- FORK InSync 178, adjustable preload, 50mm
- WHEELS: Bontrager Corvair rims
- TIRES: Bontrager Comfort w/Kevlar
- SHIFTERS: Lancaster Alivio
- FRONT DERAILLEUR: Lancaster Nexave T301
- REAR DERAILLEUR: Lancaster Deore LX
- CRANKSET: Lancaster T303 48/38/28

For those looking for a superior city bike at a reasonable price, the City Cruiser 200 is the answer. As with all City Cruiser models the 200 provides unparalleled performance and comfort. Tour Nation's patented aluminum frame is light, durable, and shock absorbing. The City Cruiser 200 provides a wider gear range than other models in this class, giving you just the right gear for pedaling on any incline. The 200's design puts you in an upright, relaxed riding position that makes pedaling easier and more enjoyable. As with all City Cruiser models, the 200 also includes semi-smooth tires to soak up the bumps while providing superior traction.

class = "combo"

Combo 750

- SIZES: (S) 17.5", (M) 20", (L) 22.5"
- FRAME Prime Aluminum. Oversized tubes.
- FORK Trek high tensile steel ATB
- WHEELS: Matrix 550 rims
- TIRES: Bontrager Select, 700x38c f/r
- SHIFTERS: SRAM Verio
- FRONT DERAILLEUR: Lancaster C051
- REAR DERAILLEUR: Lancaster TY40GS
- CRANKSET: SunRace FCM36 48/38/28

For those who need to go off-road or on, Tour Nation presents its line of Combo bikes. These hybrids combine the comfort of a mountain bike with the speed of a road bike. Each bike uses Tour Nation's patented aluminum frame system for a frame that is light, durable, and stiffer to easily generate power. The frame's medium upright position lets you enjoy the scenery while getting into shape. The Combo models use a suspension seat post to soften the bumps and bruises from rough payment and trails. All models use Lancaster derailleurs and brakes with reinforced casing for greater durability and reliability.

class = "road"

Tour 250

- SIZES: (S) 17.5", (M) 20", (L) 22.5"
- FRAME Prime SL Aluminum.
- FORK Cro-Moly
- WHEELS: Winston Select: Paired Spoke
- TIRES: IRC Duro Tour, 700x35c f/r
- SHIFTERS: Lancaster Alivio
- FRONT DERAILLEUR: Lancaster Nexave 301
- REAR DERAILLEUR: Lancaster Deore SGS
- CRANKSET: Lancaster Nexave T401 48/38/28

Go for a bike ride, come back in a month. This is the idea behind Tour Nation's line of touring bikes. The Tour 250 is a classic example of a rugged touring bike designed for days, weeks, and even months of continuous use. The Tour 250 is loaded with features for the serious cyclist, including reinforced braze-ons for pannier racks. The Tour 250 is also easy on your body with a suspension seat post, spring saddle, and adjustable high-rise seat stem, perfect for long tours and long days. All parts are engineered to the highest quality. Quick release levers for all major parts make roadside repairs a breeze.

Using IDs and Classes in a Style Sheet

- To apply a style to an element with a specified id value, use the selector
    `#id {styles}`
  where `id` is the id value and `styles` is the list of styles associated with the specific element. In Internet Explorer and Opera, the name of the attribute must be id. In Firefox and Netscape, the id can have any attribute name, but must be declared as an ID attribute in a DTD associated with the XML document.
- To apply a style to a class of elements in Internet Explorer or Opera, use
    `elem.class {styles}`
  or
    `.class {styles}`
  where `elem` is the name of the element and `class` is the value of the class attribute associated with the element. The name of the attribute must be "class".
- To apply a style to a class of elements in Firefox or Netscape, use
    `elem[att="class"] {styles}`
  or
    `[att="class"] {styles}`
  where `att` is the name of the class attribute and `class` is the value of the attribute.

Finally, some browsers, including versions of the Macintosh Safari browser, do not support the use of id selectors in style sheets attached to XML documents, even for ids declared in DTDs. For these browsers, you can treat the id selector as any other attribute. Thus, for compatibility with Safari, you would enter the selector for a modelID value of "c100" within the model element as

```
model[id="c100"] {styles}
```

Janet's document does not use id attributes; however, you will get a chance to create styles based on ids in the case problems at the end of the tutorial.

Working with Pseudo-Elements

Thus far all the selectors you've used have been based on elements that exist somewhere in the hierarchy of the XML document. However, you can also define selectors that are not actual elements but are instead abstracted from what you know of an element's content, use, or position. For example, the description element is part of the bike document, but the first letter of that description is not (there is no "first letter" element). You can work with this kind of abstracted element by treating it as a **pseudo-element**.

CSS supports a wide variety of pseudo-elements, including those that select the first letter or first line of an element's content. The syntax for creating a style declaration for a pseudo-element is

```
selector:pseudo-element {styles}
```

where `selector` is an element or group of elements within a document, `pseudo-element` is an abstract element based on the selector, and `styles` are the styles that you want to apply to the pseudo-element. Figure 5-57 lists some of the pseudo-elements supported by CSS and XML.

Pseudo-element	Description	Example
first-letter	The first letter of the element text	name:first-letter {font-size: 14pt}
first-line	The first line of the rendered element text	name:first-line {text-transform: uppercase}
before	Content directly prior to the element	name:before {content: "Special!"}
after	Content directly after the element	name:after {content: "eof"}

For example, to display the first letter of every bike description in a gold fantasy font, you would use the declaration

```
description:first-letter {font-family: fantasy; color: gold}
```

You can also use pseudo-elements to create drop-caps. To create a drop-cap, you increase the font size of an element's first letter and float it on the left margin. Drop-caps also generally look better if you decrease the line height of the first letter, enabling the surrounding content to wrap more closely around the letter. You suggest creating a drop-cap style for the description elements in Janet's document. You also think that the description text would look better if the first line appeared in small caps. To create this effect, you'll add the following style to the bike.css style sheet:

```
description:first-letter {font-size: 26pt; text-align: top;
                          float: left; line-height: 0.8;
                          margin-right: 5px}
description:first-line    {font-variant: small-caps}
```

Add these declarations to the style sheet.

To create a drop-cap for the description element:

1. Return to the **bike.css** file in your text editor, and add the following style declarations at the bottom of the file (see Figure 5-58):

```
description:first-letter {font-size: 26pt; text-align: top;
                          float: left; line-height: 0.8;
                          margin-right: 5px}
description:first-line    {font-variant: small-caps}
```

```
name.city           {color: yellow}
name[class="city"]  {color: yellow}

name.combo          {color: lightgreen}
name[class="combo"] {color: lightgreen}

description:first-letter {font-size: 26pt; text-align: top; float: left;
                          line-height: 0.8; margin-right: 5px}

description:first-line    {font-variant: small-caps}
```

2. Close the bike.css file, saving your changes.

3. Return to your Web browser, and reload the **bike.xml** file. Figure 5-59 shows the revised document displaying the drop-cap style and the new style applied to the first line of the description text.

> **Trouble?** Depending on your browser, the appearance of the drop cap may be different than in the figure.

Figure 5-59   **Final design for the bike document**

8/17/2007

Tour Nation

Bike Models

City Cruiser 100

- SIZES: (L) 16.5", (XL) 18.5", (XXL) 21"
- FRAME: Prime Aluminum Comfort Specific
- FORK: Trek high tensile steel ATB
- WHEELS: Matrix 550 rims
- TIRES: Bontrager Comfort, 26x1.95" f/r
- SHIFTERS: SRAM 5.0 Royale
- FRONT DERAILLEUR: Lancaster C051
- REAR DERAILLEUR: SRAM ESP 4.0
- CRANKSET: SunRace FCM36 48/38/28

THE CITY CRUISER 100 IS DESIGNED TO GIVE YOU THE perfect blend of comfort and performance, taking away the bumps and bruises of city roads. Our patented aluminum frame process provides a comfortable frame that is light, durable, and shock absorbing. The City Cruiser 100 includes several comfort features, like a suspension seat post, spring saddle, and adjustable high-rise seat stem. The City Cruiser 100 also includes semi-smooth tires that roll on the pavement, giving the rider plenty of traction while soaking up the bumps.

▶ **4.** Close your Web browser if you want to take a break before starting the end of session exercises.

You've completed your work on designing a CSS style sheet for Janet's bike document. She'll study your design and get back to you with any changes.

Session 5.3 Quick Check

1. What is the difference between a specific font and a generic font?
2. What is a relative unit? What are the two relative units supported by CSS?
3. How would you display the Summary element in a boldface Arial font?
4. How would you set the kerning of the Summary element to 0.4 points?
5. How would you apply a style to an element tag with the id name "Model500"? What do you have to do to apply this style in Firefox and Netscape?
6. How would you apply a style to the bike element with the class name "Mountain_Bikes"? Give the style declaration in both forms.
7. What is a pseudo-element? Give two examples of a pseudo-element.

Tutorial Summary

This tutorial covered how to create a CSS style sheet and apply it to an XML document. The first session covered the history and theory behind the development of CSS. The session then explored how to write selectors to apply styles to specific elements within a document, examining how to create inline, block, and list-item display styles and how to hide elements on a rendered page. The session concluded with a look at how to position and size elements on a rendered page. The second session looked at the various parts of the box model, including setting the margin size, padding size, and border style. The second session also covered how to apply background images to document elements. The third session looked at the multiple font and text styles supported by CSS, including those for setting font color, size, and typeface. The third session also examined how to create styles for elements of a particular id or belonging to a particular class. The tutorial concluded with a look at pseudo-elements and ways of creating drop-caps.

Key Terms

absolute position	CSS3	relative position
absolute unit	em unit	relative unit
block-level element	ex unit	scalable
box model	fixed position	selector
Cascading Style Sheets	floating	specific font
class attribute	generic font	static position
color name	hanging indent	style sheet
color value	id attribute	styles
CSS	inline element	tile
CSS1	kerning	tracking
CSS2	leading	watermark
CSS2.1	pseudo-element	

Practice

Practice the skills you earned in the tutorial using the same case scenario

Review Assignments

Data files needed for this Review Assignment: bike2txt.css, bike2txt.xml, c100.jpg, c200.jpg, combo750.jpg, paper.jpg, tnation.jpg, tour250.jpg, tri200.jpg

Janet has had time to study your document and to discuss it with others at Tour Nation. She wants to make a few changes to the page layout and design, and she wants you to create a new style sheet to match her ideas. A preview of the new design for the bike model document is shown in Figure 5-60.

Figure 5-60

Tour Nation
Bike Models

Janet Schmidtt
8/17/2007

City Cruiser 100

THE CITY CRUISER 100 IS DESIGNED TO give you the perfect blend of comfort and performance, taking away the bumps and bruises of city roads. Our patented aluminum frame process provides a comfortable frame that is light, durable, and shock absorbing. The City Cruiser 100 includes several comfort features, like a suspension seat post, spring saddle, and adjustable high-rise seat stem. The City Cruiser 100 also includes semi-smooth tires that roll on the pavement, giving the rider plenty of traction while soaking up the bumps.

SIZES: (L) 16.5", (XL) 18.5", (XXL) 21"
FRAME: Prime Aluminum Comfort Specific
FORK: Trek high tensile steel ATB
WHEELS: Matrix 550 rims
TIRES: Bontrager Comfort, 26x1.95" f/r
SHIFTERS: SRAM 5.0 Royale
FRONT DERAILLEUR: Lancaster C051
REAR DERAILLEUR: SRAM ESP 4.0
CRANKSET: SunRace FCM36 48/38/28

City Cruiser 200

FOR THOSE LOOKING FOR A SUPERIOR city bike at a reasonable price, the City Cruiser 200 is the answer. As with all City Cruiser models the 200 provides unparalleled performance and comfort. Tour Nation's patented aluminum frame is light, durable, and shock absorbing. The City Cruiser 200 provides a wider gear range than other models in this class, giving you just the right gear for pedaling on any incline. The 200's design puts you in an upright, relaxed riding position that makes pedaling easier and more enjoyable. As with all City Cruiser models, the 200 also includes semi-smooth tires to soak up the bumps while providing superior traction.

SIZES: (L) 16.5", (XL) 18.5", (XXL) 21"
FRAME: Prime Aluminum Comfort Specific.
FORK: InSync 178, adjustable preload, 50mm
WHEELS: Bontrager Corvair rims
TIRES: Bontrager Comfort w/Kevlar
SHIFTERS: Lancaster Alivio
FRONT DERAILLEUR: Lancaster Nexave T301
REAR DERAILLEUR: Lancaster Deore LX
CRANKSET: Lancaster T303 48/38/28

Combo 750

FOR THOSE WHO NEED TO GO OFF-road or on, Tour Nation presents its line of Combo bikes. These hybrids combine the comfort of a mountain bike with the speed of a road bike. Each bike uses Tour Nation's patented aluminum frame system for a frame that is light, durable, and stiffer to easily generate power. The frame's medium upright position lets you enjoy the scenery while getting into shape. The Combo models use a suspension seat post to soften the bumps and bruises from rough payment and trails. All models use Lancaster derailleurs and brakes with reinforced casing for greater durability and reliability.

SIZES: (S) 17.5", (M) 20", (L) 22.5"
FRAME: Prime Aluminum. Oversized tubes.
FORK: Trek high tensile steel ATB
WHEELS: Matrix 550 rims
TIRES: Bontrager Select, 700x38c f/r
SHIFTERS: SRAM Verio
FRONT DERAILLEUR: Lancaster C051
REAR DERAILLEUR: Lancaster TY40GS
CRANKSET: SunRace FCM36 48/38/28

To complete this task:

1. Using your text editor, open **bike2txt.xml** and **bike2txt.css** from the tutorial.05x/ review folder. Enter *your name* and *the date* in the comment section of each file and save them as **bike2.xml** and **bike2.css** respectively.

2. Go to the bike2.xml file in your text editor. Above the root document element insert a processing instruction linking the document to the bike2.css style sheet file.

3. Locate the img element directly after each name element. To each img element tag insert the attribute class="bikephoto", identifying the inline image as a photo of a particular bike model.

4. Close the file, saving your changes.

5. Go to the bike2.css file in your text editor. Directly below the comment section, insert the @namespace rule to declare the HTML namespace using the prefix "html" and the URI *http://www.w3.org/1999/xhtml*. (*Hint*: See Tutorial 2 for a discussion of style sheets and namespaces.)

6. Below the @namespace rule, insert a style to display bike photo images with a 1 pixel solid purple border and a margin of 5 pixels. Float the bike photos on the left margin. (*Hint*: The selector for the bike photos must be either html|img[class= "bikephoto"] or html\:img.bikephoto to represent the widest range of browsers.)

7. Below the style declarations for the bike photo images, set the default display style for elements in the document to block.

8. Set the width of the document element to 720 pixels, the font size to 12 points, and the width of the left margin to 10 pixels.

9. Use absolute positioning to set the left coordinates of the author and date elements to 620 pixels. Set the top coordinate of the date element to 25 pixels. For both elements, set the font size to 8 points.

10. Center the content of the title and subtitle elements. Display the subtitle element in a bold 24 point font. Use relative positioning to place the subtitle element with a top coordinate of -15 pixels.

11. Use the image file paper.jpg as the background image for the model element. Add a 1 pixel-wide solid black border around the element, and set the size of the bottom margin to 10 pixels. Only display the model element when both margins are clear of floating elements. (*Hint*: Use the clear style.)

12. Display the text of the name element in a bold white italic font, 14 points in size. Set the kerning value (the space between letters) to 10 pixels and the padding within the name element to 2 pixels. Align the text with the right margin. Add a 1 pixel solid black border around the name element.

13. Set the width of the features element to 300 pixels surrounded by a 5 pixel margin and containing 5 pixels of padding. Set the font size to 8 points on a white background. Set the border width of the features element to 1 pixel on the top and left and 3 pixels on the right and bottom. The border color should be purple, and the border style should be solid. Float the features element on the right.

14. Set the display style of the fName element to inline. Display the text of the fName element in bold purple font in uppercase letters.

15. Set the font size of the description element to 10 points. Set the padding around the element to 5 pixels.

16. Set the font family of the name, description, fName, and subtitle elements to Arial, Helvetica, and sans-serif.

17. For name elements of the city class, set the background color to the color value (128, 128, 255). For name elements of the combo class, set the background color to the value (64, 192, 64). For name elements of the road class, set the background color value to (255, 128, 128).

18. Display the first line of text from the description element in uppercase letters.

19. Close the bike2.css file, saving your styles.

20. Open bike2.xml in your Web browser, and verify that the styles and layout applied to the document resemble those shown in Figure 5-60.

21. Submit your completed work to your instructor.

Apply

Use the skills you learned in this tutorial to create a color-coded table of stock quotes

Case Problem 1

Data files needed for this Case Problem: down.gif, nasdaqtxt.css, nasdaqtxt.xml, up.gif

Hardin Financial   Kevin Summers of Hardin Financial tracks stock market data for the stock exchanges, including the NASDAQ. He is interested in the NASDAQ 100, a listing of 100 representative stocks on the NASDAQ stock exchange. A server at Hardin Financial records information for each of the 100 listings every five minutes and places that data into an XML document. Kevin wants to display the data from this document in an easy-to-read table. He thinks this can be accomplished using a cascading style sheet, and asks for your help in creating the styles. Figure 5-61 shows a diagram of Kevin's document.

Figure 5-61

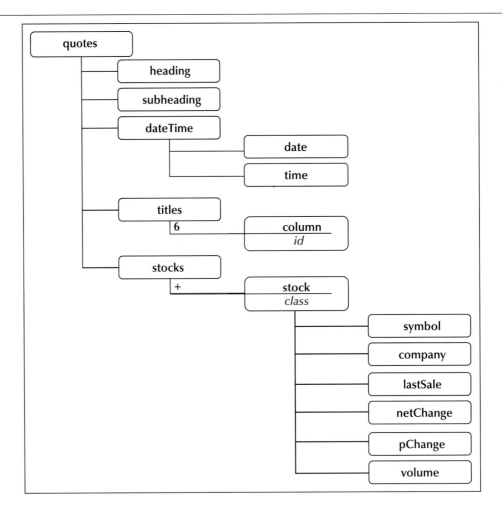

The date and time of the stock quotes are stored in the date and time elements, and the page headings are stored in the heading and subHeading elements. Kevin envisions displaying the stock data in six columns. The column titles are stored in the six column elements, with ids ranging from c1 to c6. Information for each stock is stored in the symbol, company, lastSale, netChange, pChange, and volume elements. Each stock element has a class attribute. A class value of up specifies an increased stock price, and a class value of down indicates a declining stock. A class value of unchanged means that a stock hasn't changed in value. Kevin wants all declining stocks to appear in a red font with a down arrow graphic, and increasing stocks to appear in green with an up arrow. Stocks that haven't changed in value should appear in black with no associated graphic.

Figure 5-62 shows a preview of the page you'll create for Kevin.

Figure 5-62

Symbol	Name	Last Sale	Net Change	% Change	Volume
▼ AAPL	Apple Computer, Inc.	$15.26	-0.17	-1.10%	5.548
▲ ABGX	Abgenix, Inc.	$9.22	0.06	0.66%	1.396
▼ ADBE	Adobe Systems Inc.	$23.96	-0.98	-3.93%	4.432
▼ ADCT	ADC Telecommunications, Inc.	$1.80	-0.16	-8.16%	5.980
▲ ADRX	Andrx Group	$22.19	1.05	4.97%	2.401
▼ ALTR	Altera Corp.	$11.83	-0.49	-3.98%	6.993
▼ AMAT	Applied Materials, Inc.	$14.87	-0.83	-5.29%	27.627
▼ AMCC	Applied Micro Circuits Corp.	$4.61	-0.13	-2.74%	4.126
▲ AMGN	Amgen Inc.	$45.64	0.15	0.33%	33.644
▼ AMZN	Amazon.com, Inc.	$14.46	-0.31	-2.11%	3.802
▼ APOL	Apollo Group, Inc.	$39.25	-0.05	-0.13%	2.166
▲ ATML	Atmel Corp.	$3.14	0.25	7.37%	8.349
▼ BBBY	Bed Bath and Beyond Inc.	$31.00	-1.66	-5.08%	6.928
▼ BEAS	BEA Systems, Inc.	$5.55	-0.52	-8.57%	14.196
▼ BGEN	Biogen, Inc.	$35.97	-0.22	-0.61%	3.700
▲ BMET	Biomet, Inc.	$25.93	0.42	1.65%	1.659
▼ BRCD	Brocade Communications Systems, Inc.	$18.75	-1.14	-5.73%	10.285
▼ BRCM	Broadcom Corp.	$18.76	-0.89	-4.53%	10.100
▼ CDWC	CDW Computer Centers, Inc.	$47.80	-2.22	-4.44%	1.755
▲ CEFT	Concord EFS, Inc.	$19.50	2.65	11.96%	45.162
▲ CEPH	Cephalon, Inc.	$48.00	2.36	5.17%	3.385
CHIR	**Chiron Corp.**	**$33.74**	**0.00**	**0.00%**	**3.011**

NASDAQ 100
Current quotes

11/01/2008 11:45:05

To create a style sheet for this page:

1. Using your text editor, open **nasdaqtxt.xml** and **nasdaqtxt.css** from the tutorial.05x/case1 folder: Enter *your name* and *the date* in the comment section of each file and save them as **nasdaq.xml** and **nasdaq.css** respectively.

2. Go to the nasdaq.xml file in your text editor. Take some time to review the contents of the file, becoming familiar with the file structure and data content. Note that the internal DTD for the document indicates that the id attribute of the column element contains ID data. Below the DTD, insert a processing instruction linking this file to the nasdaq.css style sheet. Close the nasdaq.xml file, saving your changes.

3. Go to the nasdaq.css file in your text editor. Set the width of the quotes element to 750 pixels, the margin around the quotes element to 20 pixels, and the font size to 12 points.

4. Display the dateTime element in a block, positioned absolutely on the page with the top coordinate set to 0 pixels and the left coordinate set to 600 pixels. Set the font size to 8 points.

5. Set the font size of the heading element to 32 points. Set the font size of the sub-Heading to 14 points, positioned relatively on the page with a top coordinate of -10 pixels. For both the heading and subHeading elements, display the text in a centered bold Arial, Helvetica, or sans-serif font within a block.

6. Display the titles element in a block with a bottom margin of 20 pixels. Display the column element as an inline element with the text displayed in underlined 8 point Courier New or monospace font.

7. Using absolute positioning, place the following elements at the following left coordinates and (in some cases) widths:

- The #c1 element (i.e., the element with the id value "c1") at 40 pixels
- The company and #c2 elements at 130 pixels
- The lastSale and #c3 elements at 430 pixels with a width of 70 pixels
- The netChange and #c4 elements at 510 pixels with a width of 80 pixels
- The pChange and #c5 elements at 590 pixels with a width of 80 pixels
- The volume and #c6 elements at 640 pixels with a width of 100 pixels

   If you are using the Macintosh Safari browser, you may find that the browser does not support the use of id selectors for the #c1 through #c6 ids. In this case, create a selector based on the value of the id attribute within the column element.

8. Display the stock element in a block with a 1 pixel-wide solid black bottom border. Display the stock text in a 10-point Courier New or monospace font.

9. Use relative positioning to place the symbol element with a left coordinate of 40 pixels.

10. Right-align the text of the following elements: lastSale, netChange, pChange, volume, #c2, #c3, #c4, #c5, and #c6.

11. Using both methods, display stock elements from the down class with a red font color. Add the background image down.gif to the element. Do not repeat (tile) the background image, and place it at the left center of the stock element. Use the same style for stock elements from the up class, except use the up.gif image file for the background, and set the font color to green.

12. Save your changes to the file.

13. Open nasdaq.xml in your Web browser, and verify that the stock quotes appear as shown in Figure 5-62.

14. Submit your completed project to your instructor.

Case Problem 2

Data files needed for this Case Problem: elemtxt.xml, pcharttxt.css

MidWest University Dr. Steve Karlson is a chemistry professor at MidWest University. Recently, he placed data regarding chemical elements in an XML document. The structure of his document is shown in Figure 5-63. Each chemical element in his document contains the atomic number, element symbol, and atomic weight. Dr. Karlson has also included three heading elements that he wants to use to label different parts of the table. Each chemical element contains an id attribute identifying the element. The first chemical element, hydrogen, is labeled e1; the second, helium, is labeled e2, and so forth.

Figure 5-63

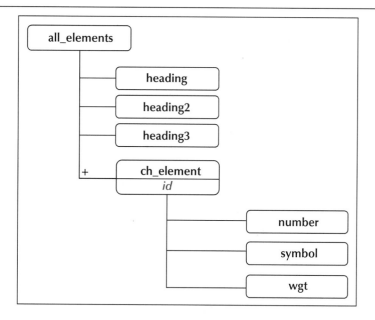

He asks for your help in creating a style sheet to display this data in the classic form of the periodic table of elements. The table you'll create is shown in Figure 5-64. To make this table, you'll place each chemical element on the document using absolute positioning.

Figure 5-64

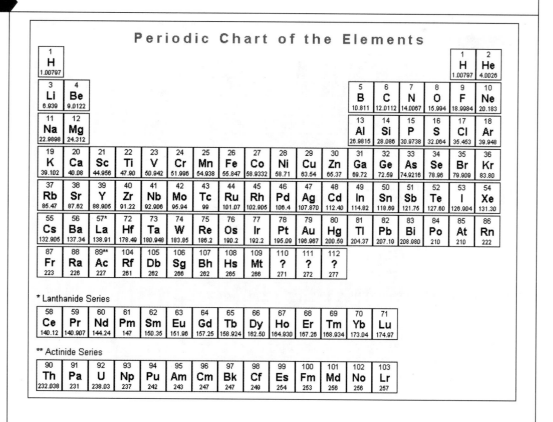

To complete this task:

1. Using your text editor, open **elemtxt.xml** and **pcharttxt.css** from the tutorial.05x/ case2 folder: Enter *your name* and *the date* in the comment section of each file and save them as **elements.xml** and **pchart.css** respectively.

2. Go to the elements.xml file in your text editor. Directly below the DTD insert a processing instruction linking this file to the pchart.css style sheet. Close the file, saving your changes.

3. Go to the pchart.css file in your text editor. Set the width of the all_elements element to 730 pixels on an ivory background. Set the font family of the element to Arial, Helvetica, or sans-serif.

4. Display the heading element in a block. Display the text of the heading element in a red 16-point bold font centered on the page. Set the kerning (letter spacing) value to 5 pixels.

5. Display the heading2 element in a block, absolutely positioned with a top coordinate of 420 pixels and a left coordinate of 10 pixels. Set the font size to 10 points. Place the heading3 element in a block absolutely positioned with a top coordinate of 500 pixels and a left coordinate of 10 pixels. Set the font size to 10 points.

6. Display the ch_element element in a block on a white background. Center the text of the element. Set the width to 40 pixels. Add a 1-pixel solid black border. Finally, position the ch_element absolutely on the page, but do not specify any page coordinates.

7. Display the number, symbol, and wgt elements in blocks. Set the font sizes to 8 points, 12 points, and 7 points respectively. Display the symbol text in a bold font.

8. Using the element ids shown in Figure 5-65, set the left coordinates of each of the elements in the periodic table.

Figure 5-65

Element ID	Left coordinate
e1, e3, e11, e19, e37, e55, e58, e87, e90	10px
e4, e12, e20, e38, e56, e59, e88, e91	50px
e21, e39, e57, e60, e89, e92	90px
e22, e40, e61, e72, e93, e104	130px
e23, e41, e62, e73, e94, e105	170px
e24, e42, e63, e74, e95, e106	210px
e25, e43, e64, e75, e96, e107	250px
e26, e44, e65, e76, e97, e108	290px
e27, e45, e66, e77, e98, e109	330px
e28, e46, e67, e78, e99, e110	370px
e29, e47, e68, e79, e100, e111	410px
e30, e48, e69, e80, e101, e112	450px
e5, e13, e31, e49, e70, e81, e102	490px
e6, e14, e32, e50, e71, e82, e103	530px
e7, e15, e33, e51, e83	570px
e8, e16, e34, e52, e84	610px
e1a, e9, e17, e35, e53, e85	650px
e2, e10, e18, e36, e54, e86	690px

If you're using the Macintosh Safari browser, you may have to create selectors based on the value of the id attribute within the ch_element element, because some versions of this browser do not support id selectors.

9. Using the element ids shown in Figure 5-66, set the top coordinates of each of the elements in the periodic table.

Figure 5-66

Element ID	Top coordinate
e1, e1a, e2	50px
e3-e10	100px
e11-e18	150px
e19-e36	200px
e37-e54	250px
e55, e56, e57, e72-e86	300px
e87, e88, e89, e104-e112	350px
e58-e71	440px
e90-e103	520px

10. Close the file, saving your changes.
11. Open elements.xml in your Web browser, and verify that the elements are displayed in the periodic table as shown earlier in Figure 5-64. (If you are running Internet Explorer you might see the ivory background only behind the page title.)
12. Submit your completed project to your instructor.

Case Problem 3

Challenge

Explore how to use the table-cell display style to create a table of room reservations

Data files needed for this Case Problem: schedtxt.css, schedtxt.xml

Cutler Convention Center   Karen Cho is the reservations coordinator for the Cutler Convention Center in Cutler, Indiana. Recently, the center's database began storing reservations for conference rooms in an XML document using a customized vocabulary. The structure of Karen's XML document is shown in Figure 5-67. Karen has created a compound document containing the h1 element from the XHTML vocabulary for the page heading and elements from her own XML vocabulary to display reservation information. The date element stores the dates for conference room reservations. The times element stores the different time blocks in which reservations can be made. Each time block is stored in the hour element. The rooms element contains reservation information on specific rooms, indicating whether the room has been reserved for the given time block or not.

Figure 5-67

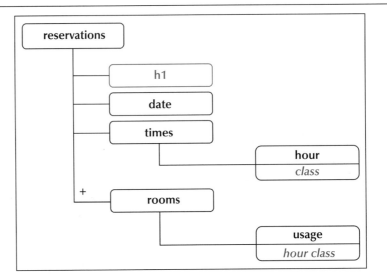

Karen wants this information displayed in a table from which she can quickly determine whether a particular room is free during a given time block. Reserved rooms and time blocks should be displayed in red table cells, while free time blocks and rooms should be displayed with a white background. Figure 5-68 shows a preview of the reservation table that Karen wants to display. Note that this figure shows the Web page in the Firefox browser.

Figure 5-68

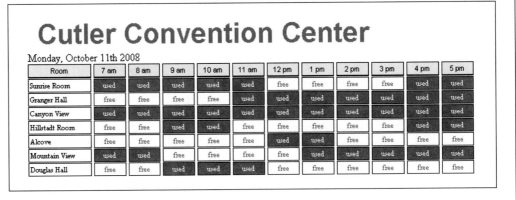

To create a style sheet for this page:

1. Using your text editor, open **schedtxt.xml** and **schedtxt.css** from the tutorial.05x/case3 folder: Enter *your name* and *the date* in the comment section of each file and save them as **schedule.xml** and **schedule.css** respectively.

2. Go to the **schedule.xml** file in your text editor. Review the contents of the file, becoming familiar with the data structure and content. Directly below the comment section, insert a processing instruction linking the document to the schedule.css style sheet. Close the file, saving your changes.

3. Go to the schedule.css file in your text editor. Directly below the comment section declare the XHTML namespace using the html namespace prefix and the namespace URI *http://www.w3.org/1999/xhtml*.

4. Set the margin around the reservations element to 15 pixels.
5. Display text for the h1 element from the XHTML namespace in a 32 points Arial, Helvetica, or sans-serif font with color value of (0, 128, 0). Set the margin around the h1 element to 0 pixels. (*Hint*: You will have to use both namespace syntaxes from Tutorial 2 for the h1 selector.)
6. Display the date element as a block element.

Explore

7. Display the hour element as a table cell (*Hint*: Use table-cell for the display style.) Display the text of the hour element in centered 8-point Arial, Helvetica, or sans-serif font on a yellow background. Set the width of the table cell to 50 pixels with a 1-pixel wide solid black border. Set the width of the bottom border to 2 pixels. Set the padding size of the hour element to 2 pixels.
8. Display the rooms and times elements as blocks.

Explore

9. Display the usage element as a table cell in an 8-point font. Add a 1 pixel solid black border with 2 pixels of padding.

Explore

10. Set the width of any element belonging to the roomname class to 100 pixels.
11. For usage elements belonging to the yes class, set the width of the element to 50 pixels on a red background. Display the text in a centered white font.
12. For usage elements belonging to the no class, set the width of the element to 50 pixels on a white background. Display the text in a centered green font.
13. Close the style sheet, saving your changes. Open schedule.xml in your Web browser, and verify that the document appears in the style shown in Figure 5-68. *Note*: Some browsers may display slight differences in the space between the table cells. At the time of this writing, the table-cell display style is not supported by all browsers. If you are running a browser like Internet Explorer, the table cells in the schedule table will not line up.
14. Submit your completed project to your instructor.

Case Problem 4

Create

st your knowledge of ascading Style Sheets designing a style eet for a culinary eb site

Data files needed for this Case Problem: mealstxt.css, mealstxt.xml

WebChef Linda Amanti works for WebChef, a Web site for recipes, cooking tips, diet advice, and articles on health and wellness. The site is moving its recipe database to a set of XML documents. So far, Linda has placed a few Chinese recipes into an XML document. The structure of the document, mealstxt.xml, is shown in Figure 5-69.

Figure 5-69

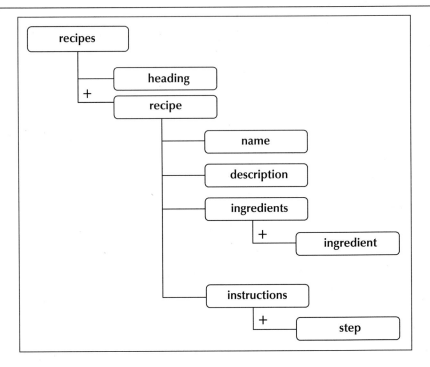

Linda wants your help in setting up a cascading style sheet to display these recipes in an interesting and informative layout. The design of the Web page is up to you.

To complete this task:

1. Using your text editor, open **mealstxt.xml** and **mealstxt.css** from the tutorial.05x/ case4 folder. Enter *your name* and *the date* in the comment section of each file, and save them as **meals.xml** and **meals.css** respectively.

2. Go to the meals.xml file in your text editor. Review the contents of the file, becoming familiar with the data structure and content. Directly below the comment section, insert a processing instruction linking the document to the meals.css style sheet. Close the file, saving your changes.

3. The design of the page is up to you. It should include the following style elements:
   - Elements in blocks, positioned on the page by floating the element or using defined page coordinates
   - Modifications of the border, padding, and margin styles for at least one element
   - Application of text and background colors.
   - Setting the font color, size, and style of text within an element
   - Applying a list item style to an element

4. Test your design in your Web browser.

5. Submit your completed project to your instructor.

Quick Check Answers

Session 5.1

1. <?xml-stylesheet type="text/css" href="styles.css" ?>.
2. document {color: red}
3. models > model
4. cName {display: inline}
5. notes {display: list-item; list-style: circle outside}
6. notes {width: 300px}
7. notes {position: absolute; top: 10px; left: 50px}
8. notes {float: left}

Session 5.2

1. Summary {background-color: rgb(255, 192, 255)
2. margin-left: 3px; margin-right: 3px;
3. Summary {border: 5px dashed red}
4. Summary {padding: 10px}
5. Document {background-image: url(paper.gif) }
6. background-repeat: repeat-y
7. background-attachment: fixed

Session 5.3

1. A specific font is one that is installed on a user's computer, such as Times New Roman, Arial, or Helvetica. A generic font is a general description of a font, allowing a user's operating system to determine which installed font best matches the description.
2. A relative unit expresses the font size relative to the size of a standard character. CSS supports two relative units: em and ex. The em unit is more useful for page design because 1 em is equal to the default font size for the browser.
3. Summary {font-weight: bold; font-family: Arial}
4. Summary {letter-spacing: 0.4pt}
5. #Model500 {styles}
   To apply this style using Firefox or Netscape you have to define the id attribute as an ID in a DTD attached to the document.
6. bike.Mountain_Bikes {styles}
   bike[class="Mountain_Bikes"] {styles}
7. A pseudo-element is a selector that is not an actual element, but is instead abstracted from what you know of an element's content, use, or position. Pseudo-elements include first-line, first-letter, before, and after.

Objectives

Session 6.1
- Learn the history and theory of XSLT
- Understand XPath and examine a node tree
- Create and attach an XSLT style sheet
- Create a root template
- Generate a result document from an XSLT style sheet

Session 6.2
- Create and apply templates to different nodes
- Extract and display the value of an element
- Extract and display the value of an attribute
- Work with XSLT's built-in templates

Session 6.3
- Set the value of an attribute in a result document
- Create conditional output using the if and choose elements
- Create an XPath expression using predicates
- Use XSLT to generate elements and attributes

Working with XSLT and XPath

Transforming an XML Document

Case

Hardin Financial

Hardin Financial is a brokerage firm with headquarters in Chicago, Illinois. Founded by Alan Hardin, the company has provided financial planning and investment services to Chicago-area corporations and individuals for 25 years. As part of its investment services business, the company advises clients on investment portfolios, so it needs to have a variety of stock market information available for its employees.

Kevin Summers, a Hardin Financial analyst, is investigating the possibility of storing stock data in XML format. He created a small test document describing the financial status of 14 stocks listed on the New York Stock Exchange. Kevin is especially interested in the different ways this data can be presented in Web documents.

Kevin heard that the content of an XML document can be transformed into a variety of publishing formats, including HTML, and he asks for your help in creating prototype documents that showcase this feature of XML.

Student Data Files

▼tutorial.06x

▽ **tutorial folder**
    stocktxt.xml
    stocktxt.xsl
    stock.css
    + 3 image files

▽ **review folder**
    stock2txt.xml
    stock2txt.xsl
    stock2.css
    + 3 image files

▽ **case1 folder**
    messtxt.xml
    messtxt.xsl
    skyweb.css
    + 10 image files

Session 6.1

Introducing XSLT

You meet with Kevin to discuss how he wants to format his stock report. He's created a sample document for you to work on. You can apply what you learn from working on this sample document to larger, more complicated projects in the future. Figure 6-1 describes the contents of Kevin's document.

Figure 6-1 ▶ **Elements in the stock document**

Element	Description
portfolio	The root element
author	The author of the document
date	The date of the document contents
time	The time the document was last updated, in 24 hour format
stock	Information for an individual stock
sName	The name of the stock, containing an attribute named symbol that stores the stock abbreviation
description	A description of the stock
category	The category for the stock: Industrials, Transportation, or Utilities
link	The URL of the stock's Web page
today	The opening, high, low, current, and volume values of the stock, stored in the following attributes: open, high, low, current, and vol
five_day	Stock activity information for the last five days
day	The stock value for each day, stored in the following attributes: open, high, low, close, vol, and date

Kevin's file contains information on 14 different stocks, including the opening value of the stock on the New York Stock Exchange, its low and high values for the day, its current value, and the number of shares traded for the day. Kevin also included the previous five days of activity for each stock. Figure 6-2 shows the structure of the file.

Structure of the stock document ◄ **Figure 6-2**

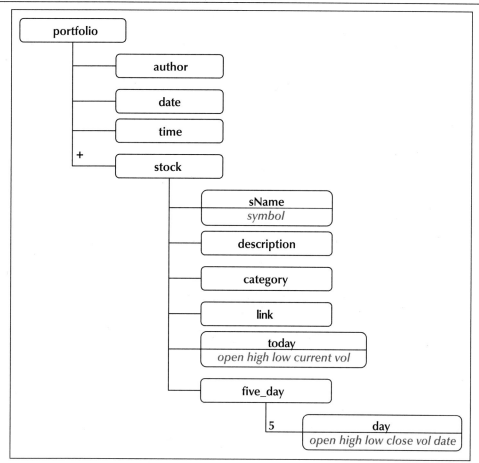

Open the document now.

To open the stock document:

1. Use your text editor to open **stocktxt.xml** from the tutorial.06x/tutorial folder. Enter **your name** and **the date** in the comment section at the top of the file, and save the file as **stock.xml**.

2. Take a few minutes to study the contents of the file. Pay careful attention to the document structure and the use of attributes to store daily information on the stock's opening and closing values, as well as the sales volume.

Figure 6-3 previews how Kevin wants the contents of the stock document to be reported. The description of the stock and the current stock values are displayed along the left page margin of the report. The five days of stock values are also placed in a separate table below the stock description. Finally, Kevin wants the stocks sorted into different stock categories (industrials, transportation, or utilities). In the sketch from Figure 6-3, Kevin has placed the Aluminum Company of America stock in the Industrials category.

Figure 6-3   **Kevin's proposed stock report**

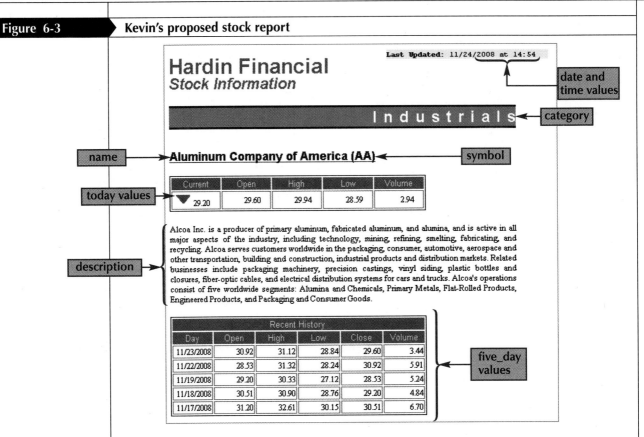

To create a report like this, you could try to combine the XML elements from Kevin's document with elements from the XHTML vocabulary in a compound document. However, Kevin doesn't want the structure of his XML document modified by adding XHTML elements. Instead, he wants a style sheet that can add elements from both XHTML and his stock vocabulary automatically into a formatted report. CSS cannot do this, but a style sheet language called XSLT can.

The History of XSL

One of the challenges of working with an XML document is presenting the XML data in a useful format, particularly for Web users. As you've seen, one method of accomplishing this is by designing a style sheet for the document using CSS. However, CSS has the following limitations:

- CSS displays element content as it appears in the XML document. Although you can apply a style, such as a font size, to content, you can't change the format of the content itself. For example, you can't specify that a date entered in an XML document as "June 28, 2008" should be displayed as "6/28/2008."
- CSS does not allow you to add additional text to element content. Although some CSS3 styles provide capability to do this, they are not well supported by current browsers.
- CSS doesn't provide easy methods to display images or insert links.
- CSS displays only element content, not element attributes.
- An element can be formatted only one way in a document. For example, you cannot display an element as a heading in one part of the page and as a table cell in another.

In an effort to overcome limitations of CSS and provide a more robust method of displaying XML data, in 1998 the W3C began developing the **Extensible Stylesheet Language**, or **XSL**. XSL allows you to transform your XML data into a variety of formats, including HTML, XHTML, Portable Document Format (PDF), Rich Text Format (RTF), and even a new XML document.

XSL is composed of the following two parts, with each part acting as a separate language:

- **XSL-FO (Extensible Stylesheet Language – Formatting Objects)** is used for the layout of paginated documents.
- **XSLT (Extensible Stylesheet Language Transformations)** is used to transform the contents of an XML document into another document format.

XSL-FO is an XML vocabulary that describes the precise layout of text on a page. It supports elements to describe pages, text blocks, horizontal rules, headers, footers, and other page elements. Support for XSL-FO in browsers is very limited at the time of this writing, and therefore Kevin does not feel that you should use it for his stock report project. Instead, you'll create the stock report document using XSLT, which enjoys wide browser support and is robust enough to handle the report that Kevin has designed for his stock data.

At the time of this writing, the most recent version of XSLT released by the W3C is XSLT 1.0. In November 2005, the W3C released a candidate recommendation for XSLT 2.0. A candidate recommendation is a stable working draft of the language that the W3C has proposed to the community for implementation experience and feedback, but which is not a final proposal for the language. Current support for XSLT 2.0 is mixed and limited, although this will certainly change in the future. In this text, unless explicitly stated otherwise, assume that all discussion of XSLT refers to the standards of XSLT 1.0.

XSLT Style Sheets and Processors

The purpose of XSLT is to transform the contents of an XML document into another output format. The output format can be almost anything, including another XML document, a simple text file, a Web page written in XHTML, or a desktop publishing format like RTF (Rich Text Format), PDF (Portable Document Format), or PostScript. Thus, XSLT provides programmers with a wide range of opportunities for displaying XML content.

To employ XSLT, you must create an **XSLT style sheet** that contains instructions for transforming the contents of an XML document into the document format of your choice. An XSLT style sheet is itself an XML document, with elements, attributes, and processing instructions from the XSLT vocabulary. XSLT style sheets have the filename extension .xsl to distinguish them from other XML documents.

An XSLT style sheet works by translating a **source document** of XML content into a **result document** written in the chosen output format. To perform this transformation, you need an **XSLT processor** that applies the style sheet to the source document to generate the result document (see Figure 6-4). The result document can be a physical document stored in a separate file, or it can be a virtual document that is generated by the XSLT processor and appears to a user only when the processor is running.

Figure 6-4 | **Transforming a source document**

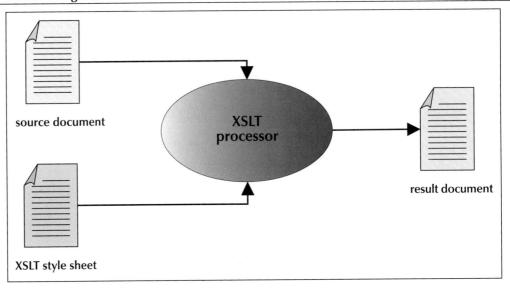

Transformations of a source document can be performed on a server or a client. In a **server-side transformation**, a server receives a request from a client to generate the result document. The server applies the style sheet to the source document and returns the result document to the client, often as a new file. In a server-side transformation, the client does not need an XSLT processor, because all of the work is done on the server. This makes the process more accessible to a wide variety of users who may not have access to an XSLT processor. A disadvantage to server-side transformations is the heavy load they can place on a server as it attempts to handle transformation requests from multiple clients.

In a **client-side transformation**, a client requests retrieval of both a source document and a style sheet from the server. The client then performs the transformation and generates its own result document. There are several client-side XSLT processors available, including the following:

- MSXML, a client-side XSLT processor, is available from Microsoft and is included with Internet Explorer 5.0 and later versions.
- TransforMiiX is a client-side XSLT processor built into the Mozilla browser engine and employed by Netscape and Firefox.
- xt is an open source XSLT processor developed by James Clark.
- Saxon is an open source XSLT processor developed by Michael Kay.
- Xalan Apache, an open source component developed by the Apache Software Foundation, is available for both the Java and C++ programming languages. At the time of this writing, the Macintosh Safari browser does not completely support XSLT 1.0. If you are using Safari, you may have to generate a result document in a separate file.

The XSLT processors built into Web browsers do not generate result documents as separate files; instead, they render a source document using the styles defined in an XSLT style sheet. Most current browsers now support an internal XSLT processor. However, if you need to support older browsers, you must generate the result document as a separate file, with the result document written in the HTML or XHTML language. At the time of this writing, the Macintosh Safari browser does not completely support XSLT 1.0. If you are using Safari, you may have to generate a result document in a separate file.

After discussing the features of XSLT with Kevin, you both decide to use XSLT to create the stock report document. Because this result document is going to be read on Hardin Financial's intranet, you want to write it in HTML format. This allows users to view the document in a Web browser, making it the most flexible format for Hardin Financial employees.

Attaching an XSLT Style Sheet

As with CSS style sheets, an XSLT style sheet is attached to an XML document using a processing instruction. The syntax of the processing instruction is

```
<?xml-stylesheet type="text/xsl" href="url" ?>
```

where *url* is the URL of the file containing the XSLT style sheet. You decide to create an XSLT style sheet named stock.xsl and attach it to the stock.xml document.

To attach an XSLT style sheet:

▶ **1.** Use your text editor to open **stocktxt.xsl** from the tutorial.06x/tutorial folder. Enter **your name** and **the date** in the comment section at the top of the file, and save the file as **stock.xsl**.

▶ **2.** Return to the **stock.xml** file in your text editor, and insert the following processing instruction directly above the opening <portfolio> tag (see Figure 6-5):

```
<?xml-stylesheet type="text/xsl" href="stock.xsl" ?>
```

Attaching the stock.xsl style sheet ◀ Figure 6-5

```
<?xml-stylesheet type="text/xsl" href="stock.xsl" ?>
<portfolio>
    <author>Kevin Summers</author>
    <date>11/24/2008</date>
    <time>14:54</time>
```

`XSLT style sheet`   `style sheet file`

▶ **3.** Close the stock.xml file, saving your changes.

Creating an XSLT Style Sheet

Now you can start creating your XSLT style sheet. Because the style sheet will be an XML document, it must follow the general structure of all XML documents. The root element of an XSLT style sheet is named stylesheet or transform (the names are synonymous). The root element must also include a version attribute with the value "1.0". In addition, in order for the document to be recognized by an XML processor as an XSLT style sheet, it must be placed in the *http://www.w3.org/1999/XSL/Transform* namespace.

Note that users employing Internet Explorer 5.0 as an XSLT processor must use the *http://www.w3.org/TR/WD-xsl* namespace.

This special namespace is required because Internet Explorer 5.0 was based on an early draft of the XSLT specifications. An error results if you attempt to use the *http://www.w3.org/1999/XSL/Transform* namespace with IE 5.0. Given that IE 5.0 is based on a draft version of XSLT, it is best if users upgrade to version 6.0, or use an XSLT processor that supports the final specification. Attempting to base a style sheet on the draft specification can lead to unpredictable results. Typically, the XSLT namespace is associated with a namespace prefix of xsl. You'll follow that convention in this and future tutorials, but as with any XML document, you are free to use a different namespace prefix.

Putting all of this together, the general structure of an XSLT stylesheet is

```
<?xml version="1.0" ?>
<xsl:stylesheet version="1.0"
    xmlns:xsl="http://www.w3.org/1999/XSL/Transform">

  Style sheet contents

</xsl:stylesheet>
```

Use this information to start creating the general structure of the stock.xsl file.

To create the XSLT stylesheet:

1. Return to the **stock.xsl** file in your text editor, and below the comment section insert the following tags (see Figure 6-6):

```
<xsl:stylesheet version="1.0"
    xmlns:xsl="http://www.w3.org/1999/XSL/Transform">

</xsl:stylesheet>
```

Figure 6-6 ▶ **Insert the root stylesheet element and XSLT namespace**

```
<xsl:stylesheet version="1.0"
    xmlns:xsl="http://www.w3.org/1999/XSL/Transform">

</xsl:stylesheet>
```

XSLT namespace

2. Save your changes to the file.

<u>Reference Window</u> **Creating an XSLT Style Sheet**

- To create an XSLT style sheet, use the general structure
  ```
  <?xml version="1.0" ?>
  <xsl:stylesheet version="1.0"
      xmlns:xsl="http://www.w3.org/1999/XSL/Transform">

      Style sheet contents

  </xsl:stylesheet>
  ```
  You can substitute the tag <xsl:transform> for the <xsl:stylesheet> tag if you prefer.

Introducing XPath

With the basic structure of the XSLT style sheet file set, you can begin working on the design of Kevin's stock report. To do this, you first need to learn how to access the different elements and attributes in the stock.xml document.

Nodes and the Node Tree

In XSLT, the content of a source document is organized into nodes, where a **node** is any of the following:

- The source document itself
- A comment statement
- A processing instruction
- A defined namespace
- An element
- The text contained within an element
- An element attribute

The following are *not* considered nodes:

- The XML declaration
- A CDATA section
- An entity reference
- A DOCTYPE declaration

Nodes are distinguished based on the objects they refer to in a document. A node for an element is called an **element node**. A node that stores element attributes is called an **attribute node.** A **text node** contains the text within an element. **Comment nodes** and **processing instruction nodes** store information about the comments and processing instructions in the source document, respectively.

The various nodes are organized into a **node tree**, with the **root node** or **document node** at the top of the tree containing all other nodes. The root node is the node that represents the source document itself; this should not be confused with the root element. Figure 6-7 shows the node tree for a sample XML document. Note that although the XML declaration in the first line of the document is not treated as a node, the other lines of code in the document have places in the node tree.

A sample node tree ◀ **Figure 6-7**

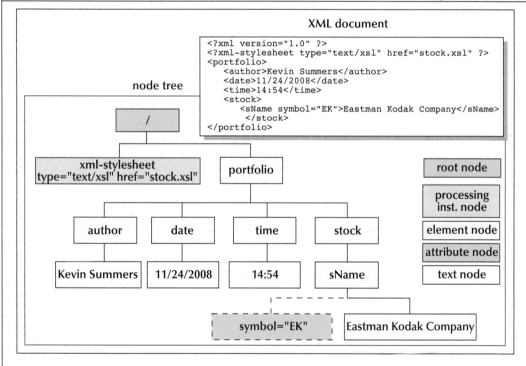

The relationship between the nodes in a node tree follows a familial structure. A node that contains other nodes is called a **parent node**, and the nodes contained in a parent node are called **child nodes**. Nodes that share a common parent are called **sibling nodes**. Note that a node can have only one parent. As you progress further down the tree, any node found at a level below another node is referred to as a **descendant** of that node. The node at the top of the branch is referred to as the **ancestor** of all nodes that lie beneath it. In the sample document shown in Figure 6-7, the portfolio node is the parent of the child nodes author, date, time, and stock. Further down the node tree is the sName node, which is a descendant of both the portfolio and stock nodes. The root node has only two child nodes: the portfolio node and the processing instruction that links the XML document to the stock.xsl style sheet.

Absolute and Relative Location Paths

The different nodes in a node tree can be referenced using **XPath**, a non-XML language that identifies different parts of an XML document. As with XSLT, the most current version of XPath at the time of this writing is XPath 1.0. However, a candidate recommendation for XPath 2.0 was released in November 2005 by the W3C, and features of XPath 2.0 will certainly be adopted by XSLT processors in the years to come. Unless otherwise stated in this manuscript, though, you should assume that all references to XPath refer to XPath 1.0.

XPath is used in conjunction with XSLT to indicate which nodes are being processed and sent to the result document. To select a node or a group of nodes from a node tree, an XPath expression defines a **location path** to the node or nodes. Location paths can be written in either absolute or relative terms.

In describing an **absolute path**, XPath begins with the root node, identified by a forward slash (/), and proceeds down the levels of the node tree until the selected node is reached. Each level is identified by additional forward slashes. The general syntax is therefore

```
/child1/child2/child3/...
```

where `child1`, `child2`, `child3`, and so forth are the descendants of the root node. For example, the absolute path to the sName node from Figure 6-7 is

```
/portfolio/stock/sName
```

For element nodes, you use the name of the element to identify the node. You can avoid listing all of the levels of a node tree by using a double forward slash (//) with the syntax

```
//descendant
```

where `descendant` is the name of the descendant node. For example, the path

```
//sName
```

refers to all sName elements in the document, no matter where they are located in the node tree. Note that a location path might point to more than one node in the source document. In such cases, the collection of nodes is referred to as a **node set**.

As you'll see later, an XSLT processor navigates through the node tree as it generates the contents of a result document. The node where the processor is focused at a given moment is called the **context node**. In place of an absolute path, you can also reference a node through a **relative path** that expresses a node's location relative to the context node. For example, you may want to work with the parent of the context node or the context node's first child or sibling. Figure 6-8 describes some of the common relative path expressions in XPath.

| Figure 6-8 | Relative path expressions |

Relative path	Description
.	Refers to the context node
..	Refers to the parent of the context node
child	Refers to the child of the context node named *child*
child1/child2	Refers to the *child2* node, a child of the *child1* node beneath the context node
../sibling	Refers to a sibling of the context node named *sibling*
.//descendant	Refers to a descendant of the context node named *descendant*

For example, if the context node from Figure 6-7 is the portfolio element, then the XPath expression

```
stock/sName
```

refers to the stock element (the child of the portfolio element) and then to the sName element (the child of the stock element). Figure 6-9 provides other examples of the relative paths in the node tree from Figure 6-7, assuming the stock element is the context node. Take some time to study these XPath expressions, since understanding relative paths is essential to understanding how to write XSLT code.

Relative path expressions   Figure 6-9

Context node	Relative path	Description
stock	.	Refers to the stock element
	..	Refers to the portfolio element, the parent of the stock element
	sName	Refers to the sName element, a child of the stock element
	../date	Refers to the date element, a sibling of the stock element
	.//sName	Refers to all descendent elements of the stock element named sName
	../..	Refers to the parent of the portfolio element (in this case the root node)

Identifying Nodes with Location Paths   Reference Window

- To create an absolute reference to a node, use the location path expression
  `/child1/child2/child3/...`
  where `child1`, `child2`, `child3`, and so on are descendants of the root node.
- To reference a node without regard for its location in the node tree, use the expression
  `//descendant`
  where `descendant` is the name of the descendant node.
- To reference the context node, use
  `.`
- To reference the parent of the context node, use
  `..`
- To reference a child of the context node, use
  `child`
  where `child` is the name of the child node.
- To reference a sibling of the context node, use
  `../sibling`
  where `sibling` is the name of the sibling node.

Referencing Node Sets

XPath also allows you to refer to a node set using the wildcard character (*). For example, the path

```
/portfolio/*
```

is an absolute reference that matches all of the children of the portfolio element. To select all of the nodes in the node tree, you can use the path

```
//*
```

In this case, the (*) symbol matches any node, and the (//) symbol sets the scope of the search to include all of the descendants of the root node. XPath allows you to combine different paths into a single expression using the (|) operator. The expression

```
/portfolio/date | /portfolio/time
```

matches both the date and time child elements of the portfolio element. Similarly, the expression

```
//sName | //author
```

selects all of the sName and author node elements in the node tree, regardless of their location.

Referencing Attribute Nodes

The XPath expressions you have seen so far have been concerned only with element nodes, but as you saw earlier, attributes, comments, text, and processing instructions are also treated as nodes. The syntax to refer to an attribute node is

```
@attribute
```

where `attribute` is the name of the attribute. For example, the sName element from Figure 6-7 has a single attribute named symbol. The absolute reference to this attribute is

```
/portfolio/stock/sName/@symbol
```

If the stock element is the context node, then the relative path to the symbol attribute is

```
sName/@symbol
```

If the sName element is the context node, then the relative path is

```
@symbol
```

To select all symbol attributes in the node tree regardless of their location, you can use the XPath expression

```
//@symbol
```

Finally, to select all attribute nodes in the node tree regardless of their location, you combine the asterisk wildcard with the (@) symbol in the following XPath expression:

```
//@*
```

Referencing Text Nodes

A text node is simply the text content of an element. There are no nodes for character or entity references. If element text contains an entity or character reference, that reference is resolved by an XSLT processor before the text node is created. Thus, there is no way of knowing whether the content of a text node originally contained entity or character references. The syntax to refer to a text node is

```
text()
```

For example, to reference the text contained with the sName element, you can use the absolute path

```
/portfolio/stock/sName/text()
```

or more generally

```
//sName/text()
```

To match all text nodes in the document no matter their location in the node tree, use

```
//text()
```

By accessing text nodes, you can use XSLT to create result documents that act upon the actual text content of elements in the source document. This subject, however, is beyond the scope of this tutorial.

Referencing Comment and Processing Instruction Nodes

Comments are treated as nodes, and can be referenced using the expression

```
comment()
```

For example, if you insert comments at the top of an XML document, those comments can be referenced using the absolute path expression

```
/comment()
```

All of the comments in a document can be referenced using the XPath expression

```
//comment()
```

The node tree includes a processing instruction node for every processing instruction in the source document, except those that occur within a DOCTYPE declaration. (The XML declaration is not treated as a processing instruction node.) To reference a processing instruction, you use the XPath expression

```
processing-instruction()
```

Thus, the absolute path to a processing instruction in the source document would be

```
/processing-instruction()
```

and you could reference all of the processing instructions in the source document with the expression

```
//processing-instruction()
```

There is usually little need for referencing comments or processing instructions in the source document until you get to more advanced XSLT applications.

You've barely scratched the surface of all that can be done with XPath. As you continue to work on XSLT style sheets in this and future tutorials, you'll return to XPath periodically to explore the various facets of this language. However, what you've learned is enough to start writing an XSLT style sheet for Kevin's stock report.

Introducing XSLT Templates

The basic building block of an XSLT style sheet is the template. A **template** is a collection of rules that define how a particular collection of nodes in a source document should be transformed in a result document. A template fills the same role that a selector fills in the Cascading Style Sheets language: it indicates which parts of a source document receive the styles defined in the style sheet. The general syntax of an XSLT template is

```
<xsl:template match="node set">

    styles

</xsl:template>
```

where *node set* is an XPath expression that references a node set from the source document and *styles* are the XSLT styles applied to those nodes. As an XSLT processor moves through the source document's node tree, it applies these styles when it encounters the nodes defined in the match attributes. The node specified in the match attribute becomes the context node for any location paths used in the template. For example, if the template is written for the stock node, then any XPath expressions in that template must be written assuming the stock node is the context node.

The Root Template

The basic template in an XSLT style sheet is the **root template**, which defines styles for the source document's root node. Because the root node refers to the source document itself, the root template sets the initial styles for the entire result document. The syntax for the root template is

```
<xsl:template match="/">

    styles

</xsl:template>
```

Note that the location path for the match attribute is set to "/", matching the XPath expression for the root node. This also makes the root node the context node for all XPath expressions within the template. The root template can be located anywhere between the opening and closing <xsl:stylesheet> tags of the XSLT document. However, it is customary to put the root template at the top of the document, directly after the opening <xsl:stylesheet> tag.

Creating a Template

- To create an XSLT template, use the syntax
  ```
  <xsl:template match="node set">
      styles
  </xsl:template>
  ```
  where *node set* is an XPath expression that references a node set from the source document and *styles* are the XSLT styles defined for the node or nodes.
- To create a root template, use the syntax
  ```
  <xsl:template match="/">
      styles
  </xsl:template>
  ```

Add a root template to the stock.xsl file.

To create the root template:

1. Return to the **stock.xsl** file in your text editor.

2. Within the stylesheet element, insert the following content (see Figure 6-10):

```
<xsl:template match="/">
</xsl:template>
```

```
<xsl:stylesheet version="1.0"
        xmlns:xsl="http://www.w3.org/1999/XSL/Transform">

<xsl:template match="/">

</xsl:template>

</xsl:stylesheet>
```

XPath expression matching the root node

Next you can populate the root template with elements and attributes from XSLT.

Literal Result Elements

A template contains two types of elements: XSLT elements and literal result elements. An XSLT element is any element that is part of the XSLT vocabulary. XSLT elements must be placed within the XSLT namespace, usually with the namespace prefix xsl. XSLT elements contain instructions to the XSLT processor regarding how to interpret the contents of the source document or how to render the contents of the result document. A **literal result element** is any element that is not part of the XSLT vocabulary and that has content to be sent to the result document. A literal result element is not acted upon by the XSLT processor but is treated instead as raw text. For example, any HTML tags in a style sheet are considered a literal result because they are ignored by XSLT processors and sent directly to the result document.

In this case, Kevin wants to create a Web page based on the contents of the stock.xml file. He shows you the initial code for the HTML file that he wants to generate:

```
<html>
<head>
   <title>Stock Information</title>
   <link href="stock.css" rel="stylesheet" type="text/css" />
</head>
<body>
   <h1>Hardin Financial</h1>
   <h2>Stock Information</h2>
</body>
</html>
```

Note that Kevin created an external CSS style sheet named stock.css to format some of the tags of his HTML file. HTML uses the link element to attach an HTML file to an external style sheet. If you want to review CSS usage, you can examine the contents of stock.css to see how the headings are formatted.

All of the HTML elements in Kevin's initial code are literal result elements, because they do not involve any of the elements associated with XSLT. Because they are to be placed directly in the result document as text, you need only add the HTML code to the root template as follows:

```
<xsl:template match="/">
   <html>
   <head>
      <title>Stock Information</title>
      <link href="stock.css" rel="stylesheet" type="text/css" />
   </head>
   <body>
      <h1>Hardin Financial</h1>
      <h2>Stock Information</h2>
   </body>
   </html>
</xsl:template>
```

Even though the HTML tags are treated as text, they must still follow basic XML syntax. For example, all two-sided tags must contain a closing tag, and all attribute values must be placed within quotes. Failure to follow XML syntax results in an error.

To populate the root template:

1. Within the root template, insert the following content (see Figure 6-11):

```
<html>
<head>
    <title>Stock Information</title>
    <link href="stock.css" rel="stylesheet" type="text/css" />
</head>
<body>
    <h1>Hardin Financial</h1>
    <h2>Stock Information</h2>
</body>
</html>
```

Figure 6-11 ▶ **Populating the root template with literal result elements**

```
<xsl:template match="/">
    <html>
    <head>
        <title>Stock Information</title>
        <link href="stock.css" rel="stylesheet" type="text/css" />
    </head>
    <body>
        <h1>Hardin Financial</h1>
        <h2>Stock Information</h2>
    </body>
    </html>
</xsl:template>
```

literal result elements

2. Save your changes to the file.

In some cases, literal result elements are themselves part of a namespace. For example, you may want to place all of the HTML elements within the HTML namespace using the prefix html. In this case, you simply include the namespace prefix with the element. Thus, you enter an h1 heading as

```
<html:h1>Hardin Financial</html:h1>
```

However, this is not necessary for the stock report. So far, you've set up the template to send HTML code to the result document. How do you let XSLT processors know to treat this text as HTML code rather than simple text? One way is by indicating the output method in the XSLT style sheet.

Specifying the Output Method

By default, an XSLT processor renders the result document as an XML file. However, most processors instead create an HTML file if the <html> tag is included as a literal result element in the root template. This is a convention followed by the programmers of XSLT processors, though, and is not part of the XSLT specifications. To ensure complete control over how processors format your source document, you can specify the output method using the XSLT element

```
<xsl:output attributes />
```

where *attributes* is the list of attributes that define the output format of the result document. Figure 6-12 describes the different attributes associated with the output element.

Attributes of the output element | Figure 6-12

Attribute	Description
method	Defines the output format using the value xml, html, or text
version	Specifies the version of the output
encoding	Specifies the character encoding
omit-xml-declaration	Specifies whether to omit an XML declaration in the first line of the result document (yes) or to include it (no)
standalone	Specifies whether a standalone attribute should be included in the output and sets its value (yes or no)
doctype-public	Sets the URI for the public identifier in the <!DOCTYPE> declaration
doctype-system	Sets the system identifier in the <!DOCTYPE> declaration
cdata-section-elements	Specifies a list of element names whose content should be output in CDATA sections
indent	Specifies whether the output should be indented to better display its structure (indentations are automatically added to HTML files without use of this attribute)
media-type	Sets the MIME type of the output

For example, to instruct XSLT processors to create HTML 4.0 files, you insert the following tag directly after the opening <xsl:stylesheet> tag:

```
<xsl:output method="html" version="4.0" />
```

On the other hand, to use your style sheet to transform one XML document into another, you add the following tag to the stylesheet file:

```
<xsl:output method="xml" version="1.0" />
```

Sometimes programmers need only a piece of an XML document, consisting of a few elements or attributes, as a result document. Such a document, called an **XML fragment**, does not include an opening XML declaration:

```
<?xml version="1.0" ?>
```

To remove this declaration from the result document, you use the following open method:

```
<xsl:output method="xml" version="1.0" omit-xml-declaration="yes" />
```

Finally, to create a plain text file, the output method is

```
<xsl:output method="text" />
```

Text files are used in cases in which the code of the result document follows neither the HTML nor the XML syntax. One format for text files is the Rich Text Format (RTF), which is supported by most word processors. To create an RTF file, you insert code for the RTF file into the style sheet. XSLT processors then pass the code through as text, without checking the document for well-formedness or validity.

The other attributes of the output element provide additional control over the format of the text and content of any XML elements that may be placed in a template file. For example, you can control the content of the DOCTYPE declaration using the doctype-public and doctype-system attributes. Naturally, this would be applicable only if the result document is an XML file. For international documents, you may need to set the encoding attribute to match the character encoding used by readers.

After discussing the importance of specifying an output method, Kevin agrees that you should add the output element to the stock.xsl style sheet, specifying that the result document should be treated as an HTML version 4.0 file.

To specify the output format of the result document:

▶ **1.** Insert the following code immediately before the opening <xsl:template> element located at the top of the stock.xsl file (see Figure 6-13):

```
<xsl:output method="html" version="4.0" />
```

Figure 6-13	Setting the output format

```
<xsl:stylesheet version="1.0"
    xmlns:xsl="http://www.w3.org/1999/XSL/Transform">
<xsl:output method="html" version="4.0" />

<xsl:template match="/">
    <html>
    <head>
        <title>Stock Information</title>
        <link href="stock.css" rel="stylesheet" type="text/css" />
    </head>
```

the result document should be formatted as an HTML Version 4.0 file

▶ **2.** Close the stock.xsl file, saving your changes.

Now that you've specified an output method, you can view the result document generated by the XSLT style sheet.

Transforming a Document

There are two ways to view a result document. One way is to use a browser that contains an XSLT processor to view the source document. Because the source document includes a processing instruction that applies the stock.xsl style sheet, the browser transforms the source document and presents the result document in the browser window. Alternatively, a user can use a third-party XSLT processor to create the result document as a separate file on their computer, and then view that file in a browser that does not contain an XSLT processor.

Transforming a Document in a Browser

Most current Web browsers contain an XSLT processor, allowing you to view the transformed document by simply opening the source document, stock.xml. The browser applies the style sheet rules defined in the stock.xsl file. Older browsers, like Netscape 6.2 or the Macintosh Safari browser, contain XSLT processors that might render the result document with some formatting errors, so you may have to test several browsers to determine which ones can reliably transform a given source document. If you are not running a current browser with a built-in XSLT processor, you do not have to complete the steps in the section, and can proceed to the next section to learn how to create a separate file using the Exchanger XML Editor.

To view the result document:

▶ **1.** Use your browser to open **stock.xml** from the tutorial.06x/tutorial folder. Figure 6-14 shows the result document created by transforming the source document.

Initial result document ◀ Figure 6-14

Hardin Financial
Stock Information

▶ **2.** Close your Web browser.

A Web browser allows you to quickly view the results of the transformation. However, if you don't have access to a browser with a built-in XSLT processor, or you are concerned that your audience does not have access to a current browser, you can create the transformed document as a separate file to be viewed in any browser. You'll do this now using the Exchanger XML Editor.

Transforming a Document in the Exchanger XML Editor

Most XSLT processors provide the capability to create the result document as a separate file. In this tutorial you'll use the Exchanger XML Editor, but you can use other processors such as Saxon, xt, or Xalan. If you have not already installed the Exchanger XML Editor, the appendix includes installation instructions and an overview of how to work with the program.

One advantage of creating a separate HTML file is that it can then be viewed in any Web browser, whether or not that browser contains an XSLT processor. However, this also means that every time you make a change to the source document or the style sheet, you have to regenerate the result document.

To generate the result document:

▶ **1.** Start the Exchanger XML Editor, and open **stock.xml** and **stock.xsl** from the tutorial.06x/tutorial folder.

Trouble? If the Exchanger XML Editor reports a schema error and a RelaxNG error, click the OK button to clear the dialog boxes and proceed.

▶ **2.** Click the stock.xml tab to make this document the active pane in the Main window.

▶ **3.** Click **Execute Advanced XSLT** from the Transform menu on the Exchanger XML Editor menu bar. The Execute XSLT dialog box opens.

▶ **4.** Click the **Current Document** option button in the Input section and select **stock.xml** from the drop-down list box.

▶ **5.** Click the **Open Document** option button in the XSL section and select **stock.xsl** from the drop-down list box.

▶ **6.** Click the **New Document** option button in the Output section. Figure 6-15 shows the completed dialog box. Click the **Execute** button to start the transformation.

Figure 6-15 ▶ **Transforming the document in the Exchanger XML Editor**

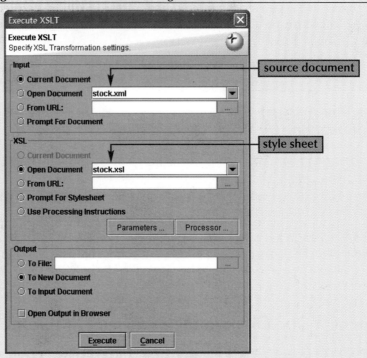

> **Trouble?** The Exchanger XML Editor will report a well-formedness error in the new document. You can ignore this error.

7. The Exchanger XML Editor runs the tranformation. Close the Execute Scenario dialog box when the tranformation is completed. The editor inserts a new document tab named New Document 1 in the Main window.

8. With the New Document 1 tab active, click **Save As** on the File menu.

9. Save the file as **stock.htm** in the tutorial.06x/tutorial folder.

10. Click **Exit** on the File menu to close the Exchanger XML Editor, without saving any other changes to the three documents.

11. Open stock.htm in your Web browser, verify that its appearance matches the page shown earlier in Figure 6-14, and close your Web browser.

12. Use your text editor to open the stock.htm file. Note that the code contained within the file matches the code defined in the stock.xsl style sheet. Close your text editor.

When you viewed the contents of the stock.htm file, you may have noticed that the XSLT processor added one extra line to the document:

```
<meta http-equiv="Content-Type" content="text/html; charset=UTF-8">
```

This code provides additional information to the browser about the content of the document and its encoding. This was added because of the output element that you added to the stock.xsl file. The meta element makes it clear to any application opening this file what type of content the file contains and how the characters are encoded.

At this point, you have not placed any content of the source document into the result document. So far you have created the literal result elements—specifically the h1 and h2 headings—formatted using styles from the stock.css style sheet. In the next session, you'll learn how to insert values from the stock.xml source document into the result document.

Session 6.1 Quick Check

1. What are XSLT, XPath, and XSL-FO?
2. What processing instruction links an XML document to an XSLT style sheet named styles.xsl?
3. In an XML document, the root element is named books and it contains one child element named book. The book element contains two child elements named author and title. What is the absolute path for the title element?
4. In the above example, what is the relative path from the author to the title element, assuming that the author element is the context node?
5. If, in the above examples, the title element contains an attribute named isbn, what is the absolute path to this attribute?
6. What XPath expression do you use to reference the author element, regardless of where it is located in the node tree?
7. What is a literal result element?
8. What XSLT element do you use to specify that the result document should be a text file? Under what circumstances might you want to create a text file and not an HTML or XML document?

Session 6.2

Extracting Element Values

In the last session you worked with Kevin to create the initial XSLT style sheet for the stock report. Because the style sheet sent only HTML code to the result document, it was not any more effective than creating a separate HTML document in a text editor. What Kevin would like to see are the values from the source document integrated with HTML code in the result document. To insert a node's value into the result document, you use the XSLT element

```
<xsl:value-of select="expression" />
```

where *expression* is an XPath expression that identifies the node from the source document's node tree. For element nodes, the value of the node is the text that the node contains. If the element node contains child elements in addition to text content, the text in those child nodes appears as well.

To see how this works, return to Kevin's proposed sketch of his Web page, shown earlier in Figure 6-3. At the top of the page, Kevin wants to display the date and time of the source document as follows:

Last Updated: *date* at *time*

where *date* and *time* are values taken from the source document's date and time elements. In the stock.xml document, the value contained in the date element is 11/24/2008, and the value contained in the time element is 14:54. Thus, to present these values in a formatted text string, you add the following expressions to the root template in the stock.xsl file:

```
Last Updated:
<xsl:value-of select="portfolio/date" />
at
<xsl:value-of select="portfolio/time" />
```

You may wonder why the XPath expression is "portfolio/date" rather than "/portfolio/date". This is because you're adding this code to the root template, and as the commands in that template are processed the context node is the root node. Thus, you can use a relative path to the date and time nodes rather than an absolute path.

Inserting a Node's Value

- To insert a node's value into the result document, use the XSLT element

  ```
  <xsl:value-of select="expression" />
  ```

  where *expression* is an XPath expression that identifies the node from the source document's node tree.

To display the values of the date and time elements:

▶ **1.** Return to the **stock.xsl** file in your text editor.

▶ **2.** Insert the following code within the body element in the root template as shown in Figure 6-16:

```
<div id="datetime"><b>Last Updated: </b>
   <xsl:value-of select="portfolio/date" /> at
   <xsl:value-of select="portfolio/time" />
</div>
```

Note that the <div id="datetime"> tag was added to format the date and time text string using a style from the stock.css style sheet, which places this text in the upper-right corner of the Web page.

Figure 6-16	Displaying the date and time element values

```
<xsl:template match="/">
   <html>
   <head>
      <title>Stock Information</title>
      <link href="stock.css" rel="stylesheet" type="text/css" />
   </head>
   <body>

      <div id="datetime"><b>Last Updated: </b>
         <xsl:value-of select="portfolio/date" /> at
         <xsl:value-of select="portfolio/time" />
      </div>

      <h1>Hardin Financial</h1>
      <h2>Stock Information</h2>
   </body>
   </html>
</xsl:template>
```

▶ **3.** Save your changes to the file.

▶ **4.** Using either your browser (if it contains a built-in XSLT processor) or the Exchanger XML Editor, generate the revised result document. If you use the editor, follow the techniques described in the last session to create a file named stock.htm containing the transformed document. Figure 6-17 shows the new Web page.

Figure 6-17	Revised result document

date and time values drawn from the source document

Last Updated: 11/24/2008 at 14:54

Hardin Financial
Stock Information

Next you want to add the names of all of the stocks in Kevin's document, displaying them as h3 headings. The HTML code for displaying each stock's name is

```
<h3>stock name</h3>
```

where `stock name` is the name of the stock. To generate this code from the root template, you add the following code:

```
<h3><xsl:value-of select="portfolio/stock/sName" /></h3>
```

If you're unclear about the location path used in this expression, refer to the source document or to the tree diagram shown earlier in Figure 6-2. Add this code now to the stock.xsl style sheet.

To display a stock name:

1. Return to the **stock.xsl** file in your text editor.

2. Insert the following code immediately after the h2 element in the root template (see Figure 6-18):

```
<h3>
   <xsl:value-of select="portfolio/stock/sName" />
</h3>
```

Display the stock name values in an h3 heading ◀ Figure 6-18

```
<h1>Hardin Financial</h1>
<h2>Stock Information</h2>
<h3>
   <xsl:value-of select="portfolio/stock/sName" />
</h3>
```

3. Save your changes to the stock.xsl file, and regenerate the result document (either within your Web browser or by using an XSLT processor such as the Exchanger XML Editor). Figure 6-19 shows the revised result document.

First stock name in the result document ◀ Figure 6-19

Hardin Financial
Stock Information

Last **Updated**: 11/24/2008 at 14:54

Aluminum Company of America

The first stock name appears in the document, but where are the others? Although the XSLT value-of element does display the node's value, if there are multiple elements in the source document that match the XPath expression, only the value of the first element appears. To apply this style to all elements in the source document, you can use another XSLT element to apply the style to all occurrences of the element.

Processing Several Elements

When several nodes in the source document match an XPath expression, you can apply the same style to each item using XSLT's for-each element. The syntax of this element is

```
<xsl:for-each select="expression">
   styles
</xsl:for-each>
```

For example, to display each stock name from the source document as an h3 heading, you can use the following code:

```
<xsl:for-each select="portfolio/stock">
   <h3><xsl:value-of select="sName" /></h3>
</xsl:for-each>
```

As the XSLT processor goes through the source document's node tree, it stops at each occurrence of a portfolio/stock node and sends the following style to the result document:

```
<h3><xsl:value-of select="sName" /></h3>
```

Note that the XPath expression in this statement uses a relative path reference to point to the sName element. In this case, the context node is the portfolio/stock node, as that is the node currently being processed in the for-each statement. One of the challenges for new XSLT programmers is to keep track of the context node; assuming an incorrect context node for a given expression is a common source of errors.

To display multiple stock names:

1. Return to the **stock.xsl** file in your text editor.

2. Replace the three lines of code used to generate the stock name with the h3 heading with the following (see Figure 6-20):

   ```
   <xsl:for-each select="portfolio/stock">
      <h3>
      <xsl:value-of select="sName" />
      </h3>
   </xsl:for-each>
   ```

Figure 6-20

Setting a style for each occurrence of the name element

```
<div id="datetime"><b>Last Updated: </b>
   <xsl:value-of select="portfolio/date" /> at
   <xsl:value-of select="portfolio/time" />
</div>

<h1>Hardin Financial</h1>
<h2>Stock Information</h2>

<xsl:for-each select="portfolio/stock">
   <h3>
   <xsl:value-of select="sName" />
   </h3>
</xsl:for-each>
```

replace the three lines to generate the h3 heading with a for-each statement

3. Save your changes to the style sheet, and regenerate the result document using your Web browser, the Exchanger XML Editor, or some other XSLT processor. Figure 6-21 shows the revised content of the result document and the first few stock names from the source document.

Hardin Financial
Stock Information

Last Updated: 11/24/2008 at 14:54

Aluminum Company of America

Unocal Corporation

General Motors Corporation

Eastman Kodak Company

Running a Style for Each Occurrence of an Item

Reference Window

- To apply a style to each occurrence of a node, use the XSLT element

```
<xsl:for-each select="expression">
    styles
</xsl:for-each>
```

where *expression* is an XPath expression that matches several nodes from the source document's node tree and *styles* are styles that are applied to each node matching that XPath expression.

You have now used the for-each element to display multiple values. A more versatile approach, however, is to create a template for nodes that are repeated throughout a document.

Working with Templates

Rather than using the XSLT for-each element, you can create a template for the sName element. An XSLT processor can then apply the template whenever it encounters the sName element in the source document. Such a template would appear as follows:

```
<xsl:template match="sName">
    <h3><xsl:value-of select="." /></h3>
</xsl:template>
```

where the match attribute now matches the sName element. Thus, each sName element in the node tree is associated with this template. Because the context node in this template is the sName element, the value of the select attribute is changed from "sName" to ".". Recall from Figure 6-8 that the "." symbol refers to the context node.

Simply creating a template does not cause processors to use it in the result document. You also must indicate where you want the template applied in the XSLT style sheet.

Applying a Template

To apply a template, use the apply-templates element with the syntax:

```
<xsl:apply-templates select="expression" />
```

where *expression* is an XPath expression for a node set in the source document. The XSLT processor then searches the XSLT style sheet for a template matching that node set. The value of the XPath expression depends on the value of the context node. For example, to apply the sName template from within the root template, you set the XPath expression to "portfolio/stock/sName" as in the following code:

```
<xsl:template match="/">
   <xsl:apply-templates select="portfolio/stock/sName" />
</xsl:template>
```

In this example, the context node is the root node. However, within a template for the stock element, the apply-templates element uses a different path to reference the sName element:

```
<xsl:template match="stock">
   <xsl:apply-templates select="sName" />
</xsl:template>
```

In both cases, the XSLT processor searches the node tree of the source document, starting with the context node and working down. If the specified path is repeated several times (as is the sName node), the template is applied for each occurrence. This is why templates can be used in place of the for-each element.

Reference Window

Applying a Template

- To apply a template, use the XSLT element
  `<xsl:apply-templates select="expression" />`
  where *expression* is an XPath expression matching a node set from the source document.

To see how this works, replace the for-each element with a template for the sName node.

To create and apply a template:

1. Return to the **stock.xsl** file in your text editor.
2. Delete the for-each construction from the root template (all of the lines shown in red in Figure 6-20), and replace it with the following line:

```
<xsl:apply-templates select="portfolio/stock/sName" />
```

3. Insert the following code immediately above the closing </xsl:stylesheet> tag:

```
<xsl:template match="sName">
   <h3>
      <xsl:value-of select="." />
   </h3>
</xsl:template>
```

Figure 6-22 shows the revised file.

Creating and applying a template | Figure 6-22

```
<xsl:template match="/">
   <html>
   <head>
      <title>Stock Information</title>
      <link href="stock.css" rel="stylesheet" type="text/css" />
   </head>
   <body>

      <div id="datetime"><b>Last Updated: </b>
         <xsl:value-of select="portfolio/date" /> at
         <xsl:value-of select="portfolio/time" />
      </div>

      <h1>Hardin Financial</h1>
      <h2>Stock Information</h2>

      <xsl:apply-templates select="portfolio/stock/sName" />

   </body>
   </html>
</xsl:template>

<xsl:template match="sName">
   <h3>
      <xsl:value-of select="." />
   </h3>
</xsl:template>
```

applying the name template →

name template →

4. Save your changes to the file, and regenerate the result document, verifying that the appearance of the result document is unchanged with the new code.

Creating the Stock Template

One of the advantages of using templates instead of the for-each element is that you can break up the nodes of a source document into manageable chunks. A template can also be called from other templates in the style sheet, making it very easy to reuse the same code in different locations in the result document. To see how this works in practice, you create a template for each stock node in the source document. Kevin has collected a lot of information about each stock, so you break that information into separate templates. You start by reporting only the stock name and description for each stock. Kevin wants the following HTML code to be generated for each stock:

```
<div>
   <h3>Stock Name</h3>
   <p>Stock Description</p>
</div>
```

where *Stock Name* is the name of each stock (drawn from the sName element) and *Stock Description* is the description of the stock (taken from the description element). The XSLT styles to generate this code are

```
<xsl:template match="stock">
   <div>
      <xsl:apply-templates select="sName" />
      <p><xsl:value-of select="description" /></p>
   </div>
</xsl:template>
```

Note that to insert the h3 heading, you simply reference the sName template that you've already added to the stock.xsl stylesheet.

To add the stock template:

1. Return to the **stock.xsl** file in your text editor.

2. Insert the following stock template between the root and sName templates:

```
<xsl:template match="stock">
   <div>
      <xsl:apply-templates select="sName" />
      <p><xsl:value-of select="description" /></p>
   </div>
</xsl:template>
```

3. Change the select attribute of the apply-templates element in the root template from "portfolio/stock/sName" to **"portfolio/stock"**. Figure 6-23 shows the new and revised style sheet code.

| Figure 6-23 | Creating the stock template |

```
            <h1>Hardin Financial</h1>
            <h2>Stock Information</h2>

            <xsl:apply-templates select="portfolio/stock" />

         </body>
      </html>
   </xsl:template>

stock
template   <xsl:template match="stock">
            <div>
               <xsl:apply-templates select="sName" />
               <p><xsl:value-of select="description" /></p>
            </div>
         </xsl:template>

   <xsl:template match="sName">
      <h3>
         <xsl:value-of select="." />
      </h3>
   </xsl:template>
```

4. Save your changes to the style sheet, and regenerate the result document in your browser, using the Exchanger XML Editor, or some other XSLT processor. Figure 6-24 shows the revised layout of the result document.

| Figure 6-24 | Stock name and description |

Hardin Financial
Stock Information

Last Updated: 11/24/2008 at 14:54

Aluminum Company of America

description → Alcoa Inc. is a producer of primary aluminum, fabricated aluminum, and alumina, and is active in all major aspects of the industry, including technology, mining, refining, smelting, fabricating, and recycling. Alcoa serves customers worldwide in the packaging, consumer, automotive, aerospace and other transportation, building and construction, industrial products and distribution markets. Related businesses include packaging machinery, precision castings, vinyl siding, plastic bottles and closures, fiber-optic cables, and electrical distribution systems for cars and trucks. Alcoa's operations consist of five worldwide segments: Alumina and Chemicals, Primary Metals, Flat-Rolled Products, Engineered Products, and Packaging and Consumer Goods.

Working with Attribute Nodes

Stocks are identified both by their stock name and their abbreviation or symbol. For example, the stock symbol for the Aluminum Company of America is "AA." Kevin wants the stock symbol to appear next to the stock name as follows:

Aluminum Company of America (AA)

The symbol is an attribute of the stock element. Recall that attributes are referenced using the expression @attribute, where attribute is the attribute's name. To add the symbol to the result document, you can modify the sName template, inserting the value of the symbol attribute. Because the symbol attribute is a child of the sName node, the XPath reference to the attribute is "@symbol". The revised template is then

```
<xsl:template match="sName">
<h3>
    <xsl:value-of select="." />
    (<xsl:value-of select="@symbol" />)
</h3>
</xsl:template>
```

Modify the sName template now, adding the value of the symbol attribute.

To display the symbol attribute value:

1. Return to the **stock.xsl** file in your text editor.

2. Insert the following code immediately above the closing </h3> tag in the sName template (see Figure 6-25):

   ```
   (<xsl:value-of select="@symbol" />)
   ```

Displaying an attribute value ◄ Figure 6-25

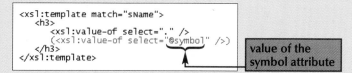

```
<xsl:template match="sName">
    <h3>
        <xsl:value-of select="." />
        (<xsl:value-of select="@symbol" />)
    </h3>
</xsl:template>
```

value of the symbol attribute

3. Save your changes to the style sheet, and regenerate the result document. Verify that the symbol for each stock appears in parenthesis after the stock name.

The stock document also contains attributes that store the daily values of each stock. For example, the opening, high, low, current, and volume values of the ALCOA stock are entered in the stock.xml file as attributes of the today element:

```
<today open="29.60" high="29.94" low="28.59" current="29.20"
vol="2.94" />
```

Kevin wants this data to appear in a table that appears directly below each stock's name in the result document. The HTML code he wants you to use for this information is

```
<table>
<tr>
    <th>Current</th>
    <th>Open</th>
    <th>High</th>
    <th>Low</th>
    <th>Volume</th>
</tr>
<tr>
```

```
        <td>current</td>
        <td>open</td>
        <td>high</td>
        <td>low</td>
        <td>volume</td>
   </tr>
   </table>
```

where *current*, *open*, *high*, *low*, and *volume* are the attribute values from the today element. You insert this code by creating two templates. The first template creates the table for the today element. The second template creates table cells for each of the five stock value attributes.

To create the current stock values table:

1. Return to the **stock.xsl** file in your text editor.

2. Insert the following template directly below sName template:

```
<xsl:template match="today">
    <table>
    <tr>
        <th>Current</th>
        <th>Open</th>
        <th>High</th>
        <th>Low</th>
        <th>Volume</th>
    </tr>
    <tr>
    </tr>
    </table>
</xsl:template>
```

3. Go to the stock template and insert the following code directly below the apply-templates element that applies the sName template. Figure 6-26 shows the new and revised code of the stock.xsl style sheet.

```
<xsl:apply-templates select="today" />
```

Figure 6-26   **Creating the today template**

```
<xsl:template match="stock">
    <div>
        <xsl:apply-templates select="sName" />
        <xsl:apply-templates select="today" />
        <p><xsl:value-of select="description" /></p>
    </div>
</xsl:template>

<xsl:template match="sName">
    <h3>
        <xsl:value-of select="." />
        (<xsl:value-of select="@symbol" />)
    </h3>
</xsl:template>

<xsl:template match="today">
    <table>
    <tr>
        <th>Current</th>
        <th>Open</th>
        <th>High</th>
        <th>Low</th>
        <th>Volume</th>
    </tr>
    <tr>
    </tr>
    </table>
</xsl:template>

</xsl:stylesheet>
```

template for the today element

Next you have to put the actual daily values into the today table. Because they all share the common code structure of

```
<td>value</td>
```

you can place this code into a separate template, matching that template to each of the stock value attributes.

To display the current stock values:

1. Below the today template, insert the following template:

```
<xsl:template match="@current|@open|@high|@low|@vol">
   <td><xsl:value-of select="." /></td>
</xsl:template>
```

Note that the match attribute in the template uses the (|) symbol to apply this template to any of the following attributes: current, open, high, low, or vol.

2. Apply this template to the daily values table by inserting the following apply-templates elements within the second table row (see Figure 6-27):

```
<xsl:apply-templates select="@current" />
<xsl:apply-templates select="@open" />
<xsl:apply-templates select="@high" />
<xsl:apply-templates select="@low" />
<xsl:apply-templates select="@vol" />
```

Stock values template ◄ Figure 6-27

```
<xsl:template match="today">
   <table>
   <tr>
      <th>Current</th>
      <th>Open</th>
      <th>High</th>
      <th>Low</th>
      <th>Volume</th>
   </tr>
   <tr>
      <xsl:apply-templates select="@current" />
      <xsl:apply-templates select="@open" />
      <xsl:apply-templates select="@high" />
      <xsl:apply-templates select="@low" />
      <xsl:apply-templates select="@vol" />
   </tr>
   </table>
</xsl:template>

<xsl:template match="@current|@open|@high|@low|@vol">
   <td><xsl:value-of select="." /></td>
</xsl:template>
```

template stock value attributes

3. Save your changes to the file, and regenerate the result document. Figure 6-28 shows the current stock values placed in a table above the first stock description.

Current stock values ◄ Figure 6-28

Aluminum Company of America (AA)

Current	Open	High	Low	Volume
29.20	29.60	29.94	28.59	2.94

Alcoa Inc. is a producer of primary aluminum, fabricated aluminum, and alumina, and is active in all major aspects of the industry, including technology, mining, refining, smelting, fabricating, and recycling. Alcoa serves customers worldwide in the packaging, consumer, automotive, aerospace and other transportation, building and construction, industrial products and distribution markets. Related businesses include packaging machinery, precision castings, vinyl siding, plastic bottles and closures, fiber-optic cables, and electrical distribution systems for cars and trucks. Alcoa's operations consist of five worldwide segments: Alumina and Chemicals, Primary Metals, Flat-Rolled Products, Engineered Products, and Packaging and Consumer Goods.

The stock document also contains daily stock values from the previous five days of activity. Kevin stored this information in his XML document as attributes of the day element. Figure 6-29 shows the structure of this fragment of the stock.xml document.

Figure 6-29
Structure of the five_day element

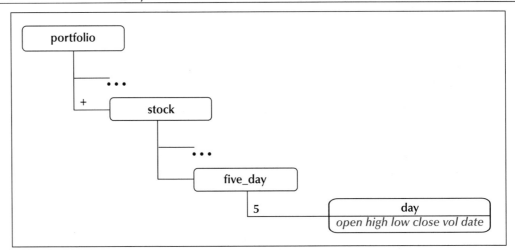

For example, these are the five-day stock values for the ALCOA stock:

```
<five_day>
    <day open="31.20" high="32.61" low="30.15" close="30.51"
        vol="6.70" date="11/17/2008">1</day>
    <day open="30.51" high="30.90" low="28.76" close="29.20"
        vol="4.84" date="11/18/2008">2</day>
    <day open="29.20" high="30.33" low="27.12" close="28.53"
        vol="5.24" date="11/19/2008">3</day>
    <day open="28.53" high="31.32" low="28.24" close="30.92"
        vol="5.91" date="11/22/2008">4</day>
    <day open="30.92" high="31.12" low="28.84" close="29.60"
        vol="3.44" date="11/23/2008">5</day>
</five_day>
```

Kevin suggests that you display these values in a table below each stock description with the stock values from each day occupying a separate table row. To create the table, you add two new templates. The first template sets up the HTML code for the entire table, formatting the table's size, border, and headings. The second template displays five separate table rows for each of the five-day values. The code for the entire table is

```
<table>
<tr>
    <th colspan="6">Recent History</th>
</tr>
<tr>
    <th>Day</th>
    <th>Open</th>
    <th>High</th>
    <th>Low</th>
    <th>Close</th>
    <th>Volume</th>
</tr>
    stock values
</table>
```

where *stock values* are five rows of values for the stock. Add this template to the stock style sheet.

To create the five-day stock table:

1. Below the today template, insert the following template for the five_day element:

```
<xsl:template match="five_day">
   <table>
   <tr>
      <th colspan="6">Recent History</th>
   </tr>
   <tr>
      <th>Day</th>
      <th>Open</th>
      <th>High</th>
      <th>Low</th>
      <th>Close</th>
      <th>Volume</th>
   </tr>
   </table>
</xsl:template>
```

Next you have to apply the five_day template, displaying the table below the stock description.

2. Navigate to the stock template, and below the paragraph that contains the stock description, insert the following code (see Figure 6-30):

```
<xsl:apply-templates select="five_day" />
```

Figure 6-30	Inserting the five-day template

```
<xsl:template match="stock">
    <div>
        <xsl:apply-templates select="sName" />
        <xsl:apply-templates select="today" />
        <p><xsl:value-of select="description" /></p>
        <xsl:apply-templates select="five_day" />
    </div>
</xsl:template>

<xsl:template match="sName">
    <h3>
        <xsl:value-of select="." />
        (<xsl:value-of select="@symbol" />)
    </h3>
</xsl:template>
```

```
<xsl:template match="five_day">
    <table>
    <tr>
        <th colspan="6">Recent History</th>
    </tr>
    <tr>
        <th>Day</th>
        <th>Open</th>
        <th>High</th>
        <th>Low</th>
        <th>Close</th>
        <th>Volume</th>
    </tr>
    </table>
</xsl:template>
```

The second template defines the HTML code for each row of the table. The HTML code for each table row is

```
<tr>
    <td>day</td>
    <td>open</td>
    <td>high</td>
    <td>low</td>
    <td>close</td>
    <td>volume</td>
</tr>
```

where *day*, *open*, *high*, *low*, *close*, and *volume* are the attribute values of the day element. These attribute values are presented using the same HTML format you've already placed in a template to display the daily stock values, meaning that you can use the earlier template here as well. This is a good example of how using templates can enable you to easily reuse the same code in different situations. Even though you're looking at attributes for a different element in a different context, you can still use the sample template.

The day template therefore appears as

```
<xsl:template match="day">
<tr>
   <xsl:apply-templates select="@date" />
   <xsl:apply-templates select="@open" />
   <xsl:apply-templates select="@high" />
   <xsl:apply-templates select="@low" />
   <xsl:apply-templates select="@close" />
   <xsl:apply-templates select="@vol" />
</tr>
</xsl:template>
```

To create and apply the day template:

1. Below the five_day template, insert the following day template:

   ```
   <xsl:template match="day">
   <tr>
      <xsl:apply-templates select="@date" />
      <xsl:apply-templates select="@open" />
      <xsl:apply-templates select="@high" />
      <xsl:apply-templates select="@low" />
      <xsl:apply-templates select="@close" />
      <xsl:apply-templates select="@vol" />
   </tr>
   </xsl:template>
   ```

2. Add **|@date|@close** to the match attribute of the stock values template.

3. Navigate to the five_day template, and above the closing </table> tag insert the following line to apply the day template:

   ```
   <xsl:apply-templates select="day" />
   ```

   Figure 6-31 shows the revised text of the style sheet.

Inserting the day template ◀ Figure 6-31

```
<xsl:template match="five_day">
    <table>
    <tr>
        <th colspan="6">Recent History</th>
    </tr>
    <tr>
        <th>Day</th>
        <th>Open</th>
        <th>High</th>
        <th>Low</th>
        <th>Close</th>
        <th>Volume</th>
    </tr>
    <xsl:apply-templates select="day" />
    </table>
</xsl:template>

<xsl:template match="day">
<tr>
    <xsl:apply-templates select="@date" />
    <xsl:apply-templates select="@open" />
    <xsl:apply-templates select="@high" />
    <xsl:apply-templates select="@low" />
    <xsl:apply-templates select="@close" />
    <xsl:apply-templates select="@vol" />
</tr>
</xsl:template>

<xsl:template match="@current|@open|@high|@low|@vol|@date|@close">
    <td><xsl:value-of select="." /></td>
</xsl:template>
```

4. Close the stock.xsl file, saving your changes.

5. Regenerate the result document, opening the stock report in your Web browser. Figure 6-32 shows the revised layout and content of the report.

Figure 6-32 Five day stock values

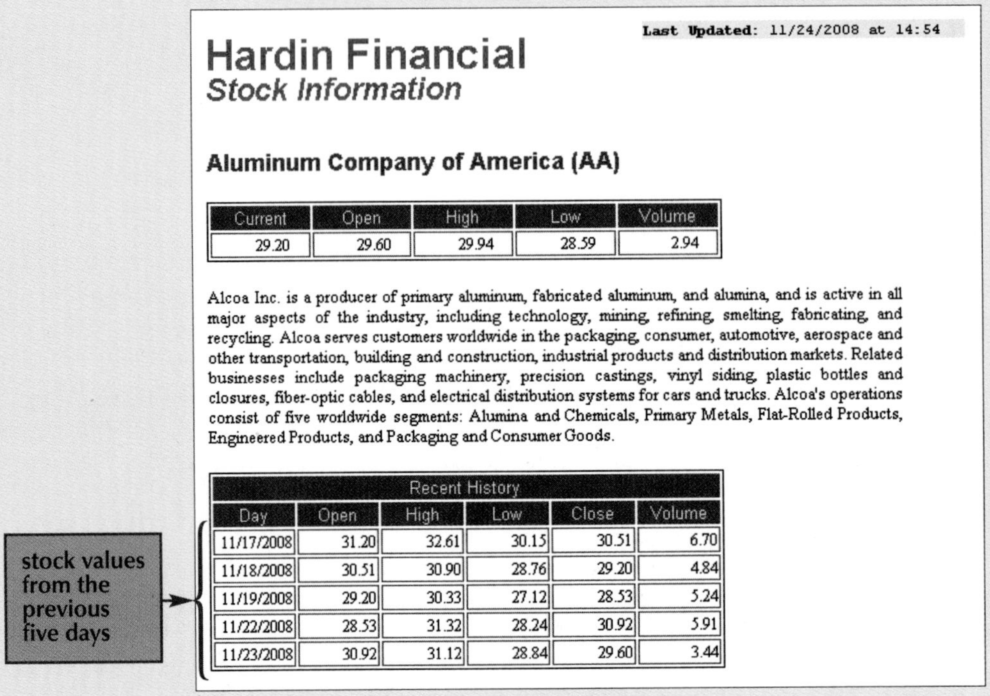

Last Updated: 11/24/2008 at 14:54

Hardin Financial
Stock Information

Aluminum Company of America (AA)

Current	Open	High	Low	Volume
29.20	29.60	29.94	28.59	2.94

Alcoa Inc. is a producer of primary aluminum, fabricated aluminum, and alumina, and is active in all major aspects of the industry, including technology, mining, refining, smelting, fabricating, and recycling. Alcoa serves customers worldwide in the packaging, consumer, automotive, aerospace and other transportation, building and construction, industrial products and distribution markets. Related businesses include packaging machinery, precision castings, vinyl siding, plastic bottles and closures, fiber-optic cables, and electrical distribution systems for cars and trucks. Alcoa's operations consist of five worldwide segments: Alumina and Chemicals, Primary Metals, Flat-Rolled Products, Engineered Products, and Packaging and Consumer Goods.

Recent History					
Day	Open	High	Low	Close	Volume
11/17/2008	31.20	32.61	30.15	30.51	6.70
11/18/2008	30.51	30.90	28.76	29.20	4.84
11/19/2008	29.20	30.33	27.12	28.53	5.24
11/22/2008	28.53	31.32	28.24	30.92	5.91
11/23/2008	30.92	31.12	28.84	29.60	3.44

6. Close your Web browser.

Using Built-In Templates

So far in this session, you've seen how to create and apply templates to a node from the source document's node tree. What happens when an XSLT processor encounters a node set that is not associated with a template? In this case, the XSLT processor applies a **built-in template** to the node. XSLT supports a built-in template for each type of node found in the node tree. For example, the built-in template for element nodes is

```
<xsl:template match="*|/">
   <xsl:apply-templates />
<xsl:template>
```

This template matches the document root and all nodes in the source document's node tree. Note that no select attribute is given for the apply-templates element. If no select attribute is specified, the XSLT processor locates all of the children of the context node and applies templates to them. The result of this built-in template is that the XSLT processor navigates the entire node tree searching for templates to apply. For example, if the structure of the source document is

```
<portfolio>
   <stock>
      <five_day>
         <day />
      </five_day>
   </stock>
</portfolio>
```

the built-in template allows you to write a template that matches the day element even if no templates are written for the five_day or stock elements.

Built-In Text Templates

You may have noticed that the text contained within an element or attribute is considered a node, but you never wrote a template to display the values of these nodes in the stock. xsl style sheet. This is because text nodes and the text values of attributes have the following built-in template:

```
<xsl:template match="text()|@*">
   <xsl:value-of select="." />
</xsl:template>
```

This template matches all text nodes and attributes and causes their values to appear in the result document. For this built-in template to be invoked, the element and attribute nodes from the source document have to be selected with a template written by the programmer. However, once you select an element or attribute node, you can display the text contained within that node without having to write a separate template for the text node.

Built-In Comment and Processing Instruction Templates

By default, the comments and processing instructions in a source document do not appear in the result document. The built-in template for these nodes is

```
<xsl:template match="comment()|processing-instruction()" />
```

Because this template does nothing, no values are sent to the result document. Note that this template element appears in a one-sided tag because it contains no content.

At this point, you've added all of the stock data that Kevin wants to show in the result document. In the next session, you'll insert attribute values and learn how to modify the appearance of the document by sorting the nodes of the node tree and creating conditional nodes.

Session 6.2 Quick Check

Review

1. An XML document contains a root element named books that has one child named book. There are several book nodes in the node tree. Within each book element are two child elements named title and author. What XSLT command do you use to display a book's title as an h1 heading? Assume that the context node is book.
2. In the previous question, if the context node points to the books element, what code do you use to display all of the book titles in the source document?
3. What command do you use to apply the category template?
4. If urlLink is an attribute of the book element that points to a Web site containing information about the book, what code do you enter to write the following tag to the result document: <a href="*urlLink*">*book*</a>. Assume that *book* is the context node for this expression.
5. What value do you enter into the match attribute of a template to apply the template to any of the following attributes: isbn, date, publisher, pages?
6. What is a built-in template?

Session 6.3

Inserting Attribute Values

Kevin carefully examined the document you created and he has a few suggestions to improve its appearance. He thinks it would be useful to change the name of each stock in the result document to a link targeting the company's home page. Using the Alcoa stock as an example, the HTML code Kevin wants added to the result document looks as follows:

```
<h3>
   <a href="http://www.alcoa.com">Aluminum Company of America</a>
</h3>
```

Kevin included the URL for the company's home page in the link element of the source document (see Figure 6-1). He thinks it should be a simple matter to place this link in the document. The following code shows Kevin's first attempt:

```
<xsl:template match="sName">
   <h3><a href="<xsl:value-of select="../link" /> ">
   <xsl:value-of select="." />
   (<xsl:value-of select="@symbol" />)
   </a></h3>
</xsl:template>
```

However, the XSLT processor returns an error message. Because Kevin's style sheet is an XML document, it must follow the syntax rules for all XML documents. One such rule is that tags must be well formed, but because the a element includes an opening bracket in the href value before the closing bracket of the a tag,

```
<a href="< ...
```

the code is rejected by the XSLT processor. To avoid generating an error in this situation, an element's attribute value can instead be written using the syntax

```
<elem attribute="{expression}">
```

where *elem* is the name of the element, *attribute* is the name of the element's attribute, and *expression* is an XPath expression that defines the value of the attribute. For example, to insert the address of the link, you add the a element and href attribute to the sName template as follows:

```
<xsl:template match="sName">
   <h3><a href="{../link}">
   <xsl:value-of select="." />
   (<xsl:value-of select="@symbol" />)
   </a></h3>
</xsl:template>
```

The value of the expression in this case is the XPath expression "../link", which points to the sibling of the sName element. An XSLT processor uses the value of this element as the value for the link's target.

Reference Window

Inserting an Attribute Value

- To insert an attribute value, use the syntax

  ```
  <elem attribute="{expression}">
  ```
  where `elem` is the name of the element in the result document, `attribute` is the name of an attribute associated with the element, and `expression` is an XPath or XSLT expression that defines the value of the attribute.

To insert links in the result document:

1. Return to the **stock.xsl** file in your text editor.

2. Locate the sName template, and directly after the opening <h3> tag insert the following code:

   ```
   <a href="{../link}">
   ```

3. Directly before the closing </h3> tag insert:

   ```
   </a>
   ```

   Figure 6-33 shows the revised code of the sName template.

Inserting an attribute value — Figure 6-33

```
<xsl:template match="sName">
   <h3>
   <a href="{../link}">
   <xsl:value-of select="." />
   (<xsl:value-of select="@symbol" />)
   </a>
   </h3>
</xsl:template>
```

4. Save your changes to the style sheet, and regenerate the result document.

5. Viewing the result document in your Web browser, verify that stock names appear as links. Click the **Aluminum Company of America** stock name and verify that it opens the Web page located at the URL *http://alcoa.com*.

   Trouble? If you don't have access to the Internet, verify that a link has been created by hovering your mouse pointer over a stock name and checking that the URL of the link appears in your browser's status bar.

Sorting Node Sets

Kevin has also noticed that the five-day table in the stock report lists the oldest stock values first and the most recent ones last. Kevin wants to see the order reversed so that the most recent stock values are listed at the top of the table. By default, node sets are processed in **document order**, the order in which they appear in the document. To specify a different order, you can use XSLT's sort element. This element can be used with either the apply-templates element or the for-each element to specify the order in which the nodes are processed and sent to the result document. The general form is

```
<xsl:apply-templates select="expression">
   <xsl:sort attributes />
<xsl:apply-templates>
```

With the for-each element the general form is

```
<xsl:for-each select="expression">
   <xsl:sort attributes />
</xsl:for-each>
```

Note that when you sort with the apply-templates element, the element tag changes from a one-sided tag into a two-sided tag. The sort element contains several attributes to control how XSLT processors sort the nodes in the source document. The syntax of the sort element is:

```
<xsl:sort select="expression" data-type="type" order="type"
          case-order="type" />
```

where the select attribute determines the criteria under which the context node is sorted, the data-type attribute indicates the type of data (text, number, or qname), the order attribute indicates the direction of the sorting (ascending or descending), and the case-order attribute indicates how to handle the sorting of uppercase and lowercase letters (upper-first or lower-first). By default, the sort element assumes that the data is in text form and that it should be sorted in ascending alphabetical order.

For example, if you wanted to sort the stocks by stock name, you use the following code in the root template:

```
<xsl:apply-templates select="portfolio/stock">
   <xsl:sort select="sName" />
</xsl:apply-templates>
```

or equivalently with the for-each element

```
<xsl:for-each select="portfolio/stock">
   <xsl:sort select="sName" />
</xsl:for-each>
```

If you don't include the select attribute, XSLT processors assume that you want to sort the values of the context node. Thus, the following code can also be used to sort the stocks by stock name:

```
<xsl:for-each select="portfolio/stock/sName">
   <xsl:sort />
</xsl:for-each>
```

To sort in descending order, add the order attribute to the sort element as follows:

```
<xsl:sort select="sName" order="descending" />
```

It is important to be cautious when using the sort element with numeric values. For example, if you try to sort the numbers 1 through 100, you end up with the sort order of 1, 10, 100, 11, 12, and so forth, as by default element content is treated as text. To sort numerically, you must include the data-type attribute. For numeric data, set the value of the data-type attribute to number:

```
<xsl:sort select="expression" data-type="number" />
```

If you need to sort by more than one factor, you must place one sort element after another. For example, to sort the stocks first by category and then by the stock name within each category, you enter the following code into the root templates:

```
<xsl:apply-templates select="portfolio/stock">
   <xsl:sort select="category" />
   <xsl:sort select="sName" />
</xsl:apply-templates>
```

Kevin wants the table of five-day stock values sorted in descending order by date. Unfortunately, there is no date data-type in XPath 1.0 (dates will be added to XPath 2.0). To get around this problem, each of the five-day values has been assigned a number, with 1 assigned to the first day in the five-day period and 5 assigned to the last day. Kevin wants the fifth day to appear first, followed by the fourth day, and so on. To sort these values, you modify the apply-templates element in the five_day template, changing it from

```
<xsl:apply-templates select="day" />
```

to

```
<xsl:apply-templates select="day">
   <xsl:sort data-type="number" order="descending" />
</xsl:apply-templates>
```

Remember that because you did not include the select attribute, the sorting is applied to the context node, which in this case is the value contained within the day element.

Sorting a Node Set

Reference Window

- To sort a node set, use the expression
  ```
  <xsl:apply-templates select="expression">
    <xsl:sort attributes />
  <xsl:apply-templates>
  ```
  or
  ```
  <xsl:for-each select="expression">
    <xsl:sort attributes />
  </xsl:for-each>
  ```
  where *attributes* is the attributes that define how the node should be sorted.
- To specify the item by which to sort, use the attribute
  ```
  <xsl:sort select="expression" />
  ```
  where *expression* references a node set in the node tree by which you want to sort the element.
- To specify that the sorting should be done numerically or alphabetically, use the attribute
  ```
  <xsl:sort data-type="type"
  ```
  where *type* is "text" or "qname" for alphabetical sorting, or "number" for numerical sorting.
- To sort in ascending or descending order, use the attribute
  ```
  <xsl:sort order="type" />
  ```
  where *type* equals "ascending" or "descending".
- In the case of text, to sort by either lowercase or uppercase letters first, use the attribute
  ```
  <xsl:sort case-order="type" />
  ```
  where *type* equals either "upper-first" or "lower-first".

To sort the rows in the five-day table:

1. Return to the **stock.xsl** file in your text editor.

2. Locate the five_day template near the bottom of the file, and replace the apply-templates element that applies the day template with the following (see Figure 6-34):
   ```
   <xsl:apply-templates select="day">
      <xsl:sort data-type="number" order="descending" />
   </xsl:apply-templates>
   ```

Figure 6-34 ▶ **Sorting the rows of the five-day table**

```
<xsl:template match="five_day">
    <table>
    <tr>
        <th colspan="6">Recent History</th>
    </tr>
    <tr>
        <th>Day</th>
        <th>Open</th>
        <th>High</th>
        <th>Low</th>
        <th>Close</th>
        <th>Volume</th>
    </tr>

    <xsl:apply-templates select="day">
        <xsl:sort data-type="number" order="descending" />
    </xsl:apply-templates>

    </table>
</xsl:template>
```

> applies the day template sorted by the descending value of the day element

Trouble? Make sure that you change the <xsl:apply-templates> tag from an empty tag to a two-sided tag by removing the (/) character at the end of the opening tag.

3. Save your changes to the style sheet, and regenerate the result document. Open the result document in your Web browser and verify that the five-day table is sorted with the most recent date (11/23/2008) placed at the top (see Figure 6-35).

Figure 6-35 ▶ **Revised five-day table**

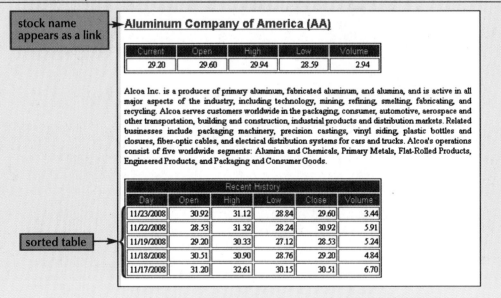

> stock name appears as a link

Aluminum Company of America (AA)

Current	Open	High	Low	Volume
29.20	29.60	29.94	28.59	2.94

Alcoa Inc. is a producer of primary aluminum, fabricated aluminum, and alumina, and is active in all major aspects of the industry, including technology, mining, refining, smelting, fabricating, and recycling. Alcoa serves customers worldwide in the packaging, consumer, automotive, aerospace and other transportation, building and construction, industrial products and distribution markets. Related businesses include packaging machinery, precision castings, vinyl siding, plastic bottles and closures, fiber-optic cables, and electrical distribution systems for cars and trucks. Alcoa's operations consist of five worldwide segments: Alumina and Chemicals, Primary Metals, Flat-Rolled Products, Engineered Products, and Packaging and Consumer Goods.

> sorted table

		Recent History			
Day	Open	High	Low	Close	Volume
11/23/2008	30.92	31.12	28.84	29.60	3.44
11/22/2008	28.53	31.32	28.24	30.92	5.91
11/19/2008	29.20	30.33	27.12	28.53	5.24
11/18/2008	30.51	30.90	28.76	29.20	4.84
11/17/2008	31.20	32.61	30.15	30.51	6.70

Defining Conditional Nodes

Kevin also wants to be able to tell, at a glance, whether a particular stock has increased or decreased from its opening value. He has created three graphics for you to use to identify a stock as increasing, decreasing, or unchanged:

- up.gif: A green triangle pointing up, indicating that the stock's value has increased since the market opened
- down.gif: A red triangle pointing down, indicating that the stock's value has declined
- same.gif: A blue line, indicating that the stock's value is unchanged

To use these graphics, the style sheet must apply different HTML code based on the performance of a stock. If the stock has increased in value, the HTML code is

```
<td><img src="up.gif">Stock Value</td>
```

If it has decreased in value, the HTML code is

```
<td><img src="down.gif">Stock Value</td>
```

If the value is unchanged, the HTML code is

```
<td><img src="same.gif">Stock Value</td>
```

where *Stock Value* is the value of the current attribute from the today element. To send text to the result document that changes based on a node's value, you need to use a conditional element. XSLT supports two kinds: if and choose.

Using the if Element

The syntax for the if element is

```
<xsl:if test="expression">
   styles
</xsl:if>
```

where *expression* is an XPath expression that is either true or false. If the expression is true, the XSLT style commands are generated by the processor; otherwise, nothing is done. For example, the following code displays the stock name only if the value of the symbol attribute is equal to 'AA':

```
<xsl:if test="@symbol = 'AA'">
   <h3><xsl:value-of select="sName" /></h3>
</xsl:if>
```

Note that the text string must be enclosed in either double or single quotes. As with other aspects of XML, comparisons are case sensitive. Be careful when comparing node sets and single values. When multiple values are involved, the expression is true if any of the values in the node set satisfy the test condition. For example, the XPath expression

```
/portfolio/stock/sName/@symbol = "AA"
```

is true as long as there is at least one symbol attribute in the node set that is equal to "AA". This means that the if condition

```
<xsl:if test="/portfolio/stock/sName/@symbol = 'AA'">
   <xsl:value-of select="/portfolio/stock/sName" />
</xsl:if>
```

displays a stock name even for those stock names whose attribute values are not equal to "AA", just as long as one stock in the node set has a symbol equal to "AA".

Using the choose Element

Unlike other programming languages, XSLT does not support an else-if construction. This means that the if element tests for only one condition and allows for only one outcome. If you want to test for multiple conditions and display different outcomes, you need to use the choose element. The syntax of the choose element is

```
<xsl:choose>
    <xsl:when test="expression1">
        styles
    </xsl:when>
    <xsl:when test="expression2">
        styles
    </xsl:when>
    . . .
    <xsl:otherwise>
        styles
    </xsl:otherwise>
</xsl:choose>
```

where *expression1*, *expression2*, and so forth are expressions that are either true or false. XSLT processors proceed through the list of when elements one at a time. When they encounter an expression that is true, they process the corresponding style and ignore the rest of the when elements. If no expressions are true, the style contained in the otherwise element is processed.

Using Comparison Operators and Functions

The equal symbol (=) in the previous code samples is an example of a **comparison operator** and is used to compare one value to another. Comparisons can be made between numbers, text strings, attribute nodes, element nodes, or text nodes. Figure 6-36 describes other comparison operators supported by XPath.

Figure 6-36	Comparison operators

Operator	Description	Example
=	Tests whether two values are equal to each other	@symbol = "AA"
!=	Tests whether two values are unequal	@symbol != "AA"
&lt;	Tests whether one value is less than another	day < 5
<=	Tests whether one value is less than or equal to another	day <= 5
>	Tests whether one value is greater than another	day > 1
>=	Tests whether one value is greater than or equal to another	day >= 1
and	Combines two expressions, returning a value of true only if both expressions are true	@symbol = "AA" and day > 1
or	Combines two expressions, returning a value of true if either expression is true	@symbol = "AA" or @symbol = "UCL"
not	Negates the value of the expression, changing true to false or false to true	not(day >= 1)

Because XML treats the left angle bracket character (<) as the opening character for an element tag, you must use the text string < for less-than comparisons. XML doesn't have a problem with the right angle bracket character (>), however. As a result, one way to avoid using the < expression is to reverse the order of a comparison. For example, instead of writing a comparison as

```
day &lt; 5
```

you write it as

```
5 > day
```

Comparison tests can be combined using the and and or operators. For example, the expression

```
day > 2 and day &lt; 5
```

tests whether the value of the day element lies between 2 and 5. Similarly, the expression

```
@symbol = "AA" or @symbol = "UCL"
```

tests whether the value of the symbol attribute is equal to "AA" or "UCL". You can reverse the true/false value of an expression using the not() function. The expression

```
not(@symbol = "AA")
```

returns a value of false if the value of the symbol attribute is equal to "AA" and true if the symbol attribute is not equal to "AA".

Applying a Conditional Node

Reference Window

- To apply a style only if a particular condition is met, use the XSLT element
  ```
  <xsl:if test="expression">
    styles
  </xsl:if>
  ```
  where expression is an expression that is either true or false.
- To apply styles under several possible conditions, use the syntax
  ```
  <xsl:choose>
    <xsl:when test="expression1">
      styles
    </xsl:when>
    <xsl:when test="expression2">
      styles
    </xsl:when>
    ......
    <xsl:otherwise>
      styles
    </xsl:otherwise>
  </xsl:choose>
  ```
  where expression1, expression2, and so forth are expressions that are either true or false. If none of the expressions is true, then the styles contained in the otherwise element are applied in the result document.

Kevin needs you to test for three possible conditions: whether the current stock value is rising, falling, or unchanged from the opening value. Therefore, you use the choose element rather than the if element to set up the conditional styles. The code to accomplish Kevin's task is:

```
<xsl:choose>
   <xsl:when test="@current &lt; @open">
      <img src="down.gif" />
   </xsl:when>
   <xsl:when test="@current > @open">
      <img src="up.gif" />
   </xsl:when>
   <xsl:otherwise>
      <img src="same.gif" />
   </xsl:otherwise>
</xsl:choose>
```

Because this new style supersedes the styles previously used for the @current value, you have to modify the code for the today template.

To sort the rows in the five-day table:

1. Return to the **stock.xsl** file in your text editor.

2. Locate the today template in the middle of the file, delete the line <xsl:apply-templates select="@current" />, and replace it with the following:

```
<td>
<xsl:choose>
   <xsl:when test="@current &lt; @open">
      <img src="down.gif" />
   </xsl:when>
   <xsl:when test="@current > @open">
      <img src="up.gif" />
   </xsl:when>
   <xsl:otherwise>
      <img src="same.gif" />
   </xsl:otherwise>
</xsl:choose>
<xsl:value-of select="@current" />
</td>
```

3. Locate the stock values template near the bottom of the file, and remove @currentl from the value of the match attribute.

   Figure 6-37 shows the revised code of the style sheet.

Inserting the five-day template | **Figure 6-37**

```
<xsl:template match="today">
    <table>
    <tr>
        <th>Current</th>
        <th>Open</th>
        <th>High</th>
        <th>Low</th>
        <th>Volume</th>
    </tr>
    <tr>
        <td>
        <xsl:choose>
            <xsl:when test="@current &lt; @open">
                <img src="down.gif" />
            </xsl:when>
            <xsl:when test="@current > @open">
                <img src="up.gif" />
            </xsl:when>
            <xsl:otherwise>
                <img src="same.gif" />
            </xsl:otherwise>
        </xsl:choose>
        <xsl:value-of select="@current" />
        </td>
        <xsl:apply-templates select="@open" />
        <xsl:apply-templates select="@high" />
        <xsl:apply-templates select="@low" />
        <xsl:apply-templates select="@vol" />
    </tr>
    </table>
</xsl:template>
```

conditional style created for the @current attribute

@current attribute removed from the match list

```
<xsl:template match="@open|@high|@low|@vol|@date|@close">
    <td><xsl:value-of select="." /></td>
</xsl:template>
```

4. Save your changes to the style sheet, and regenerate the result document. Verify that the appropriate graphic image appears in front of the current stock value indicating whether the stock value has risen, fallen, or remained unchanged from its opening value (see Figure 6-38).

Figure 6-38 | Selecting a graphic symbol

Aluminum Company of America (AA)

Current	Open	High	Low	Volume
▼ 29.20	29.60	29.94	28.59	2.94

graphic indicates falling stock value

Alcoa Inc. is a producer of primary aluminum, fabricated aluminum, and alumina, and is active in all major aspects of the industry, including technology, mining, refining, smelting, fabricating, and recycling. Alcoa serves customers worldwide in the packaging, consumer, automotive, aerospace and other transportation, building and construction, industrial products and distribution markets. Related businesses include packaging machinery, precision castings, vinyl siding, plastic bottles and closures, fiber-optic cables, and electrical distribution systems for cars and trucks. Alcoa's operations consist of five worldwide segments: Alumina and Chemicals, Primary Metals, Flat-Rolled Products, Engineered Products, and Packaging and Consumer Goods.

Working with Predicates

The stocks in Kevin's document are grouped into three categories—industrials, utilities, and transportation—and he wants the result document to organize the stocks in a similar fashion. One way to accomplish this is to use predicates. A **predicate** is part of a location path that tests for a condition and references the node set that fulfills that condition. The general syntax for a predicate is

```
node[expression]
```

where `node` is a node set from the source document's node tree, and `expression` is an expression for a condition that the node set must fulfill. The expression in the predicate can use the same conditional operators used with the if and choose elements. For example, the predicate

```
sName[@symbol = "AA" or @symbol="UCL"]
```

matches all sName elements whose symbol attribute is equal to either "AA" or "UCL". If you don't include a value for an attribute, the expression selects only those nodes that contain the attribute. For example, the expression

```
sName[@symbol]
```

selects only those sName elements that have a symbol attribute.

Predicates and Node Position

A predicate can also indicate the position of a node in the node tree. The general syntax is

```
node[position]
```

where `position` is an integer indicating the position of the node. For example, the expression

```
stock[3]
```

selects the third stock element in the source document. A union operator (|) can also be used to select multiple positions. Thus, the expression

```
stock[3|5]
```

selects the third and fifth stock elements.

Predicates and Functions

A predicate can also contain an XPath function. The two that you'll explore in this tutorial are the last() and position() functions. You'll look at other XPath functions in the next tutorial. The last() function returns the last node in the node tree. Thus, the expression

```
stock[last()]
```

returns the last stock element from the source document's node tree. The position() function returns the position value of the node. For example, the following predicate selects the second stock element:

```
stock[position()=2]
```

To select a range of positions, you can combine the position() function with a conditional operator. The following expression selects the second through fifth stock nodes:

```
stock[position()>=2 and position()&lt;=5]
```

Finally, predicates can be used in combination with any XPath expression. The following example uses a predicate to return the name of the second stock element:

```
<xsl:value-of select="stock[position()=2]/sName" />
```

Using Node Predicates

Reference Window

- To select a subset of nodes from the node tree, use the XPath expression
    node[expression]
  where *node* is a node from the source document's node tree, and *expression* is an expression for the condition that the node must fulfill.
- To process only the first node from a branch of the node tree, use the expression
    node[1]
- To process only the last node from a branch of the node tree, use the expression
    node[last()]
- To process a node from a specific location in the node's tree branch, use the expression
    node[position()=value]
  where *value* is an integer indicating the node's location in the branch.

Kevin wants to display the name of each stock category using an h2 heading. Under each heading, Kevin wants to display the stocks that belong to that category (industrials, utilities, transportation). He also wants the stocks sorted in alphabetical order by stock name within each category. The code to display the industrial stocks looks as follows:

```
<h2 class="category">Industrials</h2>
<xsl:apply-templates select="portfolio/stock[category='Industrials']">
   <xsl:sort select="sName" />
</xsl:apply-templates>
```

Add code to the style sheet to display the stocks in categories.

To display the stock names by category:

▶ **1.** Return to the **stock.xsl** file in your text editor.

▶ **2.** Go to the root template, and replace the line <xsl:apply-templates select="portfolio/stock" /> with the following code (see Figure 6-39):

```
<h2 class="category">Industrials</h2>
<xsl:apply-templates select="portfolio/
stock[category='Industrials']">
    <xsl:sort select="sName" />
</xsl:apply-templates>

<h2 class="category">Utilities</h2>
<xsl:apply-templates select="portfolio/
stock[category='Utilities']">
    <xsl:sort select="sName" />
</xsl:apply-templates>

<h2 class="category">Transportation</h2>
<xsl:apply-templates select="portfolio/
stock[category='Transportation']">
    <xsl:sort select="sName" />
</xsl:apply-templates>
```

Figure 6-39   Display stock information by categories

```
<xsl:template match="/">
    <html>
    <head>
        <title>Stock Information</title>
        <link href="stock.css" rel="stylesheet" type="text/css" />
    </head>
    <body>

        <div id="datetime"><b>Last Updated: </b>
            <xsl:value-of select="portfolio/date" /> at
            <xsl:value-of select="portfolio/time" />
        </div>

        <h1>Hardin Financial</h1>
        <h2>Stock Information</h2>
```

industrial stocks →
```
        <h2 class="category">Industrials</h2>
        <xsl:apply-templates select="portfolio/stock[category='Industrials']">
            <xsl:sort select="sName" />
        </xsl:apply-templates>
```

utility stocks →
```
        <h2 class="category">Utilities</h2>
        <xsl:apply-templates select="portfolio/stock[category='Utilities']">
            <xsl:sort select="sName" />
        </xsl:apply-templates>
```

transportation stocks →
```
        <h2 class="category">Transportation</h2>
        <xsl:apply-templates select="portfolio/stock[category='Transportation']">
            <xsl:sort select="sName" />
        </xsl:apply-templates>

    </body>
    </html>
</xsl:template>
```

▶ **3.** Close the stock.xsl file, saving your changes.

▶ **4.** Use your Web browser or XSLT processor to regenerate the result document. Verify that the stocks are now grouped into categories and that within each category stocks are listed alphabetically (see Figure 6-40).

Hardin Financial
Stock Information

Last Updated: 11/24/2008 at 14:54

category heading →

Industrials

stocks are sorted alphabetically within categories →

Aluminum Company of America (AA)

Current	Open	High	Low	Volume
▼ 29.20	29.60	29.94	28.59	2.94

Alcoa Inc. is a producer of primary aluminum, fabricated aluminum, and alumina, and is active in all major aspects of the industry, including technology, mining, refining, smelting, fabricating, and recycling. Alcoa serves customers worldwide in the packaging, consumer, automotive, aerospace and other transportation, building and construction, industrial products and distribution markets. Related businesses include packaging machinery, precision castings, vinyl siding, plastic bottles and closures, fiber-optic cables, and electrical distribution systems for cars and trucks. Alcoa's operations consist of five worldwide segments: Alumina and Chemicals, Primary Metals, Flat-Rolled Products, Engineered Products, and Packaging and Consumer Goods.

Recent History					
Day	Open	High	Low	Close	Volume
11/23/2008	30.92	31.12	28.84	29.60	3.44
11/22/2008	28.53	31.32	28.24	30.92	5.91
11/19/2008	29.20	30.33	27.12	28.53	5.24
11/18/2008	30.51	30.90	28.76	29.20	4.84
11/17/2008	31.20	32.61	30.15	30.51	6.70

5. Close your Web browser or XSLT processor.

In addition to categorizing nodes, you can use predicates for many other applications. In future tutorials you'll examine ways to write predicates to create more advanced and dynamic node structures.

Creating Elements and Attributes with XSLT

In writing the code for the stock report, you explicitly entered the HTML code for the elements and attributes of the final result document. In some cases you want to use XSLT to generate those elements and attributes dynamically, based on the content of the source document. This happens most often in situations in which you are changing the structure of an XML document by changing elements to attributes or reordering the content of the source document's node tree. To change the source document's structure, you can use XSLT to create new nodes for elements, attributes, and other node types. The following XSLT tags are used to create different objects in the result document:

- <xsl:document> for root or document nodes
- <xsl:element> for element nodes
- <xsl:attribute> for attribute nodes
- <xsl:text> for text nodes
- <xsl:comment> for comment nodes
- <xsl:processing-instruction> for processing instruction nodes
- <xsl:namespace> for namespace nodes

You investigate these different XSLT elements now, starting with the instruction to create an element node.

Creating an Element

To create an element, XSLT uses the <xsl:element> tag as follows:

```
<xsl:element name="name" namespace="uri"
    use-attribute-sets="namelist">
  styles
</xsl:element>
```

where the name attribute assigns a name to the element, the namespace attribute provides a namespace, and use-attribute-sets provides a list of attribute sets (more on this later). For example, if Kevin wanted a result document in which the sName element and symbol attribute were both entered as elements, he could write the following template for the sName element:

```
<xsl:template match="sName">
   <xsl:element name="stockName">
      <xsl:value-of select="." />
   </xsl:element>
   <xsl:element name="stockSymbol">
      <xsl:value-of select="@symbol" />
   </xsl:element>
</xsl:template>
```

When this template is applied, the source document code

```
<sName symbol="AA"> Aluminum Company of America</sName>
```

is transformed in the result document to

```
<stockName>Aluminum Company of America</stockName>
<stockSymbol>AA</stockSymbol>
```

If you need to create a one-sided element, you simply use a one-sided <xsl:element /> tag. For example, the code

```
<xsl:element name="stocks" />
```

creates the following empty element in the result document:

```
<stocks />
```

New elements can be combined with predicates, conditional statements, and the for-each element to create a subset of the original source document in a new structure. For example, to create an XML document containing a list of the stock symbols of transportation stocks, you could apply the following style sheet to Kevin's stock document:

```
<?xml version="1.0" ?>
<xsl:stylesheet version="1.0"
    xmlns:xsl="http://www.w3.org/1999/XSL/Transform">
<xsl:output method="xml" version="1.0" indent="yes" />

<xsl:template match="/">
   <xsl:apply-templates select="portfolio" />
</xsl:template>

<xsl:template match="portfolio">
   <xsl:element name="Transportation">
      <xsl:for-each select="stock[category='Transportation']">
         <xsl:sort select="sName" />
         <xsl:element name="stockSymbol">
            <xsl:value-of select="sName/@symbol" />
         </xsl:element>
```

```
        </xsl:for-each>
    </xsl:element>
</xsl:template>
</xsl:stylesheet>
```

After transforming the stock.xml document, an XSLT processor generates the following result document:

```
<?xml version="1.0" encoding="UTF-16"?>
<Transportation>
    <stockSymbol>ABF</stockSymbol>
    <stockSymbol>CNI</stockSymbol>
    <stockSymbol>R</stockSymbol>
    <stockSymbol>LUV</stockSymbol>
    <stockSymbol>UNP</stockSymbol>
</Transportation>
```

Creating Attributes and Attribute Sets

Attributes are created in XSLT using the <xsl:attribute> tag as follows:

```
<xsl:attribute name="name" namespace="URI">
    styles
</xsl:attribute>
```

where the name attribute specifies the name of the attribute and the namespace attribute indicates the namespace. If Kevin wants to create an XML document that included each transportation stock's current value as an attribute of the corresponding stock element, he could use the following style sheet:

```
<?xml version="1.0" ?>

<xsl:stylesheet version="1.0"
     xmlns:xsl="http://www.w3.org/1999/XSL/Transform">
<xsl:output method="xml" version="1.0" indent="yes" />

<xsl:template match="/">
    <xsl:apply-templates select="portfolio" />
</xsl:template>

<xsl:template match="portfolio">
    <xsl:element name="Transportation">
        <xsl:for-each select="stock[category='Transportation']">
            <xsl:sort select="name" />
            <xsl:element name="stock ">
                <xsl:attribute name="current">
                    <xsl:value-of select="today/@current" />
                </xsl:attribute>
                <xsl:value-of select="name/@symbol" />
            </xsl:element>
        </xsl:for-each>
    </xsl:element>
</xsl:template>

</xsl:stylesheet>
```

The resulting XML document contains the following code:

```
<?xml version="1.0" encoding="UTF-16"?>

<Transportation>
    <stock current="13.00">ABF</stock>
    <stock current="47.19">CNI</stock>
    <stock current="25.23">R</stock>
    <stock current="14.00">LUV</stock>
    <stock current="59.32">UNP</stock>
</Transportation>
```

Related to XSLT's attribute element is the attribute-set element, which is used to create sets of attributes to be applied to different elements within a style sheet. The syntax of the attribute-set element is

```
<xsl:attribute-set name="name" use-attribute-sets="name-list">
   <xsl:attribute name="name1">styles</xsl:attribute>
   <xsl:attribute name="name2">styles</xsl:attribute>
   ...
</xsl:attribute-set>
```

where the name attribute contains the name of the set, and *name1*, *name2*, and so on are the names of the individual attributes created within that set. You can also refer to other attribute sets by specifying their names in the *name-list* parameter, allowing you to build a collection of attribute sets by combining one with another.

The advantage of attribute sets is that a whole collection of attributes can be applied to several different elements at once. For example, the bgcolor, fgcolor, and align attributes are used in earlier versions of HTML to format Web page text. You can group these attributes into a single attribute set and apply them to different elements in the result document. The following code shows how to create an attribute set for specific values of these attributes.

```
<xsl:attribute-set name="formats">
   <xsl:attribute name="bgcolor">red</xsl:attribute>
   <xsl:attribute name="fgcolor">white</xsl:attribute>
   <xsl:attribute name="align">right</xsl:attribute>
</xsl:attribute-set>
```

To apply this attribute set to an h1 element, you use the code

```
<xsl:element name="h1" attribute-set="formats">
   Hardin Financial
</xsl:element>
```

resulting in the following HTML code being sent to the result document:

```
<h1 bgcolor="red" fgcolor="white" align="right">
   Hardin Financial
</h1>
```

Creating Elements and Attributes

- To create an element, use the XSLT element

```
<xsl:element name="name" namespace="uri"
      use-attribute-sets="namelist">
   styles
</xsl:element>
```

where the name attribute assigns a name to the element, the namespace attribute provides a namespace, and use-attribute-sets provides a list of attribute sets.

- To create a one-sided or empty element, use

```
<xsl:element attributes />
```

- To create an attribute, use

```
<xsl:attribute name="name" namespace="uri">
   styles
</xsl:attribute>
```

where the name attribute specifies the name of the attribute and the namespace attribute indicates the namespace.

- To create a set of attributes, use

```
<xsl:attribute-set name="name" use-attribute-sets="name-list">
   <xsl:attribute name="name1">styles</xsl:attribute>
   <xsl:attribute name="name2">styles</xsl:attribute>
   ...
</xsl:attribute-set>
```

where the name attribute is the name of the set and use-attribute-sets can refer to the contents of another attribute set.

Creating Comments and Processing Instructions

XSLT also includes elements to create comments and processing instructions in a result document. To create a comment, use the element

```
<xsl:comment>
   Comment Text
</xsl:comment>
```

For example, the code

```
<xsl:comment>
   Kevin Summers Stock Portfolio
</xsl:comment>
```

creates the following comment in the result document:

```
<!-- Kevin Summers Stock Portfolio -->
```

To create a processing instruction, use the element

```
<xsl:processing-instruction name="name">
   attributes
</xsl:processing-instruction>
```

where *name* is the name of the processing instruction and *attributes* are attributes contained within the processing instruction. For example, if you want to add a processing instruction to attach the result document to the styles.css style sheet, you use the code

```
<xsl:processing-instruction name="xml-stylesheet">
   href="styles.css" type="text/css"
</xsl:processing-instruction>
```

which generates the following tag in the result document:

```
<?xml-stylesheet href="styles.css" type="text.css"?>
```

The processing-instruction element contains the attributes of the processing instruction to be placed in the result document. Do not use the <xsl:attribute> tag to create the processing instruction's attribute and attribute values.

Reference Window

Creating Comments and Processing Instructions

- To add a comment to the result document, use
  ```
  <xsl:comment>
      Comment Text
  </xsl:comment>
  ```
  where *Comment Text* is the text to be placed in the comment.
- To add a processing instruction to the result document, use
  ```
  <xsl:processing-instruction name="name">
      attributes
  </xsl:processing-instruction>
  ```
  where *name* is the name of the processing instruction and *attributes* are attributes and attribute values contained in the processing instruction.

You don't have to use XSLT to create elements, attributes, comments, or processing instructions in Kevin's stock report, but you keep these features of XSLT in mind for future projects. For now, you've completed your work on the stock report. Kevin will examine the document and discuss the results with his colleagues. If he needs to make changes, he'll contact you.

Review

Session 6.3 Quick Check

1. An XML document contains the root element named books, which has a single child element named book. Each book element has two child elements named title and author. Using the XSLT's for-each element, sort the book elements in alphabetical order based on the title.
2. By default, does the <xsl:sort> element sort items numerically or alphabetically?
3. The book element has a single attribute named category. The value of category can be either fiction or nonfiction. Write an if construction that displays the book title only if it is a nonfiction book.
4. Use a choose construction that displays book titles in an h3 heading if they are fiction and an h2 heading if otherwise.
5. Correct the following expression so that it doesn't result in an error:
   ```
   test="sales < 20000"
   ```
6. What code do you use to select the first book from the XML document described in Question 1? What do you use to select the last book?
7. What code do you use to create an element named inventory that contains the value 15000?
8. What code do you use to create an empty element named inventory that contains a single attribute named amount with the value 15000?
9. What code do you use to create a processing instruction in the result document linking the result document to an XSLT style sheet named styles.xsl?

Tutorial Summary

This tutorial introduced the XSLT style sheet language and XPath, a language for describing the content and structure of XML documents. The first session covered the limits of CSS as a style sheet language for XML documents and introduced the history and features of XSLT. A basic XSLT style sheet document was created and attached to a source document. The session then introduced XPath and examined how the contents of an XML document can be viewed as a collection in a node tree. The basic building block of an XSLT style sheet, the template, was then used to create a basic result document. The result document itself was generated using a Web browser or the Exchanger XML Editor. The second session looked at methods of displaying element values in the result document. It also showed how to display several different node values, both by using the for-each construction and by adding a combination of templates to the style sheet. The session then looked at attribute nodes and methods of displaying attribute values in the result document. The session concluded with a discussion of XSLT's built-in templates. The third session examined how to set attribute values in the result document and how to create conditional output both by using the if and choose elements and by setting values with predicates. The tutorial concluded by examining how to dynamically create elements, attributes, comments, and processing instructions with XSLT.

Key Terms

absolute path
ancestor
attribute node
built-in template
child node
client-side
    transformation
comment node
comparison operator
context node
descendant
document node
document order
element node
Extensible Stylesheet
    Language

Extensible Stylesheet
    Language - Format-
    ting Objects
Extensible Stylesheet
    Language -
    Transformations
literal result element
location path
node
node set
node tree
parent node
predicate
processing instruction
    node
relative path
result document

root node
root template
server-side
    transformation
sibling node
source document
style
template
text node
XML fragment
XPath
XSL
XSL-FO
XSLT
XSLT processor
XSLT style sheet

actice the skills you
arned in the tutorial
ing the same case
enario

Review Assignments

Data files needed for this Review Assignment: down.gif, same.gif, stock2.css, stock2txt. xml, stock2txt.xsl, up.gif

Kevin Summers has worked with the stock report you generated and has made a few modifications to the source document. Kevin has removed the five-day information and replaced it with a yearly summary of each stock's high and low values, p/e ratio, earnings, and yield. Figure 6-41 shows the layout of the new source document.

Figure 6-41

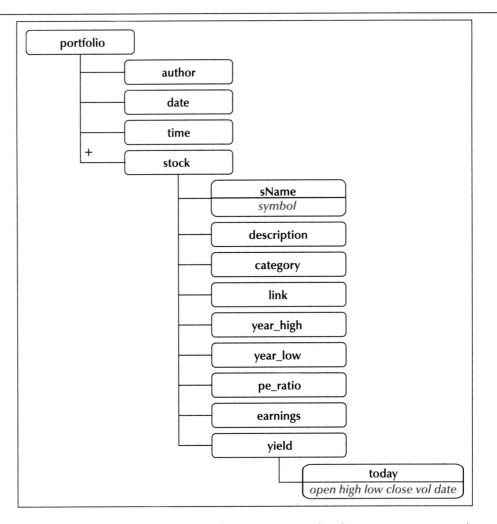

Kevin wants to try a new design, in which the current stock values appear prominently in a table at the top of the page, and summary information about each stock appears lower on the page. Figure 6-42 shows a preview of the page you'll create.

Figure 6-42

As of 11/24/2008 at 14:54

Current Stock Values

Stock	Current	Open	High	Low	Volume
▼ AA	29.20	29.60	29.94	28.59	2.94
▲ ABF	13.00	12.80	13.18	11.90	1.00
▼ AEP	34.45	36.10	36.42	34.35	2.67
▼ AZO	67.19	68.00	69.30	65.80	1.59
▼ CNI	47.19	47.70	48.14	46.63	0.35
▼ ED	37.05	37.17	37.50	36.43	1.22
▲ EK	29.84	29.40	29.84	27.83	3.16
— GM	46.67	46.67	47.00	44.53	6.08
— LUV	14.00	14.00	14.59	13.53	4.03
▼ MRO	24.08	24.15	24.63	23.70	1.84
▲ PPL	30.50	30.05	30.62	29.40	0.84
▼ R	25.23	25.62	26.29	24.93	0.26
▲ UCL	33.80	33.35	34.00	32.66	1.01
▲ UNP	59.32	59.00	59.70	58.20	1.81

Summary Information

Aluminum Company of America

Category	
	Industrials
Year High	42.00
Year Low	27.36
P/E Ratio	39.40
Earnings	0.73
Yield	2.09

Alcoa Inc. is a producer of primary aluminum, fabricated aluminum, and alumina, and is active in all major aspects of the industry, including technology, mining, refining, smelting, fabricating, and recycling. Alcoa serves customers worldwide in the packaging, consumer, automotive, aerospace and other transportation, building and construction, industrial products and distribution markets. Related businesses include packaging machinery, precision castings, vinyl siding, plastic bottles and closures, fiber-optic cables, and electrical distribution systems for cars and trucks. Alcoa's operations consist of five worldwide segments: Alumina and Chemicals, Primary Metals, Flat-Rolled Products, Engineered Products, and Packaging and Consumer Goods.

In addition to placing the current stock values at the top of the page, Kevin wants to create links between each stock's entry and the summary paragraph for that stock located further down the page. He has created a CSS style sheet named stock2.css to format the HTML elements on the Web page. Kevin decided not to include any five-day information in this version of the page.

Because creating a style sheet can be complicated, it is strongly recommended that you save your changes and generate the result document as you complete each step below to check on your progress and detect any problems early.

To complete this task:

1. Using your text editor, open **stock2txt.xml** and **stock2txt.xsl** from the tutorial.06x/ review folder. Enter *your name* and *the date* in the comment section of each file, and save them as **stock2.xml** and **stock2.xsl** respectively.

2. Go to the stock2.xml file in your text editor. Take some time to review the content of the file and its structure. Add a processing instruction after the comment section that attaches this XML document to the stock2.xsl style sheet. Close the file, saving your changes.

3. Go to the stock2.xsl file in your text editor. Below the comment section set up this document as an XSLT style sheet by adding a stylesheet root element and declaring the XSLT namespace using the namespace prefix xsl.

4. Add an output element with a method attribute that tells the XSLT processor that the result document should conform to the HTML version 4.0 format.

5. Create a root template that sends the following literal result elements to the result document:

```
<html>
<head>
    <title>Stock Information</title>
    <link href="stock2.css" rel="stylesheet" type="text/css" />
</head>
<body>
</body>
</html>
```

6. Directly after the opening <body> tag in the root template, insert the following code:

```
<div id="datetime">
    As of date at time
</div>
```

where *date* and *time* are the values of the date and time elements from the source stock2.xml file.

7. Below the root template, insert a template to produce the following HTML code:

```
<td>value</td>
```

where *value* is the value of the context node. Set the match attribute of this template to match any of the following stock value attributes in the source document: current, open, high, low, vol; or any of the following stock value elements: category, year_high, year_low, pe_ratio, earnings, and yield.

8. Above the stock values template you just created, insert a template for the stock element. Have the template write the following code:

```
<h3 id="symbol">name</h3>
```

where *symbol* is the symbol for the stock (*Hint*: Use the XPath expression sName/@symbol), and *name* is the name of the stock.

9. Below the h3 element within the stock template, add the following code:

```
<table border="10" class="summtable">
<tr>
    <th class="head2">Category</th>
    category
</tr>
<tr>
    <th class="head2">Year High</th>
    year_high
</tr>
<tr>
    <th class="head2">Year Low</th>
    year_low
</tr>
<tr>
    <th class="head2">P/E Ratio</th>
    pe_ratio
</tr>
<tr>
    <th class="head2">Earnings</th>
    earnings
```

```
    </tr>
    <tr>
       <th class="head2">Yield</th>
       yield
    </tr>
    </table>
```

where *category*, *year_high*, *year_low*, *pe_ratio*, *earnings*, and *yield* are the code you generate when you apply the stock values template you created in Step 7 to the category, year_high, year_low, pe_ratio, earnings, and yield elements.

10. Directly below the table you created in the stock template, insert the following code:

```
<p>description</p>
```

where *description* is the value of the description element.

11. Return to the root template. Directly above the closing </body> tag, insert the following code:

```
<h2 id="summary">Summary Information</h2>
stock summary
```

where *stock summary* is the code generated by applying the stock template sorted by stock symbol. (*Hint*: Use the XPath expressions portfolio/stock to match the stock element and sName/@symbol to select the sort order.)

12. Above the stock template, insert a template matching the today element. Within this template, insert the following code:

```
<tr>
    <td class="symbolcell">
    <a href="#symbol">symbol</a>
    </td>
    current
    open
    high
    low
    vol
</tr>
```

where *symbol* is the value of the symbol attribute (*Hint*: Use the XPath reference "../sName/@symbol" to match the symbol attribute) and *current*, *open*, *high*, *low*, and *vol* are lines of code returned by applying the stock values template in Step 7 to the current, open, high, low, and vol attributes.

13. Kevin wants a graphic image to appear next to the stock symbol to indicate whether the stock value is rising, falling, or unchanged from its opening value. Within the today template, directly before the opening <a> tag, insert XSLT code to write the following code:

```
<img src="down.gif />
```

if the value of the current attribute is less than the open attribute. Write the code

```
<img src="up.gif />
```

if the value of the current attribute is greater than the open attribute. Otherwise, have the XSLT processor write the code

```
<img src="same.gif />
```

14. Return to the root template and insert the following code directly above the h2 heading "Summary Information."

```
<h1>Current Stock Values</h1>
<table border="1" align="center" id="stocktable">
<tr>
   <th>Stock</th>
```

```
        <th>Current</th>
        <th>Open</th>
        <th>High</th>
        <th>Low</th>
        <th>Volume</th>
    </tr>

    today

</table>
```

where *today* is the code generated by applying the template for the today element. Sort the code returned by the today template by the value of the stock symbol (*Hint*: use the XPath reference "../sName/@symbol".)

15. Close the stock2.xsl file, saving your changes.

16. Generate your result document using either the Exchanger XML Editor, your Web browser, or another XSLT processor. Verify that the layout matches that shown in Figure 6-42, and that each link in the Stock Values table jumps the user to the corresponding stock's summary paragraph, located further down the Web page.

17. Submit your completed project to your instructor.

Case Problem 1

Data files needed for this Case Problem: m01.jpg, m13.jpg, m16.jpg, m20.jpg, m27.jpg, m31.jpg, m42.jpg, m51.jpg, m57.jpg, messtxt.xml. messtxt.xsl, skyweb.css, skyweb.jpg

SkyWeb   Dr. Andrew Weiss of Central Ohio University uses XML to store astronomical data. One of his XML files contains information on the Messier catalog, a list of deep sky objects of particular interest to astronomers and amateur observers. Figure 6-43 describes the elements and attributes in his document.

Figure 6-43

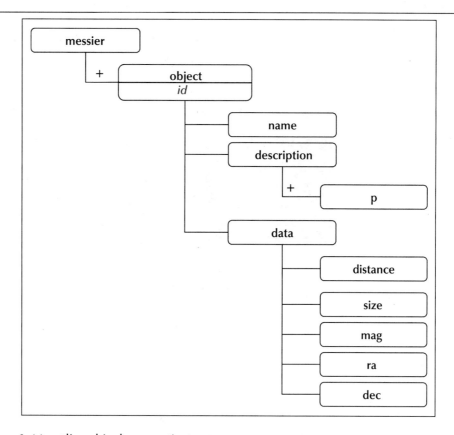

Figure 6-44 outlines his document's structure.

Figure 6-44

Element	Description
messier	The root element of the document
object	A single Messier object; the id attribute indicates the Messier catalog number
name	The name of the Messier object
description	A description of the Messier object
p	A paragraph of the object description
data	Data on the Messier object
distance	The distance to the object in light years
size	The apparent size of the object (in arc minutes)
mag	The magnitude of the object
ra	The object's right ascension in the night sky
dec	The object's declination in the night sky

Dr. Weiss needs your help in designing an XSLT style sheet that displays the contents of his source document in an easy-to-read format. A preview of the final result document is shown in Figure 6-45.

Figure 6-45

SkyWeb
The Messier Objects

The Crab Nebula (m01)

The Crab Nebula is one of the most famous supernova remnants in the night sky. The supernova was first noted on July 4, 1054, by Chinese astronomers. At its height, the supernova was about 4 times brighter than Venus and could be seen during the day for a period of more than three weeks.

The remnant of the this supernova was discovered in 1731 by the British astronomer John Bevis. Messier himself found it in 1758 while looking for Halley's comet. He soon realized it was no comet and the Crab Nebula became the first entry in Messier's famous catalog of celestial objects.

Distance (light years)	Size (arc min)	Magnitude	Right Ascension	Declination
7200	6 x 4	8.4	05:34.5	+22:01

To complete this task:

1. Using your text editor, open **messtxt.xml** and **messtxt.xsl** from the tutorial.06x/case1 folder. Enter *your name* and *the date* in the comment section of each file, and save them as **messier.xml** and **messier.xsl** respectively.

2. Go to the messier.xml file in your text editor. Review the structure and content of the file. Add a processing instruction after the comment section that attaches this XML document to the messier.xsl style sheet. Close the file, saving your changes.

3. Go to the messier.xsl file in your text editor. Below the comment section set up this document as an XSLT style sheet by adding a stylesheet root element and declaring the XSLT namespace using the namespace prefix xsl. Add an output element with a method attribute that tells XSLT processors that the result document should conform to the HTML version 4.0 format.

4. Create a root template that writes the following code to the result document:

```
<html>
<head>
   <title>The Messier Objects</title>
   <link href="skyweb.css" rel="stylesheet" type="text/css" />
</head>
<body>
   <h1 id="logo"><img src="skyweb.jpg" alt="SkyWeb" /></h1>
</body>
</html>
```

5. Create a template that writes a table cell containing information about each Messier object. The template should match the following elements: distance, size, mag, ra, and dec. The template should write the following code:

```
<td>value</td>
```
where *value* is the value of the context node.

6. Create a template for the data element that displays a table of descriptive data. The template should write the following code:

```
<table border="5">
<tr>
    <th>Distance (light years)</th>
    <th>Size (arc min)</th>
    <th>Magnitude</th>
    <th>Right Ascension</th>
    <th>Declination</th>
</tr>
<tr>
    distance
    size
    mag
    ra
    dec
</tr>
</table>
```

where *distance*, *size*, *mag*, *ra*, and *dec* contain code returned by applying the template created in Step 5 to the distance, size, mag, ra, and dec elements.

7. Above the data template, insert a template for the object element. Have the template write the following code:

```
<div>
    <h2>name (id)</h2>
    data
</div>
```

where *name* is the value of the name element, *id* is the value of the id attribute, and *data* contains the code created by applying the data template created in Step 6.

8. Directly below the h2 element in the object template, use a for-each element to insert the following code for the first paragraph in the description element:

```
<p><img src="id.jpg" />p</p>
```

where *id* is the value of the id attribute for the current Messier object, and *p* is the content of the paragraph element. (*Hint*: The XPath reference for the for-each element should be set to "description/p[1]", the XPath reference for the id attribute should be "../../@id", and the XPath reference for the paragraph should be simply the context node.)

9. Directly below the for-each element you just inserted, insert another for-each element for paragraphs in the description element whose position in the node tree is greater than 1. For each of those paragraphs write the code:

```
<p>p</p>
```

where *p* is the content of those selected paragraphs.

10. Return to the root template. Directly above the closing </body> tag, insert the following code:

```
<h1>The Messier Objects</h1>
    object
```

where *object* is the code generated by applying the object template sorted by the id attribute.

11. Close the messier.xsl file, saving your changes.

12. Generate the result document. Verify that the layout matches that shown in Figure 6-45.
13. Submit your completed project to your instructor.

Case Problem 2

Data files needed for this Case Problem: back.jpg, home.htm, links.jpg, nasa.htm, neptune.htm, rss2txt.xml, sci.css, scitimes.jpg, scitxt.xsl, side.jpg, vm.htm, whales.htm

SciNews   Lee McNeil manages the RSS news feed for SciNews, a Web site reporting the latest news in the field of science and technology. RSS is an XML vocabulary designed for the reporting and distribution of current news features across the Internet. Lee wonders whether she can create a style sheet for her RSS documents so that when opened in customers' Web browsers they appear as nicely formatted Web pages. She has asked for for your help in designing an XSLT style sheet for a sample RSS document. Figure 6-46 shows a preview of the Web page she wants you to create.

Figure 6-46

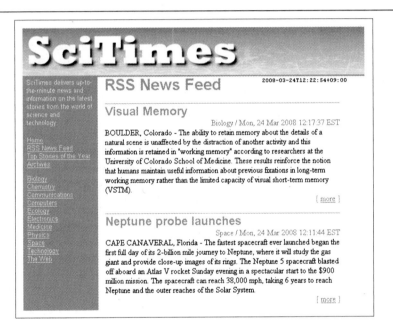

To complete this task:

1. Using your text editor, open **rss2txt.xml** and **scitxt.xsl** from the tutorial.06x/case2 folder. Enter *your name* and *the date* in the comment section of each file, and save them as **rss2.xml** and **sci.xsl** respectively.
2. Go to the rss2.xml file in your text editor. Add a processing instruction after the comment section that attaches this XML document to the sci.xsl style sheet. Close the file, saving your changes.
3. Go to the sci.xsl file in your text editor. Below the comment section set up this document as an XSLT style sheet by adding a stylesheet root element and declaring the XSLT namespace using the namespace prefix xsl. Also declare an RSS namespace having a URI of *http://purl.org/dc/elements/1.1/* and a namespace prefix of *dc*.

4. Create a root template containing the following code:

```
<html>
   <head>
      <title>title</title>
      <link rel="stylesheet" href="sci.css" />
   </head>
   <body>
   </body>
</html>
```

where *title* is the value of the title element in the source document, located as a child of the channel element.

5. RSS allows users to specify an image for the news provider using the image element. Create a template for the image element containing the following code:

```
<a href="link">
   <img src="url" alt="title" width="width" height="height"
   longdesc="description" />
</a>
```

where *link* is the value of the link element (within the image element of the source document), *title* is the value of the image's title, *width* is the value of the width element, *height* is the value of the height element, and *description* is the value of the description element.

6. Return to the root element, and apply the image template by adding the following code directly below the opening <body> tag:

```
<div id="logo">image</div>
```

where *image* is the code generated by applying the image template.

7. Directly below the code you entered in Step 6, insert the following code to display the current date and time of the RSS news feed:

```
<div id="datetime">date</div>
```

where *date* is the value of the date element. The date element must be placed in the *dc* namespace you declared in Step 3.

8. Each RSS news feed contains a short description of the news source. Display this description by adding the following code to the result document directly below the code you entered in Step 7:

```
<div id="links">
   <p>description</p>
   <p><img src="links.jpg" /></p>
</div>
```

where *description* is the value of the description element, a child of the channel element.

9. RSS news feed articles are organized into different items and placed within an item element. Create a template for the item element that generates the following code:

```
<h2>title</h2>
<p id="subjtime">subject / pubDate</p>
<p>description</p>
<p id="itemlink">[ <a href="link">more</a> ]</p>
```

where *title* is the item's title, *subject* is the item's subject, *pubDate* is the publication date and time of the item, *description* is the description of the item, and *link* is a hypertext link to the complete news story article. The *subject* and *pubDate* elements must be placed within the dc namespace you declared in Step 3.

10. Apply the item template by adding the following code to the root template, directly above the closing </body> tag:

```
<div id="news">
    <h1>RSS News Feed</h1>
    items
</div>
```

where *items* contains the code generated by applying the item template.

11. Close the sci.xsl file, saving your changes.

12. Generate the result document. Verify that the layout matches that shown in Figure 6-46. Also verify that clicking the page logo and the four article links displays Web pages for those links. (The links in the sidebar are only displayed for appearance and do not represent real links.) Depending on your browser, your result document may look slightly different from the one shown in Figure 6-46.

13. Submit your completed project to your instructor.

Case Problem 3

Data files needed for this Case Problem: acctxt.xml, checking.dtd, checktxt.xsl

Homestead School Linda Sanchez manages the accounts for Homestead School, a small parent-run school in Groveton, Pennsylvania. The database that Linda uses stores account information in an XML document. Linda has become aware that she can access this XML document, and by using an XSLT style sheet she can automate the process of creating a new XML document with the account information rearranged in a new format. Figure 6-47 shows the structure of her accounts.xml file.

Figure 6-47

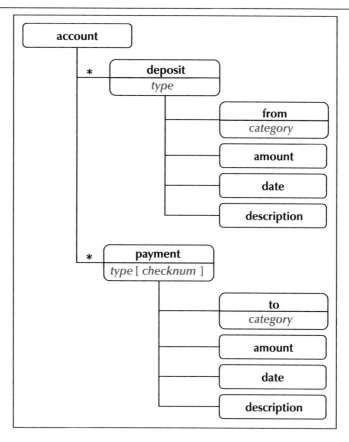

Linda wants to generate an XML document that displays only the checks written on the account. She envisions a simpler XML document with the structure shown in Figure 6-48.

Figure 6-48

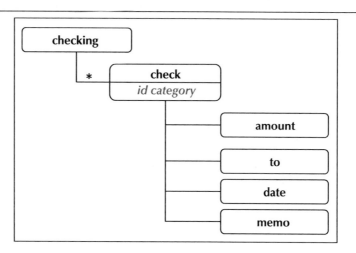

To complete this task:

1. Using your text editor, open **acctxt.xml** and **checktxt.xsl** from the tutorial.06x/case3 folder. Enter *your name* and *the date* in the comment section of each file, and save them as **accounts.xml** and **checks.xsl**, respectively.

2. Go to the accounts.xml file in your text editor. Add a processing instruction after the comment section that attaches this XML document to the checks.xsl style sheet. Close the file, saving your changes.

3. Go to the checks.xsl file in your text editor. Below the comment section set up this document as an XSLT style sheet by adding a stylesheet root element.

Explore ▶ 4. Add an output element to the stylesheet that instructs the XSLT processor that the result document is an XML version 1.0 document, that the text is indented, and that the XML document should contain a DOCTYPE system declaration pointing to the checking.dtd file.

Explore ▶ 5. Insert the root template. Within the root template, create a comment node for the result document that contains the following text:

```
Author: name
Date:   date
```
where *name* is your name and *date* is the date.

Explore ▶ 6. Create a template for the payment element, and within this template create an element named check for each payment element in the source document (*Hint*: Set the value of the select attribute in the for-each element to the value of the context node).

Explore ▶ 7. For the check element, create two attributes: one named id equal to the value of the checknum attribute, and the second named category equal to the category attribute of the to element from the source document.

8. Also within the check element, create the following four elements:

- The amount element with a value equal to the amount element from the source document
- The to element with a value equal to the to element from the source document
- The date element with a value equal to the date element from the source document
- The memo element with a value equal to the description element from the source document

9. Return to the root template. Directly below the comment node you created in Step 5, create an element node named checking. Within the checking element, apply the payment template, but use a predicate to select only those payment nodes whose type attribute is equal to check.

Explore ▶ 10. Sort the application of the payment template in descending order based on the amount element. (*Hint*: Be sure to sort the amount values numerically.).

11. Close the checks.xsl file, saving your changes.

12. Using the Exchanger XML Editor or another XSLT processor, generate the result document. Store the result document as **checking.xml** in the tutorial.06x/cases folder.

13. View the contents of the checking.xml file, and using the Exchanger XML Editor or another XML parser, verify that it is well-formed and valid based on the DTD in the checking.dtd file.

14. Submit your completed project to your instructor.

Create

*est your knowledge of
SLT style sheets by
reating a style sheet to
isplay a baseball
ox score*

Case Problem 4

Data files needed for this Case Problem: scoretxt.css, scoretxt.xml

Baseball Abstract   Roy Packard is a statistician for the *Baseball Abstract,* an online publication reporting on daily activities of major league baseball. Roy's database stores data in portable XML documents. Figure 6-49 shows the structure of one such document containing information about a recent ballgame between Minnesota and Boston.

Figure 6-49

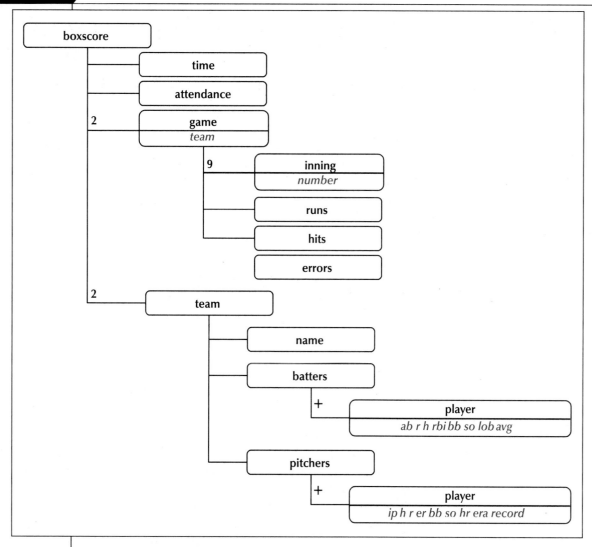

Roy wants your help in displaying information from this document in a box score report that can be displayed on the Web. Figure 6-50 shows a preview of a typical box score report for this type of data.

Figure 6-50

Minnesota at Boston

Final	1	2	3	4	5	6	7	8	9	Runs	Hits	Errors
Minnesota	1	0	0	0	0	0	0	0	2	3	6	0
Boston	0	2	0	1	0	0	1	0	x	4	10	0

Minnesota

Batters								
Player	AB	R	H	RBI	BB	SO	LOB	Avg.
L. Lawrence	4	0	0	0	0	1	0	0.255
S. Kemper	4	1	1	2	0	2	1	0.302
B. Aaron	4	1	0	0	0	0	0	0.286
C. Collins	4	0	1	1	0	2	1	0.303
D. Light	3	0	1	0	1	0	1	0.301
U. Guess	3	0	1	1	0	0	0	0.299
R. Dension	3	0	0	0	0	1	1	0.277
K. Kaufmann	2	0	1	0	0	0	0	0.252
L. Sanchez	2	0	0	0	0	0	1	0.279
J. Cho	3	1	1	0	0	1	0	0.281

Pitchers							
Player	IP	H	R	ER	BB	SO	HR	ERA
M. Li (L, 3-9)	7	8	4	3	3	4	0	3.85
R. Rawlings	2	2	0	0	0	2	0	4.20

Boston

Batters								
Player	AB	R	H	RBI	BB	SO	LOB	Avg.
J. Kasie	4	0	0	0	0	2	3	0.295
A. Wilson	4	1	2	2	0	0	1	0.268
M. Turner	4	1	2	0	0	0	1	0.316
R. Bonds	4	0	1	1	0	1	2	0.311
L. Wilkes	3	0	0	0	1	0	1	0.223
J. Hayes	3	0	1	1	0	0	0	0.251
B. Stevens	3	0	0	0	0	1	1	0.271
J. Sheridan	2	0	2	0	0	0	0	0.241
S. Stevens	1	0	0	0	0	1	0	0.302
M. Mitchell	3	1	1	0	1	0	1	0.225
A. White	2	0	1	0	1	0	0	0.281
B. Alvarez	2	1	0	0	0	1	0	0.277

Pitchers							
Player	IP	H	R	ER	BB	SO	HR	ERA
K. Mays (W, 16-2)	8	6	3	2	0	6	0	2.14
S. Wolf (S, 21)	1	0	0	0	0	3	0	3.51

Time: 2:22
Attendance: 32,018

To complete this task:

1. Using your text editor, open **scoretxt.xml** and **scoretxt.xsl** from the tutorial.06x/ case4 folder. Enter *your name* and *the date* in the comment section of each file, and save them as **score.xml** and **score.xsl** respectively.

2. Go to the score.xml file in your text editor. Review the contents of the file, becoming familiar with the data structure and content. Directly below the comment section, insert a processing instruction linking the document to the score.xsl style sheet. Close the file, saving your changes.

3. The design and layout of the result document is up to you. It should display the inning-by-inning results of the game in a tabular format, with the total runs, hits, and errors appearing at the end of the table.

4. Tables should also be created for the batting and pitching statistics of individual players.

5. The result document should also display the length of the game and the total attendance.

6. Generate a result document. Verify that the result document displays all of the import data of the box score in a readable layout.

7. Submit your completed project to your instructor.

Review

Quick Check Answers

Session 6.1

1. `<?xml-stylesheet type="text/css" href="styles.css" ?>`
   XSLT is the XSL language used to transform XML content into a presentation format. XPath is used to locate information from an XML document and perform operations and calculations upon that content. XSL-FO is used to implement page layout and design.

2. `<?xml-stylesheet type="text/xsl" href="styles.xsl" ?>`

3. /books/book/title

4. ../title

5. /books/book/title/@isbn

6. //author

7. Literal result elements are elements that are not processed by the XSLT processor but are sent as text to the result document.

8. `<xsl:output method="text" />`
   You would create a text document if you were creating a result document for a format other than HTML and XML—such as a PDF (Portable Document Format) file or an RTF file.

Session 6.2

1. `<h1><xsl:value-of select="title" /></h1>`

2. `<xsl:for-each select="book">`
   `<h1><xsl:value-of select="title" /></h1>`
   `</xsl:for-each>`

3. `<xsl:apply-templates select="category" />`

4. `<a href="{@urlLink}"><xsl:value-of select="." /></a>`

5. "@isbn|@date|@publisher|@pages"
6. A template built into the XSLT processor employed by the XSLT processor when it counters a node not associated with a template

Session 6.3

1. ```
   <xsl:for-each select="/books/book">
   <xsl:sort select="title" />
   </xsl:for-each>
   ```
2. Alphabetically
3. ```
   <xsl:if test="@category = 'Non-fiction'">
   <xsl:value-of select="title" />
   </xsl:if>
   ```
4. ```
   <xsl:choose>
   <xsl:when test="@category = 'Fiction'">
   <h3><xsl:value-of select="title" /></h3>
   </xsl:when>
   <xsl:otherwise>
   <h2><xsl:value-of select="title" /></h2>
   </xsl:otherwise>
   </xsl:choose>
   ```
5. test="sales < 20000"
6. books/book[1]
   books/book[last()]
7. ```
   <xsl:element name="inventory">
   15000
   </xsl:element>
   ```
8. ```
   <xsl:element name="inventory">
   <xsl:attribute name="amount">
   15000
   </xsl:attribute>
   </xsl:element>
   ```
9. ```
   <xsl:processing-instruction name="xml-stylesheet">
   href="styles.xsl" type="text/xsl"
   </xsl:processing-instruction>
   ```

Objectives

Session 7.1
- Create and format numbered lists
- Calculate sums and counts of nodes
- Create a spanning table cell
- Work with mathematical operators

Session 7.2
- Format numeric values
- Work with string functions
- Control the use of white space in a style sheet
- Declare and reference variables and parameters

Session 7.3
- Understand the principles of functional programming
- Create recursive templates
- Work with extensions to XSLT and XPath
- Explore developments in XPath and XSLT 2.0

Creating a Computational Style Sheet

Working with Functions, Variables, and Parameters

Case

Wizard Works

Wizard Works, Inc., located in Avondale, Kentucky, is a mail order enterprise that manufactures and sells fireworks to private users and professional entertainers. Bernard Kolbe, an account manager at Wizard Works, is responsible for tracking customer information and sales orders.

The company has begun to store sales order data in XML documents, and Bernard wants to generate reports about his customers based on the information from these documents. One such report would display orders placed by each customer, the cost of each order, and the total cost of all of the orders in the XML document.

One way to generate a report is to create an XSLT style sheet that can calculate values based on the data from the source document. Bernard has done some work with XSLT style sheets, but he doesn't yet know how to perform calculations with them. He has asked for your help in accomplishing this task.

Student Data Files

▼tutorial.07x

▽ tutorial folder
   libtxt.xsl
   orderstxt.xml
   workstxt.xsl
   works.css
   + 1 image file

▽ review folder
   cattxt.xml
   itemstxt.xsl
   sharedtxt.xsl
   items.css
   + 1 image file

▽ case1 folder
   pollstxt.xml
   pollstxt.xsl
   polls.css
   + 2 image files

▽ case2 folder
   golftxt.xml
   golftxt.xsl
   golf.css

▽ case3 folder
   filltxt.xml
   filltxt.xsl
   functtxt.xsl
   fill.css

▽ case4 folder
   autotxt.xml
   autotxt.xsl

Session 7.1

Viewing the Orders Report

When you meet with Bernard to discuss the report, he shows you an XML document named orders.xml that contains order information for a select group of Wizard Works customers. For each customer Bernard has collected address information, all of the orders submitted by the customer, and the items purchased on each order. The contents of orders.xml are described in Figure 7-1.

| Figure 7-1 | Contents of the orders document |

Element	Description
customers	The root element of the document
customer	Information about each customer; the *CID* attribute contains a customer's ID number
cName	Customer name
fName	Customer first name (optional)
lName	Customer last name
street	Customer street address
city	Customer city of residence
state	Customer state of residence
postalCode	Customer postal code
phone	Customer phone number
orders	Information for each customer order
order	Information for a specific order; the *OID* attribute contains the order ID number, and the *date* attribute indicates the date that the order was submitted
items	Information for each item in an order
item	Item ordered by a customer; the *price* attribute contains the price of the item, and the *qty* attribute contains the quantity ordered

The layout of the file is shown in Figure 7-2. Note that each customer may have submitted more than one order. For each order, Bernard has entered the items ordered, the quantity of items, and the price of each item. Each order may include several different items.

Structure of the orders document | **Figure 7-2**

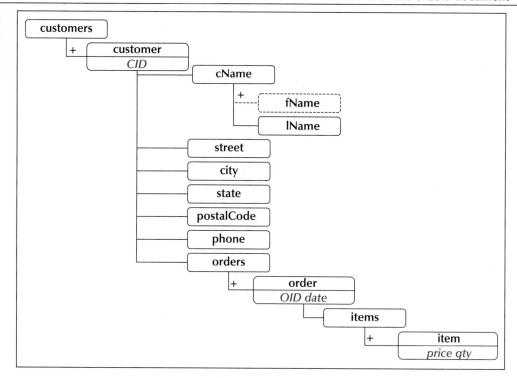

To open the orders document:

1. Use your text editor to open **orderstxt.xml** from the tutorial.07x/tutorial folder. Enter **your name** and **the date** in the comment section at the top of the file, and save the file as **orders.xml**.

2. Take some time to study the contents of the file, paying careful attention to the document structure and the values of the elements and attributes.

Bernard has started to work on the style sheet, but it only displays the raw data from the XML document. In his style sheet, Bernard created the following templates:

- The root template, which writes the opening HTML code for the Web page and displays a summary table that describes the customers contained in Bernard's report
- The customer template, which displays a table describing each customer
- The orders template, which displays a table with all of the orders made by each customer; Bernard also wants to use this template to calculate the grand totals for each customer.
- The items template, which Bernard wants to use to display the totals associated with each order
- The item template, which displays each item ordered by a customer

Currently, the style sheet contains no calculations to report the total number of items or the total cost of the orders. To see the current state of Bernard's style sheet, open the XSLT file now and attach it to the source document.

To view and apply the works style sheet:

1. Use your text editor to open **workstxt.xsl** from the tutorial.07x/tutorial folder. Enter *your name* and *the date* in the comment section at the top of the file, and save the file as **works.xsl**.

2. Review the contents of the style sheet, paying careful attention to the different templates in the document.

3. Return to the orders.xml in your text editor, and directly after the comment section insert the following processing instruction to apply the works.xsl style sheet to the orders document:

```
<?xml-stylesheet type="text/xsl" href="works.xsl" ?>
```

4. Close the orders.xml file, saving your changes.

5. Using the techniques discussed in Tutorial 6, generate the result document. Figure 7-3 shows the current layout and content of the result document.

| Figure 7-3 | Initial result document |

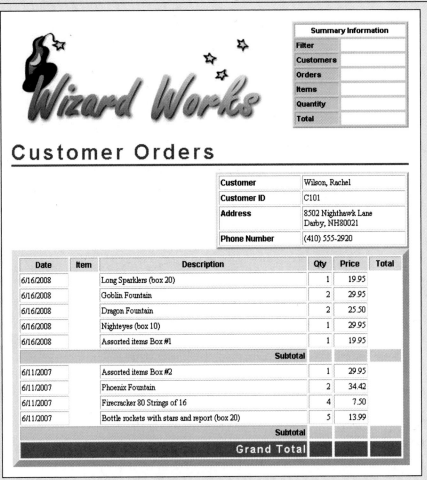

Trouble? The figures in this tutorial are based on the Internet Explorer browser running on Windows. If you are running a different browser or operating system, your result document may differ in appearance.

Bernard did a good job displaying the contents of works.xml in a readable format, but several things still need to be done. Bernard provides you with the following task list for the complete order report (see Figure 7-4):

- The Summary table at the top of the page must display the total number of customers listed in the works.xml document, the number of orders submitted, the number of items ordered, the quantity of items, and the total cost of the orders.
- The order date is to be merged into a single cell for each order, rather than duplicated in each row of the order.
- The Item column must number the items ordered by each customer.
- The total cost of each item (price multiplied by quantity) must appear in the Total column.
- The Subtotal row must display the total quantity of items ordered and the total cost.
- The Grand Total row must display the total quantity of all items ordered by each customer, along with the total cost.

Bernard's task list | Figure 7-4

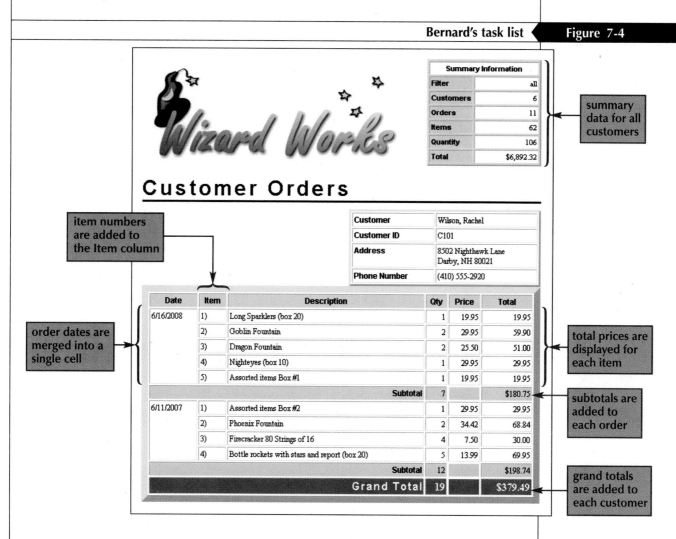

To make the necessary changes to the result document, Bernard needs to use elements and functions from both XSLT and XPath to calculate the relevant values.

Numbering Nodes

You start revising Bernard's document by adding item numbers to the Item column in each orders table. By numbering the items, Bernard will be able to see at a glance just how many items are included in a particular order. To number these items, you can use one of two approaches: XPath's position() function, or the XSLT number element. You investigate each of these methods in more detail, beginning with the position() function.

Using XPath's position() Function

The position() function was introduced along with predicates in Tutorial 6 as a way of referencing a node set that occupies a particular position in a node tree. You can also use the function to return the position of the context node in the result document. The expression is

```
<xsl:value-of select="position()" />
```

The position() function can also be used in an if element to test whether a node occupies a particular position in the result document. For example, the following XSLT if element tests whether the current node is in the third position of its node set:

```
<xsl:if test="position()=3" />
```

Values of the position() function are determined by the order in which nodes are processed in the result document; they are not based on the order of nodes in the source document. This means that if you sort the nodes in the result document, the position values are based on the sorted order of the nodes as they appear in the result document, not on the unsorted order from the source document.

Using the number Element

The position() function returns only the position of a node; for more complicated numbering schemes, you should use the XSLT number element. The number element is used either to create numbered lists or to format numeric values. The syntax of the number element is

```
<xsl:number select="expression" />
```

where *expression* is an XPath expression that indicates which nodes in the source document are being numbered. The select attribute is optional. If no select attribute is specified, the number element generates counting numbers for the current node being processed. Figure 7-5 demonstrates how to use the number element to create a numbered list of firework items. As the XSLT processor returns each firework item in the node set, it increases the numeric count for the numbered list.

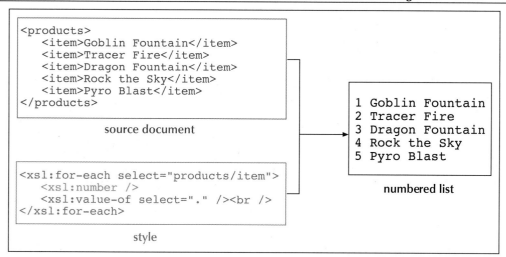

```
<products>
    <item>Goblin Fountain</item>
    <item>Tracer Fire</item>
    <item>Dragon Fountain</item>
    <item>Rock the Sky</item>
    <item>Pyro Blast</item>
</products>
```
source document

```
1 Goblin Fountain
2 Tracer Fire
3 Dragon Fountain
4 Rock the Sky
5 Pyro Blast
```
numbered list

```
<xsl:for-each select="products/item">
    <xsl:number />
    <xsl:value-of select="." /><br />
</xsl:for-each>
```
style

Unlike the position() function, the number element generates its count based on the position of an item within the source document, not the result document: This means that sorting elements does not affect the generated counting numbers. For example, the following style sorts the fireworks list in alphabetical order:

```
<xsl:for-each select="products/item">
   <xsl:sort select="." />
   <xsl:number /> <xsl:value-of select="." /> <br />
</xsl:for-each>
```

The resulting list is sorted alphabetically, but the numbering still reflects the order in which the product elements appeared in the source document:

```
3 Dragon Fountain
1 Goblin Fountain
5 Pyro Blast
4 Rock the Sky
2 Tracer Fire
```

To create a sorted list in which the counting numbers represent the sorted order, you should use XPath's position() function, as discussed above.

Specifying the Count Pattern

XSLT processors calculate the value of the number element by counting the number of previous siblings to the current node in the source document and adding one to that total. This mechanism allows you to keep a running total of two different elements within a single numbered list. Figure 7-6 demonstrates what would happen if you attempted to create a numbered list of both fountain and rocket elements in the products list.

Figure 7-6 **Numbering different items**

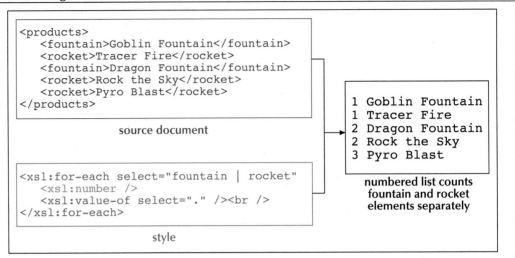

```
<products>
   <fountain>Goblin Fountain</fountain>
   <rocket>Tracer Fire</rocket>
   <fountain>Dragon Fountain</fountain>
   <rocket>Rock the Sky</rocket>
   <rocket>Pyro Blast</rocket>
</products>
```

source document

```
1 Goblin Fountain
1 Tracer Fire
2 Dragon Fountain
2 Rock the Sky
3 Pyro Blast
```

**numbered list counts
fountain and rocket
elements separately**

```
<xsl:for-each select="fountain | rocket"
   <xsl:number />
   <xsl:value-of select="." /><br />
</xsl:for-each>
```

style

Because there are two fountains in this list, they are numbered 1 and then 2. The three rockets are numbered 1, 2, and then 3. The fact that fountains and rockets are mixed in the list does not affect the numbers applied to the elements. The only thing that determines the numeric value is the number of prior siblings to the current node. To apply the same count to nodes from different elements, you add a count pattern to the number element. The syntax is

```
<xsl:number count="pattern" />
```

where *pattern* is an XPath expression that matches the nodes to be included in the running count. Figure 7-7 shows how to use the count attribute to create a numbered list of both fountain and rocket items with the numeric count increasing each time the XSLT processor encounters one of those two elements.

Figure 7-7 **Using the count attribute**

```
<products>
   <fountain>Goblin Fountain</fountain>
   <rocket>Tracer Fire</rocket>
   <fountain>Dragon Fountain</fountain>
   <rocket>Rock the Sky</rocket>
   <rocket>Pyro Blast</rocket>
</products>
```

source document

```
1 Goblin Fountain
2 Tracer Fire
3 Dragon Fountain
4 Rock the Sky
5 Pyro Blast
```

**numbered list counts
rocket and fountain
elements as one**

```
<xsl:for-each select="fountain | rocket">
   <xsl:number count="fountain | rocket" />
   <xsl:value-of select="." /><br />
</xsl:for-each>
```

style

Working with Levels

The number element keeps a running count by tracking the number of siblings prior to the node being counted. This also means that an XSLT processor restarts the numeric count if it encounters a node that has no prior siblings. In the prior examples, you considered only numbered lists in which all the items are placed in the same group. However, if you group items as fountains and rockets, an XSLT processor numbers each group separately, restarting the count each time it encounters the first item element in a new group (see Figure 7-8.) Because the Goblin Fountain item and the Tracer Fire item have no prior siblings in the source document, the counting restarts with each of them, creating two different numbered lists.

Restarting a numbered list ◄ Figure 7-8

```
<products>
    <fountains>
        <item>Goblin Fountain</item>
        <item>Dragon Fountain</item>
    </fountains>
    <rockets>
        <item>Tracer Fire</item>
        <item>Rock the Sky</item>
        <item>Pyro Blast</item>
    </rockets>
</products>
```
source document

```
<xsl:for-each select="//item">
    <xsl:number />
    <xsl:value-of select="." /><br />
</xsl:for-each>
```
style

```
1 Goblin Fountain
2 Dragon Fountain
1 Tracer Fire
2 Rock the Sky
3 Pyro Blast
```
numbered list restarts the count at each new level of item elements

You can specify a rule for counting nodes across levels by applying the level attribute to the number element. The syntax is

```
<xsl:number level="type" />
```

where *type* is single, any, or multiple. A value of single counts items at one level only (the default). A value of any counts items across different levels as if they were all siblings on the same level or within the same group. For example, in Figure 7-9, the level attribute is set to any to continue the count whenever the XSLT processor hits a new item element, no matter what level or group it has been placed within in the source document.

Figure 7-9 ▶ **Creating a numbered list for any level**

```
<products>
    <fountains>
        <item>Goblin Fountain</item>
        <item>Dragon Fountain</item>
    </fountains>
    <rockets>
        <item>Tracer Fire</item>
        <item>Rock the Sky</item>
        <item>Pyro Blast</item>
    </rockets>
</products>
```

source document

```
1 Goblin Fountain
2 Dragon Fountain
3 Tracer Fire
4 Rock the Sky
5 Pyro Blast
```

numbered list counts
item elements across
different levels

```
xsl:for-each select="//item">
    <xsl:number level="any" />
    <xsl:value-of select="." /><br />
<xsl:for-each>
```

style

Finally, a value of multiple for the level attribute counts nodes in a hierarchical list or an outline, with different levels in the source document representing different levels of numbering in the numbered list. This is particularly useful in legal documents in which sections are numbered hierarchically or with documents such as books that contain chapters, sections, and subsections. To display a hierarchical numbered list, you also need to include the count attribute to indicate which elements in the source document should be counted in the hierarchy. Figure 7-10 shows a numbered list that counts all of the group and item elements in the document. Because these elements are placed at different levels in the source document, specifying a level of multiple allows the numbered list to reflect that hierarchy.

Figure 7-10 ▶ **Creating a hierarchical numbered list**

```
<products>
    <group>
        <title>Fountains</title>
        <item><title>Goblin Fountain</title></item>
        <item><title>Dragon Fountain</title></item>
    </group>
    <group>
        <title>Rockets</title>
        <item><title>Tracer Fire</title></item>
        <item><title>Rock the Sky</title></item>
        <item><title>Pyro Blast</title></item>
    </group>
</products>
```

source document

```
1 Fountains
1.1 Goblin Fountain
1.2 Dragon Fountain
2 Rockets
2.1 Tracer Fire
2.2 Rock the Sky
2.3 Pyro Blast
```

numbered list reflects the
hierarchy of the elements in
the source document

```
<xsl:for-each select="//group | //item">
    <xsl:number level="multiple" count="group | item" />
    <xsl:value-of select="title" /><br />
</xsl:for-each>
```

style

For documents that contain features such as chapters and footnotes, footnote numbering usually starts anew with each chapter. If you want to restart the node numbering at certain points in the source document's node tree, you can add the from attribute to the number element using the syntax

```
<xsl:number from="pattern" />
```

where *pattern* is an XPath pattern that indicates where the numbering should restart. The style for an XML document that restarts the footnote numbering with each chapter element might look as follows:

```
<xsl:for-each select="//footnote">
   <xsl:number level="any" from="chapter" />
   <xsl:value-of select="." />
</xsl:for-each>
```

Typically, the from attribute is used when the level attribute is set to either any or multiple. It is seldom necessary to restart a number list when the level attribute is equal to single, because the numbering restarts by default at each new group or level.

Formatting a Numbered List

A second use of the number element is to format a number's appearance. The syntax to specify a numeric format is

```
<xsl:number format="pattern" />
```

where *pattern* is an expression that describes the format of the list. The format attribute supports the following list types:

- "1" to create a list of integers: 1, 2, 3, ...
- "a" to create an alphabetical list of lowercase letters: a, b, c, ...
- "A" to create an alphabetical list of uppercase letters: A, B, C, ...
- "i" to create a list of lowercase Roman numerals: i, ii, iii, iv, v, ...
- "I" to create a list of uppercase Roman numerals: I, II, III, IV, V, ...

To create a numbered list using uppercase letters, you use the element

```
<xsl:number format="A" />
```

The value of the format attribute can contain additional characters to further define the appearance of a list. For example, to create the sequence (a), (b), (c), (d), ..., you use the attribute

```
<xsl:number format="(a)" />
```

For large documents that contain thousands of nodes, you may need to format the appearance of larger numbers. By default, XSLT processors display numbers using a comma as a thousands separator. For example, the number 548710 appears as 548,710. If you are creating an international document, or simply wish to choose a different method of displaying large numbers, you can add the group-size and grouping-separator attributes to the number element:

```
<xsl:number grouping-size="value"
     grouping-separator="character" />
```

where the grouping-size attribute defines the number of digits in each group of numbers (the default is 3), and the grouping-separator attribute defines the character used to separate the groups (the default is a comma). For example, the style

```
<xsl:number format="1"
     grouping-size="2" grouping-separator=" " />
```

displays the number 548710 as 54 87 10.

An international document might also require a different format for alphabetical lists. You can format lists using the attributes

```
<xsl:number lang="language" letter-value="type" />
```

where the lang attribute specifies the language to be used by XSLT processors and the letter-value attribute is either alphabetic for the normal alphabetic numbering scheme, or traditional for a traditional numbering scheme. The precise implementation of these attributes depends upon the processor. Refer to the documentation for the processor you plan to use to determine how to use these attributes in your style sheets.

Formatting a Numeric Value

So far, you've looked only at how the number element can be used to generate numbered lists. You can also use the element to create and format any numeric value you specify by using the value attribute

```
<xsl:number value="expression" />
```

where *expression* is any XPath expression that returns a numeric value. For example, the following code displays the value of the postion() function using a number element, formatting the position as an uppercase Roman numeral:

```
<xsl:number value="position()" format="I" />
```

Reference Window	**Numbering Nodes**

- To display the position of the current node as it appears in the result document, use the XPath function
  ```
  position()
  ```
- To display the position of the current node as it appears in the source document, use the XSLT element
  ```
  <xsl:number />
  ```
- To define the pattern of the nodes to be included in the counting, use
  ```
  <xsl:number count="pattern" />
  ```
  where *pattern* is an XPath expression that matches the nodes to be included in the running count.
- To count nodes regardless of their place in the source document, use
  ```
  <xsl:number level="any" />
  ```
- To create a hierarchical numbered list, use
  ```
  <xsl:number level="multiple" count="pattern" />
  ```
  where *pattern* is an XPath expression matching the nodes in the different levels of the hierarchy.
- To format a list or a number, use
  ```
  <xsl:number format="pattern" />
  ```
  where *pattern* is an expression that describes the format of the list or number.

Now that you've seen the options available to you for numbering the nodes from your source document, you can focus on Bernard's order report. Recall that Bernard wanted to numerically list each item ordered by a customer, placing those numbers in the Item column. To add this feature, you'll use the number element. In the future, Bernard may want to sort the items by name or price, so you'll also use the position() function to base the numbers on the processed order of the nodes, rather than their order in the source document.

To create a numbered list:

1. Return to the **works.xsl** file in your text editor, and go to the item template located at the bottom of the file.

2. Directly after the opening <td> for the second table cell, insert the following element (see Figure 7-11):

```
<xsl:number value="position()" format="1)" />
```

Numbering the item element ◀ Figure 7-11

```
<xsl:template match="item">
    <tr>
        <td class="tdtext"><xsl:value-of select="../../@date" /></td>
        <td class="tdtext"><xsl:number value="position()" format="1)" /></td>
        <td class="tdtext"><xsl:value-of select="." /></td>
        <td><xsl:value-of select="@qty" /></td>
        <td><xsl:value-of select="@price" /></td>
        <td></td>
    </tr>
</xsl:template>
```

3. Save your changes to the file, and then use your browser, the Exchanger XML Editor, or another XSLT processor to generate the result document. The appearance of the first order table is shown in Figure 7-12.

Item numbers ◀ Figure 7-12

numbered list

Date	Item	Description	Qty	Price	Total
6/16/2008	1)	Long Sparklers (box 20)	1	19.95	
6/16/2008	2)	Goblin Fountain	2	29.95	
6/16/2008	3)	Dragon Fountain	2	25.50	
6/16/2008	4)	Nighteyes (box 10)	1	29.95	
6/16/2008	5)	Assorted items Box #1	1	19.95	
			Subtotal		
6/11/2007	1)	Assorted items Box #2	1	29.95	
6/11/2007	2)	Phoenix Fountain	2	34.42	
6/11/2007	3)	Firecracker 80 Strings of 16	4	7.50	
6/11/2007	4)	Bottle rockets with stars and report (box 20)	5	13.99	
			Subtotal		
		Grand Total			

Now, the Item column instantly shows Bernard how many items were placed on each order.

Working with XPath's Numeric Functions

The position() function is only one of several mathematical functions supported by XPath. Figure 7-13 lists the others.

Figure 7-13

XPath numeric functions

Function	Description
ceiling(*number*)	Rounds *number* up to the nearest integer
count(*node_set*)	Counts the number of nodes in *node_set*
floor(*number*)	Rounds *number* down to the nearest integer
last(*node_set*)	Returns the index of the last node in *node_set*
position()	Returns the position of the context node within the processed node set
round(*number*)	Rounds *number* to the nearest integer
sum(*node_set*)	Calculates the sum of the values of *node_set*

You apply some of these functions in the orders report, starting with the count() function.

Using the count() function

At the top of the orders report, Bernard has placed a summary table to display the total number of customers, orders, and items ordered. To calculate these values, you can use the XPath count() function, which counts the total number of nodes in a specified node set. For example, to count all of the customer elements in the source document, you can enter the following expression:

```
<xsl:value-of select="count(//customer)" />
```

Recall that the // symbol causes an XSLT processor to navigate the entire node tree, searching for element nodes named customer. Use the count() function to calculate the total number of customer, order, and item elements in the orders.xml document.

To apply the count() function:

1. Return to the **works.xsl** file in your text editor.

2. Go to the root template at the top of the document, and locate the HTML code that creates the Summary table.

3. Add the following code to the second cell of the third table row:

   ```
   <xsl:value-of select="count(//customer)" />
   ```

4. Add the following code to the second cell of the fourth table row:

   ```
   <xsl:value-of select="count(//order)" />
   ```

5. Finally, insert the following in the second cell of the fifth table row:

   ```
   <xsl:value-of select="count(//item)" />
   ```

   Figure 7-14 highlights the newly added code in the style sheet.

Counting the total number of customers, orders, and items | Figure 7-14

```
<table class="summary" border="2" cellpadding="2">
<tr>
   <th colspan="2" id="summtitle">Summary Information</th>
</tr>
<tr>
   <th>Filter</th>
   <td>
   </td>
</tr>
<tr>
   <th>Customers</th>
   <td><xsl:value-of select="count(//customer)" /></td>
</tr>
<tr>
   <th>Orders</th>
   <td><xsl:value-of select="count(//order)" /></td>
</tr>
<tr>
   <th>Items</th>
   <td><xsl:value-of select="count(//item)" /></td>
</tr>
<tr>
   <th>Quantity</th>
   <td></td>
</tr>
```

▶ **6.** Save your changes to the file, and regenerate the result document. Figure 7-15 shows the revised Summary table with the total counts of customers, orders, and items.

Revised summary table | Figure 7-15

Summary Information	
Filter	
Customers	6
Orders	11
Items	62
Quantity	
Total	

Using the sum() function

A given customer may order more than one of a particular item. The quantity actually ordered by the customer is stored in the qty attribute of the item element. Bernard wants the summary table to display the total overall quantity of items ordered, not just the number of different items. To calculate this value, you have to sum up all of the values of the qty attribute in the source document. This can be done using XPath's sum() function in the following statement:

```
<xsl:value-of select="//sum(@qty)" />
```

Add this statement to the appropriate cell in the Summary table.

To apply the sum() function:

▶ **1.** Return to the **works.xsl** file in your text editor.

▶ **2.** Add the following code to the Quantity table cell of the Summary table (see Figure 7-16):

```
<xsl:value-of select="sum(//@qty)" />
```

Figure 7-16 ▶ **Applying the sum() function**

```
<tr>
  <th>Customers</th>
  <td><xsl:value-of select="count(//customer)" /></td>
</tr>
<tr>
  <th>Orders</th>
  <td><xsl:value-of select="count(//order)" /></td>
</tr>
<tr>
  <th>Items</th>
  <td><xsl:value-of select="count(//item)" /></td>
</tr>
<tr>
  <th>Quantity</th>
  <td><xsl:value-of select="sum(//@qty)" /></td>
</tr>
```

Bernard also wants to calculate the quantity of items on each order and by each customer, and then display those values in the subtotal and grand total rows on the order report (see Figure 7-4). To calculate these values, you must specify a node set limited to a particular order or a particular customer. For example, because all items for a particular order are stored within the items element, to calculate the total quantity of various items for a particular order, you add the following element to the items template:

```
<xsl:value-of select="sum(item/@qty)" />
```

Similarly, all the items for a particular customer are grouped within the orders element. Thus, to calculate the total quantity of items ordered for a particular customer, you add the following element to the orders template:

```
<xsl:value-of select="sum(order/items/item/@qty)" />
```

Add these calculations to the items and orders templates now.

To calculate the quantity of items by order and customer:

▶ **1.** Go to the items template, and insert the following code in the second table cell (see Figure 7-17):

```
<xsl:value-of select="sum(item/@qty)" />
```

Figure 7-17 ▶ **Calculating the total quantity for items within an order**

```
<xsl:template match="items">
  <xsl:apply-templates select="item" />

  <tr>
    <th class="sub" colspan="3">Subtotal</th>
    <td class="sub"><xsl:value-of select="sum(item/@qty)" /></td>
    <td class="sub"></td>
    <td class="sub"></td>
  </tr>
</xsl:template>
```

▶ **2.** Go to the orders template, and add the following code to the second table cell of the second table row (see Figure 7-18):

```
<xsl:value-of select="sum(order/items/item/@qty)" />
```

Calculating the total quantity for all customer orders | Figure 7-18

```
<xsl:template match="orders">
   <table class="orderinfo" border="10" cellpadding="2">
   <tr>
      <th>Date</th>
      <th>Item</th>
      <th>Description</th>
      <th>Qty</th>
      <th>Price</th>
      <th>Total</th>
   </tr>

   <xsl:apply-templates select="order/items" />

   <tr>
      <th class="grand" colspan="3">Grand Total</th>
      <td class="grand"><xsl:value-of select="sum(order/items/item/@qty)" /></td>
      <td class="grand"></td>
      <td class="grand"></td>
   </tr>

   </table>
</xsl:template>
```

3. Save your changes to the style sheet, and regenerate the result document. As shown in Figure 7-19, the result document should now display the total quantity of items ordered by all customers, by each customer, and within each order.

Revised order report | Figure 7-19

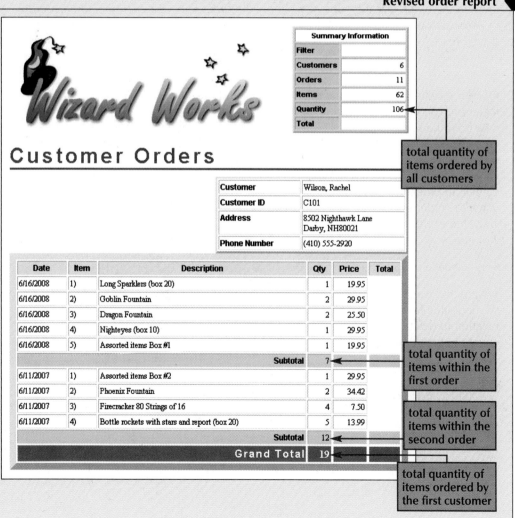

total quantity of items ordered by all customers

total quantity of items within the first order

total quantity of items within the second order

total quantity of items ordered by the first customer

Calculating Totals and Sums

- To count the number of items in a node set, use the XPath function
  ```
  count(node-set)
  ```
  where *node-set* is an XPath expression referencing a collection of nodes in the source document.
- To calculate the sum of the values stored in a node set, use
  ```
  sum(node-set)
  ```

Creating a Spanning Table Cell

Bernard has come by to study your progress. He likes the work you've done using the sum() and count() functions. As he looks over the order report, he notices that the date of the order is repeated for each item in the order. Bernard thinks this is distracting, so he wants the order date to span the rows containing the items from the order. The HTML code to create a cell spanning several table rows is

```
<td rowspan="rows">content</td>
```

where *rows* is the number of rows to be spanned by the cell and *content* is the content of the cell. In Bernard's result document, the number of rows is equal to the number of items in the order, and the content is simply the order date. For example, the first order in Bernard's order report contains five orders, so the HTML code for the order date cell should read

```
<td rowspan="5">6/16/2008</td>
```

Of course, different orders have different dates and different numbers of items ordered; therefore, you have to determine the number of items in an order, as well as the order date from the source document. Determining these values depends on the location of the context node. Each item ordered by a customer is displayed in a separate row in the order table. In the works.xsl style sheet, the item template is used to write the HTML code for these rows; therefore, the context node is the item element. To determine the date of an order, you have to go up two levels in the node tree from the item node to reach the order node, and then down one level to the date attribute (see Figure 7-2). Thus, the expression for the location path that goes from the item element to the date attribute is

```
../../@date
```

In the same way, to determine the total number of items, you have to go up two levels in the node tree from the item element to the order element, and then apply the count() function to determine the total number of items within that order. The expression to count the total number of items in the current order is

```
count(../../items/item)
```

The XSLT code to create the row spanning cell is therefore

```
<td rowspan="{count(../../items/item)}">
   <xsl:value-of select="../../@date" />
</td>
```

When a table cell spans several rows, the remaining cells in that column should be removed from the table. Because the first order date is placed in the cell that spans the rest of the rows for the customer order, you must first test whether the current row corresponds to the first item in the order. To accomplish this, you use the position() function and an if element. If the conditions of the if element are satisfied, you will write the row spanning cell containing the order date for the order. The general syntax is

```
<xsl:if test="position()=1">
   Create row spanning cell
</xsl:if>
```

Putting all of these pieces together, the revised code to display the order date in the first table cell is:

```
<xsl:if test="position()=1">
   <td rowspan="{count(../../items/item)}">
      <xsl:value-of select="../../@date" />
   </td>
</xsl:if>
```

Add this code to the item template in the works.xsl style sheet.

To create the row-spanning cell:

1. Return to the **works.xsl** file in your text editor, and go to the item template near the bottom of the file.

2. After the first <tr> tag in the template, delete the HTML code for the first table cell, and replace it with the following code (see Figure 7-20):

   ```
   <xsl:if test="position()=1">
      <td class="tdtext" rowspan="{count(../../items/item)}">
         <xsl:value-of select="../../@date" />
      </td>
   </xsl:if>
   ```

Creating a row-spanning cell | Figure 7-20

```
<xsl:template match="item">
    <tr>
        <xsl:if test="position()=1">
            <td class="tdtext" rowspan="{count(../../items/item)}">
                <xsl:value-of select="../../@date" />
            </td>
        </xsl:if>
        <td class="tdtext"><xsl:number value="position()" format="1)" /></td>
        <td class="tdtext"><xsl:value-of select="." /></td>
        <td><xsl:value-of select="@qty" /></td>
        <td><xsl:value-of select="@price" /></td>
        <td></td>
    </tr>
</xsl:template>
```

3. Save your changes to the style sheet, and regenerate the result document. Verify that the table cell containing the order date now spans all of the rows of each customer order (see Figure 7-21).

Figure 7-21

Order dates in single table cells

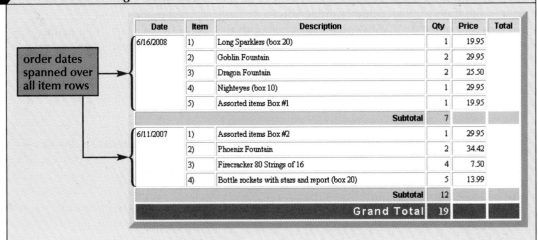

order dates spanned over all item rows

Date	Item	Description	Qty	Price	Total
6/16/2008	1)	Long Sparklers (box 20)	1	19.95	
	2)	Goblin Fountain	2	29.95	
	3)	Dragon Fountain	2	25.50	
	4)	Nighteyes (box 10)	1	29.95	
	5)	Assorted items Box #1	1	19.95	
		Subtotal	7		
6/11/2007	1)	Assorted items Box #2	1	29.95	
	2)	Phoenix Fountain	2	34.42	
	3)	Firecracker 80 Strings of 16	4	7.50	
	4)	Bottle rockets with stars and report (box 20)	5	13.99	
		Subtotal	12		
		Grand Total	19		

Working with Mathematical Operators

Bernard also wants to calculate the total cost of each item purchased: a value equal to the item's price multiplied by the quantity of items ordered. To enter this formula in the style sheet, you must use one of the six operators that XPath uses to perform basic mathematical operations. Figure 7-22 describes the different operators. If you attempt to perform a numeric calculation on a nonnumber, the processor displays the text string NaN (Not A Number).

Figure 7-22

XPath mathematical operators

Operator	Description	Example
+	Adds two numbers together	3 + 5
–	Subtracts one number from another	5 – 3
*	Multiplies two numbers together	5 * 3
div	Divides one number by another	15 div 3
mod	Provides the remainder after performing a division of one number by another	15 mod 3
–	Negates a single number	–2

In the orders.xml document, the qty attribute of the item element contains the quantity of each item ordered, and the price attribute contains the item's price. To calculate the value of the total price, you can use the multiplication operator (*) to multiply the quantity by the price. If the context node is the item element, the code to calculate the total price of the item is

```
<xsl:value-of select="@qty * @price" />
```

Add this expression to the cells in the Total column of each order table.

To calculate the total price:

1. Return to the **works.xsl** file in your text editor, and go to the item template.

2. Insert the following code within the last table cell as shown in Figure 7-23:

```
<xsl:value-of select="@qty * @price" />
```

Calculating the total cost of an item | **Figure 7-23**

```
<xsl:template match="item">
    <tr>
        <xsl:if test="position()=1">
            <td class="tdtext" rowspan="{count(../../items/item)}">
                <xsl:value-of select="../../@date" />
            </td>
        </xsl:if>
        <td class="tdtext"><xsl:number value="position()" format="1)" /></td>
        <td class="tdtext"><xsl:value-of select="." /></td>
        <td><xsl:value-of select="@qty" /></td>
        <td><xsl:value-of select="@price" /></td>
        <td><xsl:value-of select="@qty * @price" /></td>
    </tr>
</xsl:template>
```

3. If you plan to take a break at the end of this session, you may close the works.xsl file, saving your changes.

4. Regenerate the result document. As shown in Figure 7-24, the order report should now include the total price of each item ordered.

Total item costs in the order report | **Figure 7-24**

Date	Item	Description	Qty	Price	Total
6/16/2008	1)	Long Sparklers (box 20)	1	19.95	19.95
	2)	Goblin Fountain	2	29.95	59.9
	3)	Dragon Fountain	2	25.50	51
	4)	Nighteyes (box 10)	1	29.95	29.95
	5)	Assorted items Box #1	1	19.95	19.95
		Subtotal	7		
6/11/2007	1)	Assorted items Box #2	1	29.95	29.95
	2)	Phoenix Fountain	2	34.42	68.84
	3)	Firecracker 80 Strings of 16	4	7.50	30
	4)	Bottle rockets with stars and report (box 20)	5	13.99	69.95
		Subtotal	12		
		Grand Total	19		

total price of each item

5. If you want to take a break before starting the next session, you may close your Web browser or XSLT processor.

You've achieved a great deal on adding calculated values to Bernard's order report. In the next session, you'll learn how to format numeric values and text strings. You'll also learn how to calculate the total price of an order, and total all of the orders in the source document.

Session 7.1 Quick Check

Review

1. What code would you use to test whether the current node is located in the fifth position of its node set?

2. If you want to number the nodes in a node set based on their positions in the result document, should you use the number element or the XPath position() function, and why?

3. What code would you use to number the current node using lowercase Roman numerals?
4. To create a hierarchical number list, what is the value of the level attribute?
5. What code would you use to round the value of the Age element to the nearest integer?
6. The average value is defined as the sum of a collection of items divided by its count. What code would you use to display the average value of the Age element?

Session 7.2

Formatting Numbers

Bernard checked all the calculated values in the Totals column, and they appear to be correct. However, he did notice an inconsistency that he wants to remedy. Some numbers are shown with two digits to the right of the decimal point, but others have one or none at all. Bernard wants every cost value to appear as currency with two digits to the right of the decimal and including a thousands separator.

Using the format-number() Function

You can specify how processors display numbers using the XPath format-number() function. The syntax of the function is

```
format-number(value, format)
```

where *value* is the value of the number, and *format* is a pattern that indicates how the number should appear. Figure 7-25 describes the symbols that can be used in creating the number format pattern.

Figure 7-25 ▶ **Number format symbols**

Symbol	Description
#	Placeholder that displays an optional number of digits in the formatted number and is usually used as the far left symbol in the number format
0	Placeholder that displays required digits in the formatted number
.	Separates the integer digits from the fractional digits
,	Separates groups of digits in the number
;	Separates the pattern for positive numbers from the pattern for negative numbers
–	Shows the location of the minus symbol for negative numbers
%	Multiplies the number by 100 and displays the number as a percentage
‰	Multiplies the number by 1000 and displays the number as a per-mille value

For example, the pattern

```
format-number(56823.847, "#,##0.00")
```

displays the number 56,823.85. Note that the processor rounds the value if the number contains digits other than those provided by the number format. For values that can be either positive or negative, you can specify different patterns using a semicolon symbol (;) to separate the two patterns. The expression

```
format-number(-238.2, "#,##0.0;(#,##0.0)")
```

displays the number –238.2 as (238.2). Any characters not listed in Figure 7-25 appear as part of the number format. To display the number 152.25 as currency, for example, you could use the number format

```
format-number(152.25, "$#,##0.00")
```

which a processor displays as $152.25.

International Number Formats

The numbering scheme used by the format-number() function follows the American system, in which decimal places are represented by a period (.), and the thousands separator is represented by a comma (,). If you plan to create an international document, you may need to support the numbering schemes of other countries. Some European countries, for example, use a comma as the decimal point and a period to separate groups of three digits. To define a different numbering scheme, you apply the following element to the style sheet:

```
<xsl:decimal-format attributes />
```

where `attributes` is a list of attributes that define the numbering scheme that XSLT processors should employ when rendering numeric values. Because the decimal-format element defines behavior for the entire style sheet, it must be entered as a direct child of the stylesheet element and cannot be placed within a template. Figure 7-26 describes the different attributes of the decimal-format element.

Attributes of the decimal-format element ◄ **Figure 7-26**

Attribute	Description
name	Name of the decimal format; if you omit a name, the numbering scheme becomes the default format for the document
decimal-separator	Character used to separate the integer and fractional parts of the number; the default is "."
grouping-separator	Character used to separate groups of digits, the default is ","
infinity	Text string used to represent infinite values; the default is "infinity"
minus-sign	Character used to represent negative values; the default is "-"
NaN	Text used to represent entries that are not numbers; the default is "NaN"
percent	Character used to represent numbers as percentages; the default is "%"
per-mille	Character used to represent numbers in parts per 1000; the default is "‰"
zero-digit	Character used to indicate a required digit in the number format pattern; the default is "0"
digit	Character used to indicate an optional digit in the number format pattern; the default is "#"
pattern-separator	Character used to separate positive number patterns from negative number patterns in the number format; the default is ";"

To create a numbering scheme for some European countries, you can insert the following element at the beginning of the XSLT style sheet:

```
<xsl:decimal-format name="Europe"
    decimal-separator="," grouping-separator="." />
```

To use this numbering scheme in your number formats, you include the name of the scheme as part of the format-number() function. To employ the Europe scheme, you enter the number format as

```
number-format(56823.847, "#.##0,00", "Europe")
```

and the processor displays the number as 56.823,85.

Reference Window

Formatting Numeric Values

- To format a number, use the XPath function
  `format-number(value, format)`
  where `value` is the value of the number, and `format` is a pattern that indicates how the number should appear.
- To set the default number formats for the style sheet, use the XSLT element
  `<xsl:decimal-format attributes />`
  where `attributes` is a list of attributes that define the numbering scheme that XSLT processors should employ when rendering numeric values.

Bernard suggests that you display the total price values to two decimal places and include a thousands separator.

To format the total price values:

1. Return to the **works.xsl** file in your text editor, and go to the item template.

2. Modify the value of the select attribute that displays the total price so that it employs the following number format (see Figure 7-27):

   ```
   format-number(@qty * @price, '#,##0.00')
   ```

Figure 7-27   Specifying a number format

```
<xsl:template match="item">
    <tr>
        <xsl:if test="position()=1">
            <td class="tdtext" rowspan="{count(../../items/item)}">
                <xsl:value-of select="../../@date" />
            </td>
        </xsl:if>
        <td class="tdtext"><xsl:number value="position()" format="1)" /></td>
        <td class="tdtext"><xsl:value-of select="." /></td>
        <td><xsl:value-of select="@qty" /></td>
        <td><xsl:value-of select="@price" /></td>
        <td><xsl:value-of select="format-number(@qty * @price, '#,##0.00')" /></td>
    </tr>
</xsl:template>
```

Trouble? You must enclose the number format, #,##0.00, within a set of *single* quotation marks because the entire value of the select attribute is enclosed in double quotation marks.

3. Save your changes to the style sheet.

4. Regenerate the result document. Figure 7-28 shows the revised order report with the values in the total price column formatted to two decimal places.

Total price values displayed to two decimal places

Figure 7-28

Date	Item	Description	Qty	Price	Total
6/16/2008	1)	Long Sparklers (box 20)	1	19.95	19.95
	2)	Goblin Fountain	2	29.95	59.90
	3)	Dragon Fountain	2	25.50	51.00
	4)	Nighteyes (box 10)	1	29.95	29.95
	5)	Assorted items Box #1	1	19.95	19.95
		Subtotal	7		
6/11/2007	1)	Assorted items Box #2	1	29.95	29.95
	2)	Phoenix Fountain	2	34.42	68.84
	3)	Firecracker 80 Strings of 16	4	7.50	30.00
	4)	Bottle rockets with stars and report (box 20)	5	13.99	69.95
		Subtotal	12		
		Grand Total	19		

Working with Text

Just as the number-format() function provides a way of formatting the appearance of numeric values, XPath and XSLT also provide elements and functions to work with the appearance and content of text strings. You start by exploring how to work with text nodes and white space in the result document.

Text Nodes and White Space

Another issue that Bernard noticed in the document is the lack of space between each customer's state and postal code. For example, the address information for the first customer appears as

8502 Nighthawk Lane
Darby, NH80021

Notice there is no space between the state abbreviation (NH) and the postal code (80021). When you examine the code for the style sheet, the code that creates the state abbreviation and postal code is as follows:

```
<xsl:value-of select="state" /> <xsl:value-of select="postalCode" />
```

Bernard asks you why, if there is a space between the two <xsl:value-of> tags in the code, there is no space between the state and postal code in the result document.

The reason lies in how XSLT processors create and manage text nodes in the result document. An XSLT processor creates a text node whenever it encounters a value-of element in the style sheet; however, if two value-of elements are placed adjacent to one another—even if they're separated by white space in the style sheet—the XSLT processor merges them into a single text node. This is what happened with the address data, causing the state and postalCode values to appear merged into a single text string in the order report.

There are two ways of resolving this problem. One is to use a character entity to explicitly insert a white space character between the two XSLT elements. In HTML, you can insert nonbreaking spaces (spaces not susceptible to white space stripping) using the character entity . However, this character entity is not supported in XML. Instead, you can use one of the following entities to insert white space into a result document:

- Space:
- Tab: 	
- New line:

- Carriage return: 
- Nonbreaking space:

For example, to insert two nonbreaking spaces between the state and postalCode values, you could use the code

```
<xsl:value-of select="state" />  
<xsl:value-of select="postalCode" />
```

When this code is written to an HTML-formatted document, the   entity references are interpreted as nonbreaking spaces. The other way of handling this issue is to create a text node and insert it directly into the style sheet. The syntax to create a text node is

```
<xsl:text>text</xsl:text>
```

where *text* is a text string contained within the text node. Thus, to insert a blank space between two other text nodes, you could also add the following code to the address in the style sheet:

```
<xsl:value-of select="state" /><xsl:text> </xsl:text>
<xsl:value-of select="postalCode" />
```

Note that the <xsl:text> tag can contain only literal text, not other XSLT elements. It is also important to note that if the output format of the result document is HTML, Web browsers use white space stripping to remove any consecutive occurrences of white space. Thus, you cannot use the text element to create two blank spaces, but you can do so by using the   entity reference. Add two nonbreaking spaces to the addresses in the order report.

To insert nonbreaking spaces into the style sheet:

1. Return to **works.xsl** in your text editor.

2. Go to the customer template, and insert the following entity references between the values of the state and postalCode elements as shown in Figure 7-29:

   ```
     
   ```

Figure 7-29 ▶ **Inserting two nonbreaking spaces**

```
<th>Address</th>
<td><xsl:value-of select="street" /><br />
    <xsl:value-of select="city" />,
    <xsl:value-of select="state" />  <xsl:value-of select="postalCode" />
</td>
```

3. Save your changes, and regenerate the result document. Verify that two blank spaces now separate the state abbreviation and the postal code for each customer address in the order report.

Controlling White Space

The previous example highlights how problems with white space can appear unexpectedly in a result document. In addition to a lack of white space, developers can also encounter excess white space. For example, there may be unwanted spaces, extra lines, and tabs appearing in a result document. This results from occurrences of white space that are treated as text nodes by XSLT processors. Figure 7-30 highlights how a simple block of code can actually contain several "hidden" text nodes for the various spaces and line returns within the document. For example, the line return and the two blank spaces between the <tr> and <th> tags are actually treated by XSLT processors as text nodes containing the &#A;&#20;&#20; characters.

White space text nodes in the style sheet ◄ Figure 7-30

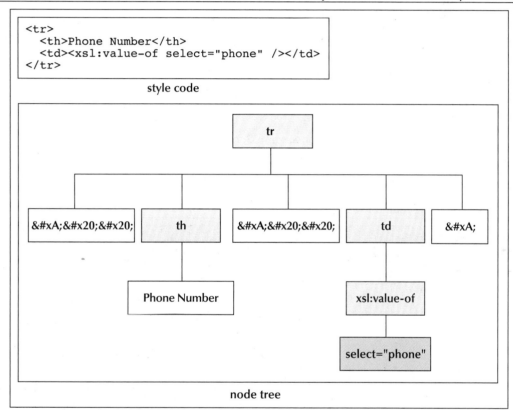

```
<tr>
  <th>Phone Number</th>
  <td><xsl:value-of select="phone" /></td>
</tr>
```
style code

node tree

This is not a problem when generating HTML files because Web browsers strip out excess white space. It can be a problem, however, if the output is written to another XML document or another format such as RTF or PDF. In these formats, the white space might be preserved and rendered in the result document, causing unexpected line returns and extra blank spaces. In these situations, a programmer may want to explicitly remove white space text nodes from the result document. This can be done by adding the following element to the top of the file as a direct child of the stylesheet element:

```
<xsl:strip-space elements="list" />
```

where *list* is a white space-separated list of elements in the source document that contain only white space characters. To remove all white space text nodes from the document, add the following element to the style sheet:

```
<xsl:strip-space elements="*" />
```

The opposite problem is to ensure that text nodes that contain only white space are not deleted. To preserve white space text nodes, use the following element:

```
<xsl:preserve-space elements="list" />
```

where once again, *list* is a white space-separated list of elements containing only white space. Thus, to preserve all white space text nodes, you add the following element to the style sheet:

```
<xsl:preserve-space elements="*" />
```

Finally, another way of working with white space characters is to use the XPath normalize-space() function. The normalize-space() function removes any leading or trailing spaces from a text string. For example, the expression

```
normalize-space("    goodbye    ")
```

returns the text string, "goodbye" without the leading or trailing spaces. The normalize-space() function is commonly used with text values such as passwords in which it is important to ensure that any inadvertent white space characters are removed.

XPath Text Functions

The normalize-space() function is one example of a function supported by XPath to manipulate text strings or to extract information from a text string. Figure 7-31 describes some of the other XPath text string functions.

Figure 7-31 ▶ **XPath 1.0 string functions**

Function	Description
concat(*string1*, *string2*, *string3*, ...)	Combines *string1*, *string2*, *string3*, ... into a single text string
contains(*string1*, *string2*)	Returns the value true if *string1* contains the text string *string2*, and false if otherwise
normalize-space(*string*)	Returns *string* with leading and trailing white space characters stripped away
starts-with(*string1*, *string2*)	Returns the value true if *string1* begins with the characters defined in *string2*, and false if otherwise
string(*object*)	Converts *object* to a text string; if *object* is not specified, the string() function returns the string value of the context node
string-length(*string*)	Returns the length of *string*; if *string* is not specified, the string-length() function returns the length of the string value of the context node
substring(*string*, *start*, *length*)	Returns a substring from *string*, starting with the character in the *start* position and continuing for *length* characters; if no length is specified, the substring goes to the end of the original text string
substring-after(*string1*, *string2*)	Returns a substring of *string1* consisting of everything occurring after the characters defined in *string2*
substring-before(*string1*, *string2*)	Returns a substring of *string1* consisting of everything occurring before the characters defined in *string2*
translate(*string1*, *string2*, *string3*)	Returns *string1* with occurrences of characters listed in *string2* replaced by characters in *string3*

One use of XPath text string functions is to extract individual values from a list. For example, the command

```
substring-before("C101 C102 C103 C104", " ")
```

locates the first blank space in the text string and extracts all the text before the first blank space. In this case, the function returns the text string C101. The substring-before() function is often used to break up strings of values into individual text strings. You do not need to use this function in the orders report.

Using Variables

The orders.xml file contains orders from individuals, businesses, and government agencies. Orders are divided into two groups that can be distinguished by their customer ID or CID. All individuals have CIDs that begin with the letter C, such C101, C102, and so forth. All businesses and government agencies have CIDs that begin with the letter B, such as B101. Bernard would like to modify his report to show only the orders from businesses and government agencies. You can use the XPath starts-with() function to identify all the customers whose CID starts with the letter B. The form of the function is

```
starts-with(@CID, "B")
```

Applying this function in a predicate, the following location path selects only those customer elements from businesses or government agencies:

```
customers/customer[starts-with(@CID, "B")]
```

One problem with this approach is that there are several places in the style sheet where such a predicate would have to be used. This means that every time Bernard wanted to change the group of customers to be displayed, he would have to locate and edit all of these predicates. In a small document, this might not be a big impediment, but in a large complicated style sheet, this would be a major task. Instead, Bernard wants to define this location path at only one point in the document and then refer to that value later in the style sheet. This can be done by creating a variable.

Declaring a Variable

A **variable** is a user-defined name that stores a particular value or object. Variables can store any of the following:

• Number
• Text string
• Node set
• Boolean value (either true or false)
• Result tree fragment

Variables are created using the XSLT element

```
<xsl:variable name="name" select="value" />
```

where *name* is the variable's name and *value* is the value or object stored by the variable. Variable names follow the same XML rules that apply to other elements: a variable name cannot start with a number, and variable names are case sensitive. XSLT variables do not act like variables you may have encountered in programming languages. The most important difference is that *the value of an XSLT variable can be set only once*. The reason for this is discussed in the next session.

The simplest use for a variable is to store a numeric value. The following code creates a variable named price, storing the value 29.95:

```
<xsl:variable name="price" select="29.95" />
```

Using a variable to store a text string is slightly different. You must enclose the text string within a second set of quotation marks. For example, to create a company variable storing the text string Wizard Works, you use the following code:

```
<xsl:variable name="company" select="'Wizard Works'" />
```

Note that if you use double quotation marks for the variable value, you have to use single quotation marks for the text string. If you omit the quotation marks around a text string, XSLT processors treat the text as the name of an element or node in the source document. Omitting the single quotation marks in the above code causes processors to look for a node named Wizard Works. If they don't find such a node, they do not report an error message, but instead assign a blank value to the company variable.

A variable can also point to a node set, such as in the following code:

```
<xsl:variable name="custList" select="customers/customer" />
```

This code creates the custList variable pointing to the node set "customers/customer".

Understanding Variable Scope

Where a variable is declared determines where it can be used. The area where a variable can be referenced is known as the variable's **scope**. Variables can have either global scope or local scope.

A variable with **global scope**, also known as a **global variable**, can be referenced from anywhere within a style sheet. To create a global variable, the variable must be declared at the top level of the style sheet, as a direct child of the stylesheet element. Because global variables are referenced anywhere in a style sheet, each must have a unique variable name.

A variable that is declared within a template, known as a **local variable**, has **local scope** and can be referenced only within that template. Unlike global variables, local variables can share the same variable name if they are declared in different templates. You can also assign the same name to a global variable and a local variable. In this case, an XSLT processor uses the local variable within the template in which it is defined, and the global variable elsewhere.

Now that you've seen how to declare a variable, you are ready to add a variable to Bernard's style sheet. Bernard wants a global variable named group that stores a node set consisting only of business or government agency customers. The code to create the group variable is:

```
<xsl:variable name="group"
    select="customers/customer[starts-with(@CID,'B')]" />
```

Because group is to be a global variable, it needs to be declared at the top of the style sheet, as a direct child of the stylesheet element.

To declare the group variable:

1. Return to **works.xsl** in your text editor.

2. Go to the top of the style sheet file, and directly below the opening <xsl:stylesheet> tag, insert the following variable declaration (see Figure 7-32):

```
<xsl:variable name="group"
    select="customers/customer[starts-with(@CID,'B')]" />
```

Declaring the group variable | Figure 7-32

```
<xsl:stylesheet version='1.0' xmlns:xsl="http://www.w3.org/1999/XSL/Transform">
<xsl:variable name="group"
    select="customers/customer[starts-with(@CID,'B')]" />
<xsl:output method="html" version="4.0" />
```

node set limited to customers whose
CID attribute starts with the letter B

Referencing a Variable

Once a variable is created, it can be referenced using the expression

$name

where name is the variable's name. For example, to display the value of the price variable, you enter the following code in the style sheet:

```
The price of the item is <xsl:value-of select="$price" />.
```

If the value of the price variable is 29.95, the processor displays the text string

```
The price of the item is 29.95.
```

If the variable contains a node set, you can use the variable reference in place of a node reference. For example, if the custList variable points to the node set customers/customer, you can create a template for this node set using the following XSLT command block:

```
<xsl:template match="$custList">
    styles
</xsl:template>
```

You've already declared the group variable in the works.xsl style sheet. Now replace all occurrences of the customer node set with a reference to the value of the group variable.

To reference the group variable:

1. Go to the root template, and within the second cell of the third table row change the value of the select attribute from select="count(//customer)" to:

```
select="count($group)"
```

2. Change the select attribute in the second cell of the fourth row from select="count(//order)" to:

```
select="count($group//order)"
```

▶ **3.** Change the select attribute in the second cell of the fifth table row from select="count(//item)" to

```
select="count($group//item)"
```

▶ **4.** Change the select attribute in the second cell of the sixth table row from select="sum(//@qty)" to

```
select="sum($group//@qty)"
```

▶ **5.** Locate <xsl:apply-templates select="customers/customer" /> tag, and change it to

```
<xsl:apply-templates select="$group" />
```

Figure 7-33 shows the revised code for the root template.

Figure 7-33	Referencing the group variable

```
<tr>
    <th>Customers</th>
    <td><xsl:value-of select="count($group)" /></td>
</tr>
<tr>
    <th>Orders</th>
    <td><xsl:value-of select="count($group//order)" /></td>
</tr>
<tr>
    <th>Items</th>
    <td><xsl:value-of select="count($group//item)" /></td>
</tr>
<tr>
    <th>Quantity</th>
    <td><xsl:value-of select="sum($group//@qty)" /></td>
</tr>
<tr>
    <th>Total</th>
    <td></td>
</tr>
</table>

<p><img src="logo.jpg" alt="Wizard Works" /></p>

<h1>Customer Orders</h1>
<xsl:apply-templates select="$group" />
</body>
</html>
</xsl:template>
```

> reference the node set defined by the group variable

▶ **6.** Save your changes to the style sheet, and use your browser or XMLSpy to regenerate the result document. Figure 7-34 displays a portion of the revised result document that shows data for Wizard Works business and government customers only. The report should contain only two customers: Miller Foods and Greenbush County.

Order report limited to business and government customers ◀ Figure 7-34

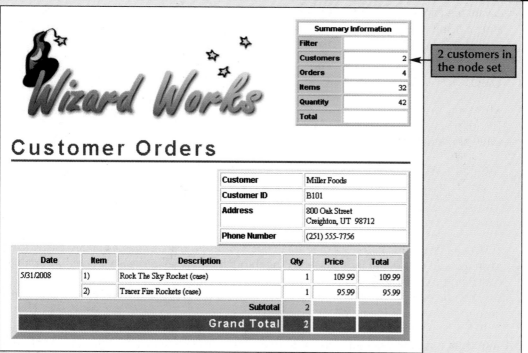

2 customers in the node set

Declaring and Referencing Variables

Reference Window

- To declare a variable, use the XSLT element
  ```
  <xsl:variable name="name" select="value" />
  ```
  where *name* is the variable's name and *value* is the value or object stored by the variable.
- To reference a variable, use the expression
  ```
  $name
  ```

From the result document, you can see that the two customers placed four orders, purchasing 32 different items. Bernard wants to see if the rest of the report is updated correctly when the value of the group variable is changed. Find out by revising the value of the group variable so that it displays only the orders of the customer whose CID equals C103.

To test the group variable:

1. Return to **works.xsl** in your text editor.

2. Change the value of the group variable's select attribute from select="customers/ customer[starts-with(@CID, 'B')]" to

   ```
   select="customers/customer[starts-with(@CID, 'C103')]"
   ```

3. Save your changes to works.xsl, and regenerate the result document. Verify that the only customer shown in the order report is Uwe Lungren, with a CID of C103.

Working with Result Tree Fragments

A variable can also store blocks of code called **result tree fragments**. The syntax for creating a result tree fragment is

```
<xsl:variable name="name">
    styles
</xsl:variable>
```

where *styles* contains the literal result and XSLT elements contained in the fragment. The following code creates a variable named dateCell that stores code for placing the value of the date attribute into a table cell:

```
<xsl:variable name="dateCell">
    <td>
        <xsl:value-of select="@date" />
    </td>
</xsl:variable>
```

Storing a code block in a result tree fragment can result in style sheets that are easier to maintain and revise. Rather than searching through a long style sheet for code, a variable containing a code block can be defined at the top of the style sheet. This block of code can then be easily repeated throughout the style sheet. To revise the code block you only need to revise the value of the variable.

Referencing a variable that contains a result tree fragment is a more complex process. You cannot use the value-of element to reference a result tree fragment because XSLT processors convert the data type of such a variable from a result tree fragment to a Boolean value, a number, or a text string. For example, you can't reference the dateCell variable using the code

```
<tr>
    <xsl:value-of select="$dateCell" />
</tr>
```

because an XSLT processor converts the reference to a text string, keeping the value of the date attribute, but losing the opening and closing <td> tags in the process. In most cases, an XSLT processor displays an error message if you attempt to reference a result tree fragment in this way. Instead, to display a result tree fragment, you create a copy. This is done through either the XSLT copy element or the copy-of element. The copy element copies the current node in the source document, but because it does not copy descendants of that node, it is known as a **shallow copy**. The syntax of the copy element is

```
<xsl:copy use-attribute-sets="list" />
```

where *list* is a white space-separated list of attribute sets (see Tutorial 6 for a discussion of attribute sets). Conversely, the copy-of element creates a **deep copy** of a selected node that includes all descendants of that node. The syntax of the copy-of element is

```
<xsl:copy-of select="expression" />
```

where *expression* is an XPath expression for a node set or a value to be copied to the result document. If the expression is a number or Boolean value, the copy-of element converts the expression to a text string, and the text is output to the result document. For example, to copy the result tree fragment stored in the dateCell variable, you apply the code

```
<tr>
    <xsl:copy-of select="$dateCell" />
</tr>
```

and an XSLT processor would write the following command block to the result document:

```
<tr>
   <td><xsl:value-of select="@date" /></td>
</tr>
```

Both the copy and copy-of elements are used primarily when transforming one XML document into another XML document. If parts of the source document's node tree will be unchanged in the result document, it is more efficient to copy those sections directly than to re-create them piece by piece by creating individual elements and attributes, as was discussed in Tutorial 6.

Reference Window

Creating a Copy of a Node Set

- To create a shallow copy of the current node (one that does not include the node's descendants), use the XSLT element
    ```
    <xsl:copy use-attribute-sets="list" />
    ```
    where *list* is a white space-separated list of attribute sets.
- To create a deep copy of a node set (including all descendants), use the element
    ```
    <xsl:copy-of select="expression" />
    ```
    where *expression* is an XPath expression for a node set of a value that should be copied to the result document.

Using Parameters

Each time Bernard wants to view the results for a particular customer, he must edit the style sheet and regenerate the result document. Bernard can avoid this by using parameters in his style sheet. A **parameter** is a variable whose value changes after its declared and whose value can be set from outside of its scope. The ability to set a parameter's value from outside its scope means that **global parameters** can have their values set from outside of the style sheet (for example, from the XSLT processor). A **local parameter** can have its value set from another template within the style sheet file. Parameters are declared using the element

```
<xsl:param name="name" select="value" />
```

where *name* is the parameter name and *value* is the parameter's default value. Note that the value of the select attribute is used only when no value has been passed to the parameter from the outside. Parameters are referenced using the same syntax that is applied to variables. For example, Bernard can use the following code to create a parameter named filter that specifies which customers appear in the orders report:

```
<xsl:param name="filter" select="'C104'" />
```

Here, the default value of the filter parameter is C104. To display information only about the customer whose CID begins with C104, you can modify the declaration for the group variable as follows:

```
<xsl:param name="filter" select="'C104'" />
<xsl:variable name="group"
    select="customers/customer[starts-with(@CID, $filter)]" />
```

The group variable then contains only the node set of that customer whose CID begins with C104. As with variables, parameter values containing text strings must be enclosed within a second set of quotation marks. If an empty text string is specified for the filter parameter's value as is done in the following code, the group variable points to all customer elements in the source document:

```
<xsl:param name="filter" select="''" />
<xsl:variable name="group"
     select="customers/customer[starts-with(@CID, $filter)]" />
```

Add the filter parameter to the works.xsl style sheet.

To declare the filter parameter:

1. Return to **works.xsl** in your text editor.

2. Insert the following element directly above the declaration for the group variable:

   ```
   <xsl:param name="filter" select="''" />
   ```

3. Change the code declaring the group variable to

   ```
   <xsl:variable name="group"
        select="customers/customer[starts-with(@CID,$filter)]" />
   ```

   Figure 7-35 shows the revised style sheet code.

Figure 7-35 ▸ **Declaring the filter parameter**

reference to the filter parameter

```
<xsl:stylesheet version='1.0' xmlns:xsl="http://www.w3.org/1999/XSL/Transform">
<xsl:param name="filter" select="''" />
<xsl:variable name="group"
     select="customers/customer [starts-with(@CID,$filter)]" />
<xsl:output method="html" version="4.0" />
```

default value for the filter parameter is set to an empty text string

Bernard wants the Summary table in the order report to indicate the value of the filter parameter so that he can see clearly what types of customers appear in the document. If no value for the Filter parameter is specified, he wants the Summary table to display the value "all" because all the customers appear in the result document. You can accomplish this by using an if element in the document, displaying the word "all" if the value of the filter parameter is an empty text string.

To display the filter value:

1. Locate the HTML code for the second table cell of the second row of the Summary table. Within the opening and closing <td> tags, insert the code (see Figure 7-36):

   ```
   <xsl:if test="$filter=''">all</xsl:if>
   <xsl:value-of select="$filter" />
   ```

Figure 7-36 ▸ **Displaying the filter value**

```
<body>
<table class="summary" border="2" cellpadding="2">
<tr>
    <th colspan="2" id="summtitle">Summary Information</th>
</tr>
<tr>
    <th>Filter</th>
    <td>
        <xsl:if test="$filter=''">all</xsl:if>
        <xsl:value-of select="$filter" />
    </td>
</tr>
```

2. Close the works.xsl file, saving your changes.

3. Regenerate the result document. The document should now display information about all of the customers in the source document, and the Filter cell in the Summary table should display the value "all".

4. Close your Web browser if you used it to view the result document.

Setting a Parameter Value

Because you defined the filter parameter globally within the style sheet, you have the ability to change its value using your XSLT processor. The ability to set a parameter's value from outside the style sheet depends upon which XSLT processor is being used. To determine how to work with parameters in your XSLT processor, you have to consult the processor's documentation. A server-side framework such as Cocoon, AxKit, or XSQL allows developers to pass a parameter's value as part of the URL for a Web page. For XSLT processors that work on the client side, such as Saxon or xt, you include the parameter's value in the command line that generates the result document.

The XSLT processors built into Web browsers do not at this time allow users to set parameter values directly. You can set parameter values by running a JavaScript program from within the browser, a technique you'll explore in Tutorial 10. The Exchanger XML Editor does include the ability to set the parameter's value interactively. You decide to show Bernard how to accomplish this.

To set the parameter value in the Exchanger XML Editor:

1. If it isn't already open, start the Exchanger XML Editor on your computer and open the **orders.xml** and **works.xsl** files from the tutorial.07x/tutorial folder. Ignore any error messages when you open the works.xsl file.

2. If necessary, make orders.xml the active pane in the document window by clicking the **orders.xml** tab.

3. Click **Transform** on the menu bar and then click **Execute Advanced XSLT** to open the Execute XSLT dialog box.

4. Click the **Open Document** option button in the Input section and then select **orders.xml** from the drop-down list box. Click the **Open Document** option button in the XSL section and select **works.xsl** from the list box.

5. Click the **Parameters** button to open the XSLT Parameters dialog box.

6. Click the **Add** button.

7. Type **filter** in the Name box, press the **Tab** key and type **C104** in the Value box. Click the **OK** button. As shown in Figure 7-37 the parameter, filter=C104 is added to XSLT parameters dialog box.

Figure 7-37 | Inserting the parameter value in the Exchanger XML Editor

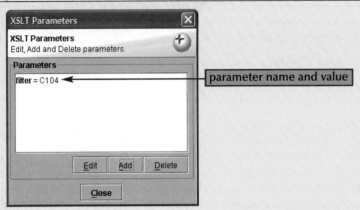

8. Click the **Close** button.

9. Click the **Execute** button and then close the Execute Scenario dialog box when the tranformation is complete. Figure 7-38 shows the generated HTML for the new document. Note that only the orders for customer C104 are contained in the document.

Figure 7-38 | HTML code for customer C104

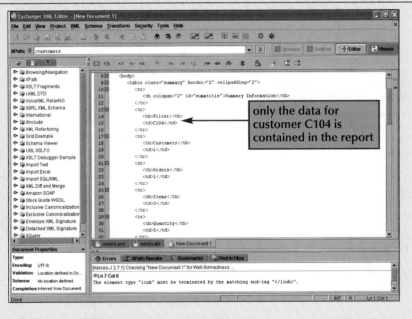

At this point, you could save the order report on this one customer as a permanent file, or regenerate the output document, specifying a new filter value and view a new order report. For now, though, exit the Exchanger XML Editor without saving the document.

10. Exit the Exchanger XML Editor without saving any changes you may have made to the source document or style sheet.

Creating and Using Parameters

- To declare a parameter, use the XSLT element
  ```
  <xsl:param name="name" select="value" />
  ```
  where `name` is the parameter name and `value` is the parameter's default value.
- To reference a parameter, use the expression
  ```
  $name
  ```
  where `name` is the name of the parameter.
- To set the value of a template parameter, use the with-param element as in the following code:
  ```
  <xsl:apply-templates select="expression">
    <xsl:with-param name="name" select="value" />
  </xsl:apply-templates>
  ```
  where `name` is the parameter's name and `value` is the value that is passed to the parameter. Note that the with-param element must be the first child of the apply-templates element.

Introducing Template Parameters

The filter parameter you just worked with is an example of a global parameter, as its value is defined outside of the style sheet and, once set, the parameter's value can be referenced anywhere within the style sheet. Parameters can also be local in scope when they're declared within a template. Such parameters are also referred to as **template parameters**. To create a local or template parameter you enter the following code:

```
<xsl:template match="node">
   <xsl:param name="name" select="value" />
   styles
</xsl:template>
```

where `name` is the parameter's name and `value` is the parameter's default value. Note that a template parameter must be the first element declared in a template before any other XSLT or literal result elements. Similar to a global parameter, the value of a template parameter can also be passed to it from outside of the template. To pass a value to a template parameter, apply the template using the code structure

```
<xsl:apply-templates select="expression">
   <xsl:with-param name="name" select="value" />
</xsl:apply-templates>
```

where `name` is the name of a parameter declared within the template and `value` is the value passed to the parameter. If you don't include the select attribute, the template uses the default parameter value. For example, in the following sample code, the customer template is called with a value of C101, which is passed to the custID parameter within that template:

```
<xsl:apply-templates select="customers/customer">
   <xsl:with-param name="custID" select="C101" />
</xsl:apply-templates>
...
<xsl:template match="customer">
   <xsl:param name="custID" />
   styles
</xsl:template>
```

When passing a parameter value, you must make sure that the value of the name attribute in the with-param element matches the name of the template parameter. If you mistype the name, an XSLT processor does not pass the value and does not return an error message indicating that a mistake was made.

You'll learn more about template parameters and how to use them effectively in the next session.

Review

Session 7.2 Quick Check

1. Your style sheet contains the code:

   ```
   <xsl:value-of select="First" /> <xsl:value-of select="Last" />
   ```

   When you view the result document, the text appears as follows with no space between the first and last name:

   ```
   JohnSmith
   ```

   How would you revise the code to correct this problem?

2. What code would you use to create a variable named NewYearsDay that stores the text string 1/1/2008?
3. How would you reference the NewYearsDay variable defined in the previous question?
4. What is a result tree fragment? What XSLT element do you use to display a result tree fragment in your result document?
5. What is variable scope? What is the difference between a global variable and a local variable? How do you declare each one?
6. How do parameters differ from variables?
7. You want to access the Date template, setting the value of the Today parameter within the template to the value 12/11/2008. What code would you use in your style sheet?

Session 7.3

Introducing Functional Programming

Bernard reviewed your work on the order report, and he is pleased with the layout of the page and the use of parameters to define the subset of customers to appear in the report. The last remaining task is to calculate the total cost of the customer orders. You've already calculated the cost of each individual item by multiplying the price of the item by the quantity ordered. Bernard needs you to write code that adds up all of those costs to arrive at overall totals for each order, each customer, and for all of the customers in the report. In other languages, this could be done using the following structure:

```
function totalCost
   total = 0
   for each item in the order
      total = (item cost) + total
   next item
   report total
end function
```

This type of structure is an example of a **loop**. As the processor repeats (or loops through) the code for each item in the order, the value of the total variable is increased by the cost of each item. The loop ends when the cost of the last item is added to the total; thus, after the loop is finished, the total contains the sum of all of the item costs. The function could then report the total.

The only problem with this approach is that it doesn't work in XSLT because variable values are fixed and cannot be updated. There would be no way of modifying the value of a totalCost variable while looping through the items in the order. In fact, loops are invalid structures in XSLT.

The Philosophy of Functional Programming

XSLT is a functional programming language. **Functional programming** relies on the evaluation of functions and expressions, rather than the sequential execution of commands. Because of this, you may find XSLT to be quite different from other computer languages you may have worked with in the past. Functional programming follows the same paradigm as mathematical functions. For example, the following statement to calculate the square root of a value is perfectly acceptable in a functional programming language because it does not alter the value of x to perform the calculation:

```
y = squareRoot(x)
```

However, the following statement found in the loop discussed above is invalid because it involves changing the value of the total variable:

```
total = (item cost) + total
```

Functional programming languages such as XSLT do not allow this kind of statement; instead, they are designed around the following principles:

- The main program consists entirely of functions with well-defined inputs.
- The results of the program are defined in terms of outputs from functions.
- There are no assignment statements; thus, when a variable is declared, its value cannot be changed.
- Because the program consists only of function calls, the order of the execution is irrelevant.

Proponents of functional programming argue that adherence to these principles results in code that is easier to maintain and less susceptible to error. It is their belief that the fact that assignment statements impose a specific order of execution on the code can lead to complications. They also believe that the fact that a variable's value can be changed means that it is necessary to understand the whole code structure in order to interpret even the simplest assignment statement. For example, the meaning of a simple statement such as x = x + 1 depends on several factors, including the initial value of x and how often the statement is run. In complex applications, it is often necessary to use sophisticated debugging tools to track the value of a variable as it changes throughout the execution of the code.

However, in functional programming, each time a function is called it does the same thing, regardless of how many times it has already been called, or the condition of other variables in the style sheet. With functional programming, it is important to think about the desired end result, rather than the sequential steps needed to achieve that effect. You've already been applying the principles of functional programming when creating and applying templates. Each template can be thought of as a function, with the input being the specified node set and the output being the result text generated by XSLT. In fact, an entire style sheet can be considered a single function with the input being the source document and the output being the result document.

The benefits of functional programming are by no means accepted universally, and many programmers believe that some tasks can be done only using assignment statements, updatable variables, and sequential commands.

Understanding Recursion

Since loops are invalid, how do you create the same effect using a functional programming language? This is done through recursion. **Recursion** is the process by which a function calls itself. Figure 7-39 shows the general syntax of a totalCost() function that uses recursion to calculate the cost of all items in an order.

| Figure 7-39 | Structure of a recursive function |

```
function totalCost (items)
    if (items exist)
        total = (cost of 1st item) + totalCost (remaining items)
    else
        report total
end function
```

the total cost function continues to call itself until no items are left

Compare this code to the loop displayed earlier. In this structure, the totalCost() function keeps calling itself, reducing the number of items remaining in the list. At some point, no items are left. When that happens, the function calculates the cost of each item, moving backwards out of the set of nested function calls until it has processed all the items in the list. It is important to include a stopping condition in a recursive structure so that there is an end to all the function calls. If you fail to include such a condition, you run the risk of endless recursion as the function calls itself indefinitely.

Although there is no function element in XSLT, you can create this kind of recursive structure using named templates.

Using Named Templates

So far, all of the templates you've created have been matched to specific nodes in the source document. A **named template** is a template that is not associated with any particular node set. Instead, it is a collection of XSLT and literal result elements that can be accessed from other templates in the style sheet. By accessing a named template, you can apply the styles defined in the template to the result document. Thus, named templates have the same utility as functions.

Creating a Named Template

A named template is created using the structure

```
<xsl:template name="name">
    styles, variables and parameters
</xsl:template>
```

where *name* is the name of the template. The template name can be any valid XML name. Within the template, you add the styles, variables, and parameters needed for the template's output. You decide to create a named template called totalCost to calculate the total cost of items purchased from Wizard Works. The initial structure of the totalCost template is

```
<xsl:template name="totalCost">
   <xsl:param name="list" />
   <xsl:param name="total" select="0" />
   XSLT elements
</xsl:template>
```

where *XSLT elements* are the elements that perform the actual calculation. At this point, you don't need to be concerned about how to calculate the total cost value. The totalCost template has two local parameters: list and total. The list parameter contains the node set of items whose total cost you wish to calculate. The total parameter contains the total cost of the items. Because its default value is zero, if the totalCost template is called without specifying a value for the total parameter, the processor assumes a value of 0. Add this template to the works.xsl style sheet.

To create a named template:

▶ **1.** Reopen the **works.xsl** file in your text editor.

▶ **2.** Go to the bottom of the file, and insert the following template directly above the closing </xsl:stylesheet> tag (see Figure 7-40):

```
<xsl:template name="totalCost">
   <xsl:param name="list" />
   <xsl:param name="total" select="0" />

   <!-- Calculate the total item cost -->
</xsl:template>
```

Inserting the totalCost template   **Figure 7-40**

```
<xsl:template name="totalCost">
   <xsl:param name="list" />
   <xsl:param name="total" select="0" />

   <!-- Calculate the total item cost -->
</xsl:template>

</xsl:stylesheet>
```

Calling a Named Template

Once a named template is created, it can be called as follows:

```
<xsl:call-template name="name">
   <xsl:with-param name="param1" select="value1" />
   <xsl:with-param name="param2" select="value2" />
   ...
</xsl:call-template>
```

where *name* is the name of the template; *param1*, *param2*, and so forth are parameters used within the template; and *value1*, *value2*, and so forth are the values passed to each template parameter. The only element that the call-template element can contain is the with-param element. If you don't specify a value for a parameter declared in a named template, the parameter assumes its default value. The name of the template must be written explicitly and cannot be contained within an expression or function.

Figure 7-41 shows the three places in the result document where Bernard wants to apply the totalCost template:

- In the Summary table, displaying the total cost of all of the items in the result document
- Within each order made by a customer, displaying the total cost of all items for that order
- In each customer's orders table, displaying the total cost of all items ordered by that customer

| Figure 7-41 | Displaying the total item costs |

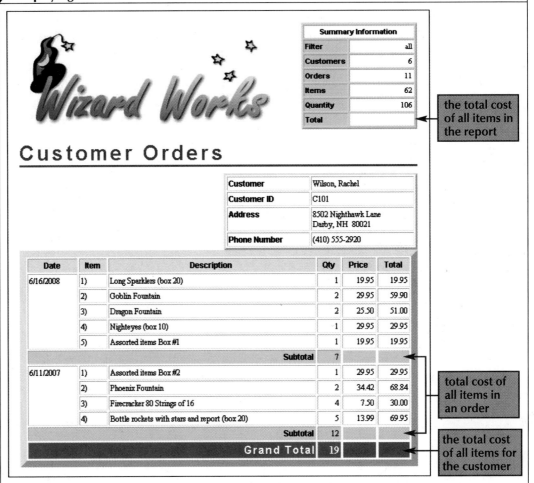

The only difference between these three situations is the collection of items. You should be able to use the totalCost template in each situation by varying the value of the list parameter. For example, to calculate the total cost of all items in the report, you can call the totalCost template using the following code:

```
<xsl:call-template name="totalCost">
   <xsl:with-param name="list" select="$group//item" />
</xsl:call-template>
```

Recall that the $group variable indicates the collection of customers that Bernard wants to appear in the report. The expression "$group//item" selects all item elements that are children of those customers. Note that because this code doesn't include the total parameter, it will have its default value of 0 when the totalCost template is applied.

Each customer's collection of orders is contained in the orders element. Therefore, to calculate the total cost of all of those items, you call the totalCost template from within the orders template using the code block

```
<xsl:call-template name="totalCost">
   <xsl:with-param name="list" select="order/items/item" />
</xsl:call-template>
```

For each orders element, a different total cost is calculated, displaying the total cost of items ordered by the customer. Finally, the items element contains the collection of all items in a specific order. To calculate the total cost of these items, you add the following code to the items template:

```
<xsl:call-template name="totalCost">
   <xsl:with-param name="list" select="item" />
</xsl:call-template>
```

In this case, a separate total cost is calculated for each collection of items elements in the source document. Add this code to the works.xsl style sheet now.

To call a named template:

▶ **1.** Go to the root template, and in the last cell of the last row in the Summary table, insert the following code (see Figure 7-42):

```
<xsl:call-template name="totalCost">
   <xsl:with-param name="list" select="$group//item" />
</xsl:call-template>
```

Calling the totalCost template from the root template ◀ Figure 7-42

```
<tr>
   <th>Quantity</th>
   <td><xsl:value-of select="sum($group//@qty)" /></td>
</tr>
<tr>
   <th>Total</th>
   <td>
      <xsl:call-template name="totalCost">
         <xsl:with-param name="list" select="$group//item" />
      </xsl:call-template>
   </td>
</tr>
</table>
```

▶ **2.** Go to the orders template, and insert the following into the last table cell:

```
<xsl:call-template name="totalCost">
   <xsl:with-param name="list" select="order/items/item" />
</xsl:call-template>
```

▶ **3.** Go to the items template, and insert the following into the last table cell:

```
<xsl:call-template name="totalCost">
   <xsl:with-param name="list" select="item" />
</xsl:call-template>
```

Figure 7-43 shows the revised code for both the Orders and Items templates.

| Figure 7-43 | Calling the totalCost template from the orders and items templates |

```
<xsl:template match="orders">
    <table class="orderinfo" border="10" cellpadding="2">
    <tr>
        <th>Date</th>
        <th>Item</th>
        <th>Description</th>
        <th>Qty</th>
        <th>Price</th>
        <th>Total</th>
    </tr>

    <xsl:apply-templates select="order/items" />

    <tr>
        <th class="grand" colspan="3">Grand Total</th>
        <td class="grand"><xsl:value-of select="sum(order/items/item/@qty)" /></td>
        <td class="grand"></td>
        <td class="grand">
            <xsl:call-template name="totalCost">
                <xsl:with-param name="list" select="order/items/item" />
            </xsl:call-template>
        </td>
    </tr>

    </table>
</xsl:template>


<xsl:template match="items">
    <xsl:apply-templates select="item" />

    <tr>
        <th class="sub" colspan="3">Subtotal</th>
        <td class="sub"><xsl:value-of select="sum(item/@qty)" /></td>
        <td class="sub"></td>
        <td class="sub">
            <xsl:call-template name="totalCost">
                <xsl:with-param name="list" select="item" />
            </xsl:call-template>
        </td>
    </tr>
</xsl:template>
```

Reference Window

Creating and Calling Named Templates

- To create a named template, insert the element
  ```
  <xsl:template name="name">
      styles, variables and parameters
  </xsl:template>
  ```
  where *name* is the name of the template.
- To call a named template, insert the element
  ```
  <xsl:call-template name="name">
      <xsl:with-param name="param1" select="value1" />
      <xsl:with-param name="param2" select="value2" />
      ...
  </xsl:call-template>
  ```
  where *name* is the name of the template; *param1*, *param2*, and so forth are parameters used within the template; and *value1*, *value2*, and so forth are the values passed to the template parameters.

Writing a Recursive Template

Now that you've created the basic structure of the totalCost template, you can write the code to perform the necessary calculations. This is done using a recursive template. **Recursive templates** are templates that call themselves, usually passing along a new parameter value with each call. A recursive template needs to contain the following features:

1. A stopping condition usually contained within an if or choose element

2. A call-template element to call the template recursively
3. One or more local parameters passed recursively to the template

Figure 7-44 displays the general form of a recursive function using an if element, while Figure 7-45 shows the general form using a choose element.

Recursive template with an if element ◄ **Figure 7-44**

```
<xsl:template name="name">
   <xsl:param name="param" select="default" />

   <xsl:if test="stopping condition not met">
      commands
      <xsl:call-template name="name">
         <xsl:with-param name"param" select="new value" />
      </xsl:call-template>
   </xsl:if>

</xsl:template>
```

Recursive template with a choose element ◄ **Figure 7-45**

```
<xsl:template name="name">
   <xsl:param name="param" select="default" />

   <xsl:choose>
      <xsl:when test="stopping condition not met">
         commands
         <xsl:call-template name="name">
            <xsl:call-template name="param" select="new value" />
         </xsl:call-template>
      </xsl:when>

      <xsl:otherwise>
         commands
      </xsl:otherwise>
   </xsl:choose>

</xsl:template>
```

In both structures, the stopping condition is tested. If the condition is not met, a few commands are run and then the function is called again (from within the recursive template) setting a new value for the template's parameter. If the stopping condition is met, the recursive template stops (in the case of using the if element) and runs another set of commands (with the choose element). Writing a recursive template can be a daunting task at first, so start by looking at a couple of examples.

Counting Numbers

Figure 7-46 shows the code for a recursive template named counting that displays a list of numbers. The template has three parameters: num, stop, and step. The num parameter contains the number to be displayed in the list, the stop parameter indicates the stopping point in the list, and the step parameter indicates how much to increase each number. In this example, the counting template is called with initial values for the num, stop, and step parameters set to 0, 30, and 3. Thus, it generates a list of numbers from 0 to 30 in steps of 3.

Figure 7-46   **A recursive template to count numbers**

```
<xsl:call-template name="counting":>
   <xsl:with-param name="num" select="0" />
   <xsl:with-param name="stop" select="30" />
   <xsl:with-param name="stop" select="3" />
</xsl:call-template
```

```
<xsl:template name="counting">
   <xsl:param name="num" />
   <xsl:param name="stop" />
   <xsl:param name="step" />

   <xsl:if test="$num &lt;= $stop">
      <xsl:value-of select="$num" /><br />
      <xsl:call-template name="counting">
          <xsl:with-param name="num" select="$num+$step" />
          <xsl:with-param name="stop" select="$stop" />
          <xsl:with-param name="step" select="$step" />
      </xsl:call-template>
   </xsl:if>

</xsl:template>
```

```
0
3
6
9
12
15
18
21
24
27
30
```

The stopping condition for the counting template is contained in the if element:

```
<xsl:if test="$num &lt;= $stop">
```

The recursive template continues as long as the value of the num parameter is less than or equal to the value of the stop parameter. If this is the case, the value of the num parameter is displayed in the result document, and the counting template is called again, this time with the value of the num parameter increased by the value of the step parameter, as indicated in the element

```
<xsl:with-param name="num" select="$num+$step" />
```

Note that even though the template does not change the value of the stop or step parameters, you still have to include their values when recursively calling the counting template; otherwise, these values are lost when the template is applied.

Calculating a Minimum Value

XPath 1.0 does not include a minimum or maximum function, but you can create your own versions using recursive templates. Figure 7-47 shows a template named minVal that displays the minimum value from a node set. This is a more complicated example than the counting numbers template, so it is helpful to examine the code in detail. The template contains two local parameters: list and min. The list parameter stores the node set to be examined, while the min parameter contains the minimum value from that node set. The default value of the min parameter is set to a very high value of 999,999,999.

A recursive template to calculate a minimum value ◀ Figure 7-47

```
<xsl:template name="minVal">
   <xsl:param name="list" />
   <xsl:param name="min" select="999999999" />

   <xsl:choose>
      <xsl:when test="$list">
         <xsl:choose>
            <xsl:when test="$list[1] &lt; $min">
               <xsl:call-template name="minVal">
                  <xsl:with-param name="list" select="$list[position() > 1]" />
                  <xsl:with-param name="min" select="$list[1]" />
               </xsl:call-template>
            </xsl:when>
            <xsl:otherwise>
               <xsl:call-template name="minVal">
                  <xsl:with-param name="list" select="$list[position() > 1]" />
                  <xsl:with-param name="min" select="$min" />
               </xsl:call-template>
            </xsl:otherwise>
         </xsl:choose>
      </xsl:when>

      <xsl:otherwise>
         <xsl:value-of select="$min" />
      </xsl:otherwise>

   </xsl:choose>

</xsl:template>
```

The minVal template uses a choose element to test whether there are any values in the list node set. This is done using the expression

```
test="$list"
```

If there are no values in the list node set, this expression returns the Boolean value false; otherwise, the expression is true. If there are values in the list, the template tests whether the first value in the list is less than the value of the min parameter, using the expression

```
test="$list[1] &lt; $min"
```

Note that the first time the template is accessed, the default value of the min parameter is 999,999,999; thus, in almost all situations, the value of the first value in the list is less than 999,999,999 (you can always increase the default value of the min parameter if necessary). If the first value is less than the current minimum, the code calls the minVal template again, using the first value as the new value for the min parameter. The node set referenced by the list parameter is reduced, set to the remaining items in the list (any item whose position() value is greater than 1). The code is

```
<xsl:call-template name="minVal">
   <xsl:with-param name="list" select="$list[position() > 1]" />
   <xsl:with-param name="min" select="$list[1]" />
</xsl:call-template>
```

If the first value is not less than the current minimum, the code calls the minVal template again, using the same current minimum value. The node set defined by the list parameter is reduced again to cover only the remaining items:

```
<xsl:call-template name="minVal">
   <xsl:with-param name="list" select="$list[position() > 1]" />
   <xsl:with-param name="min" select="$min" />
</xsl:call-template>
```

Thus, in either case the template calls itself, the number of items in the list node set is reduced, and this process continues until there are no items left. Once this happens, the stopping condition is met, and the template displays the value of the min parameter.

Explore how this works for an actual set of values. Suppose you want to find the minimum value in the following list of values:

```
<values>
  <item>10</item>
  <item>25</item>
  <item>8</item>
  <item>14</item>
  <item>26</item>
  <item>19</item>
  <item>20</item>
</values>
```

you could apply the minVal template using the following code:

```
<xsl:call-template name="minVal">
   <xsl:with-param name="list" select="values/item" />
</xsl:call-template>
```

Because no value is assigned to the min parameter, the template uses the default value of 999,999,999 as the starting value. In this case, the value 8 appears in the result document. The code used to calculate the maximum value is similar, except that you set the default maximum value to a small number, such as –999,999,999, and then test whether the first value in the list node set is greater than that number.

Calculating the Total Order Cost

Now that you've studied two examples of recursive templates, you can start writing the code for the totalCost template. The template uses the same general technique that was used in the minVal template: it starts calculating the total cost by calculating the cost of the first item in the list, and then adding that value to the total and reducing the size of the list by one item each time the template is called. The general structure is

```
<xsl:choose>
   <xsl:when test="$list">
      Calculate the first item cost
      Call the totalCost template
   </xsl:when>
   <xsl:otherwise>
      Display the total cost
   </xsl:otherwise>
</xsl:choose>
```

Note that the when element uses the same condition that was used in the minVal template example. The function continues to call itself if the list parameter is nonempty. Add this structure to the totalCost template.

To add the choose structure:

1. Go to the totalCost template at the bottom of the file.

2. Below the comment line insert the following code (see Figure 7-48):

```
<xsl:choose>
    <xsl:when test="$list">
        <!-- Calculate the first item cost -->
        <!-- Call the totalCost template -->
    </xsl:when>

    <xsl:otherwise>
        <!-- Display the total cost -->
    </xsl:otherwise>
</xsl:choose>
```

Inserting the structure of the totalCost template   **Figure 7-48**

```
<xsl:template name="totalCost">
    <xsl:param name="list" />
    <xsl:param name="total" select="0" />

    <!-- Calculate the total item cost -->
    <xsl:choose>
        <xsl:when test="$list">
            <!-- Calculate the first item cost -->
            <!-- Call the totalCost template -->
        </xsl:when>

        <xsl:otherwise>
            <!-- Display the total cost -->
        </xsl:otherwise>
    </xsl:choose>

</xsl:template>
```

To calculate the cost of the first item, you create a variable named first using the command

```
<xsl:variable name="first" select="$list[1]/@qty * $list[1]/@price" />
```

Recall that in calculating the cost of each item in the order report, you had to multiply an item's quantity by its price. You are doing the same here for the first value in the list. Once that first cost is calculated, you can then call the totalCost template again, reducing the size of the list node set by including only those items *after* the first value in the list and with a value for the total parameter that includes the cost of the first item. The command block is

```
<xsl:call-template name="totalCost">
    <xsl:with-param name="list" select="$list[position() > 1]" />
    <xsl:with-param name="total" select="$first + $total" />
</xsl:call-template>
```

The totalCost template continues to call itself until it exhausts all of the items in the list. At that point, you want to display the value of the total parameter, formatted as currency. The command to display the total parameter is

```
<xsl:value-of select="format-number($total, '$#,#00.00')" />
```

Add these commands to the appropriate places in the totalCost template.

To complete the totalCost template:

▶ **1.** Directly below the comment "Calculate the first item cost," insert the following line:

```
<xsl:variable name="first" select="$list[1]/@qty * $list[1]/
@price" />
```

▶ **2.** Below the comment "Call the totalCost template," insert the following code block:

```
<xsl:call-template name="totalCost">
   <xsl:with-param name="list" select="$list[position() > 1]" />
   <xsl:with-param name="total" select="$first + $total" />
</xsl:call-template>
```

▶ **3.** Finally, below the comment "Display the total cost," insert

```
<xsl:value-of select="format-number($total, '$#,#00.00')" />
```

Figure 7-49 shows the final code of the totalCost template.

Figure 7-49 ▶ **The completed totalCost template**

```
<xsl:template name="totalCost">
   <xsl:param name="list" />
   <xsl:param name="total" select="0" />

   <!-- Calculate the total item cost -->
   <xsl:choose>
      <xsl:when test="$list">
         <!-- Calculate the first item cost -->
         <xsl:variable name="first" select="$list[1]/@qty * $list[1]/@price" />

         <!-- Call the totalCost template -->
         <xsl:call-template name="totalCost">
            <xsl:with-param name="list" select="$list[position() > 1]" />
            <xsl:with-param name="total" select="$first + $total" />
         </xsl:call-template>

      </xsl:when>

      <xsl:otherwise>
         <!-- Display the total cost -->
         <xsl:value-of select="format-number($total, '$#,#00.00')" />

      </xsl:otherwise>
   </xsl:choose>

</xsl:template>
```

Now regenerate the result document to test whether the totalCost template correctly adds up the total cost of items purchased on each order, by each customer, and in the entire order report.

▶ **4.** Save your changes to the style sheet, and using your Web browser, the Exchanger XML Editor, or another XSLT processor regenerate the result document. Figure 7-50 shows the total cost values from the order report.

Total costs displayed in the order report   Figure 7-50

	Summary Information	
Filter		all
Customers		6
Orders		11
Items		62
Quantity		106
Total		$6,892.32

Customer Orders

Customer	Wilson, Rachel
Customer ID	C101
Address	8502 Nighthawk Lane Darby, NH 80021
Phone Number	(410) 555-2920

Date	Item	Description	Qty	Price	Total
6/16/2008	1)	Long Sparklers (box 20)	1	19.95	19.95
	2)	Goblin Fountain	2	29.95	59.90
	3)	Dragon Fountain	2	25.50	51.00
	4)	Nighteyes (box 10)	1	29.95	29.95
	5)	Assorted items Box #1	1	19.95	19.95
		Subtotal	7		$180.75
6/11/2007	1)	Assorted items Box #2	1	29.95	29.95
	2)	Phoenix Fountain	2	34.42	68.84
	3)	Firecracker 80 Strings of 16	4	7.50	30.00
	4)	Bottle rockets with stars and report (box 20)	5	13.99	69.95
		Subtotal	12		$198.74
		Grand Total	19		$379.49

> the total cost of all items in the report

> total cost of all items in an order

> the total cost of all items for the customer

Based on the order report, you can tell Bernard that the total cost of all items purchased by customers in the orders.xml file is $6,892.32. You can also report on individual customers. For example, the first customer, Rachel Wilson, purchased $379.49 worth of products, paying $180.75 on her first order and $198.74 on her second.

Working with Multiple Style Sheets

Bernard is pleased with your work on the totalCost template. In fact, he thinks it is so useful that he plans to use it in other style sheets that he is designing. Rather than typing the template code into every file, however, Bernard wants a way to store it in a single file that is accessible to all style sheets. He envisions creating a library of such templates that can be easily reused in any of his style sheets. The contents of one style sheet could then be inserted into another by including or importing the style sheet. Start on this task by looking at how to include a style sheet.

Including a Style Sheet

To include a style sheet in another style sheet, add the following element as a child of the stylesheet element:

```
<xsl:include href="url" />
```

where *url* is the URL of the style sheet to be included in the current sheet. Including a style sheet has the same effect as inserting the components of that sheet directly into the file at the point where the include element is entered. For example, to include the elements from the style sheet file library.xsl, you add the element

```
<xsl:include href="library.xsl" />
```

The include element does not perform a direct text copy. For example, it doesn't copy the opening and closing <xsl:stylesheet> tags. Instead, it copies the elements and templates within the style sheet.

When combining style sheets, you should be careful not to duplicate template names. When template names clash, XSLT processors use whichever template is defined last in the combined sheet. This means that if you do have duplicate template names, where you insert the include element impacts which template is used by the processor.

There is no limit to how many style sheets can be included in a single document. In addition, you can create a chain of included style sheets, in which style sheet A includes style sheet B, which includes style sheet C, and so forth.

Importing a Style Sheet

Alternatively, you can import the contents of a style sheet using the element

```
<xsl:import href="url" />
```

where *url* is the location of the sheet to import. Similar to the include element, the import element must be at the top level of the style sheet. However, there are a couple of differences between importing and including:

- The import element must be the *first* child of the stylesheet element, but the include element can be placed anywhere within a style sheet as long as it is a child of the stylesheet element.
- In the case of name conflicts between templates in the imported style sheet and templates in the importing sheet, the templates in the importing sheet have precedence.
- If you import several style sheets, the last one imported has the highest precedence among the imported sheets in the event of a name conflict.

The issue of precedence is important when creating a design involving multiple style sheets. A developer can create general templates in one sheet and then override those templates with specific instructions in the importing sheets.

The include and import elements are not supported by all browsers at the time of this writing. Currently neither Safari nor Netscape for the Macintosh support including or importing external style sheet files. Therefore if you need to support those browsers, you will have to avoid placing style sheet code in external files. However you can use those browsers if you generate the result document using another Macintosh-based XSLT processor like oXygen.

Including and Importing Style Sheets

- To include a style sheet, use the element
  ```
  <xsl:include href="url" />
  ```
  where *url* is location of the style sheet to be included in the current sheet.
- To import a style sheet, use
  ```
  <xsl:import href="url" />
  ```
  Now that you've seen how to insert one style sheet into another, you decide to place the
  totalCost template in its own sheet and then import it into works.xsl.

To create a template library:

1. Use your text editor to open the **libtxt.xsl** file from the tutorial.07/tutorial folder. Enter *your name* and *the date* in the comment section, and save the file as **library.xsl**.

2. Return to the **works.xsl** file in your text editor.

3. Insert the following element directly below the opening <xsl:stylesheet> tag (see Figure 7-51):

   ```
   <xsl:import href="library.xsl" />
   ```

Importing the library style sheet ◀ Figure 7-51

```
<xsl:stylesheet version='1.0' xmlns:xsl="http://www.w3.org/1999/XSL/Transform">
<xsl:import href="library.xsl" />
<xsl:param name="filter" select="''" />
<xsl:variable name="group"
    select="customers/customer [starts-with(@CID,$filter)]" />
<xsl:output method="html" version="4.0" />
```

4. Using the cut and paste features of your text editor, cut the entire code for the totalCost template located at the bottom of works.xsl and paste it into library.xsl, as shown in Figure 7-52.

Contents of the library style sheet ◀ Figure 7-52

```
<xsl:stylesheet version='1.0' xmlns:xsl="http://www.w3.org/1999/XSL/Transform">

<xsl:template name="totalCost">
    <xsl:param name="list" />
    <xsl:param name="total" select="0" />

    <!-- Calculate the total item cost -->
    <xsl:choose>
        <xsl:when test="$list">
            <!-- Calculate the first item cost -->
            <xsl:variable name="first" select="$list[1]/@qty * $list[1]/@price" />

            <!-- Call the totalCost template -->
            <xsl:call-template name="totalCost">
                <xsl:with-param name="list" select="$list[position() > 1]" />
                <xsl:with-param name="total" select="$first + $total" />
            </xsl:call-template>

        </xsl:when>

        <xsl:otherwise>
            <!-- Display the total cost -->
            <xsl:value-of select="format-number($total, '$#,#00.00')" />

        </xsl:otherwise>
    </xsl:choose>

</xsl:template>

</xsl:stylesheet>
```

5. Close both the works.xsl and library.xsl files, saving your changes.

6. Regenerate the result document, verifying that the order report is not changed by placing the totalCost template into the library style sheet.

Trouble? If you are using Safari or Netscape for the Macintosh, you may need to keep the code for the totalCost template in the works.xsl style sheet. At the time of this writing, the XSLT processors built into these browsers do not support the import element.

You show the completed work to Bernard and explain to him that he can use the contents of library.xsl in any style sheet he creates by using either the include or import element.

Working with Extension Functions

As you probably recognized when you worked with the code for the minimum template earlier in this session, it would save programmers a lot of trouble if XPath included a minimum value function. While XPath 1.0 doesn't include such a function, some XSLT processors do support extensions to the XSLT and XPath languages. XSLT allows for the following kinds of extensions:

- **Extension functions** that extend the list of functions available to XPath and XSLT expressions
- **Extension elements** that extend the list of elements that can be used in an XSLT style sheet
- **Extension attributes** that extend the list of attributes associated with XSLT elements
- **Extension attribute values** that extend the data types associated with XSLT attributes

Different XSLT processors and versions of the same processor support different extensions. For this reason, you should use extensions only when you are sure that a given document is always accessed using the same processor.

A community of XSLT developers is working on an initiative to create a standard collection of extension elements and extension functions called **EXSLT**. It is hoped that eventually all XSLT processors will support the EXSLT standard to allow for greater portability of XSLT style sheets across processors.

Defining the Extension Namespace

The first step in using extensions is to define an extension's namespace using the stylesheet element. Different extensions use different namespaces, so you must refer to the extension's documentation to determine how the extension should be applied. For example, the math functions provided by EXSLT are associated with the namespace www.exslt.org/math. To define this extension in the style sheet, you insert the following attributes into the stylesheet element:

```
<xsl:stylesheet version="1.0"
    xmlns:xsl="http://www.w3.org/1999/XSL/Transform"
    xmlns:math="http://www.exslt.org/math"
    extension-element-prefixes="math">
```

In this case, any function or element in the style sheet that contains the math prefix is recognized by the processor as an EXSLT extension.

The extension-element-prefixes attribute is used to tell the XSLT processor which prefixes to regard as prefixes for extensions. This is a way to differentiate extension namespaces from other namespaces in the style sheet. If you use several extensions in the style sheet, list all of the prefixes separated by white space in the extension-element-prefixes attribute value. For example, the code

```
<xsl:stylesheet version="1.0"
    xmlns:xsl="http://www.w3.org/1999/XSL/Transform"
    xmlns:math="http://www.exslt.org/math"
    xmlns:saxon="http://ic1.com/saxon"
    extension-element-prefixes="math saxon">
```

references two extension namespaces: math and saxon.

Using an Extension Function

Once a prefix for an extension has been defined, you can use the extension function or extension element in your style sheet, assuming that your processor supports the extension. Figure 7-53 describes some of the mathematical functions supported by EXSLT.

Math extension functions in EXSLT ◄ **Figure 7-53**

EXSLT function	Returns
math.abs(*number*)	absolute value of *number*
math.cos(*number*)	cosine of *number*
math.highest(*node-set*)	nodes with the highest value in *node-set*
math.lowest(*node-set*)	nodes with the lowest value in *node-set*
math.max(*node-set*)	maximum value from *node-set*
math.min(*node-set*)	minimum value from *node-set*
math.power(*base, number*)	value of *base* raised to the *number* power
math.random()	random number between 0 and 1
math.sin(*number*)	sine of *number*
math.sqrt(*number*)	square root of *number*
math.tan(*number*)	tangent of *number*

One of the functions created by EXSLT is the min() function to calculate the minimum value of a node set. The syntax for using the min() function is

```
min(node-set)
```

where *node-set* is the set of nodes to analyze. For example, if your XML document contains the elements

```
<values>
  <item>10</item>
  <item>25</item>
  <item>8</item>
  <item>14</item>
  <item>26</item>
  <item>19</item>
  <item>20</item>
</values>
```

you can display the minimum value using the expression

```
<xsl:value-of select="math.min(values/item)" />
```

Before using this function, you have to check to see if the processor you are using supports the extension. If you try to use the min() function in a processor that doesn't support it, an error results.

Testing Function Availability

Trying to keep track of all of the extensions supported by a given XSLT processor would be an arduous task. Instead, you can have your processor test whether it supports a particular extension function, using the function

```
function-available("prefix:function")
```

where *prefix* is the namespace prefix of the extension function and *function* is the function name. The function-available() function returns the Boolean value true if it supports the function and false if it does not. The following code uses the function-available() function to test whether the math.min() function is supported by the XSLT processor. If it isn't, the processor sets the value to a text string indicating that the extension function is required.

```
<xsl:choose>
   <xsl:when test="function-available('math.min')">
      <xsl:value-of select="math.min(values/item)" />
   </xsl:when>
   <xsl:otherwise>
      <xsl:value-of select="Extension function required" />
   </xsl:otherwise>
</xsl:choose>
```

If you do not have a named template that duplicates a given EXSLT extension function, you can typically find such a template on the Web. Be aware that some templates are not free and must be purchased before they can be used.

Writing an Extension Function

In addition to using existing extension functions, you can create your own. In MSXML, the processor used by Internet Explorer, you can write an extension in any scripting language supported by the HTML script element. These include both JavaScript and VBScript.

Extension functions for the MSXML processor are created by adding a script element at the top of the style sheet. The syntax of the script element is

```
<msxsl:script language="language" implements-prefix="prefix">
   script commands
</msxsl:script>
```

where *language* is the language of the script, *prefix* is the namespace prefix you want to assign to the extension functions you create, and *script commands* is the commands needed to create the extension function. Note that the script tag is placed in the MSXSL namespace using the msxsl namespace prefix. The prefix should be associated with the namespace urn:schemas-microsoft-com:xslt in the stylesheet element of the XSLT file.

For example, XPath does not provide a function to generate random numbers, but JavaScript does with its Math.random() function. Thus, if you wanted to create an extension function to generate random numbers with the MSXML processor, you could take advantage of that function using the following code:

```
<xsl:stylesheet version="1.0"
    xmlns:xsl="http://www.w3.org/1999/XSL/Transform"
    xmlns:jsext="http://javascript-extensions"
    xmlns:msxsl="urn:schemas-microsoft-com:xslt"
```

```
      extension-element-prefixes="jsext msxsl">
<msxsl:script implements-prefix="jsext" language="javascript">
    function random() {
        return Math.random();
    }
</msxsl:script>
```

To run the extension function, you enter the code

```
<xsl:value-of select="jsext:random()" />
```

The result document would display a random number between 0 and 1. This specific technique works only with the MSXML processor. If you are using another processor, refer to the processor's documentation to learn how to create extension functions it recognizes.

Working with Extension Elements and Attributes

In addition to extension functions, you can also use extension elements and attributes in your style sheets. Similar to extension functions, extension elements and attributes must be associated with namespaces. You must also identify which namespaces are extension namespaces using the extension-element-prefixes attribute in the stylesheet element. Using the extension-element-prefixes attribute is critical because it tells XSLT processors how to differentiate extension elements and attributes from literal result elements.

Changing a Variable's Value

XSLT's inability to change a variable's value can be frustrating. You can get around this limitation, though, by using an extension supported by the Saxon XSLT processor that allows variable values to be changed on the fly. To reference the saxon extension namespace, you insert the following attributes into the stylesheet element:

```
<xsl:stylesheet version="1.0"
    xmlns:xsl="http://www.w3.org/1999/XSL/Transform"
    xmlns:saxon="http://ic1.com/saxon"
    extension-element-prefixes="saxon">
```

To create a variable that can be assigned a value after it is declared, you enter the following extension attribute to XSLT's variable element:

```
<xsl:variable name="name" saxon:assignable="yes" />
```

where *name* is the name of the variable and the assignable attribute tells processors that this variable can be assigned a different value later in the style sheet. To assign a new value to the variable, use the extension element

```
<saxon:assign name="name" select="expression" />
```

where *name* is once again the name of the variable and *expression* is a new value assigned to the variable. For example, the following code creates a variable named CVar that stores a customer's ID:

```
<xsl:variable name="CVar" saxon:assignable="yes" select="C1" />
```

Later in the style sheet, the following code changes the value of the CVar variable from C1 to B2 using Saxon's assign element.

```
<saxon:assign name="CVar" select="B2" />
```

Creating a Loop

If you find it difficult to work with recursive templates, you can instead create loops using Saxon's while element. The syntax of the element is

```
<saxon:while test="condition">
   commands
</saxon:while>
```

where *condition* is an expression that must be true for the loop to continue and run the *commands* contained within the while element. By combining the Saxon assign and while extensions, you can create the following loop:

```
<xsl:variable name="i" select="1" saxon:assignable="yes" />
<saxon:while test="$i &lt; 5">
   The value of i is <xsl:value-of select="$i" />
   <saxon:assign name="i" select="$i+1" />
</saxon:while>
```

The result document would display the text

```
The value of i is 1
The value of i is 2
The value of i is 3
The value of i is 4
The value of i is 5
```

Testing Element Availability

As with extension functions, you can test whether a processor supports a particular extension element or attribute, using the function

```
element-available("extension")
```

where *extension* is the name of the extension element or attribute. For example, the following code tests whether a processor supports the saxon extension before attempting to run the loop:

```
<xsl:if test="element-available("saxon.while")>
   <xsl:variable name="i" select="1" saxon:assignable="yes" />|
   <saxon:while test="$i &lt; 5">
      The value of i is <xsl:value-of select="$i"/>
      <saxon:assign name="i" select="$i+1"/>
   </saxon:while>
</xsl:if>
```

You can support processors that don't recognize an extension element or attribute by using the fallback element. When a processor encounters an extension element it doesn't recognize, it searches inside of that element for the fallback element. If it finds it, it processes the code contained within that element, rather than reporting an error. The following code uses the fallback element to provide an alternate set of instructions for processors that do not support Saxon's while element:

```
<xsl:variable name="i" select="1" saxon:assignable="yes" />
<saxon:while test="$i &lt; 5">
   The value of i is <xsl:value-of select="$i"/>
   <saxon:assign name="i" select="$i+1"/>
   <xsl:fallback>
      <xsl:value-of select="This style sheet requires Saxon" />
   </xsl:fallback>
</saxon:while>
```

If the Saxon XSLT processor is used, the while loop is run; otherwise, the processor runs the fallback code and displays the text "This style sheet requires Saxon."

You discuss the issue of extensions with Bernard. At this point, he decides that he would rather stick with the basic XSLT language than insert extensions, which might not be supported by all XSLT processors.

Looking towards XSLT and XPath 2.0

In November 2005, the W3C released candidate recommendations for XSLT 2.0 and XPath 2.0. A candidate recommendation is a stable working draft of the language that the W3C has proposed to the community for implementation experience and feedback. At the time of this writing, the features of XSLT and XPath 2.0 are supported in some XSLT processors, but they are not universally supported. No Web browser currently supports version 2.0 of XSLT and XPath, and it is possible that some changes will be made to the specifications before they reach their final versions.

The Function Element

XSLT 2.0 introduces the function element, which can be used to define a style sheet function that can be called from any XPath expression used in the style sheet. The syntax of the function element is

```
<xsl:function name="name">
   parameters
   function result
</xsl:function>
```

where `name` is the name of the function, `parameters` is any local parameters used in the function, and `function result` is XSLT code that generates the result of the function. The name of the function must be qualified with a namespace prefix to distinguish it from the functions built into XPath. The declaration for the namespace should be placed in the stylesheet element. The function element itself should be entered as a child of the stylesheet element and not placed within a template. The following code uses the function element to create a function that displays the square of a given number:

```
<xsl:function name="ext:square">
   <xsl:param name="num" />
   <xsl:value-of select="$num*$num" />
</xsl:function>
```

To call this function, you add it to any element in the style sheet. For example:

```
The square of 9 is <xsl:value-of select="ext:square(9)" />
```

As with templates, functions can be recursive for more complex calculations. If a function contains more than one parameter, the order of the param elements within the function define the order in which the parameter values must be entered when the function is called.

XPath 2.0 Functions

XPath 2.0 supports a wealth of new functions for manipulating text strings and calculating values. A few of these functions are listed in Figure 7-54.

Figure 7-54 | **XPath 2.0 functions**

Function	Returns
abs(*number*)	absolute value of *number*
avg(*node_set*)	average of the values contained in *node_set*
current-date()	current date of the transformation
current-dateTime()	current date and time of the transformation
current-time()	current time of the transformation
lower-case(*string*)	*string* in lowercase
max(*node_set*)	maximum value in *node_set*
min(*node_set*)	minimum value in *node_set*
upper-case(*string*)	*string* in uppercase

Once XPath 2.0 becomes the de facto standard for XSLT processors, you will be able to calculate minimum and maximum values of node sets without having to write your own recursive functions. More elements and functions from XSLT and XPath 2.0 are presented in Appendix B and C.

At this point you've completed your work on the style sheet for Wizard Works' order report. Bernard will study what you've accomplished and get back to you with any changes or ideas for future projects.

Review

Session 7.3 Quick Check

1. What is functional programming? How do you replace loops in a functional program?
2. What is a named template? What is a recursive template?
3. What command would you use to include code from the style sheet Functions.xsl?
4. What command would you use to import code from the style sheet Functions.xsl?
5. What is the difference between importing code and including code?
6. What are extension functions? What is EXSLT?
7. You wish to use extensions supported by the Xalan processor. The namespace for Xalan is xml.apache.org/xslt. What attributes would you add to the stylesheet element to reference these extensions? Use the namespace prefix lxslt.
8. JavaScript supports a function named cos() that calculates the cosine of a number. What code would you enter to create an extension function for the MSXML processor that accesses this function? Use msxsl for the MSXML namespace prefix. Identify the extension functions you create using the namespace http://new_functions.com with the prefix newfunc.
9. Under XSLT and XPath 2.0, what code would you enter to calculate the average price of the items in the node set: //item/@price?

Review

Tutorial Summary

This tutorial examined how to use XSLT and XPath to calculate summary values for a report on customer orders. The first session looked at how to use XPath's position() function and XSLT's number element to create numbered lists of elements. It also explored how to format these numeric lists. The session concluded with the XPath sum() and count() functions and examined the different mathematical operators supported by XPath for performing more in-depth calculations. The second session continued to look at how to format numbers using the XPath format-number() function and turned to a general discussion of working with text strings, including how to control the behavior of white space in a style sheet. The second session also explored how to declare and apply variables and parameters. It discussed how the scope of variables and parameters governs their use in a style sheet. The session also provided an opportunity to apply a global parameter to a transformation using the Exchanger XML Editor. The third session introduced functional programming and explained how the functional principles of XSLT govern the way that certain calculations, such as determining the minimum value from a node set, are performed. The session also discussed how recursive templates can be used to replace loops. The tutorial concluded with a look at extensions to XSLT and XPath offered by different XSLT processors, and explored some of the functions and elements in XSLT and XPath 2.0 that will aid in the future with creating computational style sheets.

Key Terms

deep copy	global scope	recursion
EXSLT	global variable	recursive template
extension attribute	local parameter	result tree fragment
extension attribute value	local scope	scope
extension element	local variable	shallow copy
extension function	loop	template parameter
functional programming	named template	variable
global parameter	parameter	

Practice

Practice the skills you
learned in the tutorial
using the same case
scenario

Review Assignment

Data files needed for this Review Assignment: cattxt.xml, items.css, itemstxt.xsl, logo. jpg, sharedtxt.xsl

Bernard has approached you with a new task. He wants to create a report that displays the items that customers have ordered, organized by item type. As with his earlier report, he has created an XML document containing a catalog of Wizard Works products as a starting point. Figure 7-55 shows the layout of the catalog document.

Figure 7-55

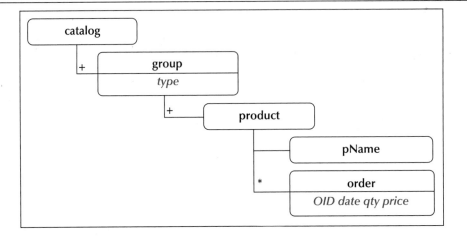

Each product is organized into one of the following six groups: Assorted, Fireworks, Fountains, Palms, Rings, and Rockets. For each item within those groups, Bernard has stored the item's name and a list of customer orders, including the order ID, the date of the order, the item's price at the time of the order, and the quantity of items ordered.

Bernard wants you to generate a report that calculates the total number of items ordered for each product. The report should also calculate the total revenue for all products within a group and for all groups in the report. Figure 7-56 shows a preview of part of the report.

Figure 7-56

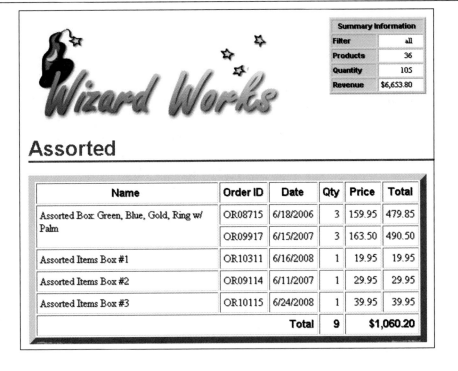

To complete this task:

1. Using your text editor, open **cattxt.xml**, **itemstxt.xsl**, and **sharedtxt.xsl** from the tutorial.07x/review folder. Enter *your name* and *the date* in the comment section of each file, and save them as **catalog.xml**, **items.xsl**, and **shared.xsl** respectively.

2. Go to the catalog.xml file in your text editor. Review the content of the file to become familiar with the data and the data structure. Add a processing instruction after the comment section that attaches this XML document to the items.xsl style sheet. Close the file, saving your changes.

3. Go to the items.xsl file in your text editor, and review the content of the style sheet and the different templates it contains. Below the output element, insert a global parameter named filter. Set the default value of this parameter to an empty text string.

4. Below the filter parameter create a global variable named productList. Set the value of the productList variable to the node set of all of the group elements in the source document whose type attribute starts with the value of the filter parameter.

5. Go to the root template and make the following changes and additions to the template:

   - Within the second cell of the second table row, display the value of the filter parameter. If the value of the filter parameter is an empty text string, display the text "all".

   - Within the second cell of the third table row, display the count of product elements within the node set referenced by the productList variable. (*Hint*: Use the node set $productList//product).

   - Within the second table cell of the fourth table row, display the sum of product quantities ordered within the node set referenced by the productList variable. (*Hint:* Use the @qty attribute to return the quantity values.)

   - Above the closing </body> tag, change the select attribute of the apply-template element so that it selects the node set referenced by the productList variable.

6. Go to the group template, and in the second cell of the last table row display the sum of the quantity of items ordered in the product/order node set.

7. Go to the order template, and make the following changes:

   - Replace the first table cell with an if element that tests whether the position of the context node is equal to 1. If so, write the following code to the result document:
     ```
     <td rowspan="orders">
        product name
     </td>
     ```
     where `orders` is the count of the number of order elements in the current order (*Hint*: Use the location path "../order" to reference the node set of orders) and `product name` is the name of the product (*Hint*: Use the location path "../pName").

   - For the last table cell, display the value of the qty attribute multiplied by the price attribute. Format this value as #,##0.00.

8. Save your changes to the items.xsl file.

9. Go to the shared.xsl file in your text editor, and create a named template called totalRevenue that calculates the total revenue for a collection of products. (*Hint*: Use the code in the totalCost template from the tutorial as a guide.) The template should contain the following code:

   - A local parameter named list to store the node set of items to be examined

   - A local parameter named total to store the total revenue of the products ordered; the default value of the total parameter should be zero.

- A choose element containing a test for whether there are items in the node set contained in the list parameter. If so, the template should recursively call itself with (1) the value of the total parameter set to the current total parameter plus the value of the first item in the list (equal to value of item's price attribute multiplied by the quantity attribute), and (2) the node set of the list parameter reduced to only those items after the first item in the current list.
- When there are no items left in the node set referenced by the list parameter, display the value of the total parameter using the format, $#,#00.00.

10. Close the shared.xsl file, saving your changes.
11. Return to the items.xsl file in your text editor, and insert an import element directly after the opening <xsl:stylesheet> tag to import the contents of the shared.xsl file into the style sheet.
12. Go to the root template and in the last cell of the last table row, call the totalRevenue template, setting the node set in the list parameter to all of the order elements within the productList variable. (*Hint*: Use the location path $productList//order.)
13. Go to the group template, and in the last cell of the last table row call the totalRevenue template, setting the list parameter to the node set product/order.
14. Close the items.xsl style sheet, saving your changes.
15. Open the catalog.xml file in your Web browser or an XSLT processor, and verify that the report now calculates the total revenue for each product in the report, the total revenue within each group, and the total revenue over all groups.
16. Open catalog.xml in the Exchanger XML Editor or another XSLT processor that supports the application of global parameters. Use the XSLT processor to set the value of the filter parameter to the text string Rings, and verify that when the result document is generated, the report is limited to those orders and items from the Rings group. (*Note:* If you are running Netscape or Safari for the Macintosh, you might have to store the contents of the shared.xsl file in the items.xsl style sheet or generate the result document using another XSLT processor.)
17. Submit the completed project to your instructor.

Apply

Use the skills you learned in this tutorial to create a horizontal bar chart

Case Problem 1

Data files needed for this Case Problem: back.jpg, logo.jpg, polls.css, pollstxt.xml, pollstxt.xsl

ElectionWeb   Abby Rosenthal is a manager for the Web site ElectionWeb, which reports on current election results for the public. With an election coming up, Abby is looking at ways in which the Web site can track and report on the different contests. Current vote totals are being written to an XML document named polls.xml. The structure of the polls document is shown in Figure 7-57.

Figure 7-57

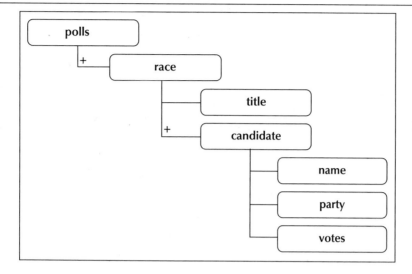

Using the data from her XML document, Abby wants to generate a report showing the vote totals, the percentage for each candidate, and a horizontal bar chart in which the length of the bar is proportional to the vote total percentages. Figure 7-58 shows a preview of the report you'll create for Abby.

Figure 7-58

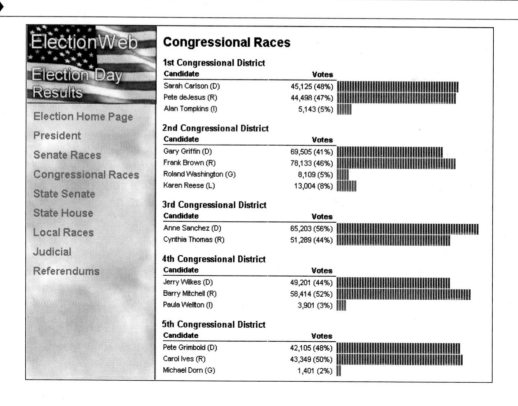

To complete this task:

1. Using your text editor, open **pollstxt.xml** and **pollstxt.xsl** from the tutorial.07x/case1 folder. Enter **your name** and **the date** in the comment section of each file, and save them as **polls.xml** and **polls.xsl** respectively.

2. Go to the polls.xml file in your text editor. Add a processing instruction after the comment section that attaches this XML document to the polls.xsl style sheet. Close the file, saving your changes.

Explore

3. Go to the polls.xsl file in your text editor. Below the output element, create a global variable named redcell that contains the following result tree fragment:

   ```
   <td class="red"> </td>
   ```
   Create two other global variables named bluecell and greencell containing the same result tree fragment, with class attribute values of blue and green respectively.

4. Go to the candidate template, and create a local variable named percent that is equal to the value of the votes element divided by the sum of the votes for all the candidates in the race. (*Hint:* The location path for all the votes for the current race is "..//votes".)

5. Go to the second table cell in the candidate template, and format the value of the votes element as #,##0.

6. After the votes total, display the value of the percent variable, formatted as (#0%).

Explore

7. Use XSLT's text element to place a space between the vote total and the vote percent.

8. Create a recursive template named showBar that contains two local parameters named cells and partyType. The cells parameter is used to store the number of table cells to display the horizontal bar chart. The default value of the cells parameter should be 0.

Explore

9. Within the showBar template, test whether the value of the cells parameter is greater than 0. If so, have the template do the following:
   - Use the choose element to test whether the value of the partyType parameter is equal to R or D. If the partyType parameter is equal to R, display the redcell result tree fragment. If the partyType parameter is equal to D, display the bluecell result tree fragment. Otherwise, display the greencell result tree fragment.
   - Use recursion to call the showBar template again with the cells parameter equal to the current value of the cells parameter minus 1 and the partyType parameter equal to its current value.

10. Go back to the candidate template. Directly before the closing </tr> tag, call the showBar template. The value of the cells parameter should be equal to the value of the percent variable multiplied by 100. The value of the partyType parameter should be equal to the value of the party element.

11. Close the polls.xsl file, saving your changes.

12. Generate the result document. Verify that the result document shows horizontal bars for each candidate in the five elections. (*Note:* Under some versions of Safari, the % symbol will not be displayed in the result document.)

13. Submit the completed project to your instructor.

Case Problem 2

Data files needed for this Case Problem: golf.css, golftxt.xml, golftxt.xsl

SportsStats SportsStats is a Web site that reports on sporting events. Peter Li is one of the statisticians at SportStats. He reports on professional golf tournaments. The scores that the company receives arrive in XML documents. Peter has created a sample XML document named golf.xml that contains scores from a professional tournament. The document stores the name, date, and location of the tournament, the pars for the 18 holes on the tournament's golf course, and the scores from a selected golfer for the 18 holes on the course over four rounds. Figure 7-59 shows the structure of the golf.xml file.

Figure 7-59

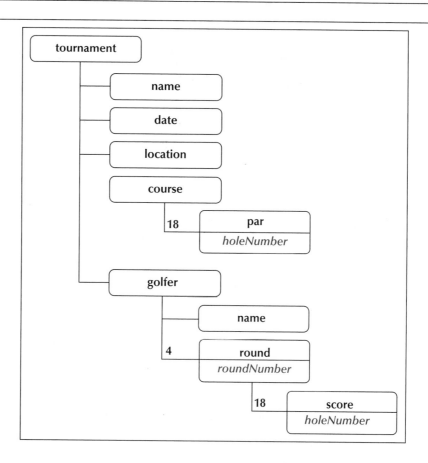

Using this information, Peter wants to create a result document showing the scorecard for the golfer in the golf.xml file. The scorecard should show the following:

- The player's total strokes for each of the four rounds of the tournament
- The par for each hole
- The player's score on each hole; a score below par should appear in red; a score above par should appear in green.
- The player's running score in relation to par for each hole; a score above par should appear with a plus symbol (i.e., +2), while a score of 0 should appear as E.
- The total scores for the front nine, back nine, and all 18 holes for each of the four rounds of the tournament

Figure 7-60 shows a preview of the result document you'll create for Peter. He has already created much of the style sheet and some of the templates but needs your help in inserting functions to calculate the various totals and subtotals for the scorecard.

Figure 7-60

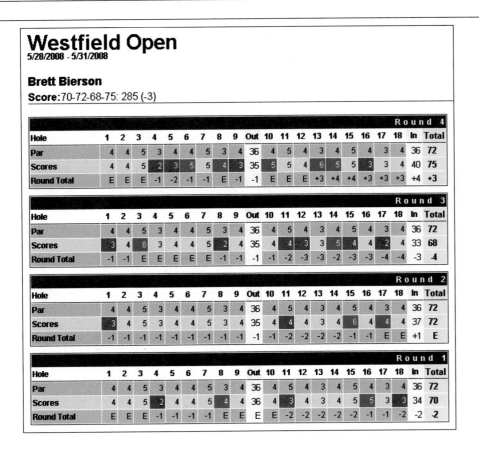

To complete this task:

1. Using your text editor, open **golftxt.xml** and **golftxt.xsl** from the tutorial.07x/case2 folder. Enter *your name* and *the date* in the comment section of each file, and save them as **golf.xml** and **golf.xsl** respectively.

2. Go to the golf.xml file in your text editor. Add a processing instruction after the comment section that attaches this XML document to the golf.xsl style sheet. Close the file, saving your changes.

3. In the golf.xsl file, go to the golfer template, and within the paragraph tags below the h3 heading, insert the following code:

    `<b>Score:</b> r1-r2-r3-r4: allRounds(parScore)`
    where `r1`, `r2`, `r3`, and `r4` are the sums of the score elements within the first, second, third, and fourth rounds; `allRounds` is the sum of the score elements from all rounds, and `parScore` is the sum of all the score elements minus 4 times the sum of all of the par elements in the source document.

4. Go to the bottom of the style sheet and insert a template named formatScore. The purpose of this template is to format the golfer's score relative to par. A value of 0 should be displayed as E, a negative value should be displayed as *-value*, and a positive value should be displayed as *+value*. Add the following to the formatHole template:

   - A parameter named scoreValue that stores the golfer's score on the selected hole
   - Insert a choose element, and test whether the value of the scoreValue parameter is equal to 0. If it is, write the text string E; otherwise, write the value of the scoreValue parameter formatted using the number format: -#;+#.

5. Above the fomatScore template insert a template named formatHole. The purpose of this template is to format the table cells containing the golfer's score for each hole on the course. Add the following to the formatHole template:

   - Two parameters named parScore and holeScore. The parScore parameter contains the par for a selected hole on the course. The holeScore parameter contains the score the golfer achieved on the hole.
   - Insert a choose element that tests whether the holeScore parameter is equal to, less than, or greater than the parScore parameter. If holeScore is less than parScore, write the following code:
     ```
     <td class="low">holeScore</td>
     ```
     where *holeScore* is the value of the holeScore parameter. If holeScore is greater than parScore, write the code:
     ```
     <td class="high">holeScore</td>
     ```
     otherwise, write the code:
     ```
     <td>holeScore</td>
     ```

6. Below the round template insert a template for the par element. The purpose of this template is to write the row that contains the pars for the 18 holes on the golf course. Add the following to the par template:

   - Write the following code to the result document:
     ```
     <td>par</td>
     ```
     where *par* is the value of the context node for the par template.
   - Add a choose element to test whether the value of the holeNumber attribute for the par element is equal to 18 or 9. If the value of the holeNumber attribute is equal to 18, write the following code:
     ```
     <td class="sub">backNine pars</td>
     <td class="final">all pars</td>
     ```
     where *backNine pars* is the sum of all par elements whose holeNumber attribute is greater than 9 and less than or equal to 18, and *all pars* is the sum of all par elements in the source document.

     If the value of the holeNumber attribute is equal to 9, write the following code:
     ```
     <td class="sub">frontNine pars</td>
     ```
     where *frontNine pars* is the sum of all par elements whose holeNumber attribute is less than or equal to 9.

7. Below the par template insert a template for the score element. The purpose of this template is to write the row containing the golfer's scores for the course's 18 holes. Add the following to the template:

   - Declare a variable named holeNum equal to the value of the holeNumber attribute.
   - Call the formatHole template you created in Step 5 using the value of the context node for the holeScore parameter, and for the parScore parameter use the value of the par element whose holeNumber attribute equals the holeNum variable.

- Insert a choose element that tests whether the value of the holeNum variables equals 18 or 9. If holeNum equals 18, write the following code to the result document:
  ```
  <td class="sub">backNine scores</td>
  <td class="final">all scores</td>
  ```
  where *backNine scores* is the sum of all score elements whose holeNumber attribute is greater than 9 and less than or equal to 18, and *all scores* is the sum of all score elements in the current round. (*Hint*: To reference the scores in the current round, use the location path: "../score".)
- If the value of the holeNumber attribute is equal to 9, write the following code:
  ```
  <td class="sub">frontNine scores</td>
  ```
  where *frontNine scores* is the sum of all score elements whose holeNumber attribute is less than or equal to 9.

8. Return to the round template and do the following:
   - Directly below the closing </th> tag for the Par table heading, apply the par template for all of the par elements in the source document. (*Hint*: Use the location path "//par" to select all of the par elements.)
   - Directly below the closing </th> tag for the Scores table heading, apply the score template for the score element.

9. Below the score template insert a template named calcScores. The purpose of this template is to write the table row containing the running total of the golfer's score against par for each round. This template uses recursion to call itself again and again until the complete table row is written. Add the following parameters and variables to the template:
   - Declare parameters named currentRound and currentHole. Do not set any default values for these parameters.
   - Declare a variable named parTotal. Set the value of the variable to the sum of all par elements whose holeNumber attribute is less than or equal to the value of the currentHole parameter.
   - Declare a variable named golferTotal. Set the value of the variable to the sum of all score elements in the current round whose holeNumber attribute is less than or equal to the value of the currentHole parameter. (*Hint*: To reference the score elements in the current round, use the XPath expression "$currentRound/score".)
   - Declare a variable named currentScore. Set the value of the variable to parTotal minus golferTotal.
   - Using a two-sided <xsl:variable> tag, declare a variable named currentScoreText, setting the value of the variable to the text string returned by calling the formatScore template you created in Step 4 using the value of the currentScore variable for the scoreValue parameter.

10. Within the calcScores template, write the following code:
    ```
    <td>currentScoreText</td>
    ```
    where *currentScoreText* is the value of the currentScoreText variable.

11. Within the calcScores template, add a choose element that tests whether the value of the currentHole variable is equal to 18 or 9. If the value of the currentHole variable is equal to 18, do the following:
    - Declare a variable named backNinePar equal to the sum of all par elements whose holeNumber attribute is greater than 9 and less than or equal to 18.
    - Declare a variable named backNineGolfer equal to the sum of all score elements in the current round whose holeNumber attribute is greater than 9 and less than or equal to 18. (*Hint*: To reference all score elements in the current round use the XPath expression "$currentRound/score".)
    - Declare a variable named backNineScore. Set the value of the variable to backNinePar minus backNineGolfer.
    - Declare a variable named backNineScoreText, setting the value of the variable to the text string returned by calling the formatScore template using the value of the backNineScore variable for the scoreValue parameter.
    - Write the following code to the result document:
      ```
      <td class="sub">backNineScoreText</td>
      <td class="final">currentScoreText</td>
      ```
      where `backNineScoreText` is the value of the backNineScoreText variable and `currentScoreText` is the value of the currentScoreText variable.
12. If the currentHole variable tested in Step 11 is equal to 9, write the following code to the result document:
    ```
    <td class="sub">currentScoreText</td>
    ```
    where `currentScoreText` is the value of the currentScoreText variable.
13. Within the calcScores template, insert an if element that tests whether the value of the currentHole variable is less than 18. If so, do the following:
    - Call the calcScores template again, setting the value of the currentRound parameter to its current value and setting the value of the currentHole parameter to its current value plus 1.
14. Return to the round template, and directly below the closing </th> tag for the Round Total table heading call the calcScores template. Set the value of the currentRound parameter to the context node. Set the value of the currentHole parameter to 1.
15. Close the golf.xsl style sheet, saving your changes.
16. Generate the result document using your Web browser or another XSLT processor. Verify that the golf scores for the four rounds match the values shown in Figure 7-60. (*Note:* At the time of this writing, Netscape for the Macintosh does not format the values correctly. If you are using this browser, you need to generate the result document using a different XSLT processor.)
17. Submit the completed project to your instructor.

Challenge

xplore how to use
SLT to calculate mini-
ums, maximums, and
andard deviations

Case Problem 3

Data files needed for this Case Problem: fill.css, filltxt.xml, filltxt.xsl, functtxt.xsl

Datalia, Inc. Datalia Inc. is one of the country's leading manufacturers of infant care products. One of these products is baby powder. Each bottle is filled automatically by a machine called a filler. The weight of each bottle filled with powder should be 400 grams; however, because of random variations in the production process, the actual weight varies.

Kemp Wilson is a quality control engineer for Datalia. Part of his job is to oversee the production process. On every shift, samples of bottle weights are taken from 24 fillers and entered automatically into an XML document. The structure of the document is shown in Figure 7-61.

Figure 7-61

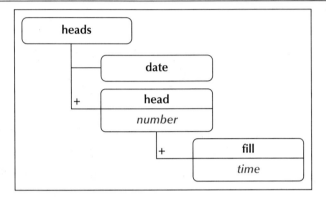

Kemp wants to summarize the sample data into a report that displays the count, average, minimum, maximum, and standard deviation from each filler sample. (The standard deviation is a statistic that measures the spread of the data values.) Kemp wants to be able to specify the number of sample values to analyze. Figure 7-62 shows a preview of the report that Kemp wants to generate.

Figure 7-62

Datalia, Inc.
Filler Sample Values

Date: 2008/08/11
Collection Time: 00:18:00 - 02:49:00

Filler Head	N	Average	Minimum	Maximum	Std. Dev
01	100	403.19	358.60	460.60	22.75
02	100	402.10	352.60	467.40	23.48
03	100	393.61	344.20	448.00	22.98
04	100	394.09	102.60	441.50	35.26
05	100	402.43	347.00	470.40	22.40
06	100	396.39	325.80	460.10	26.19
07	100	407.02	374.70	455.70	19.86
08	100	404.88	371.00	458.20	21.23
09	100	408.88	368.40	457.10	19.12
10	100	405.11	366.40	451.60	19.54

Kemp has created much of the style sheet, but needs your help writing recursive templates to calculate the summary statistics for the minimums, maximums, and standard deviations. If the filler heads are malfunctioning, this often appears with widely variable filler values and high standard deviations. The formula for the standard deviation is shown in Figure 7-63.

Figure 7-63

$$ s = \sqrt{\frac{\sum_{i=1}^{n} \left(x_i - \bar{x}\right)^2}{n-1}} $$

where x_i represents individual values, $\bar{x}$ is the average of the values, and n is the count of the values. In nonmathematical terms, to calculate the standard deviation, you calculate the difference between each value and overall average and square the difference; you sum up all of the squared differences and divide that value by the count of items minus 1; and then you determine the square root of that value.

Kemp has received a style sheet that contains a recursive template used to calculate the square root of a number to three decimal places, but he doesn't have a template to calculate the standard deviation. You'll use the squareRoot template in calculating the standard deviation statistic.

To complete this task:

1. Using your text editor, open **filltxt.xml**, **filltxt.xsl**, and **functxt.xsl** from the tutorial. 07x/case3 folder. Enter *your name* and *the date* in the comment section of each file, and save them as **fill.xml**, **fill.xsl**, and **function.xsl** respectively.

2. Go to the fill.xml file in your text editor. Add a processing instruction after the comment section that attaches this XML document to the fill.xsl style sheet. Close the file, saving your changes.

3. Go to the function.xsl file in your text editor. Create a template named average that contains a single parameter named list. The list parameter will be used to store a node set of values. Display the sum of the values in the list divided by the count of values in the list. Format the value so that it displays the average to two decimal places to the right of the decimal point.

4. Create a template named minimum to calculate the minimum value from a list of values. The template has two parameters: list and currentMin. The list parameter will contain the node set of items. Set the default value of the currentMin parameter to 999999999. Add a choose element to the template that tests whether the list parameter contains any values. If it does, do the following:

    - Declare a variable named first equal to the first value in the list.
    - If the value of the first variable is less than the currentMin parameter, then call the minimum template, setting the value of the currentMin parameter to the value of the first variable and reducing the size of the list parameter to those items whose position in the node set is greater than 1. Otherwise, call the minimum template using the current value of the currentMin parameter and continue removing the first item from the list node set.

    If the list parameter is empty of values, then display the value of the currentMin parameter to two decimal places.

Explore ▶

5. Using the minimum template as a model, create a similar template named maximum to calculate the maximum value from a list. The template should have two parameters: list and currentMax. Set the default value of the currentMax parameter to -999999999.

Explore ▶

6. Create a template named stdDev to calculate the standard deviation of values from a list. The template has three parameters named allList, list, and total. The allList parameter will contain a node set of all of the items in the list. The list parameter will contain a node set of list values that is reduced by one item each time the template is called recursively. The total parameter will contain a running total of squared differences used to calculate the standard deviation. Set the initial or default value of the total parameter to 0. Add a choose element to the stdDev template to test whether the list parameter contains any items. If so, do the following:

    - Declare a variable named first equal to the first item in the list node set.
    - Declare a variable named avg equal to the sum of the values in the allList node set divided by the count of items in the allList node set.
    - Call the stdDev template with (1) the value of the list parameter reduced by removing the first item from the list, (2) the total parameter set equal to the current value of the total parameter plus the squared difference between the first and avg variables, and (3) the value of the allList parameter set to its current value. [*Hint*: To calculate the squared difference use the expression "($first − $avg)*($first − $avg)".]

    If the list parameter is empty of values then call the squareRoot template, setting the value of the number parameter to the value of the total parameter divided by the count of items in the allList node set minus 1.

7. Close the function.xsl file, saving your changes.

8. Go to the fill.xsl file in your text editor, and create a global parameter named samples. The purpose of this parameter is to determine how many samples from each filler head to include in the report. Set the default value to 100.

9. Use the import element to import the contents of the function.xsl style sheet.

10. Create two global variables named startTime and stopTime. Set the value of the start-Time variable equal to the value of the time attribute from the first fill element in the source document. Set the value of the stopTime variable equal to the value of the time attribute from the *n*th fill element in the source document, where *n* is the value of the samples parameter.

11. Go to the root template, and within the paragraph element directly after the <br /> tag, insert the following code:

```
<b>Collection Time: </b> startTime - stopTime
```
where *startTime* and *stopTime* are the values of the startTime and stopTime variables.

12. Go to the template for the head element and add the following:
   - In the first table cell, display the value of the number attribute.
   - In the second table cell, display the count of fill elements whose position is less than or equal to the value of the samples parameter.
   - In the third table cell, display the average fill value for those fill elements whose position is less than or equal to the value of the samples parameter. (*Hint*: Call the average template using the node set for the value of the list parameter.)
   - In the fourth table cell, display the minimum fill value for those fill elements whose position is less than or equal to the value of the samples parameter.
   - In the fifth table cell, display the maximum fill value for those fill elements whose position is less than or equal to the value of the samples parameter.
   - In the sixth table cell, display the standard deviation of the fill elements whose position is less than or equal to the value of the samples parameter. (*Hint:* Call the stdDev template using the same node set for both the list and allList parameters.)

13. Close the fill.xsl style sheet, saving your changes.

14. Open fill.xml in your Web browser, and verify that it shows the descriptive statistics for 100 samples of each filler head and that your values match those shown in Figure 7-62. Depending on the speed of your browser, it may take a few seconds for the browser to calculate the values displayed in the table. (*Note:* If you are using Safari or Netscape for the Macintosh, you must place all of the templates in the same style sheet file, because the XSLT processors in these browsers do not support the use of external style sheets at the time of this writing.)

Explore

15. Open fill.xml in the Exchanger XML Editor or another XSLT processor that supports the application of global parameters and external style sheets. To limit the report to only the first 50 samples, use the XSLT processor to set the value of the samples parameter to 50 (no quotation marks). Verify that the time of the samples range from 00:18:00 to 01:24:00. The first filler head should have an average fill volume of 412.77, a minimum of 358.60, a maximum of 460.60, and a standard deviation of 27.42.

16. Submit the completed project to your instructor.

Create

Test your knowledge of XSLT style sheets by creating a style sheet to calculate the values associated with a shipping manifest

Case Problem 4

Data files needed for this Case Problem: autotxt.xml, autotxt.xsl

AutoMaze, Inc. AutoMaze is an online auto parts superstore. David Hansen manages shipping and receiving for the company. Lately, he has been using XML to store shipping manifests. The structure of a typical document is shown in Figure 7-64.

Figure 7-64

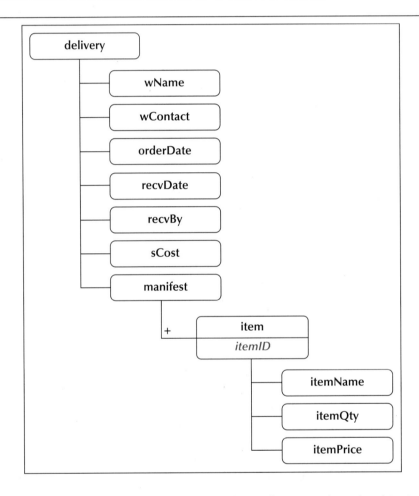

David wants you to create a style sheet that displays information from the shipping manifest document. The style sheet must include the ability to calculate the cost of items on the manifest as well as the total cost of all items.

To complete this task:

1. Using your text editor, open **autotxt.xml** and **autotxt.xsl** from the tutorial.07x/case4 folder. Enter *your name* and *the date* in the comment section of each file, and save them as **automaze.xml** and **automaze.xsl** respectively.
2. Attach the automaze.xsl style sheet to the automaze.xml file.
3. Add styles to the automaze.xsl style sheet to display the contents of the automaze.xml file. The design of the result document is up to you, but must include the following features:
   * The warehouse name and warehouse contact person
   * The date of the order, the date the items were received, and who received them

- The cost of shipping for the order
- A list of all items on the manifest, with the total item cost equal to the item quantity multiplied by the item's price
- The total cost of all items on the manifest, including the cost of shipping

4. Test your style sheet on your Web browser or an XSLT processor, and verify that all required elements are displayed and that the total cost is correctly calculated.
5. Submit the completed project to your instructor.

Quick Check Answers

Session 7.1

1. test = "position()=5"
2. The position() function, because the number element numbers items based on their position in the source document
3. <xsl:number format="i" />
4. level="multiple"
5. <xsl:value-of select="round(Age)" />
6. <xsl:value-of select="sum(Age) div count(Age)" />

Session 7.2

1. Either by enclosing the blank space within a pair of <xsl:text> elements, or by using the   entity
2. <xsl:variable name="NewYearsDay" select="1/1/2008" />
3. $NewYearsDay
4. A result tree fragment is lines of code that are stored in an XML variable. To reference a result tree fragment, you use either the <xsl:copy> or <xsl:copy-of> elements.
5. The area where a variable can be referenced is known as the variable's scope. A global variable can be referenced anywhere within the document. A local variable can be referenced only within the template in which it is defined.
6. A parameter is a variable whose value can be changed after it is declared and whose value can be set from outside of its scope.
7. <xsl:call-template name="Date">
   <xsl:with-param name="Today" select="'12/11/2008'" />
   </xsl:call-template>

Session 7.3

1. Functional programming language relies on the evaluation of functions and expressions rather than the sequential execution of commands to perform tasks. Loops are replaced by recursive functions and templates.
2. A named template is a template that is not associated with any particular element. A recursive template is a template that calls itself when it is being run.
3. <xsl:include href="Functions.xsl" />
4. <xsl:import href="Functions.xsl" />
5.
   a. The import element must be the first child of the stylesheet element, but the include element can be placed anywhere within a style sheet, as long as it is a child of the stylesheet element.

    b. In the case of name conflicts between templates in the imported style sheet and templates in the importing sheet, the templates in the importing sheet have precedence.

    c. If you import several style sheets, the last one imported has the highest precedence among the imported sheets in the event of a name conflict.

6. Extension functions are additions to XSLT and XPath that allow for the creation of new functions. EXSLT is a proposed standard collection of extension elements and functions.

7. <xsl:stylesheet version="1.0"
        xmlns:xsl="http://www.w3.org/1999/XSL/Transform"
        xmlns:lxslt="http://xml.apache.org/xslt"
  extension-element-prefixes="lxslt">

8. <xsl:stylesheet version="1.0"
        xmlns:xsl="http://www.w3.org/1999/XSL/Transform"
        xmlns:newfunc="http://new_functions.com"
        xmlns:msxsl="urn:schemas-microsoft-com:xslt"
        extension-element-prefixes="newfunc msxsl">

```
<msxsl:script implements-prefix="newfunc"
        language="javascript">
  function cos() {
    return Math.cos();
  }
</msxsl:script>
```

9. avg(//item/@price)

Objectives

Session 8.1
- Work with step patterns
- Write a step pattern to create an element group
- Create and apply a moded template

Session 8.2
- Work with ID attributes
- Create reference keys
- Generate an ID automatically
- Understand how to apply Muenchian grouping

Session 8.3
- Extract information from external source documents
- Work with lookup data
- Insert data into an XSLT style sheet
- Work with code snippets

Creating Element Groups

Working with IDs, Keys, and Groups

Case

MidWest Homes, Inc.

MidWest Homes, Inc. is an online real estate agency. The company stores realty information in an online database that can then write information about different listings into XML documents. The documents are then attached to XSLT style sheets to generate the Web pages that appear on the agency's Web site.

Web designer Lisa Riccio is working on one of the company's Web pages that displays new home listings for southern Wisconsin. To make it easier for home-buyers to locate specific properties, Lisa wants the Web page to display real estate listings organized by city. However, the contents of the source document are not organized by city, and Lisa does not have the ability to modify the source document; therefore, any changes to the Web page have to be done by modifying the style sheet. She has come to you for help in creating a style sheet that groups real estate listings by city.

Student Data Files

▼tutorial.08x

▽ **tutorial folder**

listtxt.xml
listtxt.xsl
listings.css
+ 2 XML documents
+ 1 image file

▽ **review folder**

styletxt.xml
styletxt.xsl
agencies.xml
style.css
+ 1 image file

▽ **case1 folder**

comtxt.xml
comtxt.xsl
comedy.css

▽ **case2 folder**

orderstxt.xml
flowtxt.xsl
flowers.css
+ 2 XML documents

▽ **case3 folder**

wstxt.xml
wstxt.xsl
ws.css

▽ **case4 folder**

montxt.xml
montxt.xsl
persons.xml
+ 1 image file

Session 8.1

Working with Step Patterns

You and Lisa meet to discuss her proposal to display realty listings grouped by city. She brings along a sample XML document that contains a list of homes recently placed on the market in the southern Wisconsin area. Figure 8-1 shows the content of her document.

| Figure 8-1 | Elements in the listings document |

Element	Description
listings	The root element of the document
property	Information about each property; the rln attribute stores the real estate listing number; the firm attribute contains the id of the firm selling the property; the agent attribute contains the ID of the realty agent representing the seller
street	Street address of the property
city	City in which the property is located
state	State in which the property is located
zip	Postal code of the property
price	Selling price of the property
style	Property's building style
sqfeet	Property size in square feet
bathrooms	Number of bathrooms in the property
bedrooms	Number of bedrooms in the property
garage	Size and type of garage
age	Age of the property in years
description	Description of the property

For each property, Lisa has recorded the property's address, price, style, size (in square feet), number of bathrooms, number of bedrooms, garage size and type, age, and a description. Figure 8-2 shows the structure of the document.

Structure of the listings document | Figure 8-2

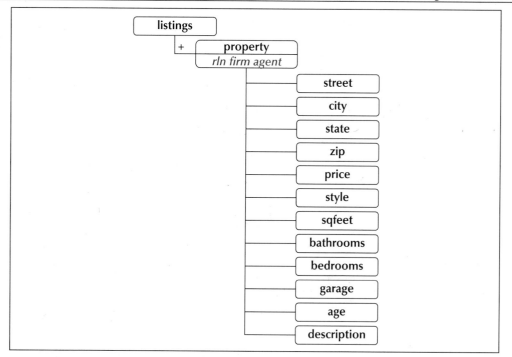

Lisa has designed a style sheet for this document. To see her progress, open the source document and the style sheet now.

To open the listings document:

1. Use your text editor to open **listtxt.xml** from the tutorial.08x/tutorial folder. Enter *your name* and *the date* in the comment section at the top of the file, and save the file as **listings.xml**.

2. Review the contents of the file, noting the document structure. Below the comment section, insert a processing instruction to attach this document to the **listings.xsl** style sheet.

3. Close the file, saving your changes.

4. Open the **listtxt.xsl** file in your text editor. Enter *your name* and *the date* in the comment section, and save the file as **listings.xsl**.

5. Use your Web browser or an XLST processor to generate the result document for the listings.xml file based on the listings.xsl style sheet. Figure 8-3 shows the appearance of Lisa's property report.

Figure 8-3 Lisa's current property report

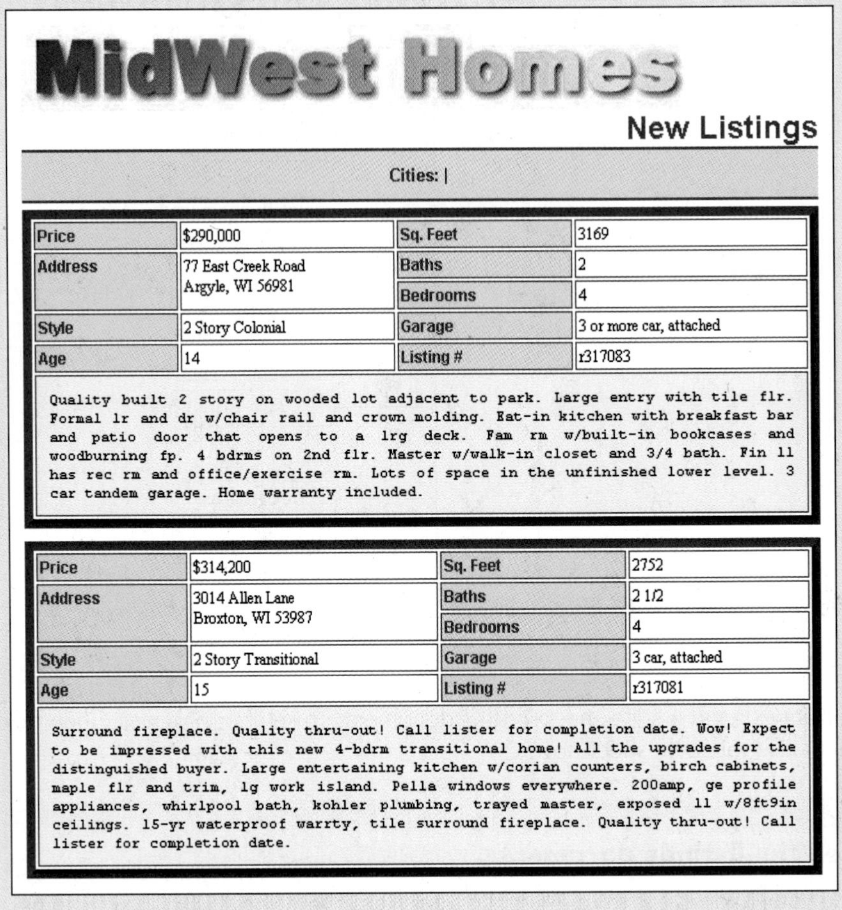
MidWest Homes

New Listings

Cities: |

Price	$290,000	Sq. Feet	3169
Address	77 East Creek Road Argyle, WI 56981	Baths	2
		Bedrooms	4
Style	2 Story Colonial	Garage	3 or more car, attached
Age	14	Listing #	r317083

Quality built 2 story on wooded lot adjacent to park. Large entry with tile flr. Formal lr and dr w/chair rail and crown molding. Eat-in kitchen with breakfast bar and patio door that opens to a lrg deck. Fam rm w/built-in bookcases and woodburning fp. 4 bdrms on 2nd flr. Master w/walk-in closet and 3/4 bath. Fin ll has rec rm and office/exercise rm. Lots of space in the unfinished lower level. 3 car tandem garage. Home warranty included.

Price	$314,200	Sq. Feet	2752
Address	3014 Allen Lane Broxton, WI 53987	Baths	2 1/2
		Bedrooms	4
Style	2 Story Transitional	Garage	3 car, attached
Age	15	Listing #	r317081

Surround fireplace. Quality thru-out! Call lister for completion date. Wow! Expect to be impressed with this new 4-bdrm transitional home! All the upgrades for the distinguished buyer. Large entertaining kitchen w/corian counters, birch cabinets, maple flr and trim, lg work island. Pella windows everywhere. 200amp, ge profile appliances, whirlpool bath, kohler plumbing, trayed master, exposed ll w/8ft9in ceilings. 15-yr waterproof warrty, tile surround fireplace. Quality thru-out! Call lister for completion date.

Currently Lisa's report displays information for each property sorted by city and price. Lisa wants to make the following changes to the result document:

- Display a list of the cities at the top of the document, including the number of properties listed within each city.
- Organize property information by city.
- Link each city in the list at the top of the document with the section of the document that describes houses available in that city.
- Display information about the realty agency and listing agent for the property below each home description.

Figure 8-4 shows a preview of the page you'll create for Lisa.

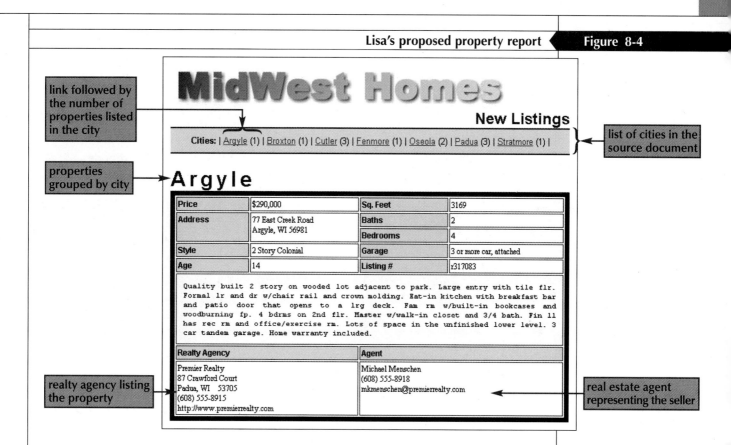

If Lisa knew which cities were in the source document, she could easily create a style sheet that groups the output based on the city names. However, because the collection of cities containing new listings varies daily, she needs to find a way of retrieving this information from the XML document itself. Fortunately, XSLT provides several ways of doing this. The first technique you'll explore involves step patterns.

Introducing Step Patterns

As you learned in Tutorial 6, a location path is an XPath expression that defines a path for processors to navigate through a source document's node tree. Up to now, you've been using location paths where the only directions processors can travel are up and down the node tree from the context node, going to either the context node's ancestors or descendants. However, XPath supports more complicated expressions called **step patterns**, allowing processors to move in almost any direction through the node tree. A step pattern is composed of an axis, a node test, and predicate. The **axis** specifies the direction in which the processor should move through the node tree, the **node test** specifies a node for the step pattern to match, and the predicate defines properties of the node to be matched. The general syntax of a step pattern is

```
axis::node-test[predicate]
```

where `axis` is the direction that the XSLT processor should move, `node-test` is the node to be matched, and `predicate` is the expression that a specific node should match. Only the `node-test` part of the step pattern is required. In previous tutorials, you used node tests and predicates in your XPath expressions. For example, the expression

```
property[city="Cutler"]
```

has a node test of

```
property
```

and a predicate of

```
city="Cutler"
```

When an XSLT processor encounters this expression, it selects all of the children of the context node that have the element name property and contain a child element named city whose value is Cutler. Note that the processor assumes that it is to move down the node tree to examine only the descendants of the context node. However, if you want to apply this pattern to siblings or ancestor elements rather than to the context node's descendants, you must work with the axis part of the step pattern.

Reference Window

Working with Step Patterns

- To create a step pattern, use the syntax
  ```
  axis::node-test[predicate]
  ```
  where *axis* defines how to move through the node tree, *node-test* specifies the node for the step pattern to match, and *predicate* further tests the nodes to see if they match a particular pattern.

Working with Axes

XPath supports 13 values for the axis part of the step pattern. Figure 8-5 describes the axis values that can be used in any XPath step pattern.

Figure 8-5

Axis values

Axis	Selects
ancestor	All nodes that are ancestors of the context node, starting with the context node's parents and moving up the node tree
ancestor-or-self	All nodes that are ancestors of the context node, starting with the context node and moving up the node tree
attribute	All of the attribute nodes of the context node
child	All children of the context node
descendant	All nodes that are descendants of the context node, starting with the node's immediate children and moving down the node tree
descendant-or-self	All nodes that are descendants of the context node, starting with the context node and moving down the node tree
following	All nodes that appear after the context node in the source document, excluding the context node's own descendants
following-sibling	All siblings of the context node that appear after the context node in the source document
namespace	All namespace nodes of the context node
parent	The parent of the context node
preceding	All nodes that appear before the context node in the source document, excluding the context node's own ancestors
preceding-sibling	All siblings of the context node that appear before the context node in the source document
self	The context node

The default value for the axis portion of the step pattern is child, which instructs processors to select the children of the context node that match the node test and predicate. Thus, from the perspective of a processor, the following two expressions are equivalent:

```
property[city="Cutler"]
child::property[city="Cutler"]
```

In both cases above, the processor selects property elements that are children of the context node (whatever that may be) and that match the specified predicate. To go in a different direction, you change the axis value. For example, the location path

```
ancestor::property[city="Cutler"]
```

selects property elements from the city of Cutler that are ancestors of the context node. To work with siblings of the context node, you use the following location path:

```
following-sibling::property[city="Cutler"]
```

This expression selects the siblings that follow the context node in the source document and that are named property and are located in the city of Cutler.

As you learned in Tutorial 6, a processor creates a node set when it evaluates a location path. The order of objects in the node set is determined by the direction the processor takes as it navigates the node tree. You can use node numbers in the predicate to select specific items from a node set. For example, the location path

```
following-sibling::property[2]
```

selects the second property element following the context node. Generally, the processor moves up and down the node tree before moving left or right. Figure 8-6 charts the effect of the different axis values on both the nodes selected and the order in which they're selected. The context node is indicated in blue and the objects in the node set are numbered, with lower node numbers selected first in the node set.

Figure 8-6 ▶ **Node numbers from different axis values**

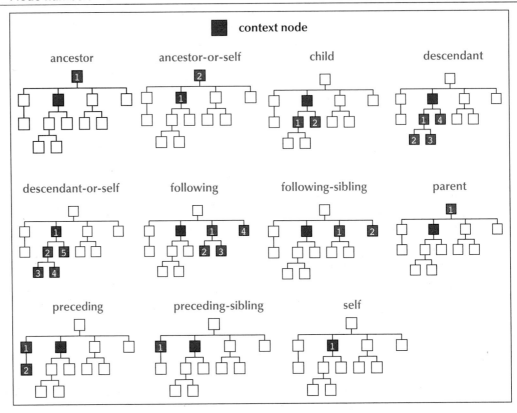

For some step patterns, processors recognize an abbreviated form. Figure 8-7 displays additional examples of step patterns in the complete syntax, including the axis, node test, and predicate, versus the familiar abbreviated form.

Figure 8-7 ▶ **Abbreviated location paths**

Step pattern	Abbreviated as
self::node()	.
parent::node()	..
child::property/child::city	property/city
child::listings/descendant::city	listings//city
property/attribute::firm	property/@firm
parent::node()/property/attribute::firm	../property/@firm

Creating a List of Unique Cities

Step patterns can provide you with great flexibility in selecting a node set. With a properly constructed step pattern, you can create node sets that can select a wide range of elements from the node tree. You can take advantage of that flexibility to create a node set containing a list of the city names found in Lisa's source document. The city names are children of the property element (see Figure 8-2). To create a node set of all of the city elements, you could use the location path

```
listings/property[city]
```

The problem with this approach is that it selects every property element that contains a city element (see Figure 8-8). Although this would certainly allow you to create a list of all of the city names, many city names would be duplicated.

Selecting all property elements containing a city node ◀ Figure 8-8

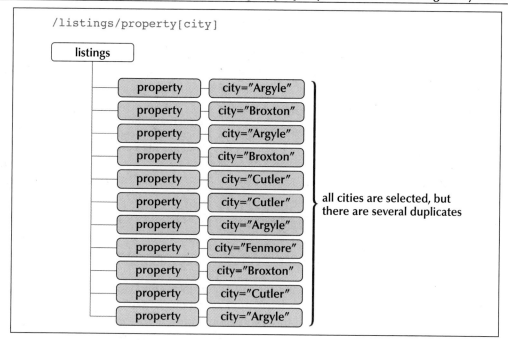

Lisa wants only one property from each city in order to create a list of the city names. One method to accomplish this is to locate all of the duplicate entries and remove them from the node set. To determine which nodes are duplicates, you can create a step pattern that instructs the processor to select only those properties that have a preceding sibling containing the same city name. To check for a preceding property with the same city name, you could use the following expression utilizing the preceding axis:

```
city=preceding::property/city
```

To create a node set based on this expression, you add it to the predicate of the following location path:

```
listings/property[city=preceding::property/city]
```

This yields the node set shown in Figure 8-9.

Figure 8-9	Selecting only duplicate city nodes

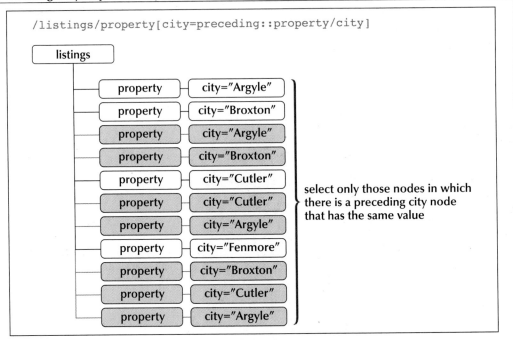

```
/listings/property[city=preceding::property/city]
```

Note that this node set consists of the second occurrence, third occurrence, and so on of each city, because only these nodes have a preceding property element with the same city name. The nodes that don't fulfill this expression represent the first occurrences of each city in the node tree. Thus, you want to reverse this node set, selecting only those properties that *do not* contain a city name duplicated in a preceding sibling. To reverse a node set, you use the XPath not() function. The expression is

```
not(city=preceding::property/city)
```

Adding this expression to a predicate results in the following location path:

```
listings/property[not(city=preceding::property/city)]
```

The property elements selected by this expression include only those properties representing the first occurrence of each city name—in other words, the nodes that are not duplicates of previous nodes. This also means that the node set contains a collection in which each city name appears only once and all city names are represented (see Figure 8-10).

Figure 8-10

Selecting only city nodes which are not duplicates

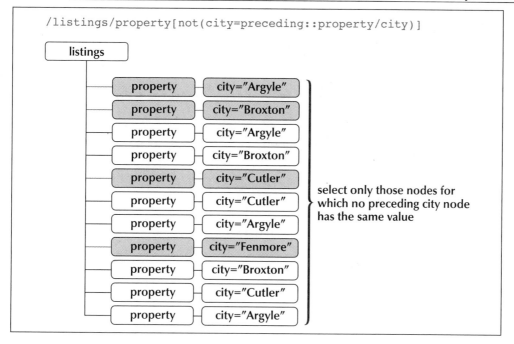

Using this location path, you can construct a template to display the city names in a list. The code is

```
<xsl:apply-templates
    select="listings/property[not(city=preceding::property/city)]">
    <xsl:sort select="city" />
</xsl:apply-templates>
```

The apply-templates element selects only those properties that represent the first occurrence of each city name. The sort element is used to sort those properties by order of their city names. To display the individual city names, you write the following code for the property element:

```
<xsl:template match="property">
  <xsl:value-of select="city" /> |
</xsl:template>
```

This template displays the city names separated by the | character. If you apply this code to all of the properties in Lisa's document, the following list of cities is generated:

```
Argyle | Broxton | Cutler | Fenmore | Oseola | Padua | Stratmore
```

Creating a List Using Step Patterns

Reference Window

- To create a list of unique values using step patterns, use the following syntax to select the first occurrence of each unique node value:

  not(*node*=preceding::*node-set*)

  where *node* is a specific node in the source document, and *node-set* is the complete set of values for that node in the source document.
- Once you generate the list of unique values, you can use the apply-templates element or the for element to write code to the result document for each unique value.

To create the city list:

1. Return to the **listings.xsl** file in your text editor.

2. Go to the root template, and add the following code directly above the closing </div> tag:

```
<xsl:apply-templates select=
    "listings/property[not(city=preceding::property/city)]">
  <xsl:sort select="city" />
</xsl:apply-templates>
```

3. Go to the bottom of the file, and insert the following template directly before the closing </xsl:stylesheet> tag:

```
<xsl:template match="property">
  <xsl:value-of select="city" /> |
</xsl:template>
```

Figure 8-11 shows the revised code in the style sheet file.

Figure 8-11 ▶ **Creating the city list template**

```
<xsl:template match="/">
  <html>
  <head>
    <title>Real Estate Listings</title>
    <link href="listings.css" rel="stylesheet" type="text/css" />
  </head>
  <body>
    <p><img src="logo.jpg" alt="Midwest Homes" /></p>
    <h2>New Listings</h2>

    <div id="city_list"><b>Cities: </b> |

    <xsl:apply-templates
        select="listings/property[not(city=preceding::property/city)]">
      <xsl:sort select="city" />
    </xsl:apply-templates>

    </div>

    <xsl:apply-templates select="listings/property">
      <xsl:sort select="city" />
      <xsl:sort select="price" />
    </xsl:apply-templates>

  </body>
  </html>
</xsl:template>
```

```
<xsl:template match="property">
  <xsl:value-of select="city" /> |
</xsl:template>

</xsl:stylesheet>
```

4. Save your changes to the file, and regenerate the result document using your Web browser, the Exchanger XML Editor, or other XSLT processor. Figure 8-12 shows the revised appearance of the properties document.

Trouble? The list of city names may appear wrapped to a second line in some browsers.

The list of city names appears as expected, but what happened to the property descriptions? The problem is that the style sheet has two property templates. The first property template contains a table describing each property, and the second template displays the list of city names associated with those properties. When an XSLT processor encounters two templates with the same name, it uses the last one defined in the style sheet, which in this case is the template you just created. One way to allow XSLT processors to distinguish between the two property templates is with moded templates.

Creating Moded Templates

Moded templates are templates that apply different styles to the same node set in the source document. The syntax for a moded template is

```
<xsl:template match="node-set" mode="mode">
    styles
</xsl:template>
```

where *node-set* is the node set in the source document, *mode* is the name of the mode, and *styles* is the XSLT code applied to that node set under the specified mode. For example, to convert the city list template you created into a moded template, you use the following template code:

```
<xsl:template match="property" mode="cityList">
```

The mode attribute distinguishes this template from the other property template in Lisa's style sheet. To apply a moded template, you simply include the mode's value in the apply-templates element as follows:

```
<xsl:apply-templates select="node-set" mode="mode">
```

When an XSLT processor encounters this element, it applies only those templates that match both the node set and the mode name. For example, you can apply the cityList template using the following code:

```
<xsl:apply-templates
    select="listings/property[not(city=preceding::property/city)]"
    mode="cityList">
```

When an XSLT processor encounters this element, it applies the template for the property node set under the cityList mode.

Creating Moded Templates

- To create a moded template, use the code
  ```
  <xsl:template match="node-set" mode="mode">
      styles
  </xsl:template>
  ```
  where *node-set* is the node set in the source document, *mode* is the name of the mode, and *styles* is the XSLT code applied to that node set under the specified mode.
- To apply a moded template, use the element
  ```
  <xsl:apply-templates select="node-set" mode="mode" />
  ```

To create a moded template:

1. Return to the **listings.xsl** file in your text editor.

2. Go to the root template, and add the following attribute to the apply-templates element that applies the template for the city list:

   mode="cityList"

3. Go to the template that creates the city list at the bottom of the style sheet, and add the following attribute to the template element:

   mode="cityList"

   Figure 8-13 shows the revised code for the style sheet.

Figure 8-13 ▶ Specifying the template mode

```
<xsl:template match="/">
  <html>
  <head>
    <title>Real Estate Listings</title>
    <link href="listings.css" rel="stylesheet" type="text/css" />
  </head>
  <body>
    <p><img src="logo.jpg" alt="Midwest Homes" /></p>
    <h2>New Listings</h2>

    <div id="city_list"><b>Cities: </b> |

    <xsl:apply-templates
        select="listings/property[not(city=preceding::property/city)]"
        mode="cityList">
      <xsl:sort select="city" />
    </xsl:apply-templates>

    </div>

    <xsl:apply-templates select="listings/property">
      <xsl:sort select="city" />
      <xsl:sort select="price" />
    </xsl:apply-templates>

  </body>
  </html>
</xsl:template>
```

```
<xsl:template match="property" mode="cityList">
  <xsl:value-of select="city" /> |
</xsl:template>

</xsl:stylesheet>
```

4. Save your changes to the style sheet file, and regenerate the result document using your Web browser or XSLT processor. Figure 8-14 shows the revised result document.

The city list and property descriptions | **Figure 8-14**

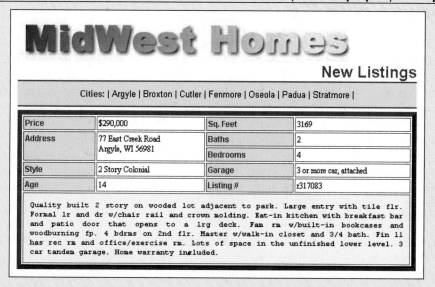

5. If you want to take a break before starting the next session, you may close your files and applications now.

You show the result document to Lisa, and she is pleased with your progress. Your next task is to group the individual property descriptions by city and to create links between the names in the city list and the property listings for each city. You'll work on this task in the next session.

Session 8.1 Quick Check

Review

1. Describe the three parts of a step pattern.
2. What location path do you use to select the context node only? Provide the extended, not the abbreviated, expression.
3. Express the following location path using step patterns:

```
/property/city
```

4. How can the following step pattern be abbreviated?

```
child::property/attribute::rln
```

5. What are moded templates?
6. What code would you use to create a moded template named propertyList for the property node?
7. What code would you use to apply the propertyList moded template to the /listings/property node set?

Working with IDs

Lisa likes what you've done so far with her property report. Next, she wants you to group the individual property descriptions by city, separating each group of cities with an h1 heading. Although you could do this using the same step pattern you developed in the previous session, this approach can be very inefficient for large documents. Lisa's current document contains only 12 property nodes to search through, but she wants to allow for documents containing tens of thousands of property listings. She wonders if this approach still works quickly and efficiently if there are so many nodes to examine.

For example, in Lisa's document, each property is identified by its real estate listing number (rln). This value is stored in the rln attribute of the property element. If Lisa wanted to locate a property with an rln of r317087, she could use the location path

```
//property[@rln="r317087"]
```

When a processor encounters this expression, it begins a search to locate every property element in the node tree with the specified rln value. If Lisa adds thousands of properties to her document, this would be a time-consuming search. Moreover, if she repeats this expression elsewhere in her style sheet, the processor repeats the search because it does not permanently store the node set for reuse elsewhere in the style sheet. Lisa can avoid this problem by storing the expression in a variable, but the problem remains that some location paths are not always very efficient in creating node sets from the source document's node tree. However, you can improve the efficiency of XSLT by declaring the ID attribute.

Declaring an ID Attribute

As you learned in Tutorial 3, XML allows you to validate the contents of an XML document by creating a DTD (document type definition). One item you can declare in a DTD is an ID attribute, which provides a way to uniquely identify a particular item from the source document. Recall that the syntax for declaring an ID attribute is either

```
<!ATTLIST element attribute ID #REQUIRED>
```

or

```
<!ATTLIST element attribute ID #IMPLIED>
```

depending on whether use of the attribute is required (#REQUIRED) or optional (#IMPLIED). If Lisa wants to declare the rln attribute as an ID and require every property element to have an rln attribute, she can create a DTD containing the following declaration:

```
<!ATTLIST property rln ID #REQUIRED>
```

One of the results of declaring an ID attribute is that processors must verify that all ID attribute values are unique, even if they are associated with different elements in the source document. If Lisa's document has two or more properties with the same rln, processors reject the document as invalid, providing a useful check for Lisa as she compiles real estate listings.

The process of ensuring unique ID values has an additional benefit: an XML processor has to create an index that matches each element with an ID attribute value. XPath allows you to search this index to create node sets, and because the index is smaller than the entire node tree, any search involving IDs is faster than a search of the node set. This becomes an important consideration for large XML documents.

Using the id() Function

The XPath function to search the ID index is

```
id(value)
```

where *value* is the value of the ID attribute. The id() function returns the element node whose attribute matches the value specified in the id() function. For example, if the rln attribute is declared as an ID attribute in a DTD, the expression

```
id("r317087")
```

returns the property element with an rln of r317087. This expression generates a node set (though less efficiently) that is identical to the one created using the expression

```
//property[rln="r317087"]
```

An important point to remember about ID attributes is that all IDs belong to the same index, even if they are associated with different attributes. Thus, a source document containing the attribute declarations

```
<!ATTLIST firm firmID ID #REQUIRED>
<!ATTLIST agent agentID ID #REQUIRED>
```

would place both the firmID and agentID attributes in a single index. This means that the following code is invalid because the ID value a2140 is repeated, even though it is the value for different attributes:

```
<firm firmID="a2140">
   <agent agentID="a2140" />
</firm>
```

Though using IDs and the id() function can accelerate searches considerably, you should be aware of some problems with this approach:

- IDs can be associated only with attributes. An index cannot be created based on the values of an element or values of the children of an element. For example, Lisa cannot use the real estate listing number as an element in her source document if she also wanted to use it as an ID.
- You must create a unique ID for each of the ID attributes, even if they are associated with different elements. This can be a time-consuming and difficult process for large documents.
- ID attributes must be valid XML names, and therefore they cannot contain spaces or begin with numbers. Because of this requirement, traditional IDs, such as Social Security numbers or ISBNs, cannot be declared as ID attributes.

Because of these limitations, ID attributes and the id() function are not always the best way to generate node sets. A more flexible and useful alternative is to create a key.

Reference Window | **Declaring and Finding an ID**

- To declare an ID attribute in the source document's DTD, use either of the following expressions:

  ```
  <!ATTLIST element attribute ID #REQUIRED>
  ```
  or
  ```
  <!ATTLIST element attribute ID #IMPLIED>
  ```
  depending on whether use of the attribute is required (#REQUIRED) or optional (#IMPLIED).
- To reference the element node containing an ID attribute with the specified value, use the XPath function

  ```
  id(value)
  ```
  where *value* is the value of the ID attribute.

Working with Keys

A **key** is an index that matches values of elements or attributes with nodes in a source document. Keys can be thought of as generalized IDs, without their limitations. Unlike IDs, keys have the following characteristics:

- Keys are declared in the style sheet, not in the DTD of the source document.
- Keys have names as well as values, allowing the style sheet author to create multiple distinct keys rather than rely on a single index.
- Keys can be associated with either attribute or element values.
- Keys can have values that are not limited to XML names (such as Social Security numbers).

As you'll see later in this tutorial, keys also have the additional advantage of being an efficient way of grouping nodes in a way that does not rely on inefficient step patterns.

Creating a Key

To create a key, add the following XSLT element at the top level of the style sheet as a child of the stylesheet element:

```
<xsl:key name="name" match="node-set" use="expression" />
```

where *name* is the name of the key, *node-set* is the set of nodes in the source document to which the key is applied, and *expression* is an XPath expression that indicates the values to be used in the key's index table. When an XSLT processor encounters a key element, it creates an index based on the values in the key. Thus, keys create the same type of indexes that are created when IDs are declared in a DTD associated with the source document.

For example, to create a key named rlns based on the rln attribute of each property element in the source document, you add the following key element to the style sheet:

```
<xsl:key name="rlns" match="//property" use="@rln" />
```

The rlns key creates an index of all of the rln attributes in the source document. Note that the expression in the match attribute acts as the context node for the expression in the use attribute. In this case, the expression @rln indicates that rln is an attribute of the property element. Because keys are not limited to attributes, you can also create a key based on the value of a child element. If you wanted to create a cityNames key based on the city associated with each property, you would create the following key element:

```
<xsl:key name="cityNames" match="//property" use="city" />
```

In this case, an index is built that contains all the unique city names in the document. The code for this key assumes that city is a child of the property element, which is true in the case of the listings.xml file.

You decide to create a key named cityNames for the property elements in the source document, based on the city in which each property is located.

To create a key:

▶ **1.** Return to the **listings.xsl** file in your text editor.

▶ **2.** Insert the following code directly below the opening <xsl:stylesheet> tag (see Figure 8-15):

```
<xsl:key name="cityNames" match="property" use="city" />
```

Adding the cityNames key ◀ Figure 8-15

```
<xsl:stylesheet version='1.0' xmlns:xsl="http://www.w3.org/1999/XSL/Transform">
<xsl:key name="cityNames" match="property" use="city" />

<xsl:template match="/">
  <html>
  <head>
    <title>Real Estate Listings</title>
    <link href="listings.css" rel="stylesheet" type="text/css" />
  </head>
```

▶ **3.** Save your changes to the file.

Using the key() Function

To reference the node set defined by a key, you use the XPath function

```
key(name, value)
```

where *name* is the name of the key and *value* is the key's value. The key() function is the equivalent of the id() function for IDs. For example, to use the rlns key to reference the property element containing the rln attribute with a value of r317087, you use the XPath function

```
key("rlns", "r317087")
```

which is equivalent to the location path

```
//property[rln="r317087"]
```

Unlike IDs, a key can point to more than one node because the key values are not required to be unique in the source document. Thus, the cityName key defined above can be used to return all property elements from specified cities. The expression

```
key("cityNames", "Cutler")
```

is equivalent to the location path

```
//property[city="Cutler"]
```

Similar to an ID index, a key returns the node set more quickly and efficiently because the XSLT processor only has to search through the key's index and not the entire node tree. The key() function can also be used with a predicate to select a specific node from a node set. For example, the expression

```
key("cityNames", "Cutler")[1]
```

selects the first property element from the city of Cutler. The key() function can also be used nested within other XPath functions. The expression

```
count(key("cityNames", "Cutler"))
```

returns the count of all property elements from the city of Cutler. The key value itself does not have to be entered explicitly; it can also be inserted as a reference to a node in the source document. For example, the code

```
<xsl:for-each select="//property">
   <xsl:value-of select="count(key('cityNames', city))" />
</xsl:value-of>
```

returns a count of the properties associated with each city. Instead of specifying a value for the city name, this code uses the value of the property's city element.

Reference Window | **Creating and Using Keys**

- To create a key, use the element
    ```
    <xsl:key name="name" match="node-set" use="expression" />
    ```
    where *name* is the name of the key, *node-set* is the set of nodes in the source document to which the key is applied, and *expression* is an XPath expression that indicates the values to be used in the index table of the key.
- To access values from the key, use the function
    ```
    key(name, value)
    ```
    where *name* is the name of the key and *value* is the key's value.

Lisa wants the city list at the top of the property report to include a count of the number of properties within each city. You decide to add this information with a key() function using the cityNames key you've already created.

To apply the key() function:

▶ 1. Go to the cityList moded template at the bottom of the style sheet.

▶ 2. Directly before the | character, insert the following code, leaving a space before the | character (see Figure 8-16):

```
(<xsl:value-of select="count(key('cityNames', city))" />)
```

Figure 8-16

Using the key() function

```
<xsl:template match="property" mode="cityList">
    <xsl:value-of select="city" />
    (<xsl:value-of select="count(key('cityNames', city))" />) |
</xsl:template>

</xsl:stylesheet>
```

▶ **3.** Save your changes to the file, and regenerate the result document using your Web browser or an XSLT processor. Figure 8-17 shows the revised city list with the count of properties displayed alongside the city name.

Displaying the count of properties associated with each city

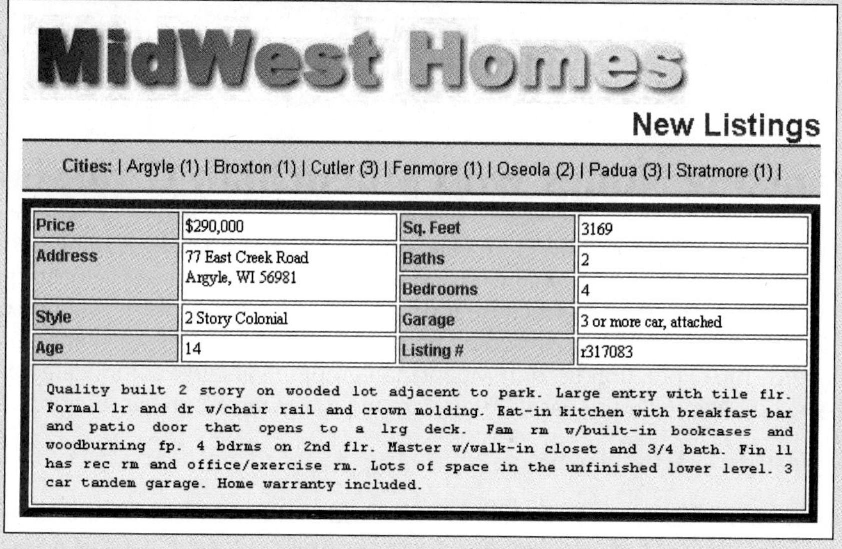

Figure 8-17

MidWest Homes
New Listings

Cities: | Argyle (1) | Broxton (1) | Cutler (3) | Fenmore (1) | Oseola (2) | Padua (3) | Stratmore (1) |

Price	$290,000	Sq. Feet	3169
Address	77 East Creek Road Argyle, WI 56981	Baths	2
		Bedrooms	4
Style	2 Story Colonial	Garage	3 or more car, attached
Age	14	Listing #	r317083

Quality built 2 story on wooded lot adjacent to park. Large entry with tile flr. Formal lr and dr w/chair rail and crown molding. Eat-in kitchen with breakfast bar and patio door that opens to a lrg deck. Fam rm w/built-in bookcases and woodburning fp. 4 bdrms on 2nd flr. Master w/walk-in closet and 3/4 bath. Fin ll has rec rm and office/exercise rm. Lots of space in the unfinished lower level. 3 car tandem garage. Home warranty included.

From the city list, Lisa can see at a glance that she has only one new listing from the city of Argyle, but three new properties listed in Padua. This is useful information, but she needs to be able to group the property descriptions by each city. Now that you've learned how to use keys and the key() function, the only feature you need to learn to create such a group involves creating IDs.

Generating IDs

So far you've used XPath to reference node sets based on either ID or key values. In some style sheets, however, you will want to do the opposite: generate an ID that identifies a specific node or node set within the source document. To create such an ID, XPath provides the function

```
generate-id(node-set)
```

where *node-set* is the node set for which you want to create an ID. If you omit a node set, the function is applied to the current context node. The generate-id() function returns an arbitrary text string starting with an alphanumeric character and followed by several more alphanumeric characters. The exact ID value is generated by the XSLT processor and depending on the processor, a different arbitrary alphanumeric string might be created for a given node set in each session in which the style sheet is accessed.

However, different node-sets always have different IDs. Thus, if two node sets share the same generated ID, they must be the same node set. Therefore, one use of the generate-id() function is to determine whether two variables refer to the same node set. For example, if a style sheet has two variables named nodes1 and nodes2, the expression

```
test="generate-id($nodes1)=generate-id($nodes2)"
```

returns a value of true if the node set referenced by nodes1 is the same as the node set referenced by nodes2.

Reference Window

Generating an ID Value

- To generate an ID value for a node set, use the XPath expression
  ```
  generate-id(node-set)
  ```
  where *node-set* is the node set for which you want to create an ID. If you omit a node set, the function is applied to the current context node.

Organizing Nodes with Muenchian Grouping

You now have enough information to create a more efficient way of grouping node sets than the mechanism you set up in the last session with step patterns. This technique is known as **Muenchian grouping** because it was first formulated by Steve Muench of the Oracle Corporation. Muenchian grouping depends on the use of the key() and generate-id() functions. The expression used in Muenchian grouping is fairly complicated at first glance, so you begin with the basics. Start with the following XPath expression:

```
node1[generate-id()=IDvalue]
```

This expression places the generate-id() function within the predicate for the *node1* node set. The node set created by this expression consists only of those nodes in *node1* whose generated ID value equals *IDvalue*. Though you can't predict what ID value will be generated by an XSLT processor, if you replace *IDvalue* in the expression with

```
node1[generate-id()=generate-id(node2)]
```

you generate a node set containing all the nodes in *node1* whose generated ID value is equal to the generated ID value for the node set *node2*. Another way to think about this is the node set defined by this expression consists of the intersection of *node1* and *node2*, containing only the nodes in *node1* that are also present in *node2*. For example, the expression

```
property[generate-id()=generate-id(//property[city="Cutler"])]
```

returns a node set of all the property elements whose generated ID equals the generated ID of Cutler properties. This is in essence the node set of all property elements from the city of Cutler (see Figure 8-18).

Selecting nodes with the generate-id() function ◀ Figure 8-18

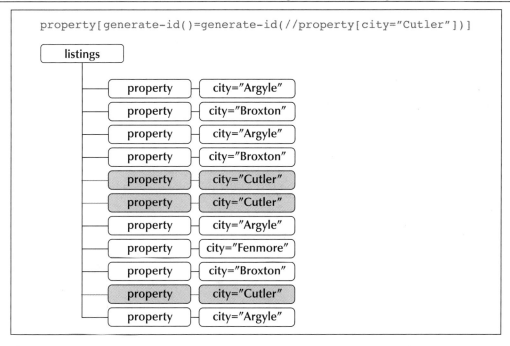

```
property[generate-id()=generate-id(//property[city="Cutler"])]
```

However, for a large source document, it is more efficient to define *node2* using keys instead of a predicate expression. You've already created the cityNames key for the list of cities, so the node set for *node2* can be defined using the XPath function key ("cityNames", "Cutler"), resulting in the following predicate (see Figure 8-19):

```
property[generate-id()=generate-id(key("cityNames","Cutler"))]
```

Selecting nodes with the generate-id() and key() functions ◀ Figure 8-19

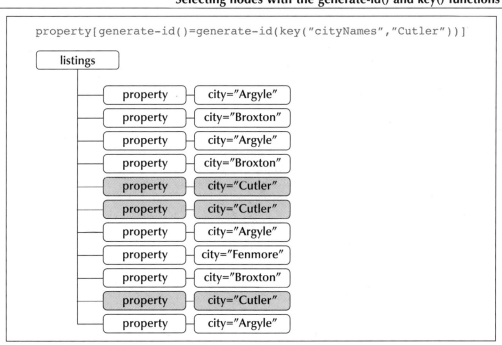

```
property[generate-id()=generate-id(key("cityNames","Cutler"))]
```

At this point, your node set selects all the Cutler properties, but you can limit *node2* to only the first property from Cutler by adding a predicate containing the node number. Thus, you change

```
key("cityNames", "Cutler")
```

to

```
key("cityNames", "Cutler")[1]
```

and the new expression

```
property[generate-id()=generate-id(key("cityNames","Cutler")[1])]
```

creates a node set that contains only the first Cutler property (see Figure 8-20).

Figure 8-20 | **Selecting the first Cutler property**

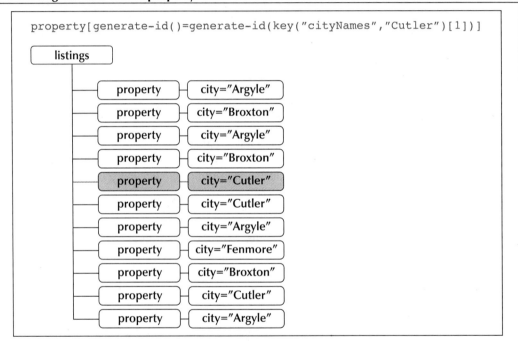

So far, this may seem like a lot of work for a node set that can be created using a far simpler location path. However, the final step in developing Muenchian grouping is to apply this expression to all of the cities in the source document—not just Cutler. To accomplish this, you replace Cutler with the city element itself:

```
property[generate-id()=generate-id(key("cityNames",city)[1])]
```

This complete expression is the Muenchian grouping that returns a node set consisting of the first property element for each city in the source document. This is the same result you obtained in the last session using step patterns (see Figure 8-21). The advantage, though, is that for larger node sets this expression is much more efficient than the step pattern.

Using Muenchian grouping to select the first property of each city ◀ Figure 8-21

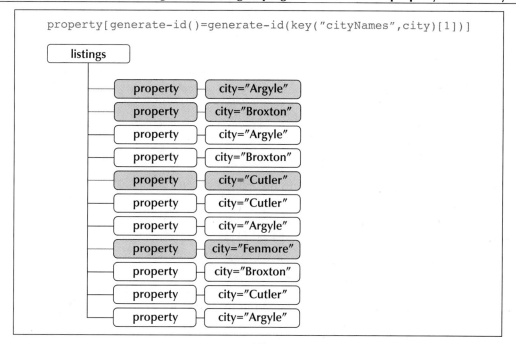

```
property[generate-id()=generate-id(key("cityNames",city)[1])]
```

listings

property	city="Argyle"
property	city="Broxton"
property	city="Argyle"
property	city="Broxton"
property	city="Cutler"
property	city="Cutler"
property	city="Argyle"
property	city="Fenmore"
property	city="Broxton"
property	city="Cutler"
property	city="Argyle"

Employing Muenchian Grouping

Reference Window

- First, create a key for the element or attribute that you want to group using the XSLT element
    ```
    <xsl:key name="name" match="node-set" use="expression" />
    ```
  where *name* is the name of the key, *node-set* is the node set that you want to group, and *expression* is an XPath expression that references the element or attribute on which to group.
- Next, add the following expression to the select attribute of a for-each or apply-templates element:
    ```
    node-set[generate-id()=generate-id(key(name,expression)[1])]
    ```
  where *node-set*, *name*, and *expression* are the same values and node sets used in creating the key. This expression returns the first occurrence of each node in *node-set* for the index defined in the key.
- Finally, within the for-each or apply-templates element, you can reference the group value using
    ```
    expression
    ```
  where *expression* is the element or attribute used to group the node set.

Now that you have seen how to create a group of property elements using Muenchian grouping, you can display the city names as h1 headings using a for-each element. You can also sort the for-each element in alphabetical order of city name. The code to do this is

```
<xsl:for-each
  select="//property[generate-id()=generate-id
(key('cityNames', city)[1])]">
  <xsl:sort select="city" />
  <h1><xsl:value-of select="city" /></h1>
</xsl:for-each>
```

In this code, the select attribute of the for-each element selects one property from each city and displays the city name within the for-each element. Add this code to the listings. xsl style sheet.

To apply Muenchian grouping:

1. Go to the root template, and *delete* the following lines of code:

```
<xsl:apply-templates select="/listings/property">
   <xsl:sort select="city" />
   <xsl:sort select="price" />
</xsl:apply-templates>
```

2. Replace the four deleted lines with the following (see Figure 8-22):

```
<xsl:for-each
   select="//property[generate-id()=generate-
         id(key('cityNames', city)[1])]">
   <xsl:sort select="city" />
   <h1><xsl:value-of select="city" /></h1>
</xsl:for-each>
```

Figure 8-22	Using Muenchian grouping to group properties by city

```
<xsl:template match="/">
   <html>
   <head>
      <title>Real Estate Listings</title>
      <link href="listings.css" rel="stylesheet" type="text/css" />
   </head>
   <body>
      <p><img src="logo.jpg" alt="Midwest Homes" /></p>
      <h2>New Listings</h2>

      <div id="city_list"><b>Cities: </b> |

      <xsl:apply-templates
            select="listings/property[not(city=preceding::property/city)]"
            mode="cityList">
         <xsl:sort select="city" />
      </xsl:apply-templates>

      </div>

      <xsl:for-each
            select="//property[generate-id()=generate-id(key('cityNames', city)[1])]">
         <xsl:sort select="city" />
         <h1><xsl:value-of select="city" /></h1>
      </xsl:for-each>

   </body>
   </html>
</xsl:template>
```

replace the apply-templates code with a for-each element

3. Save your changes to the file, and regenerate the result document in your Web browser or XSLT processor. Figure 8-23 shows the current state of the property report with the different city name headings.

MidWest Homes

New Listings

Cities: | Argyle (1) | Broxton (1) | Cutler (3) | Fenmore (1) | Oseola (2) | Padua (3) | Stratmore (1) |

Argyle

Broxton

Cutler

Fenmore

Oseola

Padua

Stratmore

Next you display the property descriptions from each city, sorted in descending order of price. Because the property descriptions have already been created in the property template, you only need to apply that template within the for-each element. The code to apply the property template is

```
<xsl:apply-templates select="key('cityNames', city)">
   <xsl:sort select="price" order="descending" />
</xsl:apply-templates>
```

Note that this code uses the cityNames key to include only those properties from a selected city. Add this code to the for-each element you created in the last set of steps.

To display the property descriptions within each city:

► 1. Return to **listings.xsl** in your text editor.

► 2. Go to the root template and within the for-each element insert the following code below the h1 heading (see Figure 8-24):

```
<xsl:apply-templates select="key('cityNames', city)">
   <xsl:sort select="price" order="descending" />
</xsl:apply-templates>
```

Figure 8-24 **Applying the property template for each city**

```
<xsl:for-each
    select="//property[generate-id()=generate-id(key('cityNames', city)[1])]">
  <xsl:sort select="city" />
  <h1><xsl:value-of select="city" /></h1>
  <xsl:apply-templates select="key('cityNames', city)">
    <xsl:sort select="price" order="descending" />
  </xsl:apply-templates>
</xsl:for-each>
```

3. Save your changes to the style sheet, and regenerate the result document. Figure 8-25 shows the property reports nested within each city and sorted in descending order of price. Verify that your property report is organized in the same way.

Figure 8-25 **Displaying property descriptions for each city**

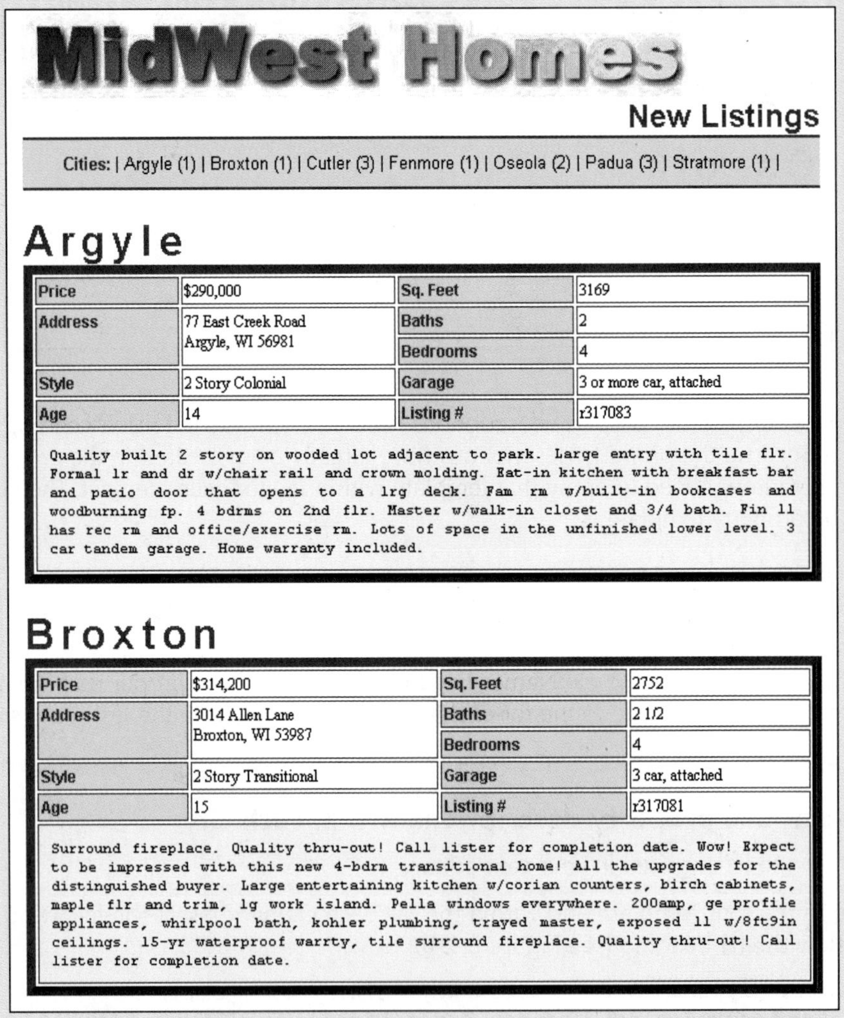

MidWest Homes

New Listings

Cities: | Argyle (1) | Broxton (1) | Cutler (3) | Fenmore (1) | Oseola (2) | Padua (3) | Stratmore (1) |

Argyle

Price	$290,000	Sq. Feet	3169
Address	77 East Creek Road Argyle, WI 56981	Baths	2
		Bedrooms	4
Style	2 Story Colonial	Garage	3 or more car, attached
Age	14	Listing #	r317083

Quality built 2 story on wooded lot adjacent to park. Large entry with tile flr. Formal lr and dr w/chair rail and crown molding. Eat-in kitchen with breakfast bar and patio door that opens to a lrg deck. Fam rm w/built-in bookcases and woodburning fp. 4 bdrms on 2nd flr. Master w/walk-in closet and 3/4 bath. Fin ll has rec rm and office/exercise rm. Lots of space in the unfinished lower level. 3 car tandem garage. Home warranty included.

Broxton

Price	$314,200	Sq. Feet	2752
Address	3014 Allen Lane Broxton, WI 53987	Baths	2 1/2
		Bedrooms	4
Style	2 Story Transitional	Garage	3 car, attached
Age	15	Listing #	r317081

Surround fireplace. Quality thru-out! Call lister for completion date. Wow! Expect to be impressed with this new 4-bdrm transitional home! All the upgrades for the distinguished buyer. Large entertaining kitchen w/corian counters, birch cabinets, maple flr and trim, lg work island. Pella windows everywhere. 200amp, ge profile appliances, whirlpool bath, kohler plumbing, trayed master, exposed ll w/8ft9in ceilings. 15-yr waterproof warrty, tile surround fireplace. Quality thru-out! Call lister for completion date.

Muenchian grouping can appear daunting at first, so take some time to examine the code you've just entered to understand how the different city groups and property descriptions within each city are generated.

Creating Links with Generated IDs

Lisa likes the work you've done in grouping the property descriptions by city. Next she wants you to create links between the names in the city list at the top of the report and the section of the report that describes the properties within that city. You can use the generate-id() function to create such links for specific locations within a Web page. In HTML, these links are created using the a element along with an ID attribute in the target of the link. The basic syntax is

```
<a href="#id">linked text</a>
...
<elem id="id">target of link</elem>
```

where *id* identifies the location of the target within the Web page, *linked text* is the text of the link, *elem* is the HTML element that acts as the link's target, and *target of link* is the content of the link's target. If the source document contains ID attributes, you can use the values of those attributes as link targets. However, if there are no appropriate link targets, you can generate your own IDs using the XPath generate-id() function. The code is

```
<a href="#{generate-id(node)}">linked text</a>
...
<elem id="{generate-id(node)}">target of link</elem>
```

where *node* is a node in the source document that uniquely identifies the target of link. The only requirement is that the node used in the link be the same as the node used in the link's target. If they are different, the generated IDs will not match. Because a generated ID is a random string that can change each time a document is opened, a link that uses a specific ID value might not work in the future. For example, an XSLT processor might generate the following HTML code to create links between a city name and the h1 heading of that city:

```
<a href="#AE1804Z">Cutler</a>
...
<h1 id="AE1804Z">Cutler</h1>
```

When a user clicks the link on the Web page, the browser jumps to the Cutler section of the property report, which has the generated ID value AE1804Z. However, the next time the style sheet is executed, a different ID might be created. For this reason, you should use generated IDs only for links and targets within the same document, and you should not write code that assumes a specific value for the generated ID.

Creating Links and Targets

Reference Window

- To generate ID values for internal targets and links, use the generate-id() function as follows:
  ```
  <a href="#{generate-id(node)}">linked text</a>
  ...
  <elem id="{generate-id(node)}">target of link</elem>
  ```
  where *node* is a node in the source document, *linked text* is the text of the link, *elem* is an HTML element that acts as the link's target, and *target of link* is the content of the link's target.

Use the generate-id() function to generate an internal link between the city names and the section of the report describing the properties listed within that city.

To create the links:

1. Return to **listings.xsl** in your text editor.

2. Go to the cityList moded template at the bottom of the file, and insert the following tag directly before the value-of element that displays the city name:

```
<a href="#{generate-id()}">
```

3. Add a closing **</a>** directly after the value-of element.

4. Go up to the root template, and within the opening <h1> tag that displays the city name, insert the following attribute:

```
id="{generate-id()}"
```

Figure 8-26 highlights the revised code in the style sheet.

| Figure 8-26 | **Create links and targets** |

```
<xsl:template match="/">
  <html>
  <head>
    <title>Real Estate Listings</title>
    <link href="listings.css" rel="stylesheet" type="text/css" />
  </head>
  <body>
    <p><img src="logo.jpg" alt="Midwest Homes" /></p>
    <h2>New Listings</h2>

    <div id="city_list"><b>Cities: </b> |

    <xsl:apply-templates
        select="listings/property[not(city=preceding::property/city)]"
        mode="cityList">
      <xsl:sort select="city" />
    </xsl:apply-templates>

    </div>

    <xsl:for-each
        select="//property[generate-id()=generate-id(key('cityNames', city)[1])]">
      <xsl:sort select="city" />
      <h1 id="{generate-id()}"><xsl:value-of select="city" /></h1>
      <xsl:apply-templates select="key('cityNames', city)">
        <xsl:sort select="price" order="descending" />
      </xsl:apply-templates>
    </xsl:for-each>

  </body>
  </html>
</xsl:template>
```

```
<xsl:template match="property" mode="cityList">
  <a href="#{generate-id()}">
  <xsl:value-of select="city" />
  </a>
  (<xsl:value-of select="count(key('cityNames', city))" />) |
</xsl:template>

</xsl:stylesheet>
```

5. Save your changes to listings.xsl, and regenerate the result document. As shown in Figure 8-27, each name in the city list should now be underlined, indicating that it acts as a link within the report.

6. Click each of the links in the city list, and verify that the Web browser jumps to the section of the report describing the new listings within that city.

7. If you wish to take a break before starting the next session, you may close your open files and applications.

You've completed the task of grouping the information in Lisa's document. In the next session, you learn how to display information from another XML file in your result document.

Session 8.2 Quick Check

Review

1. Why is this statement false: ID attributes can be duplicated as long as they are used with different elements.

2. What XPath expression would you use to select nodes whose agentID attribute equals "f102"? Assume that the agentID attribute has been defined in the document's DTD.

3. What is wrong with the following XPath expression?
`id(381-71-2905)`

4. What is a key? How does a key differ from an ID?

5. The agent element has a single child element named agentName that stores the name of the real estate agent. What code would you use to create a key named agentNames applied to the agent element with key values based on agentName?

6. What code would you use to create a node set using the agentNames key for agents named Howard?

7. What XPath expression would you enter to generate an ID based on the agentName element? Assume that agent is the context node.

8. Using Muenchian grouping, what expression would you use to create a node set for the agent element grouped by the agentName element?

Sessions 8.3

Working with Multiple Document Sources

Each listing is associated with a real estate agency and a listing agent. Lisa has stored the IDs of each using the firm and agent attributes of the property element (see Figure 8-2). The firm attribute contains the ID number for the real estate agency, and the agent attribute contains the ID number for the listing agent. Lisa has two other XML documents, firms.xml and agents.xml, that contain detailed information about each agency and agent. Figure 8-28 describes the contents of these two documents.

Figure 8-28	Contents of the agents and firms documents

Document	Element	Description
agents.xml	agents	The root element of the document
	agent	Information about each agent; the ID attribute contains the ID number of the agent
	name	The name of the agent
	phone	The phone number of the agent
	email	The agent's e-mail address
firms.xml	firms	The root element of the document
	firm	Information about each firm; the ID attribute contains the ID number of the firm
	name	The name of the firm
	street	The street address of the firm
	city	The city in which the firm is located
	state	The state in which the firm is located
	zip	The postal code of the firm
	phone	The phone number of the firm
	web	The URL of the firm's Web site

The structure of the two documents is shown in Figure 8-29.

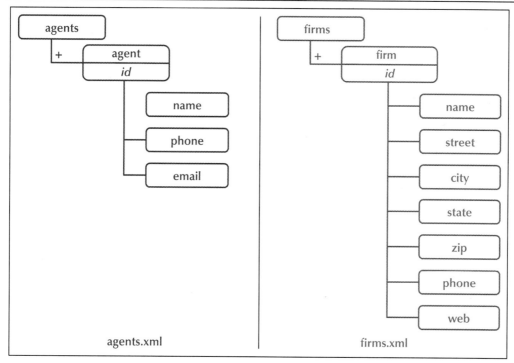

Lisa wants to display information from these two documents in the properties report. To do this, she needs you to match up the firm and agent attributes in the listings.xml file with the ID attributes in the firms.xml and agents.xml files (see Figure 8-30).

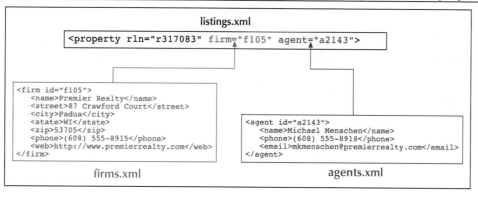

Using the document() Function

In Tutorial 7, you used the import and include elements to apply multiple style sheets to a single source document. In this case, you have the opposite task: you want to use multiple source documents in a single style sheet. To create a reference to another source document within a style sheet, you use the XPath function

```
document(object, base)
```

where *object* is either the URI of another XML source document or a node in the current source document that contains the URI of an external document that you want to access. The second parameter, *base*, is optional and fulfills the same purpose that the base element does in HTML: it defines the base URI used for resolving relative references. If no value for base is specified, the external document is assumed to be in the same folder as the style sheet. For example, the expression

```
document("firms.xml")
```

references the source document firms.xml. In some cases, the URI of the external source document is stored in an element, as in the following example:

```
<xmlDoc>firms.xml</xmlDoc>
```

To access the firms.xml document in this case, you simply reference the element containing the URI of the source document, as follows:

```
document(xmlDoc)
```

One advantage of this approach is that if you need to access different external documents or update the location of an external document, you can do so through the XML source file, leaving the style sheet unchanged. One disadvantage is that the document() function is not supported by all browsers. In particular, at the time of this writing, the Safari browser does not support the use of the document() function.

Reference Window

Accessing Data from Other Source Documents

- To create a reference to another source document within a style sheet, use the XPath function
    ```
    document(object, base)
    ```
  where *object* is either the URI of another XML source document or a node set in the current source document that contains the URI of an external document that you want to access, and *base* is an optional parameter that defines the base URI used for resolving relative references.

Once the document() function is used to reference an external file, the contents of that file are treated as a node set, with the file's root node as the root of the node tree. For example, if you want to access the city element from the firms.xml file, you use the expression

```
document("firms.xml")/firms/city
```

Note that if the external source document contains the same node names as the primary source document, the same template is applied to both documents. To avoid this problem, you can use either namespaces in the two documents to differentiate them or moded templates to apply a specific template to each node.

It is less efficient for large documents to continually call the document() function. Instead, it is common practice to create a variable for an external document, so that the document() function only has to be called once. Add two global variables to Lisa's style sheet to reference both the firms.xml and agents.xml files.

To create the document variables:

▶ 1. Return to the **listings.xsl** file in your text editor.

▶ 2. Insert the following code directly below the opening <xsl:stylesheet> tag (see Figure 8-31):

```
<xsl:variable name="agents" select="document('agents.xml')" />
<xsl:variable name="firms" select="document('firms.xml')" />
```

Creating variables for the agents.xml and firms.xml files | Figure 8-31

```
<xsl:stylesheet version='1.0' xmlns:xsl="http://www.w3.org/1999/XSL/Transform">
<xsl:variable name="agents" select="document('agents.xml')" />
<xsl:variable name="firms" select="document('firms.xml')" />

<xsl:key name="cityNames" match="property" use="city" />
```

To make it more efficient to retrieve data from these external documents, Lisa wants you to create keys based on the values of the ID attribute for the firm and agent elements. You create the following keys:

```
<xsl:key name="agentID" match="agent" use="@id" />
<xsl:key name="firmID" match="firm" use="@id" />
```

Note that the match attributes of the key elements do not reference either the agents.xml or firms.xml documents. This is because you cannot use the document() function or variables within the match attribute. However, the key can still access node sets within those documents if you set the context node to one of those external files. You'll see how to do this shortly. For now, create the agentID and firmID keys.

To create the ID keys:

▶ 1. Insert the following code directly below the firms variable (see Figure 8-32):

```
<xsl:key name="agentID" match="agent" use="@id" />
<xsl:key name="firmID" match="firm" use="@id" />
```

Defining agentID and firmID keys | Figure 8-32

```
<xsl:stylesheet version='1.0' xmlns:xsl="http://www.w3.org/1999/XSL/Transform">
<xsl:variable name="agents" select="document('agents.xml')" />
<xsl:variable name="firms" select="document('firms.xml')" />
<xsl:key name="agentID" match="agent" use="@id" />
<xsl:key name="firmID" match="firm" use="@id" />
```

▶ 2. Save your changes to the style sheet.

Looking up Data from Other Documents

Now that you've created variables and keys that reference node sets in the agents.xml and firms.xml documents, you can retrieve data from the documents for use in the property report. For each property, Lisa wants you to use the agent and firm attributes of the property element to display contact information for the agent and firm. Figure 8-33 shows a preview of a revised property report.

Figure 8-33 ▷ **Displaying firm and agent data**

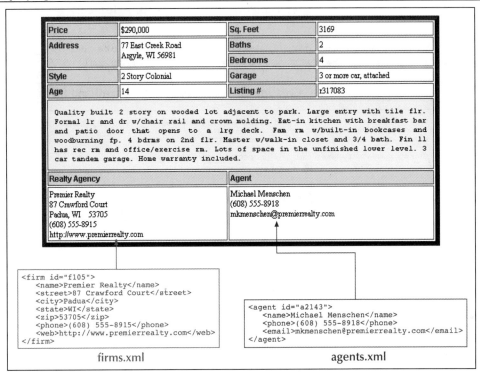

Add the table rows and table cells to the property report to display this information.

To add table rows and cells to the property report:

1. Go down to the first property template.

2. Directly above the closing </table> tag, insert the following code (see Figure 8-34):

```
<tr>
    <th colspan="2">Realty Agency</th>
    <th colspan="2">Agent</th>
</tr>
<tr>
    <td colspan="2">
    </td>
    <td colspan="2">
    </td>
</tr>
```

Adding table rows and cells to the property report ◄ Figure 8-34

```
<tr>
    <td id="description" colspan="4">
        <xsl:value-of select="description" />
    </td>
</tr>
<tr>
    <th colspan="2">Realty Agency</th>
    <th colspan="2">Agent</th>
</tr>
<tr>
    <td colspan="2">
    </td>
    <td colspan="2">
    </td>
</tr>
</table>
</xsl:template>
```

One of the challenges of working with multiple source documents is keeping track of the current source document. The **current source document** is the document that contains the context node (whatever that may be). This is particularly important when working with XPath's key() function, as that function returns node sets only from the current source document. You can't access a key index from a source document other than the current data source. Thus, to access the agentID and firmID keys you created earlier, you have to switch the context node to point to the agents.xml and firms.xml files. One way of accomplishing this is by inserting the code that displays data from the files within a for-each element. For example, the general code structure for the firms.xml document is

```
<xsl:for-each select="$firms">
    retrieve firm data
</xsl:for-each>
```

Recall that the firms variable references the firms.xml file. The firms variable points only to a single document, so this for loop is run only once. However, running the for loop changes the context node to the root node of the firms.xml document. Once this is done, you can retrieve information about the firm handling the property and display that information on Lisa's Web page.

Changing the Context Node to an External Document
Reference Window

- To change the context node to a node in an external document, use the structure
  ```
  <xsl:for-each select="$document">
      styles
  </xsl:for-each>
  ```
  where *document* is a variable that references a node set in the external document and *styles* is the XSLT styles to be applied to the node set.

The challenge is to make sure that you match up the property with the correct agency. The ID number of the firm handling the property is stored in the firm attribute of the property element, but because you switched the context node to the firms.xml document, you no longer have access to that information. To get around this problem, you can store the value of the firm attribute in a variable named fID *before* the for-each element. The complete code is therefore

```
<xsl:variable name="fID" select="@firm" />
<xsl:for-each select="$firms">
    retrieve firm data
</xsl:for-each>
```

Add this code to Lisa's style sheet.

To change the source document to the firms.xml file:

▶ **1.** Insert the following code within the first cell of the last table row (see Figure 8-35):

```
<xsl:variable name="fID" select="@firm" />
<xsl:for-each select="$firms">
   <!-- Retrieve firm data -->
</xsl:for-each>
```

Figure 8-35 ▶ **Inserting the fID variable and for-each element**

```
<tr>
    <th colspan="2">Realty Agency</th>
    <th colspan="2">Agent</th>
</tr>
<tr>
    <td colspan="2">

    <xsl:variable name="fID" select="@firm" />
    <xsl:for-each select="$firms">
        <!-- Retrieve firm data -->
    </xsl:for-each>

    </td>
    <td colspan="2">
    </td>
</tr>
</table>
</xsl:template>
```

▶ **2.** Save your changes to the file.

Once you've changed the current source document to the firms.xml file, you can use the key() function to retrieve descriptive data about the realty agency associated with the current property listing. For example, to display the name of the agency, you enter the following code:

```
<xsl:value-of select="key('firmID', $fID)/name />
```

This statement returns the name of the firm whose ID attribute equals the value of the fID variable. Use this form to display the name, address, phone number, and Web site URL of each real estate agency.

To display the firm data:

▶ **1.** Insert the following code within the for-each element you entered above, as shown in Figure 8-36:

```
<xsl:value-of select="key('firmID', $fID)/name" /> <br />
<xsl:value-of select="key('firmID', $fID)/street" /> <br />
<xsl:value-of select="key('firmID', $fID)/city" />,
<xsl:value-of select="key('firmID', $fID)/state" />   
<xsl:value-of select="key('firmID', $fID)/zip" /><br />
<xsl:value-of select="key('firmID', $fID)/phone" /><br />
<xsl:value-of select="key('firmID', $fID)/web" />
```

Retrieving the firm data ◄ Figure 8-36

```
<xsl:variable name="fID" select="@firm" />
<xsl:for-each select="$firms">
    <!-- Retrieve firm data -->
    <xsl:value-of select="key('firmID', $fID)/name" /> <br />
    <xsl:value-of select="key('firmID', $fID)/street" /> <br />
    <xsl:value-of select="key('firmID', $fID)/city" />,
    <xsl:value-of select="key('firmID', $fID)/state" />   
    <xsl:value-of select="key('firmID', $fID)/zip" /><br />
    <xsl:value-of select="key('firmID', $fID)/phone" /><br />
    <xsl:value-of select="key('firmID', $fID)/web" />
</xsl:for-each>
```

2. Save your changes to the file, and regenerate the result document using either your Web browser or your XSLT processor. Figure 8-37 shows the revised property report for the first property.

Realty agency data for the first property ◄ Figure 8-37

Argyle

Price	$290,000	Sq. Feet	3169
Address	77 East Creek Road Argyle, WI 56981	Baths	2
		Bedrooms	4
Style	2 Story Colonial	Garage	3 or more car, attached
Age	14	Listing #	r317083

Quality built 2 story on wooded lot adjacent to park. Large entry with tile flr. Formal lr and dr w/chair rail and crown molding. Eat-in kitchen with breakfast bar and patio door that opens to a lrg deck. Fam rm w/built-in bookcases and woodburning fp. 4 bdrms on 2nd flr. Master w/walk-in closet and 3/4 bath. Fin ll has rec rm and office/exercise rm. Lots of space in the unfinished lower level. 3 car tandem garage. Home warranty included.

Realty Agency	Agent
Premier Realty 87 Crawford Court Padua, WI 53705 (608) 555-8915 http://www.premierrealty.com	

Trouble? If your browser does not support the document() function, you will not see information about the agency in the table.

The code to retrieve and display data about the seller's agent is similar:

```
<xsl:variable name="aID" select="@agent" />
<xsl:for-each select="$agents">
   <!-- Retrieve agent data -->
   <xsl:value-of select="key('agentID', $aID)/name" /> <br />
   <xsl:value-of select="key('agentID', $aID)/phone" /><br />
   <xsl:value-of select="key('agentID', $aID)/email" />
</xsl:for-each>
```

In this case, the value of the agent attribute is stored in the aID variable. You then use that variable to extract the name, phone number, and e-mail address of the real estate agent with that ID. Add this code to the listings.xsl style sheet.

To display the agent data:

1. Return to the **listings.xsl** file in your text editor.

2. Insert the following code within the last table cell of the property template, as shown in Figure 8-38:

```
<xsl:variable name="aID" select="@agent" />
<xsl:for-each select="$agents">
   <!-- Retrieve agent data -->
   <xsl:value-of select="key('agentID', $aID)/name" /> <br />
   <xsl:value-of select="key('agentID', $aID)/phone" /><br />
   <xsl:value-of select="key('agentID', $aID)/email" />
</xsl:for-each>
```

Figure 8-38	Retrieving agent data

```
<td colspan="2">

<xsl:variable name="aID" select="@agent" />
<xsl:for-each select="$agents">
   <!-- Retrieve agent data -->
   <xsl:value-of select="key('agentID', $aID)/name" /> <br />
   <xsl:value-of select="key('agentID', $aID)/phone" /><br />
   <xsl:value-of select="key('agentID', $aID)/email" />
</xsl:for-each>

   </td>
  </tr>
 </table>
</xsl:template>
```

3. Close the listings.xsl file, saving your changes.

4. Regenerate the result document using your Web browser or your XSLT processor. Figure 8-39 shows the final version of Lisa's property report.

Trouble? If your browser does not support the document() function, you will not see information about the agent in the table.

5. Close your Web browser or XSLT processor.

Placing Data into a Style Sheet

In some situations, you may want to place data directly into a style sheet rather than in a secondary source document. For example, the descriptions of the different realty agencies and agents could have been inserted into the listings.xsl file. Data placed within a style sheet is known as a **data element**. Because it can be easier to manage a single file rather than several, some XML authors use data elements instead of external XML data sources.

A data element should be placed in its own namespace with a namespace prefix to distinguish it from other types of elements in a style sheet. For example, to place information about real estate agents into the listings.xsl document, Lisa could use the following code:

```
<xsl:stylesheet version="1.0"
    xmlns:xsl="http:/www.w3.org/1999/XSL/Transform"
    xmlns:data="http://www.data_elements.com">
<data:agents>
   <data:agent id="a2140">
      <data:name>Karen Fawkes</data:name>
      <data:phone>(608) 555-3414</data:phone>
      <data:email>karen_fawkes@tofferrealty.com</data:email>
   </data:agent>
   ...
</data:agents>
```

To access the style sheet data, you use the document() function with an empty text string as follows:

```
document('')
```

XSLT processors interpret the empty text string as a relative URL and access the current style sheet file. Because a style sheet file is also an XML document, the document() function creates a node set based on the elements and attributes of the style sheet. The data elements you created are also a part of that node set. Because the root element of any style sheet is the stylesheet element, you can access the data elements by starting with the stylesheet element and working down the node tree. For example, to reference the agent data elements, you can use the expression

```
document('')/xsl:stylesheet/data:agents/data:agent
```

As with other expressions, you can use predicates, step patterns, and XPath functions to refine the data elements node set.

Inserting Code Snippets

A final use of the document() function is to insert snippets of code into the result document. If your intent is to create a Web page, this code could include such elements as a standard heading or logo that applies to all of your Web documents. Because the document() function is designed to access XML documents, the only requirement is that HTML code be placed in a well-formed XHTML file.

For example, MidWest Homes uses a standard logo and heading. Rather than retyping the HTML code each time Lisa needs to create a style sheet, the heading and logo information can be stored in an XHTML file named heading.html.

To use the code from that file, Lisa needs to use the document() function to access the document and the copy-of element to insert the node set into the result document. The code appears as

```
<xsl:copy-of select="document('heading.html')" />
```

One of the advantages of creating code snippets is that they can easily be modified without having to edit the style sheets directly. If at a later time, Lisa wants to change the heading used in her documents, she needs to edit only a single file. She can leave the XSLT style sheet alone.

You've successfully completed your work on Lisa's project, and she is pleased with how you used XSLT to organize and present the property information in her source document. Lisa has some other reports she wants to create, and will discuss those projects with you later.

Review

Session 8.3 Quick Check

1. What function would you use to access the secondary source document stores.xml?
2. What is the difference between the document() function and the include or import elements?
3. If the stores.xml document contains a descendant element named "store_name", what XPath expression would you use to reference the store_name element from within your style sheet?
4. What code structure would you use to change the context node in the style sheet to the stores.xml document?
5. How would you modify the <xsl:stylesheet> element in order to use data elements in your style sheet? Assume that the data elements have the namespace *http://www.stores.com* and the namespace prefix "stores".
6. What function would you use to access data elements in your style sheet? Assume that the data elements have the namespace prefix storesNS and that you want to reference the stores/store node set.
7. What code would you use to insert a code snippet from the XHTML file logo.htm into your style sheet?

Review

Tutorial Summary

This tutorial continued work with XSLT and XPath by looking at how to efficiently group node sets in the source document. The first session returned to the topic of location paths and explored how to create more detailed and complicated expressions using step patterns. Step patterns were then used to group a node set based on the value of the city element. The session concluded with a discussion of moded templates. The second session looked at how ID attributes can be created and referenced within a style sheet. It then looked at creating and applying keys. Using both ids and keys, the second session introduced a more efficient way of grouping nodes using Muenchian grouping. The third session explored how to retrieve data from several source documents into a single style sheet. The tutorial concluded with a brief look at working with code snippets.

Key Terms

axis	data element	node test
current source	key	Muenchian grouping
document	moded template	step pattern

Practice

Practice the skills you learned in the tutorial using the same case scenario

Review Assignment

Data files needed for this Review Assignment: agencies.xml, logo.jpg, style.css, styletxt.xml, styletxt.xsl

Lisa asks you to design another style sheet for her. Many of her clients are not looking for a house in a particular geographic area as much as they are looking for one of a particular style. She wants you to create a new style sheet based on her property data that groups the property report by housing style. She has already created the style sheet for the property report, but needs your help in grouping the properties. Figure 8-40 shows a preview of the report you'll help her create.

Figure 8-40

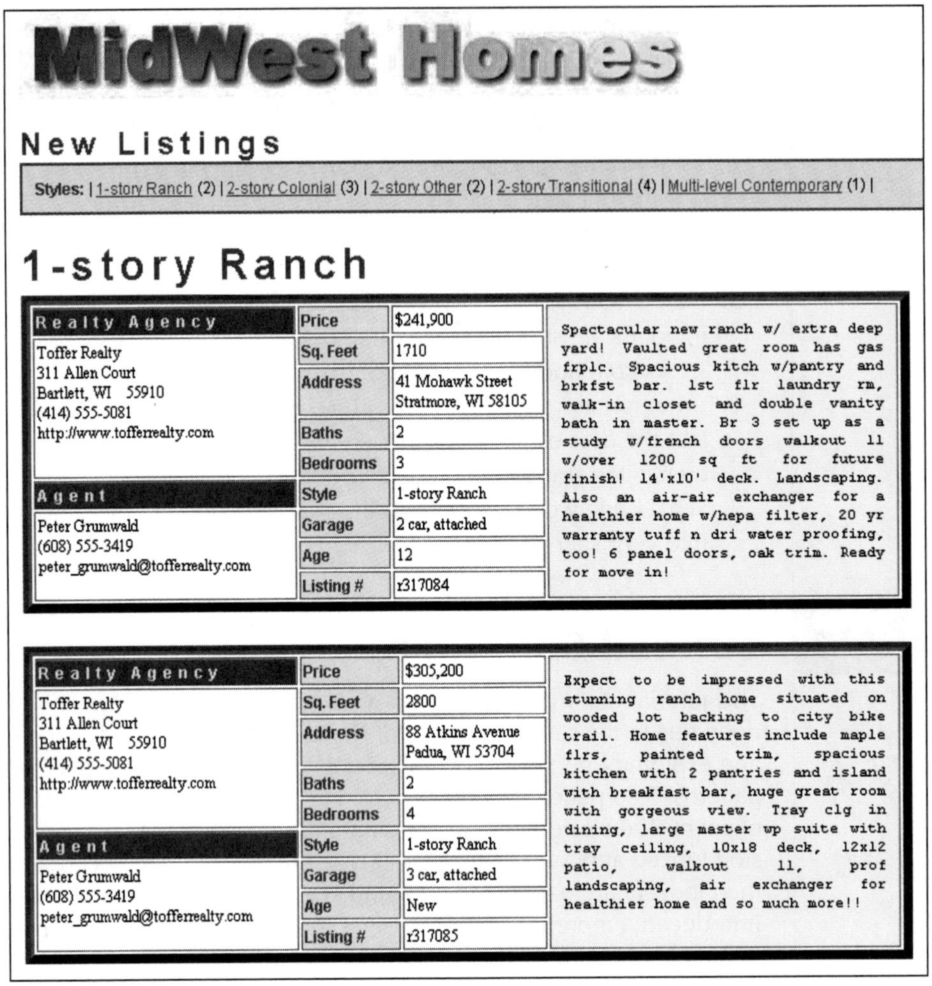

MidWest Homes

New Listings

Styles: | 1-story Ranch (2) | 2-story Colonial (3) | 2-story Other (2) | 2-story Transitional (4) | Multi-level Contemporary (1) |

1-story Ranch

Realty Agency	Price	$241,900	Spectacular new ranch w/ extra deep yard! Vaulted great room has gas frplc. Spacious kitch w/pantry and brkfst bar. 1st flr laundry rm, walk-in closet and double vanity bath in master. Br 3 set up as a study w/french doors walkout ll w/over 1200 sq ft for future finish! 14'x10' deck. Landscaping. Also an air-air exchanger for a healthier home w/hepa filter, 20 yr warranty tuff n dri water proofing, too! 6 panel doors, oak trim. Ready for move in!
Toffer Realty 311 Allen Court Bartlett, WI 55910 (414) 555-5081 http://www.tofferrealty.com	Sq. Feet	1710	
	Address	41 Mohawk Street Stratmore, WI 58105	
	Baths	2	
	Bedrooms	3	
Agent	Style	1-story Ranch	
Peter Grumwald (608) 555-3419 peter_grumwald@tofferrealty.com	Garage	2 car, attached	
	Age	12	
	Listing #	r317084	

Realty Agency	Price	$305,200	Expect to be impressed with this stunning ranch home situated on wooded lot backing to city bike trail. Home features include maple flrs, painted trim, spacious kitchen with 2 pantries and island with breakfast bar, huge great room with gorgeous view. Tray clg in dining, large master wp suite with tray ceiling, 10x18 deck, 12x12 patio, walkout ll, prof landscaping, air exchanger for healthier home and so much more!!
Toffer Realty 311 Allen Court Bartlett, WI 55910 (414) 555-5081 http://www.tofferrealty.com	Sq. Feet	2800	
	Address	88 Atkins Avenue Padua, WI 53704	
	Baths	2	
	Bedrooms	4	
Agent	Style	1-story Ranch	
Peter Grumwald (608) 555-3419 peter_grumwald@tofferrealty.com	Garage	3 car, attached	
	Age	New	
	Listing #	r317085	

The property report should also contain information on the real estate agencies and agents handling the properties. Since working on her last project, Lisa has placed all of this information within a single file. Figure 8-41 shows the structure of the new agencies file. You have to extract information from this second source document to complete the report.

Figure 8-41

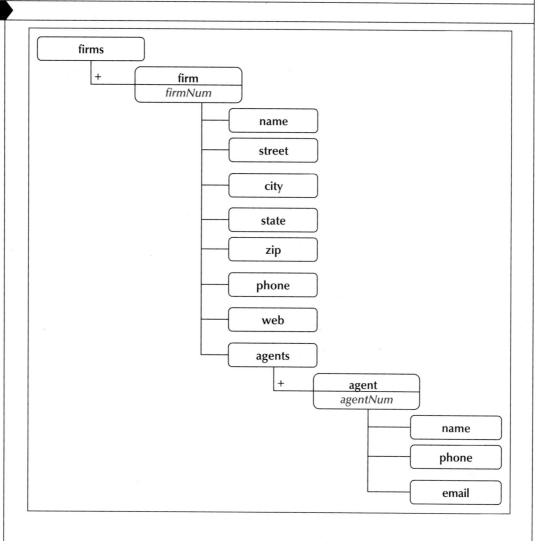

To complete this task:

1. Using your text editor, open **styletxt.xml** and **styletxt.xsl** from the tutorial.08x/review folder: Enter *your name* and *the date* in the comment section of each file, and save them as **style.xml** and **style.xsl** respectively.

2. Go to the style.xml file in your text editor. Add a processing instruction after the comment section that attaches this XML document to the style.xsl style sheet. Close the file, saving your changes.

3. Go to the style.xsl file in your text editor, and review the content of the style sheet and the different templates it contains. At the top of the file, directly below the opening <xsl:stylesheet> tag, do the following:

   • Create a variable named agencies that selects the agencies.xml file.

   • Create a key named agentID that matches the agent element, using values of the agentNum attribute to generate the key index.

   • Create a key named firmID that matches the firm element, using values of the firmNum attribute to generate the key index.

   • Create a key named styles that matches the property element, using values of the style element to generate the key index.

4. At the bottom of the style sheet, insert a moded template named styleList that matches the property element. The purpose of this template is to create a list of the different housing styles associated with the properties in the style.xml document. Have the template write the following code:

```
<a href="#id">style</a> (count) |
```
where *id* is an ID value generated automatically by the XSLT processor, *style* is the value of the style element, and *count* is the number of properties that contain that *style*. (*Hint*: Use the key() function and the styles key to retrieve the node set of properties belonging to a particular style, and use the XPath count() function to calculate the number of properties in that node set.)

5. Go to the root template. Directly above the closing </div> tag, apply the styleList moded template sorted by style. Use a step pattern to select only the first property in the source document associated with each style. (*Hint*: Use the same step pattern form used in Session 8.1 to generate the city list.)

6. Between the closing </div> tag and the closing </body> tag, insert a for-each element. The value of the select attribute for the for-each element should contain the first property in the source document associated with each housing style. Use Muenchian grouping in the expression that selects this node set. (*Hint*: Use the same type of grouping expression applied in Session 8.2 to generate the list of city headings.) Within the for-each element, add the following:

   - Sort the output by values of the style element.
   - For each style, write the following code to the result document:
     ```
     <h1 id="id">style</h1>
     ```
     where *id* is an ID value generated automatically by the XSLT processor and *style* is the value of the style element.
   - Apply a template for each property belonging to the selected housing style. (*Hint*: Use the key() function with the styles key and the value of the style element.) Sort the applied template by the sqfeet element.

7. Go to the property template. The purpose of this template is to display a table describing each property. Most of the contents of the table have already been created for you. Your task is to insert the firm and agent data into the table in the appropriate cells. To insert the firm data, insert the following below the comment "Place Firm Data Here":

   - Declare a variable named fID, selecting the value of the firm attribute.
   - Insert a for-each element, selecting the value of the agencies variable.
   - Within the for-each element, write the following code to the result document:
     ```
     name <br />
     street <br />
     city,
     state   
     zip <br />
     phone <br />
     web
     ```
     where *name*, *street*, *city*, *state*, *zip*, *phone*, and *web* are the values of the name, street, city, state, zip, phone, and web elements for the selected firm in the agencies.xml file. (*Hint*: Use the key() function with the firmID key and the value of the fID variable to select the appropriate firm element from the agencies.xml file.)

8. Insert the following below the comment "Place Agent Data Here":
   - Declare a variable named aID, selecting the value of the agent attribute.
   - Insert a for-each element, selecting the value of the agencies variable.
   - Within the for-each element, write the following code to the result document:

   ```
   name <br />
   phone <br />
   email
   ```

   where `name`, `phone`, and `email` are the values of the name, phone, and email elements for the selected agent in the agencies.xml file.

9. Save your changes to the style.xsl file.

10. Use your Web browser or your XSLT processor to generate the result document. Verify that the property report displays each property grouped by housing style, that the list of housing styles includes a count of the number of each property within each style, that links within the style list jump the browser to the appropriate style section in the report, and that the agent and firm data are correctly retrieved from the agencies.xml file.

11. Submit the completed project to your instructor.

Case Problem 1

Data files needed for this Case Problem: comedy.css, comtxt.xml, comtxt.xsl

North American Film Academy   Al Olsen of the North American Film Academy is working on a list of the greatest American film comedies. To compile the list, he sent a questionnaire to film critics, reviewers, and professors, asking them to list their 20 favorite American comedies of all time. He received 162 responses and stored the results in an XML document. Figure 8-42 shows the structure of that document.

Figure 8-42

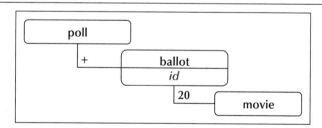

Al has placed each movie within a ballot element. The movie element contains a film name selected by the critic. He wants your help in creating a style sheet that lists the selected comedies. The list should be grouped by the names of the movies, sorted in descending order of votes. The votes are calculated by the number of times each movie name appears in the document. The list should also include the percentage of ballots that contain each movie. For example, the highest-rated comedy in Al's document is *Dr. Strangelove*, which received 95 votes and appeared on 58.64 percent of the ballots submitted. Figure 8-43 shows a preview of the movie report you'll create for Al.

Figure 8-43

The Top American Comedy Films

Number of Ballots: 162

Rank	Movie	Votes	%
1.	DR. STRANGELOVE (1964)	95	58.64%
2.	TOOTSIE (1982)	82	50.62%
3.	SINGIN' IN THE RAIN (1952)	75	46.30%
4.	THE PRODUCERS (1968)	75	46.30%
5.	DUCK SOUP (1933)	74	45.68%
6.	SOME LIKE IT HOT (1959)	72	44.44%
7.	AIRPLANE! (1980)	69	42.59%
8.	THE APARTMENT (1960)	68	41.98%
9.	CITY LIGHTS (1931)	67	41.36%
10.	THE GRADUATE (1967)	65	40.12%
11.	BLAZING SADDLES (1974)	64	39.51%
12.	M*A*S*H (1970)	64	39.51%
13.	ANNIE HALL (1977)	63	38.89%
14.	IT HAPPENED ONE NIGHT (1934)	63	38.89%
15.	THE GENERAL (1927)	63	38.89%
16.	THE GOLD RUSH (1925)	62	38.27%
17.	THE ODD COUPLE (1968)	59	36.42%
18.	THIS IS SPINAL TAP (1984)	59	36.42%
19.	YOUNG FRANKENSTEIN (1974)	59	36.42%
20.	BEING THERE (1979)	58	35.80%

Part of the style sheet has been created for you. Your job is to write the XSLT code that generates the list of movies, calculates the total votes for each, and sorts the list in descending order of votes.

To complete this task:

1. Using your text editor, open **comtxt.xml** and **comtxt.xsl** from the tutorial.08x/case1 folder: Enter *your name* and *the date* in the comment section of each file, and save them as **comedy.xml** and **comedy.xsl** respectively.

2. Go to the comedy.xml file in your text editor. Add a processing instruction after the comment section that attaches this XML document to the comedy.xsl style sheet. Take some time to examine the file, and then close the file, saving your changes.

3. Go to the comedy.xsl file in your text editor, and review the content of the style sheet and the different templates it contains. At the top of the file, directly below the opening <xsl:stylesheet> tag, create a key named movies that matches the movie element, using the value of that element to create the key index. (*Hint*: Set the value of the use attribute to the context node.)

4. Go to the root template and below the h2 heading, insert code to write the following text to the result document:

   `<p>Number of Ballots: total`
   where `total` is the total number of ballot elements in the source document.

5. Between the closing </tr> and </table> tags, insert a for-each element. In the select attribute, insert an expression that uses Muenchian grouping to select a node set containing the first occurrences of each movie. (*Hint*: Use the function key('movies', .)[1] to select individual movies.)

6. Within the for-each element you created in the last step, sort the movie list in descending order of votes for each movie, and in alphabetical order according to the movie names. (*Hint*: To sort the movies in descending order of votes, call the key() function with the movies key, using the value of the context node.)

7. Directly after the sorting of the node set (and within the for-each element), write the following code into the result document:

```
<tr>
    <td>position</td>
    <td>movie</td>
    <td class="right">count</td>
    <td class="right">percent</td>
</tr>
```

where *position* is the position of the movie in the result document, *movie* is the name of the movie, *count* is the total number of votes for the movie, and *percent* is the total number of votes for the movie divided by the total number of ballots. Use a number format to display the percent value as 0.00%. (*Hint*: To calculate the position of the movie, use the position() function applied to the context node.)

8. Finally, within the for-each element, test whether the position of the context node is divisible by 10. If it is, write the following code to the result document:

```
<tr>
    <td colspan="4"><hr /></td>
</tr>
```

(*Hint*: Use the mod operator to determine if the position value is divisible by 10.)

9. Save your changes to comedy.xsl.

10. Use your Web browser or XSLT processor to generate the result document. Verify that the movie report displays a list of 100 movie titles, sorted in descending order of votes. There should be a horizontal line separating each group of 10 movies.

11. Submit the completed project to your instructor.

Case Problem 2

Data files needed for this Case Problem: customers.xml, flowers.css, flowtxt.xsl, items.xml, orderstxt.xml

WebFlowers, Inc. Ivan Suryadi works on Web page design for WebFlowers, an online florist. Recently the company has been looking at ways to incorporate XML documents into order reports. Ivan created three sample XML documents named orders.xml, customers.xml, and items.xml. These documents contain order information and names of WebFlowers customers as well as items listed in the company's catalog. The structure of the three documents is shown in Figure 8-44.

Figure 8-44

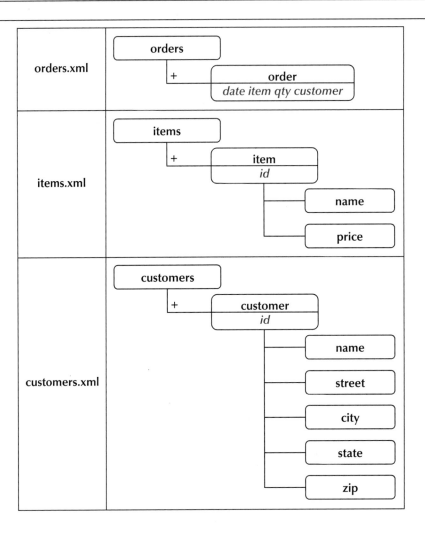

The item attribute in the orders.xml document is matched with the ID attribute in the items.xml file, and the customer attribute from orders.xml is similarly matched with the ID attribute in the customers.xml file. Ivan wants to combine information from these three documents on a single Web page that shows the order history of the company for a 5-day period. The page should display each order, the customers that submitted the order, the items purchased on each order, the quantities and prices of the items, and the total price of all of the items on the orders. The report should also include subtotals for each day and a grand total for the 5-day period. Figure 8-45 shows a preview of the page that Ivan wants to create.

Figure 8-45

Flower Orders

Date	Customer	Item	Price	Qty	Total
June-15-2008	Karen Karls 89 Mohawk Lane Madison, KY 89312	Large Flower Vase Arrangement	74.99	1	74.99
	Gary Wilkes 9837 Second Street Yale, OR 69023	One Dozen Pink Roses	62.99	1	62.99
	Home Notions 8634 Main Street Hawthorne, UT 58944	Flower Bowl	54.99	5	274.95
			Subtotal	**7**	**$412.93**
June-16-2008	Anthony Morranon 78 Alberone Avenue East Texas, OK 78121	Pedestal Bowl	49.99	1	49.99
	Andy Sertain 9317 Lawrence Street Banton, TX 65731	Yellow Daisy Vase	49.99	1	49.99
	Kitchen Wares 25 Mall Road Poulin, GA 34871	Medley Basket	54.99	4	219.96
	Michael White 111 Dixon Street North Forks, MN 61098	Pretty in Pink	49.99	1	49.99
			Subtotal	**7**	**$369.93**
June-17-2008	Maria Hoffman 8911 Third Street Oseola, WI 54871	One Dozen Pink Roses	62.99	1	62.99
	Dawson Nursing Home 311 Paulson Street Fennimore, PA 73213	Spring Fling Flowers	59.99	2	119.98
			Subtotal	**3**	**$182.97**
			Grand Total	**17**	**$965.83**

Part of the style sheet was created by Ivan and linked to the orders.xml file. Your job is to complete the style sheet by retrieving information from customers.xml and items.xml, as well as grouping the output by date.

To complete this task:

1. Using your text editor, open **orderstxt.xml** and **flowtxt.xsl** from the tutorial.08x/ case2 folder: Enter *your name* and *the date* in the comment section of each file, and save them as **orders.xml** and **flowers.xsl** respectively.
2. Go to the orders.xml file in your text editor. Add a processing instruction after the comment section that attaches this XML document to the flowers.xsl style sheet. Close the file, saving your changes. Open the **customers.xml** and **items.xml** file in your text editor, and review the contents of those files. Close the files without saving any changes you may inadvertently make.
3. Go to the flowers.xsl file in your text editor. Directly below the opening <xsl: stylesheet> tag, insert the following:
   - Declare a global variable named items that selects the items.xml file.
   - Declare a global variable named customers that selects the customers.xml file.
   - Create a key named itemID that matches the item element, using values of the ID attribute to generate the key index.

- Create a key named custID that matches the customer element, using values of the ID attribute.
- Create a key named date that matches the order element, using values of the date attribute.

Explore

4. To complete the order report, you need to create a recursive template to calculate the total cost for each day and for the 5-day period. The recursive template will be similar to the one you created in Tutorial 7, but in this case some of the values will be retrieved from the items.xml file. To calculate the total cost, insert a template named totalCost at the bottom of the style sheet and add the following:
   - Declare two template parameters named list and total. The list parameter will be used to store a list of item prices and values. The total parameter will be used to store a running total of the total item price. Set the default value of the total parameter to 0.
   - Insert a choose element that tests whether the list parameter contains an empty node set.
   - If the list parameter is not empty, declare a local variable named first that stores the first list parameter node, a variable named iID that is equal to the value of the item attribute of the first variable, and a variable named itemQty that is equal to the value of the qty attribute of the first variable.
   - Insert a for-each element that selects the value of the items variable (recall that this is a global variable that points to the items.xml file). The purpose of the for-each element is to change the context node to the items.xml file so you can retrieve the price of items ordered by the customer. Within the for-each element, declare a local variable named itemPrice that returns the price value of an item element whose ID attribute equals the iID variable. (*Hint*: Use the key() function with the itemID key and the iID variable.)
   - Call the totalCost template with the value of the list parameter set to values in the list whose position in the node set is greater than 1 and with the value of the total parameter equal to the value of the itemQty variable multiplied by the itemPrice variable plus the current value of the total parameter.
   - If the list parameter is empty, then return the value of the total parameter displayed with the number format $#,#00.00.

5. Go to the order template. The purpose of this template is to display orders for a specific date in the source document. The template also displays subtotals for all of the orders on that date. At the top of the order template, declare the following local variables:
   - A variable named cID that selects the value of the customer attribute
   - A variable named iID that selects the value of the item attribute
   - A variable named qtyValue that selects the value of the qty attribute

6. Go to the comment "Display order date." The order table contains a table cell displaying the date of the order. The cell should span the number of rows equal to the number of orders placed on that date plus 2. To create the row-spanning cell, add the following below the comment:
   - Insert an if element that tests whether the value of the position() function for the context node is equal to 1.
   - If this is the first order, then write the following code to the result document:
     ```
     <td rowspan="rows" class="date">
        date
     </td>
     ```

where *rows* is the number of rows for the date cell to span and *date* is the value of the date attribute. To calculate the value of *rows* use the date key you created in Step 3 and the value of the date attribute to return a node set of all orders from a given date. Use the count() function to count the number of nodes in this node set and add it to that value.

7. Go to the comment "Display customer information." This section of the template displays information about a customer submitting an order on that date. Below the comment, add the following:

   - Insert a for-each element that selects the value of the customers variable that you created in Step 3.
   - Within the for-each element, write the following code to the result document:

     ```
     <td>
     name <br />
     street <br />
     city,
     state   
     zip
     </td>
     ```

     where *name, street, city, state,* and *zip* are values of the name, street, city, state, and zip elements from the customers.xml file. (*Hint*: Use the custID key you created in Step 3 with the value of the cID variable you created in Step 5.)

8. Go to the comment "Display item name and price." This section of the template displays the name and price of each item. Below the comment, add the following:

   - Insert a for-each element that selects the value of the items variable.
   - Within the for-each element, write the following code to the result document:

     ```
     <td>
         name
     </td>
     <td class="num">
         price
     </td>
     ```

     where *name* and *price* are values of the name and price elements from the items.xml file. To retrieve these values use the itemID key with the value of the iID variable.

9. Go to the comment "Display cost of items ordered." This section of the template calculates the cost of each item (multiplying the item price by the quantity ordered). Below the comment, add the following:

   - Insert a for-each element that selects the value of the items variable.
   - Within the for-each element, write the following code to the result document:

     ```
     <td class="num">
         item cost
     </td>
     ```

     where *item cost* is the price of the item multiplied by the quantity ordered. To determine the item price use the itemID key and the value of the iID variable. To determine the quantity ordered use the qtyValue variable that you created in Step 5. Use the format-number() function to format the product of these two values using the number format #0.00.

10. Go to the comment "Display subtotals." This section of the template displays the subtotals for the orders on the given day. Do the following:
    - Go to the empty table cell directly below the Subtotal table cell. Within this table cell, display the sum of qty attributes for the orders on the current date. (*Hint*: Use the date key with the date attribute to return the orders for the current date. Use the sum() function to calculate the sum of the qty attributes within that node set.)
    - Within the next table cell, apply the totalCost template you created in Step 4, using the node set returned by the date key using the date attribute. You do not have to specify a value for the total parameter.
11. Go to the root template. Between the two table rows, insert code to create table rows that describe the orders taken on each date. To create the table rows, do the following:
    - Insert a for-each element that employs Muenchian grouping to select first order elements from each unique date in the source document.
    - Sort the for-each element by values of the date attribute.
    - Apply the order template by selecting the node set generated by the date key using the value of the date attribute. Sort the application of the order template by the value of the customer attribute.
12. The last table row in the root template displays the grand total of orders in the source document. Add the following to that table row:
    - Within the second table cell, display the sum of all qty attributes in the source document.
    - Within the third table cell, call the totalCost template with the list parameter equal to the node set of all order elements in the source document. You do not have to specify a value for the total parameter.
13. Close the flowers.xsl file, saving your changes.
14. Use your Web browser or XSLT processor to generate the result document. Verify that the order report displays a table of all orders in the orders.xml document grouped by date. The table should also display customer and item information taken from the customers.xml and items.xml files and correctly calculate the subtotals from each order date and the grand total of all orders.
15. Submit the completed project to your instructor.

Challenge

Explore how to use step patterns, axes, and Muenchian grouping to create a report on the history of the World Series

Case Problem 3

Data files needed for this Case Problem: ws.css, wstxt.xml, wstxt.xsl

SportStats, Inc. Steve Karsten works for SportsStats, Inc., a company that publishes statistics for a wide variety of sporting events. Steve approached you with a problem, and he needs help. He has an XML workbook that contains the results of all of the Major League Baseball World Series. The structure of the file is shown in Figure 8-46. The results of the series are contained in the series element. The year is stored in the year attribute, and the MVP of the series is contained in the mvp attribute. Each series element contains two team elements. The first team element stores information about the series winner, and the second team element stores information about the loser. Both elements are empty. The name of the team is stored in the name attribute, and the number of games the team won in the series is stored in the wins attribute.

Figure 8-46

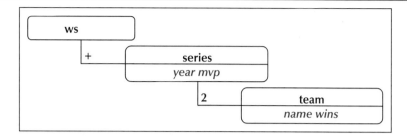

Steve needs your help to create a report of this data. There are three tables in the report. The first table should display the outcome of each World Series, sorted in descending order of date. The second table should display each club's record in the World Series, reporting the number of Series appearances, Series won, lost, and the number of games won and lost. The table should be sorted in descending order of the number of World Series appearances. The third table should report the years that each club appeared in the World Series. The table should be sorted by club name. Figure 8-47 shows a preview of the World Series report.

Figure 8-47

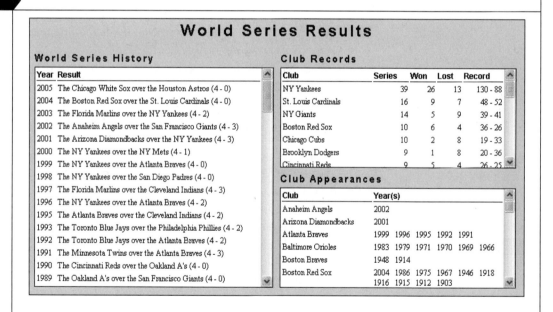

To complete this task:

1. Using your text editor, open **wstxt.xml** and **wstxt.xsl** from the tutorial.08x/case3 folder: Enter *your name* and *the date* in the comment section of each file, and save them as **ws.xml** and **ws.xsl** respectively.

2. Go to the ws.xml file in your text editor. Add a processing instruction after the comment section that attaches this XML document to the ws.xsl style sheet. Close the file, saving your changes.

3. Go to the ws.xsl file in your text editor. Directly below the opening <xsl:stylesheet> tag, add the following:
   - A key named winners that matches the first team element, using values of the name attribute to generate the key index
   - A key named losers that matches the second team element, using values of the name attribute
   - A key named teams that matches the team element, using values of the name attribute

4. Go to the first table. This table displays the yearly results of the World Series. Below the first table row, insert a for-each element that selects every series element in the source document. Add the following to the for-each element:
   - Sort the for-each element by descending order of the year attribute. Treat the year attribute value as a number.
   - Write the following code to the result document:

```
<tr>
    <td>year</td>
    <td>The name1 over the name2
        (win1 - win2)
    </td>
</tr>
```

   where *year* is the value of the year attribute, *name1* is the value of the name attribute for the first team, *name2* is the value of the name attribute for the second team, *win1* is the value of the wins attribute for the first team, and *win2* is the value of the wins attribute for the second team.

5. Go to the second table. This table displays the overall records of different clubs that have appeared in the World Series. Below the first table row of this table, insert a for-each element. The for-each element should use Muenchian grouping to select a node set of team elements, one for each club name (use the name attribute of the team element). Sort the contents of the for-each element as follows:
   - Sort the for-each element by descending order of the number of appearances of each team in the World Series. (*Hint*: Apply the count() function to the teams key, using the value of the name attribute to return the number of appearances by each team.) Treat the count value as a number.
   - Sort the for-each element by the value of the name attribute.

Explore

6. Next you have to calculate the number of games won and lost by each team throughout the entire history of the World Series. You do this by declaring variables within the for-each element:
   - Declare the teamName variable equal to the value of the name attribute.
   - Declare the gamesWon variable equal to the sum of the wins attribute for each team. (*Hint*: Use the teams key with the name attribute to create a list of the team elements for a given team. Apply the sum() function to the wins attribute of those teams.)
   - There is no attribute for the losses incurred by each team. Instead you have to count the number of wins of their opponent in the series in which they appear. There are two node sets you have to create: one for the opponents who lose the World Series and one for opponents who win the World Series.

- Declare the losses1 variable. This variable contains the node set of the opponents that lost the World Series. To create this node set, select all of the team elements in the source document whose position equals 1 and whose first following sibling has a name attribute with a value equal to the teamName variable. (*Hint:* Use the following-sibling axes to select the following sibling.)
- Declare the losses2 variable. This variable contains the node set of the opponents that won the World Series. To create this node set, select all of the team elements in the source document whose position equals 2 and whose first preceding sibling has a name attribute with a value equal to the teamName variable.
- Declare the gamesLost variable. The value of this variable is equal to the sum of the wins attribute in the losses1 node set plus the sum of the wins attribute in the losses2 node set.

7. Within the for-each element you created in Step 5, write the following code to the result document:

```
<tr>
    <td>name</td>
    <td class="num">appearances</td>
    <td class="num">wins</td>
    <td class="num">losses</td>
    <td class="num">gamesWon - gamesLost</td>
</tr>
```

where *appearances* is the count of elements in the teams key using the value of the name attribute; *wins* is the count of elements in the winners key using the value of the name attribute; *losses* is the count of elements in the losers key using the value of the name attribute; and *gamesWon* and *gamesLost* are the values of the gamesWon and gamesLost variables.

> **Explore**

8. Go to the third table. The purpose of this table is to display a list of appearances by each team in the source document. To display this information, insert a for-each element below the first table row. The for-each element should use Muenchian grouping to select each unique team name. Within the for-each element, do the following:
   - Sort the for-each element by the value of the name attribute.
   - Write the following code to the result document:
     ```
     <tr>
         <td>name</td>
         <td>
             year list
         </td>
     </tr>
     ```
     where *name* is the value of the name attribute and *year list* is a space-separated list of years in which the team appeared in the World Series.
   - To create *year list*, insert an embedded for-each element that selects the teams key using the value of the name attribute. Within the for-each element, write the code:
     ```
     year  
     ```
     where *year* is the value of the year attribute of the series element. (*Hint:* Use the parent axes to go up the node tree from the context node, and then go to the series element.)

9. Close the ws.xsl style sheet, saving your changes.

10. Use your Web browser or XSLT processor to generate the result document. Verify that the World Series report displays three tables: a table of the yearly outcomes, a table of records by club, and a table listing the appearances of each club.

11. Submit the completed project to your instructor.

Case Problem 4

Data files needed for this Case Problem: logo.jpg, montxt.xml, montxt.xsl, persons.xml

Lighthouse Charitable Trust   Denise Murchanson is the fundraising coordinator for the Lighthouse Charitable Trust, a charitable organization located in central Kentucky. One of her responsibilities is to maintain a record of donations by individuals. Denise has two XML documents. The first document, money.xml, contains a list of 60 donations given to the organization within the last two months. Each donation has a personal identification number (pin) that indicates the individual who made the donation. A second document, persons.xml, contains contact information for each individual. Each individual has a pid attribute that matches the pin value from the money.xml document. Figure 8-48 shows the structure of both documents.

Figure 8-48

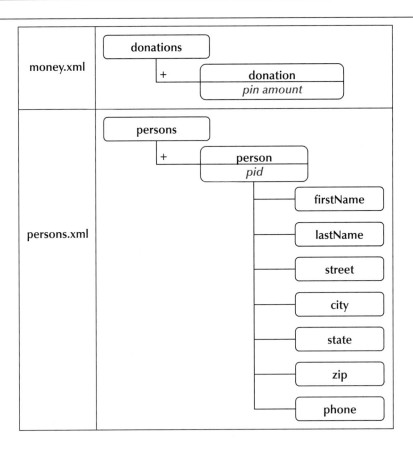

Denise wants to generate a report listing current donors, grouped by the amount of their donations. She needs you to create a style sheet that displays information about all contributors and the amount of money they donated to the trust.

To complete this task:

1. Using your text editor, open **montxt.xml** and **montxt.xsl** from the tutorial.08x/case4 folder: Enter *your name* and *the date* in the comment section of each file, and save them as **money.xml** and **money.xsl** respectively.
2. Attach the money.xsl style sheet to the money.xml file.
3. Add styles to the money.xsl style sheet to generate the contribution report. The style and layout of the report is left up to you, but it must include the following features:
   - The total amount of donations and the total number of donors must be displayed in the report.
   - Each contribution amount must be presented in a list at the top of the report. The amounts should be sorted from highest to lowest.
   - The list of contributors must be grouped by the amount of money contributed. The contribution groups should be sorted in descending numeric order.
   - Within each contribution group, the name and address of the person who contributed that amount must be displayed.
   - There should be links between the list of contribution amounts at the top of the page and the section of the report in which the contributors at that donation level appear.
   - All monetary amounts should appear in a currency format.
   - The report should calculate and display the total donations and number of contributors per group and overall.
4. Test your style sheet on your Web browser or an XSLT processor, and verify that all required elements are displayed and that the contributor list is properly grouped.
5. Submit the completed project to your instructor.

Review

Quick Check Answers

Session 8.1

1. The axis that defines how to move through the node tree, the node test that specifies the node for the step pattern to match, and the predicate that further tests the nodes to see if they match a particular pattern
2. self::node()
3. child::property/child::city
4. property/@rln
5. Moded templates are templates that apply different styles to the same node set in the source document.
6. <xsl:template match="property" mode="propertyList">
7. *styles*
8. </xsl:template>
9. <xsl:apply-templates select="/listings/property" mode="propertyList">

Session 8.2

1. You must create a unique ID for each ID attribute, even if they are associated with different elements.
2. id("f102")
3. ID values cannot begin with numbers.

4. A key is an index that matches values of either an element or an attribute with nodes in the source document. Keys are declared in the style sheet, not the DTD. Keys can have names as well as values. Keys can be associated with node sets that contain attribute and element values. Keys can have values that are not limited to XML names.

5. <xsl:key name="agentNames match="agent" use="agentName" />

6. key("agentNames, "Howard")

7. generate-id(agentName)

8. agent[generate-id()=generate-id(key("agentNames, agentName))]

Session 8.3

1. document("stores.xml")

2. The document() function is used to include several XML documents within a single style sheet. The <xsl:include> and <xsl:import> elements are used to combine several style sheets with a single XML document.

3. document("stores.xml")//store_name

4. A for element using a variable that points to the external source document

5. <xsl:stylesheet version="1.0"
   xmlns:xsl="http:/www.w3.org/1999/XSL/Transform"
   xmlns:stores=" http://www.stores.com">

6. document("")/xsl:stylesheet/storesNS:stores/store

7. <xsl:copy-of select="document('logo.htm')" />

Objectives

Session 9.1
- Work with fields, records, and recordsets
- Create a data island
- Bind Web page elements to XML fields
- Implement the dataformatas attribute

Session 9.2
- Work with attribute fields
- Move through the records in a recordset
- Work with the methods and properties of a recordset

Session 9.3
- Work with data table binding
- Display table data in pages
- Bind a Web page to a hierarchical recordset

Using XML as a Data Source

Binding Web Elements to XML with Internet Explorer

Case

Freezing Point Refrigerators

Freezing Point is a company that manufactures and sells refrigerators and other kitchen appliances. To make information easily accessible to its employees, the company maintains an intranet with Web pages containing a wide variety of corporate information.

Catherine Davis is a personnel manager at Freezing Point and has been assigned the job of putting the staff directory on the company's intranet. Her Web page needs to include each employee's name, department, position, phone number, years of service, and job status, as well as a picture of each employee.

Catherine has stored all of the information in an XML document, but she needs a way to put that information into her Web page. She doesn't want to reenter all of the information into an HTML file, because doing so would be time consuming and she might make an error in transferring the data. Catherine also doesn't want to have to edit the Web page every time employee information changes, which happens frequently. Catherine knows there is a way to display XML data in a formatted Web page. She finds this an attractive option because it means she would need to maintain only the XML document. Catherine can format the Web page herself, but she needs your help to place XML data in her report.

NOTE: The tasks in this tutorial require Internet Explorer for Windows version 5.0 or above and a working knowledge of JavaScript.

Student Data Files

▼tutorial.09x

▽ tutorial folder	▽ review folder	▽ case1 folder
fp1txt.htm	inv1txt.htm	amtxt.htm
fp2txt.htm	inv2txt.htm	autoord.xml
fp3txt.htm	inv3txt.htm	amstyles.css
+ 3 XML documents	+ 3 XML documents	
+ 3 CSS style sheets	+ 3 CSS style sheets	
+ 21 image files	+ 13 image files	

Session 9.1

Introducing Data Binding

You and Catherine meet to discuss her ideas for the staff directory Web page that will be placed on the company's intranet. She has already designed a layout for the Web page. She has inserted placeholder text into her page that she wants you to replace with data drawn from an XML document containing staff information. To see her progress, open her current Web page.

To open the staff page:

1. Use your text editor to open **fp1txt.htm** from the tutorial.09x/tutorial folder. Enter **your name** and **the date** in the comment section at the top of the file, and save the file as **fp1.htm**.

2. Open the fp1.htm file in Internet Explorer. Figure 9-1 shows the current appearance of the page.

| Figure 9-1 | Initial staff page |

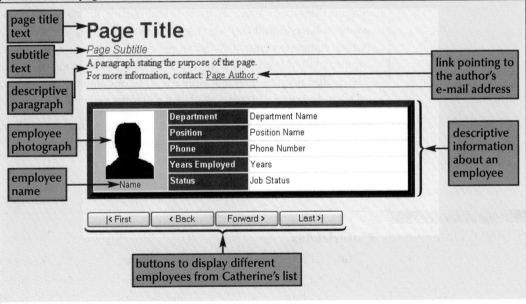

The staff page contains the following elements that need to be populated with data (see Figure 9-1):

- Title
- Subtitle
- Paragraph describing the purpose and content of the page
- Link pointing to the e-mail address of the Web page author
- Table containing an employee's name, photo, department, position, phone number, years of service, and job status

The page shows information on only one employee at a time, so in addition to the above data, the page also contains a set of buttons to allow users to move through the list of employees. The First and Last buttons move the user to the first and last employees in the list, and the Back and Forward buttons move the user forward and backward through the list one employee at a time.

Up to this point, if you've wanted to use data from an XML document in a Web page, you've either had to create a compound document combining elements from HTML and your XML vocabulary, or you've written an XSLT style sheet to display the XML data in HTML format. However, Catherine does not see how either approach will work for her document as the Web page will display information about only one employee at a time, and it will be left to the user via the Web form buttons to select which employee to display.

Another approach that you'll investigate in this tutorial and the next involves using JavaScript and some HTML elements to retrieve data from an XML document. The XML document acts as a source of data for the Web page in much the same way a database might act as a data source for an application. In this tutorial, you'll look at an approach developed specifically for the Internet Explorer browser that involves data binding.

Data binding is a process by which information in a data source is stored as an object in computer memory. Data binding can be used with a wide variety of possible data sources, from complex databases to simple text files. In this case, the data source is an XML document. Data from the XML document is bound with elements in an HTML document. When the page is rendered by a browser, the data from the XML document is automatically inserted into the Web page (see Figure 9-2.)

Data binding   **Figure 9-2**

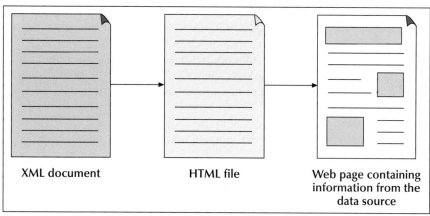

XML document   HTML file   Web page containing information from the data source

One of the advantages of data binding is that it frees data from the format in which it is displayed. For the Web, this means that the same data source can be combined with several different Web pages without forcing a Web page designer to reenter that data (see Figure 9-3). It also makes it easier to design a Web page, because a designer has to be concerned only with the appearance of the page, not with its content.

Figure 9-3 **Data binding with several Web pages**

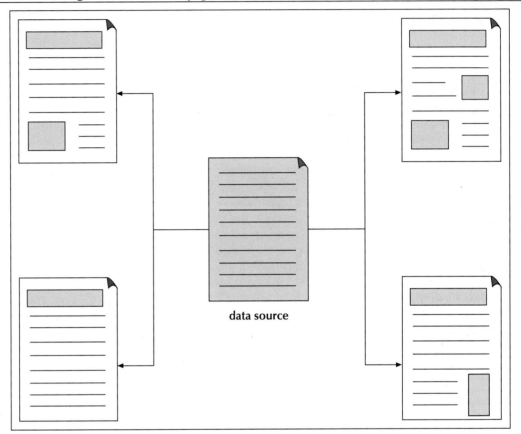

data source

You should apply the data-binding techniques discussed in this tutorial only in situations where you know users are running the Internet Explorer browser. In the next tutorial, you'll look at a more advanced solution that has wider browser support; however, if you only need to support Internet Explorer, the techniques in this tutorial are easier to implement. This is the case with Catherine's project as her Web page will only be made available to the company's intranet.

Figure 9-4 shows a preview of how Catherine wants you to use data from her XML documents to create a final Web page displaying information about the company and its employees.

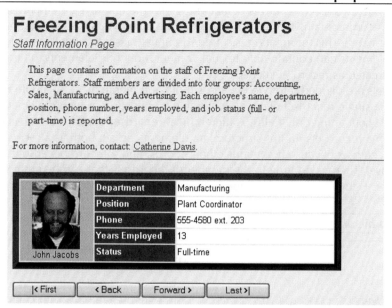

Before you can apply data binding to the staff directory Web page, you first need to look at how the data contained in an XML document is organized and referenced.

Understanding Fields, Records, and Recordsets

Data in a data source is organized by fields, records, and recordsets. For XML documents, a **field** or **field element** is an element that contains a single item of information, such as an employee's last name or age. A collection of these fields for a single entity is stored in a **record** or **record element**. Finally, a collection of records is stored within a **recordset** or **recordset element**. Figure 9-5 demonstrates how to interpret the contents of an XML document in terms of fields, records, and recordsets.

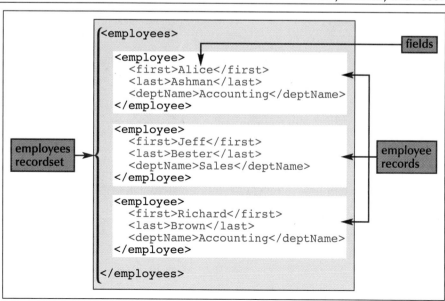

This particular XML document contains a single recordset named employees that stores three records. Each record is contained within the employee element. Each employee record contains three fields that store the employee's first and last names and department name. This information is stored in the first, last, and deptName fields. Note that field elements can contain only textual content, not child elements; otherwise, they would be treated as record elements.

Recordsets are divided into two classes: simple and hierarchical. A **simple recordset** consists of a single recordset element containing a collection of record elements, with each record containing only fields. A **hierarchical recordset** contains a collection of nested simple recordsets. In this structure, an element can act both as a recordset and a record: a recordset because it contains other records, and a record because it is a child of a recordset. There is no limit to the number of recordsets that can be nested within one another. Figure 9-6 shows examples of simple and hierarchical recordsets.

Figure 9-6 | **Simple and hierarchical recordsets**

```
<employees>

  <employee>
    <first>Alice</first>
    <last>Ashman</last>
    <deptName>Accounting</deptName>
  </employee>
  <employee>
    <first>Jeff</first>
    <last>Bester</last>
    <deptName>Saes<deptName>
  </employee>
  <employee>
    <first>Richard</first>
    <last>Brown</last>
    <deptName>Accounting</deptName>
  </employee>

</employees>
```

simple recordset

```
<employees>

  <department>
    <deptName>Accounting</deptName>
    <employee>
      <first>Alice</first>
      <last>Ashman</last>
    </employee>
    <employee>
      <first>Tom</first>
      <last>Forrest</last>
    </employee>
  </department>

  <department>
    <deptName>Sales</deptName>
    <employee>
      <first>Jeff</first>
      <last>Bester</last>
    </employee>
  </department>

</employees>
```

hierarchical recordset

The recordset on the left is a simple recordset. It contains a single recordset element named employees. The employees element contains three employee records, and each record contains three fields, storing the first, last, and deptName data. The recordset on the right is hierarchical, incorporating two levels of recordsets. The employees recordset contains records on individual departments at the company. Each of the department records also acts as a recordset containing a collection of employee records for employees in that department as well as the deptName field containing the department's name.

The distinction between simple and hierarchical recordsets is important because Internet Explorer uses different data-binding techniques depending on the type of the recordset stored in a data source. Start by exploring how to retrieve data from simple recordsets. Later in the tutorial you'll look at techniques for dealing with hierarchical recordsets.

Creating a Data Island

The first step in data binding is to attach the Web page to a data source called a **data island**. A data island refers to either an external file or data entered directly into the HTML file. The syntax to create a data island from an external file is

```
<xml id="id" src="url"></xml>
```

where *id* is an ID name assigned to the data island, and *url* is the filename and location of the data source file. For example, to create a data island named company that points to an XML document named company.xml you enter the following code into your HTML file:

```
<xml id="company" src="company.xml"></xml>
```

To insert a data island directly into an HTML file, you use the syntax

```
<xml id="id">
    data
</xml>
```

where *data* is the content of an XML document containing the data you want to access from the Web page. The following code illustrates how a data island is placed directly into an HTML file:

```
<xml id="staff">
    <?xml version="1.0"?>
    <employees>
        <employee>
            <first>Alice</first>
            <last>Ashman</last>
            <deptName>Accounting</deptName>
        </employee>
        <employee>
            <first>Jeff</first>
            <last>Bester</last>
            <deptName>Sales</deptName>
        </employee>
    </employees>
</xml>
```

The xml element can be placed within either the head or the body section of the HTML file. Note that you have to include all of the features of an XML document, including the xml declaration and the root element. Also note that you do not have to specify a separate namespace for the contents of the xml element; however, the content does have to be well formed.

It is generally not useful to insert XML code directly into an HTML file. After all, the whole philosophy of data binding is to separate data content from the Web page. By placing her data in a separate document, Catherine can update her staff listings and company information without editing the Web page itself. Similarly, she can edit the appearance of her Web page without having to worry about data content.

Creating a Data Island

- To create a data island for data stored in a separate file, insert the following element into the HTML file:

  `<xml id="id" src="url"></xml>`

  where *id* is the ID name assigned to the data island, and *url* is the filename and location of the data source file.
- To create a data island for data entered directly into an HTML file, use the following element:

  ```
  <xml id="id">
      data
  </xml>
  ```

  where *data* is the data content of the data island. For XML data, the content must be well formed.

How Data Islands Are Stored

When Internet Explorer creates a data island from either an internal or external XML source, the XML parser built into Internet Explorer reads and stores the data island as a **Data Source Object** or **DSO**. The DSO handles all of the interaction between the browser and the data island, supplying the values from the data island for each element in the Web page. In addition, you can write program code to control the actions of the DSO, such as specifying which records are displayed in the Web page at a given time. If the XML document is not well formed or valid, Internet Explorer does not create a DSO. Unfortunately, it does not report the source of the problem to the user.

It is also important to note that a DSO is created only once for each session. If the contents of the data source are modified after Internet Explorer creates the initial DSO, those changes are not reflected in the Web page until the next time the page is opened or refreshed by the browser.

Creating a Data Island

You start your work on the staff Web page by creating a data island and attaching the contents of the fpinfo.xml file to Catherine's sample page. The fpinfo.xml file contains descriptive information about the staff directory page. The contents of the file are described in Figure 9-7.

Figure 9-7 | **The contents of the fpinfo.xml file**

Element	Description
information	The root element of the document
title	The report's title
subtitle	The report's subtitle
purpose	Description of the report's purpose
author	The report's author
authorEmail	E-mail address of the report's author

Figure 9-8 shows the structure of the document.

Structure of the fpinfo document ◀ **Figure 9-8**

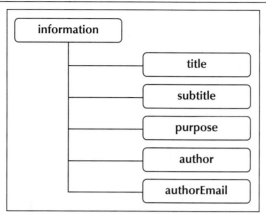

To create a data island:

1. Use your text editor to open **fpinfo.xml** from the tutorial.09x/tutorial folder.

2. Take some time to examine the contents of the file. Note that it contains a simple recordset containing five fields: title, subtitle, purpose, author, and authorEmail.

3. Close the file, but do not save any changes you may have inadvertently made to the document.

4. Return to the **fp1.htm** file in your text editor.

5. Directly above the closing </head> tag insert the following HTML code (see Figure 9-9):

```
<xml id="pageInfo" src="fpinfo.xml"></xml>
```

Creating the pageInfo data island ◀ **Figure 9-9**

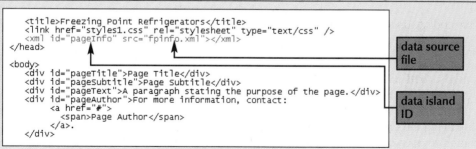

The next step is to bind elements in the staff Web page to the five fields from the fpinfo.xml document.

Binding an HTML Element to a Field

Catherine wants to display field values from the fpinfo.xml file in the Web page elements described below (see Figure 9-10):

- Page title in the title field
- Page subtitle in the subtitle field
- Paragraph describing the purpose of the page in the purpose field
- Name of the page's author in the author field
- Target of the page author link in the authorEmail field

Figure 9-10 ▶ **Fields in the staff report page**

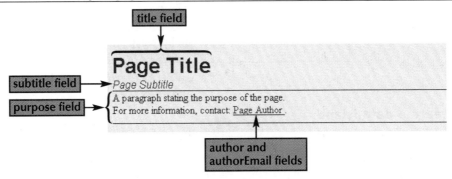

The syntax for binding an HTML element to a data field is

```
<elem datasrc="#id" datafld="field"> ... </elem>
```

where `elem` is the name of the HTML element, `id` is the ID of the data island, and `field` is the name of the field in the data source. Not every HTML element supports data binding, however, and the field value is not applied to every element in the same way. For some elements, the field value is displayed in the Web page as part of the element's content. For example, you can bind a span element to a data field, as in the following code:

```
<span datasrc="#id" datafld="field"></span>
```

This code causes Internet Explorer to write the following code to the Web page:

```
<span>field value</span>
```

where `field value` is the value of the field. Any content that might have been previously placed within the span element would be overwritten by the field value. It is important to note that Internet Explorer preserves any line breaks in the field value when displaying the text in the Web page. If you don't want to preserve any line breaks, you should remove them from the field's value, allowing multiple lines of text to wrap automatically to the next line.

Some elements, such as inline images, don't contain content; instead they are rendered in Web pages based on their attribute values. An inline image displays an image file based on the value of its src attribute, which indicates the URL of the image file to be displayed. When data binding is applied to such an element, the field value takes the place of the attribute value. For example, binding the inline image code

```
<img datasrc="#id" datafld="field" />
```

results in the following code being generated by Internet Explorer:

```
<img src="field value" />
```

In this case, *field value* is the URL of the image file that the browser displays in the Web page. Figure 9-11 describes the different HTML elements that support data binding and indicates how the field values are interpreted by Internet Explorer. In some cases, a field value is displayed in the Web page as content, while in other cases it is applied to an attribute value.

HTML elements that support data binding ◄ Figure 9-11

Element	Resulting value
link	`<a href="field value"></a>`
Java applet parameter	`<param value="field value" />`
button	`<button>field value</button>`
div container	`<div>field value</div>`
frame	`<frame src="field value" />`
inline frame	`<iframe src="field value"></iframe>`
inline image	`<img src="field value" />`
checkbox	`<input type="checkbox" checked="field value" />`
hidden field	`<input type="hidden" value="field value" />`
password field	`<input type="password" value="field value" />`
option button	`<input type="radio" checked="field value" />`
text field	`<input value="field value" />`
label	`<label>field value</label>`
marquee	`<marquee>field value</marquee>`
list box item	`<option>field value</option>`
span container	`<span>field value</span>`
text area	`<textarea value="field value"></textarea>`

Binding an HTML Element to a Field

Reference Window

- To bind an HTML element to a data field, use the syntax
  ```
  <elem datasrc="#id" datafld="field"></elem>
  ```
  where *elem* is the name of the HTML element, *id* is the ID of the data island, and *field* is the name of the field in the data source. The field value is then interpreted either as page content or as the value of an attribute associated with the element.
- The content of a data field is interpreted as a simple text string. To force the browser to interpret the text string as HTML code, add the following attribute to the element:
  ```
  dataformatas = "html"
  ```
- By default, Internet Explorer preserves any line breaks in the field's value. To remove the line breaks from the rendered page, set the value of the dataformatas attribute to "html".

Now that you've seen how to bind HTML elements and fields, you are ready to bind the fields from the fpinfo document to staff directory page.

To bind HTML elements to fields:

1. Locate the div element for the page title. Remove the placeholder text "Page Title" displayed between the opening and closing <div> tags and add the following attributes to the opening <div> tag (see Figure 9-12):

   `datasrc="#pageInfo" datafld="title"`

   Trouble? Removing the placeholder text is not strictly necessary because value extracted from the title field overwrites it; however, removing unnecessary code can make the document easier to interpret.

2. Go to the div element for the page's subtitle. Delete the placeholder text "Page Subtitle" and add the attributes `datasrc="#pageInfo" datafld="subtitle"` to the opening <div> tag.

3. Go to the div element for the description of the page. Delete the placeholder text "A paragraph stating the purpose of the page." and add the attributes `datasrc="#pageInfo" datafld="purpose"` to the opening <div> tag.

   Next you'll change the link that points to the e-mail address of the Web page author. Currently, this link points to "#", which represents the current file.

4. Go to the a element within the div element for the page author and replace the attribute href="#" with the attributes `datasrc="#pageInfo" datafld="authorEmail"`.

   Finally, bind the name of the page's author to the Author element.

5. Delete the placeholder text "Page Author" and add the attributes `datasrc="#pageInfo" datafld="author"` to the opening <span> tag. Figure 9-12 shows all of the revised HTML code.

Figure 9-12	Binding HTML elements to fields

```
    <title>Freezing Point Refrigerators</title>
    <link href="styles1.css" rel="stylesheet" type="text/css" />
    <xml id="pageInfo" src="fpinfo.xml"></xml>
</head>

<body>
    <div id="pageTitle" datasrc="#pageInfo" datafld="title"></div>
    <div id="pageSubtitle" datasrc="#pageInfo" datafld="subtitle"></div>
    <div id="pageText" datasrc="#pageInfo" datafld="purpose"></div>
    <div id="pageAuthor">For more information, contact:
        <a datasrc="#pageInfo" datafld="authorEmail">
            <span datasrc="#pageInfo" datafld="author"></span>
        </a>.
    </div>
```

6. Save your changes to the file, and reopen fp1.htm in your Internet Explorer browser. As shown in Figure 9-13, the placeholder text at the top of the page has been replaced with values drawn from the title, subtitle, purpose, and author fields in the fpinfo.xml document.

Freezing Point Refrigerators

Staff Information Page

This page contains information on the staff of Freezing Point
Refrigerators. Staff members are divided into four groups: Accounting,
Sales, Manufacturing, and Advertising. Each employee's name, department,
position, phone number, years employed, and job status (full- or
part-time) is reported.

For more information, contact: Catherine Davis .

▶ **7.** Move the mouse pointer over the link for Catherine Davis, and verify that the status bar displays the URL *mailto:cdavis@freezingpoint.com*.

▶ **8.** If you want to take a break before starting the next session, you may close any open files or applications.

Catherine's Web page still has placeholder text in the staff information table. To replace that text, you must bind the relevant tags with an XML document describing company employees. You'll do that in the next session.

Using the dataformatas Attribute

By default, the contents of an XML element are interpreted by Internet Explorer as literal text. However, there may be situations when you wish to store HTML code in an XML element. For example, rather than using two elements for the author name and e-mail address, Catherine could have included both pieces in a single element using the following CDATA section:

```
<name>
  <![CDATA[
    <a href="mailto:cdavis@freezingpoint.com">
    Catherine Davis</a>
  ]]>
</name>
```

However, if you had bound this element to an HTML element using the code

```
Questions? Contact <span datasrc="#pageInfo" datafld="name">
</span>
```

Internet Explorer would still interpret the contents of the name element as literal text and would *not* have rendered them as a link. In fact, Internet Explorer would have displayed the actual HTML as text within the Web page:

```
Questions? Contact <a href="mailto:cdavis@freezingpoint.com">Catherine
Davis</a>
```

To get around this problem, you can specify that Internet Explorer interpret the content of an element as HTML code rather than literal text by using the dataformatas attribute. The syntax is

```
dataformatas="type"
```

where *type* is either "text" (the default) or "html". Thus, to force the browser to interpret the field value in the above example as HTML code rather than literal text, you add the dataformatas attribute to the span element as follows:

```
Questions? Contact <span datasrc="#pageInfo" datafld="name"
dataformatas="html"></span>
```

Internet Explorer then displays the author's name as a link. You can also use the dataformatas attribute to remove line breaks from the field's value by setting the dataformatas attribute value to "html". Note that the only HTML elements that support the dataformatas attribute are button, div, label, marquee, and span.

Using the $TEXT Field

Up to this point, you've used field names to reference specific fields in the XML document. You can also bind elements to records. Because a record contains a collection of fields, the DSO stores the values of those fields in a single pseudo-field named $TEXT. The $TEXT field contains the character data from all of the fields in a record, not including attribute values. For example, for the record

```
<employee>
    <first>Alice</first>
    <last>Ashman</last>
</employee>
```

the value of the $TEXT field is Alice Ashman, taking its value from the values of both the first and last fields. Thus, if you want to bind an HTML element to the employee record, you enter the following code:

```
The employee's name is <span datasrc="#pageInfo" datafld="$TEXT"></
span>.
```

and the text in the Web page would be rendered as

```
The employee's name is Alice Ashman.
```

The $TEXT field name is useful when you need to work with all of the field values as a single text string. It is also useful for binding element attributes to HTML tags, as you'll see later in the tutorial.

You've successfully completed the first stage of working with Catherine's Web page. In the next session, you'll bind more elements to her document, and you'll learn how to display multiple records in a single page.

Review

Session 9.1 Quick Check

1. Define the following terms:
   a. data binding
   b. field
   c. record
   d. recordset
2. What is the difference between a simple recordset and a hierarchical recordset?
3. What is a data island?
4. What HTML code would you enter to create a data island named compInfo that is connected to the company.xml file?
5. What HTML code would you enter to bind a span element to the cName field in the compInfo data island?

6. How is a field value applied to an inline frame?

7. What is the $TEXT field?

Session 9.2

Binding to an XML Attribute

In the last session, you learned how to bind data from a single record to a Web page. However, Catherine also wants to display information about company employees. She has stored that data in an XML document named emp1.xml. Figure 9-14 describes the contents of the document.

The contents of the emp1.xml file ◀ **Figure 9-14**

Element	Description
staff	The root element of the document
employee	Information about an employee; the status attribute indicates the employee's employment status (Part-time or Full-time)
name	The employee's name
department	The employee's department
position	The employee's job title
phone	The employee's phone number
years	The number of years the employee has worked for the company
photo	The filename of an image file containing the employee's photograph

The structure of the document is shown in Figure 9-15.

Structure of the emp1 document ◀ **Figure 9-15**

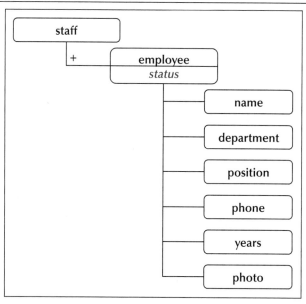

Unlike the fpinfo.xml file, the emp1.xml file contains several records: one for each employee. For each employee record, Catherine has recorded the employee's name, department, position, office phone number, the number of years employed by Freezing Point, and the filename of an image file displaying the employee's photo. Thus, you'll have to work with multiple records to display all of the records in this recordset. To start, add a second data island to the fp1.htm file to access this data source.

To create a data island for the emp1.xml file:

▶ 1. Use your text editor to open **emp1.xml** from the tutorial.09/tutorial folder.

▶ 2. Examine the contents of the file. Note that it contains a simple recordset containing records for 20 different employees. Close the file, but do not save any changes you may have made to the document.

▶ 3. Return to the **fp1.htm** file in your text editor.

▶ 4. Directly above the closing </head> tag insert the following xml element (see Figure 9-16):

```
<xml id="staffInfo" src="emp1.xml"></xml>
```

| Figure 9-16 | Creating the staffInfo data island |

```
<title>Freezing Point Refrigerators</title>
<link href="styles1.css" rel="stylesheet" type="text/css" />
<xml id="pageInfo" src="fpinfo.xml"></xml>
<xml id="staffInfo" src="emp1.xml"></xml>
</head>
```

Figure 9-17 shows how Catherine wants the different elements in the staff table bound to fields from the emp1.xml document. All of the fields in the table are represented by elements in the emp1.xml document except for the status field. In the emp1.xml file, job status is stored as an attribute of the employee element. How do you bind an HTML element to an attribute?

| Figure 9-17 | Fields in the staff information table |

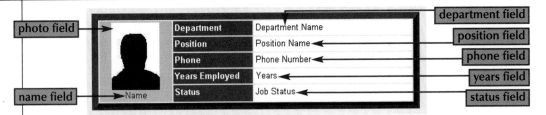

Attributes are treated by the DSO as fields. If the attribute is part of a record element like the employee element, it is easy to bind the attribute values to a Web page. For example, the following code has an ID attribute as part of the employee element:

```
<employee ID="E304">
   <name>Alice Ashman</name>
   <deptName>Accounting</deptName>
</employee>
```

This code is interpreted by the DSO exactly as if the ID attribute had been placed in its own element, as in the following code:

```
<employee>
    <ID>E304</ID>
    <name>Alice Ashman</name>
    <deptName>Accounting</deptName>
</employee>
```

The situation becomes a bit more complicated if the attribute is not part of a record element but is instead placed into a field element, as in the following code:

```
<employee>
    <name ID="E304">Alice Ashman</name>
    <deptName>Accounting</deptName>
</employee>
```

In this case, the attribute is still treated by the DSO as a field element, but the field element containing the attribute becomes a record element. A DSO treats the above code as follows:

```
<employee>
    <name>
        <ID>E304</ID>
        Alice Ashman
    </name>
    <deptName>Accounting</deptName>
</employee>
```

This leaves the text "Alice Ashman" unassociated with a field. However, because you can use the $TEXT field to reference all of the character data within an element, the DSO interprets this code as follows:

```
<employee>
    <name>
        <ID>E304</ID>
        <$TEXT>Alice Ashman</$TEXT>
    </name>
    <deptName>Accounting</deptName>
</employee>
```

As a result of the way that DSOs interpret attribute values, they treat simple recordsets as hierarchical recordsets, which can complicate data binding. For this reason, it is a good idea not to use attributes in field elements if you plan to do data binding. In the emp1. xml document, the status attribute is part of the employee record element, not one of the field elements, so you can interpret it as a separate field and attach it to the appropriate table cell in the staff information table. Since the td element does not support data binding, you'll use span elements within each of the table cells to bind those cells to the appropriate fields.

To bind the staff table to the employee fields:

1. Go down the file to the table section, and locate the inline image for the employee photo. Replace the attribute src="photo.jpg" with the attribute

   `datasrc="#staffInfo" datafld="photo"`

2. Go to the following span element, remove the "Name" placeholder text, and add the attributes `datasrc="#staffInfo" datafld="name"` to the opening <span> tag.

3. Go to the department span element, remove the "Department Name" placeholder text, and add the attributes `datasrc="#staffInfo" datafld="department"` to the opening <span> tag.

4. Go to the position span element, remove the "Position Name" placeholder text, and add the attributes `datasrc="#staffInfo" datafld="position"` to the opening <span> tag.

5. Go to the phone span element, remove the "Phone Number" placeholder text, and add the attributes `datasrc="#staffInfo" datafld="phone"` to the opening <span> tag.

6. Go to the span element for years employed, remove the "Years" placeholder text, and add the attributes `datasrc="#staffInfo" datafld="years"` to the opening <span> tag.

7. Finally, go to the job status span element, remove the "Job Status" placeholder text, and add the attributes `datasrc="#staffInfo" datafld="status"` to the opening <span> tag. Figure 9-18 highlights the revised code.

Figure 9-18	Binding the elements from the staff table

```
<table cellpadding="2">
    <tr>
        <td rowspan="5" id="photo">
            <img datasrc="#staffInfo" datafld="photo" alt="" /><br />
            <span datasrc="#staffInfo" datafld="name"></span>
        </td>
        <th>Department</th>
        <td><span datasrc="#staffInfo" datafld="department"></span></td>
    </tr>
    <tr>
        <th>Position</th>
        <td><span datasrc="#staffInfo" datafld="position"></span></td>
    </tr>
    <tr>
        <th>Phone</th>
        <td><span datasrc="#staffInfo" datafld="phone"></span></td>
    </tr>
    <tr>
        <th>Years Employed</th>
        <td><span datasrc="#staffInfo" datafld="years"></span></td>
    </tr>
    <tr>
        <th>Status</th>
        <td><span datasrc="#staffInfo" datafld="status"></span></td>
    </tr>
</table>
```

8. Save your changes to the file, and reopen fp1.htm in your Web browser. Figure 9-19 shows the revised Web page with information for the first employee displayed in the staff table.

Figure 9-19	Data from the first employee record

Working with a Data Source Object

Most HTML tags can display field values only one record at a time. Catherine's Web page is an example of this, displaying information on only the first employee. However, Catherine wants to be able to navigate through the contents of her staff directory. To do this, you can take advantage of data-access technology supported by Microsoft called **ActiveX data objects** or **ADO**. ADO allows you to work with a Data Source Object by either applying a **method** (a command to perform an operation on an object) or changing one of the **properties**, or characteristics, of the DSO. For client-side applications using Internet Explorer, you can work with the methods and properties of the DSO with JavaScript. Start by examining how to use JavaScript to apply a method to a recordset contained within a DSO.

Applying a Method to a Recordset

The syntax for applying a JavaScript method to a recordset is

```
id.recordset.method()
```

where `id` is the ID of the data island in the Web document and `method` is the name of a method supported by ADO to modify the recordset. Several methods can be applied to DSOs, but you'll concentrate only on those that allow you to navigate through the records in a recordset. These methods are listed in Figure 9-20.

JavaScript methods of the recordset object ◀ Figure 9-20

recordset method	Moves to
id.recordset.moveFirst()	the first record in the *id* recordset
id.recordset.movePrevious()	the previous record
id.recordset.moveNext()	the next record
id.recordset.moveLast()	the last record in the *id* recordset
id.recordset.move(*i*)	record number *i* in the *id* recordset (record numbering starts with the number 0)

For example, if you wanted to display the last record in the staffInfo DSO, you would run the following method:

```
staffInfo.recordset.moveLast()
```

To move to the first record in the same Data Source Object, you would use the method

```
staffInfo.recordset.moveFirst()
```

The other methods listed in Figure 9-20 can be applied in a similar way. There are several ways to run these methods. In Catherine's staff report, you'll run these methods using the form buttons on the Web page. To run a method when a form button is clicked, you add the following code to the HTML file:

```
<button onclick="command"> ... </button>
```

where *command* is a JavaScript command to be run in response to the action of clicking the button. For example, to move to the last record in the staffInfo recordset, you use the code

```
<button onclick="staffInfo.recordset.moveLast()"> ... </button>
```

Moving Through a Recordset with JavaScript

- To move to the next record in a recordset, use the JavaScript method
    id.recordset.moveNext()
  where *id* is the ID of the data island.
- To move to the previous record, use
    id.recordset.movePrevious()
- To move to the first record, use
    id.recordset.moveFirst()
- To move to the last record, use
    id.recordset.moveLast()
- To move to a specified record, use
    id.recordset.move(*i*)
  where *i* is the record number (recording numbering starts with an index value of 0).

Now that you've seen how DSOs can be manipulated using different JavaScript methods, you are ready to apply these methods using the form buttons on Catherine's staff page. You'll insert code to move to the first, last, next, and previous records in the recordset.

To move through the staffInfo recordset:

1. Return to the **fp1.htm** file in your text editor, and go to the first button element at the bottom of the file. Within the opening <button> tag, insert the attribute

   `onclick="staffInfo.recordset.moveFirst()"`

2. Within the opening <button> tag for the back button, insert

   `onclick="staffInfo.recordset.movePrevious()"`

3. To the forward <button> tag, add

   `onclick="staffInfo.recordset.moveNext()"`

4. Finally, add the following attribute to the last <button> tag:

   `onclick="staffInfo.recordset.moveLast()"`

   Figure 9-21 shows the revised code of the fp1.htm file.

Adding recordset methods to the button elements ◄ **Figure 9-21**

```
<p>
   <button onclick="staffInfo.recordset.moveFirst()">
      |&lt; First
   </button>
   <button onclick="staffInfo.recordset.movePrevious()">
      &lt; Back
   </button>
   <button onclick="staffInfo.recordset.moveNext()">
      Forward &gt;
   </button>
   <button onclick="staffInfo.recordset.moveLast()">
      Last &gt;|
   </button>
</p>
</body>
</html>
```

5. Save your changes to the file, and reload or refresh the fp1.htm file in your Internet Explorer browser. Verify that the four buttons located below the table allow you to move backwards and forwards through the records in the staffInfo recordset. Figure 9-22 shows the contents of the last record.

The last record in the staffInfo recordset ◄ **Figure 9-22**

Trouble? If Internet Explorer displays a yellow bar at the top of the page restricting access to the active content on the page, click the bar, select Allowed Blocked Content on the pop-up menu, and click Yes.

Working with Data Source Object Properties

Catherine is thrilled with your work implementing the button feature. However, she did discover one small problem that needs to be addressed. When she navigated to the last button and clicked the Forward button, the Web page displayed a blank record with a missing inline image.

You explain to Catherine that this is the result of the Web page trying to access a record that doesn't exist. Catherine understands your explanation but is concerned that users will find this effect disconcerting. She would like you to revise the page to prohibit users from moving outside the boundaries of the recordset. If a user attempts to move before the first record, Catherine would like the last record displayed, and if they attempt to move beyond the last record, she would like the first record to be displayed. In this way, users can loop through the entire recordset.

To do this, you need to determine which record a user is currently viewing; this is accomplished by working with the properties of the Data Source Object. DSO properties are described with the syntax

```
id.recordset.property
```

where *property* is one of the Data Source Object properties supported by the ADO associated with recordsets. Figure 9-23 describes some of the properties that allow you to determine the position of the record currently displayed in a Web page.

Figure 9-23	JavaScript properties of the recordset object

Recordset property	Returns
id.recordset.BOF	A Boolean value (true or false) indicating whether the current record position is at the beginning of the DSO *before* the first record
id.recordset.EOF	A Boolean value indicating whether the current record position is at the end of the DSO *after* the last record
id.recordset.Index	The index number of the current record in the DSO recordset (the first record has an index value of 0)
id.recordset.RecordCount	The total number of records in the DSO recordset

Two properties are of most use to you: the BOF (beginning of file) property and the EOF (end of file) property. The BOF property returns a value of true if the DSO is at the beginning of the file before the first record in the recordset. Similarly, the EOF property returns a value of true if the DSO is at the end of the file after the last record in the recordset. Otherwise, both properties return a value of false, indicating that one of the records in the recordset is currently active. You can use these properties to determine whether a user is attempting to move off of the list of records. To prevent this from happening, you can add an if statement to the Back and Forward buttons in the staff Web page. For example, if you revise the code for the Back button to

```
staffInfo.recordset.movePrevious();
if (staffInfo.recordset.BOF) staffInfo.recordset.moveLast()
```

the browser moves to the previous record, but if that moves the user before the first record, the user is automatically jumped to the last record. In the same way, you can revise the code for the Forward button to

```
staffInfo.recordset.moveNext();
if (staffInfo.recordset.EOF) staffInfo.recordset.moveFirst()
```

This code moves the user to the next record in the recordset. If that action moves the user after the last record, the user is automatically jumped to the first record in the recordset. Add both of these commands to the appropriate button elements in the staff info Web page.

To modify the features of the Back and Forward buttons:

▶ **1.** Locate the <button> tag for the Back button.

▶ **2.** After the movePrevious() method, within the set of double quotation marks, type a semicolon (**;**), and then type the following command, as shown in Figure 9-24:

```
if (staffInfo.recordset.BOF) staffInfo.recordset.moveLast()
```

The semicolon is necessary in JavaScript to separate one command from another.

▶ **3.** Go to the next button element, and after the moveNext() method, within the set of double quotation marks, type a semicolon and insert the following command:

```
if (staffInfo.recordset.EOF) staffInfo.recordset.moveFirst()
```

Figure 9-24 shows the revised code.

Testing the position of the current record ◀ **Figure 9-24**

```
<p>
   <button onclick="staffInfo.recordset.moveFirst()">
      |&lt; First
   </button>
   <button onclick="staffInfo.recordset.movePrevious();
                    if (staffInfo.recordset.BOF) staffInfo.recordset.moveLast()">
      &lt; Back
   </button>
   <button onclick="staffInfo.recordset.moveNext();
                    if (staffInfo.recordset.EOF) staffInfo.recordset.moveFirst()">
      Forward &gt;
   </button>
   <button onclick="staffInfo.recordset.moveLast()">
      Last &gt;|
   </button>
</p>
</body>
</html>
```

▶ **4.** Close the file, saving your changes and then reload or refresh **fp1.htm** in your Web browser.

▶ **5.** Click the **Last >|** button to go to the last record in the recordset, and then click the **Forward >** button. Verify that you jumped to the first record in the recordset, displaying information on Alice Ashman.

▶ **6.** Click the **< Back** button, and verify that you jumped to the last record, displaying information on Shirley Winston.

▶ **7.** You've completed your work on the fp1.htm file. If you want to take a break before starting the next session you may close any open files or applications.

Catherine is pleased with the changes you have made. In the next session, you'll continue to work with Catherine's employee data to learn how to display multiple records in a single table and how to work with hierarchical recordsets.

Session 9.2 Quick Check

Review

1. How are attributes that are part of record elements treated in a Data Source Object?
2. Describe what happens to the data structure when an attribute is added to a field element.
3. What JavaScript command would you use to display the last record from a data island named CInfo?

4. What command would you use to display the previous record from the CInfo recordset?
5. What command would you use to display a record with the index number 5 from the CInfo recordset?
6. What recordset property indicates whether the current record is past the last record in the recordset?
7. What recordset property returns the index number of the current recordset?

Session 9.3

Binding a Table to Data

Catherine has put together a draft of another page she would like you to develop. The code you worked with in the last session had the limitation of displaying data from one record at a time. Catherine wants to create a page where she can view all of the staff records at a glance, without having to scroll through several pages of records. She has already created the Web page and inserted two xml elements in her file to connect the document to the fpinfo.xml and emp1.xml documents. She has also bound several Web page elements to corresponding elements in the fpinfo.xml document. Your job is to display staff information in her new sample page.

To open the revised staff page:

1. Use your text editor to open **fp2txt.htm** from the tutorial.09x/tutorial folder. Enter **your name** and **the date** in the comment section at the top of the file, and save the file as **fp2.htm**.

2. Open the **fp2.htm** file in your Internet Explorer browser. Figure 9-25 shows the initial appearance of the page.

   The Web page contains buttons to display the table by pages. You'll learn about pages and how to use them later in the session.

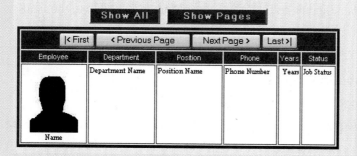

Freezing Point Refrigerators
Staff Information Page

This page contains information on the staff of Freezing Point
Refrigerators. Staff members are divided into four groups: Accounting,
Sales, Manufacturing, and Advertising. Each employee's name, department,
position, phone number, years employed, and job status (full- or
part-time) is reported.

For more information, contact: Catherine Davis.

Currently, the Web table displays a single sample row, but Catherine wants the table to display content from all of the records in the XML document. This can be done using **data table binding**, in which each record is displayed in a different row of a table. The syntax for binding an entire table to a recordset is

```
<table datasrc="#id">
   <tr>
      <td><span datafld="field1"></span></td>
      <td><span datafld="field2"></span></td>
      ...
   </tr>
</table>
```

where *id* is the ID of the data island and *field1*, *field2*, and so on are the fields from the recordset within that data island. Even though a single element from the table is bound to a single field element, the browser repeats the table row for each record in the recordset. The datasrc attribute is placed in the table element, and the datafld attributes are placed in individual table cells. As with the table in the last session, the td element doesn't support data binding, so you must enclose the text of each table cell using a span element or any other HTML element that supports data binding.

Reference Window

Binding a Table to Data

- To bind a Web table to a recordset, use the general form

```
<table datasrc="#id">
    <tr>
        <td><span datafld="field1"></span></td>
        <td><span datafld="field2"></span></td>
        ...
    </tr>
</table>
```

where *id* is the ID of the data island and *field1*, *field2*, and so on are the fields from the recordset.

Use table data binding to bind the cells in Catherine's table to the fields in the staffInfo data source.

To apply table data binding:

1. Return to the **fp2.htm** file in your text editor.

2. Go to the table element, and within the opening <table> tag insert the attribute

   `datasrc="#staffInfo"`

3. Locate the <img> tag in the first cell of the third row and replace the src="photo. jpg" attribute with the attribute `datafld="photo"`

4. Delete the "Name" placeholder text and add the attribute `datafld="name"` to the opening <span> tag.

5. Continue through the rest of the table as you did in the last session, deleting the placeholder text for Department Name, Position Name, Phone Number, Years, and Job Status, and adding datafld attributes to the corresponding <span> tags that point to the department, position, phone, years, and status fields. Figure 9-26 shows the revised code.

Binding the table elements to the staffInfo data source ◄ **Figure 9-26**

```
<table datasrc="#staffInfo">
  <thead>
  <tr>
      <th colspan="6">
          <button>|&lt; First</button>
          <button>&lt; Previous Page </button>
          <button>Next Page &gt;</button>
          <button>Last &gt;|</button>
      </th>
  </tr>
  <tr>
      <th class="th1"><span>Employee</span></th>
      <th class="th1"><span>Department</span></th>
      <th class="th1"><span>Position</span></th>
      <th class="th2"><span>Phone</span></th>
      <th class="th3"><span>Years</span></th>
      <th class="th4"><span>Status</span></th>
  </tr>
  </thead>

  <tr><td style="text-align: center">
      <img datafld="photo" alt="" /><br />
      <span datafld="name"></span>
      </td>
      <td>
        <span datafld="department"></span>
      </td>
      <td>
        <span datafld="position"></span>
      </td>
      <td>
        <span datafld="phone"></span>
      </td>
      <td style="text-align: right">
        <span datafld="years"></span>
      </td>
      <td>
        <span datafld="status"></span>
      </td>
  </tr>
</table>
```

▶ **6.** Save your changes to fp2.htm, and use your Internet Explorer browser to reload or refresh the file. Figure 9-27 shows the completed Web page with all of the records from the emp1.xml document displayed in the table.

Viewing the entire recordset in a single table ◄ **Figure 9-27**

Employee	Department	Position	Phone	Years	Status
Alice Ashman	Accounting	Administrative Assistant	555-4580 ext. 581	5	Part-time
Jeff Bester	Sales	Sales Manager	555-4580 ext. 411	3	Full-time
Richard Brown	Manufacturing	Shop Manager	555-4580 ext. 193	15	Full-time
Maureen Charnas	Advertising	Advertising Executive	555-4580 ext. 804	1	Full-time

|< First   < Previous Page   Next Page >   Last >|

Working with Table Pages

Catherine realizes that as she adds more records to her XML document, the table in the Web page will become increasingly long and unwieldy. With that in mind, Catherine would like to give users the option of limiting the number of records displayed at any one time to three. Users could then move forward or backward through the recordset, three records at a time. This technique of breaking up the recordset into manageable chunks is called **paging**.

Specifying the Page Size

To create a table page, you add the datapagesize attribute to the opening <table> tag. The syntax for this attribute is

```
datapagesize="number"
```

where *number* is the number of records you want displayed in a single page. Add this attribute to the table element now.

To define the page size:

1. Return to the **fp2.htm** file in your text editor.

2. Insert the attribute **datapagesize="3"** to the opening <table> tag as shown in Figure 9-28.

Figure 9-28 ▶ Setting the data table page size

```
<table datasrc="#staffInfo" datapagesize="3">
  <thead>
  <tr>
      <th colspan="6">
          <button>|&lt; First</button>
          <button>&lt; Previous Page </button>
          <button>Next Page &gt;</button>
          <button>Last &gt;|</button>
      </th>
  </tr>
```

3. Save your changes to the file, and reload or refresh fp2.htm in your Web browser. Verify that only the first three records are displayed in the Web table (see Figure 9-29).

Displaying the first page of the staffInfo recordset ◄ **Figure 9-29**

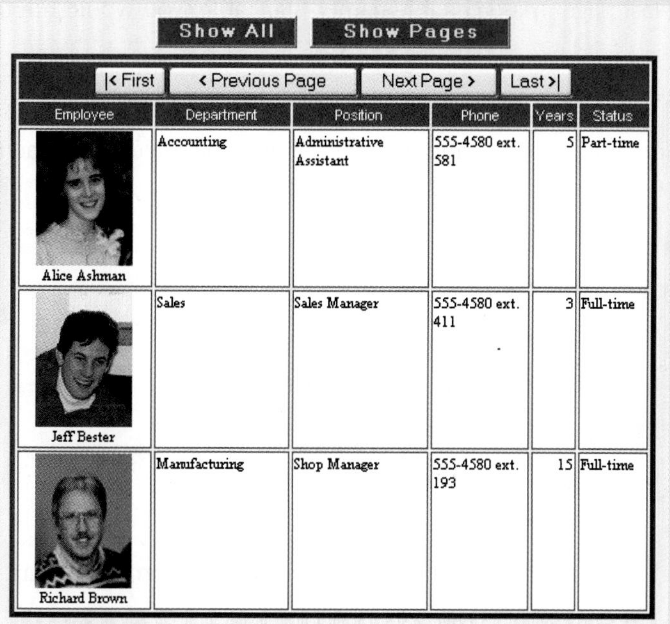

As in the last session, you now have to add commands to enable navigation from one page to another in the Web table.

Navigating a Table Page

Before you can write a command to page through the different groups of records in the table, you must first assign a unique identifier to the table using the ID attribute. The syntax for assigning an ID attribute to a table element is

```
<table id="id"> ... </table>
```

where *id* is the unique ID for the table object. This step is necessary because the commands to navigate the table pages act on the table itself and not the recordset displayed within the table. Figure 9-30 describes the methods and properties associated with table pages.

Table methods and properties ◄ **Figure 9-30**

Table method/property	Description
id.firstPage()	Displays the first page in the *id* table
id.previousPage()	Displays the previous page in the table
id.nextPage()	Displays the next page in the table
id.lastPage()	Displays the last page in the table
id.datapagesize=*n*	Sets the number of pages in the *id* table to *n* pages

To run these commands, you can add a JavaScript command to the onclick attribute of each button element as you did for the buttons in Catherine's original page. For example, to move to the last page in a data table named staffTable, you would run the following command:

```
staffTable.lastPage()
```

Complete the following steps to add the appropriate table methods to the four buttons located above the table in Catherine's Web page.

To page through the data table:

1. Return to the **fp2.htm** file in your text editor.

2. Go to the table element, and insert the attribute

   `id="staffTable"`

3. Go to the button element for the "First" button, and insert the attribute

   `onclick="staffTable.firstPage()"`

4. Go to the button element for the "Previous Page" button, and insert the attribute

   `onclick="staffTable.previousPage()"`

5. Go to the button element for the "Next Page" button, and insert the attribute

   `onclick="staffTable.nextPage()"`

6. Go to the button element for the "Last" button, and insert the attribute

   `onclick="staffTable.lastPage()"`

   Figure 9-31 shows the revised code in the file.

Figure 9-31 **Paging through the data table**

```
<table datasrc="#staffInfo" datapagesize="3" id="staffTable">
  <thead>
  <tr>
     <th colspan="6">
        <button onclick="staffTable.firstPage()">|&lt; First</button>
        <button onclick="staffTable.previousPage()">&lt; Previous Page </button>
        <button onclick="staffTable.nextPage()">Next Page &gt;</button>
        <button onclick="staffTable.lastPage()">Last &gt;|</button>
     </th>
  </tr>
```

7. Save your changes to the file, and reload fp2.htm in your Internet Explorer browser.

8. Click the **First**, **Previous Page**, **Next Page**, and **Last** buttons and verify that they allow you to move through the data table three records at a time.

Catherine also wants to provide users with the option of switching between a view of all records in the table and a view that displays the table by pages. To do this, you add commands to the buttons she has already created to change the datapagesize attribute of the table. To show all of the records in the recordset, you must set the value of the page size to a very high value and then instruct the browser to move to the first page in the table. If you don't include the command to show the first page, Internet Explorer increases the page size, but the pages prior to the current page are not displayed in the browser. The complete command to accomplish this task is

```
staffTable.datapagesize=999999;
staffTable.firstPage()
```

To restore the page size to three, use the command

```
staffTable.datapagesize=3;
```

The two buttons that Catherine created for this purpose are located just above the Web page table. Modify these buttons now to allow users to switch between a page view and a full view of the data table records.

To switch between a page view and a full view:

1. Return to the **fp2.htm** file in your text editor.

2. Go to the Show All <button> tag, and insert the attribute

   `onclick="staffTable.datapagesize=999999; staffTable.firstPage()"`

3. Go to the next button element, and insert the attribute

   `onclick="staffTable.datapagesize=3"`

   Figure 9-32 shows the revised code in the document.

Switching the table view   Figure 9-32

```
<div id="pageData">

    <div id="pageTitle" datasrc="#pageInfo" datafld="title"></div>
    <div id="pageSubtitle" datasrc="#pageInfo" datafld="subtitle"></div>
    <div id="pageText" datasrc="#pageInfo" datafld="purpose"></div>
    <div id="pageAuthor">For more information, contact:
        <a datasrc="#pageInfo" datafld="authorEmail">
            <span datasrc="#pageInfo" datafld="author"></span>
        </a>.
    </div>

    <p>
        <button onclick="staffTable.datapagesize=999999; staffTable.firstPage()">
        Show All
        </button>
        <button onclick="staffTable.datapagesize=3">Show Pages</button>
    </p>
</div>
```

4. Save your changes, close the file, and reload fp2.htm in your Internet Explorer browser.

5. Click the **Show All** and **Show Pages** buttons, and verify that the view of the table records switches from a paged view to a full view and back.

Working with Hierarchical Recordsets

Catherine has gotten some feedback on her staff Web page. Although many employees appreciate what she has done, some have suggested that she organize the employee list by department. She has done that by creating a new XML document that groups the employee elements within the department element. Figure 9-33 shows the layout of her new document, stored in the emp2.xml file.

Figure 9-33 ▶ **Structure of the emp2 document**

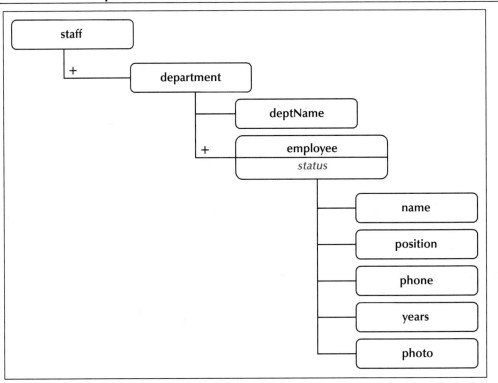

Up to this point, you've worked with simple recordsets. Figure 9-33 shows a hierarchical recordset, in which the department recordset is nested within the staff recordset. The department recordset contains the deptName field, displaying the name of the department, and the employee record element, containing descriptions of each employee in the department placed within the name, position, phone, years, and photo fields and the status attribute.

Catherine has written another version of the staff directory Web page to work with this new layout. Open this page now.

To open the revised page:

▶ **1.** Use your text editor to open the **emp2.xml** file from the tutorial.09x/tutorial folder. Scroll through the document noting the structure of the document and the content of the fields. Close the file without saving any changes.

▶ **2.** Use your text editor to open **fp3txt.htm** from the tutorial.09x/tutorial folder. Enter *your name* and *the date* in the comment section at the top of the file.

▶ **3.** Below the xml element at the top of the file, insert the following xml element to create a data island for the emp2.xml data source (see Figure 9-34):

```
<xml id="staffInfo" src="emp2.xml"></xml>
```

Creating the staffInfo data source for the emp2 document ◀ **Figure 9-34**

```
<body>
    <xml id="pageInfo" src="fpinfo.xml"></xml>
    <xml id="staffInfo" src="emp2.xml"></xml>

    <div id="pageData">

        <div id="pageTitle" datasrc="#pageInfo" datafld="title"></div>
        <div id="pageSubtitle" datasrc="#pageInfo" datafld="subtitle"></div>
        <div id="pageText" datasrc="#pageInfo" datafld="purpose"></div>
        <div id="pageAuthor">For more information, contact:
            <a datasrc="#pageInfo" datafld="authorEmail">
                <span datasrc="#pageInfo" datafld="author"></span>
            </a>.
        </div>

        <p>
            <button>Next Department</button>
        </p>
    </div>
</body>
```

▶ **4.** Save the file as **fp3.htm**, and open the file in your Internet Explorer browser. Figure 9-35 shows the initial appearance of the revised staff directory.

The initial fp3 Web page ◀ **Figure 9-35**

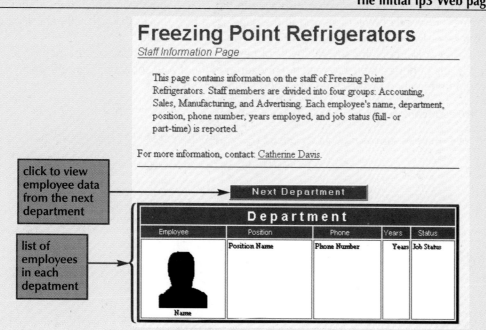

In this page, Catherine wants the data table to display information on all employees from a given department. Catherine has provided a button labeled "Next Department" that users can click to go from one department record to the next. Thus, this Web page works with the two recordsets in different ways. The records in the department recordset are displayed in the Web table, and to go from one department to another in the staff recordset, users use the Next Department button outside of the Web table.

Start by looking at how to populate the employee records in the Web table. The code to display the records from a nested recordset element follows the general structure

```
<table datasrc="#id" datafld="record">
   <tr>
      <td><span datafld="field1"></span></td>
      <td><span datafld="field2"></span></td>
      ...
   </tr>
</table>
```

where id is the ID of the data island, $record$ is the name of the record element within the recordset, and $field1$, $field2$, and so on are fields within the inner record. Note that the main difference between this table format and the table format for a simple recordset like those you worked on earlier is that here you must include the name of the record element in the table element. Once that is done, any fields within the Web table are displayed based on the currently selected record. For example, to bind the employee fields displayed in Figure 9-33 to a table, you enter the following code:

```
<table datasrc="#staffInfo" datafld="employee">
   <tr>
      <td><span datafld="name"></span></td>
      <td><span datafld="position"></span></td>
      . . .
   </tr>
</table>
```

The actual employee information displayed in the table depends on which department record is currently being displayed in the page. As a user moves through different department records, the values displayed in the Web table are updated in response.

If a recordset contains several levels of nested record elements, you must include several levels of nested tables to match. For example, the layout shown in Figure 9-36 would be matched by the series of nested tables shown below:

```
<table datasrc="#id" datafld="recordset1">
<tr>
   <td><table datasrc="#id" datafld="recordset2">
      <tr>
         <td><table datasrc="#id" datafld="records">
            <tr>
               <td><span datafld="field1"></span></td>
               <td><span datafld="field2"></span></td>
               <td><span datafld="field3"></span></td>
            </tr>
            </table>
         </td>
      </tr>
      </table>
   </td>
</tr>
</table>
```

Several layers of nested record elements ◀ **Figure 9-36**

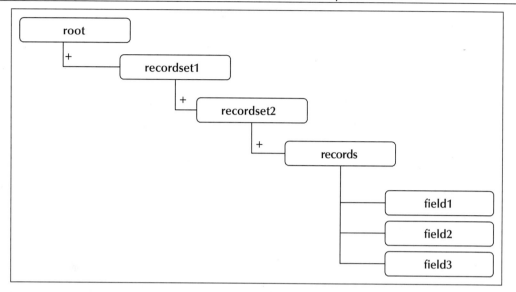

Working with a Hierarchical Recordset

Reference Window

- To display data from a hierarchical recordset in a table, use the general form

```
<table datasrc="#id" datafld="record">
  <tr>
    <td><span datafld="field1"></span></td>
    <td><span datafld="field2"></span></td>
    ...
  </tr>
</table>
```

where *id* is the name of the data island, *record* is the name of the record element found within a nested recordset, and *field1*, *field2*, and so on are fields within the nested record.

Complete the data table in Catherine's staff directory by adding the data fields for the employee record element and the field describing each employee.

To complete the data table:

▶ **1.** Return to the **fp3.htm** file in your text editor, and go to the table element.

▶ **2.** Within the opening <table> tag insert the following attributes:

```
datasrc="#staffInfo" datafld="employee"
```

3. Following the same process you used for Catherine's other Web pages, delete the image name and all of the placeholder text in the table and add datafld attributes, binding the different table elements to the photo, name, position, phone, years, and status fields. Figure 9-37 highlights the revised code for the data table.

| Figure 9-37 | Binding table elements to the staffInfo data source |

```
<table datasrc="#staffInfo" datafld="employee">
  <thead>
  <tr>
     <th id="mainhead" colspan="5">
        <span>Department</span>
     </th>
  </tr>
  <tr>
     <th class="th1"><span>Employee</span></th>
     <th class="th1"><span>Position</span></th>
     <th class="th2"><span>Phone</span></th>
     <th class="th3"><span>Years</span></th>
     <th class="th4"><span>Status</span></th>
  </tr>
  </thead>

  <tr><td style="text-align: center">
        <img datafld="photo" alt="" /><br />
        <span datafld="name"></span>
     </td>
     <td>
        <span datafld="position"></span>
     </td>
     <td>
        <span datafld="phone"></span>
     </td>
     <td style="text-align: right">
        <span datafld="years"></span>
     </td>
     <td>
        <span datafld="status"></span>
     </td>
  </tr>
</table>
```

4. Save your changes to the file, and reload fp3.htm in your Internet Explorer browser. As shown in Figure 9-38, the Web page now displays the employee list for the first department record in the emp2.xml file.

Figure 9-38 Employees from the first department record

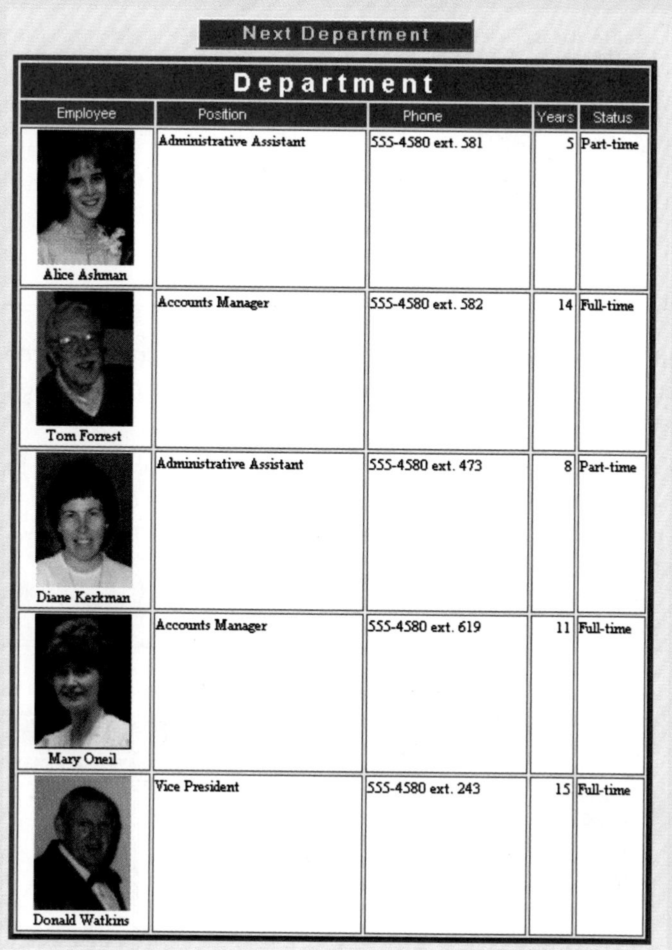

Catherine notes that the employee table does not specify the name of the department. This information is stored in the deptName field; however, that field is part of the department record—not the employee record. Add this field to the Web table.

To display the department name:

1. Return to the **fp3.htm** file in your text editor.
2. Go to the first th element within the Web table, and delete the placeholder text "Department".
3. Within the opening <span> tag insert the following attributes (see Figure 9-39):

```
datasrc="#staffInfo" datafld="deptName"
```

| Figure 9-39 | Retrieving the deptName field |

```
<table datasrc="#staffInfo" datafld="employee">
  <thead>
  <tr>
      <th id="mainhead" colspan="5">
          <span datasrc="#staffInfo" datafld="deptName"></span>
      </th>
  </tr>
  <tr>
      <th class="th1"><span>Employee</span></th>
      <th class="th1"><span>Position</span></th>
      <th class="th2"><span>Phone</span></th>
      <th class="th3"><span>Years</span></th>
      <th class="th4"><span>Status</span></th>
  </tr>
  </thead>
```

If you omit the datasrc attribute, Internet Explorer assumes that the deptName field is part of the employee record element and is thus not able to display the field value.

4. Save your changes to the file, and reload fp3.htm in your Internet Explorer browser. As shown in Figure 9-40, the table should now display the heading "Accounting," indicating that the employees shown are from the Accounting Department.

| Figure 9-40 | Displaying the accounting department name |

To show employee data from other departments, you move to the next record in the department recordset. Because the department recordset also acts as a record within the staff recordset, you can use the same JavaScript methods you used with the fp1.htm file to move from one record to another. Thus, to move to the next department, you run the command

```
staffInfo.recordset.moveNext()
```

There is only one button in Catherine's Web page to navigate through the recordset, so when users reach the last record, Catherine would like them sent back to the first record. You'll use the following code to add the desired functionality to the Next Department button:

```
staffInfo.recordset.moveNext();
if (staffInfo.recordset.EOF) staffInfo.recordset.moveFirst()
```

Add this code to the button now.

To display data from other departments:

▶ **1.** Return to the **fp3.htm** file in your text editor.

▶ **2.** Go to the button element for the Next Department button, and insert the following attributes within the opening <button> tag (see Figure 9-41):

```
onclick="staffInfo.recordset.moveNext();
if (staffInfo.recordset.EOF) staffInfo.recordset.moveFirst()"
```

Moving to the next department record ◀ **Figure 9-41**

```
<p>
    <button onclick="staffInfo.recordset.moveNext();
                    if (staffInfo.recordset.EOF) staffInfo.recordset.moveFirst()">
        Next Department
    </button>
</p>
</div>
```

▶ **3.** Close the fp3.htm file, saving your changes.

▶ **4.** Reload fp3.htm in your Internet Explorer browser. Verify that by clicking the **Next Department** button, the browser displays the employee data and department name of the next department record in the data source (Sales). Figure 9-42 displays the employee records from the Manufacturing Department.

Employees of the Manufacturing department ◀ **Figure 9-42**

▶ **5.** Close your browser.

Catherine is pleased with the final version of her staff Web page. By using a hierarchical recordset, Catherine was able to organize the employee data in a reasonable and useful way. She'll get back to you if she needs any more work done on this issue.

Review

Session 9.3 Quick Check

1. Where should you put the datasrc attribute if you want to use table binding?
2. What is paging?
3. How would you set the size of a table to five pages?
4. A table object has the ID PTable. What command would you use to display the last page in the table?
5. What command would you use to change the page size of PTable to six?
6. How do you display several levels of nested recordsets within a Web page?

Review

Tutorial Summary

This tutorial looked at how to use XML as a data source in Web documents. The focus of the tutorial was on a proprietary approach supported by the Internet Explorer browser that involves treating XML documents as collections of records and fields. The first session covered how to create data islands connected to internal and external XML data sources. It explored how to bind Web page elements to fields in the data source and how to treat the field values as either text or HTML code. The second session looked first at how to treat XML attributes as fields. It then examined the methods and properties of recordsets in order to write JavaScript code to navigate through the different records within a recordset. The third session explored how to display multiple records within a Web table using data table binding. It also looked at how to display a data table in a collection of distinct pages. The session concluded by examining how to display content from a hierarchical recordset.

Key Terms

ActiveX data object	DSO	property
ADO	field	record
data binding	field element	record element
data island	hierarchical recordset	recordset
Data Source Object	method	recordset element
data table binding	paging	simple recordset

Review Assignment

**Data files needed for this Review Assignment: fpc1000.jpg, fpc1020.jpg, fpc1050.jpg,
fpc1070.jpg, fpc1090.jpg, fpc2000.jpg, fpc2020.jpg, fpc2050.jpg, fpc3000.jpg, fpc3050.
jpg, fpc3070.jpg, fpc3090.jpg, inv1txt.htm, inv2txt.htm, inv3txt.htm, model.jpg, refg1.
xml, refg2.xml, sinfo.xml, styles1.css, styles2.css, styles3.css**

Catherine has been using the staff page you designed for a few weeks now. Her associates at Freezing Point Refrigerators have seen her work and would like to use data binding with some of their XML documents. Jason Lewis maintains a Web page describing
the various refrigerators sold by the company. Jason has collected the following information on each refrigerator model: the model name, the selling price, the refrigerator's
cubic capacity, the refrigerator's dimensions, whether the model is energy efficient or
not, and whether the freezer unit is located above or side by side with the main unit.
Jason has also organized the refrigerator models into two types: those that are designed
to fit into cabinet spaces and those that are freestanding. Using this data he has created
two documents. The first, refg1.xml, organizes this data into a simple recordset. The second, refg2.xml, uses a hierarchical recordset. Figure 9-43 displays the structures of both
documents.

Figure 9-43

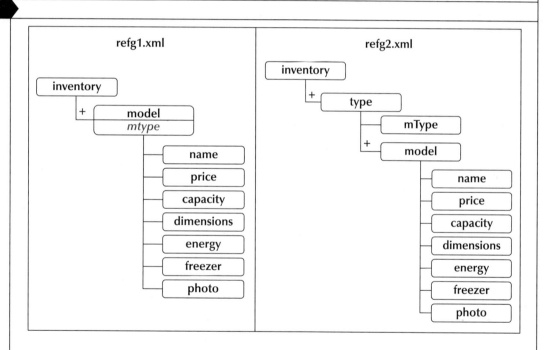

Jason has created another document named sinfo.xml containing information about the
company that Jason wants to include in any Web page he creates. Like the fpinfo.xml file
used in the staff directory Web page, this document contains a few fields organized in a
simple recordset.

Jason would like to create three Web pages to display information about the different Freezing Point Refrigerator models. The first, inv1.htm, should display each refrigerator model on a separate page. The second, inv2.htm, should display all of the refrigerator models in a single table that can be broken into individual pages. The third, inv3.htm, should display the model data broken down by model type. Figure 9-44 shows a preview of the inv1.htm file. The other Web pages employ a table design similar to that used in Freezing Point Refrigerator's staff directory Web page.

Figure 9-44

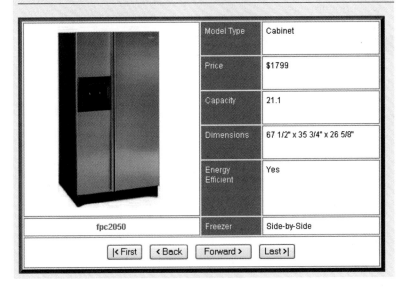

Jason has already created the basic format for these three pages. He needs your help in binding those pages with the contents of his XML documents and inserting commands to navigate through the records in the recordsets.

To complete this task:

1. Using your text editor, open **inv1txt.htm**, **inv2txt.htm**, and **inv3txt.htm** from the tutorial.09x/review folder. Enter *your name* and *the date* in the comment section of each file, and save them as **inv1.htm**, **inv2.htm**, and **inv3.htm** respectively.
2. Go to the **sinfo.xml**, **refg1.xml,** and **refg2.xml** files in your text editor. Take some time to review the contents and structure of these three files. Close the files without saving any changes you may inadvertently make.
3. Go to the inv1.htm file in your text editor. Create two data islands in the head section of the document. The first, named sInfo, should point to the contents of the sinfo.xml file. The second, named refInfo, should point to the contents of the refg1.xml file.

4. Bind the text of the page's title, subtitle, and purpose to the contents of the title, subtitle, and purpose fields in the sInfo data island. Bind the target of the author's link to the value of the authorEmail field of the sInfo data island. Bind the text of the author's name to the author field.

5. Within the table describing an individual refrigerator model, bind each of the following items to fields in the refInfo data island:
   - Bind the inline image to the photo field.
   - Bind the model type to the mType field.
   - Bind the refrigerator price to the price field.
   - Bind the capacity and dimensions of the refrigerator to the capacity and dimensions fields.
   - Bind the contents of the mName span element to the name field.
   - Bind the energy efficiency and freezer type to the energy and freezer fields.

6. Add the following JavaScript commands to the buttons located at the bottom of the Web table:
   - If a user clicks the First or Last button, display the first or last records in the refInfo recordset.
   - If a user clicks the Forward button, display the next record in the refInfo recordset. If this causes the Data Source Object to move beyond the last record in the recordset, display the first record.
   - If a user clicks the Back button, display the previous record in the refInfo recordset. If this causes the Data Source Object to move before the first record in the recordset, display the last record.

7. Save your changes to the inv1.htm file. Open the file in your Internet Explorer browser, and verify that the contents of the sInfo data island are displayed at the top of the page, that information about each refrigerator is displayed in the table, and that you can move through the contents of the refInfo data island by clicking the buttons on the Web page.

8. Go to the inv2.htm file in your text editor. Add data islands named sInfo and refInfo to the head section of the document pointing to the sinfo.xml and refg1.xml files. Bind the page's title, subtitle, purpose, author name, and author link to the appropriate fields in the sInfo data island.

9. Set the data page size for the table to 4. Set the data source for the whole table to the refInfo data island. Bind the contents of the last row of the table to the following fields in the refg1.xml document: name, price, mType, capacity, dimensions, energy, and freezer. Also bind the inline image in the last table row to the photo field.

10. Add the following JavaScript commands to the buttons on the Web page:
   - If the user clicks the First, Previous Page, Next Page, or Last Page buttons, display the first, previous, next, or last page of records in the table.
   - If the user clicks the Show All button, set the data page size to an extremely high number.
   - If the user clicks the Show Pages button, set the data page size to 4.

11. Save your changes to inv2.htm. Open the file in your Internet Explorer browser, and verify that all of the fields from the sinfo.xml and refg1.xml documents are displayed in the Web page. Further verify that the Web page buttons allow you to move through the Web table page by page and that you can switch between a paged view and a complete view of the Web table records.

12. Go to the inv3.htm file in your text editor. Add data islands named sInfo and refInfo2 to the head section of the document pointing to the sinfo.xml and refg2.xml files. Bind the page's title, subtitle, purpose, author name, and author link to the appropriate fields in the sInfo data island.

13. Set the data source of the Web table to the refInfo2 data island. Set the data field of the table to the model field. Bind the contents of the Web table to the following fields in the refinfo2.xml document: mType, photo, name, price, capacity, dimensions, energy, and freezer. The mType field should be displayed in the table's first row.

14. Add an onclick attribute to the Cabinet Refrigerators option button to run a JavaScript command that displays the first record in the refInfo2 data island.

15. Add an onclick attribute to the Freestanding Refrigerators option button to run a JavaScript command that displays the last record in the refInfo2 data island.

16. Save your changes to inv3.htm. Open the file in your Internet Explorer browser, and verify that all of the fields from the sinfo.xml and refg2.xml documents are displayed in the Web page. Also verify that you can switch from cabinet to freestanding refrigerators by clicking the option buttons above the Web table.

17. Submit the completed project to your instructor.

Case Problem 1

Apply

Use the skills you learned in this tutorial to create a shipping manifest report for a hierarchical recordset

Data files needed for this Case Problem: amstyles.css, amtxt.htm, autoord.xml

AutoMaze, Inc. David Hansen manages shipping and receiving for AutoMaze, an auto parts superstore. The company stores shipping manifests in XML documents and then makes them accessible to employees via the company's intranet. David is exploring ways to bind the XML data to a Web page. He has a sample shipping manifest stored in the autoord.xml file. The structure of this file is shown in Figure 9-45.

Figure 9-45

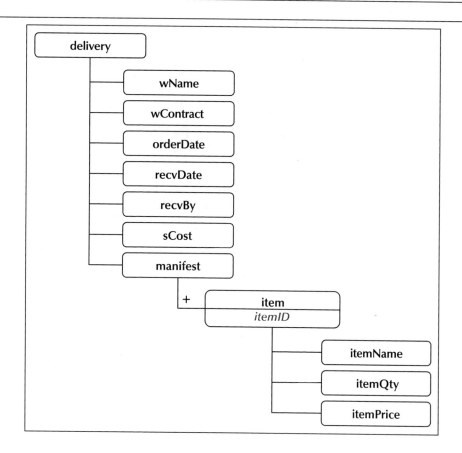

A preview of the Web page you'll create for David is shown in Figure 9-46. David has already created a draft of this page; your job is to insert the data binding.

Figure 9-46

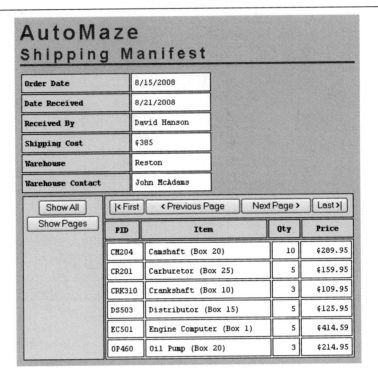

To complete this task:

1. Using your text editor, open **amtxt.htm** from the tutorial.09x/case1 folder. Enter **your name** and **the date** in the comment section of the file, and save it as **am.htm**.

2. Go to the **autoord.xml** file in your text editor. Examine the content and structure of the document. Close the file without saving any changes you may inadvertently make.

3. Return to the **am.htm** file in your text editor. Add a data island named orderInfo to the head section of the document, attaching the Web page to the autoord.xml file.

4. Go to the first Web table. Within this table, bind the span elements within the table cells to the following fields in the orderInfo data source: orderDate, recvDate, recvBy, sCost, wName, and wContact.

5. Go to the second Web table. This table is used to display the items on the shipping manifest. Bind this table to the manifest field in the orderInfo data source.

6. Within the second Web table is a nested table (used for the hierarchical recordset). Set the ID of this table to "orders", and set the data page size to 6. Bind the table element to the item field in the orderInfo data source.

7. Within the nested table, bind the span elements to the itemID, itemName, itemQty, and itemPrice fields.

8. Go to the button elements at the top of the second Web table. Add the following JavaScript commands:
   - If the user clicks the Show All button, set the data page size property of the orders table to 999999 and display the first page of the table.
   - If the user clicks the Show Pages button, set the data page size property of the orders table to 6 and display the first page of the table.
   - If the user clicks the First button, go to the first page in the orders table.

- If the user clicks the Previous Page button, go to the previous page in the orders table.
- If the user clicks the Next Page button, go to the next page in the orders table.
- If the user clicks the Last button, go to the last page in the orders table.

9. Save your changes to the am.htm file, and open the file in your Internet Explorer browser. Verify that you can view the items in the shipping manifest by pages or all at once and that you can use the Web buttons to move through the items in the hierarchical recordset.

10. Submit the completed project to your instructor.

Apply

Use the skills you earned in this tutorial o populate a Web orm from an XML ata source

Case Problem 2

Data files needed for this Case Problem: bwills.jpg, chlist.xml, chstyles.css, czims.jpg, emcd.jpg, photo.jpg, rshapiro.jpg, slisttxt.htm, taaron.jpg, tdavis.jpg

Reunions, Inc. Cindy Carlson works for Reunions, Inc., a company that promotes and organizes parties, reunions, receptions, and other special events. Cindy has been developing a class reunion Web page for Central High School. Cindy's idea is to have several computer terminals located at the class reunion site allowing participants to access online information about the party and their classmates. Cindy has already collected information about the class reunion participants, and she has stored that data in an XML document named chlist.xml. The structure of the XML document is shown in Figure 9-47.

Figure 9-47

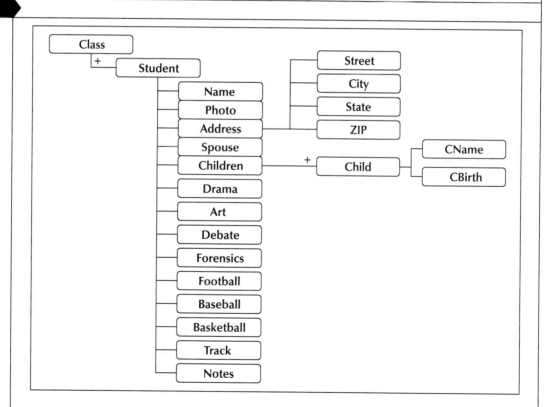

Cindy's document is organized in a hierarchical recordset with several nested levels. Her document includes information on each ex-student's name, address, and children; activities they were involved with in school; special notes about their high school experiences; and a current photo. Figure 9-48 shows a preview of the page that Cindy wants you to create.

Figure 9-48

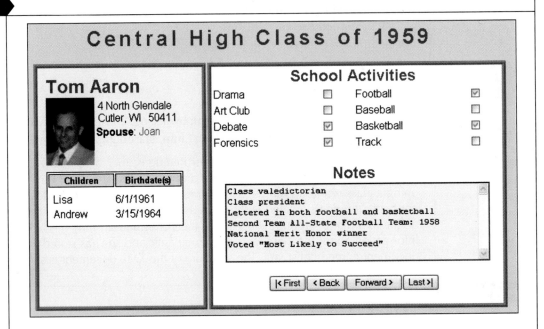

Cindy has already created a draft of the Web page, but she needs your help in binding the contents of her XML document to the HTML file.

To complete this task:

1. Using your text editor, open **slisttxt.htm** from the tutorial.09x/case2 folder. Enter *your name* and *the date* in the comment section of the file, and save it as **slist.htm**.

2. Go to the **chlist.xml** file in your text editor. Examine the content and structure of the document. Close the file without saving any changes you may inadvertently make.

3. Return to the **slist.htm** file in your text editor. Add a data island named studInfo to the head section of the document, attaching the Web page to the chlist.xml file.

4. Go the second div element (containing the ID value sName) and bind the contents of this element to the Name field from the studInfo data source.

5. Bind the inline image of the reunion participant to the Photo field.

6. Go to the table element below the inline image, and bind the table to the Address field in the studInfo data source. Within this table, bind the span elements for the Street, City, State, and ZIP text strings to the Street, City, State, and ZIP fields. (*Hint*: You have to bind this data as a hierarchical recordset.)

7. Bind the span element containing the spouse's name to the Spouse element in the studInfo data source.

Explore

8. Go to the next table, which contains a list of the participant's children. This table element contains two additional nested tables within it. First bind the outermost table element with the cTable ID to the Student field in the studInfo data source. Then go to the next table element and bind that table to the Children field in the studInfo data source. Finally, within this table is the last nested table. Bind that table element to the Child field in the studInfo data source and within that nested table, bind the span elements for the CName and CBirthdate to the CName and CBirth fields.

Explore

9. Go to the next table (found within the rightBox div element). Bind the check boxes in the table to the Drama, Football, Art, Baseball, Debate, Basketball, Forensics, and Track fields in the studInfo data source.

Explore

10. Go to the textarea element, and bind the element to the Notes field in the studInfo data source.

11. Add the following commands to the buttons at the bottom of the page:
    - If the user clicks the First or Last buttons, display the first or last record in the studInfo recordset.
    - If the user clicks the Forward button, display the next record in the studInfo recordset. If this causes the browser to move past the last record, display the first record.
    - If the user clicks the Back button, display the previous record in the studInfo recordset. If this causes the browser to move before the first record, display the last record.

12. Save your changes to the slist.htm file, and open the file in your Internet Explorer browser. Verify that clicking the Web form buttons moves you through the records in the recordset. Also verify that the check boxes and text area elements display values taken from the data source.

13. Submit the completed project to your instructor.

Case Problem 3

Challenge

Explore how to use data binding to display stories from an RSS news feed

Data files needed for this Case Problem: mm.jpg, moneytxt.htm, mstyles.css, news1. htm, news2.htm, news3.htm, news4.htm, rss2.xml, side.jpg

Money Managers   Marie Ruiz oversees the intranet for Money Managers, a financial consulting firm. One of her responsibilities is to manage RSS news feeds containing some of the most recent financial news stories of interest to her colleagues. Marie would like to treat the RSS document as a data source and use Internet Explorer to display news articles as records on the company Web site. She needs your help in setting up the code for the news feed Web page. Figure 9-49 shows a preview of the completed Web page.

Figure 9-49

Figure 9-50 shows the structure of a typical RSS document. Note that the document is a hierarchical recordset with news stories stored in the item element located several levels down in the hierarchy. Thus, any code you enter has to work with the hierarchical nature of this data. The RSS document also contains several namespaces. To reference these elements you have to include the namespace prefix along with the element name.

Figure 9-50

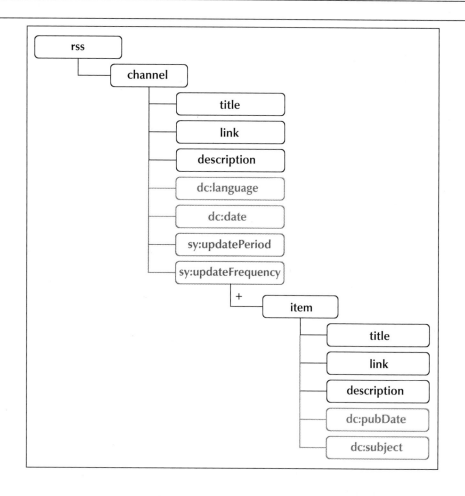

To complete this task:

1. Using your text editor, open **moneytxt.htm** from the tutorial.09x/case3 folder. Enter *your name* and *the date* in the comment section of the file, and save it as **money.htm**.

2. Go to the **rss2.xml** file in your text editor. Take some time to examine the contents and structure of the file. Close the document without making any changes.

3. Return to the money.htm file in your text editor. Add a data island named news to the head section of the document, attaching the Web page to the rss2.xml file.

4. Go to the datetime div element, and within the element insert a table element. Bind the table element to the channel field within the news data source. Add a single row to the table, and within the table row insert a single table cell containing a span element bound to the dc:date field.

5. Go to the links div element. Within this element, bind the table element to the channel field within the news data source. Bind the description span element to the description field. Set the data format of the description field to "html" to remove the line breaks from the description text.

6. Go to the news div element. Within this element, insert a table element bound to the channel field in the news data source. Within the table, insert a single table row containing a single table cell. The table cell should contain an h1 heading and, within the h1 heading, a span element displaying the contents of the title field.

Explore

7. Add a second table row to the table you created in Step 6. Within this row, insert a single table cell containing a table element. Bind the table element to the item field in the news data source. Within this nested table, insert a single table row containing one table cell. The table cell should contain the following code:

```
<h2>title</h2>
<p id="subjtime">subject / pubDate</p>
<p>description</p>
<p id="itemlink">[ <a href="link">more</a> ]</p>
```

where *title* is the value of the title field, *subject* is the value of the dc:subject field, *pubDate* is the value of the dc:pubDate field, *description* is the value of the description field, and *link* is the value of the link field. The *title*, *subject*, *pubDate*, and *description* fields must all be placed within span elements. Set the data format of the description field to "html".

8. Save your changes to the money.htm file, and open the file in your Internet Explorer browser. Verify that the news articles, titles, and descriptions are displayed in the Web page. Verify that clicking the **more** link below each news story opens a Web page containing that story.

9. Submit the completed project to your instructor.

Create

Test your knowledge of data binding by binding a travel itinerary for a travel agency

Case Problem 4

Data files needed for this Case Problem: castles.jpg, hebrides.jpg, highland.jpg, lake. jpg, scottxt.htm, tour.xml

Tour Scotland, Inc. Ian Findlay is the owner of the touring agency Tour Scotland, Inc., which organizes tours to Scotland and the British Isles for travelers from all over the world. He stores information about the various tours offered by his agency in an XML document. He needs your help in binding the data from his document to a Web page. Figure 9-51 shows the structure of Ian's document, tour.xml.

Figure 9-51

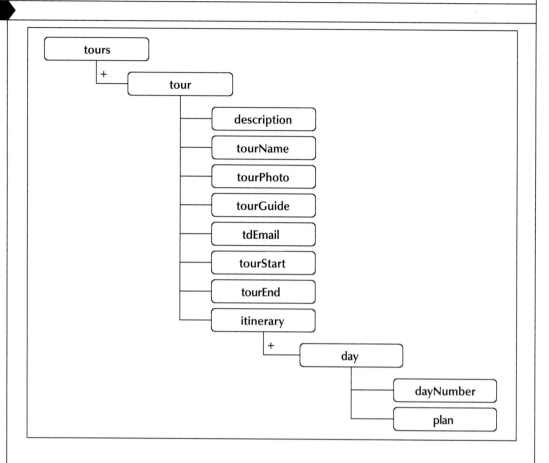

The description field contains a section of HTML code that Ian wants you to insert directly into the document. The itinerary field contains a nested recordset describing the events of each day of the tour. There are four tours in his file: the Lake District tour, the Hebrides tour, the Highland tour, and the Castles of Scotland tour. Ian has not created a Web page for his data yet. He has left the design up to you.

To complete this task:

1. Using your text editor, open **scottxt.htm** from the tutorial.09x/case4 folder. Enter *your name* and *the date* in the comment section of the file, and save it as **scotland.htm**.
2. Go to the **tour.xml** file in your text editor. Take some time to examine the contents and structure of the file. Close the document without making any changes.
3. Return to the scotland.htm file in your text editor. Add a data island named tourInfo to the head section of the document, attaching the Web page to the tour.xml file.
4. The Web page should display information about a single tour at a time, and the itinerary for each tour should be displayed as a table in the Web page.
5. The page should display an image from the selected tour (the image source file is indicated in the photo field).

6. The page should display a link to the e-mail address of the tour guide (found in the tdEmail field).
7. The information from the description field should be displayed in the Web page using the HTML formatting codes indicated in the tour.xml document.
8. The rest of the tour information should be displayed elsewhere in the Web page using whatever styles and formatting you choose.
9. The page should include navigation buttons to move through the tours in the XML document.
10. When you're finished, open the scotland.htm file in Internet Explorer, and verify that you can view information about the different records in the Tour Scotland tour list.
11. Submit the completed project to your instructor.

Quick Check Answers

Session 9.1

1.
   a. Data binding is a process by which information in a data source is stored as an object in computer memory.
   b. A field is an element that contains a single item of information.
   c. A record is a collection of fields for a single entity.
   d. A recordset is a collection of records.
2. A hierarchical recordset can contain nested recordsets. A simple recordset cannot.
3. A data island is the data attached to a Web page through the process of data binding.
4. <xml id="compInfo" src="company.xml"></xml>
5. <span datasrc="#compInfo" datafld="cName"></span>
6. As the value of the src attribute
7. The $TEXT field contains the character data from all of the fields in a record, not including attribute values.

Session 9.2

1. As fields
2. The field element becomes a record element with the attribute becoming one of the fields of the record element. The text in the field can be accessed only through the $TEXT field name.
3. CInfo.recordset.moveLast()
4. CInfo.recordset.movePrevious()
5. CInfo.recordset.move(5)
6. EOF
7. Index

Session 9.3

1. within the opening <table> tag
2. breaking up a recordset into manageable chunks called pages
3. Include the datapagesize="5" attribute in the table tag.
4. PTable.lastPage()
5. PTable.datapagesize=6
6. If the recordset contains several levels of nested recordsets, you must include several levels of nested tables to match.

Objectives

Working with the Document Object Model

Creating Interactive Documents Using JavaScript and XML

Case

The Lighthouse Charitable Trust

Susan Martinez is the fundraising coordinator for The Lighthouse, a charitable organization located in central Kentucky. One of her responsibilities is to maintain a contact list of donors and the amount of money each has contributed to the organization. Susan has stored this information in an XML document and created an XSLT style sheet to view that information.

Susan wants to create an interactive Web page that allows her to view the contents of her XML document in a variety of ways. She also wants the ability to insert new records into the XML document via a custom Web form rather than modifying the source document. To do this, she needs a program that can access and modify the contents of both her XML document and her XSLT style sheet. She's asked for your help in writing such a program.

NOTE: The tasks in this tutorial require Internet Explorer for Windows version 5.0 or above or Firefox version 1.5 or above and a working knowledge of JavaScript.

Student Data Files

▼tutorial.10x

▽ tutorial folder	▽ review folder	▽ case1 folder
clisttxt.htm	granttxt.htm	reptxt.htm
clist.css	grants.css	headtxt.xsl
clist.xml	grants.xml	stocks.xml
clist.xsl	grants.xsl	stock.css

Session 10.1

Introducing the Document Object Model

You sit down with Susan at The Lighthouse office to discuss her proposal to create an online contributions report. She has already created a sample XML document containing a list of contributions. Figure 10-1 shows the structure of her XML file. For each contribution, she has recorded the name and address of the donor, the date of the contribution, and the amount given.

Figure 10-1 | Structure of the clist.xml document

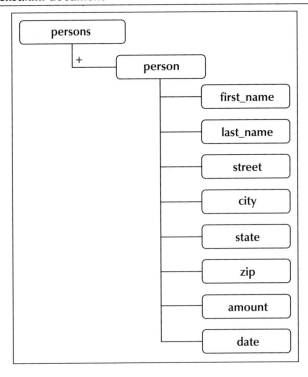

Susan also created an XSLT style sheet to display this contribution data in a Web table. Figure 10-2 shows the result document that is created by applying her style sheet to her source document.

Contribution list Web table ◄ **Figure 10-2**

Contributor List			Total: $3,450
Date	**Name**	**Address**	**Amount**
2008-09-03	Rainey, Genny	657 Dawson Lane Youngston, KY 88873	$50
2008-09-02	Lu, Basilia	851 Flad Court Jasper, KY 88633	$500
2008-08-31	Levesque, Kris	542 Upton Avenue Delphi, KY 88793	$100
2008-08-31	Mckinnon, Livia	557 Ivy Avenue Jasper, KY 88960	$50
2008-08-30	Damico, Petronila	44 Stewart Street Drake, KY 88604	$250
2008-08-30	Ingersoll, Lynwood	723 Jackson Avenue Delphi, KY 88802	$500
2008-08-28	Warren, Hugh	585 Lindon Court Wheaton, KY 88877	$50
2008-08-27	Thomas, Tom	Rigel Avenue Drake, KY 89411	$100
2008-08-25	White, Jeri	Hawkes Lane Delphi, KY 89211	$150
2008-08-25	Bones, Steve	900 Lawton Street Wheaton, KY 89211	$50
2008-08-23	Wilkes, Alan	321 Ashburn Jasper, KY 89831	$150
2008-08-23	Thu, Uma	25 Longton Lane Delphi, KY 89011	$100
2008-08-23	Li, Howard	4312 East Oak Avenue Youngston, KY 89318	$250
2008-08-23	Browne, Cynthia	71 Circuit Court Wheaton, KY 89321	$50
2008-08-22	Windt, Gary	55 Hawking Street Delphi, KY 89011	$1,000
2008-08-22	Sanchez, Andrew	891 Lindon Lane Delphi, KY 89011	$50
2008-08-22	Whitney, Jane	87 Hilltop Drive Jasper, KY 89381	$50

Before proceeding with her project, you decide to explore the documents that Susan has already created.

To view the source document and style sheet:

► **1.** Use your text editor to open **clist.xml** from the tutorial.10x/tutorial folder. Take some time to review the content and structure of the file. Close the file without making any changes to the document.

► **2.** Use your text editor to open **clist.xsl** from the tutorial.10x/tutorial folder. Review the templates and style elements used in the document. Once again, close the document without saving any changes you may have inadvertently made to the file.

Until now, you've used XML and XSLT to create static result documents. If you wanted to change the contents or layout of a result document, you had to revise either the source document or the style sheet code using a text editor or an XML editor such as XMLSpy. Static result documents require users to have a working knowledge of XML and XSLT to make changes. For users not well-versed in those languages, however, you can create a **front-end application** to perform the task of revising the style sheet or source document through an easy-to-use interface. For example, a Web form could be used to allow users to enter new data or specify the changes they want to make to the style sheet. This is what Susan has in mind for her Web page.

Susan wants your help with creating a Web form that displays the contribution list and supports the following features:

- Input fields to add new contributions and contributors to the table
- Option buttons to sort the contributions list by date, amount given, donor name, and city of residence
- An input box in which she can enter an expression to filter the contributions list, displaying only those contributions that satisfy a particular condition, such as contributions of $500 or more

Figure 10-3 shows a preview of the Web page that Susan has in mind.

Figure 10-3 ▷ **Susan's proposed contribution report**

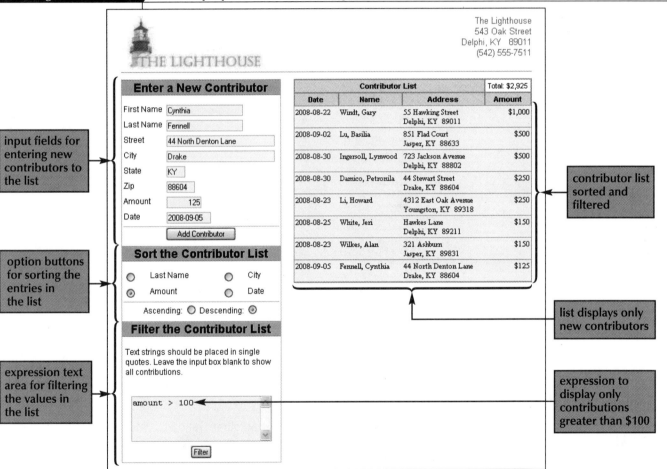

input fields for entering new contributors to the list

option buttons for sorting the entries in the list

expression text area for filtering the values in the list

contributor list sorted and filtered

list displays only new contributors

expression to display only contributions greater than $100

Susan has already entered the initial HTML code for her Web page. Open the file she created and explore it now.

To open the contribution report page:

▶ **1.** Use your text editor to open **clisttxt.htm** from the tutorial.10x/tutorial folder. Enter *your name* and *the date* in the comment section at the top of the file and save the file as **clist.htm**.

▶ **2.** Take some time to review the contents and structure of the HTML file.

3. Open the clist.htm file in your Web browser. Figure 10-4 shows the current appearance of the page.

Initial Web page ◄ **Figure 10-4**

The Lighthouse
543 Oak Street
Delphi, KY 89011
(542) 555-7511

THE LIGHTHOUSE

Enter a New Contributor

First Name
Last Name
Street
City
State
Zip
Amount
Date

Add Contributor

Sort the Contributor List

○ Last Name   ○ City
○ Amount   ◉ Date

Ascending: ○ Descending: ◉

Filter the Contributor List

Text strings should be placed in single quotes. Leave the input box blank to show all contributions.

Filter

Trouble? To complete all of the assignments in this tutorial you should be running Windows Internet Explorer 5.0 or higher or Firefox 1.5 or higher. If you are running an earlier browser version or a different browser, you might not be able to complete all of the tasks in this tutorial.

At present, Susan has inserted only the HTML code for the Web form controls. To complete her Web page, you need to add code to load the contents of the clist.xml file, apply the clist.xsl style sheet, and display the resulting content on her Web page. Your code also needs to include commands that modify the contents of both the XML document and XSLT style sheet in response to user requests.

The W3C DOM

To modify an XML or XSLT document, you need to be able to access the document and its contents. This is done through a **Document Object Model** or **DOM**, which is a systematic framework for working with the content and structure of a document. Just as it did in writing the specifications for XML and HTML, the World Wide Web Consortium (W3C) has developed specifications for a Document Object Model, called the **W3C DOM**, designed for markup languages such as XML and HTML. The W3C DOM is not a programming language; rather, it describes the interface between a programming language and document content. In this tutorial, you'll use the JavaScript programming language, but the techniques you will employ can be easily applied to other languages, such as Java or ASP. Once programmers understand the W3C DOM, they may need to use different programming languages for different tasks, but they do not need to change their basic programming models.

There are four specifications, or levels, in the W3C DOM, labeled DOM Level 0 through DOM Level 3. Figure 10-5 summarizes the aspects of each DOM.

Figure 10-5 ▶ **DOM Levels**

DOM	Description	Browser support
DOM Level 0	**DOM Level 0** is roughly equivalent to the programming model developed in the mid 1990's by Netscape Navigator 3.0 and Internet Explorer 3.0 for use with HTML documents. DOM Level 0 is sometimes referred to as the **basic model** and is of interest to programmers who need a DOM that is compatible with early browser versions and who work primarily with HTML.	Excellent: should be supported by all browsers and recent browser versions
DOM Level 1	**DOM Level 1** finalized by the W3C in 1998, provides the model for representing basic document content. The DOM Level 1 specification is broken into two parts: Core and HTML. The Core specification provides a set of instructions for interacting with any structured document including XML, XHTML, or HTML. The HTML specifications provide additional instructions for interacting with HTML documents.	Excellent: should be supported by all current browsers and recent browser versions
DOM Level 2	**DOM Level 2** released in November 2000, extended DOM Level 1 by providing support for namespaces, Cascading Style Sheets, and user-initiated actions, such as mouse clicks and key strokes. DOM Level 2 also provides more methods for manipulating the content and structure of a source document. DOM Level 2 is divided into six specifications: Core, Views, Events, Style, Traversal and Range, and HTML.	Very good: most (but not all) Level 2 specifications are supported by current browsers
DOM Level 3	**DOM Level 3**, released in April 2004, provides a framework for working with document loading and saving, as well as for working with DTDs and document validation. DOM Level 3 is divided into five specifications: Core, Load and Save, Validation, Events, and XPath.	Minor: most current browsers provide little or no support

Most of your work on Susan's contribution report follows the specifications of DOM Level 1 and DOM Level 2. Note that browser support for DOM Level 2 is very good at the time of this writing, though there are some gaps in coverage from different browsers. Browser support for the W3C DOM is constantly changing and improving. Several sites on the Web provide current DOM compatibility tables for the different browsers. You can also review material on each browser's Web site to determine its current level of support.

Internet Explorer and the W3C DOM

Internet Explorer works with XML documents through its internal XML parser, MSXML. MSXML has undergone several revisions since it was first introduced in Internet Explorer 4.0 (see Figure 10-6). Note that because MSXML is separate from Internet Explorer, you cannot determine the MSXML version in use simply by examining the version number of the Internet Explorer browser. Later in this section, you'll explore how to use JavaScript to determine which version of MSXML a browser is using.

Versions of MSXML ◄   **Figure 10-6**

MSXML version	Description
MSXML 1.0	The first version of MSXML, shipped with Internet Explorer 4.0; built on **MS DOM**, a Microsoft Document Object Model that predates the standards set in the W3C DOM
MSXML 2.0	Released with Internet Explorer 5.0; provides partial support for the W3C DOM and XSL patterns
MSXML 2.6	Released with Windows 2000; provides support for the W3C DOM, XSL patterns, XPath and SAX version 2
MSXML 3.0	Released in November 2000; provides support for the W3C DOM, XSLT, XPath, namespaces, and SAX version 2
MSXML 4.0	Released in October 2001, renamed Microsoft XML Core services; improved the performance of the MSXML parser and added support for XSD schemas, improved HTTP data access, and improved DOM-SAX integration
MSXML 5.0	Released in 2003 with Office 2003; designed specifically for use with the Microsoft Office suite, adding support for XML digital signatures
MSXML 6.0	Released in 2005 with SQL Server 2005; enhanced to eliminate security threats; some insecure features, such as DTDs and inline schemas, are turned off by default

Some users may have multiple versions of MSXML installed on their systems. Starting with version 3.0, Microsoft allowed MSXML to work in either replace mode or side-by-side mode. In **replace mode**, any version references of the MSXML parser are updated so that only the latest version of the parser is used. This may cause programs written for specific versions of MSXML to fail. In **side-by-side mode**, versions of the MSXML parser can be installed without affecting other previously installed versions. This allows multiple versions of the parser to coexist without error. The application accessing the MSXML parser decides which version of MSXML to use for a particular task. Note that MSXML 4.0 can be used only in side-by-side mode and must be installed separately from the Windows operating system and Internet Explorer. All of the tasks in this tutorial can be accomplished using MSXML 2.6 and above. If you're running Windows XP or Internet Explorer 5.0 or above, MSXML 2.6 is installed by default.

Mozilla and the W3C DOM

Mozilla-based browsers (primarily Netscape 6.0 and above and Firefox) also support the W3C Document Object Model through DOM Level 2. Because these browser versions were developed after the W3C specifications were written, they follow the official specifications more closely than Internet Explorer. As with any JavaScript program, you have to test your code against multiple browsers and multiple versions of the same browser. Later versions of Firefox and Netscape provide fuller and more bug-free support for the W3C DOM than earlier versions, but if you have to support a wide audience of users, you may have to write your code to fit the lowest common denominator.

Creating a Cross-Browser Solution

Because there are some fundamental differences between Internet Explorer and the Mozilla-based browsers in implementing the Document Object Model, any program code that you write has to first determine which browser is in use. One approach is to use **object detection**, in which a user's browser is queried as to whether it supports a particular JavaScript object or object property. By determining what objects the browser recognizes, you can determine what browser the user is running. You can store this information in a Boolean variable using the conditional operator

```
var browser = object ? true:false;
```

where *browser* is the name of the Boolean variable that reports whether a particular browser is in use and *object* is the name of a JavaScript object or object property supported by that browser. For this project, you need two Boolean variables: one named IE that has a value of true if the browser is Internet Explorer version 5.0 or above, and another named MOZ that has a value of true if a Mozilla-based browser is in use. The code to create the IE variable is

```
var IE = window.ActiveXObject ? true:false;
```

The code to create the MOZ variable is

```
var MOZ = document.implementation.createDocument ? true:false;
```

As you'll see shortly, the ActiveXObject object is associated only with the Internet Explorer browser and the document.implementation.createDocument object is supported by Mozilla-based browsers (but not by Internet Explorer at the current time). Once the IE and MOZ variables have been created, you can run code specific to Internet Explorer and Mozilla-based browsers using the following structure:

```
if (IE) {
   Internet Explorer code
} else if (MOZ) {
   Mozilla code
}
```

Because IE and MOZ are Boolean variables limited to values of true and false, the if statements in the above code only run the appropriate code if the IE or MOZ variables have the value true. Add these variables to the clist.htm file.

To create the IE and MOZ variables:

1. Return to the **clist.htm** file in your text editor.

2. Directly above the closing </head> tag insert the following script element and JavaScript code (see Figure 10-7):

   ```
   <script type="text/javascript">
   var IE = window.ActiveXObject ? true:false;
   var MOZ = document.implementation.createDocument ? true: false;
   </script>
   ```

| Figure 10-7 | Creating the IE and MOZ variables |

```
<title>Contributors List</title>
<link href="clist.css" rel="stylesheet" type="text/css" />
<script type="text/javascript">
 var IE = window.ActiveXObject ? true:false;
 var MOZ = document.implementation.createDocument ? true: false;
</script>
</head>
```

Trouble? JavaScript is case sensitive, so the code you entered must match the code shown in Figure 10-7 including the use of upper- and lowercase letters.

3. Save your changes to the file.

Alternatives to the W3C DOM

As you'll see later, the W3C Document Object Model represents the contents of an XML document in a hierarchical tree structure. Through this tree structure, you can access the different parts of an XML document to modify, delete, or add new data. One problem with this approach is that it is memory intensive. Typically, the amount of memory required to create this tree structure is 10 times the size of the source document. This means, for example, that a 100 KB file can require 1 MB of memory for processing. This can be a major hurdle for large source documents.

An alternative to a Document Object Model is the **Simple API for XML**, or **SAX**, which handles XML information in a single unidirectional data stream. Because SAX does not load an entire document into memory during processing, it is ideal for larger documents that could overwhelm computers with limited memory. You will not be using SAX in Susan's project, so your work will be limited to the W3C DOM.

Creating a Document Object

Now that you have an overview of Document Object Models and their browser support, you can begin working on Susan's Web page. Your first task is to create a document object. A **document object** is an object that can store the contents and structure of a document. At present, Internet Explorer and Mozilla-based browsers use different methods to create document objects, so any code needs to accommodate these differences to be cross-browser compatible. Start by looking at the Internet Explorer approach.

Creating a Document Object in Internet Explorer

Internet Explorer creates document objects using **ActiveX**, a Microsoft technology that can be used to create interactive content for the Web. To create a document object, you enter the JavaScript command

```
docObj = new ActiveXObject(PID);
```

where *docObj* is the variable name of the document object and *PID* is the program ID that indicates the type of document object to be created. Each version of MSXML supports a different program ID for creating document objects. The following program IDs are currently supported by different versions of MSXML:

- Msxml2.DOMDocument.5.0
- Msxml2.DOMDocument.4.0
- Msxml2.DOMDocument.3.0
- MSXML2.DOMDocument
- Microsoft.XMLDOM

Note that for the latest versions of MSXML, the version number is attached to the program ID. For example, to create a document object named XMLdoc in MSXML 3.0, you run the following command:

```
XMLdoc = new ActiveXObject("Msxml2.DOMDocument.3.0");
```

With so many possible program IDs, you may wonder which one to choose, especially if you don't know what version of MSXML a given user may be running. Generally it is best to use the most recent version of MSXML supported by a user's browser, as that version is presumably the most efficient, the fastest, and the most compatible with the latest DOM standards. One way to ensure that you are using the most recent version is to query the browser using each program ID. To do this, you can put the different program IDs into an **array**, which is a collection of data values organized under a single name. The following code creates an array named DOMPID that contains the different program IDs supported by MSXML:

```
var DOMPID = ["Msxml2.DOMDocument.5.0", "Msxml2.DOMDocument.4.0",
              "Msxml2.DOMDocument.3.0", "MSXML2.DOMDocument",
              "Microsoft.XMLDOM"];
```

Notice that the program IDs in the array are listed starting with the most recent MSXML version. To determine which of the program IDs to use in your code, you loop through the content of the array and stop when you reach a program ID that is supported by the browser. The code to loop through the DOM PID array is

```
function getPID(pArray) {
    var PIDStr = "";
    var PIDFound = false;
    for (i=0; i<pArray.length && !PIDFound; i++) {
        try {
            var objectXML=new ActiveXObject(pArray[i]);
            PIDStr=pArray[i];
            PIDFound=true;
        } catch (objException) {
        }
    }
    return PIDStr;
}
```

This function uses a for loop to go through the list of progIDs in an array named pArray. For each progID, the function uses a try...catch command block to catch errors generated by using an unsupported progID value. The first progID value that does not result in an error is returned by the function. Because the program ID values are placed in the array with the most recent values listed first, the program ID returned by this function represents the most current version of MSXML of the versions defined in the array.

You could then call the getPID() function from within the JavaScript command to create the document object as follows:

```
XMLdoc=new ActiveXObject(getPID(DOMPID));
```

Because the getPID() function returns the most recent MSXML program ID, the XMLdoc document object is created using the most current version of MSXML available on the user's browser.

Rather than entering the DOMPID array and the getPID() function into the clist.htm file, Susan has created a JavaScript file named library.js that contains this array and function. You can create a link to this external script file and use it to create the XMLdoc document object for Susan's Web page.

To create a document object in Internet Explorer:

▶ 1. Use your text editor to open the **library.js** file from the tutorial.10x/tutorial folder. Take some time to review the contents of this file. Your work throughout the remainder of the tutorial uses the functions and variables created in this file.

2. Close the library.js file without saving any changes you may have inadvertently made to the file.

3. Return to the **clist.htm** file in your text editor. Directly above the script element you inserted earlier, insert the following link to the external library.js file:

```
<script type="text/javascript" src="library.js"></script>
```

4. Go to the internal script element, and directly above the closing </script> tag insert the following code to declare the XMLdoc variable and to store a document object in it:

```
var XMLdoc; //Source XML document
```

5. Insert the following function at the bottom of the script element to create the XMLdoc variable:

```
function init() {
    if (IE) {
        XMLdoc=new ActiveXObject(getPID(DOMPID));
    }
}
```

6. Add the event handler **onload="init()"** to the opening <body> tag to run the init() function when the page is initially loaded by a browser. Figure 10-8 highlights the new code added to the clist.htm file.

Creating a document object in Internet Explorer — Figure 10-8

```
<title>Contributors List</title>
<link href="clist.css" rel="stylesheet" type="text/css" />
<script type="text/javascript" src="library.js"></script>

<script type="text/javascript">
var IE = window.ActiveXObject ? true:false;
var MOZ = document.implementation.createDocument ? true: false;

var XMLdoc; //Source XML document

function init() {
    if (IE) {
        XMLdoc=new ActiveXObject(getPID(DOMPID));
    }
}

</script>

</head>

<body onload="init()">
    <form name="webform" id="webform">
```

Note that the command to create the document object is run only if the IE variable equals true—that is to say, only if the current browser is Internet Explorer. Next, you have to enter commands to create the document object for Mozilla-based browsers.

Creating a Document Object in Mozilla

Mozilla-based browsers such as Netscape and Firefox do not support ActiveX objects. To create a document object you run the createDocument() method of the document. implementation object. The syntax of the command is

```
docObj = document.implementation.createDocument(uri,root,doctype);
```

where `uri` is the URI of the document's namespace, `root` is the qualified name of the document's root element, and `doctype` is the type of document to create. Currently, there is no JavaScript support for the `doctype` parameter in any Mozilla-based browser, so you should enter a value of null.

For example to create a document object belonging to a namespace with the URI *http://lhouse.org* and having the root element persons, you enter the code

```
XMLdoc = document.implementation.createDocument("http://lhouse.
org","persons",null);
```

and JavaScript creates an XML document containing the following content:

```
<a0:persons xmlns:a0="http://lhouse.org" />
```

The a0 namespace prefix is automatically generated by the browser. In many cases you don't specify a namespace or a root element. In these situations, you enter empty text strings for the given parameter values as follows:

```
XMLdoc = document.implementation.createDocument("","",null);
```

For Susan's document, you'll create a document object, but you won't specify a namespace or a root element.

Reference Window

Creating a Document Object

Internet Explorer

- To create a document object, use the JavaScript command
    docObj = new ActiveXObject(*progID*);
  where *docObj* is the variable name of the document object and *progID* is the program ID that indicates the type of document object to be created. For the MSXML parser in Internet Explorer, you can use the following program IDs (listed in descending order of MSXML version): Msxml2.DOMDocument.5.0, Msxml2.DOMDocument.4.0, Msxml2.DOMDocument.3.0, Msxml2.DOMDocument, and Microsoft.XMLDOM.

Mozilla

- To create a document object, use the JavaScript command
    docObj = document.implementation.createDocument(*uri,root,doctype*);
  where *uri* is the URI of the document's namespace, *root* is the qualified name of the document's root element, and *doctype* is the type of document to create. For empty document objects, enter
    docObj = document.implementation.createDocument("","",null);

To create a document object in Mozilla:

1. Below the if statement you entered in init() function, insert the following lines of code (see Figure 10-9):

```
else if (MOZ) {
    XMLdoc = document.implementation.createDocument("","",null);
}
```

| Figure 10-9 | Creating a document object in Mozilla |

```
function init() {
    if (IE) {
        XMLdoc=new ActiveXObject(getPID(DOMPID));
    }
    else if (MOZ) {
        XMLdoc = document.implementation.createDocument("","",null);
    }
}
```

2. Save your changes to the **clist.htm** file, and reload the file in your Web browser. Verify that no errors are reported by the browser. At this point, you will not see any differences in the rendered Web page.

You've created document objects for both types of browsers. At this point, both document objects are empty. Your next step is to load those documents with the content of the clist.xml file.

Loading a File into a Document Object

To load an XML file into a document object, you first need to determine whether to load the file asynchronously or synchronously. An **asynchronous load** does not require the application loading the file to wait for it to finish loading before proceeding through the lines in the program code, and a **synchronous load** causes the application to stop until the file is completely loaded. The default is an asynchronous load in order to speed up processing time, but in some circumstances you may want to perform a synchronous load to avoid a situation in which your application attempts to perform an operation on an incompletely loaded file. This is a particular concern for large files or when retrieving files through a slow Internet connection. To specify that a document object should be loaded synchronously, you use the command

```
docObj.async=false;
```

where *docObj* is the document object into which you want to load the file. Next, you load the file into the document object using the method

```
docObj.load(url);
```

where *url* is the URL of the file to be loaded into the document object.

Loading a File into a Document Object	Reference Window

- To load a file into a document object, you first have to specify whether to load the file asynchronously or synchronously. To perform a synchronous load, use the command
     `docObj.async=false;`
  where *docObj* is the document object.
- To perform an asynchronous load use
     `docObj.async=true;`
- To load a file into the document object, use
     `docObj.load(url);`
  where *url* is the URL of the file to be loaded.

Because you need to load several files into different document objects in the course of creating Susan's contribution report, you can store the commands for loading a document synchronously in the following function:

```
function loadDoc(docObj, url) {
   docObj.async=false;
   docObj.load(url);
}
```

Thus, to load the clist.xml file synchronously into the XMLdoc document object, you run the following command from within the init() function:

```
loadDoc(XMLdoc, "clist.xml");
```

Add this function to the clist.htm file.

To create the loadDoc() function:

1. Insert the following function directly above the init() function:

```
function loadDoc(docObj, url) {
    docObj.async=false;
    docObj.load(url);
}
```

2. Add the following command to the init() function as shown in Figure 10-10.

```
loadDoc(XMLdoc, "clist.xml");
```

Figure 10-10	Creating the loadDoc() function

```
function loadDoc(docObj, url) {
    docObj.async=false;
    docObj.load(url);
}

function init() {
    if (IE) {
        XMLdoc=new ActiveXObject(getPID(DOMPID));
    }
    else if (MOZ) {
        XMLdoc = document.implementation.createDocument("","",null);
    }

    loadDoc(XMLdoc, "clist.xml");
}
```

3. Save your changes to the file, and reload the **clist.htm** file in your Web browser. Verify that no JavaScript errors are reported. You will not see any changes to the file's appearance, but this is a good check to ensure that you have not made an error in entering the code.

   Trouble? If a JavaScript error is reported, examine the code in your document and compare it to the previous figures. Make sure that you are not missing any quotation marks and that the use of upper- and lowercase letters matches the code.

If your XML code is not stored in an external file, Internet Explorer also supports the loadXML() method, which loads a text string as an XML document. For example, to load the XML code

```
<person>
   <name>Jo Wilcox</name>
</person>
```

into the XMLdoc document object, you use the following commands:

```
XStr="<person><name>Jo Wilcox</name></person>";
XMLdoc.loadXML(XStr);
```

Other browsers such as Netscape or Firefox do not support the loadXML() method, so you should only use it for situations in which you know your users are running Internet Explorer.

Transforming a Document with Internet Explorer

At this point, your code instructs the browser to load the source document into computer memory, but does not yet apply the transformation from Susan's style sheet to create a result document displaying the contribution list. Internet Explorer and Mozilla-based browsers support two different techniques for loading and applying XSLT transformations. You'll start by looking at Internet Explorer's approach.

Loading a Style Sheet Object

Because XSLT style sheets are also XML documents, you need to create a document object using ActiveX; however, the program IDs for XSLT style sheets differ from those for source documents. This is because ActiveX uses two different methods for retrieving document content. Source documents like the clist.xml file follow a **rental-threaded model** in which the content is accessed by the XML processor using a single sequence of instructions, or **thread**. This is preferable for most XML documents because it uses memory more efficiently. XSLT style sheets such as the clist.xsl file can also employ a **free-threaded model** in which the content is accessed by the processor through multiple input threads. The following program IDs identify a free-threaded ActiveX document object:

• Msxml2.FreeThreadedDOMDocument.5.0
• Msxml2.FreeThreadedDOMDocument.4.0
• Msxml2.FreeThreadedDOMDocument.3.0

As with the program IDs for the source document object, these IDs are stored in the following array in the library.js file:

```
var FreeThreadPID = ["Msxml2.FreeThreadedDOMDocument.5.0",
                     "Msxml2.FreeThreadedDOMDocument.4.0",
                     "Msxml2.FreeThreadedDOMDocument.3.0"];
```

You can create a document object for the style sheet using the getPID() function you used for the XMLdoc object:

```
XSLTdoc=new ActiveXObject(getPID(FreeThreadPID));
```

You can also create style sheet documents using the same program IDs you used for the source document. However, using the free-threaded model has the advantage that it allows your style sheets to be used with template and processor objects—a topic you'll explore shortly. This is not the case with style sheet objects created using the rental-threaded model. Thus, for Susan's project you'll create the style sheet object for the clist.xsl file using a free-threaded model.

To create the XSLTdoc style sheet object:

1. Return to the **clist.htm** file, and directly below the command declaring the XML-doc variable, insert the following command:

   ```
   var XSLTdoc; //XSLT style sheet document
   ```

2. Go to the init() function, and directly below the command creating the XMLdoc document object for Internet Explorer, insert the following:

   ```
   XSLTdoc=new ActiveXObject(getPID(FreeThreadPID));
   ```

> **3.** Add the following command to the end of the init() function to load the clist.xsl file into the XSLTdoc object (see Figure 10-11):
>
> ```
> loadDoc(XSLTdoc, "clist.xsl");
> ```

Figure 10-11 **Loading a style sheet object in Internet Explorer**

```
var XMLdoc; //Source XML document
var XSLTdoc; //XSLT style sheet document

function loadDoc(docobj, url) {
    docobj.async=false;
    docobj.load(url);
}

function init() {
    if (IE) {
        XMLdoc=new ActiveXObject(getPID(DOMPID));
        XSLTdoc=new ActiveXObject(getPID(FreeThreadPID));
    }
    else if (MOZ) {
        XMLdoc = document.implementation.createDocument("","",null);
    }

    loadDoc(XMLdoc, "clist.xml");
    loadDoc(XSLTdoc, "clist.xsl");
}
```

Transforming a Document

Once a style sheet file is loaded, Internet Explorer supports two methods of applying the style sheet directly to the source document: transformNode() and transformNodeToObject(). The transformNode() method creates a text string containing the code of the result document and has the following syntax:

```
docObj.transformNode(styleObj)
```

where *docObj* is either a document object or a node within a document, and *styleObj* is a document object containing a style sheet. In the following code, the browser uses the transformNode() method to create a text string containing the text of the code resulting from applying the XSLTdoc transformation to the XMLdoc source document:

```
resultStr = XMLdoc.transformNode(XSLTdoc);
```

Once the text string is generated, it can be inserted directly into the Web page and rendered by the browser. If you don't want the result document to be written into a text string, you can use the transformNodeToObject() method, which stores the result in another document object. The syntax is

```
docObj.transformNodeToObject(styleObj, resultObj)
```

where *resultObj* is a document object that stores the result of applying the *styleObj* style sheet to the *object* document object or node. The advantage of creating a result object is that you can write code to further manipulate the contents and structure of that object. If this is not an issue for your project, you may find it simpler to send the result to a text string using the transformNode() method.

Creating a Template Object

One problem with the transformNode() and transformNodeToObject() methods is that they can be drags on resources because a processor must compile the style sheet object each time the transformation is run. For a large and complicated style sheet or for programs that need to run several transformations, Microsoft suggests storing the compiled style sheet in a **template object**, which increases the efficiency of the program because the cached style sheet can be accessed repeatedly without being recompiled. This assumes, however, that the style sheet object is created using the free-threaded model. Template objects are created as ActiveX objects with one of the following program IDs:

- Msxml2.XSLTemplate.5.0
- Msxml2.XSLTemplate.4.0
- Msxml2.XSLTemplate.3.0

Reference Window

Using Style and Template Objects in Internet Explorer

- To create a style sheet object, use
  ```
  styleObj = new ActiveXObject(progID);
  ```
  where *styleObj* is the variable name of the document object and *progID* is one of the following program IDs (listed in descending order of MSXML version): Msxml2.FreeThreadedDocument.5.0, Msxml2.FreeThreaded.4.0, or Msxml2.FreeThreaded.3.0.
- To create a text string containing the result of transforming a source document, use
  ```
  docObj.transformNode(styleObj)
  ```
  where *docObj* is the source document object.
- To create a document object containing the result of transforming a source document, use
  ```
  docObj.transformNodeToObject(styleObj, resultObj)
  ```
  where *resultObj* is the result document object.
- To create a template object, use
  ```
  templateObj = new ActiveXObject(progID);
  ```
  where *templateObj* is the variable name of the document object and *progID* is one of the following program IDs (listed in descending order of MSXML version): Msxml2.XSLTemplate.5.0, Msxml2.XSLTemplate.4.0, or Msxml2.XSLTemplate.3.0.
- To store a style sheet in a template object, use
  ```
  templateObj.stylesheet = styleObj;
  ```

You decide to create a template object for Susan's program. Susan has already stored the template program IDs in an array named TemplatePID that you can access using the getPID() function.

To create the template object:

1. Directly below the command to declare the XSLTdoc variable, insert the following command:

   ```
   var XSLTemp; //IE template document
   ```

2. Go to the init() function, and directly below the command to create the XSLTdoc document object for Internet Explorer, insert the following code (see Figure 10-12):

   ```
   XSLTemp=new ActiveXObject(getPID(TemplatePID));
   ```

Figure 10-12	Creating a template object in Internet Explorer

```
var XMLdoc; //Source XML document
var XSLTdoc; //XSLT style sheet document
var XSLTemp; //IE template document

function loadDoc(docObj, url) {
    docObj.async=false;
    docObj.load(url);
}

function init() {
    if (IE) {
        XMLdoc=new ActiveXObject(getPID(DOMPID));
        XSLTdoc=new ActiveXObject(getPID(FreeThreadPID));
        XSLTemp=new ActiveXObject(getPID(TemplatePID));
    }
    else if (MOZ) {
        XMLdoc = document.implementation.createDocument("","",null);
    }

    loadDoc(XMLdoc, "clist.xml");
    loadDoc(XSLTdoc, "clist.xsl");
}
```

Creating a Processor Object

One of the advantages of the template object is that it allows you to work directly with the XSLT processor. From the processor you can specify the source document, run transformations, and, most importantly, set values for any global parameters defined in the style sheet. To create and use a **processor object**, you follow four steps:

1. Insert a free-threaded style sheet into the template object.
2. Create an XLST processor based on the template.
3. Specify an input source document for the processor.
4. Transform the source document based on the style sheet.

The command to insert a style sheet into a template is

templateObj.stylesheet=*styleObj*;

where *templateObj* is the template object and *styleObj* is a free-threaded style sheet object. To create an object to represent the processor, you run the JavaScript command

processorObj = *templateObj*.createProcessor();

where *processorObj* is a JavaScript object representing the XSLT processor and *templateObj* is a template object. For example, the following command creates a processor object named XSLTProc based on the XSLTemp object:

XSLTProc = XSLTemp.createProcessor();

Finally, you specify the input source document and use the transform() method to run the XSLT transformation using the commands

processorObj.input = *docObj*;
processorObj.transform();

where *docObj* is the source document for the transformation. The results of the transformation are stored within the processor object. Add a function to the clist.htm file named doTransform() that creates the processor object and runs the transformation under Internet Explorer.

To create the processor object:

1. Directly below the command to declare the XSLTemp variable, insert the following command:

```
var XSLTProc; //XSLT processor object
```

2. Directly above the init() function insert the following doTransform() function:

```
function doTransform() {
    if (IE) {
        XSLTemp.stylesheet=XSLTdoc;
        XSLTProc=XSLTemp.createProcessor();
        XSLTProc.input=XMLdoc;
        XSLTProc.transform();
    }
}
```

3. Add the following command to the end of the init() function to run the doTransform() function when the page is loaded (see Figure 10-13):

```
doTransform();
```

Creating a processor object in Internet Explorer   Figure 10-13

```
var XMLdoc; //Source XML document
var XSLTdoc; //XSLT style sheet document
var XSLTemp; //IE template document
var XSLTProc; //XSLT processor object

function loadDoc(docobj, url) {
    docobj.async=false;
    docobj.load(url);
}

function doTransform() {
    if (IE) {
        XSLTemp.stylesheet=XSLTdoc;
        XSLTProc=XSLTemp.createProcessor();
        XSLTProc.input=XMLdoc;
        XSLTProc.transform();
    }
}

function init() {
    if (IE) {
        XMLdoc=new ActiveXObject(getPID(DOMPID));
        XSLTdoc=new ActiveXObject(getPID(FreeThreadPID));
        XSLTemp=new ActiveXObject(getPID(TemplatePID));
    }
    else if (MOZ) {
        XMLdoc = document.implementation.createDocument("","",null);
    }

    loadDoc(XMLdoc, "clist.xml");
    loadDoc(XSLTdoc, "clist.xsl");

    doTransform();
}
```

The final part of the transformation is to retrieve the transformation output and display it in the Web page. To retrieve the result of the transformation use the command

```
resultObj = processorObj.output;
```

where `resultObj` is the object that displays the output from the transformation. Susan placed a div element in her Web page with the id "ctable". You can reference this element using the following JavaScript expression:

```
document.getElementById("ctable")
```

Currently, the div element contains no content. To insert the output code into that object, you can use the innerHTML property. The innerHTML property is a JavaScript property that specifies what HTML code should be placed within an HTML element. The code to place the results of the XSLT transformation in the ctable element is

```
var contTable = document.getElementById("ctable");
contTable.innerHTML = XSLTProc.output;
```

After running these commands, the contribution list should display the results of the transformation within the Internet Explorer browser. Add these commands to the doTransform() function.

To display the results of the transformation:

1. Go to the doTransform() function and insert the following command at the top of the function:

   ```
   var contTable = document.getElementById("ctable");
   ```

2. Add the following command at the bottom of the function as shown in Figure 10-14:

   ```
   contTable.innerHTML = XSLTProc.output;
   ```

Figure 10-14	Setting the output destination of the transformation

```
function doTransform() {
    var contTable = document.getElementById("ctable");
    if (IE) {
        XSLTemp.stylesheet=XSLTdoc;
        XSLTProc=XSLTemp.createProcessor();
        XSLTProc.input=XMLdoc;
        XSLTProc.transform();

        contTable.innerHTML = XSLTProc.output;
    }
}
```

3. Save your changes to the file, and reload **clist.htm** in your Internet Explorer Web browser, allowing blocked content if necessary. As shown in Figure 10-15, the Web page should now display the list of contributors to The Lighthouse.

Contribution list in Internet Explorer | Figure 10-15

The Lighthouse
543 Oak Street
Delphi, KY 89011
(542) 555-7511

THE LIGHTHOUSE

Enter a New Contributor

First Name
Last Name
Street
City
State
Zip
Amount
Date

Add Contributor

Sort the Contributor List

○ Last Name   ○ City
○ Amount   ◉ Date

Ascending: ○ Descending: ◉

Filter the Contributor List

Text strings should be placed in single quotes. Leave the input box blank to show all contributions.

Filter

Contributor List			Total: $3,450
Date	Name	Address	Amount
2008-09-03	Rainey, Genny	657 Dawson Lane Youngston, KY 88873	$50
2008-09-02	Lu, Basilia	851 Flad Court Jasper, KY 88633	$500
2008-08-31	Levesque, Kris	542 Upton Avenue Delphi, KY 88793	$100
2008-08-31	Mckinnon, Livia	557 Ivy Avenue Jasper, KY 88960	$50
2008-08-30	Damico, Petronila	44 Stewart Street Drake, KY 88604	$250
2008-08-30	Ingersoll, Lynwood	723 Jackson Avenue Delphi, KY 88802	$500
2008-08-28	Warren, Hugh	585 Lindon Court Wheaton, KY 88877	$50
2008-08-27	Thomas, Tom	Rigel Avenue Drake, KY 89411	$100
2008-08-25	White, Jeri	Hawkes Lane Delphi, KY 89211	$150
2008-08-25	Bones, Steve	900 Lawton Street Wheaton, KY 89211	$50
2008-08-23	Wilkes, Alan	321 Ashburn Jasper, KY 89831	$150
2008-08-23	Thu, Uma	25 Longton Lane Delphi, KY 89011	$100
2008-08-23	Li, Howard	4312 East Oak Avenue Youngston, KY 89318	$250
2008-08-23	Browne, Cynthia	71 Circuit Court Wheaton, KY 89321	$50
2008-08-22	Windt, Gary	55 Hawking Street Delphi, KY 89011	$1,000
2008-08-22	Sanchez, Andrew	891 Lindon Lane Delphi, KY 89011	$50
2008-08-22	Whitney, Jane	87 Hilltop Drive Jasper, KY 89381	$50

You've now transformed the source document and displayed the results in Susan's Web page using Internet Explorer. Next, you'll explore how to do the same thing under Mozilla.

Working with Processor Objects in Internet Explorer | Reference Window

- To create a processor object, use
  ```
  processorObj = templateObj.createProcessor();
  ```
  where *processorObj* is the processor object and *templateObj* is a template object.
- To specify the source document for the processor, use
  ```
  processorObj.input = docObj;
  ```
  where *docObj* is the source document object.
- To run the transformation (applying the template to the source document), use
  ```
  processorObj.transform();
  ```
- To save the output from the transformation, use
  ```
  resultObj = processorObj.output;
  ```
  where *resultObj* is the object that receives the output from the transformation.

Transforming a Document with Mozilla

Mozilla-based browsers such as Netscape and Firefox use a different, though similar, approach to loading style sheets and performing transformations. Mozilla doesn't make a distinction between rental- and free-threaded models for inputting data into style sheet objects; instead, you use the same method you employed earlier to create the XMLdoc object. For the XSLTdoc object this would be

```
XSLTdoc = document.implementation.createDocument("","",null);
```

Add this command to the init() function.

To create the XSLTdoc object in Mozilla:

 1. Return to the **clist.htm** file in your text editor.

 2. Go to the init() function, and insert the following command as shown in Figure 10-16:

```
XSLTdoc = document.implementation.createDocument("","",null);
```

Figure 10-16 **Loading a style sheet object in Mozilla**

```
function init() {
    if (IE) {
        XMLdoc=new ActiveXObject(getPID(DOMPID));
        XSLTdoc=new ActiveXObject(getPID(FreeThreadPID));
        XSLTemp=new ActiveXObject(getPID(TemplatePID));
    }
    else if (MOZ) {
        XMLdoc = document.implementation.createDocument("","",null);
        XSLTdoc = document.implementation.createDocument("","",null);
    }

    loadDoc(XMLdoc, "clist.xml");
    loadDoc(XSLTdoc, "clist.xsl");

    doTransform();
}
```

Creating a Processor Object

Similar to Internet Explorer, Mozilla supports an XSLT processor object from which you can insert source documents, apply style sheet transformations, and set parameter values; it does not, however, rely on template objects. To create a processor object, use the following object constructor:

```
processorObj = new XSLTProcessor();
```

To store a style sheet document in an XSLT processor, use the following importStylesheet() method:

```
processorObj.importStylesheet(styleObj);
```

where *styleObj* is the document object containing the style sheet. Thus, to create an XSLT processor and import a style sheet, you run the following code for Mozilla-based browsers:

```
XSLTProc = new XSLTProcessor();
XSLTProc.importStylesheet(XSLTdoc);
```

Add these commands to the doTransform() function.

To create a processor object in Mozilla:

▶ **1.** Go to the doTransform() function and the insert the following code as shown in Figure 10-17:

```
else if (MOZ) {
    var XSLTProc= new XSLTProcessor();
    XSLTProc.importStylesheet(XSLTdoc);
}
```

Note that these commands are only run if the browser in use is a Mozilla-based browser.

Creating a processor object in Mozilla ◀ Figure 10-17

```
function doTransform() {
    var contTable = document.getElementById("ctable");
    if (IE) {
        XSLTemp.stylesheet=XSLTdoc;
        XSLTProc=XSLTemp.createProcessor();
        XSLTProc.input=XMLdoc;
        XSLTProc.transform();

        contTable.innerHTML = XSLTProc.output;
    }
    else if (MOZ) {
        var XSLTProc= new XSLTProcessor();
        XSLTProc.importStylesheet(XSLTdoc);
    }
}
```

▶ **2.** Save your changes to the file.

Working with Processor Objects in Mozilla

Reference Window

- To create a processor object, use

    `processorObj = new XSLTProcessor();`
  where `processorObj` is the processor object.
- To import a style sheet into a processor, use

    `processorObj.importStylesheet(styleObj);`
  where `styleObj` is the document object containing the style sheet.
- To run a transformation, placing the result into a document object, use

    `resultObj = processorObj.transformToDocument(docObj);`
  where `resultObj` is the document object storing the transformation result and `docObj` is the source document for the transformation.

Running a Transformation

Next you have to run the transformation with the XSLT processor. Mozilla supports two different methods for running a transformation: transformToDocument() and transformToFragment(). The transformToDocument() method runs the transformation and creates a new document object from the result. It has the syntax

`resultObj = processorObj.transformToDocument(docObj);`

where `resultObj` is the document object storing the transformation result and `docObj` is the source document for the transformation. The transformToFragment() method takes the transformation result and creates a **document fragment** (a piece of a complete document object) that can then be appended to another document object. The syntax of the transformToFragment() method is

```
resultFragment = processorObj.transformToFragment(docObj, resultObj);
```

where `resultFragment` is the document fragment, `docObj` is the source document, and `resultObj` is the document object that stores the contents of the result fragment. Unless you need to create an entire result document, creating a fragment usually involves less overhead. For Susan's project, you can create a result fragment using the XMLDoc document as follows:

```
ResultDoc = XSLTProc.transformToFragment(XMLDoc, document);
```

The second parameter value of the transformToFragment() method, document, represents the HTML document being displayed in the browser. By running this command, you create the ResultDoc document fragment and store it in the current HTML document. However, simply storing the fragment in the HTML document does not tell the browser exactly where to place it. To do that, you have to specify its location either as a text string contained within an object (as you did with Internet Explorer) or as a new object within the HTML document. You'll look at the text string method in this session and explore how to create and append new objects in the next session.

Converting a Document Object or Fragment to a Text String

To convert a document object or a fragment to a text string in Mozilla, you create a **serializer object,** which contains a textual representation of the contents of a document object or fragment. To create a serializer object in Mozilla, you use the object constructor

```
serialObj = new XMLSerializer();
```

where `serialObj` is the serializer object that will contain the text of the document object or fragment. To serialize a specific document object or fragment, you apply the serializeToString() method

```
xStr = serialObj.serializeToString(resultObj);
```

where `xStr` is a text string containing the code of the `resultObj` document. Once the text string is generated in this fashion, you can use the innerHTML property to write it to a specific object on the Web page. Putting all of this together, the following code demonstrates how you transform and display the contribution list under a Mozilla-based browser:

```
var Resultdoc = XSLTProc.transformToFragment(XMLdoc, document);
var Xserial = new XMLSerializer();
var Xstr = Xserial.serializeToString(Resultdoc);
contTable.innerHTML = Xstr;
```

The first line in this command block creates the result document fragment by running the transformation. The next two lines serialize the result document to generate the Xstr variable, containing the text string of the document's content. Finally, the last line inserts this text into the inner HTML code of the contribution list table. Add this code to the clist.htm file.

To display the results of the transformation:

▶ 1. Insert the following code in the doTransform() function as shown in Figure 10-18:

```
var Resultdoc = XSLTProc.transformToFragment(XMLdoc, document);
var Xserial = new XMLSerializer();
var Xstr = Xserial.serializeToString(Resultdoc);

contTable.innerHTML = Xstr;
```

Transforming and displaying the result document ◀ **Figure 10-18**

```
function doTransform() {
    var contTable = document.getElementById("ctable");
    if (IE) {
        XSLTemp.stylesheet=XSLTdoc;
        XSLTProc=XSLTemp.createProcessor();
        XSLTProc.input=XMLdoc;
        XSLTProc.transform();

        contTable.innerHTML = XSLTProc.output;

    }
    else if (MOZ) {
        var XSLTProc= new XSLTProcessor();
        XSLTProc.importStylesheet(XSLTdoc);

        var Resultdoc = XSLTProc.transformToFragment(XMLdoc, document);
        var Xserial = new XMLSerializer();
        var Xstr = Xserial.serializeToString(Resultdoc);

        contTable.innerHTML = Xstr;
    }
}
```

▶ 2. Save your changes to the file, and open the **clist.htm** file in your Netscape or Firefox browser. Verify that the browser now displays the contribution list as it did earlier in Figure 10-15 for the Internet Explorer browser.

▶ 3. If you want to take a break before starting the next session, you may close any open files or applications.

You show Susan the results of your work. She's very pleased that you were able to use JavaScript to load and display the results of her XSLT style sheet. She is also interested to hear your discussion about the Document Object Model. Next, she wants you to work with the document object in order to add new entries to the contribution list and to display the contribution list in different ways.

Session 10.1 Quick Check

Review

1. What is a Document Object Model? What is the W3C DOM?
2. What JavaScript command would you use to create a document object named XDoc for an XML source document? Provide answers for both Internet Explorer and Mozilla. Assume a program ID of Microsoft.XMLDOM for the Internet Explorer solution.
3. What JavaScript command would you use to create a document object named XStyle for an XSLT style sheet? Provide a solution for both Internet Explorer and Mozilla. Assume a program ID of Msxml2.FreeThreadedDOMDocument.3.0 for the Internet Explorer solution.
4. What JavaScript code would you use to synchronously load the file source.doc into the XDoc document object?
5. What single JavaScript command would you use to transform the XDoc document object into a result string under Internet Explorer? Use the XStyle document object as the style sheet.

6. Under Internet Explorer, what JavaScript command would you use to create a template object named XTemplate? Use a program ID of Msxml2.XSLTemplate.3.0. What command would you use to load the XStyle style sheet into the template?

7. What JavaScript code would you use to create a processor object named Xprocessor? Provide a solution for both Internet Explorer and Mozilla. For Internet Explorer, assume that the name of the template object is XTemplate.

Session 10.2

Working with the Document Object

You spent much of the first session loading and transforming the source document object and the XSLT style sheet. In this session, you'll start to work with the content and structure of those documents. You'll start by looking at some of the properties and methods associated with the document object. In the last session, you used the load() method to load a file into a document object and the async property to determine whether that loading was done synchronously or asynchronously. Figure 10-19 and Figure 10-20 list several other properties and methods associated with the document object.

| Figure 10-19 | Properties of the document object |

Property	Description
docObj.async	Specifies whether *docObj* is loaded asynchronously (true) or synchronously (false)
docObj.defaultView	Returns the object displaying *docObj* (usually references the browser window)
docObj.docType	Returns *docObj*'s document type declaration (DTD)
docObj.documentElement	Returns the element node representing *docObj*'s root element
docObj.implementation	Returns the DOM implementation associated with *docObj*
docObj.parseError	Returns a parse error object containing information about the latest error returned by the parser as it attempts to load *docObj* [MSXML only]
docObj.preserveWhiteSpace	Specifies whether *docObj* preserves white space (true) or not (false) [MSXML only]
docObj.readyState	Returns an integer indicating the state of *docObj* as it is retrieved by the XML processor (1 = the document is loading, 2 = the document has been loaded and is being parsed, 3 = the document has been loaded and parsed, 4 = the retrieval is complete and the document is available) [MSXML only]
docObj.validateOnParse	Specifies whether the parser should validate *docObj* (true) or not (false) [MSXML only]

Methods of the document object | Figure 10-20

Method	Description
docObj.abort()	Aborts the asynchronous download of *docObj* [MSXML only]
docObj.getElementById(*id*)	References the element within *docObj* with the ID *id*
docObj.getElementsByTagName(*tag*)	References the list of elements within *docObj* with the tag name *tag*
docObj.load(*url*)	Loads *docObj* using data from the file located at *url*
docObj.loadXML(*xml*)	Loads the *xml* text string into *docObj* [MSXML only]
docObj.onreadystatechange()	Indicates that the ready state property of *docObj* has changed [MSXML only]
docObj.save(*object*)	Saves *docObj* to the object *object* [MSXML only]

To access a document's root element, you use the documentElement property. For example, to access the root element of Susan's clist.xml document from the last session, you enter the following expression:

```
XMLdoc.documentElement
```

The documentElement property is only one way of accessing the contents of the document object. You'll take a look at other approaches, starting with an overview of how the contents of the document object are organized in the Document Object Model.

Viewing the Node Tree

Similar to XPath and XSLT, the W3C Document Object Model organizes the contents of the document object in a hierarchal node tree. Figure 10-21 shows a sample node tree for a typical XML document.

A sample node tree | Figure 10-21

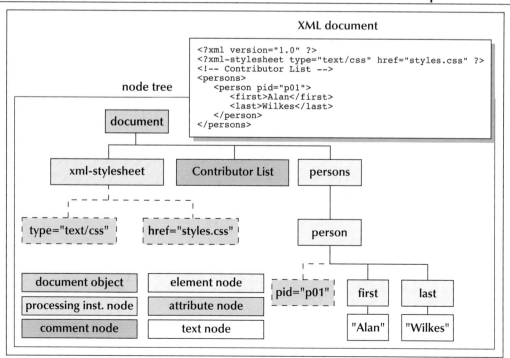

As with XPath, the W3C DOM node tree expresses the relationship between the various nodes in familial terms. A node that contains other nodes is a **parent node**, and the nodes it contains are **child nodes**. Nodes that share the same parent are **sibling nodes**. Nodes can contain different types of content. For example, **element nodes** refer to elements from the Document Object Model, and **text nodes** refer to the actual text content of element nodes. **Attribute nodes** refer to the attributes contained within elements or processing instructions. Attribute nodes are an exception to the familial structure. Although an attribute is associated with an element, the attribute node and its values are not part of the node tree. The W3C DOM includes special methods to deal with attributes, which are discussed in the third session of this tutorial.

Accessing Element Nodes by Tag Name

There are several ways of navigating through the elements contained in a document object. One of the most useful methods is the getElementsByTagName() method. The syntax of the method is

```
docObj.getElementsByTagName(tag)
```

where *docObj* is the document object and *tag* is the element's tag name. For example, to access all person elements from the XMLdoc document object, you enter the following expression:

```
XMLdoc.getElementsByTagName("person")
```

The getElementsByTagName() method returns a list sorted in the order that the elements appear in the XML document. To access a particular element node from this list, you add the index number of the element using the expression

```
docObj.getElementsByTagName(tag)[index]
```

where the first occurrence of the <element> tag has an *index* of 0, the second occurrence has an *index* of 1, and so forth. Thus, to reference the first person element in the clist.xml file, you use the expression

```
XMLdoc.getElementsByTagName("person")[0]
```

The getElementsByTagName() method does not support the use of namespaces. With MSXML, you can resolve this problem by using qualified tag names, as in the following expression:

```
docObj.getElementsByTagName(prefix:tag)
```

where *prefix* is the namespace prefix. Note that this approach fails if a default namespace is used, because there is no namespace prefix. Thus, you should avoid using the getElementsByTagName() method under MSXML when default namespaces are used with the element.

Mozilla-based browsers such as Firefox and Netscape follow the W3C specification and support namespaces using the following method:

```
docObj.getElementsByTagNameNS(uri,tag)
```

where *uri* is the URI of the namespace in which the element should reside and *tag* is the local name of the element. Because this method does not require the namespace prefix, it works equally well for default namespaces.

Using Familial Relations

Each node in a node tree can also be treated as a **node object** with its own collection of properties and methods. You can take advantage of the familial structure of a node tree to reference other nodes based on their relationship to a given node object. For example, to reference the first child node of any node object you enter the expression

```
nodeObj.firstChild
```

where *nodeObj* is a node from the document's node tree. Thus, to reference the first child node of the first person element in the clist.xml file, you enter the following expression:

```
XMLdoc.getElementsByTagName("person")[0].firstChild
```

Child nodes can also be referenced by their position in a list of child nodes for each node object. To reference the list of child nodes, use the childNodes property as follows:

```
nodeObj.childNodes
```

To reference a specific node in this list, you use the same index numbering you used for the getElementsByTagName() method. Thus, the expression

```
nodeObj.childNodes[index]
```

returns the child node of the node object with the index value *index*. The expression

```
XMLdoc.getElementsByTagName("person")[0].childNodes[1]
```

returns the second child node of the first person element in the XMLdoc document object. Node objects also support properties to access parent and sibling nodes. Figure 10-22 describes the different properties and methods for navigating node trees.

Referencing nodes in a node tree | **Figure 10-22**

Expression	Returns
docObj.getElementsByTagName(*tag*)	A list of element nodes with the tag name *tag* from the document object *docObj*
docObj.getElementsByTagName(*uri*, *tag*)	A list of element nodes with the tag name *tag* and belonging to a namespace with the URI *uri*
nodeObj.childNodes	A list of child nodes of the node object *nodeObj*
nodeObj.firstChild	The first child of *nodeObj*
nodeObj.lastChild	The last child of *nodeObj*
nodeObj.hasChildNodes()	A Boolean value indicating whether *nodeObj* has any child nodes
nodeObj.nextSibling	The node immediately following *nodeObj* in the node tree
nodeObj.previousSibling	The node immediately preceding *nodeObj* in the node tree
nodeObj.parentNode	The parent node of *nodeObj*
nodeObj.ownerDocument	The document object containing *nodeObj*
nodeObj.text	The text content of *nodeObj* and its descendant nodes [MSXML only]
nodeObj.xml	The XML text string associated with *nodeObj* and its descendants [MSXML only]

Reference Window

Navigating a Node Tree

- To reference an element node based on its tag name, use
    `docObj.getElementsByTagName(tag)`
  where `docObj` is the document object and `tag` is the element's tag.
- To reference an element node within a namespace, use
    `docObj.getElementsByTagNameNS(uri,tag)`
  where `uri` is the URI of the namespace and `tag` is the local name of the element without any namespace prefix.
- To reference the first and last child of a node object, use
    `nodeObj.firstChild`
    `nodeObj.lastChild`
  where `nodeObj` is the node object.
- To reference the list of child nodes, use
    `nodeObj.childNodes`
- To reference the parent of the node object, use
    `nodeObj.parentNode`

Node Types, Names, and Values

As you navigate a node tree, you may need some way of extracting information from each node you encounter. The following properties return a node object's type, name, and value, respectively:

`nodeObj.nodeType`
`nodeObj.nodeName`
`nodeObj.nodeValue`

The nodeType property returns an integer indicating whether the node refers to an element node, attribute node, comment node, and so forth. The nodeName property returns the name of the node; for element nodes, this is the tag name associated with the element. The nodeValue property returns the node's value. Figure 10-23 summarizes the values of these properties for different node types.

Figure 10-23 ▶ **Node types, names, and values**

Node	nodeType	nodeName	nodeValue
Element	1	*tag name*	null
Attribute	2	*attribute name*	*attribute value*
Text	3	#text	*text*
CDATA section	4	#cdata-section	*cdata-section text*
Entity reference	5	*entity reference name*	null
Entity	6	*entity name*	null
Processing instruction	7	*target*	*entire content excluding the target*
Comment	8	#comment	*comment text*
Document	9	#document	null
Document type	10	*document type name*	null
Document fragment	11	#document-fragment	null
Notation	12	*notation name*	null

Note that element nodes do not have values. If you want to change the text contained in an element, you must modify the nodeValue property of the text node contained within the element. For example, if you want to change the element

```
<name>Li</name>
```

to

```
<name>Lee</name>
```

you use the following code:

```
lastName=docObj.getElementsByTagName("name")[0];
lastName.firstChild.nodeValue="Lee";
```

In this example, the firstChild property points to the text node because it is the first (and only) child of the last element. (It is assumed for simplicity that this name element is the first name element in the document object and that the name element contains no child nodes other than the text node "Li"). If an element contains other child nodes, you have to reference the specific child node containing the element's textual content. For example, to change the content

```
<name><first>Howard</first><last>Li</last></name>
```

to

```
<name><first>Howard</first><last>Lee</last></name>
```

you run the following code:

```
pName=docObj.getElementsByTagName("name")[0];
lName=pName.childNodes[1];
lName.firstChild.nodeValue="Lee";
```

If you are working only with MSXML, you can also change the text contained in an element by using the text property. The syntax of this property is

```
nodeObj.text=text;
```

where text is the text of the node's content and its child nodes. For example, to change the text of the last element to "Lee," you use the following code:

```
last.text="Lee";
```

Note that the text property is supported only by MSXML and is not part of the official specifications for the W3C DOM.

Reference Window

Changing the Content of an Element Node

- To change the content of an element, use
  ```
  nodeObj.firstChild.nodeValue=text;
  ```
  where *nodeObj* is the node object for the element node and *text* is the text to be stored in the element.
- If the element contains several child nodes, use
  ```
  nodeObj.childNodes[index].nodeValue=text;
  ```
  where *index* is the index number associated with the text node.
- With MSXML, you can also change the content of an element node using
  ```
  nodeObj.text=text;
  ```

White Space Nodes

Under the W3C DOM, a text node might contain only white space characters, such as blank spaces, line returns, or tabs. Although they do not contain any printable characters, these **white space nodes** are still treated as text nodes (see Figure 7-30 for an earlier presentation of white space nodes within the context of the XML code). This means that the code sample

```
<name><first>Howard</first><last>Li</last></name>
```

has a different representation in the node tree than the code

```
<name>
    <first>Howard</first>
    <last>Li</last>
</name>
```

because the second code sample contains white space nodes for both the line returns and the blank spaces between the element nodes. This causes some cross-browser compatibility problems because Internet Explorer and MSXML do not recognize white space nodes as part of the node tree. To resolve this problem, you can remove the white space nodes from a document object before doing any processing on the document's content. You'll explore how to remove and add nodes to the node tree next.

Adding and Removing Nodes

Susan would like the ability to add new contributors to the contribution list. JavaScript supports several methods for creating new nodes and then appending them to any document. For example, to create an element node, you use the command

```
nodeObj = docObj.createElement(tag);
```

where *nodeObj* is the new element node, *docObj* is the document object containing the new node, and *tag* is the tag name associated with the element. To create a text node, use

```
nodeObj = docObj.createTextNode(string);
```

where *string* is the text string contained in the text node. The following code creates an element node named lastName and a text node containing the text string "Lee":

```
newName = XMLdoc.createElement("lastName");
nameText = XMLdoc.createTextNode("Lee");
```

Figure 10-24 lists the other methods used to create different node objects.

Figure 10-24 Creating node objects ◄ | Figure 10-24

Method	Creates
docObj.createAttribute(*attribute*)	An attribute node named *attribute*
docObj.createAttributeNS(*uri, qName*)	An attribute node in the *uri* namespace with the qualified name *qName*
docObj.createCDATASection(*text*)	A CDATA section containing the text string *text*
docObj.createComment(*text*)	A comment node containing the text string *text*
docObj.createDocumentFragment()	An empty document fragment
docObj.createElement(*tag*)	An element node with the tag name *tag*
docObj.createElementNS(*uri, qName*)	An element node in the *uri* namespace with the qualified name *qName*
docObj.createEntityReference(*entity*)	An entity reference named *entity*
docObj.createProcessingInstruction(*target, text*)	A processing instruction node with a target named *target* and the text string *text*
docObj.createTextNode(*text*)	A text node containing the text string *text*

Creating a Node Object

Reference Window

- To create an element node, use
    `docObj.createElement(tag)`
  where `docObj` is the document object in which the element is stored and `tag` is the tag name associated with the element.
- To create a text node, use
    `docObj.createTextNode(text)`
  where `text` is the text string contained in the text node.
- To create a comment node, use
    `docObj.createComment(text)`
  where `text` is the text string contained in the comment.
- To create an attribute node, use
    `docObj.createAttribute(attribute)`
  where `attribute` is the name of the attribute.

Creating a node object does not place it into the node tree of the document. To do that, you must append or insert the node object into the document's node tree. One method to attach a node object is the appendChild() method

`parent.appendChild(child);`

where `parent` is the parent node and `child` is the child node. The following code appends one of the text nodes created above to an element node, creating an element containing textual content:

`newName.appendChild(nameText);`

The resulting XML code for this new element is

`<lastName>Lee</lastName>`

Figure 10-25 describes some of the other methods for inserting and removing nodes.

Figure 10-25 ▶ **Inserting and removing nodes**

Method	Description
parent.appendChild(*child*)	Appends the child node *child* to the parent node *parent*
nodeObj.cloneNode(*deep*)	Clones the contents of *nodeObj*; if *deep* has the Boolean value true, all descendant nodes and their contents are also copied; if *deep* has the Boolean value false, no descendant nodes are copied
parent.insertBefore(*new*, *old*)	Inserts the *new* child node before the *old* child node
parent.removeChild(*nodeObj*)	Removes *nodeObj* from the parent node
parent.replaceChild(*new*, *old*)	Replaces the *old* child node with the *new* child node

Creating a Document Fragment

You can use these methods to create document fragments. To see how this works in practice, Figure 10-26 shows how you can use the W3C DOM to append the following document fragment to the root element of a document:

```
<person>
   <first>Anne</first>
   <last>Davis</last>
</person>
```

Figure 10-26 ▶ **Creating a document fragment**

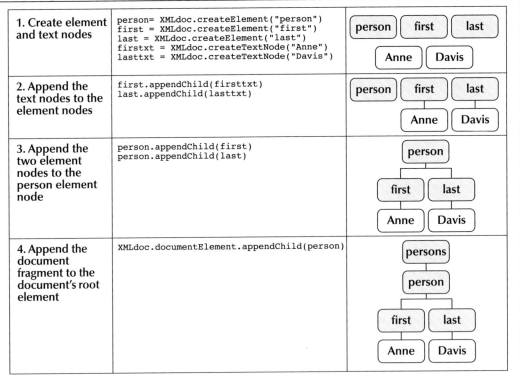

By using the methods and properties of node objects, you can create elaborate document fragments that can contain several levels of elements. However, in many cases it is quicker and easier to copy a preexisting structure from a document and then modify it as needed. This is done using the expression

nodeObj.cloneNode(*deep*)

where *nodeObj* is the node to be copied and *deep* is a Boolean value specifying whether to create a copy of the node and its descendants (true) or to copy just the node itself (false). Figure 10-27 shows how to use the cloneNode() method to create another document fragment for the XMLdoc document.

Cloning a document fragment Figure 10-27

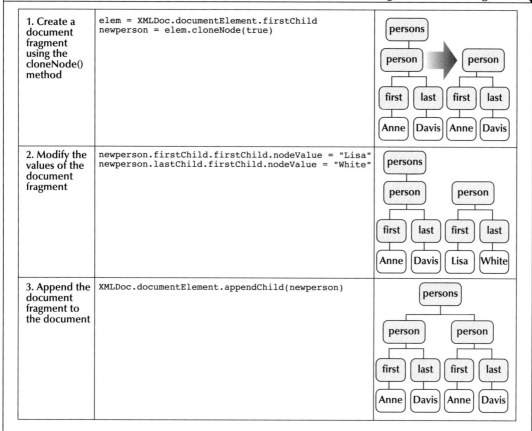

1. Create a document fragment using the cloneNode() method	`elem = XMLDoc.documentElement.firstChild` `newperson = elem.cloneNode(true)`	
2. Modify the values of the document fragment	`newperson.firstChild.firstChild.nodeValue = "Lisa"` `newperson.lastChild.firstChild.nodeValue = "White"`	
3. Append the document fragment to the document	`XMLDoc.documentElement.appendChild(newperson)`	

In the first step, you use the cloneNode() method to copy the person element and all of its descendant nodes. In the second step, you modify the values of the text nodes in the document fragment. Note that to change the content of the element, you have to move down the node tree to the text nodes and change their values using the nodeValue property. In the last step, you append the document fragment to the root element of the document. At this point, the XML code for the document looks as follows:

```
<persons>
   <person>
      <first>Anne</first>
      <last>Davis</first>
   </person>
   <person>
      <first>Lisa</first>
      <last>White</first>
   </person>
</persons>
```

Attaching and Removing a Node Object

- To append a node object to a parent node, use
    parent.appendChild(*child*)
  where *parent* is the parent node and *child* is the child node to be appended.
- To remove a node object from a parent node, use
    parent.removeChild(*child*)
- To replace one child node with another, use
    parent.replaceChild(*new*, *old*)
  where *new* is the new child node and *old* is the child node to be replaced.
- To copy a document fragment, use
    nodeObj.cloneNode(*deep*)
  where *nodeObj* is a node object and *deep* is a Boolean value that if true copies *nodeObj* and all of its descendant nodes, and if false does not copy the descendant nodes.

Removing White Space Nodes

Because MSXML and the W3C specifications differ on how to handle white space nodes, it is often advantageous to remove white space nodes from a node tree unless they are essential to the code being written. The following function can be applied to remove white space nodes from any node object and its descendants:

```
function removeWhiteSpaceNodes(node) {
   var noWhiteSpace = /\S/;
   for (var i=0; i < node.childNodes.length; i++) {
      testNode = node.childNodes[i];
      if (testNode.nodeType==3 &&
          !noWhiteSpace.test(testNode.nodeValue)) {
         node.removeChild(testNode);
         i--;
      }
      if (testNode.nodeType==1) {
         removeWhiteSpaceNodes(testNode);
      }
   }
}
```

The code used in this function is beyond the scope of this tutorial, so this discussion will not go into it in great detail. The function uses a single parameter named node that refers to a particular node object. It then loops through all of the descendant nodes of that node object. For each descendant node it tests whether the node object is a text node and whether it contains only white space characters; if so, it removes the node object from the node tree using the removeChild() method. Susan has added this function to the library.js file and you'll use it in the next section.

Adding New Records to the Contribution List

At this point, you've learned enough about modifying the contents and structure of a document object to add new records to the contribution list in The Lighthouse Web page. Susan's Web form contains data entry fields to enter the values for the new contributors. Figure 10-28 shows the part of her Web form related to data entry.

Adding a new contributor record ◄ **Figure 10-28**

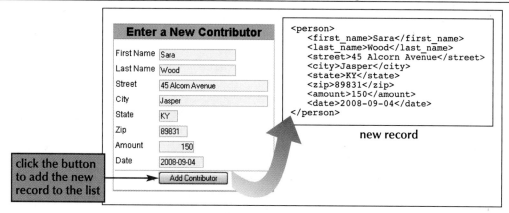

Enter a New Contributor

First Name Sara

Last Name Wood

Street 45 Alcorn Avenue

City Jasper

State KY

Zip 89831

Amount 150

Date 2008-09-04

click the button
to add the new
record to the list → Add Contributor

```
<person>
   <first_name>Sara</first_name>
   <last_name>Wood</last_name>
   <street>45 Alcorn Avenue</street>
   <city>Jasper</city>
   <state>KY</state>
   <zip>89831</zip>
   <amount>150</amount>
   <date>2008-09-04</date>
</person>
```

new record

Because of the number of child elements involved in adding a new person to her document, it is easiest to clone a preexisting person node and then edit its values to reflect the values entered into the Web form. The code to create a clone of the first person element is

```
var old=XMLdoc.getElementsByTagName("person")[0];
var clone=old.cloneNode(true);
removeWhiteSpaceNodes(clone);
```

Note that you run the removeWhiteSpaceNodes() function to remove any white space nodes that may be contained within the clone object. Add this code to the clist.htm file, placing it within a function named addRecord().

To create the addRecord() function:

1. Return to the **clist.htm** file in your text editor.

2. Directly above the init() function insert the following code, as shown in Figure 10-29:

```
function addRecord() {
    var old=XMLdoc.getElementsByTagName("person")[0];
    var clone=old.cloneNode(true);
    removeWhiteSpaceNodes(clone);
}
```

Inserting the addRecord() function ◄ **Figure 10-29**

```
function addRecord() {
    var old=XMLdoc.getElementsByTagName("person")[0];
    var clone=old.cloneNode(true);
    removeWhiteSpaceNodes(clone);
}

function init() {
    if (IE) {
        XMLdoc=new ActiveXObject(getPID(DOMPID));
        XSLTdoc=new ActiveXObject(getPID(FreeThreadPID));
        XSLTemp=new ActiveXObject(getPID(TemplatePID));
    }
    else if (MOZ) {
        XMLdoc = document.implementation.createDocument("","",null);
        XSLTdoc = document.implementation.createDocument("","",null);
    }

    loadDoc(XMLdoc, "clist.xml");
    loadDoc(XSLTdoc, "clist.xsl");

    doTransform();
}
```

Now that you have removed any white space nodes, every person element has eight child nodes containing the contributor's first name, last name, street, city, state, zip, amount of contribution, and date of contribution. To reference the text values contained in these elements, you use the expression

```
clone.childNodes[index].firstChild.nodeValue
```

where *index* ranges from 0 (for the first_name element) to 7 (for the date element). Remember that the text of an element is enclosed in a text node, which, in this case, is the first (and only) child of the node. To change the text value, you use the expression

```
clone.childNodes[index].firstChild.nodeValue=text
```

where *index* is the index value and *text* is the text value. Your current task involves retrieving the text values from the values of the text entry fields in Susan's Web form. In general, the value of a text entry field can be referenced as

```
document.form.elements[index].value
```

where *form* is the name of the Web form and *index* is the index number of the form element. In Susan's document, the name of the Web form is webform and the data input elements for the first, last, street, city, zip, amount, and date fields are stored in the first eight elements of the form. For example, the reference for the first_name input box is

```
document.webform.elements[0].value
```

and for the date input box, the reference is

```
document.webform.elements[7].value
```

By fortunate coincidence, the index numbers for the element nodes and the input boxes on the Web form match (this is not usually the case), so you can insert values from the input boxes into the element nodes using the following for loop:

```
for (i=0; i<=7; i++) {
    clone.childNodes[i].firstChild.nodeValue=document.webform.
elements[i].value;
}
```

Add this code to the addRecord() function.

To insert the new record values:

1. Add the following code to the addRecord() function, as shown in Figure 10-30:

```
for (i=0; i<=7; i++) {
    clone.childNodes[i].firstChild.nodeValue=document.webform.
elements[i].value;
}
```

Figure 10-30	Adding a new record to the document object

```
function addRecord() {
    var old=XMLdoc.getElementsByTagName("person")[0];
    var clone=old.cloneNode(true);
    removeWhiteSpaceNodes(clone);

    for (i=0; i<=7; i++) {
        clone.childNodes[i].firstChild.nodeValue=document.webform.elements[i].value;
    }
}
```

2. Save your changes to the file.

The final step in the addRecord() function is to append this document fragment to the root element of the contribution list and then rerun the XSLT transformation to display the revised XML document content in the Web page. The code is

```
XMLdoc.documentElement.appendChild(clone);
doTransform();
```

Susan also wants the values in entry fields in the Web form to be cleared once a new record is added to the list. She's added the following function to the library.js file to perform this action:

```
function resetForm() {
    for (i=0; i<=7; i++) {
        document.webform.elements[i].value="";
    }
}
```

You'll run this function after performing the transformation of the source document. Complete the addRecord() function by adding these commands.

To display the revised source document:

1. Add the following code to the addRecord() function:

```
XMLdoc.documentElement.appendChild(clone);
doTransform();
resetForm();
```

2. Add the following event handler to the input element for the Add Contributor button (see Figure 10-31):

```
onclick="addRecord()"
```

The finished addRecord() function | **Figure 10-31**

```
function addRecord() {
    var old=XMLdoc.getElementsByTagName("person")[0];
    var clone=old.cloneNode(true);
    removeWhiteSpaceNodes(clone);

    for (i=0; i<=7; i++) {
        clone.childNodes[i].firstChild.nodeValue=document.webform.elements[i].value;
    }

    XMLdoc.documentElement.appendChild(clone);
    doTransform();
    resetForm();
}
```

```
<tr>
    <td colspan="2" class="buttoncell">
        <input type="button" value="Add Contributor" onclick="addRecord()" />
    </td>
</tr>
</table>
```

3. Save your changes to the file, and reopen **clist.htm** in your Web browser.

4. Enter the following data for a new contributor:

First Name: **Sara**

Last Name: **Wood**

Street: **45 Alcorn Avenue**

City: **Jasper**

State: **KY**

ZIP: **89831**

Amount: **150**

Date: **2008-09-04**

5. Click the **Add Contributor** button.

6. Verify that the browser adds Sara Wood to the list of contributors and erases the values in the text entry fields (see Figure 10-32).

Figure 10-32	Adding a new record to the contribution list

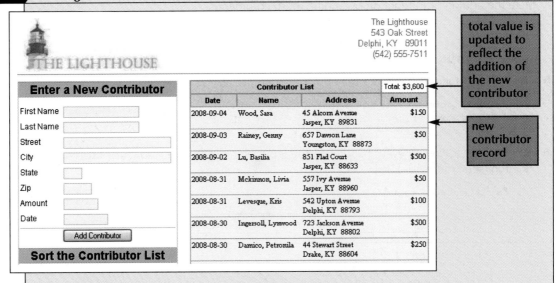

Trouble? Depending on your version of Internet Explorer and MSXML, the list of contributors might appear in a slightly different order.

At this point, you've made a change to the document object, but the modification is limited to the image of the document as it is stored in the processor's memory. If you exit the Web page, or reload it with your browser, the changes are lost. You'll explore how to make permanent changes to the document object in the next session.

Working with Attribute Nodes

By default, the contribution list on Susan's Web page is sorted in descending order of date. Susan wants to have the ability to sort the data by the contributor's last name, city of residence, amount donated, or by date. In addition, she wants to be able to sort the data in either ascending or descending order. To do this, you need to modify the contents of the clist.xsl style sheet. MSXML requires you to reload the style sheet into memory every time you modify its contents. You'll place the commands to do this in a function named sortList(). Start creating this function now.

To insert the sortList() function:

▶ **1.** Return to the **clist.htm** file in your text editor.

▶ **2.** Directly above the doTransform() function insert the following code (see Figure 10-33):

```
function sortList() {
   if (IE) {
      XSLTdoc=new ActiveXObject(getPID(FreeThreadPID));
      loadDoc(XSLTdoc, "clist.xsl");
   }
}
```

Inserting the sortList() function ◀ **Figure 10-33**

```
function loadDoc(docobj, url) {
    docobj.async=false;
    docobj.load(url);
}

function sortList() {
   if (IE) {
      XSLTdoc=new ActiveXObject(getPID(FreeThreadPID));
      loadDoc(XSLTdoc, "clist.xsl");
   }
}
```

Note that you reload the XSLT style sheet only for the Internet Explorer browser. Mozilla-based browsers do not require you to reload the style sheet when you make changes to it.

Setting Attribute Values

The contribution list is sorted within the clist.xsl style sheet using the sort element. To change the sort order, you need to change the attribute values within the <xsl:sort> tag. Figure 10-34 shows how the attributes should be changed to reflect the option buttons clicked by a user.

Modifying the sort order ◀ **Figure 10-34**

```
                                 <xsl:apply-templates select="$group">
  ⊙ Last Name   ○ City             <xsl:sort select="last_name" data-type="text" order="descending" />
  ○ Amount      ○ Date          </xsl:apply-templates>


                                 <xsl:apply-templates select="$group">
  ○ Last Name   ⊙ City             <xsl:sort select="city" data-type="text" order="descending" />
  ○ Amount      ○ Date          </xsl:apply-templates>


                                 <xsl:apply-templates select="$group">
  ○ Last Name   ○ City             <xsl:sort select="amount" data-type="number" order="descending" />
  ⊙ Amount      ○ Date          </xsl:apply-templates>


                                 <xsl:apply-templates select="$group">
  ○ Last Name   ○ City             <xsl:sort select="date" data-type="text" order="descending" />
  ○ Amount      ⊙ Date          </xsl:apply-templates>


                                 <xsl:apply-templates select="$group">
  Ascending: ⊙ Descending: ○      <xsl:sort select="date" data-type="text" order="ascending" />
                                 </xsl:apply-templates>


                                 <xsl:apply-templates select="$group">
  Ascending: ○ Descending: ⊙      <xsl:sort select="date" data-type="text" order="descending" />
                                 </xsl:apply-templates>
```

To change the attribute values of the sort element, you first create a reference to it in the node tree of the XSLTdoc document object, storing the reference in a variable named sortNode. There is only one sort node in the clist.xsl file, but it belongs to the XSLT namespace. Thus, for Internet Explorer browsers you have to reference the sort element using the qualified name with the xsl namespace prefix:

```
var sortNode=XSLTdoc.getElementsByTagName("xsl:sort")[0]
```

Because Mozilla-based browsers follow the W3C specification for namespaces, you use the namespace-aware method as follows:

```
var xNS="http://www.w3.org/1999/XSL/Transform";
var sortNode=XSLTdoc.getElementsByTagNameNS(xNS, "sort")[0]
```

Recall that "http://www.w3.org/1999/XSL/Transform" is the URI for the XSLT namespace. Add this code to the sortList() function.

To create the sortNode object:

1. Directly below the command to load the XSLTdoc object, insert the following code:

   ```
   var sortNode=XSLTdoc.getElementsByTagName("xsl:sort")[0]
   ```

2. Below the command block for Internet Explorer, insert the following command block for Mozilla (see Figure 10-35):

   ```
   else if (MOZ) {
       var xNS="http://www.w3.org/1999/XSL/Transform";
       var sortNode=XSLTdoc.getElementsByTagNameNS(xNS, "sort")[0]
   }
   ```

| Figure 10-35 | Referencing the sort element |

```
function sortList() {
    if (IE) {
        XSLTdoc=new ActivexObject(getPID(FreeThreadPID));
        loadDoc(XSLTdoc, "clist.xsl");
        var sortNode=XSLTdoc.getElementsByTagName("xsl:sort")[0]
    }
    else if (MOZ) {
        var xNS="http://www.w3.org/1999/XSL/Transform";
        var sortNode=XSLTdoc.getElementsByTagNameNS(xNS, "sort")[0]
    }
}
```

Determining the Sort Order

Now that you have a reference to the sort element, the next step is to modify that element's attribute values. In the W3C DOM, attributes are considered nodes, but they are not part of the node tree of the document. To work with attributes, you use the methods described in Figure 10-36.

Method	Description
nodeObj.getAttribute(*attribute*)	Returns the value of *attribute*
nodeObj.getAttributeNS(*uri, attribute*)	Returns the value of *attribute* within the namespace *uri*
nodeObj.getAttributeNode(*attribute*)	Returns the *attribute* node
nodeObj.getAttributeNodeNS(*uri, attribute*)	Returns the *attribute* node from within the namespace *uri*
nodeObj.removeAttribute(*attribute*)	Removes the *attribute*
nodeObj.removeAttributeNS(*uri, attribute*)	Removes the *attribute* within the namespace *uri*
nodeObj.removeAttributeNode(*attribute*)	Removes the *attribute* node
nodeObj.removeAttributeNodeNS(*uri, attribute*)	Removes the *attribute* node within the namespace *uri*
nodeObj.setAttribute(*attribute, value*)	Adds new *attribute* or changes the value of an existing attribute to *value*
nodeObj.setAttributeNS(*uri, attribute, value*)	Adds or modifies the *attribute* within the namespace *uri*
nodeObj.setAttributeNode(*attribute*)	Adds the *attribute* node
nodeObj.setAttributeNodeNS(*uri, attribute*)	Adds the *attribute* node within the namespace *uri*

To change the attribute values of the sort element, you use the setAttribute() method. For example, the following code changes the values of the select, data-type, and order attributes to "amount", "number", and "ascending", respectively:

```
sortNode.setAttribute("select", "amount");
sortNode.setAttribute("data-type", "number");
sortNode.setAttribute("order", "ascending");
```

This has the same effect as entering the following sort element into the style sheet:

```
<xsl:sort select="amount" data-type="number" order="ascending" />
```

Working with Attributes

Reference Window

- To return the value of an attribute, use
    `nodeObj.getAttribute(attribute)`
  where `nodeObj` is the node object containing the attribute and `attribute` is the name of the attribute.
- To set the value of an attribute, use
    `nodeObj.setAttribute(attribute, value)`
  where `value` is the attribute's value.
- To remove an attribute, use
    `nodeObj.removeAttribute(attribute)`

On Susan's Web form, the values of the select, data-type, and order attributes depend on which option button is clicked. To determine whether an option button is clicked, you use the JavaScript expression

```
document.form.radio[index].checked
```

where *form* is the name of the Web form, *radio* is the name of the group of option buttons, and *index* is the index number of a specific option button within the group. If this expression returns the Boolean value true, the button has been clicked. Susan's Web form contains two groups of option buttons, named sort and order. The first sort button refers to the last_name field, the second button refers to the city field, the third button refers to the amount field, and the fourth button refers to the date field. Thus, to determine whether a user has checked the sort button for the last_name field, you enter the following expression:

```
document.webform.sort[0].checked
```

Once you determine which sort option button has been clicked, you store the name of the field in a variable named select. The following code uses a set of if...else if statements to determine the value of the select variable:

```
if (document.webform.sort[0].checked) select="last_name";
else if (document.webform.sort[1].checked) select="city";
else if (document.webform.sort[2].checked) select="amount";
else select="date";
```

Of the four fields for sorting the contribution list, only the amount field is sorted as a number—the other three fields are sorted as text. Thus, you can create a second variable named datatype that determines whether to sort the list in numeric order or in alphabetical order. The code is

```
if (document.webform.sort[2].checked) datatype="number";
else datatype="text"
```

Finally, you determine whether a user wants the contribution list to be sorted in ascending or descending order. The following code checks whether the first order option button is selected. If it is selected, the value of the order variable is set to ascending; otherwise, the order variable is set to descending:

```
if (document.webform.order[0].checked) order="ascending";
else order="descending";
```

Add the code to determine the sort order to the sortList() function.

To determine the sort order:

▶ **1.** At the bottom of the sortList() function, insert the following code (see Figure 10-37):

```
if (document.webform.sort[0].checked) select="last_name";
else if (document.webform.sort[1].checked) select="city";
else if (document.webform.sort[2].checked) select="amount";
else select="date";

if (document.webform.sort[2].checked) datatype="number";
else datatype="text"

if (document.webform.order[0].checked) order="ascending";
else order="descending";
```

Determining the sort order ◄ **Figure 10-37**

```
function sortList() {
    if (IE) {
        XSLTdoc=new ActiveXObject(getPID(FreeThreadPID));
        loadDoc(XSLTdoc, "clist.xsl");
        var sortNode=XSLTdoc.getElementsByTagName("xsl:sort")[0]
    }
    else if (MOZ) {
        var xNS="http://www.w3.org/1999/XSL/Transform";
        var sortNode=XSLTdoc.getElementsByTagNameNS(xNS, "sort")[0]
    }

    if (document.webform.sort[0].checked) select="last_name";
    else if (document.webform.sort[1].checked) select="city";
    else if (document.webform.sort[2].checked) select="amount";
    else select="date";

    if (document.webform.sort[2].checked) datatype="number";
    else datatype="text"

    if (document.webform.order[0].checked) order="ascending";
    else order="descending";
}
```

▶ **2.** Save your changes to the file.

Finally, you use the setAttribute() method to place the values of the selected datatype and order variables into the attributes of the sortNode object:

```
sortNode.setAttribute("select", select);
sortNode.setAttribute("data-type", datatype);
sortNode.setAttribute("order", order);
```

You then call the sortList() function from the doTransform() function so that any transformations done to the source document are based on the selected options in Susan's Web form. You also want to rerun the transformation each time one of the option buttons is clicked, so you have to add event handlers to the six option buttons on the form.

To complete the sortList() function:

▶ **1.** Add the following code to the sortList() function (see Figure 10-38):

```
sortNode.setAttribute("select", select);
sortNode.setAttribute("data-type", datatype);
sortNode.setAttribute("order", order);
```

The completed sortList() function ◄ **Figure 10-38**

```
function sortList() {
    if (IE) {
        XSLTdoc=new ActiveXObject(getPID(FreeThreadPID));
        loadDoc(XSLTdoc, "clist.xsl");
        var sortNode=XSLTdoc.getElementsByTagName("xsl:sort")[0]
    }
    else if (MOZ) {
        var xNS="http://www.w3.org/1999/XSL/Transform";
        var sortNode=XSLTdoc.getElementsByTagNameNS(xNS, "sort")[0]
    }

    if (document.webform.sort[0].checked) select="last_name";
    else if (document.webform.sort[1].checked) select="city";
    else if (document.webform.sort[2].checked) select="amount";
    else select="date";

    if (document.webform.sort[2].checked) datatype="number";
    else datatype="text"

    if (document.webform.order[0].checked) order="ascending";
    else order="descending";

    sortNode.setAttribute("select", select);
    sortNode.setAttribute("data-type", datatype);
    sortNode.setAttribute("order", order);
}
```

2. Go to the doTransform() function, and insert the following command as shown in Figure 10-39:

```
sortList(); //set the style sheet sort options
```

| Figure 10-39 | Calling the sortList() function |

```
function doTransform() {
    var contTable = document.getElementById("ctable");
    sortList(); //set the style sheet sort options

    if (IE) {
        XSLTemp.stylesheet=XSLTdoc;
        XSLTProc=XSLTemp.createProcessor();
        XSLTProc.input=XMLdoc;
        XSLTProc.transform();

        contTable.innerHTML = XSLTProc.output;
    }
    else if (MOZ) {
        var XSLTProc= new XSLTProcessor();
        XSLTProc.importStylesheet(XSLTdoc);

        var Resultdoc = XSLTProc.transformToFragment(XMLdoc, document);
        var Xserial = new XMLSerializer();
        var Xstr = Xserial.serializeToString(Resultdoc);

        contTable.innerHTML = Xstr;
    }
}
```

3. Go to each of the six option button input elements in the clist.htm file, and insert the event handler **onclick="doTransform()"** as shown in Figure 10-40.

| Figure 10-40 | Running the doTransform() function |

```
<h3>Sort the Contributor List</h3>

<table>
<tr>
    <td><input type="radio" name="sort" onclick="doTransform()" /></td>
    <td>Last Name</td>
    <td><input type="radio" name="sort" onclick="doTransform()" /></td>
    <td>City</td>
</tr>
<tr>
    <td><input type="radio" name="sort" onclick="doTransform()" /></td>
    <td>Amount</td>
    <td>
        <input type="radio" name="sort" checked="checked" onclick="doTransform()" />
    </td>
    <td>Date</td>
</tr>
<tr>
    <td colspan="4" class="buttoncell">
        Ascending:
        <input type="radio" name="order" onclick="doTransform()" />
        Descending:
        <input type="radio" name="order" checked="checked" onclick="doTransform()" />
    </td>
</tr>
</table>
```

4. Save your changes to the file, and reload **clist.htm** in your Web browser. Verify that as you click the six option buttons in the Web form the contents of the contribution table are sorted in the appropriate order (see Figure 10-41).

A sorted contribution list ◄ **Figure 10-41**

Enter a New Contributor

First Name

Last Name

Street

City

State

Zip

Amount

Date

Add Contributor

Contributor List			Total: $3,450
Date	Name	Address	Amount
2008-08-22	Windt, Gary	55 Hawking Street Delphi, KY 89011	$1,000
2008-08-30	Ingersoll, Lynwood	723 Jackson Avenue Delphi, KY 88802	$500
2008-09-02	Lu, Basilia	851 Flad Court Jasper, KY 88633	$500
2008-08-23	Li, Howard	4312 East Oak Avenue Youngston, KY 89318	$250
2008-08-30	Damico, Petronila	44 Stewart Street Drake, KY 88604	$250
2008-08-23	Wilkes, Alan	321 Ashburn Jasper, KY 89831	$150
2008-08-25	White, Jeri	Hawkes Lane Delphi, KY 89211	$150
2008-08-23	Thu, Uma	25 Longton Lane Delphi, KY 89011	$100
2008-08-27	Thomas, Tom	Rigel Avenue Drake, KY 89411	$100
2008-08-31	Levesque, Kris	542 Upton Avenue Delphi, KY 88703	$100

Sort the Contributor List

○ Last Name   ○ City

◉ Amount   ○ Date

Ascending: ○ Descending: ◉

list sorted in descending order of amount

Trouble? Depending on your version of Internet Explorer and MSXML, the list of contributors might be sorted in a slightly different order.

5. If you want to take a break before starting the next session, you may close any open files and applications.

You show Susan the progress you've made on adding new records and sorting the contribution list. She's very pleased with your progress. In the next session, you'll explore how to create a filter for the contribution list so that it displays only contributions that match a specified set of criteria.

Session 10.2 Quick Check

Review

1. What expression would you use to create a reference to all element nodes named city in a document object named xDoc?
2. What expression would you use to reference the second occurrence of the city element node?
3. How does MSXML differ from the W3C DOM in how it handles white space nodes?
4. Create an element node named region and a text node containing the text string "Midwest". Assume that both nodes belong to the xDoc document object. Store the nodes in variables named newRegion and regionText respectively.
5. Enter code using the newRegion and regionText variables to create the following document fragment, and append the fragment to the root element of the xDoc document fragment:

   ```
   <region>Midwest</region>
   ```

6. What code would you enter to clone the second child node of the root element of the xDoc document object?
7. The city element within the xDoc document object contains an attribute named cid. What command would you enter to set the value of the cid attribute for the first city element to c001?
8. What command would you enter to remove the cid attribute from the first city element?

Session 10.3

Filtering the Source Document

The last feature that Susan wants you to add to her form is a filter to display only those records that match specified criteria. In the clist.xsl style sheet, the list of displayed records is determined by the value of the following group parameter:

```
<xsl:param name="group" select="//person" />
```

The default value of the group parameter includes all of the person elements in the source document. If you want to display a different set of records, you need to modify the parameter's value. For example, if the group parameter is set as follows:

```
<xsl:param name="group" select="//person[amount > 100]" />
```

then the style sheet displays only contributions with amounts greater than $100. Susan wants to be able to set the value of the group parameter using the text area box in the Web form (see Figure 10-42).

Figure 10-42	Filtering the contribution list

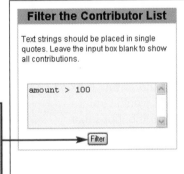

Filter the Contributor List

Text strings should be placed in single quotes. Leave the input box blank to show all contributions.

```
amount > 100
```

clicking the filter button applies the expression to the value of the group parameter

[Filter]

only contributions greater than $100 are displayed

Contributor List			Total: $2,800
Date	Name	Address	Amount
2008-09-02	Lu, Basilia	851 Flad Court Jasper, KY 88633	$500
2008-08-30	Damico, Petronila	44 Stewart Street Drake, KY 88604	$250
2008-08-30	Ingersoll, Lynwood	723 Jackson Avenue Delphi, KY 88802	$500
2008-08-25	White, Jeri	Hawkes Lane Delphi, KY 89211	$150
2008-08-23	Wilkes, Alan	321 Ashburn Jasper, KY 89831	$150
2008-08-23	Li, Howard	4312 East Oak Avenue Youngston, KY 89318	$250
2008-08-22	Windt, Gary	55 Hawking Street Delphi, KY 89011	$1,000

To do this, you'll create a function named filterList() that sets the value of the group parameter based on the expression entered in the text area box. The text area box has the field name of filter, so you can extract its value using the following expression:

```
document.webform.filter.value;
```

If this value is blank (meaning that no expression has been entered into the text area box), you set the value of the filter variable to "//person" to select all person elements; otherwise, the filter variable is set to "//person[*filterStr*]", where *filterStr* is the XPath expression entered in the filter text area box. The initial code for the filterList() function is therefore

```
function filterList() {
   var filterStr = document.webform.filter.value;
   if (filterStr=="") filter="//person"
   else filter="//person["+filterStr+"]";
}
```

Add the filterList() function to the clist.htm file.

To insert the filterList() function:

1. Reopen the **clist.htm** file in your text editor.

2. Above the doTransform() function, insert the following code (see Figure 10-43):

```
function filterList() {
    var filterStr = document.webform.filter.value;
    if (filterStr=="") filter="//person"
    else filter="//person["+filterStr+"]";
}
```

Creating the filterList() function ◄ Figure 10-43

```
function filterList() {
    var filterStr = document.webform.filter.value;
    if (filterStr=="") filter="//person"
    else filter="//person["+filterStr+"]";
}

function doTransform() {
    var contTable = document.getElementById("ctable");
    sortList(); //set the style sheet sort options
```

Working with Parameters in Internet Explorer

Next you have to change the value of the group parameter in the clist.xsl style sheet to match the value of the filter variable. Internet Explorer and Mozilla-based browsers differ in how they work with style sheet parameters, so as you did in the first session, you'll explore both techniques separately. You'll start with Internet Explorer.

Setting a Parameter Value

One of the advantages of having created the processor object in the first session is that it now allows you to work directly with style sheet parameters. Parameter values are set in MSXML using the addParameter() method

```
processorObj.addParameter(parameter, value, uri)
```

where `processorObj` is a processor object, `parameter` is the name of the style sheet parameter, `value` is the value passed to the parameter, and `uri` is an optional value that specifies the namespace URI for the parameter. The value used with the addParameter() method can be a text string, a number, a Boolean value, or a node set. For example, the expression

```
XSLTProc.addParameter("maxValue", 100)
```

sets the value of the maxValue parameter to 100. If you want to set the value of a style sheet parameter to a text string, you enter an expression such as

```
XSLTProc.addParameter("custName", "Wood, Sara")
```

which sets the value of the custName parameter to the text string, "Wood, Sara". For Susan's style sheet, you want to set the value of the group parameter to a node set defined by an XPath expression. If you wanted to display only those contributors who gave more than $100 to The Lighthouse, you might be tempted to set the value of the group parameter by specifying the XPath expression in the parameter value:

```
XSLTProc.addParameter("group", "//person[amount > 100]")
```

However, this would be incorrect. The problem with this approach is that MSXML interprets the parameter value as a text string, not as an XPath expression defining a node set. To overcome this problem, you have to convert the XPath expression into a collection of nodes in the source document.

Setting Style Sheet Parameters

Internet Explorer

- To set the value of a style sheet parameter, use
  ```
  processorObj.addParameter(parameter, value, uri)
  ```
  where *processorObj* is a processor object, *parameter* is the name of the style sheet parameter, *value* is the value passed to the parameter, and *uri* is an optional value that specifies the namespace URI for the parameter. The value can be a text string, a number, a Boolean value, a node object, or a node set.

Mozilla

- To set the value of a style sheet parameter, use
  ```
  processorObj.setParameter(uri, parameter, value)
  ```
  If the parameter is not part of a namespace, you may use null for *uri*.

Selecting a Node Set

MSXML supports two methods for creating node sets from XPath expressions. The first, selectSingleNode(), selects the first node within a document or node object that matches a specified XPath expression. The syntax of the selectSingleNode() method is

```
object.selectSingleNode(xpath)
```

where *object* is a document or node object and *xpath* is an XPath expression. For example, the following expression selects the first person within the XMLdoc document object whose amount value exceeds $100:

```
XMLdoc.selectSingleNode("//person[amount > 100]")
```

The second method, selectNodes(), selects a collection of all the nodes that match the XPath expression. The syntax of the selectNodes() method is

```
object.selectNodes(xpath)
```

Thus, the expression

```
XMLdoc.selectNodes("//person[amount > 100]")
```

selects all persons who contributed more than $100. For Susan's document, if you wanted to change the value of the group parameter to a node set of persons who gave more than $100 to the charity, you could store the node set in a variable and pass that variable to the parameter. The code to accomplish this is

```
var xNodes = XMLdoc.selectNodes("//person[amount > 100]");
XSLTProc.addParameter("group", xNodes);
```

More general code using the filter variable we created earlier is

```
var xNodes = XMLdoc.selectNodes(filter);
XSLTProc.addParameter("group", xNodes);
```

Add this command to the filterList() function.

To set the value of the group parameter:

▶ **1.** Add the following code to the end of the filterList() function:

```
if (IE) {
   var xNodes = XMLdoc.selectNodes(filter);
   XSLTProc.addParameter("group", xNodes);
}
```

To keep the XSLT processor in active memory, you have to add it as a parameter in the function statement.

▶ **2.** Insert the following parameter in the filterList() function statement:

XSLTProc

Finally, you want to run the filterList() function every time the source document is transformed so that the result document reflects the XPath expression entered in the text area box.

▶ **3.** Go to the doTransform() function, and insert the following code directly above the command to run the transformation under Internet Explorer:

```
filterList(XSLTProc); //set the style sheet parameter value
```

Figure 10-44 highlights the changes to the filterList() and doTransform() functions.

Setting the value of the group parameter | **Figure 10-44**

```
function filterList(XSLTProc) {
    var filterStr = document.webform.filter.value;
    if (filterStr=="") filter="//person"
    else filter="//person["+filterStr+"]";

    if (IE) {
        var xNodes = XMLdoc.selectNodes(filter);
        XSLTProc.addParameter("group", xNodes);
    }
}

function doTransform() {
    var contTable = document.getElementById("ctable");
    sortList(); //set the style sheet sort options

    if (IE) {
        XSLTemp.stylesheet=XSLTdoc;
        XSLTProc=XSLTemp.createProcessor();
        XSLTProc.input=XMLdoc;
        filterList(XSLTProc); //set the style sheet parameter value
        XSLTProc.transform();
```

As a test, Susan would like to see the list of contributors from the city of Delphi who gave $100 or more to The Lighthouse. You'll add an event handler to the Filter button on the Web form so that it transforms the source document when clicked.

To test the filterList() function:

▶ **1.** Go to the input element for the filter button, and insert the event handler **onclick="doTransform()"** as shown in Figure 10-45.

Figure 10-45 Calling the doTransform() function

```
<h3>Filter the Contributor List</h3>

<table>
<tr>
   <td>
      <p>Text strings should be placed in single quotes.
         Leave the input box blank to show all contributions.</p>
      <p style="text-align: center">
         <textarea name="filter" id="filter" rows="4" cols="14"></textarea><br />
         <input type="button" value="Filter" onclick="doTransform()" />
      </p>
   </td>
</tr>
</table>
```

▶ **2.** Save your changes to the file, and reload **clist.htm** in your Internet Explorer browser.

▶ **3.** Type **amount >= 100 and city = 'Delphi'** in the text area box at the bottom of the form, and click the **Filter** button. As shown in Figure 10-46, five records are displayed in the contribution list.

Figure 10-46 Filtering the contributor list

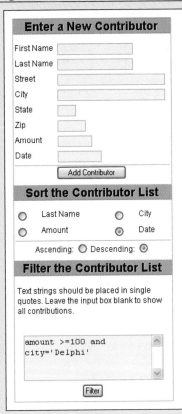

From the Web form Susan can instantly see that five people from Delphi contributed $100 or more to The Lighthouse. The amount of contributions from that group totaled $1850. Now she wants you to create a similar solution for Mozilla-based browsers.

Working with Parameters in Mozilla

The Mozilla equivalent of the addParameter() method is the setParameter() method. The syntax of this method is

```
processorObj.setParameter(uri, parameter, value)
```

where *processorObj* is a processor object, *uri* is the namespace of the parameter, *parameter* is the name of the parameter, and *value* is the parameter value. If the parameter is not part of a namespace, you can use the value null for the namespace URI. As with the addParameter() method, the value used with the setParameter() method can be a text string, a number, a Boolean value, or a node set.

Like MSXML, any XPath expression must be converted from text strings into node sets before they can be applied to a parameter; however, Mozilla does not support the select-Nodes() method. Instead, you have to create an **XPathEvaluator object** to evaluate the XPath expression. The advantage of the XPathEvaluator object is that it allows programmers to convert an XPath expression into a wide variety of formats and outputs. To create an XPathEvaluator object you use the object constructor

```
evalObj = new XPathEvaluator();
```

where *evalObj* is the XPathEvaluator object. For example, the following code creates an XPathEvaluator object named xEval:

```
var xEval = new XPathEvaluator();
```

To apply the XPathEvaluator object to an XPath expression, you use the evaluate() method

```
evalObj.evaluate(xpath, object, nsResolver, result, resultObj)
```

where *xpath* is the XPath expression, *object* is a document or node object that the XPath expression is applied to, *nsResolver* is a function that resolves any namespace prefixes returning the URI of the namespace, *result* is an integer or name that specifies the type of result to be returned from the evaluation, and *resultObj* is a result object that stores the results of the evaluation. You can set *nsResolver* to null if there is no need to resolve a namespace prefix. Also, if you are storing the results of the evaluate() method in a result object, you can also set *resultObj* to null. Figure 10-47 summarizes the different types of result objects that can be returned by the evaluate() method.

Figure 10-47 ▶ **XPath result types**

Result type	Value	Returns
XPathResult.ANY_TYPE	0	A result containing whatever type naturally results from evaluation of the expression; if the result is a node-set then UNORDERED_NODE_ITERATOR_TYPE is always the resulting type
XPathResult.NUMBER_TYPE	1	A single number; useful for XPath expressions that return numeric values such as the count() function
XPathResult.STRING_TYPE	2	The result stored as a text string
XPathResult.BOOLEAN_TYPE	3	A single Boolean value; useful for XPath expressions that return logical values
XPathResult.UNORDERED_NODE_ITERATOR_TYPE	4	A node set containing all the nodes matching the expression; the nodes may not necessarily be in the same order that they appear in the document
XPathResult.ORDERED_NODE_ITERATOR_TYPE	5	A node set containing all the nodes matching the expression, arranged in document order
XPathResult.UNORDERED_NODE_SNAPSHOT_TYPE	6	A node set containing snapshots of all the nodes matching the expression; any modifications to the node set in the document do not affect the nodes in the snapshot, and the nodes may not necessarily be in the same order that they appear in the document
XPathResult.ORDERED_NODE_SNAPSHOT_TYPE	7	A node set containing snapshots of all the nodes matching the expression, in document order
XPathResult.ANY_UNORDERED_NODE_TYPE	8	A single node matching the expression; not necessarily the first node in the document that matches the expression
XPathResult.FIRST_ORDERED_NODE_TYPE	9	The first single node matching the expression

In most cases, you can set the result type to XPathResult.ANY_TYPE or 0, and Mozilla generates the correct result object based on the XPath expression. For example, to create a node set based on the XPath expression "//person[amount > 100]" as you did with Internet Explorer, you enter either of the following commands:

```
xNodes = xEval.evaluate("//person[amount > 100]", XMLdoc, null,
0, null);
```

or

```
xNodes = xEval.evaluate("//person[amount > 100]", XMLdoc, null,
XPathResult.ANY_TYPE, null);
```

In either case, Mozilla returns a node set based on the XPath expression. For Susan's document, you simply substitute the value of the filter variable for the XPath expression as follows:

```
xNodes = xEval.evaluate(filter, XMLdoc, null, 0, null);
```

Note that the XPathEvaluator object and the evaluate() method are part of the W3C DOM Level 3 specification. At the time of this writing, only Firefox version 1.5 supports the use of the XPathEvaluator object with style sheet parameters. For other browsers, you can still modify the parameter value by modifying the value of the parameter's select attribute using the techniques discussed in the previous section.

Evaluating XPath Expressions

Internet Explorer

- To select a single node based on an XPath expression, use
  object.selectSingleNode(*xpath*)
  where *object* is a document or node object and *xpath* is an XPath expression.
- To select multiple nodes based on an XPath expression, use
  object.selectNodes(*xpath*)

Mozilla

- To create an XPathEvaluator object, use the object constructor
  evalObj=new XPathEvaluator();
  where *evalObj* is an XPathEvaluator object used to evaluate XPath expressions.
- To evaluate an XPath expression, use
  evalObj.evaluate(*xpath*, *object*, *nsResolver*, *result*, *resultObj*)
  or
  resultObj=*evalObj*.evaluate(*xpath*, *object*, *nsResolver*, *result*, null)
  where *xpath* is the XPath expression, *object* is a document or node object to which the XPath expression is applied, *nsResolver* is a function that resolves any namespace prefixes returning the URI of the namespace, *result* is an integer or name that specifies the type of result to be returned from the evaluation, and *resultObj* is a result object that stores the results of the evaluation.

Complete the filterList() function by adding commands to set the value of the group parameter in Mozilla.

To complete the filterList() function:

1. Return to the **clist.htm** file in your text editor.

2. Add the following commands to the end of the filterList() function:

```
else if (MOZ) {
   xEval = new XPathEvaluator();
   xNodes = xEval.evaluate(filter,XMLdoc,null,0,null);
   XSLTProc.setParameter(null,"group",xNodes);
}
```

3. Call the filterList() function for Mozilla browsers by adding the following command, as shown in Figure 10-48:

```
filterList(XSLTProc); //set the style sheet parameter value
```

Figure 10-48	The completed filterList() function

```
function filterList(XSLTProc) {
    var filterStr = document.webform.filter.value;
    if (filterStr=="") filter="//person"
    else filter="//person["+filterStr+"]";

    if (IE) {
        var xNodes = XMLdoc.selectNodes(filter);
        XSLTProc.addParameter("group", xNodes);
    }
    else if (MOZ) {
        xEval = new XPathEvaluator();
        xNodes = xEval.evaluate(filter,XMLdoc,null,0,null);
        XSLTProc.setParameter(null,"group",xNodes);
    }
}

function doTransform() {
    var contTable = document.getElementById("ctable");
    sortList(); //set the style sheet sort options

    if (IE) {
        XSLTemp.stylesheet=XSLTdoc;
        XSLTProc=XSLTemp.createProcessor();
        XSLTProc.input=XMLdoc;
        filterList(XSLTProc); //set the style sheet parameter value
        XSLTProc.transform();

        contTable.innerHTML = XSLTProc.output;
    }
    else if (MOZ) {
        var XSLTProc= new XSLTProcessor();
        XSLTProc.importStylesheet(XSLTdoc);

        filterList(XSLTProc); //set the style sheet parameter value
        var Resultdoc = XSLTProc.transformToFragment(XMLdoc, document);
        var Xserial = new XMLSerializer();
        var Xstr = Xserial.serializeToString(Resultdoc);
```

▶ **4.** Save your changes to the file, and open clist.htm in your Firefox browser. Verify that you can use the Filter button to display contributions that match specified criteria.

Trouble? At the current time, the XSLT processor in Netscape for Windows does not support setting the value of style sheet parameters to node sets. If you need to support this browser, you can set the value of the group parameter using the setAttribute() method described in the previous session. Set the value of the select attribute of the first (and only) param element to the value of the filter variable. You do not have to change the filter variable from a text string to a node set.

▶ **5.** You're finished working with Susan's application. You may close any open files or applications at this point.

Debugging Techniques

When you write scripts that load and modify XML documents, you occasionally run into documents that fail to load. Many browsers now support debugging consoles to help you locate the source of the trouble. You can also retrieve error information from the XML processor. Both MSXML and Mozilla provide objects to handle errors that may occur while processing XML documents.

Error Handling in Internet Explorer

MSXML places information about loading errors into a **parseError object**. You can extract information from this object to learn the reasons why MSXML failed to load a document. Figure 10-49 describes the properties of the parseError object.

MSXML parseError object ◄ **Figure 10-49**

Property	Description
parseError.errorCode	The error code of the parse error
parseError.filepos	The absolute file position where the parse error occurred
parseError.line	The line number of the parse error
parseError.linepos	The position of the character within the line where the parse error occurred
parseError.reason	A text string detailing the reason for the parse error
parseError.srcText	The full text of the line containing the parse error; an empty string is returned if an error is caused by XML that is not well-formed and cannot be assigned to a specific line
parseError.url	The URL of the XML document containing the parse error

   To determine whether MSXML encountered an error when loading an XML document, you can examine the value of the parseError.errorCode property. If this value is 0, then no error has occurred. A nonzero errorCode value indicates the presence of an error; you then have to investigate the other properties of the parseError object to determine the source of the error.

   To see how the parseError object works, a sample document has been prepared for you that attempts to load two XML documents. The first document, error1.xml, contains an ending tag that does not match the starting tag for an element. The second document, error2.xml, contains an unclosed element.

To view the parseError demo:

▶ 1. Using your Internet Explorer browser, open **demo_parseerror.htm** from the tutorial.10x/tutorial folder.

▶ 2. Click the option buttons on the form to attempt to load the two sample XML documents error1.xml and error2.xml. The page displays the error codes associated with attempting to load either of these files (see Figure 10-50).

Viewing the properties of the parseError object ◄ **Figure 10-50**

The parseError Object

Click the radio buttons below to open different XML documents using MSXML. Any errors opening the document will be displayed using properties of the parseError object.

⦿ error1.xml	
○ error2.xml	

parseError.errorCode	-1072896659
parseError.filepos	272
parseError.line	12
parseError.linepos	3
parseError.reason	End tag 'person' does not match the start tag 'first_name'.
parseError.srcText	
parseError.url	file://C:\tutorial.10x\tutorial\error1.xml

▶ 3. Close the file.

   Note that if a document has more than one error, the parseError object returns information only on the last error detected by the XML parser.

Error Handling in Mozilla

If a Mozilla-based browser fails to load a document, the browser loads a different XML document containing information about the error. You can then view or parse the contents of this document to interpret the reason for the failure. The error document has a root element named parseerror. Thus, to test whether an error has occurred under Mozilla, you can examine the documentElement.tagName property of the document you're trying to load. If the tag name is <parseerror>, a loading error has occurred. You would then examine the contents of the error document to determine the nature and cause of the error.

A demo document for Mozilla browsers has also been provided to show how errors are reported in the error document. Open the demo page now.

To view the error document demo:

▶ 1. Using your Mozilla-based browser, open **demo_mozillaerror.htm** from the tutorial.10x/tutorial folder.

▶ 2. Click the option buttons on the form to attempt to load the error1.xml and error2.xml documents. The code of the error document is displayed in the accompanying text area box (see Figure 10-51).

Figure 10-51	**Viewing the contents of the error document**

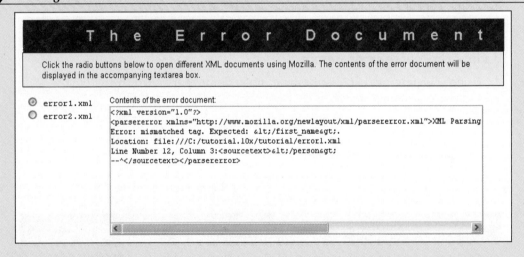

▶ 3. Close the file.

Saving an XML Document

You performed all of the work you did on Susan's document on the client side of the application with your Web browser. This limits your ability to save your work locally. Any modifications you make to the source document or to the style sheet are applied only during your current browser session. This is done for security reasons, because if Java-Script had the capability to save files on a user's local computer, it would enable programmers to easily spread viruses across the Web without easy detection.

MSXML does support the save() method to save document objects to external objects. The syntax of the save() method is

```
docObj.save(location)
```

where *location* is one of the following:

- A filename
- The name of another document object
- An ASP (Active Server Pages) response object
- A custom COM object that supports persistence

If your program is running on a Web server, you can use this method to save the file. However, the save method does not work when it is run from a client computer, due to the security reason discussed above. Note that the save() method is not part of the W3C DOM and thus is not supported by browsers other than Internet Explorer.

Working with AJAX

Because security issues limit your ability to save your document changes locally, you have to save those changes to a secure Web server. One of the most useful approaches to communicating between a client browser and a Web server is AJAX. **AJAX**, or **Asynchronous JavaScript and XML**, refers to the use of HTML, XML, XSLT, and JavaScript to enable fast, efficient communication between applications running on a user's browser and data stored and updated on a secure Web server. Because this tutorial focuses on client-side applications of XML and the Document Object Model, you will not apply AJAX methods to Susan's Web page. However, you will investigate how such an application could be created and implemented.

The Principles of AJAX

The first person to coin the AJAX acronym was Jess James Garrett in an article entitled "AJAX: A New Approach to Web Applications," which was posted in February 2005, on the Web site for the Adaptive Path consulting firm. It would be incorrect to say that either Garrett or Adaptive Path invented AJAX. When Garrett wrote his article, Google had already developed AJAX-style applications such as Google Suggest, Google Maps, and GMail. Another online service, Flickr was just starting up, providing a source for digital photo sharing. America Online's AIM Mail, was another service that used AJAX principles. What Garrett's article did was focus attention on this new approach to Web interactivity.

In the **classic Web application model** as discussed by Garrett, a user interacts with a Web server through a Web page running on their browser. The Web page might contain a Web form in which the user enters some specific pieces of information, such as a purchase order or the posting of a message. The user's action triggers an HTTP request back to the Web server. The server takes this information, perhaps runs some scripts, queries a server-side database, and generates a new Web page that is then sent back to the user's browser (see Figure 10-52). Thus, the level of information is organized in complete pages: one page to request information and another page to report on the results of that request.

Figure 10-52	Classic Web application model

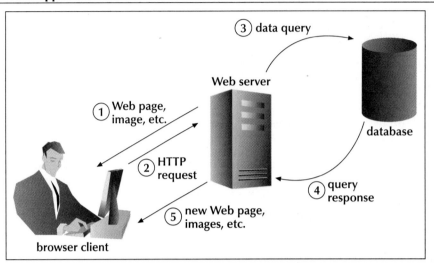

The problem with this approach is shown in Figure 10-53: the whole communication is by its nature synchronous. The user sends a request and must wait for a response from the server before proceeding. In addition, while the user is waiting for a response in the form of a new Web page, the current Web page is unavailable.

Figure 10-53	Synchronous communication

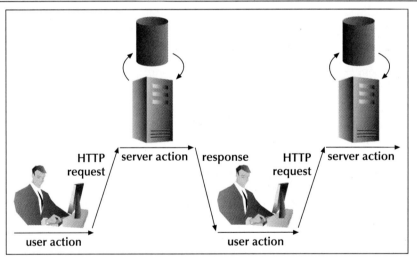

The **AJAX Web application model** adds an intermediary between the user and the server-side system, which is called an AJAX engine. The **AJAX engine** is responsible for communicating with the server and for relaying any information from the server to the user interface. The AJAX engine is any JavaScript function or object that can call for and receive data from the Web server. The user interface interacts with the AJAX engine using code written in JavaScript, but the engine communicates with the server using the same HTTP requests that the classic model employs (see Figure 10-54).

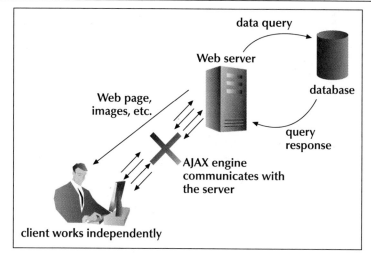

The important difference is that the AJAX engine can be placed within a portion of the Web page—for example, in an inline frame. This means that information can be retrieved from the server not in entire pages, but in smaller, more manageable pieces. This has the benefit of lessening the load on the server, which should presumably speed up communication. Moreover, because the AJAX engine, not the entire browser, is communicating with the server, a user is free to interact with the rest of the browser client as the AJAX engine works in the background. The asynchronous nature of AJAX therefore also speeds up the client's browsing experience, as he or she does not have to wait on the server to attend to other tasks (see Figure 10-55).

Asynchronous communication ◀ **Figure 10-55**

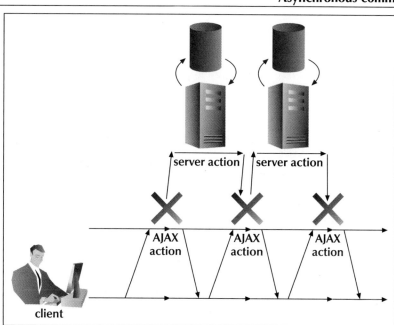

In short, AJAX is a way of developing Web applications that involve asynchronous communication, allowing a user to request information from the server while remaining free to do other things in the client browser. It employs JavaScript as the scripting language for handling the interchange of information, and can package the data received in XML document fragments that are easily processed by JavaScript.

Figure 10-56 shows how AJAX works with a search engine on the Google Web site called Google Suggest. As a user types each new character into the search phrase, an AJAX engine working in the background sends the updated phrase to the Web server. A list of topics related to the phrase, sorted by relevance, is displayed in the input box almost as fast as the user is typing. Because the communication is asynchronous, the user does not have to wait for the server to respond while typing, and because the server is dealing with small pieces of information, it can respond more quickly to each new keystroke.

| Figure 10-56 | AJAX implementation in Google Suggest |

1. the user is presented with an input box in which to type a search phrase

2. as the user types the phrase, the AJAX engine communicates with the server, constantly updating the list of relevant items displayed in the input box

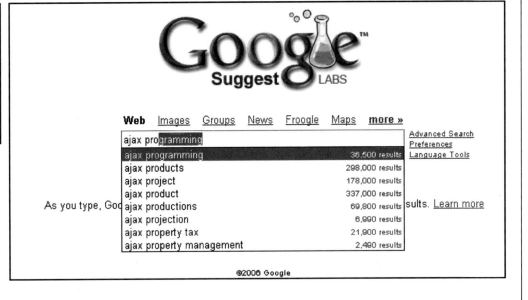

If Susan were to apply AJAX to her contribution report, she would have a system in which the filtering and sorting of the list could be done in real time with the database information on the server.

The XMLHttpRequest Object

To create an AJAX-style Web application, you first have to create the AJAX engine, which sets up communication between the client browser and the Web server. This is done by creating an object to handle the HTTP requests between the client and the server. This object class was introduced in Internet Explorer 5 as an ActiveX object called an **XMLHttp object**. A comparable implementation for Firefox, Netscape, and Safari is called the **XMLHttpRequest object**. These objects are not part of the W3C Document Object Model, but have become the de facto standards due to their near universal support in current versions of all major browsers.

To create an XMLHttpRequest object in Internet Explorer, you use the same ActiveX object constructor employed in creating the XML document:

```
reqObj = new ActiveXObject(progID);
```

where *reqObj* is the XMLHttpRequest object and *progID* is one of the following program IDs:

- Msxml2.XMLHttp.5.0
- Msxml2.XMLHttp.4.0
- Msxml2.XMLHttp.3.0
- Msxml2.XMLHttp
- Microsoft.XMLHttp

As with creating ActiveX document objects, you can place these program IDs in an array and use a JavaScript function to loop through the different program IDs, selecting the most recent ID supported by the user's browser.

To create an XMLHttpRequest object in Mozilla or Safari, you use the following object constructor:

```
reqObj = new XMLHttpRequest();
```

For a cross-browser Web page, you can use object detection to determine which approach to take for your user's browser. The following code is one such way of creating a cross-browser XMLHttpRequest object:

```
var IE = ActiveXObject ? true: false;
var MOZ = window.XMLHttpRequest ? true: false;

if (IE) {
   var reqObj = ActiveXObject(getPID(HTTPPID));
}
else if (MOZ) {
   var reqObj = new XMLHttpRequest();
}
```

This code assumes that the program IDs for the ActiveX XMLHttpRequest have been placed in an array named HTTPPID and that the getPID() function loops through that array, retrieving the most recently supported version. After the XMLHttpRequest object is created, the objects, properties, and methods applicable to it are essentially the same across browsers; thus, this is the only cross-browser code that you have to worry about in an AJAX application.

| **Creating an XMLHttpRequest Object**

Internet Explorer

- To create an XMLHttpRequest object, use
    `reqObj = new ActiveXObject(progID);`
  where *reqObj* is the XMLHttpRequest object and *progID* is an ActiveX program ID for XMLHttpRequest objects.

Mozilla and Safari

- To create an XMLHttpRequest object, use
    `reqObj = new XMLHttpRequest();`

Working with the Request Object

Figure 10-57 describes the methods associated with the XMLHttpRequest object.

Figure 10-57 | **Methods of the XMLHttpRequest object**

Method	Description
reqObj.abort()	Stops the current request
reqObj.getAllResponseHeaders()	Returns the complete set of HTTP headers as a text string
reqObj.getResponseHeader(*label*)	Returns the string value of a single HTTP header, where *label* is the header label
reqObj.open(*method, url, async, user, pwd*)	Opens the request using the specified *method* directed towards a server program at the URL *url*; the *async* argument specifies whether the call is asynchronous (true) or synchronous (false), and *user* and *pwd* are optional parameters used to supply a username and password to the server program
reqObj.send(*content*)	Transmits the request along with optional *content* such as a text string or a document object
reqObj.setRequestHeader(*label, value*)	Assigns a *label/value* pair to the request header

The most commonly used methods are open() and send(). Start by looking at the open() method. To open communication between an AJAX engine and a Web server, you use the method

```
reqObj.open(method, url, async, user, pwd)
```

where `method` is the method used to open the connection, `url` is the URL of the Web server program receiving the request, `async` is a Boolean value indicating whether the call is asynchronous (true) or synchronous (false), and `user` and `pwd` are optional parameters used to authentic the request by supplying a username and password to the server program. The most commonly used values for the `method` argument are GET and POST. You use GET on operations that are primarily data retrieval requests, and POST on operations that both send data to and receive data from the server. Note that the GET and POST methods must be entered in uppercase letters.

For security reasons, you can't specify a URL that calls pages on third-party domains—you can use only the domain that is serving up the page containing the script. This means that client-side scripts cannot fetch Web service data from data sources other than the server that originated the page. In addition, you open a request on the user's local machine—you can't specify a value for the `url` argument that begins with FILE: (for a local file).

The following examples use the open() method to open communications with an XMLHttpRequest object:

```
reqObj.open("GET", "http://www.lhouse.org/clist.xml", true);
reqObj.open("GET", "reports.html", false);
reqObj.open("POST", "show-accounts.php", true, "davis", "GRxu32");
```

The first example opens the connection using the GET method to access an XML document on the server from the *www.lhouse.org* domain. The connection is asynchronous. The second example uses the GET method to open a connection to the reports.html Web page. Note that the URL uses a relative path, not an absolute one, relying on the assumption that the Web page containing the AJAX engine is in the same domain as the reports. html file. The connection is synchronous, so the function calling this XMLHttpRequest object halts until the object provides some response. Finally, the third example shows how to use the POST method to access a PHP script. The connection is asynchronous, and in this case the code includes a username and password required to open the connection.

Once an asynchronous connection is opened, you have to monitor the state of the connection to determine when the server is ready to receive data. This is not an issue with synchronous communications, which halt all operations until a response is given. Figure 10-58 describes the properties of the XMLHttpRequest object, which can be used to assess the ongoing state of the request object.

Properties of the XMLHttpRequest object   ◄   **Figure 10-58**

Property	Description
*reqObj*onreadystatechange	Event handler for an event that fires at every state change in the *reqObj* request object
reqObj.readyState	Integer describing the current ready state of the request object where 0 = uninitialized 1 = loading 2 = loaded 3 = interactive 4 = complete
reqQbj.responseText	String version of data returned by the request object
reqObj.responseXML	DOM-compatible document object of data returned by the request object
reqObj.status	Numeric code returned by the request object, such as 404 for Not Found or 200 for OK
reqObj.statusText	String message accompanying the status code

The first property you will look at is the onreadystatechange property. This property is used to associate an event handler function with a request object, and is fired whenever the readyState of the request object changes. The request object has five possible states: 0 for an unitialized request (before any connection is initiated between the AJAX engine and the server); 1 for loading the request object; 2 for the request object having finished loading; 3 for currently interacting with the request object; and 4 for the completion of the request object. A state of 4 indicates that the transaction between the server and the AJAX application is complete and thus ready for additional commands.

The following code shows how to open an asynchronous request and then monitor the connection to determine when the connection is complete:

```
reqObj.open("GET", "http://www.lhouse.org/clist.xml", true);
reqObj.onreadystatechange = monitorReq;

function monitorReq() {
   if (reqObj.readyState == 4) {
      response received
      run commands to process the response
   }
}
```

After the open() method opens the communication with the server and you have determined that the initial communication between the AJAX engine and the server has been successfully completed, the send() method is then employed to send the request to the server. The syntax of the send() method is

```
reqObj.send(content)
```

where *content* is any optional content you want sent with the request, such as a document object or text string. Some requests, such as a GET request, do not require any content, in which case you set the *content* value to null:

```
reqObj.send(null)
```

At this point, the request is sent to the server, which can then process the request and return information back to the AJAX engine. As this is proceeding, you can still use the onreadystatechange property and the readyState property to monitor the connection between the AJAX engine and the programs running on the server.

Once a successful response has been received from the server, you can then look at the content sent from the server back to the AJAX engine. You can use two properties of the request object to view this information. One, the responseText property, returns the information as a text string. The other, the responseXML property, returns the information as an XML document. This is the preferred approach, because you can use the DOM techniques discussed in this tutorial to view, navigate, and manipulate the contents of the XML document—after all, the X in AJAX stands for XML!

Occasionally errors occur in communication between the server and the AJAX engine. Thus, before processing any information received from the server, you have to check the status code of the transaction. This is done using the status property of the request object. Figure 10-59 lists some of the possible status code values. A status code value of 200 indicates that the transaction has been successfully completed.

Figure 10-59 ▷ **Status code values**

Status code	Status code text
100	Continue
200	OK
302	Found
400	Bad Request
404	Not Found
408	Request Timeout
500	Internal Server Error

Working with the XMLHttpRequest Object

- To open a request, use

     `reqObj.open(method, url, async, user, pwd)`

  where `reqObj` is the request object, `method` is the method used to open the connection, `url` is the URL of the Web server program receiving the request, `async` is a Boolean value indicating whether the call is asynchronous (true) or synchronous (false), and `user` and `pwd` are optional parameters used to authenticate the request by supplying a username and password to the server program.

- To send a request, use

     `reqObj.send(content)`

  where `content` is any optional content to be sent with the request, such as a document object or text string.

- To check for a change in the ready state status of the request object, use the event handler

     `reqObj.onreadystatechange`

- To return the ready state status of the request, use

     `reqObj.readyState`

- To access a text string returned by the request object, use

     `reqObj.responseText`

- To access an XML document returned by the request object, use

     `reqObj.responseXML`

Conclusion

AJAX promises to offer faster and more efficient communication between client browsers and Web servers. Because it builds on current and well-supported technology such as JavaScript, HTML, XSLT, and XML, it is also well supported in the browser community. Susan immediately sees how she could use AJAX to create a client/server application in which she updates the contribution list on her browser and communicates with the server to save, update, and retrieve changes made to that list.

However, AJAX is not the solution to every client/server challenge. Critics point out the following problems with an AJAX-centric approach:

- AJAX breaks the behavior of the browser's back button, because you cannot easily go back to information previously rendered on the Web page.
- You cannot bookmark a specific state of an AJAX application, because information is not exchanged at the page level.
- Users may be confused by slow communication between the AJAX engine and the server.
- ActiveX and JavaScript must be enabled by users, which may violate security protocols instituted by some systems managers.
- Though well-supported, AJAX applications still must be tested for browser compatibility.
- AJAX applications are not always well designed for users with special needs and disabilities.

In the end, the best solution is often to develop applications that combine the best features of the traditional Web application model and the AJAX application model. This is something that you and Susan will work on in future projects for The Lighthouse.

Review

Session 10.3 Quick Check

1. You want to set the value of the customerID style sheet parameter to the text string cid41002. Enter the code to do this in both MSXML and Mozilla. Assume that the name of the XSLT processor is xProc.
2. Write code to convert the XPath expression "//customers" to a node set. Assume that the document object's name is xDoc and that you want to reference the first single node in xDoc that matches this expression. Provide a solution for both MSXML and Mozilla.
3. Repeat the previous question, except write code that creates a node set for all nodes that match the XPath expression.
4. Describe how MSXML and Mozilla differ in handling document load errors. How would you examine the error response from either one to determine whether an error has occurred?
5. Why can't you use the document object's save() method to save XML documents to a local computer?
6. What command do you use to create an XMLHttpRequest object? Provide an answer for both MSXML and Mozilla.
7. What XMLHttpRequest object property do you use to determine whether communication with the server has been successfully completed? What property do you use to determine whether a file transaction has been successfully completed?

Review

Tutorial Summary

This tutorial examined how to work with JavaScript and the document object to load, transform, and edit XML source documents and style sheets. The first session began with the history of the W3C Document Object Model, comparing the features and browser support of different levels of the W3C DOM. It then examined how to create cross-browser code to create and load document objects. The first session also looked at how to load and apply XSLT style sheets to source documents and examined some of the properties and features of the XSLT processor object. The second session looked more closely at the structure and content of document objects. It explored how to navigate a document object's node tree and how to create and insert new element nodes and text nodes. The session also covered attribute nodes and explored how to modify style sheet attributes to change the appearance of rendered page content. The third session began by using JavaScript to modify the values of style sheet parameters. It also looked at how to convert XPath expressions in nodes and node sets. The third session then covered the error-handling techniques in both MSXML and Mozilla. The tutorial concluded with a brief overview of saving XML documents and using AJAX to facilitate asynchronous communication between client browsers and Web servers.

Key Terms

ActiveX	document object	SAX
AJAX	Document Object	serializer object
AJAX engine	Model	sibling node
AJAX Web application	DOM	side-by-side mode
model	element node	Simple API for XML
array	free-threaded model	synchronous load
Asynchronous JavaScript	front-end application	template object
and XML	node object	text node
asynchronous load	object detection	thread
attribute node	parent node	W3C DOM
child node	parseError object	white space node
classic Web application	processor object	XMLHttp object
model	rental-threaded model	XMLHttpRequest object
document fragment	replace mode	XPathEvaluator object

Review Assignment

Data files needed for this Review Assignment: grants.css, grants.xml, grants.xsl, granttxt. htm, library.js, logo.jpg

Susan's next task is to create a report of the grants that The Lighthouse provides for groups working in the state. She has placed the grant information in an XML document named grants.xml, recording the titles and addresses of the organizations receiving money, as well the amounts, the dates the grants were released, and the grant categories (Culture, Education, or Human Services). Figure 10-60 shows the structure of the grants. xml file.

Figure 10-60

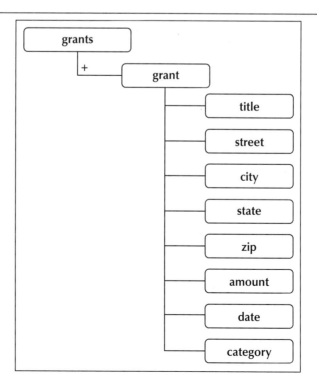

Susan has also created an XSLT style sheet named grants.xsl to display these grants in a table, and she has started work on a Web page to display this table. As with the contributions data, Susan wants to be able to sort, filter, and add new grant information from within her Web page. Figure 10-61 shows a preview of the page she wants you to create.

Figure 10-61

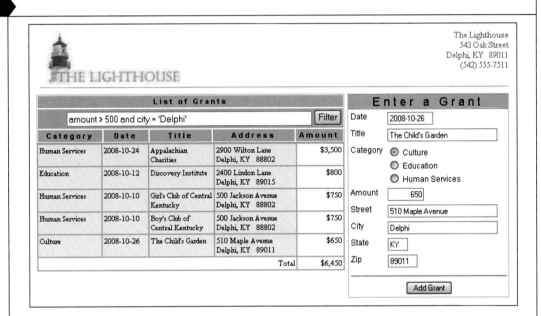

In this report, Susan wants to have the ability to sort the table by clicking on the table headings. For example, if a user clicks the amount heading, Susan wants the column sorted by amount given to the different agencies. Clicking the amount heading again toggles the sort order between ascending and descending order. The headings are formatted as links. To cause a link to run JavaScript code, you enter the following code in the link tag:

```
<a href="javascript:code"> ... </a>
```

where *code* is the JavaScript code run when a user clicks the link. Susan's form also contains several option buttons used to specify the grant category. To determine whether an option button has been clicked, use the JavaScript expression

```
document.form.option[i].checked
```

where *form* is the name of the Web form, *option* is the name of the group of option buttons on the form, and *i* is the index number of a particular option button within the group. The first option button has an index value of 0, the second button has an index value of 1, and so forth. This expression returns a Boolean value of true if the option button has been checked by the user. In Susan's Web page, the name of the form is dataform and the name of the option button group containing the grant categories is category.

To aid you in developing this report, Susan has already created an external JavaScript file named library.js containing many functions that you'll use in developing her report. Note that many of the tasks to complete this report follow the same code and structure you used to create the contributions report. Thus, you can refer back to that earlier code for assistance.

To complete this task:

1. Using your text editor, open **granttxt.htm** from the tutorial.10x/review folder. Enter *your name* and *the date* in the comment section, and save the file as **grants.htm**.
2. Use your text editor to explore the contents of the grants.xml, grants.xsl, and library.js files. You do not have to make any changes to these documents.
3. Return to the grants.htm file in your text editor. Within the head section, insert a script element linked to the library.js file. Insert a second script element and declare the following global variables:
   - The IE variable containing a Boolean value that is true if a user's browser supports ActiveX objects
   - The MOZ variable containing a Boolean value that is true if a user's browser supports the W3C DOM
   - The xmlFile variable containing the text string grants.xml, and the xsltFile variable containing the text string grants.xsl
   - Variables named xmlDoc, xsltDoc, xTemplate, and xProcessor. These variables store the XML document, XSLT document, XSLT template, and XSLT processor objects. Do not set initial values for these variables.
   - Variables named selectValue, currentSelect, currentDataType, and currentOrder. The selectValue and currentSelect variables store the value of the select attribute used to sort the grants list. The currentDataType stores the data type of the sorted list. The currentOrder variable specifies whether the list is sorted in ascending or descending order. Set the initial value of the selectValue, currentSelect, currentDataType, and currentOrder variables to date, date, text, and descending, respectively.
4. Create a function named loadDoc() used to load document objects from external files. The function has two parameters named document and file. The first line of the function should set the async property of the document object to false. The second line should load the contents of the file parameter into the document object.

5. Create a function named init(). The purpose of this function is to initially load the document and template objects under both Document Object Models. Add the following commands to the function:

   - If the user's browser is Internet Explorer, use the getPID() function from the library.js file to load document objects into the xmlDoc and xsltDoc variables (use DOMPID and FreeThreadPID, respectively, for the parameter values of the get-PID() function Also use the getPID() function to load a template object into the xTemplate variable (use TemplatePID for the parameter value).

   - If the user is running a Mozilla-based browser, load document objects into the xmlDoc and xsltDoc variables using the createDocument() method employed by those browsers.

   - After the document and template objects have been created, run the loadDoc() function to store the contents of the grants.xml and grants.xsl files in the xmlDoc and xsltDoc variables. Use the xmlFile and xsltFile variables to specify the filenames of the source document and XSLT style sheet.

6. Create a function named filterGrants(). The purpose of this function is to filter the values displayed in the table based on a filter text string entered into the Web form. The function has a single parameter named xProcessor, used to represent the XSLT processor object. Add the following commands to the function:

   - If the value of the filter input box is equal to an empty text string, set the value of the currentFilter variable to "//grant"; otherwise, set the value of the currentFilter parameter to: "//grant[*filter*]" where *filter* is the text string entered into the filter input box. (*Hint*: Reference the value of the filter input box using the expression: document.dataform.filter.value.)

   - If the user is running Internet Explorer, select the nodes specified by the value of the currentFilter variable and store the node set in a variable named xNodes. Set the value of the group parameter in the xProcessor object to the value of the xNodes variable.

   - If the user is running a Mozilla browser, create an XPathEvaluator object named xEval. Evaluate the node set specified by the currentFilter variable, and store the node set in a variable named xNodes. Set the value of the group parameter in the xProcessor object to the value of the xNodes variable.

7. Create a function named sortGrants(). The purpose of this function is to sort the grants list based on the table heading clicked by the user on the Web form. Add the following commands to the function:

   - If the user is running Internet Explorer, load an XSLT document object into the xsltDoc variable using the getPID() function from the library.js file and with a parameter value of FreeThreadPID. Run the loadDoc() function using xsltDoc and xsltFile as the parameter values. Declare a variable named sortNode that references the first xsl:sort element in the xsltDoc document object.

   - Otherwise, if the user is running a Mozilla-based browser, declare a variable named xNS that stores the namespace of the XSLT style sheet (*http://www.w3.org/1999/XSL/Transform*). Declare a variable named sortNode that references the first sort element in the xsltDoc document object belonging to the xNS namespace.

- Determine how the grant list should be sorted by adding an if structure to the function. If the value of the selectValue variable equals the value of the currentSelect variable, then test whether the value of the currentOrder variable equals ascending. If so, set the value of the currentOrder variable to descending; otherwise, set the value of the currentOrder variable to ascending. If the value of the selectValue variable does not equal the value of the currentSelect variable, then set the value of the currentSelect variable to the value of the selectValue variable, but do not change the value of the currentOrder variable.
- If the currentSelect variable equals amount, then set the value of the currentDataType variable to number; otherwise, set the value of currentDataType to text.
- Set the value of the select, data-type, and order attributes of the sortNode element to currentSelect, currentDataType, and currentOrder respectively.

8. Create a function named transformDoc(). The purpose of this function is to transform the source document based on the XSLT style sheet and then to display the result text in the Web page. Add the following commands to the function:
   - Create a variable named grantTable that references the element in the current document with the gRows ID.
   - Run the sortGrants() function.
   - If the user is running Internet Explorer, then: (1) Set the style sheet used by the xTemplate object to the xsltDoc style sheet; (2) Create a processor named xProcessor from the xTemplate object; (3) Run the filterGrants() function using xProcessor as the parameter value; (4) Set the input property of the xProcessor object to the xmlDoc document object; (5) Run the transformation using the xProcessor object; and (6) Write the output from the xProcessor object to the inner HTML of the grantTable object.
   - If the user is running a Mozilla-based browser, then: (1) Create an XSLT processor named xProcessor; (2) Import the xsltDoc style sheet into the xProcessor object; (3) Run the filterGrants() function using xProcessor as the parameter value; (4) Transform the xmlDoc document into a document fragment within the current HTML document using the xProcessor object, then store the fragment in a variable named resultDoc; (5) Create an XMLSerializer object named xSerial; (6) Serialize the contents of resultDoc, storing the text string in a variable named xStr; and (7) Write the content of the xStr variable into the inner HTML of the grantTable object.

9. Go to the init() function, and add a command to the end of the function to run the transformDoc() function.

10. Create a function named addGrant(). The purpose of this function is to insert a new grant record into the source document object. Add the following commands to the function:
    - Create a variable named oldGrant that stores the first element in the xmlDoc document with the tag name <grant>.
    - Clone the oldGrant element and all of its descendants into a variable named clone.

- Use the removeWhiteSpaceNodes() function from the library.js file to remove all white space nodes from the clone object.
- Set the content contained in the clone object's first child node to the value of the title field from the Web form. (*Hint*: To reference the content of the clone object's first child node use the expression clone.childNodes[0].firstChild.nodeValue. To reference the value of the title field use the expression document.dataform.title.value.) Using the same process, set the value of the content contained in the clone object's second through seventh child nodes to the values of the street, city, state, zip, amount, and date fields, respectively.
- If the first category option button on the Web form is checked, set the value of the content contained in the clone object's eighth child node to Culture. If the second category option button is checked, set the value to Education. Finally if the third category option button is checked, set the value to Human Services.
- Append the clone object to the root element of the xmlDoc document.
- Run the transformDoc() function.
- Run the resetForm() function from the library.js file to reset the contents of the Web form.

11. Go to the opening <body> tag in the document, and insert an event handler to run the init() function when the page is initially loaded.

12. Locate the <input> tag for the Filter button and insert an event handler to run the transformDoc() function when the button is clicked. (*Note*: Do not confuse the <input> tag for the Filter input box with the <input> tag for the Filter button.)

13. Locate the <a> tag for the Category table heading. Change the value of the href property from # to the following two JavaScript commands:
    - Set the value of the selectValue variable to Category.
    - Run the transformDoc() function.

14. Locate the <a> tag for the Date table heading, and change the href attribute so that the browser sets the value of the selectValue variable to date and runs the transformDoc() function when the heading is clicked. Do the same for the remaining links in the table heading row, setting the value of the selectValue variable to: title, city, and amount, respectively.

15. Go to the bottom of the document, and add an event handler to the Add Grant button, running the transformDoc() command when the button is clicked.

16. Save your changes to the file and open grants.htm in your Web browser. Verify that the grant list is properly displayed in the Grant table and that you can add new grants to the list by filling out the Web form and clicking the Add Grant button. Verify that you can filter the contents of the grant list by entering an XPath expression in the Filter input box and clicking the Filter button. Finally, verify that you can sort the contents of the grant list by clicking one of the five table headings, and that if you click the same heading twice in a row, the sort order toggles between ascending and descending order. (*Note*: You must be running Firefox version 1.5 or higher or Internet Explorer for Windows to see the completed project in action.)

17. Submit the completed project to your instructor.

Apply

Use the skills you learned in this tutorial to combine multiple style sheets in an online stock report

Case Problem 1

Data files needed for this Case Problem: current.xsl, down.gif, fiveday.xsl, headtxt.xsl, library.js, overview.xsl, reptxt.htm, same.gif, stock.css, stocks.xml, up.gif, yearly.xsl

Hardin Financial Kevin Summers, a financial analyst for Hardin Financial, asked for your help in creating a stock report. Kevin placed information about stocks in an XML document named stocks.xml. He has also created several XSLT style sheets to display this stock information. Figure 10-62 summarizes the contents of these style sheets.

Figure 10-62

File	Displays
current.xsl	Current stock values
fiveday.xsl	Five-day stock values
heading.xsl	A selection list containing the symbols of each stock in the report
overview.xsl	Descriptive information about the stock
yearly.xsl	Yearly summary information about the stock

Kevin would like to give users the ability to choose the style of the stock report and to select the stock or stocks to be displayed in the report. Figure 10-63 shows a preview of the report that Kevin wants your help in creating.

Figure 10-63

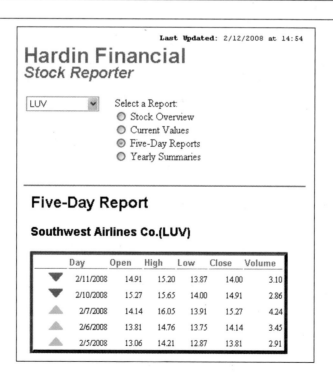

To select the stock, Kevin wants a selection list populated with the symbols of each of the 14 stocks in the stocks.xml document. Each time a user selects a different symbol from the selection list, the report should display information on the selected stock. There are several JavaScript expressions that can be used to work with selection lists that you need to complete this and future assignments. To determine which item was chosen from the selection list, use the following expression:

```
document.form.list.selectedIndex
```

where *form* is the name of the Web form, and *list* is the name of the selection list. To determine the value of the selected option in the list box, use the expression

```
document.form.list.options[i].value
```

where *i* is the index number of the selected option in the list box (determined by the selectedIndex property). Finally, to determine the text associated with the selected option, use the expression

```
document.form.list.options[i].text
```

On Kevin's Web page, the name of the Web form is stockform, and the name of the drop-down list box is symbol. The report style applied to the selected stock is chosen from the group of option buttons. Clicking a different option button applies a different style sheet to the source document. Refer to the Review Assignment for techniques to determine which option button has been checked by a user. In Kevin's form the option button group is named reports.

Kevin has also supplied you with an external JavaScript file, library.js, that contains several JavaScript functions that you'll use on this project.

To complete this task:

1. Using your text editor, open **reptxt.htm** and **headtxt.xsl** from the tutorial.10x/case1 folder. Enter *your name* and *the date* in the comment section of each file, and save them as **report.htm** and **heading.xsl** respectively.
2. Use your text editor to explore the contents of the current.xsl, fiveday.xsl, heading.xsl, library.js, overview.xsl, and yearly.xsl files. When finished, close the files without saving any changes.
3. Return to the report.htm file in your text editor. Within the head section, insert a script element linked to the library.js file. Insert a second script element, and declare the following global variables:
    - The IE variable containing a Boolean value that is true if the user's browser supports ActiveX objects
    - The MOZ variable containing a Boolean value indicating whether the user's browser supports Mozilla
    - Variables named xmlDoc and xsltDoc, used to store the document objects for the source document and style sheet. You do not have to set initial values for these variables.

4. Create a function named createXDoc(). The purpose of this function is to create and load an XML or XSLT file into a document object. The function has two parameters: xFile and PID. Add the following commands to the function:

   - If the user is running Internet Explorer, create an ActiveX document object named xDoc, using the program ID from the PID parameter. Otherwise, if the user is running a Mozilla-based browser, create a document object named xDoc.
   - Run the loadDoc() function from the library.js file, using xDoc and xFile as the parameter values.
   - Return the xDoc variable from the function.

Explore

5. Create a function named init(). The purpose of this function is to set up the initial Web page, loading the contents of the heading.xsl style sheet. Add the following commands to the function:

   - Create a variable named headingElem that references the element in the Web page document with the ID of heading. This element is where you'll store the content of the Web page heading.
   - Call the createDoc() function using parameter values of stocks.xml and DOMPID to create a document object. Store the object returned by this function in the xmlDoc variable. Call the createDoc() function again using parameter values of heading.xsl and DOMPID. Store the object returned by the function in the xsltDoc variable.
   - For Internet Explorer browsers, use the transformNode() method to transform the contents of the xmlDoc document using the xsltDoc style sheet. Store the text returned by this method in the inner HTML of the headingElem object.
   - For Mozilla-based browsers, do the following: (1) Create an XSLT processor named xProcessor; (2) Import the xsltDoc style sheet into the processor; (3) Transform the xmlDoc document into a result fragment named resultFragment, storing the fragment in the current HTML document; and (4) Append resultFragment as a child of the headingElem object.

6. Create a function named chooseReport(). The purpose of this function is to determine which of the style sheets to use in the stock report. The function has no parameters. Add the following commands to the function:

   - Create a variable named xsltFile. This variable specifies the name of the XSLT style sheet used in the report. Set its initial value to an empty text string.
   - If the first reports option button is checked, set the value of the xsltFile variable to overview.xsl. If the second option button is checked, the value of xsltFile should be current.xsl. If the third or fourth option button is checked, set the value of xsltFile to fiveday.xsl or yearly.xsl respectively.
   - Return the value of the xsltFile variable.

7. Create a function named chooseStock(). The purpose of this function is to determine which of the stocks to display in the report. The function has no parameters. Add the following commands to the function:
   - Determine the value of the selected index in the symbol selection list. Store the index in the sIndex variable.
   - Determine the value of the selected option. Store the value in the stockSymbol variable.
   - If stockSymbol equals all_stocks set the value of the filterStr variable to "//stock"; otherwise set the value of the filterStr variable to
     ```
     //stock[name/@symbol='stockSymbol']
     ```
     where *stockSymbol* is the value of the stockSymbol variable.
   - Return the value of the filterStr variable.

8. Create a function named showReport(). The purpose of this function is to run the transformation and show the results for a selected stock report and a selected stock. The function has no parameters. Add the following commands:
   - Create an object named reportElem that references the element in the Web document with the ID stock_report. This element is where you'll store the report results.
   - Call the chooseReport() function, storing the value returned by the function in the reportFile variable. Call the chooseStock() function, storing the value returned by the function in the stock variable.
   - If reportFile or stock equals an empty text string, set the inner HTML of the reportElem object to an empty text string; otherwise, run the commands in the following bulleted points.
   - Call the createXDoc() function using reportFile and FreeThreadPID as the parameter values. Store the document object created by this function in the reportXSLT variable.
   - If the user is running Internet Explorer, then: (1) Create a template object named xTemplate; (2) Store the reportXSLT style sheet in the template; (3) Create a processor object named xProcessor based on the template; (4) Input the xmlDoc document object into the processor; (5) Set the value of the stocklist parameter in the processor to the nodes in the xmlDoc selected by the value of the stock variable; (6) Run the transformation under the processor; and (7) Store the output from the transformation in the inner HTML of the reportElem object.
   - If the user is running a Mozilla-based browser, then: (1) Create a processor object named xProcessor; (2) Import the reportXSLT style sheet into the processor; (3) Create an XPathEvaluator object to evaluate the node set defined by the stock variable, then store the node set in the xNodes variable; (4) Set the value of the stocklist parameter to the xNodes node set; (5) Use the transformToDocument() method to transform xmlDoc, storing the document object in the resultDoc variable; (6) Serialize the contents of the resultDoc document object, storing the text string in the xStr variable; and (7) Set the inner HTML of the reportElem object to the value of the xStr variable.

9. Go to the opening <body> tag, and add an event handler to run the init() function when the page loads.

10. Close the report.htm file, saving your changes.

11. Open the heading.xsl file in your text editor. Go to the opening <select> tag for the symbol selection list. Insert an event handler to run the showReport() function when the value of this selection list changes. (*Hint*: Use the onchange event handler.)

12. Go to the four <input> tags for the four reports option buttons in the form. To each option button, add an event handler to run the showReport() function when the button is clicked.

13. Close the heading.xsl file, saving your changes. Open report.htm in your Web browser. Verify that you can display different reports by selecting different stock symbols from the selection list and report styles from the option buttons on the form.

14. Submit the completed project to your instructor.

Apply

Use the skills you learned in this tutorial to create an interactive basketball box score and game log

Case Problem 2

Data files needed for this Case Problem: boxscore.xsl, game.css, game.xml, gamelog. xsl, gametxt.htm, library.js, plays.txt, scoretxt.xsl, title.xsl

Sports Stats Alison Crawley is a Web page designer for Sports Stats, a Web site for sports statistics and information. The company is looking at using XML documents to store information about basketball games for upcoming tournaments. Alison wants to create a Web site on which she can enter play-by-play information about the games. Figure 10-64 shows a preview of the type of page that Alison has in mind.

Figure 10-64

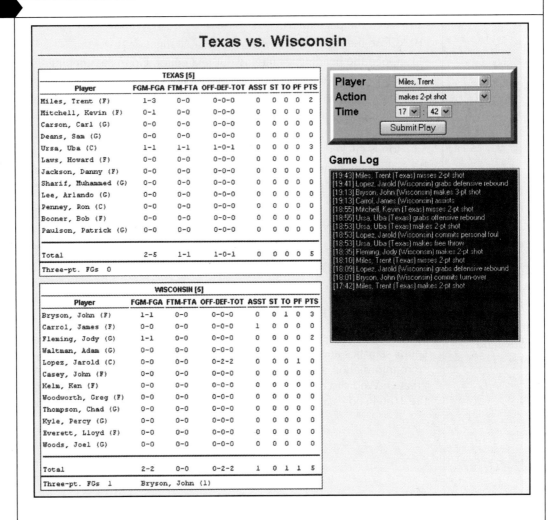

Alison envisions being able to select the name of a player, the play involving the player, and the time that the play occurred from drop-down list boxes. She would then be able to click a Submit Play button to enter the play into an XML document. The details of that play would be appended to the source document as a child of the plays element. Figure 10-65 shows the structure of the source document. Information about each play is stored in the time, player, action, and team attributes to identify when the play occurred, which players were involved, the nature of the play, and which team was involved. Initially, there are no play elements in the source document. These will be added only through the use of the Web form.

Figure 10-65

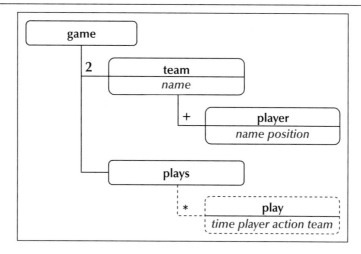

Once a new play has been added to the source document, Allison then wants the box score and game log updated to reflect the addition of the new play. Figure 10-66 summarizes the different style sheets that Allison has created for use with the source document.

Figure 10-66

File	Description
boxscore.xsl	Summarizes the plays in a box score
gamelog.xsl	Displays a game log of the plays in a drop-down list box
scoring.xsl	Displays form controls listing the players on each team, the possible plays they can be involved in, and the time that the plays occur
title.xsl	Displays the names of the teams in the game

Note that this project uses drop-down list boxes. If you're not sure how JavaScript works with drop-down list boxes, review the discussion in Case Problem 1. All of the drop-down list boxes are found on the sForm Web form. The player who participated in a play is stored in the player selection list. The action committed by a player is stored in the action selection list. The time that the play occurred is stored in the min and sec selection lists.

To complete this task:

1. Using your text editor, open **gametxt.htm** and **scoretxt.xsl** from the tutorial.10x/ case2 folder. Enter *your name* and *the date* in the comment section of each file and save them as **game.htm** and **scoring.xsl**, respectively.
2. Use your text editor to explore the contents of the boxscore.xsl, gamelog.xsl, library. js, title.xsl, and scoring.xsl. Take some time to understand the purpose of each file and how the code within the files works. Close the files without saving any changes you may make.

3. Return to the report.htm file in your text editor. Within the head section, insert a script element linked to the library.js file. Insert a second script element, and declare the following global variables:

   - The IE and MOZ variables containing Boolean values indicating whether the user's browser supports the Internet Explorer or Mozilla-based browsers.
   - Variables named xmlFile, xsltFile1, xsltFile2, xsltFile3, and xsltFile4, used to store the file names of the source document and style sheets. Store the following values in these variables respectively: game.xml, title.xsl, scoring.xsl, boxscore.xsl, and gamelog.xsl.
   - Variables named xmlDoc, xsltDoc1, xsltDoc2, xsltDoc3, and xsltDoc4, used to store document objects for the source document and style sheets. You do not have to set initial values for these variables.

4. Create a function named createXDoc(). The purpose of this function is to create and load an XML or XSLT file into a document object. The function has two parameters: xFile and PID. Add the following commands to the function:

   - If the user is running Internet Explorer, create an ActiveX document object named xDoc, using the program ID from the PID parameter. Otherwise, if the user is running a Mozilla-based browser, create a document object named xDoc.
   - Run the loadDoc() function from the library.js file, using xDoc and xFile as the parameter values.
   - Return the xDoc variable from the function.

5. Create a function named runTransform(), used to transform source documents and return the result document as a text string. The function has two parameters named xDoc and xsltDoc. Add the following commands to the function:

   - If the user is running Internet Explorer, use the transformNode() method of the xDoc object to transform the source document using the xsltDoc style sheet object. Store the resulting document text in the resultStr variable.
   - If the user is running a Mozilla-based browser, do the following: (1) Create a processor object named xProcessor; (2) Import the xsltDoc style sheet into the processor; (3) Transform the xDoc document into a document object with the variable name, resultDoc; and (4) Serialize the contents of the resultDoc document, storing the text in the resultStr variable.
   - Return the value of the resultStr variable.

6. Create a function named init() used to set up the initial appearance of the Web page. The function has no parameters. Add the following commands to the function:

   - Create the titleElem variable that points to the element in the Web page document with the ID title. Create other variables named scoringElem, boxscoreElem, and gamelogElem that point to elements with the IDs scoring, boxscore, and gamelog, respectively.
   - Call the createXDoc() function using xmlFile and DOMPID as the parameter values. Store the document object returned by the createXDoc() in the xmlDoc variable. In the same way, store style sheet document objects in the xsltDoc1, xsltDoc2, xsltDoc3, and xsltDoc4 variables using xsltFile1, xsltFile2, xsltFile3, and xsltFile4 as the first parameter value of the createXDoc() function and DOMPID as the second parameter value.

- Call the runTransform() function using xmlDoc as the first parameter value and xsltDoc1 as the second parameter value. Store the text string returned by this function in the inner HTML of the titleElem object. In the same way, call the runTransform() function three more times using xmlDoc as the first parameter value and xsltDoc2, xsltDoc3, and xsltDoc4 as the second parameter values. Store the text returned by the function in the inner HTML of the scoringElem, boxscoreElem, and gamelogElem objects, respectively.

7. Create the addPlay() function. The purpose of this function is to update the contents of the source document by adding the new play specified by the user. The function has no parameters. Add the following commands:
   - Create variables named boxscoreElem and gamelogElem referencing elements in the Web document with the IDs boxscore and gamelog, respectively.
   - Create a new play element in the xmlDoc document object, and store the element node in the newPlay variable.
   - Retrieve the selected index from the min selection list, storing the value in the minIndex variable. Retrieve the selected index from the sec selection list, storing the value in the secIndex variable. Retrieve the selected index from the action selection list, storing the value in the actIndex variable. Finally, retrieve the selected index from the player selection list, storing the value in the playerIndex variable.
   - Retrieve the text of the selected option from the min selection list whose index value equals minIndex. Store the text in the minute variable. Retrieve the text of the selection option from the sec selection list whose index equals secIndex. Store the text in the second variable.
   - Create a variable named time with a value equal to *minute:second*, where *minute* is the value of the minute variable and *second* is the value of the second variable.
   - Retrieve the text of the selected option from the player selection list whose index equals playerIndex. Store the text in the player variable. Store the value of the selection option in the team variable. Retrieve the text of the selected option from the action selection list using the actIndex variable, and store the text in the action variable.
   - Set the value of the time attribute in the newPlay element to the value of the time variable. Set the value of newPlay's player attribute to the value of the player variable. Set the value of newPlay's team attribute to the value of the team variable. Finally, set the value of newPlay's action attribute to the value of the action variable.
   - Append the newPlay element as a child of the first plays element in the xmlDoc document. Note that you do not have to specify a namespace for this new element.
   - Run the runTransform() function using xmlDoc and xsltDoc3 as the parameter values, and store the text string returned by the function in the inner HTML of the boxscoreElem object. Run the runTransform() again using xmlDoc and xsltDoc4 as the parameter values. Store the text string generated by the function in the gamelogElem object.

8. Go to the opening \<body\> tag, and add an event handler to run the init() function when the page loads.

9. Close the game.htm file, saving your changes.

10. Go to the scoring.xsl file in your text editor. Locate the <input> tag for the Submit Play button, and add an onclick event handler to the tag that runs the addPlay() function when the button is clicked.

11. Close the scoring.xsl file, saving your changes.

12. Open game.htm in your Web browser. A sample of game events is stored in the plays.txt file. Practice entering these plays in the Web form, and verify that the box score and the game log is updated correctly to reflect the sequence of new plays.

13. Submit the completed project to your instructor.

Challenge

Explore how to load different source documents into a Web report to create an interactive calendar

Case Problem 3

Data files needed for this Case Problem: 20080919.xml, 20080920.xml, 20080921.xml, 20080922.xml, 20080923.xml, lab.css, lab.xsl, labtxt.htm, library.js

MWU Computer Lab   Ian Bishop is the coordinator of Mid-West University's computer labs. One of his jobs is to handle reservations requests from instructors for each of the six computers. Reservations are granted in 1-hour slots, starting from 9 a.m. and going to 4 p.m., Mondays through Fridays.

Lately Ian has been looking at ways of putting the scheduling system in an online Web page available on the school's network. He placed schedule information for each day in a separate XML file with filenames from 20080919.xml through 20080923.xml, representing dates from 9/19/2008 through 9/23/2008. The structure of the five schedule documents is shown in Figure 10-67.

Figure 10-67

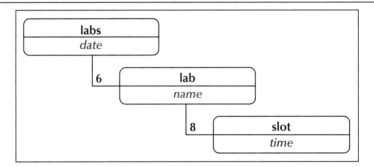

In this project, you'll use the Web form to specify which source document you want to display on the Web page. This is done by using an input field that allows you to navigate your computer's folder tree to locate the XML document. The input field returns the complete path to the source document. Because this project assumes that the source documents are all placed in the same folder as the Web page file, a function named extractFName() has been written for you to remove the extraneous path information, leaving only the filename of the source document.

Once the schedule document is loaded, Ian wants to display the lab schedule from that day in a Web table and allow users to reserve rooms and times via a Web form. If a slot is free, the lab schedule table should display the text "free"; otherwise, the lab schedule should display the name of the group reserving the space. Figure 10-68 shows a preview of the page that Ian needs your help to complete.

Figure 10-68

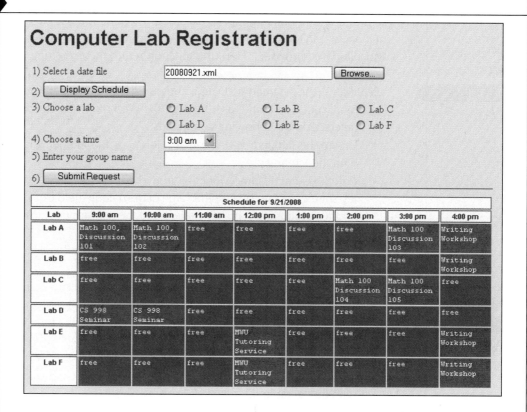

Computer Lab Registration

1) Select a date file   `20080921.xml`   Browse...

2) [Display Schedule]

3) Choose a lab   ○ Lab A   ○ Lab B   ○ Lab C
                ○ Lab D   ○ Lab E   ○ Lab F

4) Choose a time   `9:00 am ▼`

5) Enter your group name   [   ]

6) [Submit Request]

				Schedule for 9/21/2008				
Lab	**9:00 am**	**10:00 am**	**11:00 am**	**12:00 pm**	**1:00 pm**	**2:00 pm**	**3:00 pm**	**4:00 pm**
Lab A	Math 100, Discussion 101	Math 100, Discussion 102	free	free	free	free	Math 100 Discussion 103	Writing Workshop
Lab B	free	free	free	free	free	free	free	Writing Workshop
Lab C	free	free	free	free	free	Math 100 Discussion 104	Math 100 Discussion 105	free
Lab D	CS 998 Seminar	CS 998 Seminar	free	free	free	free	free	free
Lab E	free	free	free	MWU Tutoring Service	free	free	free	Writing Workshop
Lab F	free	free	free	MWU Tutoring Service	free	free	free	Writing Workshop

Ian wants the reservation table to prohibit users from reserving rooms that are already filled up. If the room is free, the table should be updated to display the new room reservation.

To complete this task:

1. Using your text editor, open the file **labtxt.htm** from the tutorial.10x/case3 folder. Enter **your name** and **the date** in the comment section of the file, and save it as **lab.htm**.

2. Review the contents of the lab.xsl and library.js files as well as one of the schedule documents. Close the files without saving any changes.

3. Return to the lab.htm file in your text editor. Within the head section, insert a script element linked to the library.js file. Insert a second script element and declare the following global variables:
   - The IE and MOZ variables containing Boolean values indicating whether the user's browser supports the Internet Explorer or Mozilla-based browsers.
   - The xmlFile, xsltFile, xmlDoc, and xsltDoc variables storing the filenames and document objects for the source document and XSLT style sheet documents. Set the initial value of the xsltFile variable to lab.xsl. Do not set initial values for the other variables.

4. Create a function named createXDoc(). The purpose of this function is to create and load an XML or XSLT file into a document object. The function has two parameters: xFile and PID. Write the function so that it creates and loads the document object under either Internet Explorer or a Mozilla-based browser. Return the document object created by the function.

5. Create a function named runTransform(), used to transform a source document and return the result document as a text string. The function has two parameters named xDoc and xsltDoc. Write the function so that it runs under Internet Explorer or Mozilla-based browsers. Have the function return the text string of the result document.

Explore

6. Create a function named getDate(). The purpose of this function is to load a source document specified by the user through the Web form. The function has no parameters. Add the following commands:
   - Create the labElem variable that references the element in the Web document with the labtable ID.
   - Call the extractFName() function from the library.js file to extract the file name of the source document. Use the value of the datefile field from the signup Web form for the function's parameter value. Store the text string returned by the function in the xmlFile variable.
   - Use the createXDoc() function to create and load the xmlDoc and xsltDoc document and style sheet objects.
   - Use the runTransform() function to run the XSLT transformation with xmlDoc and xsltDoc, storing the resulting text string in the inner HTML of the labElem object.

Explore

7. Create a function named addRequest(). The purpose of this function is to add a room reservation to the source document if possible and to notify the user of a conflict if it is not. There are no parameters to this function. Add the following commands:
   - Create the labElem variable that references the element in the Web document with the labtable ID.
   - Labs are indicated by six lab option buttons on the form. If the first lab option button is checked, set the value of the labIndex variable to 0, if the second lab option button is checked set the labIndex value to 1, and so forth. (*Hint*: See the Review Assignment for a discussion of how to work with Web form option buttons in JavaScript.)
   - Store the index of the selected option in the time selection list in the timeIndex variable. (*Hint*: See Case Problem 1 for a discussion of how to work with Web form selection lists in JavaScript.)
   - Store the value of the group input box in the group variable.
   - Create the lab node to reference the lab element from the xmlDoc document object whose index value equals labIndex. (*Hint*: Use the getElementsByTag-Name() method to create a list of lab elements in the xmlDoc document.)
   - Remove all white space nodes from the lab node using the removeWhiteSpaceNodes() function in the library.js file.
   - Create the slot node that references the child node of the lab node whose index equals timeIndex.
   - If the node value of the first child of the slot node equals free then: (1) Set the value of the first child of the slot node to the value of the group variable; (2) Call the runTransform() function using the xmlDoc and xsltDoc objects, storing the result text string in the inner HTML of the labElem object; and (3) Display the alert message "Reservation placed." Otherwise, display the alert message "Slot is already reserved." (*Hint*: To create an alert message, use the JavaScript alert() method.)

8. Go to the <input> tag for the Display Schedule button, and add an event handler to run the getDate() function when the button is clicked.

9. Go to the <input> tag for the Submit Request button, and add an event handler to run the addRequest() function when the button is clicked.

10. Save your changes to lab.htm.

11. Open the lab.htm file in your Web browser. Verify that you can insert schedule requests by doing the following:
    - Click the Browse button and locate the **20080921.xml** file in your tutorial.10x/case3 folder. Click the **Open** button to place the complete path to this file in the datefile input field.
    - Click the **Display Schedule** button to display the lab schedule for this date.
    - Click the **Lab B** option button, and select **11:00 am** from the time drop-down list box. Type **Web Publishing** in the group input box.
    - Click the **Submit Request** button, and verify that you receive an alert message indicating that the request has been entered and that the request now appears in the lab schedule.
    - Click the **Submit Request** button again, and verify that you receive an alert message indicating that this slot has been filled.

12. Submit the completed project to your instructor.

Case Problem 4

Create

Test your knowledge of working with the Document Object Model and running transformations using JavaScript by creating an interactive inventory form

Data files needed for this Case Problem: jazz.xml, jazztxt.htm, jazztxt.xsl, specials.txt

The Jazz Warehouse Richard Brooks of the Jazz Warehouse has asked for your help in designing a data entry Web form for monthly specials offered by the company. Monthly specials are currently stored in the jazz.xml document. The structure of this document appears in Figure 10-69.

Figure 10-69

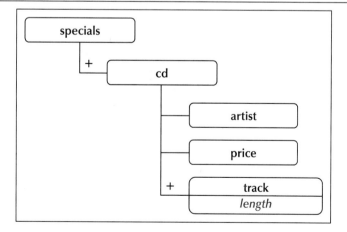

Richard wants a Web page on which he can enter the CD name, artist, price, and each of the tracks on the CD along with the track lengths. He needs the page to work for both Internet Explorer and Mozilla-based browsers.

To complete this task:

1. Using your text editor, open **jazztxt.xsl** and **jazztxt.htm** from the tutorial.10x/case4 folder. Enter **your name** and **the date** in the comment section of each file, and save them as **jazz.xsl** and **jazz.htm** respectively.
2. Go to the jazz.xsl style sheet, and create a style sheet that displays the contents of the jazz.xml document in an easy-to-read format.
3. Go to the jazz.htm file, and add JavaScript commands to create an interactive Web form to view and insert new monthly specials. The design of the Web page is up to you, but it must include the following features:
   - A section of the page that displays the current specials
   - Input boxes where users can enter a CD title, artist, and price
   - A button that users can click to enter the new CD into the source document
   - Input boxes where users can enter the track names and lengths for the new CD
   - A button that users can click to enter the new track into the source document for the new CD
   - A submit button where users can submit the new CD and track information. The Web page should automatically display the updated specials list.
4. Test your form by entering the new CDs listed in the specials.txt file.
5. Submit your completed project to your instructor.

Quick Check Answers

Session 10.1

1. The Document Object Model is a systematic framework for working with the content and structure of a document as a collection of objects. The W3C DOM is the specifications for a DOM put out by the W3C. It is not a programming language; rather, it describes the interface between a programming language and document content.

2. Internet Explorer: XDoc = new ActiveXObject("Microsoft.XMLDOM");'
   Mozilla: XDoc = document.implementation.createDocument("","",null);

3. Internet Explorer: XStyle = new ActiveXObject("Msxml2.
                         FreeThreadedDOMDocument.3.0");'
   Mozilla: XStyle = document.implementation.createDocument("","",null);

4. XDoc.async = false;

5. XDoc.transformNode(XStyle)

6. XTemplate = new ActiveXObject("Msxml2.XSLTemplate.3.0");
   XTemplate.stylesheet = XStyle;

7. Internet Explorer: XProcessor = XTemplate.createProcessor();
   Mozilla: XProcessor = new XSLTProcessor();

Session 10.2

1. xDoc.getElementsByTagName("city")

2. xDoc.getElementsByTagName("city")[1]

3. MSXML ignores the presence of white space nodes. The W3C DOM does not ignore white space nodes.

4. newRegion = xDoc.createElement("region");
   regionText = xDoc.createTextNode("Midwest");

5. newRegion.appendChild(regionText);
   xDoc.documentElement.appendChild(newRegion);

6. xDoc.documentElement.childNodes[1].cloneNode(true);

7. cityNode = xDoc.getElementsByTagName("city")[0];
   cityNode.setAttribute("cid", "c001");

8. cityNode.removeAttribute("cid");

Session 10.3

1. Internet Explorer: xProc.addParameter("customerID", "'cid41002'");
   Mozilla: xProc.setParameter(null, "customerID", "'cid41002'");

2. Internet Explorer: xDoc.selectSingleNode("//customers");
   Mozilla: xEval = new XPathEvaluator();
                       xEval.evaluate("//customers", xDoc, null, 9, null);

3. Internet Explorer: xDoc.selectNodes("//customers");
   Mozilla: xEval = new XPathEvaluator();xEval.evaluate("//customers", xDoc,
                       null, 5, null);

4. MSXML stores errors in the parseError object. Mozilla stores errors in an XML error document object. To determine whether an error has occurred in MSXML, check whether the value of parseError.errorCode equals 0. If it does, no error has occurred. To determine whether an error has occurred in Mozilla, examine the documentElement.tagName property of the document you're trying to load. If the tag name is <parseerror>, an error has occurred.

5. To prevent viruses from writing files to the local computer, JavaScript does not allow the save() method to be used.

6. Internet Explorer: new ActiveXObject(*progID*);
                        where *progID* is an ActiveX program ID for XMLHttpRequest objects
   Mozilla: new XMLHttpRequest();

7. Use the readyState property to determine whether the communication with the server has been successfully completed. Use the status property to determine the status of the file transaction.

Objectives

- Install the Exchanger XML Lite software
- Run the Exchanger XML Lite program

Installing Exchanger XML Lite

Using Exchanger XML Lite Software

Case

Introducing Exchanger XML

Exchanger XML Lite is an XML development environment created by Cladonia, used for designing and editing professional applications involving XML, XML Schema, XSL/XSLT, and other XML-based technologies. In this book, you are encouraged to install and use **Exchanger XML Lite**, a free application which can be downloaded from the Web. Using the Exchanger XML Editor, you can validate XML documents against DTDs and schemas and perform XSLT transformations.

For a complete list of features supported by each edition of Exchanger XML Lite, please refer to the Cladonia Web site at http://www.exchangerxml.com or at http://www.freexmleditor.com.

Installing Exchanger XML Lite

To install the free edition of Exchanger XML you must download and run the installation file. Because the installation file is relatively large, you will probably want to use a high-speed connection to retrieve the file. Your instructor might also make this file available to you on a local server.

To download the installation file:

1. Use your Web browser to go to the Web site at **http://www.freexmleditor.com/**.

   Trouble? The Web is constantly changing, so it is possible that the URL for the download page will have changed. If so, go to the Cladonia home page at www.exchangerxml.com.

2. Click the **Download Now** link.

   Trouble? If the Web page displays a different version of the software, click the link for that version.

3. You are shown a page with downloadable files for different operating systems. Click the link for your operating system. You will also have to choose whether or not to download a version of the software with the Java Virtual Machine. Note that the Exchanger XML Editor requires that you have Java 1.4 or higher installed on your system. Contact your instructor or resource person to determine if you have to install Java and a Java Virtual Machine on your computer.

4. Save the installation file locally on your computer so that you can run it later.

Once you save the installation file, you can run the setup program to put Exchanger XML Lite on your computer.

To install Exchanger XML Lite:

1. Double-click the icon for the installation file from the download folder. An installation wizard appears outlining the steps required for installing the software.

2. Click the **Next** button to start installing the software. In the first step of the wizard, choose the version of the Java Virtual Machine you want to use and click the **Next** button.

   Trouble? If no Java Virtual Machines are listed, you will have to download a version of Exchanger XML that includes a JVM.

3. Select a folder to contain the application files or accept the default folder location. Click the **Next** button.

4. Select a location for the program icons and then click the **Next** button.

5. Click the **Install** button to install Exchanger XML.

6. You are prompted whether to register XML file types with Exchanger XML. If you want the XML files to be opened in Exchanger XML by default, click the **Yes** button.

7. Click the **Done** button to complete the installation.

8. Save the installation file.

The Exchanger XML Editor is now ready to perform the validation and transformation tasks described in this book. Exchanger XML has a wealth of useful tools for creating, transforming, and validating XML documents. Only a small subset of these features is used in this manuscript. You are encouraged to explore these tools for more advanced projects.

XSLT Elements and Attributes

The following table describes the different XSLT elements and attributes supported in XSLT 1.0 and 2.0. Currently, XSLT 2.0 is a W3C Candidate Recommendation and may change before final release.

The following data types are used in the attribute values:

- *Boolean*   A Boolean expression returning the value true or false
- *char*   A single character
- *elements*   A white space separated list of elements
- *encoding*   A character encoding type
- *expr*   An XPath expression
- *format-pattern*   A format pattern
- *id*   An identifier
- *int*   An integer value
- *lang-code*   A language code text string
- *media*   A media type such as text, video, screen, etc.
- *name*   An unqualified name
- *node-set*   A node-set reference
- *numeric-expr*   A numeric expression
- *number*   A numeric value
- *Qname*   A qualified XML name with a required namespace prefix
- *qname*   A XML name with an optional namespace prefix
- *qnames*   A white-space delimited list of qualified names
- *pattern*   A string expression pattern
- *prefix*   A namespace prefix
- *prefixes*   A white space separated list of namespace prefixes
- *regex*   A regular expression
- *regexFlag*   A regular expression flag
- *regexFlags*   A white space separated list of regular expression flags
- *sequence*   A sequence type
- *string*   A text string
- *uri*   A namespace URI
- *url*   A location URL

Note that not all elements and attributes are supported by all browsers and XSLT processors. Check with your browser and XSLT processor documentation to determine level of support.

Optional attributes are placed within square brackets [ ].

Element	Description	Version

xsl:analyze-string
  select="*string*"
  regex="*regex*"
  [flags="*regexFlags*"]
	Splits a text string, *string*, into substrings that either match or don't match the regular expression, *regex*; the match specifications are indicated by *regex flags*	2.0

xsl:apply-imports	Applies the definition and rules of an imported style sheet in situations where the current style sheet would normally have precedence	1.0

xsl:apply-templates
  select="*node-set*"
  [mode="*qname*"]
	Applies a template to the nodes in node-set using the mode *qname*	1.0

xsl:attribute
  name="*qname*"
  [namespace="*uri*"]
	Creates an attribute node named qname under the namespace *uri*	1.0

xsl:attribute-set
  name="*string*"
  [use-attribute-sets="*qnames*"]
	Defines and names a set of zero or more xsl:attribute elements, where *string* is the name of the attribute set and *qnames* is a list of one or more attribute set names	1.0

xsl:call-template name="*qname*"	Calls and applies the template *qname* to the source document	1.0

xsl:character-map
  name="*qname*"
  [use-character-maps="*qnames*"]
	Defines a set of characters to be mapped to text strings when the result document is generated, where *qname* is the name of the character map and *qnames* is a list of character map names	2.0

xsl:choose	Used with the xs:when and xsl:otherwise elements to create conditional tests	1.0
xsl:comment	Creates a comment node	1.0
xsl:copy [use-attribute-sets="qnames"]	Copies the current node, where *qnames* is a list of attributes to be applied to the generated node	1.0

xsl:copy-of
  select="*expr*"
  [copy-namespace="yes | no"]
  [type="*qname*"]
  [validation="strict | lax | preserve | strip"]
	Copies the current node and its descendants, where *expr* identifies the nodes to be copied, the copy-namespace attribute indicates whether to copy the namespace, *qname* defines the type of node, and the validation attribute specifies the validation to be applied to the copy	2.0

xsl:decimal-format
  [name="*qname*"]
  [zero-digit ="*char*"]
  [decimal-separator="*char*"]
  [grouping-separator="*char*"]
  [minus-sign="*char*"]
  [pattern-separator="*char*"]
  [percent="*char*"]
  [per-mille="*char*"]
  [infinity="*string*"]
  [NaN="*string*"]
	Defines the format to be used when converting numbers into text strings, where the name attribute assigns a name to the format and the remaining attributes defines characters or text strings for zero digits, decimal separators, grouping separators, minus signs, pattern separators, percent signs, per-mille signs, infinity symbols, and Not A Number symbols	1.0

Element	Description	Version

xsl:document
  [validation="strict | lax | preserve | strip"]
  [type="qname"]
	Creates a document node with the validation attribute specifying a validation to be applied to the document and the type attribute defining the document type	2.0

xsl:element
  name="qname"
  [namespace="uri"]
  [inherit-namespace="yes | no"]
  [use-attribute-sets="qnames"]
  [type="qname"]
  [validation="strict | lax | preserve | strip"]
	Creates an element node named qname; other attributes can be entered to specify the element's namespace, attribute sets, element type, and type of validation	1.0

xsl:fallback	Provides alternate code to be processed if an XSLT processor does not support an element	1.0
xsl:for-each select="expr"	Specifies a set of items to be processed, specified in expr; by default, items are sorted in document order	1.0

xsl:for-each-group
  select="expr"
  [group-by="expr"]
  [group-adjacent="expr"]
  [group-starting-with="expr"]
  [group-ending-with="expr"]
	Groups items in the sequence defined by the select attribute; the group-by attribute groups items based on the value in expr; the group-adjacent, group-starting-with, and group-ending-with attributes group items based on adjacent, starting, or ending values	2.0

xsl:function
  name="Qname"
  [as="sequence"]
  [override="yes | no"]
	Defines a function using the qualified name Qname, where the as attribute defines the sequence type and the override attribute determines whether the function should override any built-in functions with the same name	2.0

xsl:if test="Boolean"	Specifies a condition for performing an operation	1.0
xsl:import href="uri"	Imports a style sheet located at uri into the current style sheet	1.0

xsl:import-schema
  [namespace="uri"]
  [schema-location="uri"]
	Makes type definitions and element and attribute declarations available for use in the current style sheet, where the namespace attribute specifies the URI of the schema namespace and the value for schema-location is the location of the schema	2.0

xsl:include href="uri"	Includes a style sheet located at uri in the current style sheet	1.0

xsl:key
  name="qname"
  match="pattern"
  [use="expr"]
	Creates a key named qname matching the node set defined in pattern and using the values defined in expr	1.0

xsl:matching-substring	Appears within the xsl:analyze-string element to process substrings matching the regular expression defined in the regex attribute	2.0

Element	Description	Version

xsl:message
  [select="*expr*"]
  [terminate="yes | no"]
	Sends a message, *expr*, to the XSLT processor; if the terminate attribute value is yes, the transformation ends with an error message	2.0

xsl:namespace
  name="prefix"
  [select="expr"]
	Creates a namespace node for an element where *prefix* is the namespace prefix and *expr* provides the content of the namespace instruction	2.0

xsl:namespace-alias
  stylesheet-prefix="*prefix*"
  result-prefix="*prefix*"
	Tells the XSLT processor to use an alias for a namespace, where the stylesheet-prefix attribute specifies the prefix for the alias and result-prefix holds the prefix of the namespace that should be used in place of the alias	2.0

xsl:next-match	Tells the XSLT processor to process the current node using the next best matching template; the xsl:next-match element must be placed within the xsl:template element	2.0
xsl:non-matching-substring	Appears within an xsl:analyze-string element to process substrings that do not match the regular expression defined in the regx attribute	2.0

xsl:number
  [select="*expr*"]
  [level="single | multiple | any"]
  [count="*pattern*"]
  [from="*pattern*"]
  [value="*numeric-expr*"]
  [format="*format-pattern*"]
  [ordinal="*string*"]
  [lang="*lang-code*"]
  [letter-value="alphabetic | traditional"]
  [grouping-separator="*char*"]
  [grouping-size="*int*"]
	Inserts a number from the select attribute into the result document or creates a numbered list using the level, count, and from attributes, or formats a numeric value using the value, format, ordinal, lang, letter-value, grouping-separator, and grouping-size attributes	1.0

xsl:otherwise	Appears within the xsl:choose element to specify instructions to be run if none of the expressions held in test attributes is evaluated as true	1.0

xsl:output
  [name="*qname*"]
  [method=xml | text | html | xhtml"]
  [media-type="*media*"]
  [version="*number*"]
  [encoding="*encoding*"]
  [byte-order-mark="yes | no"]
  [normalize-form="NFC | NFD | NKFD |
    fully-normalized | none"]
  [use-character-maps="*qnames*"]
  [indent="yes | no"]
  [doctype-public="*string*"]
  [doctype-system="*uri*"]
  [omit-xml-declaration="yes | no"]
  [standalone="yes | no"]
  [undeclared-prefixes="yes | no"]
  [escape-uri-attributes="yes | no"]
  [include-content-type="yes | no"]
  [cdata-section-elements="*qnames*]
	Used to define the format of the result document; the name attribute provides the name for the output definition, and the remaining attributes control how the format is applied	1.0

Element	Description	Version

xsl:output-character
  character="*char*"
  string="*string*"
	Used within the xsl:character-map element to define a mapping between a character, *char*, and a text string, *string*	2.0

xsl:param
  name="*qname*"
  [select="*expr*"]
  [as="*sequence*"]
  [required = "yes | no"]
  [tunnel="yes | no"]
	Declares a parameter named *qname* for a style sheet, template, or the xsl:function element; the default value of the parameter is *expr*; the tunnel attribute indicates whether the parameter is a tunnel parameter and thus automatically passed on by the called template to any further templates that it calls	1.0

xsl:perform-sort [select="expr"]	Sorts a sequence identified by *expr* or by xsl:sort elements placed within the xsl:perform-sort element	2.0
xsl:preserve-space elements="elements"	Specifies the elements whose white space nodes should be preserved within the source document	1.0

xsl:processing-instruction
  name="name"
  [select="expr"]
	Creates a processing instruction node with the target equal to the value of the name attribute, or by evaluating the values contained in the select attribute	1.0

xsl:result-document
  [href="*uri*"]
  [format="*qname*"]
  [type="*qname*"]
  [validation="strict | lax | preserve | strip"]
  [method="xml | text | html | xhtml"]
  [media-type="*media*"]
  [output-version="*number*"]
  [encoding="*encoding*"]
  [byte-order-mark="yes | no"]
  [normalize-form="NFC | NFD | NKFC | NKFD |
    fully-normalized | none"]
  [use-character-maps="*qnames*"]
  [indent="yes | no"]
  [doctype-public="*string*"]
  [doctype-system="*uri*"]
  [omit-xml-declaration="yes | no"]
  [standalone="yes | no"]
  [undeclare-prefixes="yes | no"]
  [escape-uri-attributes="yes | no"]
  [include-content-type="yes | no"]
  [cdata-section-elements="*qnames*"]
	Creates a result document node associated with the *uri* specified in the href attribute; the format of the result document is determined in the remaining attributes as well as any validation applied to the result document	2.0

xsl:sequence select="*expr*"	Adds the sequence defined by expr to the sequence nodes to such sequences	2.0

Element	Description	Version

xsl:sort
  [select="*expr*"]
  [data-type="text | number"]
  [order="ascending | descending"]
  [stable="yes | no"]
  [lang="*lang*"]
  [case-order="upper-first | lower-first"]
	Sorts a sequence of items by evaluating the values in *expr*; the remaining attributes define the rules for the sort order	1.0

xsl:strip-space elements="*elements*"	Specifies the elements whose white space nodes should be removed within the source document	1.0

xsl:stylesheet
  version="*number*"
  [id="*id*"]
  [xpath-default-namespace="*uri*"]
  [input-type-annotations="preserve | strip |
    unspecified"]
  [default-validation="preserve | strip"]
  [extension-element-prefixes="*prefixes*"]
  [exclude-result-prefixes="*prefixes*"]
	Creates the root element of an XSLT style sheet, holding all global parameters and template elements	1.0

xsl:template
  match="*pattern*"
  [mode="*qname*"]
  [priority="*number*"]
  [name="*qname*]
  [as="*sequence*]
	Declares a template for elements matching *pattern*; the mode and name attributes define a mode and name for the template, respectively; the priority attribute defines the priority of the template when more than one template matches *pattern*; the as attribute defines the template's sequence	1.0

xsl:text [disable-output-escaping="yes | no"]	Creates a text node; if the disable-output-escaping attribute equals yes, the text is output without escaping special characters such as "<"	1.0

xsl:transform
  version="*number*"
  [id="*id*"]
  [xpath-default-namespace="*uri*"]
  [input-type-annotations="preserve | strip |
    unspecified"]
  [default-validation="preserve | strip"]
  [extension-element-prefixes="*prefixes*"]
  [exclude-result-prefixes="*prefixes*"]
	Acts as an alias for the xsl:stylesheet element, creating the root element of an XSLT style sheet, holding all global parameters and template elements	1.0

xsl:value-of
  [select="*expr*"]
  [separator="*string*"]
  [disable-output-escaping="yes | no"]
	Creates a text node containing the value defined by *expr* or the value contained within the xsl:value-of element; if a sequence of values is generated, the separator between those values is defined by *string*	1.0

xsl:variable
  name="*qname*"
  [select="*expr*"]
  [as="*sequence*"]
	Declares an XSLT variable named *qname*; the value of the variable is defined either by *expr* or by the content contained within the xsl:variable element	1.0

Element	Description	Version
xsl:when test="*Boolean*"	Appears within the xsl:choose element to specify what processes should be run when the test attribute returns the value true	1.0

xsl:with-param
  name="*qname*"
  [select="*expr*"]
  [as="*sequence*"]
  [tunnel="yes | no"]
	Specifies the value to be passed to a template parameter, *qname*, using the xsl:call-template element; the value of the parameter is defined by either the select attribute or the content of the xsl:param element	1.0

XPath Reference

This appendix summarizes the main features of XPath 1.0 and 2.0, discussing location paths, operators, special characters, and XPath functions. Currently, XPath 2.0 is a W3C Candidate Recommendation and may change before final release.

Location Paths

A location path is an expression that selects a node set from an XML document. Location paths are expressed as step patterns using the syntax

axis:*node-test*[*predicate*]

where *axis* defines how the processor should move through the document node tree, *node-test* matches different kinds of nodes, and *predicate* tests the matched node for particular values or content. Only *node-test* is required. If no *axis* is specified, the XSLT processor uses the child axis.

The following axis values are supported by XPath 1.0 and 2.0.

Axis	Selects	Version
ancestor	The ancestors of the context node	1.0
ancestor-or-self	The context node and the ancestors of the context node	1.0
attribute	The attributes of the context node	1.0
child	The children of the context node	1.0
descendant	The descendants of the context node	1.0
descendant-or-select	The context node and the descendants of the context node	1.0
following	The nodes (aside from attribute and namespace nodes) that follow the context node in document order and that are not descendants of the context node	1.0
following-sibling	The siblings of the context node that follow the context node in document order	1.0
namespace	The namespace nodes on the context node	1.0
parent	The parent of the context node	1.0
preceding	The siblings of the context node (aside from attribute and namespace nodes) that precede the context node in document order and that are not ancestors of the context node	1.0
preceding-sibling	The siblings of the context node that precede the context node in document order	1.0
self	The context node	1.0

The following node-test values are supported by XPath 1.0 and 2.0.

Node-Test	Matches	Version
*	Any element or attribute nodes	1.0
attribute("*name*")	All *name* attribute nodes	2.0
attribute("*name*", "*type*")	All *name* attribute nodes of type *type*	2.0
attribute()	All attribute nodes	2.0
attribute(*, "*type*")	All attribute nodes of type *type*	2.0
comment()	All comment nodes	1.0
document-node()	All document nodes	2.0
document-node(element("*name*"))	All document nodes containing a *name* element	2.0
document-node(element("*name*", "*type*"))	All document nodes containing a *name* element of type *type*	2.0
document-node(element(*, "*type*"))	All document nodes containing an element of type *type*	2.0
document-node(schema-element("*name*"))	All document nodes containing an element declaration within the schema *name*	2.0
element("*name*")	All *name* element nodes	2.0
element("*name*", "*type*")	All *name* element nodes of type *type*	2.0
element()	All element nodes	2.0
element(*, "*type*")	All element nodes of type *type*	2.0
name	Elements or attributes named *name*	1.0
node()	Nodes of all types	1.0
processing-instruction("*target*")	Processing instruction nodes with target *target*	1.0
processing-instruction()	All processing instruction nodes	1.0
schema-attribute("*name*")	All attribute nodes based on an attribute declaration within the schema *name*	2.0
schema-element("*name*")	All element nodes based on an element declaration within the schema *name*	2.0
text()	All text nodes	1.0

Location paths can also be expressed using the following abbreviations.

Abbreviation	Location Path	Selects
.	self::node()	The context node
..	parent::node()	The parent of the context node
//	/descendant-or-self::node()	The descendants of the context node
@	attribute::	An attribute of the context node

XPath Operators

Each XPath expression includes operators organized into the following categories:

- Comparison operators for comparing values and expressions
- Logical operators for returning Boolean values
- Node set operators for manipulating node sets
- Numerical operators for returning numeric values

Type	Operator	Example	Description
Comparison	=	exp1 = exp2	Returns true if exp1 is equal to exp2
	!=	exp1 != exp2	Returns true if exp1 is not equal to exp2
	<	< exp1 exp2	Returns true if exp1 is less than exp2
	<=	exp1 <= exp2	Returns true if exp1 is less than or equal to exp2
	>	exp1 > exp2	Returns true if exp1 is greater than exp2
	>=	exp1 >= exp2	Returns true if exp1 is greater than or equal to exp2
Logical	or	exp1 or exp2	Returns true if either exp1 or exp2 is true
	and	exp1 and exp2	Returns true only if both exp1 and exp2 are true
Node Set	|	node1 | node2	Creates a union of node1 and node2
	/	node1/node2	Selects the immediate children of node1 named node2
	//	node1//node2	Selects the descendants of node1 named node2
	.	.	Returns the current context node
	*	node1/*	Selects all children of node1 regardless of name or type
	@	node1/@att	Returns the attribute att from node1
Numerical	+	exp1 + exp2	Adds the value of exp1 to exp2
	-	exp1 - exp2	Subtracts exp2 from exp1
	*	exp1 * exp2	Multiplies exp1 by exp2
	div	exp1 div exp2	Divides exp1 by exp2
	mod	exp1 mod exp2	Returns the remainder after dividing exp1 by exp2
	-	-exp1	Negates the value of exp1

XPath Functions

The following table lists the functions supported by XPath 1.0 and 2.0. Parameters of these functions can take the following data types:

Boolean	A Boolean expression returning the value true or false
char	A single character
date	A date value
dateTime	A date and time value
day	A day value
dayTimeDuration	A duration over a day and time
element	An element node
elements	A white space separated list of elements
encoding	A character encoding type
expr	An XPath expression
format-pattern	A format pattern
id	An identifier
int	An integer value
ints	A string of integer values
item	A general data type
items	A collection of *item* data types
lang-code	A language code text string
media	A media type such as text, video, screen, etc.
name	An unqualified name
node	A node reference
node-set	A node set reference
numeric-expr	A numeric expression
number	A numeric value
Qname	A qualified XML name with a required namespace prefix
qname	An XML name with an optional namespace prefix
qnames	A white space delimited list of qualified names
pattern	A string expression pattern
prefix	A namespace prefix
prefixes	A white space separated list of namespace prefixes
regex	A regular expression
regexFlag	A regular expression flag
regexFlags	A white space separated list of regular expression flags
sequence	A sequence type
string	A text string
time	A time value
uri	A namespace URI
url	A location URL
yearMonthDuration	A duration over a month and year

Note that not all XPath functions and parameters are supported by all browsers and XSLT processors. Check with your browser and XSLT processor documentation to determine levels of support. Optional parameter values are placed within square brackets [ ].

Function	Description	Version
abs(*number*)	Returns the absolute value of *number*	2.0
adjust-date-to-timezone(*date*, [*dayTimeDuration*])	Adjusts the *date* value to the time zone specified by *dayTimeDuration*; if no *dayTimeDuration* value is specified, adjusts *date* to the default time zone	2.0
adjust-dateTime-to-timezone(*dateTime*, [*dayTimeDuration*])	Adjusts the *dateTime* value to the time zone specified by *dayTimeDuration*; if no *dayTimeDuration* value is specified, adjusts *dateTime* to the default time zone	2.0
adjust-time-to-timezone(*time*, [*dayTimeDuration*])	Adjusts the *time* value to the time zone specified by *dayTimeDuration*; if no *dayTimeDuration* value is specified, adjusts *time* to the default time zone	2.0
avg(*items*)	Returns the average value of the items in *items*	2.0
base-uri(*node set*)	Returns the base URI of *node set*	2.0
boolean(*expr*)	Returns the Boolean value of *expr*	1.0
ceiling(*number*)	Rounds *number* up to the nearest integer	1.0
codepoint-equal(*string1*, *string2*)	Returns true if *string1* is equal to *string2* according to Unicode codepoint collation	2.0
codepoints-to-string(*ints*)	Returns the result of converting a sequence of integers, *ints*, into the corresponding Unicode characters and concatenating the results into a text string	2.0
collection(*string*)	Returns a sequence of nodes indicated by *string*	2.0
compare(*string1*, *string2*, [*string3*])	Compares *string1* and *string2* using the collation specified in *string3*, returning 0 if they are equal, 1 if *string1* is greater than *string2*, and -1 if *string1* is less than *string2*; if no *string3* is specified, the default collation is used	2.0
concat(*string1*, *string2*, ...)	Concatenates *string1*, *string2*, etc. returning a single text string	1.0
contains(*string1*, *string2*)	Returns true if *string2* is contained within *string1*	1.0
count(*items*)	Counts the number of items in *items*	1.0
current()	Returns the current item being processed within an xsl:for-each or xsl:template element	1.0
current-date()	Returns the current date for the transformation	2.0
current-dateTime()	Returns the current date and time for the transformation	2.0
current-group()	Returns the items in the current group, when grouping within an xsl:for-each-group element	2.0
current-grouping-key()	Returns the value used to group items within an xsl:for-each-group element using the group-by or group-adjacent attribute values	2.0
current-time()	Returns the current time for the transformation	2.0
data()	Returns a sequence of values from an item sequence	2.0
dateTime(*date*, *time*)	Returns a *dateTime* value for a specified *date* and *time*	2.0
day-from-date(*date*)	Returns a *day* value for a specified *date*	2.0
day-from-dateTime(*dateTime*)	Returns a *day* value for a specified *date* and *time*	2.0
day-from-duration(*dayTimeDuration*)	Returns a *day* value using a specified *dayTimeDuration*	2.0
deep-equal(*item1*, *item2*, [*string*])	Compares *item1* to *item2*, returning true if the expressions are equal; if *item1* and *item2* represent node sets, they are compared based on their name and content; a default collation is used unless a different collation is specified by *string*	2.0
default-collation()	Returns the URI of the default collation	2.0
distinct-values(*item*, [*string*])	Removes duplicates from *item* using the default collation unless a different collation is specified by *string*	2.0
doc(*uri*)	Returns a document node from *uri*	2.0

Function	Description	Version
doc-available(*uri*)	Returns true if the document node from *uri* is available	2.0
document(*uri1*, [*uri2*])	Returns a document node for the document at *uri1* relative to the base URI, *uri2*; if no *uri2* value is specified, the document node is returned relative to the base URI for the style sheet	1.0
element-available(*string*)	Returns true if the *string* element is available to the XSLT processor	1.0
empty(*item*)	Returns true if *item* represents an empty sequence	2.0
ends-with(*string1*, *string2*)	Returns true if *string1* ends with *string2*	2.0
error()	Halts the transformation, raising an error	2.0
exactly-one(*items*)	Returns *items* if it contains exactly one item	2.0
exists(*item*)	Returns true if *item* is not an empty sequence	2.0
false()	Returns the Boolean value false	1.0
floor(*number*)	Rounds *number* down to the nearest integer value	1.0
format-date(*date*, *string*)	Formats the *date* value based on the formatting code in *string*	2.0
format-dateTime(*dateTime*, *string*)	Formats the *dateTime* value based on the formatting code in *string*	2.0
format-number(*number*, *string*)	Formats the *number* value based on the formatting code in *string*	1.0
format-time(*time*, *string*)	Formats the *time* value based on the formatting code in *string*	2.0
function-available(*string*)	Returns true if the *string* function is available to the XSLT processor	1.0
generate-id([*node-set*])	Generates an ID value for the specified *node-set*; if no *node-set* value is specified, generates an ID for the context node	1.0
hours-from-dateTime(*dateTime*)	Calculates the hours component from the *dateTime* value	2.0
hours-from-duration(*dayTimeDuration*)	Calculates the hours component from the *dayTimeDuration* value	2.0
hours-from-time(*time*)	Calculates the hours component from the *time* value	2.0
id(*item*)	Returns the node set of elements containing the id values specified in *item*; if *item* is a text string, the id values are treated as a white space separated list; if *item* is a node set, then each node is treated as containing a separate id value	1.0
idref(*item*)	Returns the node set of elements containing the idref values specified in *item*; if *item* is a text string, the idref values are treated as a white space separated list; if *item* is a node set, then each node is treated as containing a separate idref value	2.0
implicit-timezone()	Returns the current timezone used by the processor	2.0
in-scope-prefixes(*element*)	Returns the prefixes of the in-scope namespace for *element*	2.0
index-of(*item1*, *item2*)	Returns a sequence of positive integers from *item1* given the positions within the sequence *item2*	2.0
insert-before(*item1*, *int*, *item2*)	Inserts *item2* into the *item1* sequence before the *int* position	2.0
key(*string*, *item*)	Returns the node set using the *string* key based on the values of *item*	1.0
lang(*string*)	Returns true if the language of the context node matches the *string* language	1.0
last()	Returns the index of the last item in the sequence or node set currently being processed	1.0
local-name([*node-set*])	Returns the local name of *node-set*; if *node-set* is not specified, returns the local name of the context node	1.0
local-name-from-QName(*Qname*)	Returns the local part of the qualified name *Qname*	2.0
lowercase(*string*)	Converts *string* to lowercase characters	2.0
matches(*string*, *regex*, *regexFlag*)	Returns true if *string* matches the regular expression *regex* based on the flags in *regexFlag*	2.0
max(*item*)	Returns the maximum value from the *item* sequence or node set	2.0

Function	Description	Version
min(*item*)	Returns the minimum value from the *item* sequence or node set	2.0
minutes-from-dateTime(*dateTime*)	Calculates the minutes component from the *dateTime* value	2.0
minutes-from-duration (*dayTimeDuration*)	Calculates the minutes component from the *dayTimeDuration* value	2.0
minutes-from-time(*time*)	Calculates the minutes component from the *time* value	2.0
month-from-date(*date*)	Calculates the month component from the *date* value	2.0
month-from-dateTime(*dateTime*)	Calculates the month component from the *dateTime* value	2.0
month-from-duration(*dayTimeDuration*)	Calculates the month component from the *dayTimeDuration* value	2.0
name([*node-set*])	Returns the full name of *node-set*; if no node-set is specified, returns the full name of the context node	1.0
namespace-uri([*node*])	Returns the URI of *node*; if no node is specified, returns the URI of the context node	1.0
namespace-uri-for-prefix (*string*, *element*)	Returns the namespace URI for the prefix *string* in the element *element*	2.0
namespace-uri-from-QName(*QName*)	Returns the namespace URI from the qualified name *QName*	2.0
nilled(*node*)	Returns true if *node* is an element node that is nilled	2.0
node-name(*node*)	Returns the name of *node* as a qualified name	2.0
normalize-space([*string*])	Normalizes *string* by removing leading and trailing white space; if no *string* is specified, normalizes the content of the context node	1.0
normalize-unicode([*string*])	Normalizes *string* using Unicode normalization; if no *string* is specified, normalizes the content of the context node	2.0
not([*Boolean*])	Changes the logical value of *Boolean* from false to true or true to false; if no *Boolean* value is specified, returns the value false	1.0
number([*item*])	Converts *item* to a number where *item* is a text string or a nodeset; if no *item* value is specified, converts the value of the context node	1.0
one-or-more(*items*)	Returns *items* only if it contains one or more items	2.0
position()	Returns the position of the context node within the node set being processed	1.0
prefix-fromQName(*QName*)	Returns the namespace prefix from the qualified name *QNam*	2.0
QName(*uri*, *string*)	Returns a qualified name with the namespace URI *uri* and the local name *string*	2.0
remove(*item*, *int*)	Returns the sequence from *item* after removing the object at the *int* position	2.0
replace(*string1*, *string2*, *string3*)	Replaces in *string1* each occurrence of characters that match *string2* with *string3*	2.0
resolve-QName(*string*, *element*)	Returns a qualified name from a text string *string* using the in-scope namespace for *element*	2.0
resolve-uri(*uri1*, *uri2*)	Resolves *uri1* based on the base URI specified in *uri2*	2.0
reverse(*items*)	Reverses the sequence of items in *items*	2.0
root([*node*])	Returns the root node of *node*; if no *node* is specified, returns the root of the context node	2.0
round(*number*)	Rounds *number* to the nearest integer	1.0
round-half-to-even(*number*, *int*)	Rounds *number* to *int* decimal places	2.0
seconds-from-dateTime(*dateTime*)	Calculates the seconds component from the *dateTime* value	2.0
seconds-from-duration (*dayTimeDuration*)	Calculates the seconds component from the *dayTimeDuration* value	2.0
seconds-from-time(*time*)	Calculates the seconds component from the *time* value	2.0
starts-with(*string1*, *string2*)	Returns true if *string1* starts with *string2*	1.0

Function	Description	Version
static-base-uri()	Returns the base URI of the element in which the function is called	2.0
string([*item*])	Converts *item* to a text string; if no *item* is specified, converts the value of the context node	1.0
string-join(*string1, string2, ..., string*)	Concatenates *string1, string2*, etc. into a single text string using *string* as the separator	2.0
string-length(*string*)	Returns the number of characters in *string*	1.0
string-to-codepoints(*string*)	Returns a sequence of Unicode code points based on the content of *string*	2.0
subsequence(*item, int1,* [*int2*])	Returns a subsequence from *item* where *int1* is the position of the first object to be returned and *int2* indicates the number of objects; if no *int2* value is specified, returns all items from *int1* to the end of the sequence	2.0
substring(*string, int1,* [*int2*])	Returns a substring from *string* where *int1* is the position of the first character to be returned and *int2* indicates the number of remaining characters; if no *int2* value is specified, returns all characters from *int1* to the end of the string	1.0
substring-after(*string1, string2*)	Returns a substring from *string1* that occurs after the first occurrence of *string2*	1.0
substring-before(*string1, string2*)	Returns a substring from *string1* that occurs before the first occurrence of *string2*	1.0
sum(*items*)	Calculate the sum of the numeric values in *items*	1.0
system-property(*string*)	Returns information about the system property *string*	1.0
timezone-from-date(*date*)	Calculates the time zone component from the *date* value	2.0
timezone-from-dateTime(*dateTime*)	Calculates the time zone component from the *dateTime* value	2.0
timezone-from-time(*time*)	Calculates the time zone component from the *time* value	2.0
tokenize(*string, regex*)	Splits *string* into a collection of substrings at each location in *string* that matches the regular expression *regex*	2.0
trace(*item, string*)	Debugs the processing of *item*, returning the error message *string* if an error is discovered	2.0
translate(*string1, string2, string3*)	Substitutes *string3* characters into *string1* at every occurrence of *string2*	1.0
true()	Returns the Boolean value true	1.0
unordered(*items*)	Returns the items in *items* in implementation-dependent order	2.0
unparsed-entity-public-id(*string*)	Returns the public ID of the unparsed entity *string*	2.0
unparsed-entity-uri(*string*)	Returns the URI of the unparsed entity *string*	1.0
unparsed-text(*uri,* [*encoding*])	Returns the content of the text file held at *uri*, using the encoding *encoding*	2.0
unparsed-text-available(*uri,* [*encoding*])	Returns true if there exists text content at *uri*, using the encoding *encoding*	2.0
uppercase(*string*)	Converts *string* to uppercase characters	2.0
year-from-date(*date*)	Calculates the year component from the *date* value	2.0
year-from-dateTime(*dateTime*)	Calculates the year component from the *dateTime* value	2.0
year-from-duration(*yearMonthDuration*)	Calculates the year component from the *yearMonthDuration* value	2.0
zero-or-one(*items*)	Returns *items* only if it contains zero or one item	2.0

DTD Reference

This appendix summarizes the syntax rules for document type definitions (DTDs). The rules are divided into the following categories:

- elements
- attributes
- notations
- parameter entities
- general entities

Declarations can be placed either in external files or as internal subsets of the source document. Note that at the time of this writing, some browsers do not support entities placed in external files.

Element Declarations

Element declarations provide the rules for the element instances found in the source document. Element declarations determine what kind of content can be stored within an element and provide information on the general structure of the element. Since DTDs do not support namespaces, any namespace prefixes must be included in the element name just as they appear within the source document.

Declaration	Declares
<!ELEMENT *element* EMPTY>	element containing no content
<!ELEMENT *element* ANY>	element containing any content
<!ELEMENT *element* (#PCDATA)>	element containing parsed character data
<!ELEMENT *element* (*child1*, *child2*, ...)>	element containing child elements child1, child2, ... etc. in the specified order
<!ELEMENT *element* (*child1* | *child2* | ...)>	element containing a choice of child elements: *child1* or *child2* and so forth
<!ELEMENT *element* (#PCDATA | *child1* | *child2* | ...)*>	element contains parsed character data and/or a collection of child elements

DTDs support the following symbols to indicate the occurrences of child elements within an element node:

Symbol	Description
child?	child occurs zero or one time
*child**	child occurs zero or more times
child+	child occurs one or more times

Attribute Declarations

Attribute declarations define the attributes associated with elements in the source document. The general form of an attribute declaration is

```
<!ATTLIST element att type default>
```

where `element` is the name of the element containing the attribute, `att` is the name of the attribute, `type` is the attribute's data type, and `default` indicates whether the attribute is required and whether it has a default value. Several attribute declarations can be combined into a single statement using the syntax

```
<!ATTLIST element att1 type1 default1
                  att2 type2 default2
                  att3 type3 default3>
```

where `att1`, `type1`, and `default1` are the rules associated with the first attribute, `att2`, `type2`, and `default2` are the rules associated with the second attribute, and so forth.

The following table lists the different data types supported by DTDs:

Data Type	Description
(*value1* | *value2* | ...)	Attribute value must equal *value1* or *value2* and so forth
CDATA	Simple character data
ID	A unique ID value within the source document
IDREF	A reference to a unique ID value
IDREFS	A white space separated list of references to unique ID values
ENTITY	A reference to a declared unparsed external entity
ENTITIES	A white space separated list of references to declared unparsed external entities
NMTOKEN	A name token value
NMTOKENS	A white space separated list of name token values
NOTATION (*notation1* | *notation2* | ...)	Attribute data type must be a notation from the list notation1, notation2, and so forth

The following table lists the default values supported by DTDs:

Default Value	Description
#REQUIRED	A value must be supplied for the attribute
#IMPLIED	A value for the attribute is optional
"default"	A value for the attribute is optional; if no value is provided, the attribute's value is assumed to be default
#FIXED "*default*"	The attribute's value is fixed to default

Notation Declarations

Notation declarations are used to provide information to an XML application about the format of unparsed document content. The notation declaration provides instructions to processors about how the unparsed content should be interpreted. The following table lists the notations supported by DTDs:

Declaration	Declares
<!NOTATION *notation* SYSTEM "*uri*">	A system location for the notation where *notation* is the name assigned to the notation and *uri* is the URI of the system location
<!NOTATION *notation* PUBLIC "*id*" "*uri*">	A public location for the notation where *id* is the public location; if the processor does not recognize the public ID, the URI of the system location is provided

Parameter Entity Declarations

Parameter entities are entities used to store DTD code that can then be inserted into other declarations in the DTD. When the DTD is parsed, the code stored in the parameter entity is placed into the DTD. The source of the parameter entity value can be either a text string or a reference to an external file. Parameter entities allow programmers to simplify large

DTDs by reusing common pieces of code. The following table describes parameter entity declarations:

Declaration	Declares
<!ENTITY % *entity* "*value*">	A parameter entity named entity containing the DTD code value
<!ENTITY % *entity* SYSTEM "*uri*">	A system location at the URI uri for the parameter entity
<!ENTITY % *entity* PUBLIC "*id*" "*uri*">	A public location for the entity with the public ID value id; if the processor does not recognize the public ID, a system URI is provided

To reference a parameter entity, use the following expression in the DTD:

`%entity;`

where `entity` is the name assigned to the parameter entity.

General Entity Declarations

Parameter entities are entities used to store text for element content and attribute values. When the source document is parsed, the value of the general entity is placed into the source document. Entity values can be specified either as text strings or as references to external files.

Declaration	Declares
<!ENTITY *entity* "*value*">	A general entity named entity containing the literal text value
<!ENTITY *entity* SYSTEM "*uri*">	A system location at the URI uri for the general entity
<!ENTITY *entity* PUBLIC "*id*" "*uri*">	A public location for the entity with the public ID value id; if the processor does not recognize the public ID, a system URI is provided
<!ENTITY *entity* SYSTEM "*uri*" NDATA *notation*>	A general entity for unparsed data placed at the system location uri using the notation notation
<!ENTITY *entity* PUBLIC "*id*" "*uri*" NDATA *notation*>	A general entity for unparsed data placed at the public location with the public ID id, the system location uri, and using the notation notation

To reference a general entity, use the following expression in the source document:

`&entity;`

where `entity` is the name assigned to the general entity.

XML Schema Reference

This appendix summarizes the built-in data types, elements, and facets used in the W3C XML Schema language.

XML Schema Built-In Data Types

The following table describes the built-in data types supported by XML Schema. The facets column indicates the facets that can be applied to each data type to create a custom data type. To learn more about facets, see the XML Facets table at the end of the appendix.

Datatype	Contains	Supported Facets
xs:anyURI	A standard URI or URL	xs:enumeration, xs:length, xs:maxLength, xs:minLength, xs:pattern, xs:whitespace
xs:base64Binary	Base64-encoded binary data	xs:enumeration, xs:length, xs:maxLength, xs:minLength, xs:pattern, xs:whitespace
xs:boolean	A Boolean value (true, false, 1, or 0)	xs:pattern, xs:whitespace
xs:byte	A signed 8-bit value between -128 and 127	xs:enumeration, xs:fractionDigits, xs:maxExclusive, xs:maxInclusive, xs:minExclusive, xs:minInclusive, xs:pattern, xs:totalDigits, xs:whitespace
xs:date	A Gregorian calendar date in the format *yyyy-mm-dd* where *yyyy* is the 4-digit year, *mm* is the 2-digit month, and *dd* is the 2-digit day of the month	xs:enumeration, xs:maxExclusive, xs:maxInclusive, xs:minExclusive, xs:minInclusive, xs:pattern, xs:whitespace
xs:dateTime	A Gregorian calendar date and 24-hour time in the format *yyyy-mm-ddThh:mm:ss* where *hh* is the 2-digit hour, *mm* is the 2-digit minute, and *ss* is the 2-digit second	xs:enumeration, xs:maxExclusive, xs:maxInclusive, xs:minExclusive, xs:minInclusive, xs:pattern, xs:whitespace
xs:decimal	Decimal numbers with arbitrary lengths; the decimal separator is always "."; there is no thousands separator	xs:enumeration, xs:fractionDigits, xs:maxExclusive, xs:maxInclusive, xs:minExclusive, xs:minInclusive, xs:pattern, xs:totalDigits, xs:whitespace
xs:double	A 64-bit floating number	xs:enumeration, xs:maxExclusive, xs:maxInclusive, xs:minExclusive, xs:minInclusive, xs:pattern, xs:whitespace
xs:duration	A time duration in the format *PyYmMdDhHmMsS* where *y, m, d, h, m,* and *s* are the duration values in years, months, days, hours, minutes, and seconds	xs:enumeration, xs:maxExclusive, xs:maxInclusive, xs:minExclusive, xs:minInclusive, xs:pattern, xs:whitespace
xs:ENTITIES	A white space separated list of unparsed entity references as defined in a DTD linked to the source document	xs:enumeration, xs:length, xs:maxLength, xs:minLength, xs:whitespace
xs:ENTITY	A reference to an unparsed entity as defined in a DTD linked to the source document	xs:enumeration, xs:length, xs:maxLength, xs:minLength, xs:pattern, xs:whitespace

Datatype	Contains	Supported Facets
xs:float	A 32-bit floating number	xs:enumeration, xs:maxExclusive, xs:maxInclusive, xs:minExclusive, xs:minInclusive, xs:pattern, xs:whitespace
xs:gDay	A recurring time in which the period (one month) and duration (one day) are fixed	xs:enumeration, xs:maxExclusive, xs:maxInclusive, xs:minExclusive, xs:minInclusive, xs:pattern, xs:whitespace
xs:gMonth	A recurring time in which the period (one year) and duration (one month) are fixed	xs:enumeration, xs:maxExclusive, xs:maxInclusive, xs:minExclusive, xs:minInclusive, xs:pattern, xs:whitespace
xs:gMonthDay	A recurring time in which the period (one year) and the duration (one day) are fixed	xs:enumeration, xs:maxExclusive, xs:maxInclusive, xs:minExclusive, xs:minInclusive, xs:pattern, xs:whitespace
xs:gYearMonth	A recurring time in which the period (one month) is fixed	xs:enumeration, xs:maxExclusive, xs:maxInclusive, xs:minExclusive, xs:minInclusive, xs:pattern, xs:whitespace
xs:hexBinary	Binary content coded in hexadecimals	xs:enumeration, xs:length, xs:maxLength, xs:minLength, xs:pattern, xs:whitespace
xs:ID	An ID value as defined in a DTD linked to the source document	xs:enumeration, xs:length, xs:maxLength, xs:minLength, xs:pattern, xs:whitespace
xs:IDREF	A reference to ID values as defined in a DTD linked to the source document	xs:enumeration, xs:length, xs:maxLength, xs:minLength, xs:pattern, xs:whitespace
xs:IDREFS	A white space separated list of IDREFs as defined in a DTD linked to the source document	xs:enumeration, xs:length, xs:maxLength, xs:minLength, xs:pattern, xs:whitespace
xs:int	A 32-bit signed integer ranging from -2147483648 to 2147483647	xs:enumeration, xs:fractionDigits, xs:maxExclusive, xs:maxInclusive, xs:minExclusive, xs:minInclusive, xs:pattern, xs:totalDigits, xs:whitespace
xs:integer	A signed integer of arbitrary length	xs:enumeration, xs:fractionDigits, xs:maxExclusive, xs:maxInclusive, xs:minExclusive, xs:minInclusive, xs:pattern, xs:totalDigits, xs:whitespace
xs:language	An RFC 1766 language code value	xs:enumeration, xs:length, xs:maxLength, xs:minLength, xs:pattern, xs:whitespace
xs:long	A 64-bit signed integer	xs:enumeration, xs:fractionDigits, xs:maxExclusive, xs:maxInclusive, xs:minExclusive, xs:minInclusive, xs:pattern, xs:totalDigits, xs:whitespace
xs:Name	Name text corresponding to the XML 1.0 names standard	xs:enumeration, xs:length, xs:maxLength, xs:minLength, xs:pattern, xs:whitespace
xs:NCName	An unqualified XML name	xs:enumeration, xs:length, xs:maxLength, xs:minLength, xs:pattern, xs:whitespace
xs:negativeInteger	A strictly negative integer of arbitrary length	xs:enumeration, xs:fractionDigits, xs:maxExclusive, xs:maxInclusive, xs:minExclusive, xs:minInclusive, xs:pattern, xs:totalDigits, xs:whitespace
xs:NMTOKEN	An XML 1.0 name token	xs:enumeration, xs:length, xs:maxLength, xs:minLength, xs:pattern, xs:whitespace
xs:NMTOKENS	A white space separated list of XML 1.0 name tokens	xs:enumeration, xs:length, xs:maxLength, xs:minLength, xs:pattern, xs:whitespace
xs:nonNegativeInteger	An integer of arbitrary length with a positive or zero value	xs:enumeration, xs:fractionDigits, xs:maxExclusive, xs:maxInclusive, xs:minExclusive, xs:minInclusive, xs:pattern, xs:totalDigits, xs:whitespace

Datatype	Contains	Supported Facets
xs:nonPositiveInteger	An integer of arbitrary length with a positive or zero value	xs:enumeration, xs:fractionDigits, xs:maxExclusive, xs:maxInclusive, xs:minExclusive, xs:minInclusive, xs:pattern, xs:totalDigits, xs:whitespace
xs:normalizedString	A normalized text string in which carriage returns, line feeds, and tabs have been removed	xs:enumeration, xs:length, xs:maxLength, xs:minLength, xs:pattern, xs:whitespace
xs:NOTATION	A notation as defined in the DTD linked to the source document	xs:enumeration, xs:length, xs:maxLength, xs:minLength, xs:pattern, xs:whitespace
xs:postiveInteger	A strictly positive integer of arbitrary length	xs:enumeration, xs:fractionDigits, xs:maxExclusive, xs:maxInclusive, xs:minExclusive, xs:minInclusive, xs:pattern, xs:totalDigits, xs:whitespace
xs:QName	An XML qualified name	xs:enumeration, xs:length, xs:maxLength, xs:minLength, xs:pattern, xs:whitespace
xs:short	A 32-bit signed integer ranging from -32768 and 32767	xs:enumeration, xs:fractionDigits, xs:maxExclusive, xs:maxInclusive, xs:minExclusive, xs:minInclusive, xs:pattern, xs:totalDigits, xs:whitespace
xs:string	Any text string	xs:enumeration, xs:length, xs:maxLength, xs:minLength, xs:pattern, xs:whitespace
xs:time	A time value in the format *hh:mm:ss* where *hh* is the 2-digit hour, *mm* is the 2-digit minute, and *ss* is the 2-digit second	xs:enumeration, xs:length, xs:maxLength, xs:minLength, xs:pattern, xs:whitespace
xs:token	A tokenized text string that does not contain carriage returns, line feeds, tabs, or leading or trailing blanks	xs:enumeration, xs:length, xs:maxLength, xs:minLength, xs:pattern, xs:whitespace
xs:unsignedByte	An 8-bit unsigned value ranging from 0 to 255	xs:enumeration, xs:fractionDigits, xs:maxExclusive, xs:maxInclusive, xs:minExclusive, xs:minInclusive, xs:pattern, xs:totalDigits, xs:whitespace
xs:unsignedInt	A 32-bit unsigned integer value ranging from 0 to 4294967295	xs:enumeration, xs:fractionDigits, xs:maxExclusive, xs:maxInclusive, xs:minExclusive, xs:minInclusive, xs:pattern, xs:totalDigits, xs:whitespace
xs:unsignedLong	A 64-bit unsigned integer value	xs:enumeration, xs:fractionDigits, xs:maxExclusive, xs:maxInclusive, xs:minExclusive, xs:minInclusive, xs:pattern, xs:totalDigits, xs:whitespace
xs:unsignedShort	A 16-bit unsigned integer value ranging from 0 to 65535	xs:enumeration, xs:fractionDigits, xs:maxExclusive, xs:maxInclusive, xs:minExclusive, xs:minInclusive, xs:pattern, xs:totalDigits, xs:whitespace

XML Schema Elements

The following table lists the elements supported in XML Schema, their attributes, and their content. Note that the syntax of an XML Schema element may differ depending on the context in which it is used in the schema; thus, multiple entries may appear in the table for the same element.

The data type for each attribute value is indicated in quotes following the attribute name. Attributes limited to a built-in data type are entered using the expression

```
att = xs:type
```

where `att` is the name of the attribute and `type` is the name of the built-in data type. Thus, the expression

```
id = "xs:ID"
```

indicates that values of the id attribute must be entered following the syntax rules of the xs:ID data type. Some attribute values are confined to specified values or to a list of possible data types. Enumerated values are placed within the choice expression

```
att=("value1" | "value2" | "value3")
```

where *value1*, *value2*, *value3*, etc. are the possible values or built-in data types that can be associated with the attribute's value. For example, the expression

```
minOccurs = ("0" | "1")
```

limits the values of the minOccurs attribute to either "0" or "1". Some attributes have default values, indicated using the expression

```
att="type" : "default"
```

where *type* is a data type or value and *default* is the default value assigned to the attribute. For example, the following expression sets the data type of the fixed attribute to xs:boolean with a default value of "false":

```
fixed="xs:boolean" : "false"
```

Note that XML Schema elements can also contain any attribute associated with a non-schema namespace. This allows compound documents to contain XML Schema and non-XML Schema attributes and elements.

The Content column indicates the type of content that can be placed within each element. The number of times each element can be contained is specified using the symbols ? (for zero or one), * (for zero or more), and + (for one or more). For example, the expression

```
xs:annotation?
```

indicates that the element can contain zero or one xs:annotation element. Lists of elements are placed within parentheses and separated by commas as follows:

```
(xs:annotation?, xs:element*)
```

In the above expression, the element may contain zero or one occurrence of an xs:annotation element along with zero or more occurrences of an xs:element element. Multiple occurrences of elements are indicated using the expression

```
(elem1 | elem2 | elem3)*
```

where *elem1*, *elem2*, *elem3*, etc. are the elements that can occur multiple times in any order within the schema element. Thus, the expression

```
(xs:appinfo | xs:documentation)*
```

indicates that the element can contain multiple occurrences of the xs:appinfo and xs:documentation elements in any order. Finally, the expression

```
({any})*
```

indicates that any element from another namespace can be used as content.

Element	Description	Content

xs:all
  id = xs:ID
  maxOccurs = "1":"1"
  minOccurs = ("0"|"1"):"1"
	Compositor placed outside of a group, describing an unordered group of elements	(xs:annotation?,
		xs:element*)

xs:all id = xs:ID	Compositor placed within a group, describing an unordered group of elements	(xs:annotation?, xs:element*)
xs:annotation id = xs:ID	Descriptive information about the schema for electronic or human agents	(xs:appinfo | xs:documentation)*

xs:any
  id = xs:ID
  maxOccurs = xs:nonNegativeInteger |
           ("unbounded") : "1"
  minOccurs = xs:nonNegativeInteger: "1"
  namespace = (("##any" | "##other") |
          list of (xs:anyURI |
          ("##targetNamespace" |
          "##local"))) : "##any"
  processContents = ("skip" | "lax" |
          "strict") : "strict"
	Wildcard that allows the insertion of any element belonging to a list of namespaces (if specified)	(xs:annotation?)

xs:anyAttribute
  id = xs:ID
  namespace = (("##any" | "##other") |
        list of (xs:anyURI |
        ("##targetNamespace" |
        "##local"))) : "##any"
  processContents = ("skip" | "lax" |
        "strict") : "strict"
	Wildcard that allows the insertion of any attribute belonging to a list of namespaces (if specified)	(xs:annotation?)

xs:appinfo source = xs:anyURI	Structured information for use by the XML application	({any})*

xs:attribute
  default = xs:string
  fixed = xs:string
  id = xs:ID
  name = xs:NCName
  type = xs:QName
	Global attribute definition or a reference	(xs:annotation?,
		xs:simpleType?)

xs:attribute
  default = xs:string
  fixed = xs:string
  form = ("qualified" | "unqualified")
  id = xs:ID
  name = xs:NCName
  ref = xs:QName
  type = xs:QName
  use = ("prohibited" | "optional" |
      "required")
	Local attribute definition or a reference to an attribute definition	(xs:annotation?,
		xs:simpleType?)

xs:attributeGroup
  id = xs:ID
  name = xs:NCName
	Global attribute group definition	(xs:annotation?,
		((xs:attribute | xs:attributeGroup)*,
		xs:anyAttribute?))

xs:attributeGroup
  id = xs:ID
  ref = xs:QName
	Reference to a global attribute group	(xs:annotation?)

Element	Description	Content

xs:choice
  id = xs:ID
  maxOccurs = xs:nonNegativeInteger |
        ("unbounded") : "1"
  minOccurs = xs:nonNegativeInteger: "1"
	Compositor outside of a group, defining a group of mutually exclusive elements or compositors	(xs:annotation?, (xs:element | xs:group | xs:choice | xs:sequence | xs:any)*)

xs:choice id = xs:ID	Compositor within a group, defining a group of mutually exclusive elements or compositors	(xs:annotation?, (xs:element | xs:group | xs:choice | xs:sequence | xs:any)*)

xs:complexContent
  id = xs:ID
  mixed = xs:Boolean
	Definition of a complex content model derived from a complex type	(xs:annotation?, (xs:restriction | xs:extension))

xs:complexType
  abstract = xs:boolean : "false"
  block = ("#all" | list of ("extension" |
       "restriction"))
  final = ("#all" | list of ("extension" |
       "restriction"))
  id = xs:ID
  mixed = xs:boolean : "false"
  name = xs:NCName
	Global definition of a complex type	(xs:annotation?, (xs:simpleContent | xs:complexContent | xs:group | xs:all | xs:choice | xs:sequence)?, (xs:attribute | xs:attributeGroup)*, xs:anyAttribute?)))

xs:complexType
  id = xs:ID
  mixed = xs:boolean : "false"
	Local definition of a complex type	(xs:annotation?, (xs:simpleContent | xs:complexContent | xs:group | xs:all | xs:choice | xs:sequence)?, (xs:attribute | xs:attributeGroup)*, xs:anyAttribute?)))

xs:documentation
  source = xs:anyURI
  xml:lang = xml:lang
	Descriptive information about the schema for electronic or human agents	({*any*})*

xs:element
  abstract = xs:boolean : "false"
  block = ("#all" | list of ("extension" |
       "restriction" | "substitution"))
  default = xs:string
  final = ("#all" | list of ("extension" |
       "restriction"))
  fixed = xs:string
  id = xs:ID
  name = xs:NCName
  nillable = xs:boolean : "false"
  substitutionGroup = xs:QName
  type = xs:QName
	Global definition of an element type	(xs:annotation?, (xs:simpleType | xs:complexType)?, (xs:unique | xs:key | xs:keyref)*)

Element	Description	Content
xs:element 　block = ("#all" | list of ("extension" | 　　　　　"restriction" | "substitution")) 　default = xs:string 　fixed = xs:string 　form = ("qualified" | "unqualified") 　id = xs:ID 　maxOccurs = ("0" | "1") : "1" 　minOccurs = ("0" | "1") : "1" 　name = xs:NCName 　nillable = xs:boolean : "false" 　ref = xs:QName 　type = xs:QName	Local definition of an element or a reference to a global element definition	(xs:annotation?, (xs:simpleType xs:complexType)?, (xs:unique | xs:key | xs:keyref)*)
xs:extension 　base = xs:QName 　id = xs:ID	Extension of a simple content model	(xs:annotation?, ((xs:attribute | xs:attributeGroup)*, xs:anyAttribute?))
xs:extension 　base = xs:QName 　id = xs:ID	Extension of a complex content model	(xs:annotation?), ((xs:group | xs:all, xs:choice | xs:sequence)?, ((xs:attribute | xs:attributeGroup)*, xs:anyAttribute?)))
xs:field 　id = xs:ID 　xpath = xs:token	Definition of a field to use with a uniqueness constraint	(xs:annotation?)
xs:group 　name = xs:NCName	Global elements group declaration	(xs:annotation?, (xs:all | xs:choice | xs:sequence))
xs:group 　id = xs:ID 　maxOccurs = (xs:nonNegativeInteger | 　　　　　"unbounded") : "1" 　minOccurs = xs:nonNegativeInteger : "1" 　ref = xs:QName	Reference to a global elements group declaration	(xs:annotation?)
xs:import 　id = xs:ID 　namespace = xs:anyURI 　schemaLocation = xs:anyURI	Import of the contents of an XML Schema file from a specified namespace	(xs:annotation?)
xs:include 　id = xs:ID 　schemaLocation = xs:anyURI	Inclusion of the contents of an XML Schema file	(xs:annotation?)
xs:key 　id = xs:ID 　name = xs:NCName	Definition of a key	((xs:annotation?), (xs:selector, xs:field+))
xs:keyref 　id = xs:ID 　name = xs:NCName 　refer = xs:QName	Definition of a key reference	((xs:annotation?), (xs:selector, xs:field+))
xs:list 　id = xs:ID 　itemType = xs:QName	List derived by transforming simple data types into a white space separated list of values	((xs:annotation?), (xs:simpleType ?))

Element	Description	Content

xs:notation
  id = xs:ID
  name = xs:NCName
  public = xs:token
  system = xs:anyURI
	Declaration of notation	(xs:annotation?)

xs:redefine
  id = xs:ID
  schemaLocation = xs:anyURI
	Inclusion of an XML Schema allowing for the override of simple and complex type definitions	(xs:annotation |
		(xs:simpleType | xs:complexType |
		xs:group | xs:attributeGroup))*

xs:restriction
  base = xs:QName
  id = xs:ID
	Derivation of a complex content model by restricting the attributes and child elements in complex element types	(xs:annotation?,
		(xs:group | xs:all | xs:choice |
		xs:sequence)?,
		((xs:attribute |
		xs:attributeGroup)*,
		xs:anyAttribute?))

xs:restriction
  base = xs:QName
  id = xs:ID
	Derivation of a simple data type by restricting the values of the data type through facets	((xs:annotation?),
		(xs:simpleType ?,
		(xs:minExclusive |
		xs:minInclusive |
		xs:maxExclusive |
		xs:maxInclusive |
		xs:totalDigits | xs:fractionDigits |
		xs:length | xs:minLength |
		xs:maxLength | xs:enumeration |
		xs:whiteSpace |xs:pattern)*))

xs:restriction
  base = xs:QName
  id = xs:ID
	Derivation of a simple content model by restricting the values of the data type through facets	(xs:annotation?, (xs:simpleType?,
		(xs:minExclusive |
		xs:minInclusive |
		xs:maxExclusive |
		xs:maxInclusive | xs:totalDigits |
		xs:fractionDigits | xs:length |
		xs:minLength | xs:maxLength |
		xs:enumeration | xs:whiteSpace |
		xs:pattern)*)?, ((xs:attribute |
		xs:attributeGroup)*,
		xs:anyAttribute?))

xs:schema
  attributeFormDefault = ("qualified" |
                    "unqualified") :
                    "unqualified"
  blockDefault = ("#all" | list of
             ("extension" | "restriction" |
              "substitution")) : ""
  elementFormDefault = ("qualified" |
                    "unqualified") :
                    "unqualified"
  finalDefault = ("#all" | list of ("extension" |
             "restriction"))
                    : ""
  id = xs:ID
  targetNamespace = xs:anyURI
  version = xs:token
  xml:lang = xml:lang
	Root element of XML Schema	((xs:include | xs:import |
		xs:redefine | xs:annotation)*,
		(((xs:simpleType |
		xs:complexType |
		xs:group | xs:attributeGroup) |
		xs:element | xs:attribute |
		xs:notation), xs:annotation*)*)

xs:selector
  id = xs:ID
  xpath = xs:token
	Definition of the element on which a uniqueness constraint or reference is checked	(xs:annotation?)

Element	Description	Content
xs:sequence id = xs:ID	Compositor within a group defining an ordered group of elements	(xs:annotation?, (xs:element | xs:group | xs:choice | xs:sequence | xs:any)*)

xs:sequence
  id = xs:ID
  maxOccurs = (xs:nonNegativeInteger |
      "unbounded") : "1"
  minOccurs = xs:nonNegativeInteger : "1"
	Compositor outside of a group defining an ordered group of elements	(xs:annotation?,
		(xs:element | xs:group |
		xs:choice | xs:sequence |
		xs:any)*)

xs:simpleContent id = xs:ID	Declaration of a simple content model	((xs:annotation?), (xs:restriction | xs:extension))
xs:simpleType id = xs:ID	Local definition of a simple type	(xs:annotation?, (xs:restriction | xs:list | xs:union))

xs:simpleType
  final = ("#all" | ("list" | "union" |
      "restriction"))
  id = xs:ID
  name = xs:NCName
	Global declaration of a simple type	(xs:annotation?, (xs:restriction |
		xs:list | xs:union))

xs:union
  id = xs:ID
  memberTypes = list of xs:QName
	Union of simple data types	((xs:annotation?),
		(xs:simpleType *))

xs:unique
  id = xs:ID
  name = xs:NCName
	Definition of a simple or compound constraint	((xs:annotation?),
		(xs:selector, xs:field+))

XML Schema Facets

The following table lists all of the XML Schema facets that can be used to define custom data types. Facets can contain only the xs:annotation element.

Facet	Description

xs:enumeration
  id = xs:ID
  value = anySimpleType
	Restricts a data type to a finite set of values

xs:fractionDigits
  fixed = xs:boolean : "false"
  id = xs:ID
  value = xs:nonNegativeInteger
	Specifies the number of fractional digits of a numerical data type

xs:length
  fixed = xs:boolean : "false"
  id = xs:ID
  value = xs:nonNegativeInteger
	Specifies the length of a value

xs:maxExclusive
  fixed = xs:boolean : "false"
  id = xs:ID
  value = anySimpleType
	Specifies the maximum value of a numerical data type (exclusive)

xs:maxInclusive
  fixed = xs:boolean : "false"
  id = xs:ID
  value = anySimpleType
	Specifies the maximum value of a numerical data type (inclusive)

Facet	Description

xs:maxLength
  fixed = xs:boolean : "false"
  id = xs:ID
  value = xs:nonNegativeInteger
	Sets the maximum length of a value or text string

xs:minExclusive
  fixed = xs:boolean : "false"
  id = xs:ID
  value = anySimpleType
	Specifies the minimum value of a numerical data type (exclusive)

xs:minInclusive
  fixed = xs:boolean : "false"
  id = xs:ID
  value = anySimpleType
	Specifies the minimum value of a numerical data type (inclusive)

xs:minLength
  fixed = xs:boolean : "false"
  id = xs:ID
  value = xs:nonNegativeInteger
	Sets the minimum length of a value or text string

xs:pattern
  id = xs:ID
  value = anySimpleType
	Defines a regular expression pattern for a text string

xs:totalDigits
  fixed = xs:boolean : "false"
  id = xs:ID
  value = xs:positiveInteger
	Specifies the total number of digits in a numerical data type

xs:whitespace
  fixed = xs:boolean : "false"
  id = xs:ID
  value = ("preserve" | "replace" | "collapse")
	Defines white space behavior in a numerical data type

Task Reference

TASK	PAGE #	RECOMMENDED METHOD/NOTES
Absolute path, described in XPath	XML 306	`/child1/child2/child3/...` where *child1*, *child2*, *child3*, and so forth are the descendants of the root node
Absolute position, set with CSS	XML 247	`position: absolute`
ANY content, declare in a DTD	XML 96	Use the declaration: `<!ELEMENT element ANY>`
Attribute list, declare in a DTD	XML 105	See Reference Window: Declaring an Attribute List
Attribute, add to an element	XML 20	`<element_name attribute="value">` where *attribute* is the name of the attribute, and *value* is the attribute's value. A single element can have several attributes.
Attribute, declare in a schema	XML 155	See Reference Window: Declaring an Attribute
Attribute node, create in JavaScript	XML 599	`docObj.createAttribute(attribute)` where *docObj* is the document object containing the new attribute, and *attribute* is the name of the attribute node

Attribute node, create in XSLT	XML 349	`<xsl:attribute name="name" namespace="uri">`
		`    styles`
		`</xsl:attribute>`
		where *name* specifies the name of the attribute and *uri* indicates the namespace

Attribute node, reference in XPath	XML 308	`@attribute` where *attribute* is the name of the attribute
Attribute node, remove an	XML 609	`nodeObj.removeAttribute(attribute)` where *nodeObj* is the node object containing the attribute and *attribute* is the attribute node
Attribute node, set value of	XML 609	`nodeObj.setAttribute(attribute, value)` where *nodeObj* is the node object containing the attribute, *attribute* is the attribute node, and *value* is the value stored in the attribute

Attribute set, create an	XML 350	`<xsl:attribute-set name="name" use-attribute-sets="name-list">`
		`    <xsl:attribute name="name1">styles</xsl:attribute>`
		`    <xsl:attribute name="name2">styles</xsl:attribute>`
		`    ...`
		`</xsl:attribute-set>`
		where *name* is the name of the set, *name1*, *name2*, etc. are the names of the individual attributes created within that set, and *styles* are XSLT styles applied to each attribute in the set

Attribute value, insert into an XSLT style sheet	XML 334	`<elem attribute="{expression}">` where *elem* is the name of the element in the result document, *attribute* is the name of an attribute associated with the element, and *expression* is an XPath expression that defines the value of the attribute
Background color, set with CSS	XML 254	`background-color: color` where *color* is either a color name or a color value

TASK	PAGE #	RECOMMENDED METHOD/NOTES
Background image, set with CSS	XML 262	See Reference Window: Setting a Background Image
Block element, set width with CSS	XML 242	`width: value` where *value* is expressed as a percentage of the width of the parent element, or in absolute units
Border color, set with CSS	XML 257	`border-color: top right bottom left` where *top*, *right*, *bottom*, and *left* are the color values or color names applied to the corresponding borders
Border style, set with CSS	XML 257	`border: width style color` where *width* is the width of the borders, *style* is the border style, and *color* is a color name or color value applied to the borders
Border width, set with CSS	XML 257	`border-width: top right bottom left` where *top*, *right*, *bottom*, and *left* are the widths of the corresponding borders

CDATA section, create a	XML 26	`<![CDATA[`
		`    character data`
		`]]>`
		where character data is the block of character text.

Character content, declare in a DTD	XML 96	Use the declaration: `<!ELEMENT element (#PCDATA)>`
Character reference, insert a	XML 23	See Reference Window: Inserting a Character Reference
Child element, apply CSS style to	XML 235	`parent > child {style1:value1; style2:value2; ... }` where *parent* is the parent element; *child* is the child element that receives the style; *style1*, *style2*, etc. are CSS style attributes; and *value1*, *value2*, etc. are the values applied to those attributes
Child elements, declare in a DTD	XML 98	Use the declaration: `<!ELEMENT element (child_elements)>` where *child_elements* is a list of the elements contained by *element*.
Child node, append to parent	XML 599	`parent.appendChild(child)` where *parent* is the parent node and *child* is the child node
Child node, reference a specific	XML 595	`nodeObj.childNodes[index]` where *nodeObj* is a node from the document's node tree and *index* is the index number of a specific child node
Child nodes, reference a collection of	XML 595	`nodeObj.childNodes` where *nodeObj* is a node from the document's node tree

TASK	PAGE #	RECOMMENDED METHOD/NOTES

Choice element, apply in an XSLT style sheet	XML 340	```xml
		<xsl:choose>
		    <xsl:when test="expression1">
		        styles
		    </xsl:when>
		    <xsl:when test="expression2">
		        styles
		    </xsl:when>
		
		    . . .
		
		    <xsl:otherwise>
		        styles
		    <xsl:otherwise>
		</xsl:choose>
		``
		where *expression1*, *expression2*, etc. are expressions that are either true or false and *styles* are styles that applied for each expression that is true

Class, apply a style to with CSS	XML 298	See Reference Window: Using IDs and Classes in a Style Sheet
Color, set with CSS	XML 281	`color: color` where *color* is either a color name or a color value
Comment, insert a	XML 13	`<!-- comment text -->` where *comment text* is the text of the comment.

Comment node, create a	XML 351	```xml
		<xsl:comment>
		    Comment Text
		</xsl:comment>
		``
		where *Comment Text* is the text of the comment

Comment node, reference in XPath	XML 309	`comment()`

Condition section, create in a DTD	XML 127	To ignore declarations in a DTD, use the structure:
		`<![IGNORE    declarations ]]>`
		To include declarations in a DTD, use the structure:
		`<![INCLUDE    declarations ]]>`

Count nodes in a node set, use XPath to	XML 384	`count(node-set)` where *node-set* is the location path of the node set to be counted
CSS style sheet, attach a	XML 233	`<?xml-stylesheet type="text/css" href="url" ?>` where *url* is the URL of the file containing the style sheet
Data field, bind an element to a	XML 521	`<elem datasrc="#id" datafld="field"> ... </elem>` where *elem* is the name of the HTML element, *id* is the ID of the data island, and *field* is the name of the field in the data source
Data field, set data format attribute	XML 523	`dataformatas="type"` where *type* is either "text" (the default) or "html"
Data island, create from an external file	XML 518	`<xml id="id" src="url"></xml>` where *id* is an ID name assigned to the data island, and *url* is the filename and location of the data source file

TASK	PAGE #	RECOMMENDED METHOD/NOTES

Data island, create within an HTML file	XML 518	`<xml id="id">`
		  `data`
		`</xml>`
		where *id* is an ID name assigned to the data island, and *data* is the data stored in the data island

Data, place within a style sheet	XML 492	See Reference Window: Placing Data Within a Style Sheet
Data type, derive a new	XML 181	See Reference Window: Deriving New Data Types
Data type, derive a pattern	XML 186	See Reference Window: Deriving a Patterned Data Type
Decimal format, use XSLT to specify a	XML 393	`<xsl:decimal-format attributes />` where *attributes* is a list of attributes that define the numbering scheme that the XSLT processor should employ when rendering numeric values
Default attribute value, declare in a DTD	XML 112	See Reference Window: Specifying an Attribute Default
Descendant node, reference in XPath	XML 306	`//descendant` where *descendant* is the name of the descendant node
Display block, use CSS to	XML 237	`display: block`
Display inline, use CSS to	XML 237	`display: inline`
Display table cell, use CSS to	XML 237	`display: table-cell`
Document object, convert to text string with Mozilla	XML 590	`xStr = serialObj.serializeToString(resultObj);` where *xStr* is a text string containing the code of the *resultObj* document and *serialObj* is a serializer object
Document object, create in Internet Explorer	XML 575	`docObj = new ActiveXObject(PID)` where *docObj* is the variable name of the document object and *PID* is the program ID that indicates the type of document object to be created

Document object, create in Mozilla	XML 577	`docObj =`
		`document.implementation.createDocument`
		`(uri,root,doctype)` where *uri* is the URI of the document's namespace, *root* is the qualified name of the document's root element, and *doctype* is the type of document to create

Document object, load file into	XML 579	`docObj.load(url)` where *docObj* is the document object and *url* is the URL of the file to be loaded into the document object
Document object, load file synchronously	XML 579	`docObj.async=false` where *docObj* is the document object
Document, create a reference with XPath	XML 484	`document(object, base)` where *object* is either the URI of another XML source document or a node in the current source document that contains the URI of an external document, and *base* is the base URI used for resolving relative references
DTD, declare a	XML 95	See Reference Window: Creating a DOCTYPE Declaration
Element choice, declare in a DTD	XML 99	See Reference Window: Specifying a Sequence or Choice of Child Elements

TASK	PAGE #	RECOMMENDED METHOD/NOTES

Element containing attributes and child elements, declare in a schema	XML 162	Use the structure:
		`<xs:element name="name">`
		    `<xs:complexType>`
		        `<xs:compositor>`
		            `elements`
		        `</xs:compositor>`
		    `</xs:complexType>`
		    `attributes`
		`</xs:element>`
		where *name* is the element name, *compositor* defines the structure of the child elements, and *attributes* is a list of the attributes associated with the element

Element containing attributes and simple content, declare in a schema	XML 156	Use the structure:
		`<xs:element name="name">`
		    `<xs:complexType>`
		        `<xs:simpleContent>`
		            `<xs:extension base="type">`
		                `attributes`
		            `</xs:extension>`
		        `</xs:simpleContent>`
		    `</xs:complexType>`
		`</xs:element>`
		where *name* is the element name, *attributes* is the list of attributes, and *type* is the data type of the text content of the element

Element containing only child elements, declare in a schema	XML 159	Use the structure:
		`<xs:element name="name">`
		    `<xs:complexType>`
		        `<xs:compositor>`
		            `elements`
		        `</xs:compositor>`
		    `</xs:complexType>`
		`</xs:element>`
		where *name* is the element name, *elements* is a list of the child elements, and *compositor* is sequence, choice, or all.

Element node, create in JavaScript	XML 598	`nodeObj = docObj.createElement(tag)` where *nodeObj* is the new element node, *docObj* is the document object containing the new node, and *tag* is the tag name associated with the element

Element node, create in XSLT	XML 348	`<xsl:element name="name" namespace="uri"`
		        `use-attribute-sets="namelist">`
		    `styles`
		`</xsl:element>`
		where *name* is a name for the element, *uri* specifies the element's namespace, and *namelist* is a list of attribute sets

Element sequence, declare in a DTD	XML 99	See Reference Window: Specifying a Sequence or Choice of Child Elements
Element, create a closed	XML 15	`<element_name>Content<element_name>` where *element_name* is the name of the XML element, and *Content* is the element's content.
Element, create a root	XML 18	The top level element in any XML document is the root element.

TASK	PAGE #	RECOMMENDED METHOD/NOTES
Element, create an empty	XML 19	`<element_name/>` where *element_name* is the name of the XML element.
Element, float with CSS	XML 248	`float: margin` where *margin* is either left or right
Element, position with CSS	XML 247	`position: type; top:value; left:value` where *type* indicates the type of positioning applied to the element, and the top and left attributes indicate the coordinates of the top and left edges of the element
Element, set height with CSS	XML 243	`height: value` where *value* is the height of the element, specified either as a percentage of the parent element or in absolute units
Element, stack with CSS	XML 250	`z-index: value` where *value* is a positive or negative integer or "auto"
Elements, apply CSS style to several	XML 235	`element1, element2, ... {style1:value1; style2:value2; ... }` where *element1*, *element2*, etc. are elements in the document that receive the style; *style1*, *style2*, etc. are CSS style attributes; and *value1*, *value2*, etc. are the values applied to those attributes
Elements, declare in a DTD	XML 96	Use the declaration: `<!ELEMENT element content-model>` where *element* is the element's name and *content-model* specifies what type of content the element contains.
Elements, reference by tag name	XML 593	`docObj.getElementsByTagName(tag)` where *docObj* is the document object and *tag* is the element's tag name
Elements, reference by tag name within a namespace	XML 594	`docObj.getElementsByTagNameNS(uri,tag)` where *docObj* is the document object, *uri* is the URI of the namespace in which the element should reside, and *tag* is the local name of the element
EMPTY content, declare in a DTD	XML 97	Use the declaration: `<!ELEMENT element EMPTY>`

Empty element, declare in a schema	XML 156	Use the structure:
		`<xs:element name="name">`
		`    <xs:complexType>`
		`        attributes`
		`    </xs:complexType>`
		`</xs:element>`
		where *name* is the element name and *attributes* is a list of attributes

Entity, declare a general parameter	XML 122	See Reference Window: Declaring and Using a General Parameter Entity
Entity, use a	XML 122	See Reference Window: Declaring and Using a Parameter Entity
Enumerated attribute, declare in a DTD	XML 108	Use the attribute type: `attribute (value1 | value2 | value3 | ...)` where *value1*, *value2*, *value3*, and so forth are the enumerated values of the attribute.
External document, change the context node to an	XML 487	See Reference Window: Changing the Context Node to an External Document
Flat Design, create	XML 192	Declare all elements of the instance document globally in the schema.

TASK	PAGE #	RECOMMENDED METHOD/NOTES
First child, reference a	XML 595	`nodeObj.firstChild` where `nodeObj` is a node from the document's node tree
Font family, set with CSS	XML 264	`font-family: fonts` where `fonts` is a comma-separated list of specific and generic fonts
Font size, set with CSS	XML 268	`font-size: value` where `value` is the font size in relative or absolute units
Font style, set with CSS	XML 270	`font-style: type` where `type` is normal, italic, or oblique
Font weight, set with CSS	XML 270	`font-weight: weight` where `weight` is the level of bold formatting applied to the font
For-each element, apply a	XML 321	See Reference Window: Running a Style for Each Occurrence of an Item
Format number, use XPath to	XML 392	`format-number(value, format)` where `value` is the value of the number, and `format` is a pattern that indicates how the number should appear
Hide element, use CSS to	XML 239	`display: none`
Hierarchical recordset, work with a	XML 545	See Reference Window: Working with a Hierarchical Recordset
ID, apply a style to with CSS	XML 2	`#id {styles}`
ID, generate with XPath	XML 471	`generate-id(node-set)` where `node-set` is the node set for which the ID is generated
ID, search for with XPath	XML 467	`id(value)` where `value` is the value of the ID attribute

If element, apply in an XSLT style sheet	XML 339	`<xsl:if test="expression">`
		    `styles`
		`</xsl:if>`
		where `expression` is an XPath expression that is either true or false, and `styles` are the styles to be applied if `expresson` is true

Implied attribute value, declare in a DTD	XML 111	Use the keyword, #IMPLIED, in the attribute declaration.
Kerning, set with CSS	XML 273	`letter-spacing: value` where `value` is the size of the space between individual letters
Key, create a	XML 470	`<xsl:key name="name" match="node-set" use="expression" />` where `name` is the name of the key, `node-set` is the set of nodes in the source document to which the key is applied, and `expression` is an XPath expression that indicates the values to be used in the key's index table
Key, reference using XPath	XML 470	`key(name, value)` where `name` is the name of the key and `value` is the key's value
Leading, set with CSS	XML 273	`line-height: value` where `value` is either a specific length, a percentage of the font size, or a number representing the ratio of the line height to the font size
Links, create with generated IDs	XML 479	See Reference Window: Creating Links and Targets

TASK	PAGE #	RECOMMENDED METHOD/NOTES

List data type, derive in a schema	XML 175	Use the command structure:
		`<xs:simpleType name="name">`
		    `<xs:list itemType="type" />`
		`</xs:simpleType>`
		where *name* is the name assigned to the data type, and *type* is the data type of the base type.

List style image, set with CSS	XML 240	`list-style-image: url(url)` where *url* is the URL of an image file containing the marker image
List style position, set with CSS	XML 240	`list-style-position: position` where *position* is either inside or outside.
List style type, set with CSS	XML 241	`list-style-type: type` where *type* defines the marker that appears with each list item
Location path, write in XPath	XML 307	See Reference Window: Identifying Nodes with Location Paths
Margin, set with CSS	XML 256	`margin: top right bottom left` where *top*, *right*, *bottom*, and *left* are the sizes of the corresponding margins
Mixed content, declare in a DTD	XML 103	Use the declaration: `<!ELEMENT element (#PCDATA|child1|child2|..)*>` where *element* is the parent element, and *child1*, *child2*, and so forth are the names of the child elements.
Mixed content, specify in a schema	XML 164	Add the mixed="true" attribute to a complex type element declaration.
Moded template, apply a	XML 464	`<xsl:apply-templates select="node-set" mode="mode">` where *node-set* is the node set in the source document and *mode* is the name of a moded template

Moded template, create a	XML 464	`<xsl:template match="node-set" mode="mode">`
		    styles
		`</xsl:template>`
		where *node-set* is the node set in the source document, *mode* is the name of the mode, and *styles* is the XSLT code applied to that node set under the specified mode

Modifying symbols, apply to a declaration	XML 102	See Reference Window: Applying Modifying Symbols to a Declaration
Muenchian grouping, group with	XML 475	See Reference Window: Employing Muenchian Grouping

Named attribute group, create in a schema	XML 191	Use the command structure:
		`<xs:attributeGroup name="name">`
		    attribute declarations
		`</xs:attributeGroup>`
		where *name* is the name of the attribute group, and *attribute declarations* are the declarations for the individual attributes in the group.

Named complex type, create in a schema	XML 190	Add the name="*name*" attribute to the element type declaration.

Named model group, create in a schema	XML 190	Use the command structure:
		`<xs:group name="name">`
		    element declarations
		`</xs:group>`
		where *name* is the name of the group, and *element declarations* are the declarations for the individual elements in the group.

TASK	PAGE #	RECOMMENDED METHOD/NOTES

Named template, call a	XML 415	`<xsl:call-template name="name">`
		    `<xsl:with-param name="param1" select="value1" />`
		        `<xsl:with-param name="param2" select="value2" />`
		`...`
		`</xsl:call-template>`
		where *name* is the name of the template; *param1*, *param2*, etc. are parameters used within the template; and *value1*, *value2*, etc. are the values passed to each template parameter

Named template, create a	XML 413	`<xsl:template name="name">`
		    `styles, variables and parameters`
		`</xsl:template>`
		where *name* is the name of the template and *styles*, *variables*, and *parameters* are the styles, variables, and parameters contained in the named template

Namespace, apply to a style selector	XML 63	To apply a namespace to a selector in a CSS style sheet, use the form: `prefix|selector {attribute1:value1;…}` where *prefix* is the namespace prefix, *selector* is the selector that the namespace is applied to, and *attribute1:value1*, etc. are the style attributes and values.
Namespace, apply to a style selector using an escape character	XML 65	To apply a namespace to a selector in a CSS style sheet using an escape style, use: `prefix\:selector {attribute1:value1; …}` where *prefix* is the namespace prefix, *selector* is the selector that the namespace is applied to, and *attribute1:value1*, etc. are the style attributes and values.
Namespace, apply to an attribute	XML 57	Insert the namespace prefix before the attribute name as follows: `prefix:attribute="value"`

Namespace, apply to an element	XML 58	Insert the namespace prefix before the element name as follows:
		`<prefix:element>`
		    `content`
		`</prefix:element>`

Namespace, declare in a CSS style sheet	XML 63	To declare a namespace within a CSS style sheet, add the following rule to the style sheet file: `@namespace prefix url(uri);` where prefix is the namespace prefix and uri is the URI of the namespace. Both the prefix and URI must match the prefix and URI used in the XML document.
Namespace, declare in a document prolog	XML 57	Within the XML document, insert the command: `<?xml:namespace ns="URI" prefix="prefix"?>` where *URI* is the namespace URI, and *prefix* is the namespace prefix.
Namespace, declare in an element	XML 57	Within an element, insert the attribute: `xmlns:prefix="URI"` where *URI* is the namespace URI, and *prefix* is the namespace prefix.
Namespace, use with DTDs	XML 68	Use the namespace prefixes in the element and attribute declarations as if they were part of the element and attribute names.
Node name, return the	XML 596	`nodeObj.nodeName` where *nodeObj* is a node from the document's node tree

TASK	PAGE #	RECOMMENDED METHOD/NOTES
Node set, select with Internet Explorer	XML 616	`object.selectNodes(xpath)` where `object` is a document or node object and `xpath` is an XPath expression
Node set, create a copy of a	XML 405	See Reference Window: Creating a Copy of a Node Set
Node set, number a	XML 382	See Reference Window: Numbering Nodes
Node set, sort a	XML 337	See Reference Window: Sorting a Node Set
Node type, return the	XML 596	`nodeObj.nodeType` where `nodeObj` is a node from the document's node tree
Node value, insert into an XSLT style sheet	XML 318	See Reference Window: Inserting a Node's Value
Node value, return the	XML 596	`nodeObj.nodeValue` where `nodeObj` is a node from the document's node tree
Node, copy a	XML 600	`nodeObj.cloneNode(deep)` where `nodeObj` is the node to be copied and `deep` is a Boolean value specifying whether to create a copy of the node and its descendants (true) or to copy just the node itself (false)
Node, remove a	XML 602	See Reference Window: Attaching and Removing a Node Object
Normalize text, use XPath to	XML 398	`normalize-space(text)` where `text` is the text string to be normalized
Occurrence of an element, specify in a schema	XML 160	Add the minOccurs="*value*" maxOccurs="*value*" attributes to a simple type element declaration indicating the minimum and maximum times the element can occur.
Output method, specify for an XSLT style sheet	XML 312	`<xsl:output attributes />` where `attributes` is the list of attributes that define the output format of the result document
Overflow, set with CSS	XML 243	`overflow: type` where `type` is visible (the default), hidden, scroll, or auto
Padding, set with CSS	XML 260	`padding: top right bottom left` where `top`, `right`, `bottom`, and `left` are the padding values for the corresponding sides of the block element
Parameter value, set in Internet Explorer	XML 615	`processorObj.addParameter(parameter, value, uri)` where `processorObj` is a processor object, `parameter` is the name of the style sheet parameter, `value` is the value passed to the parameter, and `uri` is an optional value that specifies the namespace URI for the parameter
Parameter value, set in Mozilla	XML 616	`processorObj.setParameter(uri, parameter, value)` where `processorObj` is a processor object, `uri` is the namespace of the parameter, `parameter` is the name of the parameter, and `value` is the parameter value
Parameter, declare in XSLT	XML 405	`<xsl:param name="name" select="value" />` where `name` is the parameter's name and `value` is the parameter's default value
Parameter, set the value of a	XML 409	See Reference Window: Creating and Using Parameters
Position of node in a node set, use XPath to return the	XML 376	`position()`
Predicate, apply to a node set	XML 345	See Reference Window: Using Node Predicates

TASK	PAGE #	RECOMMENDED METHOD/NOTES

Processing instruction node, create a	XML 351	`<xsl:processing-instruction name="`*name*`">`
		    attributes
		`</xsl:processing-instruction>`
		where *name* is the name of the processing instruction and *attributes* are attributes contained within the processing instruction

Processing instruction node, reference in XPath	XML 309	`processing-instruction()`
Processor object, create in Internet Explorer	XML 584	*processorObj* `= ` *templateObj*`.createProcessor();` where *processorObj* is a JavaScript object representing the XSLT processor and *templateObj* is a template object
Processor object, create in Mozilla	XML 588	*processorObj* `= new XSLTProcessor();` where *processorObj* is a JavaScript object representing the XSLT processor
Processor object, import style sheet using Mozilla	XML 588	*processorObj*`.importStylesheet(`*styleObj*`)` where *processorObj* is a JavaScript object representing the XSLT processor and *styleObj* is the document object containing the style sheet
Processor object, transform with Internet Explorer	XML 587	See Reference Window: Working with Processor Objects in Internet Explorer
Pseudo-element, apply a style to a	XML 309	*selector*`:`*pseudo-element* `{`*styles*`}` where *selector* is an element or group of elements within a document, *pseudo-element* is an abstract element based on the selector, and *styles* are styles applied to the pseudo-element
Recordset, navigate with JavaScript	XML 530	See Reference Window: Moving Through a Recordset with JavaScript
Relative position, set with CSS	XML 246	`position: relative`
Required attribute value, declare in a DTD	XML 111	Use the keyword, #REQUIRED, in the attribute declaration.

Restricted data type, derive in a schema	XML 181	Use the command structure:
		`<xs:simpleType name="`*name*`">`
		    `<xs:restriction base="`*type*`">`
		        `<xs:`*facet1* `value="`*value1*`" />`
		        `<xs:`*facet2* `value="`*value2*`" />`
		        `<xs:`*facet3* `value="`*value3*`" />`
		    `</xs:restriction>`
		`</xs:simpleType>`
		where *name* is the name assigned to the data type, *facet1*, *facet2*, *facet3*, etc. are constraining facets, and *value1*, *value2*, *value3*, etc. are values for each constraining facet.

Root template, create a	XML 310	`<xsl:template match="/">`
		    styles
		`</xsl:template>`
		where *styles* are the XSLT elements and literal result elements found in the root template

Russian Doll Design, create a	XML 193	Declare the root element of the instance document globally in the schema; nest all other element declarations within that declaration.
Schema, apply to a document with a namespace	XML 200	See Reference Window: Applying a Schema to a Document with a Namespace

TASK	PAGE #	RECOMMENDED METHOD/NOTES
Schema, apply to a document without a namespace	XML 166	See Reference Window: Applying a Schema to a Document without a Namespace
Schema, create a	XML 152	See Reference Window: Creating a Schema
Schema, importing a	XML 205	Add the following element as a child of the root schema element: `<xs:import namespace="uri" schemaLocation="schema" />` where *uri* is the URI of the imported schema's namespace and *schema* is the name and location of the schema file.
Schema, including a	XML 205	Add the following element as a child of the root schema element: `<xs:include schemaLocation="schema" />` where *schema* is the name and location of the schema file.

Schema, target a namespace in a	XML 196	Add the following attributes to the root schema element:
		 `prefix:xmlns="uri"`
		 `targetNamespace="uri"`
		 where *prefix* is the prefix of the XML Schema namespace and *uri* is the URI of the schema's target. If no *prefix* is specified, XML Schema is the default namespace of the schema file.

Schema, use built-in data types	XML 172	See Reference Window: Applying Built-in XML Schema Data Types
Selector, apply CSS styles to a	XML 235	`selector {style1:value1; style2:value2; ... }` where *selector* specifies the elements in the document that receive the style; *style1*, *style2*, etc. are CSS style attributes; and *value1*, *value2*, etc. are the values applied to those attributes.
Serializer object, create in Mozilla	XML 590	`serialObj = new XMLSerializer();` where *serialObj* is the serializer object that contains the text of the document object or fragment
Simple type element, declare in a schema	XML 153	Use the command: `<xs:element name="name" type="type"/>` where *name* is the name of the simple element and *type* is the data type.
Single node, select with Internet Explorer	XML 616	`object.selectSingleNode(xpath)` where *object* is a document or node object and *xpath* is an XPath expression
Step pattern, define with XPath	XML 455	`axis::node-test[predicate]` where *axis* is the direction that the XSLT processor should move, *node-test* is the node to be matched, and *predicate* is the expression that a specific node should match
Step pattern, group with a	XML 461	See Reference Window: Creating a List Using Step Patterns
String Attribute, declare in a DTD	XML 107	Use the attribute type: `attribute CDATA`
Style sheet, link to	XML 34	See Reference Window: Attaching an XML Document to a Style Sheet
Sum values in a node set, use XPath to	XML 385	`sum(node-set)` where *node-set* is the location path of the node set to be summed
Table, bind to data	XML 536	See Reference Window: Binding a Table to Data
Table, specify page size of	XML 538	`datapagesize="number"` where *number* is the number of records to display in a single page
Template object, create in Explorer	XML 583	See Reference Window: Using Style and Template Objects in Internet Explorer

TASK	PAGE #	RECOMMENDED METHOD/NOTES
Template object, insert style sheet into with Internet Explorer	XML 584	`templateObj.stylesheet=styleObj;` where `templateObj` is the template object and `styleObj` is a free-threaded style sheet object
Template parameter, pass a value to	XML 409	See Reference Window: Creating and Using Parameters
Template, apply a	XML 321	`<xsl:apply-templates select="expression" />` where `expression` is an XPath expression for a node set in the source document

Template, create for a node set	XML 310	`<xsl:template match="node-set">`
		    `styles`
		`</xsl:template>`
		where `node-set` is an XPath expression selecting a node or node set from the source document and `styles` are the XSLT styles defined for the node or nodes

Text node, create	XML 598	`nodeObj = docObj.createTextNode(string)` where `nodeObj` is the new text node, `docObj` is the document object containing the new node, and `string` is the text string contained in the text node
Text node, create a	XML 396	`<xsl:text>text</xsl:text>` where `text` is a text string contained within the text node
Text node, reference in XPath	XML 308	`text()`
Text, align with CSS	XML 272	See Reference Window: Aligning Content Horizontally and Vertically
Text, decorate with CSS	XML 276	See Reference Window: Decorating Text
Token attribute, declare in a DTD	XML 111	Use the attribute type: *attribute token* where *token* is one of the tokenized types.
Tracking, set with CSS	XML 273	`word-spacing: value` where `value` is the size of the space between individual words
Transform to object, run in Internet Explorer	XML 582	`docObj.transformNodeToObject(styleObj,resultObj)` where `docObj` is either a document object or a node within a document and `resultObj` is a document object that stores the result of applying the `styleObj` style sheet

Transformation to document, run in Mozillla	XML 589	`resultObj =`
		`processorObj.transformToDocument(docObj);`
		where `processorObj` is a processor object, `resultObj` is the document object storing the transformation result, and `docObj` is the source document for the transformation

Transformation to fragment, run in Mozilla	XML 590	`resultFragment =`
		`processorObj.transformToFragment(docObj, resultObj);`
		where `processorObj` is a processor object, `resultFragment` is the document fragment, `docObj` is the source document, and `resultObj` is the document object that stores the contents of the result fragment

Transformation, run in Internet Explorer	XML 582	`docObj.transformNode(styleObj)` where `docObj` is either a document object or a node within a document, and `styleObj` is a document object containing a style sheet

TASK	PAGE #	RECOMMENDED METHOD/NOTES

Union data type, derive in a schema	XML 176	Use the command structure:
		`<xs:simpleType name="name">`
		  `<xs:union memberTypes="type1 type2 type3..."/>`
		`</xs:simpleType>`
		where *name* is the name assigned to the data type, and *type1*, *type2*, *type3*, and so forth are the different data types being united.

Unparsed entity, use a	XML 130	See Reference Window: Declaring an Unparsed Entity
Variable, declare in XSLT	XML 399	`<xsl:variable name="name" select="value" />` where *name* is the variable's name and *value* is the value or object stored by the variable
Variable, reference in XSLT	XML 401	`$name` where *name* is the variable's name
Venetian Blind Design, create	XML 193	In the schema, use named complex types, model groups, and attribute groups to declare the various elements of the instance document.
Visibility, set with CSS	XML 238	`visibility: type` where *type* is visible, hidden, collapse, or inherit (the default)
Web browser, display an XML document in a	XML 29	Open the XML document in the Web browser. Most current browsers will show the document in a hierarchical tree. Older browsers will only show the element values.
White space, preserve in result document	XML 398	`<xsl:preserve-space elements="list" />` where *list* is a white space-separated list of elements in the source document that contain only white space characters
White space, strip from result document	XML 397	`<xsl:strip-space elements="list" />` where *list* is a white space-separated list of elements in the source document that contain only white space characters
XML, create a declaration	XML 12	See Reference Window: Creating an XML Declaration
XML document, save with Internet Explorer	XML 625	`docObj.save(location)` where *location* is a filename, the name of document object, an Active Server Page response object, or a custom COM object that supports persistence
XMLHttpRequest object, create in Mozilla	XML 629	`reqObj = new XMLHttpRequest();` where *reqObj* is the XMLHttpRequest object
XMLHttpRequest object, create in Internet Explorer	XML 629	`reqObj = new ActiveXObject(progID);` where *reqObj* is the XMLHttpRequest object and *progID* is a program ID for an ActiveX request object
XMLHttpRequest object, open	XML 630	`reqObj.open(method, url, async, user, pwd)` where *reqObj* is the request object, *method* is the method used to open the connection, *url* is the URL of the Web server program receiving the request, *async* is a Boolean value indicating whether the call is asynchronous (true) or synchronous (false), and *user* and *pwd* are optional parameters used to authenticate the request by supplying a username and password to the server program
XMLHttpRequest object, send	XML 632	`reqObj.send(content)` where *reqObj* is the request object and *content* is any optional content you want sent with the request

TASK	PAGE #	RECOMMENDED METHOD/NOTES
XMLHttpRequest object, work with	XML 633	See Reference Window: Working with the XMLHttpRequest Object
XPath expresson, evaluate in Mozilla	XML 619	`evalObj.evaluate(xpath, object, nsResolver, result, resultObj)` where `evalObj` is an XPathEvaluator object, `xpath` is the XPath expression, `object` is a document or node object to which the XPath expression is applied, `nsResolver` is a function that resolves any namespace prefixes returning the URI of the namespace, `result` is an integer or name that specifies the type of result to be returned from the evaluation, and `resultObj` is a result object that stores the results of the evaluation
XPathEvaluator object, create in Mozilla	XML 619	`evalObj = new XPathEvaluator();` where `evalObj` is the XPathEvaluator object
XSLT style sheet, attach an	XML 303	`<?xml-stylesheet type="text/xsl" href="url" ?>` where `url` is the URL of the file containing the XSLT style sheet

XSLT style sheet, general form of an	XML 303	`<?xml version="1.0" ?>`
		`<xsl:stylesheet version="1.0"`
		`    xmlns:xsl="http://www.w3.org/1999/XSL/`
		`Transform">`
		`   style sheet contents`
		`</xsl:stylesheet>`
		where `style sheet contents` is the templates, XSLT elements, and literal result elements found in the XSLT style sheet

XSLT style sheet, import an	XML 424	`<xsl:import href="url" />` where `url` is the URL of the style sheet to be imported into the current style sheet
XSLT style sheet, include an	XML 424	`<xsl:include href="url" />` where `url` is the URL of the style sheet to be included in the current style sheet

Glossary/Index

Note: Boldface entries include definitions.

Special Characters

* (asterisk), XML 101

+ (plus sign), XML 101

? (question mark), XML 101

A

absolute path An XPath location path that begins with the root node and proceeds down through the node tree. XML 306

absolute position A CSS style that places an element at defined coordinates within its parent element. XML 245–246

absolute unit A size measure expressed in one of the following units: millimeter, centimeter, inch, point, pica, or pixel. XML 242, XML 266

ActiveX A Microsoft technology that can be used to create interactive content for the Web. XML 575

ActiveX Data Object (ADO) A Microsoft data-access technology that works with a Data Source Object by either applying a method or changing one of the DSO's properties. XML 529–533

    applying methods to recordsets, XML 529–531

    properties, XML 531–533

ADO. See ActiveX Data Object (ADO)

AJAX. See Asynchronous JavaScript and XML (AJAX)

AJAX engine A JavaScript function or object that is responsible for communicating with the server and relaying any information from the server to the user interface. XML 626–628

AJAX Web application model A model of data exchange in which an AJAX engine acts as an intermediary between the user and the server-side system. XML 626–628

aligning elements, XML 270–272

all compositor, XML 159

ancestor A node that contains several levels of nodes beneath it in the node tree. XML 305

anonymous complex type A complex type that contains no name attribute. XML 190

ANY content, XML 97

array, XML 576

asterisk (*), modifying symbol, XML 101

Asynchronous JavaScript and XML (AJAX) A collection of technologies using HTML, XML, XSLT, and JavaScript to enable fast, efficient communication between applications running on a user's browser and data stored and updated on a secure Web server. XML 625–633

    principles, XML 625–628

    XMLHttpRequest object, XML 629–633

asynchronous load The loading of a file that does not require the application loading the file to wait for it to finish loading before proceeding through the lines in the program code. XML 579

attribute An item describing a feature or characteristic of an element. XML 19–21, XML 104–116, XML 162–164. See also specific attributes

    associating with elements, XML 155–157

    attribute defaults, XML 111–112

    attribute types, XML 106–111

    binding to XML attributes, XML 525–528

    CDATA, XML 106–197

    creating with XSLT, XML 347–348, XML 349–351

    declaring, XML 154–155

    defaults, XML 111–112

    DTD declarations, XML D2–3

    enumerated types, XML 107–108

Exchanger XML, XML 113–115

    inserting values, XML 334–335

    namespaces, XML 61–62

    namespaces and DTDs, XML 115–116

    referencing, XML 157–159

    setting values, XML 607

    specifying use, XML 157

    tokenized types, XML 108–111

    XSLT, XML B1–7

attribute default, XML 111–112

attribute node A node containing an element attribute. XML 305, XML 325–332, XML 594, XML 606–613

    referencing, XML 308

    setting attribute values, XML 607–608

    sort order, determining, XML 608–613

attribute-list declaration A declaration of the attribute associated with an element. XML 104–106

axis The part of a step pattern that specifies the direction in which a processor should move through the node tree. XML 455, XML 456–458

B

background

    color, XML 254–255

    images, XML 260–263

base type One of 19 fundamental built-in XML Schema data types that are not defined in terms of other types. XML 167

binding

    data tables, XML 534–537

    HTML elements to fields, XML 520–524

    to XML attributes, XML 525–528

block. See block element

block element Element that groups page content into distinct sections such a headings and paragraphs. XML 237

    handling content overflow, XML 243–245